MW00776552

HANS JÜRGEN SYBERBERG AND HIS FILM OF WAGNER'S *PARSIFAL*

Solveig Olsen

University Press of America,® Inc.
Lanham · Boulder · New York · Toronto · Oxford

Copyright © 2006 by
University Press of America,® Inc.
4501 Forbes Boulevard
Suite 200
Lanham, Maryland 20706
UPA Acquisitions Department (301) 459-3366

PO Box 317
Oxford
OX2 9RU, UK

Library of Congress Control Number: 2005935785
ISBN 0-7618-3376-5 (paperback : alk. ppr.)

In memory of my parents,

Martha Anna Olsen, née Liebich
and
Oskar Martinus Olsen

Contents

Preface

This book serves as the first introduction in English to one of Germany's most interesting and controversial filmmakers, Hans Jürgen Syberberg. Not only a film-maker, he has also published profusely, written and directed stage performances, created installation art, while also maintaining a comprehensive Internet site. The study aims at general readers as well as scholars with more specialized expertise. It is divided into three sections.

Part One (chapters 1–5) offers a biographical overview of Syberberg's early years. It proceeds in roughly chronological order, interspersing discussions of his films and most important publications up to 1981. The discussions approach the films descriptively and factually. This is necessary in part due to the widespread misrepresentation of Syberberg's oeuvre in his homeland, in part as the base for a gradual increase in interpretation and assessment. Each book and each film in his "German Cycle" receives a more thorough treatment than the earliest works, with a chapter devoted to the *Hitler* film. It contains some observations not mentioned in other studies, calling for a reevaluation.

Part Two (chapters 6–11) focuses on *Parsifal*. It too has elicited much critical literature, but no studies have addressed the incorporation of Syberberg's main aesthetic views and philosophy. Trying to fit the film into prevailing classifications of theory, scholars and reviewers have failed to recognize the foundation on which Syberberg builds, maybe because it is unexpected and much older than anticipated. Also another factor has blinded many critics. *Parsifal* is a film of an opera written and composed by Richard Wagner. Not only several films of the German Cycle feature him through music or in person, but he was also considered practically *the* national composer during the Third Reich. Not surprisingly, many Wagner studies after 1945 have focused on his anti-Semitism. Syberberg's preoccupation with topics and figures belonging to a painful past has been seen widely as an expression of an ideologically based sympathy with that past. Hence the strange film of *Parsifal*, which challenged the comprehension of scholars and journalists alike, was conveniently labeled politically suspect. This study hopes to clear up that misunderstanding. It is a complex work. One often overlooks the fact that an opera is neither a drama nor a concert composition. In an opera, text and music interact and must be studied together. They constitute two of the main components of the composition. To that come the other elements that transform it to a *Gesamtkunstwerk*, a total work of art. They include the directing, acting, dancing, stage design, etc. This mainly visual component contains enough flexibility to influence the meaning of the whole. Syberberg's film does not change the music or alter the dialogue, but it takes advantage of the flexibility available in the visual treatment. Through it Syberberg can often translate the music, adding dimensions not found in stage versions. More importantly, taking his cues from text and music, he reveals possibilities embedded in the work by Wagner. They are usually ignored, often because the composer's stage instructions contradict them. And finally, through his setting and directing Syberberg imbues the work with a surprising interpretation. Step by step, the chapters on *Parsifal* focus on the visual treatment, pointing out the salient details which have not been discussed elsewhere, not even in Syberberg's book to the film.

Part Three (chapters 12–15) examines Syberberg's biography and oeuvre after 1982. *Parsifal* forms a turning point in the cinematic category. Edith Clever, who portrays Kundry in that film, continues as the sole actress in a series of monologues for stage and film, each being discussed in turn. One chapter discusses in depth his book of 1990, which unleashed a furor. Again a close reading unveils a continuation of the author's philosophy and compositional principle, now applied to a text. His artistic output shifts later to installation art with film, of which the major works have been exhibited internationally. The last chapter focuses on his recent projects, including still ongoing restoration work in his childhood village and the materials on his Internet site. Part Three concludes with a separate unit of endnotes, bibliography, and index. Unless noted, translations in the text are mine.

Readers may wonder why a book about a filmmaker does not contain illustrations from his films. There are three reasons: The length of the book; the difficulty in obtaining permission to use photos from the films; and the availability of ample pictorial materials, even film excerpts, on Syberberg's home page, http://www.syberberg.de.

The challenges posed by *Parsifal* prompted the studies leading to this book. The fact that Syberberg remains controversial and that the essential features in *Parsifal* and his other works have gone unrecognized indicates the need for this project. It hopes to facilitate the readers' appreciation of Syberberg's artistic legacy, especially of his *Parsifal*.

Solveig Olsen
Denton, Texas
Sept. 15, 2005

Part 1

Chapter 1

The Early Years.

The information for this book derives from Syberberg's films and printed sources, such as published interviews with him, his own books and articles, literature about him, and from the Internet, including his own home page (www.syberberg.de). In spite of the publicity surrounding him during his career, Syberberg remains an intensely elusive man who divulges only select bits of information to the public. Until or unless he decides to publish his memoirs, we have to settle for the available data. An article in *The New York Times* confirms that such papers exist: "He sits in his Munich garden typing page after page of his autobiography, which he then puts in a trunk to await a more favorable age."[1] He is still active, entitling us to expect more material for a biography in the future.

Hans Jürgen Syberberg was born on December 8, 1935 to Hans-Helmuth and Ruth Syberberg in Nossendorf. It is a village with fewer than 1,000 inhabitants in the northeastern part of Germany now called Mecklenburg-Vorpommern. The numerous photographs on the home page and in an early autobiography include a portrait of his mother, a beautiful young woman with blue or grey eyes, an oval face, and her light brown hair gathered in a classic style in the back.[2] She came from Allenstein in East Prussia, today Olsztyn in Poland. Another picture in the same text shows the father as a cavalry officer in 1918 during World War I. He fought long enough to be distinguished with the Iron Cross. Born in 1897, he was considerably older than his wife. Syberberg describes him as quite a ladies' man and hunter, his mother being the most precious trophy. She was still quite young when the father brought her to his estate in Nossendorf. She had been married before and brought a daughter, Doris, into the household. Their new attempt at matrimony did not last either. The mother left after a short time, presumably because she "tired of her husband's roving eye."[3] The baby son stayed with the father. For a while, little Doris also remained in Nossendorf before she rejoined her mother. After the divorce, the boy was cared for by nannies until the father remarried. On a few occasions the son was able to visit his mother and half-sister. With amusement he reminisces how she objected to the father's new wife, a situation he did not find particularly painful himself, not knowing his family's history at the time.[4] Although Syberberg has included autobiographical information in most of his publications, he has treated his parents' divorce with reticence. Not until 2004 did he reveal on his Internet site that the mother's successor, Inga, was instrumental in Mrs. Syberberg's departure, who may not have left voluntarily. Nor has he discussed his extended family. Only one of his mother's sisters, Greten, is mentioned by name, since she lived with them for a while. Apparently the family had little contact with the father's brother, the playwright and novelist Rüdiger Syberberg.

Although Syberberg's parents had made their home in the northeast, another picture in the same collection of photos indicates the grandfather's earlier ties to the grain business in the western part of the country. The illustration shows large letters spelling "Mühlenwerke Syberberg" on top of a gigantic grain mill in Mühlheim on the Rhine. Barges on the river could unload their cargo directly into the building. The grandfather, Johannes Syberberg, sold this business before it was destroyed through bombardment during Worl War II. The grain business also sustained the Syberberg family living in the old Prussian northeast, where the boy spent the first part of his childhood in the village of Nossendorf. It lies about halfway between Güstrow and Greifswald. In this flat and fertile land the young boy grew up surrounded by grain fields, orchards and groves. His books describe a carefree existence in close contact with nature and a rural culture still distinct from the lifestyle of the cities. The Syberbergs belonged to the landed upper class that disappeared later in the "Peasants' and Workers' State" of the German Democratic Republic. In 1926 the father purchased an old estate that had been consolidated from three farms two hundred years earlier. Linden trees shaded the front courtyard leading to the manor house. From his room on the second floor the boy could observe the storks nesting on the huge thatch-roofed, half-timbered cattle and grain barn that was torn down later. An equally large stable and other outbuildings framed the cobblestoned courtyard. Across an old pond stood the church with its cemetery that the boy passed daily on his way to school. In the Syberberg home a certain formality reigned, and even as a young child the writer-filmmaker learned that children should be seen but not heard at the table. So he had ample opportunity to eat in silence while studying the huge painting that adorned a wall in the diningroom. It was a copy of Rubens' *Meleager and Atalanta*, that the parents had acquired on their honeymoon trip. Later the family was separated from the painting and considered it lost. But in 2001 Syberberg went on a search mission and was able to buy it back. As a child he did not care about the painting and strict table manners at home. He much preferred to eat with the children of the farmworkers in their cozy kitchens than face the strict table manners at home. But obviously some parts of the house exuded a warm ambience. For example the "ladies' room," or living room, appears in later photos with an inviting sofa group, paintings on the walls, and a seven-armed candelabra on one of the cabinets. The main building could easily accommodate the family, household staff, and visitors. And once lost, it became the paradise of which memories are made.

As a child, Syberberg was hardly aware of the political development. His father disdained the Nazis and soon paid the price. For years he had served Nossendorf and the surrounding community as chief administrator, *Amtsvorsteher*. He had also just been reelected mayor in 1933 when he was faced with the demand to join the party. He refused. It did not take long before he was removed from office by order of the county commissioners. They, of course, were members of the Nazi party. Soon all civil servants and public officials had to be members in order to keep their positions.[5] The father actually incurred some risk when he later hired a former inmate of a concentration camp. Thousands of politically suspect people had been imprisoned in 1933, so many, in fact, that the first concentration camps had to be built to handle the numbers. However, Mr. Syberberg experienced no repercussions from people in the community. In the Nossendorf area, non-conformists would occasionally be harassed by gangs of the SA, but by and large, the residents could continue their lives with minimal disruptions.

Even when World War II broke out, this rural idyll remained relatively unaffected for several years. Of course propaganda filled the airwaves of the "people's radio," the only allowed kind of broadcasting receiver. But Syberberg's father listened to BBC on the hidden old set, and the boy detected the father's anguish and tension. Soon prisoners of war began to arrive at the area farms, where they replaced the drafted men. It seemed to the boy that the native inhabitants gradually became as unfree as the Frenchmen, Belgians and Poles who plowed their fields. As the Russian army approached in 1945, Syberberg's childhood world vanished in chaos and terror. The family estate was overrun with refugees from the east fleeing toward the west ahead of Stalin's soldiers. Still worse, a German military unit intending to defend the village set up headquarters there. Syberberg's stepmother realized that armed resistance was not only futile; it also meant certain doom for all the civilians gathered on her property. So she resolutely hung a white sheet from a second-floor window, signaling surrender. An SS-officer promptly arrested her for treason. He was about to shoot her behind the barn when two civilians intervened and argued for mercy. Mrs. Syberberg survived. Fortunately for the family, the German soldiers on their property did not stay to face the Russians. The father learned from his illegal radio that the advancing Russian army had reached Demmin, only six kilometers away. He took the risk and informed the German commanding officer about it in the middle of the night. In fifteen minutes, the soldiers emptied all available vehicles and took off toward the west. At daybreak, civilians discovered the piles of goods left behind. Everything vanished quickly, much to the relief of the Syberbergs. Later that day the Russians arrived. They knew about Mr. Syberberg's political views and that he had treated the prisoners of war well. This recognition assured his survival. While his life was spared, the family's belongings did not fare so well. The father had foreseen the need for a hiding place for the most important personal documents. As chaos engulfed Nossendorf, only these papers remained undetected. They had been hidden behind a false wall under the staircase. Most precious among them were the photo albums with family mementos. Everything else in sight was ransacked, destroyed, or looted. Mrs. Syberberg had, for example, attempted to salvage the family silverware. Unfortunately, the freshly dug ground betrayed the hiding place, and not a single spoon escaped the looters. But plunder was the smallest of the scourges befalling the area. As most East Germans experienced it, the "liberation" consisted of a prolonged vendetta of rape, murder, torture, plunder, and destruction. Untold numbers opted for suicide or were murdered, filling the river and trees with dead bodies. The reputation of the Soviet army proved true, as the people in Nossendorf, especially the women, would soon learn. Syberberg's early publications do not discuss the terrors experienced during those weeks, but the nightmare continued to haunt him for years. Not until 1981 did he begin to hint at these events and the silence about them.

Somehow life continued under Soviet occupation. The boy found new friends among the children of the refugees, who now had nowhere else to go. The family was fortunate to keep two rooms in the manor house, but had to share bath and kitchen facilities with the new residents. At school a new and attractive teacher introduced young Syberberg to Goethe's *Faust* and the music by Bach and Mozart. Whether due to his infatuation with the teacher or due to corrective hindsight, Syberberg describes this literature and music as a new and artificial homeland replacing the lost world of his naïve childhood. The real world was becoming increasingly difficult. It did not take long for communist control to impose a new social order. In the ensuing reforms, landowners bore the brunt of the early expropriations. Later the land was reapportioned into agricultural cooperatives. The father now had to participate in the redistribution of his land. He was no longer a landowner, but an agricultural laborer. The family's circumstances had changed drastically, and in 1947 the little household moved to Rostock on the Baltic coast. On his first visit back to Nossendorf after the reunification, the son found an apple tree still standing on land that had belonged to the family estate. "The apples tasted exactly the same as when I was a boy—a dream of childhood through taste," he said (Rockwell, C15). A dream only. For years that was the closest he could come to the world of his past. He was unable to return to a time and place of pastoral innocence as a Tolstoy could, both because his personal paradise no longer existed, the buildings were owned by somebody else, and, more importantly, because the years of his early childhood were a horrible time for most people. Thus he had to come to grips with being exiled from his lost paradise, while still harboring the hope of acquiring the property in the future. This experience repeats, of course, the archetypal predicament of humanity. Not surprisingly, it recurs as a theme in his cinematic oeuvre. It was also the driving force behind his attempts to buy back the ruined remains of the estate. Only in October 2002 did he finally succeed, as will be discussed later.

The next five or six years after the move were spent in Rostock. Syberberg soon experienced difficulties getting admitted to the college-preparatory program in school. The new socialist order imposed quotas for admission according to social criteria. It granted priority to the previously underprivileged, that is, to the children of peasants and blue-collar workers. The offspring of professionals and independent business owners were restricted to a modest percentage of the total enrollment. With his background, Syberberg was not even qualified for consideration. Only through the intervention of connections was he finally accepted into the college-preparatory track. He was reminded time and again of his stigma. Every new form to fill out, every new questionnaire meant exclusion or second class status because of his parents' previous social standing. No doubt this discrimination threw a shadow over his childhood. It goes without saying that the most zealous Stalinists among his teachers had been equally eager in their political correctness during the Nazi years. This became clear to young Syberberg quite soon. The proof came when a teacher rejected his composition on the topic of "howling with the wolves." The student had treated the topic literally, as a fable: Through life-saving mimicry a wolf hound is accepted by a pack of wolves and becomes their leader. Perhaps his story was too transparent. Years later, Syberberg wrote about this episode to include a different point. Combined with the howling-with-the-wolves idea is the notion of a wolf in sheep's clothing.[6] He has returned to this phrase repeatedly over the years. In the context of the school experience, the teachers were leading dogs and wolves in sheep's clothing. The boy from Nossendorf had difficulty in adjusting to the expected conformity. But to some extent he succeeded. For example, he did win praise for his photo submission "Nie wieder Krieg" (Never Again War), and he got some pictures published in such official East German outlets as *Die junge Welt.* "My fascism was the early phase of the GDR, and my Hitler was Stalin," he confesses. Taking himself to task for this conformism, Syberberg asks, "So after all, career, conformist under the reds instead of the browns, Gulag instead of Auschwitz?"[7] Feeling compromised by his adjustment, he establishes parallels of guilt between himself, the Germans under Hitler, and the contemporary residents of East and West Germany. But, he also accentuates the difference and the limits of his collaboration. While in school in Rostock, he had refused to sign a petition demanding the expulsion of two students. Their crime consisted in being members of the Evangelical Youth Organization. He did not know them and did not care about church, nor did his action prevent the outcome. However, the situation provoked his conscience. By that time Syberberg was old enough to analyze an issue. Having been treated with discrimination, he now began to internalize the rejection, gaining independence of mind in the process.

Much of the young boy's spare time was spent listening to classical music on the radio. Although his parents appreciated the arts, they did not share their son's attachment to music. And he always found time for his beloved Karl May books. These popular travel and adventure novels have captivated German readers of all ages for over a hundred years. There are still at least 67 volumes of Karl May's books in print, and the young reader in Rostock devoured them all.

During these years young Syberberg also discovered the world of theater and cinema. Of course the Rostock film fare consisted mainly of East German and Russian productions. Most of them were politically tendentious, while others dealt with literary or cultural topics.[8] Syberberg's interest in movies and film aesthetics grew out of his early exposure to photography. Already as a boy in Nossendorf he would snap away with his father's camera. Then he would sort and gather the photos in series to create stories. Photography became his primary hobby and gradually an all-consuming passion. He soon borrowed his father's 8-mm wind-up Agfa-movex and embarked upon his first little film projects. Obviously, a noisy camera that had to be rewound every fifteen seconds left something to be desired, even for an inexperienced amateur. But these attempts in black and white served as an introduction to what later should become a career. In those early years, professional equipment was unavailable to a schoolboy. At long last a better camera materialized in the form of an Eumig. This 8-mm camera could run for two and a half minutes on flashlight batteries. Not exactly Hollywood standards, but still an improvement. Undoubtedly the father's new profession provided encouragement for the son's hobby. After the loss of his home and livelihood, the elder Syberberg studied photography at a vocational school. Here he learned alongside teenagers through the apprentice and journeyman stages towards a master's licence as *Fotomeister*. Not only did he share this interest with his son, but also a professional library on photography as well as a studio and darkroom. Emboldened by this encouragement, the young boy sought and obtained permission to film public theater performances in Rostock. With his access to the theaters he would also organize photo sessions of the actors in the basement. These local celebrities posed willingly for the young amateur, helping him gain experience in portrait photography as well as practice in filming the performances. He selected productions that promised to remain significant, such as plays by famous authors, for example Chechov, or performances starring renowned actors or those directed by professionals the boy admired. When Bertolt Brecht's assistant, Benno Besson, directed Molière's *Don Juan* in Rostock, the boy again received permission to film during the performances. This contact with Besson soon took him to East Berlin. He had just turned seventeen when in the winter of 1952–53 he showed Besson and Bertolt Brecht his film of the *Don Juan* production. Brecht liked the idea of documentary recordings and allowed Syberberg to film his next productions in Berlin. They were Brecht's own *Puntila and His Servant Matti*, *Mother Courage*, and *The Mother*, based on Gorki's novel, with Brecht's Berliner Ensemble. Brecht's wife, the legendary Helene Weigel, played the mother. Young Syberberg filmed from one of the theater boxes during the performances, doing the best he could with his primitive equipment. By now he had devised a way to muffle the noisy camera so that he would not disturb the audience. A camera hood made of an insulated carton with strategic holes allowed him to work inobtrusively. Unfortunately, his camera could not record sound. Another drawback was the interference by the supervising Ruth Berlau, a long-time assistant who had accompanied Brecht and his wife throughout their years in exile. She tried to take away the camera during a performance while Syberberg held on to it. Needless to say, their relationship soured after that. She did not allow him to turn the camera on Brecht, so he concentrated on the actors. The young boy was excited about his contact with Brecht, an internationally recognized author and theorist. "It was not a question of liking him. I adored him," Syberberg reminisces years later, admiring how Brecht's theater challenged the system and transgressed conventions, just as Wagner had done in music. "So I had two fathers who already had difficulties," he adds, "Two quite different and difficult fathers, but in cinema, I think I'm a little outside them too."[9]

In April 1953 he again traveled to Berlin, this time to film a special performance of Brecht's production of Goethe's *Urfaust*. The play is not performed often today, since Goethe revised and expanded this early work into his two-part magnum opus *Faust*, completing the second part shortly before his death. The

resulting film excerpts are therefore a rarity, in part also because they are probably the only documentary of Brecht's Ensemble on its own stage. Furthermore, they record Brecht's contribution to a debate raging in East Germany about the Faust theme, which, in Goethe's version, had long been considered an almost canonized text of the national literature.[10] The discussion escalated with Hanns Eisler's libretto *Johann Faustus*, which the political leaders and the media, mainly *Neues Deutschland*, condemned as anti-national. It culminated with Brecht's staging of the *Urfaust*. The two scenes that caused the furor were Mephisto's appearance as Faust advising a student and the episode in Auerbach's cellar tavern. The situation demonstrated to young Syberberg how threatened free artistic expression is under an authoritarian regime. It also showed how precarious Brecht's own position was, because by the time the young boy arrived in Berlin with his camera, the authorities had closed down Brecht's production. The performance that Syberberg filmed in April 1953 was a closed event arranged especially for the recording. The lack of an audience allowed him to work on the stage at times. Here he concentrated on scenes with Käthe Reichel, who played Gretchen, the student portrayed by Heinz Schubert, who years later would figure prominently in his *Hitler* film, and Norbert Christian, Brecht's Mephisto. The latter, whom he already knew from Rostock, became his mentor during his stays in Berlin. At the time Syberberg could not do anything with these rolls of film. But years later, in 1970, they served as the raw material for his film documentary *Nach meinem letzten Umzug* (After My Last Move), and again in 1993, for the video version *Syberberg filmt bei Brecht*.

While Syberberg visited Berlin, he took advantage of the relatively easy access to West Berlin. There he became acquainted with the cinema of other countries. Especially three French masterpieces impressed him: *Orpheus* and *The Beauty and the Beast* by Jean Cocteau and *The Children of Paradise* by Marcel Carné. He states that they "definitely influenced" him.[11] Interestingly, he gives the last title as *Kinder des Olymp*, (Children of Olymp), in spite of the "paradise" in the original French title, *Les enfants du paradis*. Perhaps the movie ran under the title he mentions. But the concept of paradise is so central to his oeuvre that one wonders about the change. Paradise evokes different connotations than does Olymp. One may assume that the change is a deliberate attempt to manipulate the concepts and offer hints to alert readers. These three French movies had been recommended to him by Norbert Christian. So it was Brecht's Mephisto who tempted him into seeing them and thus influenced him deeply.

Later in 1953 Syberberg traveled to Berlin for different reasons. After the gradual deterioration of socio-economic conditions in the German Democratic Republic, thousands of workers in East Berlin had gone on strike on June 16 and 17, taking to the streets. When the East German police could not subdue them, two Soviet tank divisions clashed with the insurgents in a bloody confrontation. Similar unrest erupted and was brutally crushed in a number of cities. The repercussions were predictably harsh. A trial broadcast on the radio propelled Syberberg to leave East Germany. As he told it, "At one moment the judge broke into the defense attorney's speech and screamed,'If you say one more word in mitigation, I'll put *you* in the dock.' That was it for me".[12] In September he joined the thousands who sought refuge in the West. Officially he was just traveling to East Berlin on the written invitation of the Berliner Ensemble to show Brecht the film clips of the *Urfaust* made in the spring. Bringing along a small suitcase, he looked inconspicuous enough to pass from East to West Berlin by streetcar without complications. That suitcase contained his rolls of film and still photos from his childhood and teens. He requested asylum in West Berlin, passed through eight camps, and could finally settle in Petershagen near Minden in West Germany. His comments on the years there indicate they were a lonely time. Without family or friends, he decided to prepare for life by completing secondary school, the *Gymnasium*. In spite of a setback in the series of final exams, he succeeded in graduating with the *Abitur*, the ticket for admission to a university. In 1956 his parents also left East Germany, and as most in their predicament, brought with them only what they could carry. In many respects, the Syberberg family shared the lot of millions of Germans. After a series of political systems and uprooted once more, they had to start life all over again, preparing for the future while coming to grips with the past. At least for the student, the educational pursuit was eased with stipends from the West German authorities. As an East German he enjoyed the same privileges and financial aid as the students born on the western side of the German-German border.

During his first couple of years in the West, the young man enjoyed the freedom to travel. He spent his vacations exploring several countries, among them Belgium, France, and Italy. With only thirty-two marks at his disposal, he tramped all the way to Naples, Paestum, and Capri, sleeping under the open sky and surviving on bread and water. At this time he may have dreamed of becoming a writer. His experiences in Italy resulted in a semi-autobiographical manuscript that he tried to publish. In three letters of 1955 to a publisher, he describes this and two other manuscripts.[13] The second is a novella dealing with struggle against tyranny. The undefined setting could be both the Third Reich and Eastern Europe under communism. The third story is set in Renaissance Italy and concerns a conflict between love and freedom. The letter of March 27, 1955 praises the novella genre as "das schönste Gefäß für prosaische Gedanken," (the most beautiful vehicle [or form] for thoughts in prose), requiring a high measure of concentration and artistic energy. The third letter also makes clear that he had decided on university studies and a major. At the age of twenty he headed for the University of Munich.

At the university, Syberberg majored in art history and German literature. One of his most influential teachers was Professor Hans Sedlmayr, an art historian who died in 1984. The filmmaker had planned a documentary about him, but had to abandon the project for lack of funding. Although Syberberg mentions him in *Der Wald steht schwarz und schweiget*, he does not name the titles of the books by Sedlmayr that in all likelihood proved significant for his own work.[14] They are *Die Entstehung der Kathedrale* (The Origin of the Cathedral) and *Verlust der Mitte* (Loss of the Center).[15] Central in Syberberg's films are the concepts of an "inner sanctuary" and the individual as a microcosmic center. Both ideas are important for the understanding of his films and books.

As a student Syberberg probably read Richard Wagner's publications on aesthetic topics. Of course he encountered Wagnerian music much earlier, but his university studies provided the impetus for examining the composer's theoretical texts, although he claims he had no "contact" with him until 1972 while working on his film about King Ludwig.[16] At whatever time this exposure occurred, he must have been intrigued by some similarities in the ideas of Wagner and Brecht. For example, they both believed in using the stage to produce social change, and they both produced epic theater. Wagner and Brecht join a long list of German creative authors who discussed aesthetics. One can hardly study German literature without also dealing with aesthetics and art history. Syberberg's choice of academic majors was a natural combination, at least from a German perspective.

In 1962 Syberberg completed his doctoral dissertation on the Swiss dramatist Dürrenmatt (1921–90), *Interpretationen zum Drama Friedrich Dürrenmatts*. The study was published by UNI-Druck in Munich in 1963 and is now in its fourth edition. Besides being a respected contribution to scholarship, as evidenced by its success in print, it also presents the earliest documentation for the consistency in Syberberg's evolving thought and art. The book concentrates on two plays by Dürrenmatt, *The Visit of an Old Lady* and *Romulus the Great*. They are intended to serve as models for understanding the connection between contemporary literature and culture. The author subdivides the analysis in two sections, one a linear, "horizontal" examination of plot or content, and the other a point-oriented, "vertical" discussion of structure restricted in scope to select scenes. The latter approach of immanent analysis held more attraction for the writer, to judge from the space allotted to it. This is also the method he chose later for his films with Fritz Kortner. Many of the features he scrutinizes in the book reappear transformed in his other work. That applies to the absurd and grotesque elements, the technique of ambiguity and alienation (Dürrenmatt calls it distancing), and the function of the dialogues. He pays special attention to the juxtaposition of opposites to reveal their Janus-like complementarity or hidden identity. In this context Syberberg discusses laughter and tears with reference to the ancient Greek satyr play (58–59). Other topics are the ugly and the beautiful as well as the process of overcoming, in which the tragic element reveals itself in the comical. All these observations are pertinent to his films. And so is the demonstration of how, in both Dürrenmatt plays, various elements mix dialectically and fuse to a new unity. Most interestingly, already here Syberberg identifies the criterion for a modern work of art as the ability to "evoke the spark of the religious" concealed in the work itself (142). This is what he sets out to accomplish in the film on Parsifal years later.

As motto for the book Syberberg chose two quotations on Sisyphos; the first from the *Odyssey*, the second from Albert Camus' *Myth of Sisyphos*. Discussing his dissertation Syberberg once stated that it had "something" to do with Dürrenmatt, and then he added, "but it was really a study of the Sisyphos myth."[17] He selected Camus' passage containing the apparently paradoxical statement that, on the one hand, the myth is tragic because the hero is aware of the futility of his efforts; on the other hand, that Sisyphos is happy as he returns to the valley to resume his struggle.

The two quotations about the hero's never-ending challenge could also serve the author in the following years. He knew that what he wanted to achieve would be an incessant up-hill battle. Nonetheless, he responded with impatient affirmation. With the completion of his dissertation, Dr. Syberberg turned to the camera.

In *Syberbergs Filmbuch* the author describes his years at the university as a hell of artistic inactivity and a period of incubation (111). "Incubation" is an interesting word. One assumes that it refers to the young man's gradual maturation and preparation for his vocation, much as a chick in an egg or a premature baby nurtured in an incubator. In that case the term possesses a positive connotation. But incubation also denotes the period between the contraction and the outbreak of a disease. Syberberg is playing on the ambiguity of the word. He wrote the comment in 1976 after ten years as an independent moviemaker. Passionate about his career and surrounded by controversy, he may have compared his situation with an affliction. He had "succumbed" to the lures of film as art and had contracted an incurable disease. He knew of several literary precedents for using illness as a metaphor for a creative "condition," Thomas Mann's *Doktor Faustus* being one of them. But also Richard Wagner, who occupies a prominent place in Syberberg's work, wrote in his youth a short story with such a theme. In "A Pilgrimage to Beethoven" the narrator relates how the overwhelming effect of a Beethoven concert made him fall ill.[18] When the fever subsided, he had become a musician. Another example is the actor-director-author Fritz Kortner. As a fifteen-year old he attended a performance of a Schiller play in Vienna and "woke up the next day with a raging fever and the conviction that he had to become an actor."[19] Art acts as magic, then, or a virus, or at least as a catalyst resulting in a predicament with lasting effects. In Syberberg's case this predicament was a total devotion to the arts, above all film.

Chapter 2

Name Recognition

Unlike most graduates with a doctoral degree in the humanities, Syberberg did not seek employment in academia or government service. Although he was to publish profusely in the years to come, his early career was devoted to filmwork. But how does one go about becoming a filmmaker? As everyone knows, the production of a feature-length movie usually costs a fortune. Some help was available, since (West) Germany in the sixties subsidized the arts liberally, and moviemakers could apply for public funding for their projects. Most of these grants came in the form of loans. But the competition was fierce, as a new generation of talented people crowded the field. Syberberg needed some professional experience before he could qualify for financial support. This experience he gained as a freelance filmmaker for the Bavarian Broadcasting Corporation. For a few years he produced 185 short features for television, most of them ranging in length from three to thirty minutes. But at least one from 1966, about the artist Wilhelm Kobell, is 63 minutes long. It was a hectic period. He was responsible for all aspects of the production and would proceed nonstop from one project to the next. These short films were tailored to the needs of television programming, such as seasonal themes or interviews. The people he interviewed included Fritz Kortner, August Everding, Erwin Piscator, and Friedrich Dürrenmatt. One of the seasonal productions exhibits features that anticipate Syberberg's films in the future. He got the opportunity to create an Easter program. He used pictures from the Gothic period showing various stages of the Passion of Christ. This was accompanied by a soundtrack combining passages from the Bible, music from J. S. Bach's Passion, and quotations from the memoirs of Rudolf Höss, the com mandant of Auschwitz (Stone, 1). This montage of shocking combinations attracted attention. In those days, German television allotted also considerable air-time to current cultural affairs. Knowing there existed a demand for this kind of short features, Syberberg could therefore still indulge in his love for the theater and the arts. While often covering opening nights and glittering gala events with celeb rities, he also tried to convey the artistic effort by filming the rehearsals, capturing art in the making. Syberberg refers to this time as important years of apprenticeship (*Filmbuch*, 63, 111). The phrase evokes Goethe's *Wilhelm Meisters Lehrjahre* and *Wilhelm Meisters Wanderjahre*, two novels dealing with the formative years of the protagonist. The choice of words indicates Goethe's influence on Syberberg's own development, and the developmental or transitional nature of these early years.

This phase ended gradually as Syberberg began to create feature-length productions, the first one about and with Fritz Kortner. He interviewed him and

August Everding in 1963 for a short program that also included a theater rehearsal. The following year he covered a premiere of a play directed by Kortner. Two years later Syberberg returned to create a program saluting him on his 75th birthday in 1967. But now, in 1965, he made the documentary *Fritz Kortner probt Kabale und Liebe, Fünfter Akt, siebte Szene* (Fritz Kortner Rehearses *Intrigue and Love*, Act Five, Scene Seven). The title is taken from the filmography in Syberberg's *Filmbuch*. The video version bears the slightly different title *Fünfter Akt, siebente Szene: Fritz Kortner inszeniert Kabale und Liebe*. In the credits repeated at the end of the video version, the film is identified as "Eine Sendung von Hans Jürgen Syberberg für das Studienprogramm des Bayerischen Rundfunks" (A broadcast by HJS for the Educational Program of the Bavarian Broadcasting Corporation). The company appears to have commissioned the film and provided the funds for it, but the result met with the board's disapproval. The director, a Dr. Münster, made it clear that he would not tolerate anything like it in the future (*Filmbuch*, 64). The filmmaker does not explain the reason for the objections. Perhaps it stemmed from an earlier encounter with Kortner's work. In 1961, during an icy phase of the Cold War, Kortner had made a film for television, *Die Sendung der Lysistrata* (Lysistrata's Mission), based on Aristophanes. Due to its pacifistic tendencies, the company refused to broadcast it, but could not prevent its success in movie theaters.[1] Syberberg's choice of wording for his own film, a *Sendung*, may have provoked the reaction. It is a polyvalent word. But since Syberberg's documentary features Kortner and defines itself by the same word that Kortner had used in the title of his rejected film, the board members may have interpreted the action as a provocation, at least as a subversive declaration of allegiance to Kortner.

Most biographical sketches on Syberberg either skip this work or barely mention it. Their reason may be that it is "only" a documentary. Friedrich Schiller provided the text, and Fritz Kortner directed the actors, reducing the contribution of the filmmaker. In this case his role consisted of choosing the subject matter and directing a small team with three cameras yielding sixteen hours' worth of material, and finally, editing. Not such a small task after all! As will be seen later, even the documentaries form part of a greater pattern in Syberberg's work. It is not clear if he had conceived the plan for a coherent pattern at the outset of his career, but the decision must have been made quite early.

The film concentrates on Fritz Kortner, who was born in Vienna as Fritz Nathan Kohn (1892–1970). In the years between World War I and 1933 he established himself as one of the outstanding actors and directors of German theater and cinema in Berlin. Especially his stage interpretations of the classics secured him a prominent place. His accomplishments include both books and a long list of movies to which he contributed as an actor and/or director and/or scriptwriter. Perhaps American viewers remember him best from an early role as Dr. Schön opposite Louise Brooks as Lulu in Pabst's *Pandora's Box* of 1929. Among the movies he made during his exile in Hollywood one finds *The Strange Death of Adolf Hitler* and *The Hitler Gang*, a theme that was to recur in Syberberg's oeuvre years later. Unlike most Jewish refugees, Kortner returned to Germany in 1947 to star in *The Challenge*, which had "a disturbing subject—the disillusion of a German-Jewish professor who returns from exile in America to work in a post-war German university, although advised not to do so."[2] Kortner himself had no illusions, but he commanded such a formidable position in his field that the public paid attention whenever he spoke his mind, which he often did. He could also be outspoken in a confrontational way. Immediately before the filming of the Schiller rehearsal he had caused a "scandal" with a comment on concentration camps and anti-Semitism directed against the actor who played Wurm. Although Syberberg does not mention what prompted this outburst, the Wurm-affair of the nineteenth century comes to mind. At that time an actor named Wurm gained notoriety for his anti-Semitic portrayals through caricaturizing stereotypes.[3] Since Schiller's character Wurm is one of the villains of the play, the name may have provided Kortner with enough offensive material to provoke his actor to anger. The ensuing tension was still palpable when the filming began. Syberberg describes the focusing on the dynamic Kortner as a "lion hunt," himself being only an unknown beginner armed with a camera. Kortner interested him both in his own right as an artist, and as a representative of his era, profession, and background. Syberberg has repeatedly referred to Brecht and Kortner as two masters who became his most influential teachers and, one may add, two complementary role models.

One objective of this film is clearly to portray Kortner in the act of interpretation. And since Syberberg's earliest attempts recorded Brecht's production of Goethe's *Urfaust*, he may have wanted to find an equally creative director rehearsing a play by Schiller, the other of the two semi-gods of the German literary Parnassos. He achieved an interesting symmetry of complementary characters and texts. Both plays were also written when their authors were in their mid-twenties. Schiller's title uses the word *Kabale* mainly but not exclusively in the current French meaning of "intrigue." Also in Syberberg's overall scheme, semantic polyvalence plays an important role. Thus both the Jewish Kabbalah and the Hermetic tradition reverberate faintly behind the play's title. In a related way numerous themes and motifs that recur in later works can be found in this early film, many appearing only once in embryonic form as words or names in the play or in Syberberg's report about this project in his *Filmbuch* (64–70). The most conspicuous among the themes is that of *Liebestod*, the shared death of two lovers. They are Louise Millerin, the daughter of a musician, and Ferdinand von Walter, the son of the Duke of Hesse. The Duke has just sold seven thousand of his subjects as soldiers to the British king for his war against the American insurgents. But Syberberg does not show all this; he concentrates on just the second-to-last scene in which the deceived lovers, played by Christiane Hörbiger and Helmut Lohner, drink the poison before learning the truth. Most spectators in a German audience would have read the play in school and be familiar with the context. This allows the unseen portion of the play to inform the featured selection. And of course, Syberberg chose a seminal scene that throws light on the entire play. In brief, he offers an application of the theory presented in his dissertation. His "vertical" method of analysis provides an excellent tool for a critical examination of the film.

Another objective aims at recording a creative process. It includes Kortner's splintering of the characters as distinct figures, while the camera captures his expressive face. As he goes about directing, he slips into the role of the poet and conjures up his presence. All the while he demonstrates and tries out interpretations, assuming the roles of both young lovers. The characters acquire shifting voices and manifestations. As ideas they retain a verbal identity, but their embodiment on stage takes on fleeting appearances. This low-level demiurgic process of recreation with division of characters will return in a number of films.

The filmed rehearsals continued over several days, with some breaks between sessions also being recorded. The longest of the rehearsal sessions in the film concentrates on Ferdinand's reaction to his father's shameful deed ("Murderer!"), and the dying Louise's plea to him to forgive his father. In the context of the play, the theme of forgiveness applies to a narrow field, the deception and death of the lovers. When viewed against the foil of Kortner, however, it assumes broader significance. He belonged to the ranks of victims, while the actors were heirs to a painful legacy as Gentile Germans. Kortner's reminiscences between sessions, such as the comments on Gustav Gründgens, give contours to this dimension of the film.

Miss Hörbiger's participation in the Schiller production was a serendipitous find for Syberberg, since her name and family background fit right into his cinematic plans. She is in her own right a respected Austrian actress from stage, cinema, and television.[4] Her family tree constitutes a dynasty of famous actors: Her sisters, Maresa Hörbiger and Elisabeth Orth, her parents, Paula Wessely and Attila Hörbiger, both popular during the Nazi years, and uncle, Paul Hörbiger. Years later, Syberberg included the grandfather, Hanns Hörbiger, as a character in a film. Kortner must have found it intriguing that Christiane alias Louise is the one to utter the plea for forgiveness. After all, her family had once enjoyed a privileged status while others, like Kortner, fled the country to survive.

Fritz Kortner probt Kabale und Liebe introduces one of two film categories that dominate Syberberg's oeuvre: the documentary and the fictional tale. The former usually takes the form of a portrait through interviewing or observing the individual in action. The director calls them "non-fiction" films. Both categories use an aesthetic vocabulary that suggests a deliberate place and function for each work in a larger plan. Such a procedure is, of course, unusual in any age, and has therefore gone largely unrecognized.

Syberberg's next two films are also documentaries. One of them again features Kortner: *Fritz Kortner spricht Monologe für eine Schallplatte* (Fritz Kortner Recites Monologues for a Record) runs ninety minutes according to the *Filmbuch*. It does not mention two short films extracted from the long version: *Fritz Kortner spricht Shylock* (Fritz Kortner Recites Shylock), eleven minutes, and *Fritz Kortner spricht Faust* (Fritz Kortner Recites Faust), also eleven minutes. Both are included in John Sandford's article on Syberberg in *Cinegraph*. This documentary was made in cooperation with Preiser Records that marketed the phonograph version. It is simply what the title implies: the actor-director speaking into a microphone placed on a table in front of him, on the same stage in the Munich Kammerspiele used for the Schiller rehearsal. The viewer witnesses a study in concentration and intensity, a tour de force revealing a sorcerer's art, the transformation of an old man into a succession of characters. They include Shylock, a character from Fritz Kortner's play *Zwiesprache* (Dialogue), Richard III, and Goethe's Faust just before his death. Again, several of the selections herald motifs to come in later films. This was a rare opportunity for Syberberg to record a Shylock in German. Dustin Hoffman could portray this character in New York and be applauded, but most German actors today would not dare approach the role. However, before 1933, when *The Merchant of Venice* still claimed a place in the German repertory, Kortner played the most famous Shylock in Europe. And now, as a Jew addressing a post-Holocaust German audience, Kortner-Shylock feels no compunction about exacting his pound of flesh. Between recordings, the film shows him discussing the character and his position in society. "Da kann ich noch mitfühlen," he adds (I can still empathize with [him]). Of all possible excerpts, Syberberg made him recite the revenge passage in the third act that begins with "To bait fish withal" in reference to the flesh. As the monologue changes in tone, Shylock asks, still in German, "I am a Jew. Hath not a Jew eyes?" And further on, "If you prick us, do we not bleed?" He ends with, "The villainy you teach me I will execute; and it shall go hard but I will better the instruction." The German translation lets Kortner render the concluding words with "ich will es meinen Meistern zuvortun." The word *Meister* is of special interest to Syberberg, as one discovers gradually. Kortner's passionate recital of the revenge passage forms a distinct counterpoint to the theme of forgiveness in the Schiller rehearsal. Syberberg reintroduces a segment of the Shylock-passage later in a most unexpected context.

The film does not show only Fritz Kortner. Sitting at the recording table with him is August Everding (1929–99), who had previously studied under him and later succeeded him as director. This relationship resembles that of the magus Faust and his famulus Wagner. The two men exchange interesting transitional comments and discussions between the monologues. Everding soon advanced to one of the leading positions in German theater. In 1969 he was invited to direct *The Flying Dutchman* in Bayreuth, followed by *Tristan* in 1974. As the president of the German Stage Association and the writer of a culture column in the *Welt am Sonntag*, he surprised the nation in 1996 by doing something thoroughly un-German: When the Bavarian legislature refused to renovate and subsidize Everding's beloved Prinzregenten Theater in Munich, he outfoxed the system by founding the Bavarian Stage Academy, for which he knew there would be public funding, and located the school in the theater turned academy. Then he also succeeded in attracting donations from private sponsors for the refurbishing of the decrepid Art Nouveau building. Its famous interior is a smaller adaptation of Wagner's festival theater in Bayreuth.[5] The public promptly celebrated the wily Everding as "August the Great." Kortner too would have applauded, had he been alive to see it.

Upon its first release, the film elicited a mixed reaction ranging from vilification to highest recognition. One reviewer even accused Syberberg of lying to the public about Kortner actually making a recording. He assumed Kortner only pretended to be recording (*Filmbuch* 161). Syberberg could afford to shrug off remarks like that, since the project netted him a DM 70,000 federal film award. In 1968 the film earned him two silver ribbons of the German Film Awards, one for the directing and one for the film overall. That meant visibility, recognition, and the prerequisites for competing for funds in the future. Both Kortner films were reissued together on a video cassette in 1993.

The next film followed in such quick succession that the sequence cannot be ascertained from printed sources. The *Filmbuch* mentions the second Kortner-project of 1966 only briefly and immediately after the discussion of the first one. Then follows a description of the difficulties surrounding a film on Romy Schneider, also from 1966. However, in the filmography in the back of the book and later listings, the production year for the Schneider documentary appears as 1965, placing it as number two in the list. One would conclude, then, that Syberberg wants *Romy: Anatomie eines Gesichts* (Romy: Anatomy of a Face) to be considered at least simultaneous with the second Kortner-film. The legal conflicts surrounding its final form delayed the premiere on television, making it difficult to ascertain exact dates. But a review in *Der Spiegel* of February 6, 1967 leads the reader to assume that the shooting took place in February the year before, with the premiere on television given as January 21, presumably of 1967. The original ninety-minute version aired only once. Then it was reduced to sixty minutes to meet the demands of the Bavarian Broadcasting Corporation and Miss Schneider's manager, Harry Meyen, who insisted on numerous changes and cuts so as to create an idealized portrait of her. The original version was too revealing. Schneider's lawyers prevailed over Syberberg's protests and the changes were made. They included the addition of a photo of her with her son on the lap. The child had not been born when the film was shot. After this Syberberg withdrew his name from the final, abridged version. Having disavowed the abridged *Romy*, he excluded the work from his oeuvre for a long time. Only in 1998 did the discarded materials resurface, and the original version could be restored. The film assumes the fate of Binah in the Kabbalah. There the Queen of Heaven is expelled or somehow lost from her abode, much like Sophia of the Gnostics and Brünnhilde of pre-Christian European lore. The amputated version presents the actress almost as the Holy Virgin ("Ma-donnenbild Romys," "als Mutter mit Kind") in an intact setting that did not resemble her real life and person. The first version had portrayed her truthfully, Syberberg claims, as a sad and vulnerable human being, living abroad amid several cultures and languages. The distorted version presents a wholesome movie idol fit for German television consumption. According to the review in *Der Spiegel*, one omitted episode that the filmmaker particularly wanted to retain, showed the actress in a relaxed mood after champagne had loosened her tongue. With a Sammy Davis record playing, she is telling a joke about a German Jewish emigré in New York who still kept a picture of Hitler on the wall as a form of *Heimweh*, or home-sickness.[6] Syberberg could have played on several meanings of *Heimweh*, but Meyen would have nothing of it. Such a remark, he thought, would only damage Schneider's public image. Syberberg maintains he fought for his work as a "lion for its cub" (*Filmbuch*, 73), and learned a lesson or two about the movie and television business. In this description of a mundane disagreement, Syberberg again chooses his words to support the themes continuing throughout his works. The screen image and the printed word both contribute their share.

Romy Schneider was a popular movie actress born Rosemarie Albach-Retty (1938–82). She followed in the footsteps of her famous mother, Magda Schneider (1908–96), whose screen career culminated in the thirties and forties. The mother-daughter team played together in several movies. And in *Liebelei* (Flirtation) Romy played the same role that her mother had portrayed years before. To an older German audience, the name of one of them always conjures up the memory of the other. The mother's generation of screen and stage artists claims a special place in Syberberg's cinematic world. He already introduced it with Brecht and Kortner.

With her name, Rosemarie (Rose of Heaven, Virgin Mary), shortened to Romy, the young actress endeared herself to millions, above all in the role of Sissy, the title heroine in several movies about Empress Elisabeth of Austria. This empress is mostly remembered in connection with King Ludwig II of Bavaria, a distant cousin of hers. He adored her. But she married the young emperor, and Ludwig remained a bachelor. Thus faintly the Ludwig-theme enters the world of Syberberg's films, much like a new musical fragment in an ouverture. Similarly, Schneider's work with other directors informs Syberberg's oeuvre in subtle ways. Helmut Käutner, for instance, who would later act in one of Syberberg's films, directed *Monpti* in 1957. Romy Schneider and Horst Buchholz play the lead roles, while Käutner appears in a small part. Soon after, in 1960, Schneider played Myrrhine in the already mentioned *Die Sendung der Lysistrata* under the direction of Fritz Kortner. And in 1972 she returned to the role of Sissy in Visconti's *Ludwig*. Syberberg's own film on King Ludwig appeared the same year. It would seem, then, that Syberberg chooses his subject matters and cast members with an eye to possible connections. In his cinematic cosmos, the stars move in orbits with numerous conjunctions.

Still dependent on television and not yet an independent producer, Syberberg did not have full control over the Romy Schneider project. He was therefore forced to accept the compromises and could not prevent the final version from being shown. This experience prompted him to establish a production company of his own, Syberberg Filmproduktion, and a corporation, TMS Film. The second documentary on Kortner, which may have been filmed before or almost concurrently with the Schneider-film, launched the production company.

The following year, 1967, Syberberg again returned to a subject he had worked with for television. In 1965 he had interviewed Count Konrad Pocci, and the materials resulted in two short features of resp. 25 and 21 minutes' length. It is not clear if the full-length documentary was created from the same materials or grew out of new interviews. *Die Grafen Pocci: Einige Kapitel zur Geschichte einer Familie* (The Counts Pocci: Some Chapters in the History of a Family) is 92 minutes long and the fourth non-fiction film. There also exists an abridged version of twenty-eight minutes, *Konrad Albert Pocci, der Fußballgraf vom Ammerland: Das vorläufig letzte Kapitel einer Chronik der Familie Pocci* (Konrad Albert Pocci, the

Soccer Count of Ammerland: the Last Chapter, for the Time Being, of a Chronicle
of the Dynasty Pocci). It is Syberberg's first movie in color. It features a dynasty as
well as an individual. The film begins and ends with the portrait of Konrad Albert
Pocci, the last scion of an aristocratic family and an unusual representative of his
class. And in that lies a major attraction for Syberberg.

In the film, Pocci lives on the family estate of Ammerland on the Starnberg
Lake, where in 1886 King Ludwig II had drowned under unexplained
circumstances. Instead of repairing the old dilapidated castle, the count accepts its
decline as part of the "gentle law" of nature and of his own philosophy, in which
noblesse oblige has assumed a new meaning. He has become a farmer and caretaker
of his land. His love concerns nature, not buildings. This individualist (some would
call him an excentric) thinks nothing of driving into Munich in his all-purpose farm
vehicle and take in at the fanciest hotel. Except for an occasional game of soccer or
a session with his percussion instruments, he lives a quiet life in harmony with the
surrounding forest and fields. Devoid of political ambition or thirst for publicity, he
prefers a productive existence on the periphery of society.

Among the ancestors, the grandfather stands out. Franz Pocci was a contemporary of Ludwig II and Richard Wagner, their benevolent antipode at the royal
court in Munich. Under Ludwig I he had served as master of ceremonies and court
jester.[7] A dilettante in the best sense, he composed, sketched, and wrote, especially
for children. Among his literary output one finds plays for marionette and puppet
theaters. Syberberg refers to marionettes on several occasions, and introduces
marionettes, puppets and dolls in some of his films.

Neither quietism nor mystic inwardness suffices to describe this movie,
although these elements are present. Nor does the Bavarian dialect and setting
qualify it for the *Heimat-Film* label. It presents an unsentimental, untimely, and
timeless wisdom, as well as a heritage in the process of change: the decline,
Untergang, of the aristocracy and everything for which it stands. It has simply
become a photogenic postromantic relic with crumbling castles of no social
significance. Recognizing this, Konrad Pocci, or rather Syberberg, seeks nobility
in the human heart and harmony with nature. This is conveyed in a visual narrative
divided into segments or chapters. Syberberg also makes use of montage. In both
content and technique the film bears an unmistakable Syberberg stamp. But to judge
from the paucity of literature on this movie, it appears to have met with indifference
outside of Bavaria.

During the late sixties Syberberg concentrated all his energy on moviemaking.
Only in the seventies did he begin the dialogue with the public through the printed
medium again. He had now settled permanently in Munich. One would have
expected him to embrace the cinematic program set forth in the "Oberhausen
Manifesto" from the early sixties. It was natural for his generation to affirm the new
and experimental, considering the censorship of German film production, first
under Hitler, then under Allied occupation. But Syberberg chose to go his own way
artistically while remaining engaged socially. He and his cineaste colleagues lived
in an intellectual climate vibrant with social, political, and aesthetic polemics. In

1968 the tension erupted in student and worker revolts all over Western Europe, and to some extent in the US, where the emphasis shifted to protests against the Vietnam War. For West German filmmakers, Munich had become a center of creativity and debate, although not as dominant as pre-war Berlin had been or old-time Hollywood in the US. The emerging new generation became known as the makers of the New German Cinema. They were outspoken, critical, and talented. In spite of numerous shared characteristics, Syberberg distinguished himself as an individualist from the beginning. Thomas Elsaesser states that the "early films of Syberberg or Herzog, for instance, were to a remarkable degree objects *sui generis*, outside any recognizable tradition of film-making either commercial or avant-garde".[8] Elsaesser may be thinking of Syberberg's visual technique here, for in content the films between 1968 and 1970 clearly did respond to outside impulses. But the fact that places them in a category apart is Syberberg's aesthetic program. As he has stated on several occasions, "Form ist Moral (form is morality). For years this enigmatic pronouncement could hardly be interpreted by observers as anything more than an artist's reluctance to settle for compromises and, so his detractors claimed, display his arrogance. Only in retrospect, after *Parsifal*, can one perceive dimly what he meant.

The most important source of information about these early years of professional life is *Syberbergs Filmbuch* of 1976, in which he takes stock of ten years of creative activity. Most published studies on Syberberg rely heavily on this source. However, they do not pay much attention to the sections dealing with his thoughts on film and aesthetics, probably because they failed to see anything worthwhile in them. Syberberg achieved that effect deliberately. As the omniscient narrator he often offers bits and pieces on a given topic and scatters them so as to distract the reader. Repeatedly obliterating his footprints, as it were, he forces the reader to follow the discussion closely and flip back and forth to collect the pieces. But in the end one is still left with an incomplete puzzle game. This exasperating method led to predictable results: misunderstanding or neglect of the issues most important to him. In those passages where Syberberg discusses a topic uninterruptedly, the text often fails to convey his ideas clearly. It is the same principle at play; he attempts to communicate but is unwilling to share everything with everybody. He offers hints rather than elucidation. On the other hand, minor or peripheral issues are debated clearly and often passionately. In Germany his persona has become associated with his assertive, uncompromising views on such exoteric issues. Even they are often misunderstood and distorted by the press, while the central concerns, especially those on form and morality, have gone unnoticed.

The following remarks will concentrate on only a few of Syberberg's state-ments about his early non-fiction films and aesthetics. Again, the vocabulary anticipates motifs and themes characteristic of later work, such as dreams or naïveté, or names such as Georges Méliès, Albrecht Dürer, and Caspar David Friedrich. Read without the benefit of hindsight, much of this is bewildering. At times he deliberately confuses the public. For instance, the following statement invites the reader to jump to conclusions: "I must love my object or topic to be able to present it; that excludes polemical and agitation films and leaves plenty for other directors to do."[9] Of course this sentence became a scandalon after his *Hitler*-film a few years later. Many asked if he admired the dictator. This illustrates the kind of misunderstanding Syberberg provokes knowingly. The accusers overlooked the fact that this film does not portray the historical Hitler as much as the Hitler potential in every human being. Still, the director leaves room for confusion and has continued to do so in many publications. He masters the art of speaking out of both corners of his mouth, knowing full well that the critics will only perceive what they want or recognize. Applying his infamous statement to the four films introduced so far, one understands that the individuals portrayed mean more to him than revealed in the chapters on each of them. Kortner, Schneider, and Pocci are all representatives of their world, which they preserve and enhance through their life or art. Syberberg cares about the past and does not want it obliterated and forgotten. Rather, this heritage should be remembered, even if it hurts, and, as necessary, be transmuted into a better world for the future.

The criteria distinguishing the documentaries from fiction-movies are discussed in five points in the *Filmbuch* (55–60). The already mentioned love for the subject must present it honestly and free of distortions and with historical loyalty and veracity. Syberberg uses the word *Treue* here, which in its older form covered both loyalty and truthfulness, as the English cognate still does in *true love*. He also emphasizes the craft involved, much as a member of the old guilds would take pride in his work, fusing skills and art in the service of a higher objective. This point leads to the inherent "balance" of the product. To achieve this equilibrium, a film may contain repetitions and variations on a theme, in order to present several sides of an important idea (57). The procedure accounts for the length of his later films. One recognizes in this statement also a characteristic of his output as a whole, in which numerous quotations and self-quotations form a pattern. The fifth point focuses on the choice of the topic, which has to possess representative qualities.

To Syberberg film is "the continuation of life by other means, thus not a mirror or reproduction" (56). This view applies also to the documentaries, but in them he at least tries to observe the traditional unities of place and time. The self-imposed restriction is intended primarily, one assumes, to maintain the link with an Aristotelian tradition. And finally, all his films reveal a metaphysical perspective, "Es geht hier um die Darstellung eines Makrokosmos am Mikrokosmos" (It is about presenting a macrocosm through a microcosm, 56). Each of them would, then, contain on a small scale the salient features of the overall oeuvre, perhaps in the form of a *mise en abyme* component or a sefirotic repeat borrowed from the Kabbalah. The untimely choice of words reveals the affinity for the metaphysical tradition as a vehicle for aesthetic expression.

The documentaries do not show as readily as the fiction films Syberberg's involvement in all aspects of their production. But, although others supplied much of the dialogue (literary texts and voices), Syberberg selected the topic, guided the statements through his questions, chose the literary selections in the Kortner-films, and gave the material its form. In brief, he wrote much of the scripts. This he continued to do also with his fiction films. From the beginning, then, he joined the ranks of German film authors or *auteurs*. As scriptwriter, director, and producer he gained control, and more importantly, the artistic liberty to give form to his ideas without interference.

As a film author Syberberg does not invent his stories entirely. He usually borrows ideas from one or more literary and historical sources and adapts them for his purposes. This he did also in 1968 with *Scarabea: Wieviel Erde braucht der Mensch?* (Scarabea: How Much Land Does a Person Need?). The subtitle refers to Leo Tolstoy's nine-part story of 1886 that offered the basic fable: Pahóm, a Russian peasant, makes a deal with the Bashkirs that would let him acquire as much land as he can walk around in one day. Although warned in a dream that the Bashkir chief is really the Devil tempting him, the man becomes greedy, overexerts himself, and collapses in exhaustion at sunset. All the land he now needs is the six feet for his grave. Syberberg transposes the plot to present-day Sardinia. The peasant has become the innkeeper Bach from Homburg, played by Walter Buschhoff. He travels as a tourist to Sardinia, where local bandits engage him in a deal. The tempter is now a beautiful woman. But in the course of the events, the visitor gains enough insights to undergo a transformation. No longer does he thirst after land and a profitable hotel business. He would really prefer to settle among the natives and share their simple life in what looks to him like a paradise.

Mythic symbolism permeates Sardinian traditions suggesting archetypal significance. For instance, a slaughter scene evokes a pagan sacrifice. To the blood and gore Syberberg adds sex and mother's milk (a circle of dancing women spray the tourist with their milk). Also important structurally are the dream passages and the movie-within-the-movie. This *mise en abyme* segment introduces the most obvious element of parody, showing a movie team shooting a western in the ruins of a chapel. In addition to the movie industry, other targets of parody are modern attitudes, mass tourism, and materialism. These aspects of modern society mingle with Sardinian customs, older German culture in the form of literary quotations, and ancient myth. All this in a landscape where other teams had filmed stories from the Bible. Many German critics found this too much to stomach. By far the most revolting scenes were the slaughter-sacrifice that made some viewers faint, and the maggots in a horse carcass. Syberberg practices his own version of Brechtian alienation here. Many of the critics voiced their objection and refused to acknowledge the mythic dimension. Clearly, the basic plot did not suffice in the eyes of the director, since Tolstoy had already earned credit for the invention. Syberberg's fondness for Tolstoy grew from more than literary admiration. Not only did this aristocrat and mystic withdraw to his country estate to live closer to nature in his old age; he was also a heretic. This can best be gleaned from his writings *My Confession*, *My Religion*, and the posthumous *Memoirs of a Madman*. His views brought about a rupture with the Orthodox Church.[10] Although the Tolstoy text does not display a mystical orientation apart from the dream, Syberberg adds a related dimension with symbolism, creating so to speak mythic shadows for modern characters and events. Even the vermin in the cadaver displays links with the esoteric tradition. A related example taken from modern literature might be the intestinal cancer in Umberto Eco's novel *Foucault's Pendulum*. The notion is familiar to afficionados of metaphysical lore. It continues the motif introduced in the Schiller-rehearsal with the name Wurm, German for "worm," which is a linguistic variant of the serpent and dragon in Western traditions. Syberberg also includes the word in his clips from *Urfaust*, where Gretchen refers to her baby as her little *Wurm* in the prison scene. He will reintroduce the *Wurm* in all its semantic variations in later films. Also the numerous lion references recur in Leo Tolstoy's name, which in turn links up with the motif of nobility in Syberberg's own system of myth. One finds another aristocrat among the actors. Furthermore, the heretical element surfaces in the name of the leading actress, Nicoletta Macchiavelli, recalling the author of *The Prince*. The title character embodies the strongest mythical presence both in character and name. Reminiscent of Hermes-Tadzio in Thomas Mann's *Death in Venice*, Scarabea beckons the tourist to join a different world. The name evokes the scarab, a beetle venerated in ancient Egypt as a symbol of eternal life. Amulets shaped as scarabs were often placed in the bandage wrappings of mummies to assure safe passage for the soul of the departed. But the mythic symbolism in the movie was lost on many German moviegoers. The movie elicited strong reactions with more rejection than approval at home, and with praise in Switzerland and Austria. There was no denying its merit as a work of art, earning the director the German Critics' Award and another award at the film festival of San Sebastian. The film was first released in Munich on January 1, 1969.

One detects a critical stance in all of Syberberg's films, not explicitly towards the subject, but against certain flaws in contemporary society. Some of his literary characters, for instance the lovers in *Kabale und Liebe*, function as puppets speaking for Syberberg. In *Scarabea* he resorted to parody. In the following movie this criticism becomes blunt and direct. With an English title, *Sex-Business Made in Pasing* of 1969 concentrates on the German movie industry. As with the earlier documentaries, Syberberg's subject represents something besides himself. The porno filmmaker Alois Brummer exemplifies the malaise of German cinema, and it in turn reflects German society. The economy of West Germany of the sixties had recovered from the effects of World War II. As prosperity had spread throughout society, a succession of trends accompanied the growing affluence. Starting with the gluttony wave celebrating good cuisine after years of deprivation and rationing, one soon witnessed the car wave followed by the travel wave, and finally, the sex wave. The Pill and changing attitudes transformed the tone of the media. Even respectable news magazines and family-oriented journals began to display unprecedented amounts of mostly female skin on their cover pictures. And the movie industry led the way. But after the advent of television, German cinema began to experience a steady decline in the number of patrons. As profits dwindled, the industry decided that sex was the solution to the problem. Sexually oriented fare had previously been relegated to the red-light districts, but now softcore movies began to fill the boulevard theaters. Alois Brummer was one of those directors who amassed a fortune by supplying the movie distributors with the kind of product they wanted.

This trend corrupted the market-driven German film industry, and Syberberg attacks that condition. Again he concentrates on one individual with interviews and observation of Brummer directing a Bavarian porno project. In one scene Brummer discusses how the cowgirl, *das Cowgirl*, is seduced by a count and then explains the adventures of the seven daughters of the countess. Never mind the formula: Cinema as entertainment had been brought to its lowest possible denominator. Alois Brummer is disarmingly frank about his objectives and lack of artistic pretension. Syberberg treats him kindly.

Here and there the visual narrative is interrupted by printed information and statistics on the German cinema industry, underscoring the documentary nature of the film. In this it resembles the structure of silent movies with their screens of titles and captions.

The English title appears incongruous at first glance. But along with the Bavarian cowgirl it also satirizes the German eagerness to copy anything coming out of Hollywood, preferably the worthless products. Only a few years later some of the most respected German directors catered so blatantly to the English-speaking market that they created their German movies with English dialogue from the beginning. Syberberg chose only an English title. His satire did not go far enough, it seems. His film was censored in Paris because it includes clips from Brummer's movies. Five years later, a more lenient attitude allowed Brummer's own movies to be shown there. *Sex-Business Made in Pasing* met with much public and critical acclaim in Germany. But while it netted the director additional honors, among them the German Film Award in 1970 (silver ribbon), it also earned him the status of a *persona non grata* with the powerful German movie industry.

This tension had consequences for the next film project, the second with Christian Blackwood behind the camera. *San Domingo* appeared in 1970. The plot is based on Heinrich von Kleist's story "The Engagement in St. Domingo." His two young lovers, the Swiss Gustav von der Ried and the mulatto Toni, meet and die on the Caribbean island of St. Domingo during the revolution of 1803. Participants and victims, they are caught in a net of violence, intrigue, deception, and misunderstanding. As in *Kabale und Liebe,* truth prevails too late to save them. Syberberg would resort to other texts by Kleist for later works.

The director had originally wanted to set the plot in the former German colonies in Africa (*Filmbuch*, 52). This would have connected the plot with the German history of the Second Reich, when Bismarck led Germany to "acquire" colonies overseas. History plays a prominent role in Syberberg's work, but this time he reduced it to a brief remark in print. He opted instead for a setting fraught with tension much closer in time and space: contemporary Bavaria. A young boy from an affluent family meets the daughter of a German woman and a black American occupation soldier in an environment of rebellious outsiders, mostly the underground scene of alienated youth, drug users, leather-clad motorcycle gangs prone to violence, political activists, and budding terrorists. These years marked the Baader-Meinhof gang's decline from idealists to criminals, at the same time as the Red Cells, sometimes with the blessing of the East German Secret Service, began to infiltrate Western Europe and spread their terrorism. The movie concludes with a warning by Eldridge Cleaver against ignoring the troubled young if anarchy is to be avoided. More than a diagnosis, *San Domingo* sadly enough became prophetic.

Again one recognizes many typical themes. Among them are a decadent society ripe for revolution and destruction; a young naïve fool who perishes through intrigues, much like Wagner's Siegfried (one could compile a list of parallels with the *Nibelungen Ring*), and a mixture of languages, most conspicuously Bavarian dialect. As Syberberg himself pointed out, faces again serve as landscapes revealing inner storms and sunny moments. Also worth mentioning are the use of alienation and an ensemble mixing professional and amateur actors. The director refers to the latter as lay people, *Laien*, as if contrasting them with the initiated members of a religious order or closed society. The theme of nobility recurs with some scenes playing close to King Ludwig II's Neuschwanstein, and in veiled form through the name of the leading actor, Michael König. *König* means "king."

The movie had its premiere on October 11, 1970 in Munich. While young audiences flocked to see it, the reviewers found much to criticize. The appeal to rebellious youth and the alternate culture was condemned as opportunism and speculation. The critics also did not care for the attempt to merge documentary reporting with a love story adapted from literature. Nonetheless, the movie received recognition as well. This time two of the cast members earned top honors at the German Film Awards: the camera man, Christian Blackwood, received the gold ribbon for photography, and the same honor went to Amon Düül II for his music. For later projects Syberberg chose mainly music by eighteenth and nineteenth century composers. He would also abandon contemporary plots in favor of stylized art cinema with a more clearly pronounced Janus-faced orientation towards past and present.

For the first time with this film Syberberg bypassed the established distribution system of the movie industry. He knew he had not ingratiated himself with his previous film and anticipated the revenge of the system. That his strategy raised eyebrows transpires in the reviews of *San Domingo*. Many German critics commented sarcastically on his unorthodox procedure. To an outsider, the structure of German film subsidies at that time appeared admirable. Those working inside the system knew first hand the cost in accommodation and the pressure to conform to a market-oriented business. Syberberg was not the only film director to challenge the industry. The director Jean-Marie Straub, for instance, found that avant-garde and nonconformist filmmakers were soon frozen out of funding and the distribution network. The only outlets for their films, Straub stated, "is Channel Three on television. It is obvious, a film made outside the system will never get inside. The system takes revenge."[11] And these directors were at the mercy of television if they hoped to recoup at least part of their expenses and present their work publicly. The situation provoked counter measures. Together with a handful other filmmakers, among them Herzog, Fassbinder, and Reitz, Syberberg took the initiative to create an alternative support system. In Munich they established the Arri Cinema as an outlet to the public, soon followed by similar enterprises in Hamburg, Berlin, and other cities. They now had to handle all aspects of publicity and distribution themselves, and apparently succeeded beyond expectation. Many private owners, and even chains, of movie theaters began to accept their films. This almost American spirit of enterprise continued with the establishment of the *Filmverlag der Autoren* (publishing house for film authors), in close cooperation with *Arbeitsgemeinschaft Kino*, an organization of movie theaters specializing in art cinema. For a short while, this enterprise coordinated all the movies ignored by the established distribution system. In discussing these accomplishments of the break-away group, Syberberg calls the targeted spectators "the remnant of our audience" (*Filmbuch*, 104). The movie patrons who had not yet been lost to television or mindless, titillating entertainment were for the most part well educated. Syberberg compares this minority with the public that had previously supported the national theaters for which the German literary giants had written their plays. This may sound elitist, but it also evokes a minority of a different kind. In his book on heretics and poets, Eitel Timm describes Sebastian Franck's *catholica* or community of believers as "der kleine Rest" (the little remnant), which is not tied to time or place, but forms a spiritual, invisible body.[12] This idea of an invisible church of dissenters characterizes the history of heresy. Syberberg operates with a similar concept and vocabulary. He also uses another expression on the same page that strengthens the association with religious nonconformism. He refers to the success of the Arri Cinema as a breakthrough, *Durchbruch* (104). The word sounds innocent enough, but political, literary, and metaphysical echoes reverberate throughout the passage. For instance, the breakthrough is what the protagonist in Thomas Mann's *Doktor Faustus* is striving for and achieves at an exorbitant cost. He succeeds as the Devil specifies, at the price of isolation and renunciation of everything dear to most people. Clearly, Syberberg identifies with the transgressor, or at least with his position, and knows the risks. His stand in relation to prevailing views, regardless of issue, resembles that of the heretic who removes himself beyond the confines of orthodoxy, or that of a prophet the majority prefers to ignore. They would rather consider him a Don Quixote beating windmills. Syberberg probably considers himself a Sisyphos pushing boulders.

With the passion of youth and conviction the director made himself the spokesman for his own and the dissenters' views. During his initial, close cooperation with the break-away film authors, he returned to the printed word as a supplementary mode of dialogue. The flood of articles all concern the situation of German cinema and its society. One of them accompanied the release of *San Domingo* and became a manifesto for the new movement, "An die Kinobesitzer und die Presse anstelle eines sogenannten Werberatschlags'"(To the Cinema Owners and the Press in lieu of a Socalled Advertisement Tip), reprinted first in the *Filmbuch* (223–24). Here he describes the malaise of the German cinema and the measures taken by his group, and concludes with an invitation to other filmmakers to join them in an attempt to revitalize cinema. Although not stated explicitly, cinema always means film as art. And as Syberberg would make clear over the years, art has a very special mission in his sick society. But to the targets of his criticism he seemed merely confrontational and provocative. Also of little consequence, since in 1970 his aesthetics had not yet been recognized by the public. However, he was intent on pursuing his program. That meant to stay put and continue the struggle. He was by now a family man with an Austrian-born wife, Helga Elisabeth, and a little daughter, Amelie. Protective of their privacy and safety, he does not divulge much about them to the public. With the success of his early movies, Syberberg was soon able to buy a townhouse in the part of Munich called Schwabing, known as the artists' quarter. With its enclosed garden in the back, it would later serve him as his own refuge, ghetto, and private paradise.[13] A few years later, he added a room-sized lean-to winter garden, enabling the family to enjoy a verdant view year round. This miniature paradise soon became the favorite room of the house. To the transplant from the north, Munich had become home, although it never ceased to feel like an exile.

In 1970 Syberberg could look back on seventeen years of creative work, starting with the film recordings of the Brecht performances. Most artists measure their career from the time when they begin to earn a living with their art. By such counting one would reach back to 1965 and the release of the first Kortner film. Or perhaps 1963 when Syberberg started his freelance work for television. After all, during the ten years preceeding 1963 the filmmaker was not professionally active. But he seems to include the amateur recordings of Brecht as an introduction to his career. At the age of thirty-four he returned to the early attempts. By now Brecht was dead and the reels had increased in value as documentaries. Syberberg edited the old materials in 1971, added sound in the form of voice-over, transferred it all to 35 mm film, and called it *Nach meinem letzten Umzug* (After My Last Move). He presented it to the public during the 1972 international film festival in Berlin at the concurrent "Internationales Forum des Jungen Films." The timing of this release seems carefully calculated. He made his debut at the age of seventeen, and waited for seventeen years, until he was thirty-four, before returning to the work. The numbers 17 and 34 are important in numerology.[14] In 1993 an edited version came out on video, now called *Syberberg filmt bei Brecht* (Syberberg Films at Brecht['s Theater]).

The video version includes clips from three plays plus a lecture by the Germanist Professor Dr. Hans Mayer. The first play is Brecht's *Puntila and His Servant Matti*, presented as silent film with captions and an occasional voice-over by Syberberg. In addition to two title screens, thirty-four captions accompany the moving pictures. The selections concentrate on the wedding scene. This section ends with a switch to Syberberg himself addressing the viewers, while a small television set shows the talking head of Dr. Mayer. This head soon fills the screen, reminiscing and lecturing about Brecht and the next selection, Goethe's *Urfaust*. Dr. Mayer had worked with Brecht on this production. He was thus in a unique position to enliven an academic presentation with personal experience. He returns later with some comments on Mephistopheles' transformations halfway through *Urfaust* and again at the end of the segment, with brief sound clips used to supplement Syberberg's voice-over. The third unit presents excerpts from *The Mother* by Brecht and Gorki, in memory of Helene Weigel, who played the title role. Besides being the leading actress of the Berliner Ensemble, she was also married to Brecht. This part of the film runs without interrupting captions, and Syberberg's spoken commentary drifts across many topics, as he does in his books. The film concludes with some silent montage producing unexpected interaction between characters in *Puntila* and *Urfaust*.

One additional theme begins to emerge in Syberberg's work around this time: democracy. Like a negative, it had not been developed yet in his films, only its precursor, the revolution, and its decline or distortion as mindless, manipulative society. Among the comments on the Brecht filming in the *Filmbuch,* Brecht is quoted as stating that he was all in favor of the democratization of art; but knowledge is necessary to understand art, thus he was in favor of the greater distribution of knowledge (62). The quotation appears in the margin and out of context. Its only overt connection to the narrative is Brecht himself, since Syberberg does not discuss the political or aesthetic views of the playwright in the book, nor does he refer to the quotation later. The cryptic statement is probably included because it expresses an opinion shared by Brecht and Syberberg alike. That Brecht favored democratization of art, one takes for granted. Every artist wants to reach an audience. Brecht cultivated the persona of a proletarian in solidarity with the masses. But he also made the statement that fodder comes before morality. Poor people who struggle for survival are not yet ready for the luxury of art. According to Brecht, art would not provide the kind of stimulation that someone with an empty stomach could appreciate. Certain basic needs must be met first. But even that would not suffice, if we understand the quotation correctly. Knowledge is a prerequisite for the appreciation of art. Unless the public has reached a level of receptivity and discrimination, the artist's message cannot be understood. Obviously, Brecht esteemed art and its mission highly, but found the masses insufficiently "educated" to benefit from his art. His theater is intended to function as a catalyst for critical thought. In that respect it shares several similarities with Schiller's vision of the stage as a *moralische Anstalt* (moral institution). But Brecht does not see this as a reality yet. One is led to surmise that Brecht aims at two objectives: both "educating" the people with thought-provoking entertainment, and, in the meantime, addressing a limited audience in an undemocratic fashion. In other words, operating on two levels. Syberberg adopted this *modus operandi.* It functions, for instance, in his numerous critical comments on democracy. A Neoplatonist at heart, he knows that it always has fallen short of its ideal. He distinguishes between democracy as an ideal and the flawed "socalled democracy" in our present world. "Democratization of art" in his Germany has meant a vulgarization and demeaning of the ideal. And in politics, democracy often means only a market-oriented economy, a prostitution of the ideal that makes him bristle. His discussion of the Brecht-film does not develop this topic, but the quotation identifies a concern to which he will return in later publications.

Some reviews treated the film kindly, recognizing its historical importance. But Syberberg may have miscalculated the West German public's interest in Brecht.

After all, unlike the Jewish refugees from Nazi Germany, the playwright had fled due to his communist sympathies. Having to appear later before the House Committee on Un-American Activities, he left his exile in the US and returned to settle in Soviet-occupied East Berlin. The fact was neither forgotten nor forgiven in American-dominated West Germany. Consequently, the reception of Syberberg's documentary ranged from lukewarm interest to indifference. But Brecht's life and work continued to appeal to Syberberg, now also for personal reasons. Not only Brecht's non-conformist views during the *Faust*-debate, but also his need to adapt and choose texts that were acceptable politically and meaningful artistically assumed a new significance for Syberberg. For by now he too faced powerful opposition. Due to the rejection of those movie critics whose ire he had provoked before, his own struggle intensified.

Syberberg had attacked the entire German movie industry, not just the critics. But in the early seventies it appears that the counter attacks came primarily from the reviewers. If a critic published a negative assessment with well-founded arguments, Syberberg probably accepted it tacitly, because that kind of responsible critiquing does not provoke any comments from him. It is the tendentious and malicious treatment by the German press he presents in his *Filmbuch*, contrasting it with the positive reception abroad, especially in France. He names names and quotes extensively, exposing examples of journalism at its worst. Even if one should distrust the one-sided presentation, one cannot help concluding that the profession of German movie reviewers includes many unworthy of the title. Syberberg's excerpts expose their sins, consisting of "inaccuracies," distortions, sarcasms, and tendentious omissions. In several cases, the journalists wrote reviews of films they had not seen. And quite often they would copy from each other. The cliché about writing with "passion and poison-pen" describes the situation well. In the early stages of the feud, the critics resorted to boycott through this kind of reviews. In the eighties, their continued retaliation took the form of silence, a more potent strategy.

Syberberg coined a flippant term for his predicament, *zwischen Buff und Puff*, or between the would-be-expert and the whorehouse. The brothel (*Puff*) mentality of the German movie industry had already received a broadside in *Sex-Business Made in Pasing*. The ambiguous term could equally well relate to the alchemical puffer, an unworthy, greedy practitioner of the art who is blind to the spiritual dimension of the pursuit. The other word, *Buff*, is a loanword from English (opera buff, afficionado), but pronounced with a German *u*, as in *pussycat*, to rhyme with *Puff*. Syberberg shifts the emphasis from the dillettante enthusiast to the clique-and-claque follower. He mentions in passing the Jockey Club influence as an example from the nineteenth century, evoking a parallel with Richard Wagner's fiasco in Paris (*Filmbuch* 113). The composer had refused to move the bacchanal ballet in *Tannhäuser* from the first to the second act just to accommodate the members of the Jockey Club. They would habitually dine in the club and arrive as a group at the opera in time to ogle the ballet, which traditionally appeared in the second act. Their noisy disapproval of Wagner's audacity spelled disaster for the production.

Many modern readers might not recognize the Jockey Club as a reference to Wagner, but think merely of an exclusive group of insiders. The comparison illustrates the correlation between Syberberg's films and books. In both modes of expression he pursues the same objectives and with similar means. In this case, the Jockey Club recalls Wagner, but in veiled form. Only those familiar with Wagner's biography will recognize it. Of course the term also refers to the reviewers, the *Buffs*, who boycott the director's work. Besides, the *Buff* resembles the *Büffel*, which besides "buffalo" also means a "boor." By extension, the term establishes a base for comparison between the film director and the composer.

Both in word and image Syberberg operates with polyvalence. He develops a net of references that trigger associations. These again intersect and link up in numerous combinations, creating surprising connections and coherence. The general reader will often not be familiar with his frame of reference and therefore fail to see the subtext. For example, in the same sentence where the Jockey Club appears one also finds "poisoning of the wells" (113). The reader assumes that the attackers accuse the author of poisoning the wells in the sense of dirtying the nest or harming the community. History adds a nuance: In the Middle Ages, epidemics were often attributed to "poisoning of the wells" at the hands of the Jewish minority, and persecution resulted. By applying the old scape-goat expression, Syberberg aligns himself with the persecuted minority. Stretching his frame of reference, he asks rhetorically in the same passage if some phenomena in contemporary German cinema may not betray the *Spitze einer Eiszeitgesellschaft*, (the tip of an ice age society). This is a peculiar fusion of metaphors and incomprehensible unless one remembers the support for Hanns Hörbiger's cosmic ice theories in Nazi Germany and its use in Syberberg's films to come. Thus the phrase does not refer only to a frozen, dead civilization as opposed to a flourishing culture, but also to the ideological virus of the past still endemic in German society.

This style of discourse-through-association sometimes leads to thought connections that the author may or may not have intended. For example, the rhyme of *Buff* and *Puff* brings to mind a third German word, *Muff*, which means "mustiness." It was heard frequently during the revolt of 1968 when the students demanded university reforms and the removal of academic "mustiness," such as undemocratic structure and procedures. Syberberg experienced this unrest at close hand in Munich. But a likelier source for *Muff* might be its repeated use in Ernst Bloch's mini-chapter by that title and in his essay on Karl May, both in his *Erbschaft dieser Zeit,* known in English as *Heritage of Our Times.*[15] Syberberg quotes Bloch's writings frequently, considering him a kindred spirit. The passage called "Mustiness" is an elegant aperçu discussing a suffocating legacy that children absorb. They "suffer until they become like their father" (12). Even the rebel who refuses to go along must breathe in the stale air. Syberberg encountered lots of such stale air and mustiness, but he refrains from using the word in this context.

The textual examples mentioned above illustrate Syberberg's prose. This style does not lend itself to perusal or superficial reading. It demands readers willing to reflect on the statements. It provokes a dialogue in every paragraph, and not the least, it calls for rereading and reordering of passages, so as to restructure the text into a coherent whole that makes sense to the reader. This challenge to the readers parallels the demands on the viewers. His films have found many viewers who recognize them as works of art functioning on several rungs of complexity. But the German movie critics have displayed little inclination to grapple with such aesthetic challenges. They have therefore largely ignored or rejected his works. This has not been the case abroad. The discrepancy in reception was already quite pronounced with Syberberg's next movie.

Chapter 3

International Renown

Ludwig

In his *Filmbuch* Syberberg returns repeatedly to the topic of the German cinematic crisis and his efforts to overcome it. This includes his efforts to gain acceptance for German film abroad. That his own movies enjoyed success outside Germany is a matter of record. The way he presents his struggles and the crisis in the book could easily lead the readers to assume that he contributed greatly to the hard-won international recognition of the younger German filmmakers. He undoubtedly shares in the credit, but forgets to mention that he belongs to a generation of highly talented directors. His own success resulted from a calculated strategy, he informs the readers. Trying to be different, he decided on a very "German" subject, he states in his *Filmbuch* (102). He bristles at the "grotesque" insinuations by some voices at home that the New German Cinema achieved success abroad easily. On the contrary, he claims, his generation had to carry the cross of a painful legacy that had created a world-wide anti-German bias (100).

Syberberg's resolve to embark upon his planned program meant a "radically new beginning" (55). In retrospect, one recognizes that his use of *radical* has retained a connection with the Latin origin, *radix*, meaning "root." It points here primarily but not exclusively to the root or history of the German malaise. This radically new beginning started in 1972 in Paris with the premiere of his *Ludwig: Requiem für einen jungfräulichen König* (Ludwig: Requiem for a Virginal King). It was instantly recognized for what it is: unabashedly different, artificial, and yes, thoroughly German, an art film that soon gained a cult following. It played to a full house in Paris for six months until the owner of the cinema mysteriously declared bankrupt, closed down, remodeled, and reopened the establishment as a four-screen theater. The legal maneuvering cheated Syberberg of much of the profits from that run, but the success of the movie everywhere else abroad must have consoled its maker (*Filmbuch*, 99).

For its initial release Syberberg had chosen the Marais cinema in Paris. The reason for his choice may lie in the address: 41, rue du Temple. The name derives from the medieval "Temple," the French headquarters of the Knights Templar, located in the Marais neighborhood. Syberberg's work abounds in oblique references to knights and the Knights Templar. This order of warrior monks had been founded to guard the Temple in Jerusalem during the crusades. It flourished for about 200 years until the French king, Philip IV, in conspiracy with Pope Clement V, arrested all the members of the order who were on French soil in a swift, surprise move. The leaders had gathered at their headquarters in Paris for an important meeting in 1307. As Stephen Howarth reports, many of them were burned at the stake as heretics, the order was dissolved, and its properties and wealth confiscated.[1] With the martyrdom began the mystique of the Knights Templar, which has lasted until this day. The Freemasons, for instance, claim to be the spiritual descendants of this order. Even the Nazis found the Knights Templar myth irresistible. When one considers that Hitler outlawed Freemasonry in his Reich, it becomes clear that the mystique has appealed to a wide spectrum of philosophical persuasion. Syberberg is no exception.

At first, one is hard pressed to see any obvious link between Ludwig II of Bavaria and the Parisian grounds of the Temple. But the king adored anything French, and in his more excentric years often imagined conversing with deceased members of the royal French household, some of whom were incarcerated in the restored Temple before being executed during the French Revolution. Like them, Ludwig also became a martyr during political upheaval, and the hushed-up circumstances of his drowning engendered a mystique as pervasive as that of the Templars.

Also another aspect of Syberberg's work comes to mind: his fascination with faces as landscapes. Already his documentary on Romy Schneider has as its subtitle *Anatomy of a Face*. Consistently, and also in *Ludwig*, the director lets the camera focus on the face, capturing every nuance of expression. In the case of the Knights Templar, the mystery surrounding a cherished face or head featured prominently during their trial. The prosecutors accused them of venerating an idol, known in subsequent literature as the Baphomet. Recent research has linked this mystery with the Shroud of Turin, purported to show the face of Christ. It was presumably in the possession of the family of Geoffrey de Charney, one of the highest ranked Templars burned for heresy (Howarth, 310–11). Whatever the merit of such assumptions and theories, legend is stronger than fact, and Syberberg uses related imagery linking Ludwig to this treasured face.

As Christ suffered the Passion, so also Ludwig is presented as a suffering king. He repeatedly laments that he cannot stand the demands of his position and wishes to be relieved of his public office. Similarly, Amfortas in *Parsifal* longs for release from his inherited duty to display the Grail, and even the Bible lets Christ pray on the Mount of Olives, "Remove this cup from me." In other words, the Passion is a shared motif. Another reference to Christ occurs in the visual arrangement of a tableau. Ludwig is seated, while his lover, Count Dürckheim, is kneeling at his side, resting his head against the king's chest. The pose echoes that of Christ and John, the beloved disciple, as it appears in numerous medieval artworks. One such sculpture can be seen in the Museum Mayer van den Bergh in Antwerp. Similar biblical associations arise with other details in the film, such as the foot-washing, the song of the traitor, the prophesy, the pronouncement "Es ist vollbracht," (It is finished) as in John 20.30, and a resurrection. One last and coincidental link deserves mentioning: the trials. Christ's death by execution resulted from a trial. Many of the Knights Templar suffered a similar fate in Paris. Likewise, royal prisoners suffered in the Temple during the Revolution. Even the maker of a film about King Ludwig, who had become the martyred victim of a furtive revolution, suffered from a questionable lawsuit involving the Marais theater. These references can easily strike one as blasphemous, but they nonetheless continue Syberberg's opinion in his book on Dürrenmatt that a spiritual component is a criterion of true art. This kind of faintly religious framework does not have to refer to Christ or be biblical in a literal sense. When, for instance, Ludwig on one of his nocturnal sleigh rides requests a drink of water at a farm house, he impresses a sleepy little girl as an otherworldly apparition. Reminiscing in her old age, this person compares him with the archangel Michael. Such allusions belong to the subtext.

So what is the movie like? Much has been written about it, but the readers are still in the dark. For the most part, interpreters attempt to view it from the perspective of German history, encouraged by Syberberg's own emphasis on the word "German" and by the films that followed. *Ludwig* has become known as the first part of the director's "German Trilogy," with the other two sections being *Karl May* and *Hitler: A Film from Germany*. Naturally, many discussions tend to treat the films about King Ludwig and May as stages in a story about German history leading to the disaster that Hitler represents. And justifiably so. But a better term would be the "German Cycle," since the group of films exceeds three in number.

Syberberg described his choice as a "very German subject matter." *German* has of course been a semantic can of worms for hundreds of years. The word does not define a specific nation in political terms, in spite of numerous attempts to attribute that meaning to it. The old word for "German" or *deutsch* was *tiudisc*, meaning "of the people." Grimm's dictionary defines it both as *teutonicus, germanus* and as *gentilis, popularis, vulgaris.* Thus Syberberg may not think only of his fellow modern compatriots, but also of humanity in broader terms. And the German disaster of the twentieth century certainly affected untold millions of non-Germans, as well. So, while the term *German* possesses national, even nationalistic, overtones in everyday language, one must remain aware of Syberberg's inclination to use words in their polyvalent capacity. The archaic meanings also echo through the current definitions. One might therefore find it helpful to view *Ludwig* both as a political or national statement and as a psychological study. With this in mind, the following comments approach the film diegesically.

The running time for this fiction film is two hours and fifteen minutes. It is divided into two main sections, each with its separate subtitle: "Teil 1: Der Fluch" (Part 1: The Curse) and "Teil 2: Ich war einmal" (Part 2: Once Upon a Time I Was). The main title, the first subtitle, and Syberberg's name appear up front, the rest of the credits at the end. Somehow, then, Syberberg remains close to the curse. The content is further subdivided into more than thirty independent units with titles or headlines. Reminiscent of Brecht's theater and the era of silent movies, this arrangement consists of separate, static episodes of various lengths. Much like facets on a gem stone, they present several aspects of the topic, but they do not add up to a coherent story. The following descriptions serve as representative examples.

Several early scenes depict the young king's interest in handsome men. As he had dropped Baron Hirschfeld from favor earlier, he himself experiences rejection in scene five, "The King loves de Varicourt and is disappointed by him." As a silent part of the narrative, the ritual footwashing in the background adds a glimpse of tradition, fixes the time to Maundy Thursday of Easter Week, and recalls the Last Supper with impending betrayal of Christ.

Two consecutive episodes feature Empress Elisabeth of Austria. As sister-mother-confidante and possibly lover, she serves as a fictional soundingboard and solace for the king, who pours out his heart to her. Typical of numerous anachronisms in the film, Ludwig dreams of counter measures to prevent the outbreak of World War I, which the prescient king knows is coming. He also knows that this catastrophe will crush the Second Reich that he had witnessed Bismarck found, and that it will abolish the Bavarian monarchy, which is his legacy. These disasters form part of a future that the norns had pronounced to him in the initial "curse." He is powerless to prevent the future from happening. Elisabeth, who in popular lore is considered Ludwig's only and unhappy love for a woman, conjures up associations with Wagner's *Tristan and Isolde* and even more so with Elisabeth in *Tannhäuser.* Syberberg establishes these connections through text and music from the former opera, and through the visible stage backdrops from the latter, and of course through the name. That link puts Ludwig in the position of Tannhäuser, drawing up a cluster of additional connotations. Add to this the fact that Elisabeth wears the collar and hairstyle typical of Elizabeth I of England, a detail that evokes also that monarch as well as her invisible antipode, Mary Stuart. Both queens became as romanticized in the history of their countries as King Ludwig in Bavaria. Besides, Elizabeth I was unmarried, and therefore known as the "virgin queen." Since Ludwig II also remained single, one may see in the similarity in marital status one of Syberberg's reasons for calling him a "virgin king." Actually, he uses the adjective "virginal," *jungfräulich.* However, this virginity does not imply chastity. So why did the director endow the king with the epithet? The older form of the nominal root was in the Middle Ages *juncfrouwe,* which meant primarily a young, unmarried woman of noble rank. More strongly than the modern adjective, its archaic definition would evoke the gender-based usage, emphasizing the feminine side of the king's personality. If one also accepts a spiritual dimension to the king's aspirations (not his conversations with the "spirits" of deceased persons), then one can draw on the semantics of the mystical tradition as well. Meister Eckhart, for example, wrote a famous sermon on the soul as virgin and wife, "Jesus Entered."[2] He associates *virginal* with *ledic* (free, unmarried, void, and disengaged from attachment). Although Meister Eckhart's context is religious, one might transfer the usage to the king's increasing "detachment" from people and affairs of state. Actually, his preoccupation with building a series of enchanting hide-aways is compared by Syberberg to a quest for paradise. A misguided quest, to be sure, since he tried to realize his dreams in this world. A spiritual paradise has no location (*topos*) and must remain a u-*top*-ia. But even if condemned as selfish and excentric, these projects testify to a vision of perceived beauty and imagination. Because he was a king, Ludwig possessed the means to pursue such a quest, at least until he was stopped. A very different link for *virginal* might be the king's birthday. He was born on August 25, that is, under the sign of Virgo. And now the movie leads this Virgin

King to Empress Elisabeth (Sissi), dressed as the British Virgin Queen, in what resembles ironically an alchemical *conjunctio*. The association with the Elizabethan age is strengthened by her reference to Shakespeare in terms that anticipate the prayer at the end of the film. Needless to say, neither Elisabeth nor Ludwig play their roles in the usual documentary fashion. But with the empress, Syberberg also establishes an invisible connection to his documentary on Romy Schneider. Her role as Empress Elisabeth in the Sissi-films forever merged the image of the role with that of the actress in the minds of German movie goers. Sissi and Romy became inseparable. Thus Syberberg could count on an automatic associative link in his German viewers without referring to his own work with overt means. And as the actress portraying the empress in *Ludwig* also plays one of the norns, one begins to glimpse the multi-layered network of characters, allegories, and correspondences. Nothing is as simple as it appears at first glance.

Ludwig's visit to the studio of the sculptress Elisabet Ney presents another confidante with the same name, a similar function, and several hidden connotations.[3] Without the identifying title preceding the episode, the viewer would not have guessed that this austere, chaste-looking woman was an artist. There actually existed a historical connection between the king and the sculptress in that he commissioned her to make a full-sized standing sculpture of him. A plaster copy of this sculpture can been seen in the Elisabet Ney Museum in Austin, Texas, where the artist spent the final years of her life. With her move to the United States and her creativity, Elisabet Ney combines several motifs in the film. None of these come to the fore as clearly as the artist's ability to act as a prophet and priest. Syberberg seems to suggest a link between an artist's creativity and a divinely inspired knowledge of the human predicament and ultimate truths. The artist assumes an oracular function. Actually, such a pronouncement is put in the mouth of one of Ney's contrapuntal contrasts in the film, the actress Mme Bulyowski: "Then the artist turns into a priest, art into liturgical worship, and the stage into a pulpit."[4] This Wagnerian view is a cherished notion in Syberberg's work. And since his Ludwig is at heart an artist, he has also gained insight into what the norns hold in store for him and his country. In the film, his visit to Elisabet Ney imitates Orestes' visit to his sister Iphigenie in Goethe's *Iphigenie auf Tauris*. The furies had punished Orestes by haunting him for murdering his mother, Clytaemnestra. His arrival in Tauris and clandestine mission plunge his priestess sister into inner turmoil. Distraught, she remembers the ancient song about the Fates, "das Lied der Parzen," at the end of act 4. The poem warns humans to fear the gods, especially those humans elevated to exalted positions. The gods can easily hurl them down into the darkest depths, as happened to the Titans. This poem, which the priestess-artist Elisabet Ney recites and which recurs in several scenes, becomes an oracle with gloomy prospects for Ludwig. More so due to the contrast to Goethe's play. As with Kortner's Schiller rehearsal, so also here a German audience would know the content of the play and its ending. Thanks to Iphigenie, Orestes is healed and is able to "save the image of the sister," which refers both to the temple statue of the goddess, his sister, and the feminine side of his own psyche. History (and the movie) denies Ludwig such a happy ending. And by extension, the Song of the Fates warns that the gods not only smite the exalted humans, but also inflict the same cruelty on their descendants. On one level of discourse, this is the lot Syberberg sees for his nation in its present situation.

The second part of the film begins with a long fugal episode, a *mise en abyme* segment named "Nightmare of a King." While two of the other titles include French phrases, this headline is the only title in English. The use of English continues in the second, fourth, and sixth takes as voice-over of distorted radio announcements for Superman, Tarzan, and the Lone Ranger. Belonging to different times and the realm of imagination, the names anticipate acoustically several other links to America that will soon appear visually. Seemingly unrelated to anything, they introduce three soldiers in various uniforms of the nineteenth century. At this point the sequence assumes the appearance of a staged revue, continuing with a Bavarian couple dressed in *Dirndl* and *Lederhosen* dancing the *Schuhplattler*. Before the viewer can speculate on the clash between this kitschy folklore and the preceding military presence, the performers change again. Now a beer hall entertainer, Lola Montez, presents her song-and-dance number. The historical dancer Lola Montez was a would-be Madame Pompadour who had charmed Ludwig's grandfather, Ludwig I. She was forced out of Bavaria in the revolutionary turmoil in Munich in 1848–49. She spent her final years in the United States. In Syberberg's line-up, she takes her place among the political forces trying to change the state of affairs. This Lola is dressed in a translucent fishbone skirt à la Pompadour, similar to what Marlene Dietrich wears as Lola-Lola in *The Blue Angel*. The revealing bodice of shiny scales adds a kinky note, while establishing several other strains of associations. The actress first appears in the "Curse" as one of the norns. She still wears as an ornament the scissors that the norn would use to cut the thread of life. In the "Curse" segment a walking figure wearing a similar scaled bodice exhales smoke through her nostrils like a dragon. She seems to represent a chtonic element, perhaps the maternal python monster overcome by the sun god in Delphi. That might link her in a mother-son relationship with King Ludwig, whom Syberberg describes as the "Sun King of Bavaria" in one of the episodes. Of course the epithet refers to Louis XIV as well. The scaled bodice also anticipates the breastplates of armors in *Parsifal* years later. But to the cinematic Ludwig, the scaled bodice, and the two wearers of such outfits, are insignificant. The viewer recognizes, however, that the dragon forces may have been banned to the netherworld and made powerless, but they are still stirring, as the dancer demonstrates. And Ludwig will also experience a fall similar to that of the Delphic Python and Orestes' family, as he hears again and again, while the norns keep changing their manifestations.

The revue as play-within-the-play continues. In the next number, a Prussian soldier on a bicycle in front of Neuschwanstein pedals around aimlessly for a while and disappears.The proximity of the Prussian helmet and the fairytale castle underscores the political reality: the subjugation of Bavarian autonomy under Prussian-imperial hegemony under Bismarck. The bicycle adds another dimension.

Both the wheels of the bicycle and the rounds that the rider makes accentuate the symbol of the circle. Among other things, the circle expresses the course of time, as measured on a traditional clock face and in the apparent movement of the constellations, especially the zodiac. The juxtaposition of the circular movement and the stationary castle brings together the concepts of time and space. Not so much their hidden relationship from a physicist's and a mystic's viewpoints as their connection to Ludwig's position. His personal space (castle and country) has experienced a decline in power and status, while Prussia has risen to the summit. But its symbol, the helmet, is carried around on the wheels of time. In due course, it too will slip past its zenith and down towards its demise. Time, after all, means the cycle of life with death waiting. Still familiar are its ancient depictions as the Wheel of Fortune and Chronos-Cronos-Saturn-Grim Reaper with the sickle. The fate experienced by Bavaria will, then, as a matter of course also befall Prussia. The verbal oracles had already intimated such downfalls. Now visual language varies the idea. That includes the old pun on *revolution* as a revolt and as a complete perambulation around a circle.

The mournful priestess (Ney) who presides over the next number is interrupted by a midget emerging from under her long garments. This court jester attracts everybody's attention with a loud "yahoo!" before starting his performance of cartwheels. Instead of a Harlequin cap he wears Richard Wagner's signature beret. Of course the composer is present throughout the film, mostly through his music on the soundtrack or in the conversations of others. Here he appears in person before the rulers and the politicians, and they see him as a very small entertainer of primitive tricks. This projection results from the suspicious record of his earlier revolutionary involvement in Dresden as well as his behavior in Munich. And now his cartwheels suggest that he too will experience cycles of ups and downs, and furthermore, that he as a court jester is fully aware of this human predicament.

Of the numerous other segments in this *divertimento*, two especially point to Syberberg's future works. After the king's insane brother, two anachronistic characters entertain the crowd until being chased away: Hitler and SA leader Ernst Röhm dance the rhumba in the wackiest episode of the film. Hitler appears as stiff as a puppet, while Peter Kern as Röhm gives one of the movie's few funny performances. In real life, Röhm was one of the first casualties in Hitler's consolidation of power. During the enforced exit of these two dancers, a Bavarian courtier with a raised arm chasing them out remains ambiguous. Does his posture mean a threatening shooing gesture, or is it a Hitler salute? In this episode, the two possibilities would be mutually exclusive, but the pose clearly anticipates the future. The ambiguity alludes to counterpoint at work.

The following nightmare scene contrasts with the loud and vulgar modernity of the rhumba dancers. With tinkling water supplementing the music of the soundtrack, Karl May slowly makes his entry. His identity is concealed behind the theater mask of the ancient Greek blind seer Tiresias. One soon recognizes him thanks to his supporting companion, the handsome Apache Winnetou. After all, Winnetou is one of Karl May's most popular fictional heroes. By far not so well known are May's play and novels from his late years, all of them with an esoteric bent. His oracular pronouncements in the film are fictitious, but nonetheless appropriate for the old May and useful for Syberberg's film plans.[5] As May-Tiresias addresses King Ludwig, he points out that, because the king knows Wagner's work, he must be aware of "the unholy potential of his people as well." Since May and the other performers appear to Ludwig in his nightmare, their statements and intentions have already moved through his subconscious. But the king ignores the old man, leaving the viewers unsure if he has paid any attention to his warnings.

The periodic close-ups of the king's eyes underscore the psychological nature of the parade of performers. Their voices and figures soon assume a mythic dimension. As Eric Santner points out in one of the few helpful studies of the film, Syberberg tends to endow any historical or political facts that he alludes to with the form and value of allegorical events, as they are "played out between forces and polarities that, according to Syberberg and his particular form of Freudianism, occupy the deep psychological and ideological core of real historical events. From the very beginning of the cycle, Syberberg engages in a dramaturgy of a metaphysically conceived political unconscious" (111). The metaphysical and psychological aspects of *Ludwig* have received less attention in the secondary literature than the political dimension. But Santner at least, encouraged by Syberberg's own references in the *Filmbuch* to his *Trauerarbeit* (work of mourning), examines the concept of grief in the light of Alexander and Margarethe Mitscherlich's book *The Inability to Mourn*, first published in 1967. Of special interest are the blockage and suppression of trauma that prevent the process of healing. The psychological phenomena that prompted the examination of the Mitscherlich team also inform Syberberg's German Cycle. After the German collapse in 1945, the victorious Allies, especially the American occupation forces, imposed a reeducation program on the German population known as dena-zification. Also, in many cases the confrontation with the facts of history produced unintended results, such as denial or refusal to identify with the perpetrators. And often, with blockage. In numerous other cases personal trauma and suffering also resulted in such blockage. The painful past was suppressed and forgotten. But suppressed trauma tends to interfere with the mind sooner or later, causing melancholy and endangering the health of the organism. This difficulty of many older Germans to come to grips with their past provides the cue to much in Syberberg's work. Both Santner and other interpreters therefore attempt to situate his oeuvre in the post-war category of *Trauerarbeit*. But the reviewers seem to sense that *Ludwig* defies any easy classification. For one thing, the historical king died in 1886. That precludes a clear connection to Nazism and the debacle of the twentieth century. The difficulty with fitting the film into a preconceived notion of melancholy and a national malaise has caused most reviews to see in Ludwig only the madness that later infected the nation and the character as being complicitous with, or representative of, that development. And consequently, they avoid discussing the complexities of structure and imagery that cannot be explained or recognized in terms of prevailing film theory. Syberberg operates with a multi-level frame of references that will only become recognizable gradually in the following works. For example, the emphasis on psychological affliction rests on the nexus of melancholy in alchemy and psychology and the semantic origins of being de-ranged (*ver-rückt*) in the Kabbalah. The connection only surfaces in *Parsifal*. For other details one finds parallels in music, for instance the repeated deaths of the king. Syberberg probably found part of this idea in King Ludwig's published correspondence or in Peter Wapnewski's studies about Wagner. In reference to the composer's death, Wapnewski reports that Ludwig considered the demise of "the Worshiped One to be also the last hour of his own life."[6] The emotional, empathetic effect of Wagner's death, the drowning, the beheading, they all kill a part of this cinematic Ludwig, with the last one being the most unexpected. Here he dies in full royal regalia under the guillotine, with his severed head shown to the crowd: a sacrifice marking the end of an era. The revered head and the method of execution allude to the events in Paris, only to reappear in Syberberg's *Parsifal* later.

A dead king is a useful king. Or at least profitable, considering how many tourists his castles attract. He may have been a dream king in the sense that he lived in a dream-like fantasy world, and also as a figure out of a dream world in the eyes of his adoring peasants. But in his death he became a myth, fashioned by the forces that killed him. These forces also project him as a harmless child-sized fairytale Ludwig. At least that is how the viewers see him after the resurrection. This diminutive Ludwig as a bearded child was inspired by the picture on a postcard. The story about it is mentioned in the *Filmbuch* (234–35) and by the circus director in *Hitler*. One learns that the cabaret artist and filmmaker Karl Valentin owned this kitschy card as part of his postcard collection. When Hitler wanted to buy it from him, he refused, resisting the dictator's offer and conditions. Thus again, the Hitler theme informs the Ludwig story, but now silently and imperceptibly. It also hints at the motif of resisting, versus yielding to, temptation, as it recurs in *Hierneis* and *Parsifal*. The child-as-adult had already appeared in the first unit of the film. Reappearing at the end but looking like the king when he died, the child seems to signal an overlapping of beginning and end. What looks like the end may really be only a stage in a circular movement.

The concluding scene finally assumes the semblance of a mass for the dead, during which the crowd piously offers a prayer. A pre-Vatican II German missal refers to such a prayer at the bier or at the casket as a *tumba* prayer, *tumba* being Latin for "bier." It can be no coincidence that *tumba* rhymes with *rhumba*. (Incidentally, *tumb* is also an archaic German word meaning "dumb" or "stupid," as in *der tumbe Parzival*). This episode is appropriately named with a Latin phrase taken from a requiem, "Requiescat in pace," (May he rest in peace). The prayer that the crowd recites is a distorted version of "Our Father." In spite of the Latin title suggesting a Catholic mass, Syberberg adds the Protestant ending to the prayer, which in King James' version of the Bible reads, "For Thine is the kingdom, and the power, and the glory, for ever. Amen" (Matt 6.13). The Catholic version of the prayer omits this ending. Martin Luther's choice of nouns here are *Reich*, *Kraft*, and *Herrlichkeit*. Blasphemously, Syberberg retains the syntax and replaces the vocabulary with *Sehnsucht* (longing), *Heimweh* (homesickness), and *Wahnsinn* (madness). To whom is the prayer addressed? Is it really the same God Father the Christians have in mind? Obviously not, since the nouns characterize Ludwig, not the Christian God. The Second *Reich* was not Ludwig's; it was firmly in the hands of Bismarck and the emperor during Ludwig's lifetime. By comparison, during the First *Reich*, which broke apart under Napoleon I, Ludwig might have realized his desired rule as a feudal lord. And the unwelcome, plebeian forces of the Third Reich still belonged to a nightmarish future. Similarly, the *power* and the *glory* eluded him. But *Sehnsucht*, *Heimweh*, and *Wahnsinn* describe Ludwig as his persona presents him. And since this aristocrat aspired to a social order of the past, he saw himself as the *Landesvater* of his subjects. In feudal times he would have been the lord and father of his kingdom. Our Father, King Ludwig! The elevation to mock-divine status, *Vergöttlichung*, was already anticipated in the peasant woman's reminiscence about the impression he had made on her in her childhood —an apparition like an archangel. Now he is being remembered and revered precisely for those qualities that doomed him as a ruler. And it goes without saying that the distorted prayer also characterizes the thinking of the king's subjects.

Upon closer inspection, the three noun substitutions become problematic. They are all compounds with the potential for more meanings than their usual definitions suggest. *Sehnsucht* (longing) consists of *sehnen* (to long for, yearn for) and *Sucht* (addiction, illness, obsession). The entry for *Sucht* covers 38 columns in Grimm's dictionary, indicating a broad spectrum of semantic nuances and etymology.[7] The usage includes shades with physiological, spiritual, and ethical overtones. Of interest is the first definition, consisting of three Latin equivalents: *morbus, passio, cupiditas*. *Passio* is the English "passion," both as suffering and as goal-fixated desire. Considering the spiritual echoes of the subtext, this longing or *Sehnsucht* could denote, among other things, the archetypal longing for a return to paradise and the acceptance of suffering to fulfill one's mission. The second noun, *Heimweh* (homesickness), belongs to the same context: *Heim* (home, place of origin) and *Weh* (woe, pain). As nostalgia it means "pining to return home," implying that one is far removed from this desirable abode. As with *Sehnsucht*, *Heimweh* expresses a longing and could serve as a modifyer for *exile*. And at least theoretically, one might also read it as "pain caused by one's place of origin." The emphasis shifts from the longing to return home to suffering inflicted by one's home or people. Such reading against the grain gains plausibility within the framework of Syberberg's *Trauerarbeit*. He and many thoughtful Germans of his generation have suffered through the trauma of a painful legacy as Germans. And, as already mentioned, his work of mourning addresses the need to unlock the psychological blockage of many suppressed memories and feelings. The third word, *Wahnsinn* (madness), is the most complex. *Sinn* covers the range of the English "sense," while *Wahn* and the related verbs *wahnen* and *wähnen* could fill a dictionary of their own. Like *Sucht*, *Wahn* also comprises 38 columns in Grimm! It too has undergone shifts in meanings. The older usage ranges from hope, expectation, assumption via striving and desire to the modern belief, superstition, and imagination. In all nuances, the word expresses a contrast to knowledge or truth, as something subjective and uncertain compared to facts. The current meanings of *Wahnsinn* are "madness" and "insanity." However, the voice reciting the three exchanged words in the mock-prayer pronounces them with double stress (*Sehn-Sucht, Heim-Weh, Wahn-Sinn*), inviting a consideration of each component, as if to break up the prevailing meaning. Through such refraction, the entire list of archaic, newer, and theoretical semantic combinations come into play. This relativizes the meanings. One could imagine a common denominator for all three words in longing or desire. Syberberg's choices denote a condition of psychological tension and displacement, a description of the early stage in a process. By comparison, the kingdom, power, and glory refer to a desired state or goal. A Kabbalist will recognize the compound words, especially *Wahnsinn*, as related to the concept of being deranged and displaced (deranged: *verrückt, wahnsinnig*), central to the idea of the spiritual mission of every person. This topic will be discussed later.

Another noteworthy feature of the film is its structure. Already mentioned are the static and episodic nature of the plot, the use of titles, and the allegorical overlay. Also the sporadic punning, e.g. on revolution, perhaps even on *Sehnsucht* as *sehen-Sucht* and *Seen-Sucht* (*sehen*: to see, *Seen*: seas, lakes). But more important is the function of music in the film. Most of Syberberg's own references to this film occur in an essay, "Film als Musik der Zukunft: Eine Ästhetik" (Film as Music of the Future: an Aesthetics), reprinted in his *Filmbuch* (9–21). As usual, he offers hints, but no coherent explication. He points to Wagner's *Nibelungenring* as the frame for *Ludwig*, and characterizes the relationship between music and cinematic composition as a symbiosis (14–15). His stated intention is to create "new magic worlds" ruled by laws that are closer to music than any other art. From that one concludes that the predominantly Wagnerian music accompanying the visuals does not serve only as a background soundtrack. Like text and image, the sound also carries meaning. In a dense web of references, it provides leitmotifs, quotations, counterpoints, and often substitutes for dialog. With the title implying a requiem, one expects a musical structure resembling a mass for the dead. This surfaces towards the end of the movie, but the mass is otherwise better expressed by the visual arrangements and occasional bits of dialogue. The form best suited to describe the film as a whole is the fugue. With the "Curse" outlining the human predicament much as the subject of a fugue, several "voices" carry the initial or basic tune through a series of transformations and interaction in overlay, as in counterpoint. Quite often, a subsequent presentation of the basic subject has changed so much in the metamorphosis so as to be unrecognizable. Concurrently with it, one hears or sees yet another version, also transformed and playing in counterpoint, so that the overall impression looks entirely new and unrelated to the original idea. The most common forms of contrapuntal changes of the basic subject are its inversion (upside-down), retrograde or crab (backwards), and inverted crab. Syberberg does not always place the division between these stages neatly between tableaux, but lets them sometimes occur in the middle of a scene. And thanks to the symbiosis of sound and image, the visual narrative can assume the characteristics of music. For example, the scene of Ludwig with his lover, Josef Kainz, in the photographic studio records two photo takes in quick succession. The first shows the king standing and Kainz sitting, the second reverses their positions. The shift in vertical relations amounts to a fugal inversion. At the same time, the topic of photography recurs in various forms: Ludwig informs Sissi that he has taken up photography, and later the tourists in his castle snap away. Several episodes share a subdued, monochrome coloring, such as all sepia tints or shades of red. Through the color signal one can follow a gradual debasement of photography, first as a record of truth (documentation), then as a commercial tool, as a toy, and in the service of lies and plebeian voyeurism.

There are usually at least two "voices" at play simultaneously, sound and image. Sometimes their counterpoints crowd the field, as when one hears two concurrent soundtracks, such as dialogue and music, or one sees two separate visual presentations at the same time. This happens, for example, during the king's vision of the tourists. They appear as moving hordes in tones of red on the backdrop (one of Syberberg's famous backdrop, or frontal, projections) while the king sits agonizing at his desk in the foreground. Another fugal characteristic is the episode *(Zwischenspiel, divertimento)* as the nightmare revue. Yet another is the *stretto* audible when a mournful figure soliloquies before Wagner's grave stone for a moment. An echo rejoins his (her?) voice with a few seconds' delay as if to interrupt her words. Uncertain if this apparition is the priestess-artist emerging from the composer's grave or the king himself, one only registers the androgyny of this enigmatic speaker. Finally, even the king's multiple deaths become contrapuntal variations on a theme.

Syberberg did not select the fugue as his preferred art form simply to display his virtuosity. Several reasons come to mind, one of them being the fugue as a psychological term. The second definition of "fugue" in Webster's (2nd ed.) reads, "in psychiatry, a state of psychological amnesia during which a patient seems to behave in a conscious and rational way, although upon return to normal consciousness he cannot remember the period of time nor what he did during it; temporary flight from reality." It would appear, then, that Syberberg employs the principle of the fugue as a therapeutic device, partly to describe a mental state, partly to enter and unlock this condition, so as to restore memory and induce healing. This therapy aims, of course, primarily at the Germans, but secondarily at all humanity in a secularized age oblivious of its spiritual roots.

Of course Syberberg is not the only moviemaker to present German topics. Nor is he the only creator of a cinematic trilogy. Fassbinder, for example, comes to mind. And it was from Fassbinder's group of coworkers that Syberberg borrowed several of the cast members for *Ludwig*, among them Dietrich Lohmann behind the camera; Peter Kern for three roles; Peter Moland; Ingrid Caven, who had been married to Fassbinder; and Harry Baer (Harry Zöttl) as Ludwig. Baer had starred in Fassbinder's early movie success, *Katzelmacher,* of 1969. Their collaboration continued over many years, eight times with Baer as the assistant director and fourteen times as actor. And shortly after Fassbinder's death in 1982, Baer published a biography about him.[8] One of his later films is *Frost* by Fred Kelemen in 1997. And like Baer, so also Peter Kern worked with other directors besides Fassbinder. In 1974 he starred in Wim Wenders' *False Move*, and, skipping to a more recent movie, in *Alma* by Josh Sobol in 1996. He has also tried his hand at directing, for instance with *Crazy Boys* and *Street Kid,* and *Haider lebt* in 2002. Several of these actors had belonged for years to Fassbinder's tight-knit "family," which he ruled with artistic talent, immense dynamics, and charisma, energy, tyranny, and manipulation. Some of them had joined this on-again-off-again commune as revolutionary idealists, e.g. Harry Baer. Although the leader and his entourage remained an anti-establishment counterculture, they more and more began to look like the drug-, sex-, and booze-saturated underworld of any society. Especially as Rainer Werner Fassbinder learned to accommodate himself to the money-granting sections of bureaucracy, the idealistic spirit evaporated. This shared background stands in sharp contrast to Syberberg's own life. But it serves as an undeclared foil for his *Ludwig*. His cinematic revolutionaries do not move among the downtrodden, but in court and parliament. However, regardless of their roles, the actors from Fassbinder's group retain a trace of their own persona. In musical terms, one could call it overtones, an ever so faint echo in a different octave. This dimension supports the subtext of revolution as a turning of the wheel. Better than most actors, those from Fassbinder's ranks convey this dynamic. These artists are a talented line-up of actors and crew. Most of the time, though, Syberberg does not allow them to truly act. They appear stiff and restrained, as if their characters function in counterpoint to Wagner's music, which bathes the audience in soul and passion. Only when one hears the rhumba, a non-Teutonic rhythm, does Peter Kern as Röhm display a decadent *joi de vivre.*

The film takes place in an artificial environment evoking the king's dream world. Unmistakably, many of the settings resemble an opera stage, with some episodes borrowed from a musical revue. Although the actors speak their lines, Wagner provides most of the music, transforming the performance into a tragic opera.

Ludwig was immediately recognized as a work of art, a couragous and untimely attempt to infuse a medium of entertainment with qualities associated with serious music and "high" art. It premiered on television (ZDF) late at night and reached movie theaters soon after. Its success brought Helmut Käutner's *Ludwig II* of 1954 back to the screen as well. A few months later followed Visconti's lavish *Ludwig* movie, starring Romy Schneider as Sissi. As expected, the ensuing Ludwig mania prompted comparisons and widespread discussions. One of Syberberg's admirers was the prominent French politician Valéry Giscard d'Estaing, at that time finance minister in the Pompidou government. In the United States, Francis Ford Coppola assumed the distribution of the film. It has been shown mostly at special screenings.[9] *Ludwig* secured Syberberg an international reputation. Even at home, he was honored with the German Film Award for 1972 (gold ribbon) for *Ludwig* as the best film of the year, and with a second gold ribbon for the script. It is still popular as a cult film.

The German fascination with King Ludwig is by no means over. Perhaps inspired by Syberberg's approach, Stephan Barbarino wrote the libretto to the "first Bavarian musical," *Ludwig: Sehnsucht nach dem Paradies* (Ludwig: Yearning for Paradise) with music by Franz Hummel. Opening in 1999 and housed in its own festival house on the shore of the Forggen Lake near Neuschwanstein, this enterprise completes the marketing of the king as a commodity. It went bankrupt in 2003 and was purchased by a handful investors.

Theodor Hierneis

Later in 1972 came *Theodor Hierneis, oder wie man ehem. Hofkoch wird* (Theodor Hierneis, or How One Becomes a Former Royal Cook). It too became a sensation in Paris. This time the occasion was celebrated with a banquet for 250 guests at the German House. And befitting the topic of a royal cook, the lavish menu consisted of courses that Hierneis had prepared for King Ludwig. The only exception was a dessert after a recipe by Mrs. Syberberg.

With its ninety minutes, *Hierneis* is one of the shortest feature films by Syberberg. Even so, the television version further reduced it to sixty minutes. It constitutes in some respects a compendium to and continuation of *Ludwig*, in other respects it differs noticeably. As all of Syberberg's non-fiction films, it is not "just" a documentary. *Hierneis* was the first of Syberberg's movies to be accompanied by a book. It consists actually of two books bound in one volume, with the first half supplying the bibliographical information: *Ein Mundkoch erinnert sich an Ludwig II* (A Royal Cook Remembers Ludwig II [Munich: Heimeran, 1973]). The real Mr. Hierneis had published his memoirs under the title *Der König speist* (The King Dines) with the same publisher in 1953, shortly before his death. Syberberg edited and republished the text, adding a profusion of illustrations, both historical and stills from the film. The second half of the book, beginning with page 100, contains the film script. Drawing heavily on Mr. Hierneis' autobiography as a textual source, the Hierneis of the movie reminisces while taking the audience on a tour through Ludwig's properties. Played by Walter Sedlmayr, he is the only character, except for a brief appearance of a group of tourists with their guide. Sedlmayr also played in several of Fassbinder's films. His untimely death in 1990 attracted a great deal of media attention.[10]

The characterization of *Hierneis* as a compendium to and continuation of *Ludwig* takes its cue from both obvious and more subtle connections between the two films. First of all, as a young kitchen apprentice in King Ludwig's household, Hierneis had ample opportunity to observe people and events at court. As a mature man he now shares his memories with the viewers. This accounts for some overlap, but not duplication with *Ludwig*, in part because the perspective comes "from below," belonging to a "little man." Syberberg resorts to this angle again later with two characters in the *Hitler* film. Perhaps Brecht provided the inspiration for this play on perspective. His unfinished novel *Die Geschäfte des Herrn Julius Caesar* (The Affairs of Mr. Julius Caesar) also approached Caesar through sources viewing him from below.[11] As can be expected, the memories of Theodor Hierneis dwell on impressions, observations, and interests as they relate to himself. He functions as a subjective filter. His often prosaic, even banal, comments contrast with the spectacular surroundings which Syberberg had withheld from the viewers in the *Ludwig* film. There one only saw a few of them as artists's reproductions blown up on background projections. One might call that a world seen through art and imagination, supplemented by Wagner's music. After all, in Ludwig's world, life imitated art. Hierneis' creativity, on the other hand, is restricted to the culinary arts, and no music succeeds in throwing a spell over his practical mind. The most memorable sound effects in *Hierneis* are the hoarse cries of an eagle and the narrator's unsuccessful attempt to call up an echo in the mountains. In this film too such details function as vehicles of allegory. The Third Reich revived the emblematic function of the eagle. Knowing Syberberg's fondness of imagery, a German viewer will quickly wonder if there exists a connection between Hierneis and the Nazi symbol. The lack of an echo suggests an eager but unsuccessful approach by Hierneis. The missing resonance probably does not point to his career in business during the Third Reich. Something else must cause the void, something in the man himself. Perhaps his name provides a clue. *Hirn* means "brain" and *Eis* is "ice." His brain, or mind, is surrounded by ice. In the following years, Syberberg repeatedly played with ice and cold conditions as metaphors for a Nazi mentality and a frozen stage in understanding and personal development. And yes, Hierneis, who profited from crime in the past, is still not honest about his knowledge, or worse, his role.

Syberberg claims in the *Hierneis* book that he had planned to introduce the kitchen apprentice as a character in *Ludwig*. He was intended to represent the organizing employees seeking better working conditions. Reading a proclamation, the young boy was supposed to identify himself by name and position, and then say he would later as a retiree also publish his experiences (177). This peculiar case of prognosis is fulfilled in the equally paradoxical subtitle, about how one becomes a former royal cook. This mixture of past experience, present tense, and future prospects parodies the somber oracles pronounced in *Ludwig*. But rarely would a young boy of humble origin have attained the status or insight of a prophet. Such exceptions to the rule, Syberberg would possibly argue, were Wagner, May, and Hitler, who all aspired to the status of prophet. Hierneis remained an insignifant man by historical standards. Even as a mature man, he garbles his statements, displaying his limitations. The planned episode with the kitchen apprentice was omitted from the final version of *Ludwig*, one reads, mainly because the real Hierneis developed into a bourgeois devoid of any revolutionary aspirations. So, although the character proved unsuitable for the motif of revolution in the film, Syberberg could still mention the planned incident in the book and thus retain the cyclic occurrence of the motif.

Hierneis refers by name to many characters who appeared in *Ludwig*. For viewers familiar with that film, the names conjure up faces and presences. Memory can supply the frame of reference. In a reverse move, Ludwig's real environment appears belatedly in the *Hierneis* film, only after the viewers have been forced to imagine what it actually looked like. Similarly, Hierneis will mention places of which a visual presentation follows much later. The interplay between "real" vision, imagination, and memory assumes the dynamics of a quasi-musical pattern. Another example of contrapuntal composition reveals itself in the movement of water. It may descend from the heavens as rain, shoot upwards in fountains, move placidly horizontally as an underground lake in the grotto, or even drip as a leak from an artificial lake in the king's roof garden. The main structural principle of *Ludwig* also informs *Hierneis*.

One of the characters Hierneis recalls by name is the lackey Mayr. In *Ludwig* he had shared a face with the hairdresser Hoppe and SA leader Röhm, all three roles being played by Peter Kern (*Kern* = kernel, core, nucleus). As the lackey, the character also dons a black mask that makes him unrecognizable, adding a fourth manifestation to the actor's persona. As individuals, the characters become interchangeable and indistinguishable from each other. This loss of individual contours is carried on in Mayr's last scene where he anticipates Hierneis. Both men were possibly co-conspirators, perhaps merely manipulated and powerless pawns, but in any case, underlings paid handsomely to keep quiet about the king's demise. And just as Hierneis later, the talkative Mayr reveals more than he intends.

The plot of *Hierneis* is a guided tour of King Ludwig's world, at least on one level of discourse. That makes Hierneis the tour guide, *Fremdenführer* or *Führer* for short. Nowhere in the book or film does one learn how the cook-turned-businessman fared under the other *Führer*. His material success indicates that he certainly suffered no harm. Considering his career in the Bavarian royal household after Ludwig's death and subsequently at the imperial court in Berlin, one may surmise that he later, as a delicatessen owner and caterer in Munich, also served the new rulers with equal dedication. But for now he is our *Führer* and we, the viewers, the ogling followers. We belong to the privileged visitors, to be sure, and are not to be confused with the horde of curious tourists crowding the king's chambers. Or can one be so sure? The viewers may not be willing to acknowledge the noisy crowd as alter egos, but would rather pretend that the chains of shifting identities apply only to the cinematic world. One could always rationalize and point to the aesthetic handling of repeated motifs, such as the tourists in tones of red in *Ludwig* and now the crowd invading his private quarters. Surely, we are not such voyeurs. And following Hierneis on his tour, we object to calling him a *Fremdenführer*. Maybe *cicerone*, but not *Führer*. Too uncomfortable.

Maybe the readers can perceive Syberberg's subversive agenda. By drawing the viewers into a world they have grown up to love, he works on activating subconscious responses, softening the defensive walls, reviving links of associations, and in the process, confronting the viewers with repressed truths or at least possibilities. As Hierneis, many of the director's compatriots also knew more than they would acknowledge. And Hierneis alludes too often to the generous support launching him and his fellow court servants on their successful careers. Was it blackmail or precautionary bribes? This jovial and decent-looking man hides a dark secret. He may be a victim of circumstances, but he is by no means innocent. With numerous slips and unintended hints, he reveals his weakness without admitting complicity. Syberberg invites his viewers to witness this balancing act, hoping they will recognize the parallels with their own situation. Such a recognition would be an indispensable first step towards overcoming their temporary amnesia, or fugue.

Unlike the stage of art and artifice in *Ludwig, Hierneis* leads us through the king's real world, to the extent a film can present it. And considering the guide's practical mind, it is only fitting that the music remains absent. That means, then, that Wagner's presence is visual, not audible. Now the viewers are shown the real-life recreations of the opera backdrops and architecture that inspired Ludwig's environment. For example, the lake in the grotto at Linderhof was fashioned after the stage decorations in Wagner's *Tannhäuser,* replete with electric light effects, cockle shell boat, and swans. Or the singers' hall at Neuschwanstein, modeled on a similar hall at Wartburg, where Tannhäuser competed with other troubadours. And perhaps most closely, the Hunding's cabin, modeled on the Hundingshütte backdrop in the *Walküre.* The visual cornucopia provides the same type of associative web as in *Ludwig.*

A separate track or subject is the text, which takes the form of a monologue of sorts   (Hierneis supposedly addresses the viewers as his audience) flowing incessantly. Seemingly a commentary on the visible environment, the lectures tend to trail off into reminiscences, sometimes revealing the layers of discourse. In his *Filmbuch* Syberberg characterizes the language in *Hierneis* as a score in words (22). The dynamics of language replaces the music and lively action. Most conspicuous is the contrapuntal difference between royal elegance and the unpoetic speech, be it in style or topic. Another feature typical of later work occurs in Hierneis' description of the tree serving as a center post in Hunding's cabin. The mythic Tree of Life in Germanic lore, the Yggdrasil, was an ash. When the king copied Wagner's backdrop of the tree for a mountain retreat, he had a spacious hall built around a real tree. And Hierneis reminisces, "Aha, das war die Esche, die eine Linde war" (Oh yes, that was the ash that [really] was a lindentree). Without further comment, the caption to the illustration in the book to the film identifies the tree as a beech (124). It is an insignificant discrepancy in itself, but it introduces a discordant note into the composition of words. In future films, for instance *Winifred Wagner*, such corrective measures will intrude into the cinematic narrative in the form of title screens temporarily interrupting the image.

The memories one hears are unreliable, but the true version exists somewhere, or at least a more complete version, as one must conclude from Hierneis' hints. Towards the end, the observant viewers begin to suspect that the narrator may truly believe in his love for King Ludwig and Bavaria, not realizing his betrayal. He has, after all, sold his soul for his business. As Syberberg has remarked on several occasions, his *Hierneis* requires the active, critical participation by the spectators to be appreciated. Many of the reviews also stress this. Nine translations of French reviews are included in the *Filmbuch*.

Theodor Hierneis first appeared on West German television on October 1, 1972. It received the Adolf Grimme Prize in 1973, and also in the same year, the German Film Award (gold ribbon) as best film in its category, while the actor, Walter Sedlmayr, received the same honor for his performance.

About the same time Syberberg wrote an essay, "Über ausländische Filme im deutschen Fernsehen" (About Foreign Movies on German Television) that reappeared in the *Filmbuch* (106). It deplores the trend of television companies buying up the rights to new movies at film festivals and points out the consequences for movie theaters and film production. Apparently Syberberg started early to publish his views on cinema and art. Many of these articles are difficult to trace today, but a few early ones were collected and reappeared with this essay.

Karl May

In spite of its related subject and acclaimed aesthetics, the Hierneis film is not considered to be an autonomous part of Syberberg's German Trilogy, although it obviously fits into the bigger German Cycle. One might call it an appendix to *Ludwig*. The second place in the trilogy belongs to *Karl May*, which opened in October 1974 at the Arri Cinema in Munich. It was financed in part by ZDF Television, in part by Syberberg's company from earnings on *Ludwig*. The video version retains the original length of 187 minutes, but the movie theater copies were reduced to 135 minutes.

As many of Syberberg's movies, so also *Karl May* is a portrait, but not in his usual documentary style of interviews, as with Pocci, or reminiscing lectures, as with Hierneis. This is an "almost normal" biographical recreation of May's last twelve years. The historical Karl May (1842–1912) is as unknown to Americans as he is a cherished national icon to Germans, especially young readers and movie goers. A self-made man, he rose from poverty to riches as the writer of adventure and travel stories. Many of them were made into movies. His mature years were overshadowed by media attacks and ongoing lawsuits, from which he could vindicate himself only shortly before his death. Syberberg concentrates on these years of conflict.

May, known to his admirers as the Mayster, was the prolific author of novels, short stories, poems, essays, and a play. The historical-critical edition of his works comprises ninety-nine volumes.[12] Up until about 1900, May's fame rested primarily on his Wild West stories and adventure books set in the Orient, with the most beloved characters being Old Shatterhand, Winnetou, Kara Ben Nemsi, and Hadschi Halef Omar. Some of the shorter narratives are humorous, among them "Professor Vitzliputzli." After the turn of the century, his books became increasingly allegorical, such as *Ardistan und Dschinnistan*, with the former name referring to a state of moral inferiority and the latter to a land of human perfection. His autobiography, *Mein Leben und Streben* (My Life and Striving), appeared in 1910.

If May's life had been a simple success story, it would not have interested Syberberg. His life and person must serve as an *exemplum*. That is, for all Germans, one assumes, remembering the reference to *German* and the German Trilogy. And of course Karl May's story is also germane to the quest of all humanity. This becomes increasingly clear in May's comments on the *Menschheitsseele* (soul of humanity): His aspirations and struggle exemplify the human desire for higher goals. Inversely, such aspirations could easily end in disaster, as the film warns in subtle and overt ways.

Karl May's beginning did not augur a life of fame. Born into poverty in Saxony, blind until the age of four, he experienced several scrapes with the law in his youth. Only after repeated prison terms did he in his thirties turn to writing in earnest. Much of this early work was published in magazines under a pseudonym and is generally characterized as colportage or worthless pulp. Like Balzac, May was incredibly industrious, often writing through the night. The mixture of talent and tenacity resulted in gradual success as a writer. Ernst Bloch describes him as a " yearning bourgeois conformist who was himself a boy [and who] pierced the mustiness of the age" (156). In the German version the mustiness reads as *Muff*. But in some respects May continued to live on the fringe of societal norms. For example, he used a questionable doctoral title, pretended to have visited the far-away sites of his stories numerous times (which he had not at the time), and encouraged the readers' belief that he actually was the first-person narrator writing from personal experience. And he marketed this fraudulent image as if he believed it himself. Participating in spiritistic seances, hearing voices, carrying on conversations with imaginary people, yes, he offered many reasons for attack and ridicule when the tide turned against him. He was a troubled man living in two worlds. One of the better studies on this topic is Axel Mittelstaedt's "Zur Charakterentwicklung Karl Mays."[13] To some extent, this simultaneous existence in reality and the realm of imagination marks May as a parallel to King Ludwig. But with mounting adversity in part caused by his "dishonesty," he decided to become a new person. And this is the real struggle that Syberberg focuses on. As one of the opponents remarks, without their attacks, May would not have embarked on his painful transformation. This process starts with the rejection of blackmail from a journalist and the divorce from his wife of many years, Emma. It continues with a new marriage to Klara, the widow of his best friend, and concludes with an apotheosis at the time of his death. In the struggle to overcome his human frailties, May becomes the representative pilgrim who ascends from his Ardistan to an ethically defined Dschinnistan. Hence, the plot of the movie consists mainly of this internal change with the external setbacks spurring him on.

Obviously, this plan does not offer much lively action in the usual movie sense. The public probably expected something else. After all, the name Karl May stands for adventures abroad, exotic environments, suspense, and entertainment. Instead, the internalized action requires the viewers to activate their imagination, much as the adventure books expect of the readers. That runs contrary to the potential of film as a visual medium. Nonetheless, for Syberberg the view inwards plays its part here, with a stated intention being to show the "inner world" (*Filmbuch*, 39). The reviews and scholarly studies published in German do not appreciate this deviation from expectation. And the few attempts in the film to show May in an exotic setting do not meet their approval for lack of realism. For example, the beginning of the movie presents May on his trip to the Near and Far East in 1899–1900, a blissful time he characterizes as paradise. Lush palms partially cover the background, which one recognizes from *Ludwig*. He is taking leave from a friend, whose parting words of admiration should soothe the psyche of any recognition seeker. The scene is, of course, a studio take using Syberberg's background projection technique. Only gradually do viewers realize that much of this scene takes place in May's imagination. The last doubt is swept away when the accompanying sound of tropical birds also suddenly fills his living room at home later.The artificiality of the exotic surrounding contrasts with the realism of his environment at home, revealing the internal and external worlds in which he lives. But the critics want more. Annette Deeken, for example, complains that the palm tableau does not come alive: "And it would have to give the impression of being alive, if a dream should be shown, in other words, be made visible."[14]

Neither Deeken nor any of the other critics consulted here have explicitly reacted to a circumstance which probably contributed to the frosty reception of *Karl May* in Germany. So acute is their discomfort in addressing the issue that it gets the silent treatment. In a series of films identified as German and culminating with *Hitler*, one expects the topic of the Holocaust and German-Jewish relations to be included. One can recognize the theme in *Hitler*. It is unnoticeable in *Ludwig*. But not to be ignored is the cinematic Ludwig's aspiration to an *imitatio Christi*, including the last words on the cross, "It is finished" (John 20.30). Jesus of Nazareth had of course a Jewish mother. A fact not touched upon in the film, but a matter of historical record may also be pertinent here: It was King Ludwig who forced Wagner to accept a Jewish conductor, Hermann Levi, for his *Parsifal*. One might say that in *Ludwig* the Jewish theme remains either peripheral or veiled. Expecting a fugal continuation of the theme, one would anticipate a transformation in counterpoint. It would have to fit into a series of several changes, such as basic form, inversion, crab, and inverted crab. Their interplay would translate into a variety of visual and audible equivalents: positive versus negative or distortion, descent versus ascent or lateral or no move, etc. One might, for example, expect an inversion of the protagonist's relation to someone Jewish. And Ludwig's promotion of and support for Levi actually does find a negative counterpart in the relationship between May and the blackmailer Lebius, who speaks with a presumably Yiddish accent. If the historical Lebius had not played such a prominent part in the war of the press against May, Syberberg might have had to invent him. But in post-Holocaust Germany, a Jewish character who is not a victim or a saint easily becomes a cause for scandal. And Lebius is an unsavory character. One cannot, though, describe the constellation of May and Lebius as good versus evil. Both men display too many shortcomings for that. One might rather view them as opposing forces in the dialectic of the plot. The grappling of thesis with antithesis produces a synthesis superior to either one of them. Lebius is portrayed by Willy Trenk-Trebitsch, who had to flee Germany during the Third Reich. True to fugal form, the theme is also presented in a different "voice," which is faint and abbreviated, but in counterpoint to Lebius. The actor Peter Kern, whom the readers remember from three different roles at Ludwig's court, now plays an admiring teenager, George Grosz, who visits May to pay his respects. The historical artist Grosz (1893–1959) became famous as a satirist and member of the Dada movement. Syberberg would certainly have been aware of his collaboration with Brecht on stage settings in 1927.[15] As so many others, Grosz left the country in 1933. One recognizes also an "overtone," in the figure of Karl May's friend Richard Plöhn, who died in 189. His widow later married May. While the friends were all alive as a foursome, they had purchased a cemetery plot, planning to be buried near each other. And in 1912 Karl May was laid to rest at the side of his friend. When the Nazis in 1942 wanted to commemorate the centennial of May's birth with a ceremony at the grave, they discovered that he shared a grave plot with a half-Jew. The organizers abandoned their plans for a ceremony.[16] Although Grosz and Plöhn appear only briefly in the film, their real-life biographies reverberate from a distance and inform the composition ever so faintly.

Karl May viewed the struggle to overcome his human flaws in mystical terms. Thus the paradisiacal state towards which he strove is a regained innocence and a metaphysical task to be carried out for all humanity. *Edelkitsch* (presumptuous trash) is a frequent sneer by critics for this quest in his later books. But Syberberg takes him seriously. He sees in May's yearning something Faustian. Besides, Goethe, the author of the best known German *Faust*, created also another famous embodiment of pure longing in his Mignon, a sad, enigmatic, and androgynous character in *Wilhelm Meisters Lehrjahre.* Syberberg evokes Mignon and Goethe with his Penelope, the servant in May's household. She functions as a projection of the protagonist's inner state. At the same time, she too remains an unacknowledged Anima. And as a foreigner far from home, she evokes the Kabbalistic *he* or Shekhinah in exile on earth.

In some scenes May's inner world becomes the whole world. At other times the external world can also shrink to a map, a globe, a miniature version of May's childhood village, and miniature battlefields with tin soldiers. A common form of such small-scale-versions of the embedding work or *mise en abyme* is the play-within-the-play.[17] It occurs in the film on several occasions. For example, when May answers questions from a class of schoolboys, he wears a costume made famous in his books. A quick disappearance into a side room allows a change of outfit. Obviously, this is not just a question-and-answer session, but a performance in which May presents his literary persona as himself. On another occasion the viewers follow Mrs. May and her friend into a carnival fair to share with them a peek at the newfangled wonders of motion pictures. The cameras show clips from the earliest films of Lumière and Méliès. The film-within-the-film was already anticipated in *Ludwig* when the king and Kainz in the photographer's studio move jerkily as if appearing in an early silent movie.

Another reminder of the film on Ludwig is the protagonist's visit in an artist's studio. As Elisabet Ney before, so also this artist carries out a priestly function in a subservient fashion. Alexander (Sascha) Schneider (1870–1927) "translates" May's spiritual striving and insights in his paintings, perhaps not as an oracle, but at least as a medium. Thomas Ostwald thinks that his fame today rests primarily on his illustrations in May's books.[18]   All his work, incidentally, displays a programmatic tendency, focusing on heroic, nude men and light symbolism (Jeziorkowski, 184). In spite of its spiritual subject matter, one cannot help seeing the formal neoclassicism as a precursor of Nazi art, as, for example, in his *Kriegergestalten und Todesgewalten* (Warrior Figures and Forces of Death"), published in 1915 during World War I. There is, however, a direct correlation between Schneider's symbolic paintings hanging in Karl May's home and the various stages in May's struggle.

In *Ludwig* May appeared as the blind seer Tiresias, and Elisabet Ney as a priestess-soothsayer. When he is now presented as the main character and artist, Karl May seems at first more preoccupied with his own problems than with oracular statements for the public. But as he learns to view himself as Everyman, he aspires to a wider perspective. And one of the statements in the film assumes oracular status in hindsight: "Wehe, wenn der Falsche kommt!" (Woe, if the wrong man comes). And the wrong man really did come. Legend reports that this man was greatly impressed with May's last public lecture given in Vienna. His name was Adolf Hitler. Played by Rainer von Artenfels, this young fellow with glittering eyes is seen leaving a men's shelter, where he lives, for May's lecture. This speech was never written down or recorded, but it became known as "Empor ins Reich der Edelmenschen" (Up and towards the realm of noble humans). It supposedly attracted an audience of several thousand enthusiastic admirers. Syberberg does not attempt to invent any part of this lecture, but lets the episode end as May walks onto the stage. This time the viewers have to imagine with their inner eye yet another play-within-the-play. The occasion serves, of course, as a link to the next film. It also affords the actor André Heller to appear briefly as the organizer of the event. He, too, will return in *Hitler*. But Syberberg has not abandoned the theme of prophesy: Another oracle comes from the mouth of a woman in black, Bertha von Suttner (a cameo appearance of Lil Dagover). Becoming increasingly more pacifistic over the years, May had for some time corresponded with Bertha von Suttner (1843–1914), who had earned the Nobel Prize for Peace in 1905. Their conversation behind the stage just before the famous speech ends with Suttner's gloomy premonitions. She detects a dangerous unrest and threatening energy in society. "I do not like their faces," she remarks, as if referring to the young man with the funny moustache in the audience. Two years later World War I erupted, followed by civil war, inflation, instability, and Hitler's ascent.

The friendship with Bertha von Suttner developed by necessity late in May's life. He did not seem capable before then to view women as equal human beings in non-sexist terms. To be sure, he could be a loving husband and generous friend, but the woman remained an inferior other, a servant, helper, wife, or secretary, who always agreed with him or had no opinion. One example of his earlier attitude hails from 1904. A lady named Marie Silling had written a scathing review of his book *Et in terra pax* (And Peace on Earth) in the *Dresdener Anzeiger*. It provoked him to publish a rejoinder in which he expresses his dismay that the detractor is a sixty-year old spinster and not an opponent worthy of debate who would be "intellectually muscular and capable of resistance" (Ostwald, 236–37). This response suggests that he had not yet reached the goal of his inner development. That late stage only coincides with his stay in Vienna to meet the emperor and to deliver the speech in March 1912. And evoking King Ludwig's repeated demise, there the film lets him die his first death, in the Kapuzinergruft, the crypt of canopic jars of the Habsburg emperors. There he kneels to pay his respects to the image of a crowned skull, Death, Lord of all mortal creation. Upon this final peace and insight follows his physical death a week later at home in a strongly allegorical episode. It would require a separate chapter to discuss the details of the imagery. Let it suffice to point out that these details recur periodically in the following films in fugal variations. Music plays an important part in *Karl May*, as well. This time it is supplied by d'Albert, J. S. Bach, Busoni, Chopin, Gounod, Liszt, and Mahler.

Syberberg's own comments on *Karl May* appeared in two publications. The first is an article that appeared in *Die Zeit*, "Ein deutsches Heldenleben: Karl May" (A German Heroic Life: Karl May).[19] It attempts to present the film as a faithful portrait of May, with half of the accompanying photographs underscoring the historical "veracity." For example, one still from the movie is printed next to a photo of May from 1912. They look like mirror images or the butterfly wings of a Rohrschach test. Two others juxtapose an authentic May portrait and its recreation in the film. A step further goes the montage of a face consisting half-and-half of May and the actor. This fusion changes direction as the text begins to emphasize the Everyman nature of May. Continuing the literary hint in the title, it also describes his life in the vocabulary of literary history: "His life: . . . a Siegfried speaking Saxon dialect, the proletarian Parsifal, the new Münchhausen; a Faust from Radebeul near Dresden, more foolish than Simplicissimus, . . . Kitsch for some, dreamkitsch, at least a narrator of fairytales, for others the last great mystic we had" (79). A fool and a magus, then, and everything in between. Syberberg hints at the notion of a narrator of fairytales in the subtitle of the movie, with one important qualification. The full title appears as *Es war im Lande Sachsen ein Mann der hieß Karl May* (There Was in the State of Saxony a Man Whose Name Was Karl May). The choice of words and folksy syntax approximates the beginning of a fairytale. Except that such a stock phrase always includes the word "once," "Es war *einmal*" (*Once* upon a time there was). One remembers that the second part of *Ludwig* carries the subtitle "Ich war einmal" (Once Upon a Time I Was). In Syberberg's view Karl May was not a unique phenomenon happening only once, although his life reads like a fairytale. His life and struggle represent the lot of every human being. And thus, the article points out, the movie is "a film about ourselves." Asking why the books of Karl May could remain so tremendously popular up to the present, the text suggests that they contain something, much like fairytales, that is embedded in everybody already. This something acts as a sounding board for May, the musician.

Syberberg's other text on *Karl May* appeared in the *Filmbuch* (36–46), which also includes twelve French reviews (183–97) and the related essay "Warum Ufa-Stars?" (224–25). The last title refers to UFA, or Universum Film A.G., the leading German movie production company between 1917 and 1945.[20] Most people associate it primarily with the films of the Nazi years, but, as the author reminds his readers, UFA did not begin with the Third Reich (225). The elderly members of the cast of *Karl May* should, he hopes, make the public remember German film history, and " that means, finally to acknowledge our history, which also is film history, and no longer suppress it" (225). And he adds, "ohne Geschichte gibt es keine Kultur" (without history there is no culture).

Syberberg had resorted to actors of the older generation before, the most prominent one being Kortner. This time they dominate the cast. Lil Dagover (1887–1980) appears as Bertha von Suttner. A leading role in *The Cabinet of Dr. Caligari* of 1920 made her a star. Of interest in her long career are her film roles as Sissi in *Elisabeth von Österreich* of 1931, as Madame Pompadour in *Das Schönheitspflästerchen* of 1936 (King Ludwig would have been her fan!), and her stage role in *Kabale und Liebe* at the beginning of World War II. After the war and "denazification," she continued to be professionally active and remained popular as the Grand Old Lady of German film.[21]

The choice of Kristina Söderbaum as Emma May raised many eyebrows. This star remains associated with roles in movies directed by her husband, Veit Harlan, with the most notorious being *Jew Süß* of 1940. Their success and political correctness up until 1945 resulted in a prohibition against making movies for the husband after the war. Only following several trials and after the verdict was overturned, did Söderbaum act again.[22] Her performance in *Karl May* was a comeback after many years' absence from the screen. Most of her early roles depict her as a childwoman who ends her life by drowning. Syberberg's selection of her as Emma May is therefore in keeping with her star persona: a gullible and simple-minded woman spurned by her husband.

Karl May's second wife, Klara, is played by Käthe Gold (1907–97). Fritz Kortner remarks in his memoirs that she, too, flourished during the Third Reich. He personally had only seen a pale reflection of the legend. But, he continues, Brecht had assured him that Gold had played "das einzige wirkliche Gretchen" (the only real Gretchen [in Goethe's *Faust*].[23] She continued to act in Vienna until the age of eighty.[24] With this career, she too fits into Syberberg's line-up of connected roles and "correspondences." Besides, both she, her character, and Emma May have names with esoteric connotations.

In a contrapuntal fashion, Willy Trenk-Trebitsch (1902–83) as Lebius also adds invisible dimensions to Syberberg's oeuvre. He belonged to the original cast of

Brecht/Weill's *Three Penny Opera*, which saw more than a thousand performances in Berlin, starting in 1928. Numerous members of that cast fled the country in the thirties, and at least one, Kurt Gerron, died in a concentration camp. Several sound recordings from 1930 are still available with Trenk-Trebitsch in the role of Mr. Peachum and Lotte Lenya as Jenny. As for Mr. Peachum, he plays both sides of the fence while trying to bring down Mack the Knife, not unlike Lebius in his dealings with May.[25] During his exile, Trenk-Trebitsch also played in Kortner's movie *The Strange Death of Adolf Hitler*. The actor did not, however, appear in Pabst's film version of *The Three Penny Opera* of 1930, a movie that resulted in a lawsuit between Pabst and Brecht and provoked Brecht to write his famous essay "The Three Penny Opera Case." This text on film aesthetics has played a role in the debate on cinema far beyond Germany's borders.[26] It also inspired Syberberg's thought on film. Besides, Brecht has remained important to him.

A friend of Karl May in the movie is Dittrich, played by Attila Hörbiger. One of his actress daughters, Christiane Hörbiger, appeared in *Fritz Kortner probt Kabale und Liebe* of 1965. Both Hörbiger and his equally famous wife, Paula Wessely, belonged to the privileged elite of actors in the Third Reich. It may strike one as ironic, then, that Attila Hörbiger starred as Nathan the Wise at the Vienna Burgtheater, with Christiane playing Recha, Nathan's adopted daughter (Löffler, 23). Lessing's play *Nathan der Weise* has a Jewish title character and disappeared from the repertory in all countries under Hitler's control.

Helmut Käutner portrays Karl May. Käutner (1908–80) was, like Kortner, a multi-talented director, actor, writer, and more, with a long list of awards to his credit.[27] Unlike many colleagues in the field, he managed, with a few setbacks now and then, to remain active professionally in the Third Reich without compromising his name, and was thus allowed to continue his work under Allied occupation after 1945. American viewers may remember his international successes *The Devil's General* of 1954–55 and *The Captain of Köpenick* of 1956. Among his other movies, two in particular must have intrigued Syberberg, *Ludwig II.: Glanz und Elend eines Königs* of 1954 (Ludwig II: Glory and Misery of a King) and *Monpti* of 1957. Although his role as Karl May does not bring him in contact with King Ludwig, Käutner's professional background connects him thematically to him and thus to Syberberg's Trilogy. In a similar way, his *Monpti* establishes an invisible link to Syberberg's early film on Romy Schneider, who also stars in Käutner's movie.

The preceding comments should make it clear that Syberberg chooses his actors with care. Regardless whether they play a character or present themselves in a documentary portrait, they all have backgrounds that add a subtle dimension to his oeuvre. The predominantly geriatric cast of *Karl May* could, however, have contributed to the movie's lack-luster performance at the box-office. Presumably also the lack of superficial suspense, the broken taboo, and the complex of associations with the UFA past failed to elicit the desired response. To some extent, the reviews in Germany can be blamed for creating a cool reception, but not all critics gave the thumb-down. The French reviews reprinted in the *Filmbuch* are, of course, all positive, and so were several in Germany (Kastner, 270). Bazon Brock, for example, found kind words for the film.[28] Brock praises it for presenting a "fulfilled utopia of the good life," speaking of May's death (186). This art professor may be the only observer to point out the complementarity of May and his opponent Gerlach, thus recognizing the necessity of the struggle for May's transformation.

The movie had its opening night in Vienna on 17 Oct. 1974, with Austrian Chancellor Bruno Kreisky in the audience. The following day it was released in Hamburg and Munich (Kastner 270). The film festival at San Sebastian of 1975 was apparently the first of many special event showings. Even before the release, the *Karl May* script by Syberberg received an award of 250,000 DM from the German Federal Ministery of Interior. And in 1975 the German Film Award (gold ribbon) went to Helmut Käutner for his role and to Nino Borghi for the props.

A year later, in March 1976, Syberberg's trip to California introduced the film to an American audience. It also inspired another article, "Drei Tage in Hollywood" (Three Days in Hollywood), reprinted in his *Filmbuch* (228–31). He had been invited to show *Karl May* at the Filmex 1976 as one of three German entries among 100 movies at the festival. He marveled at the great contrasts around him: The refuge for many artists fleeing Nazi-occupied Europe, the prostitution of cinematic art for the sake of profits, a tough business climate triggering risk-taking and resilience, and still, a miracle of creativity. He was gratified by the informed discussions that followed the performances and rejoyced in words of recognition by leading filmmakers and critics. A travel report interspersed with reflections, one might conclude, a simple narrative. Yet one cannot help noticing all the contradictory details resembling contrapuntal elements, such as his reference to Karl May as a "loyal, sincere German and mountebank from Saxony" (229). Even a travel report turns into a quasi-musical composition. Perhaps because the German State Department paid for the trip, this essay refrains from the usual attacks on the German film business.

Winifred Wagner

The following year brought a return to the documentary format with *Winifred Wagner und die Geschichte des Hauses Wahnfried 1914–1975* (Winifred Wagner and the history of the house Wahnfried 1914–1975). Most English literature about this film refers to it as *The Confessions of Winifred Wagner*. It is a five-hour interview with the seventy-eight year old Winifred Wagner filmed over five days in April 1975. Perhaps it would be more correct to characterize it as a monologue or oral memoir, since Mrs. Wagner does all the talking except for an occasional prompt or question. Syberberg had for some time carried around the idea of filming documentaries of elderly Germans who had made contributions to the world of arts. These interviews would serve as a record of living history. And his list included the name of Winifred Wagner. While he was immersed in research for his upcoming project, the composer Richard Wagner began to loom ever larger as the link between all his films from *Ludwig* and on. The Syberbergs knew Eva Wagner, and she in turn persuaded her famous grandmother to agree to a filmed interview. The old lady was the daughter-in-law of the composer. With this documentary, the moviemaker hit a raw nerve in his compatriots and elicited tremendous interest abroad. It became a *cause celèbre* and a scandal that caused a rift between him and the Wagner family. To understand this reaction, one needs to remember Syberberg's cinematic program, the importance of Richard Wagner in German cultural history, and how his descendants carried on his legacy.

The composer and writer Richard Wagner (1813–83) obtained the patronage of King Ludwig II and settled down in Bayreuth in northern Bavaria. His villa, Wahnfried, was a gift from the king. Thanks to generous support from the monarch he realized his utopian dream of building an opera house and establishing a quasi-sacral music festival at which only the "canonical" of his operas were, and still are, performed. Hence, among Wagnerians, the name Bayreuth denotes to some extent the city as the festival site, but more so the Wagner family as caretakers of a legacy. Since the composer's death, the members of this family have always been celebrities, making the "house Wahnfried" a dynasty of special guardians.

The composer moved into Wahnfried with his second wife, Cosima Liszt von Bülow Wagner (1837–1930). She assumed charge of the festival after his death. She brought with her two daughters from her first marriage and had three children by the composer. The only son, Siegfried Wagner (1869–1930), born when his father was fifty-six, eventually took over the direction of the festival after his mother became too old. A long-time bachelor, he married at forty-five. His seventeen-year old bride was the English-born Winifred, who gave birth to four children in quick succession. After Siegfried Wagner's death in 1930, his young widow Winifred (1897–1980) assumed the main responsibility for the festival enterprise. During the Third Reich, her daughter Friedelind (1918–91) emerged as the black sheep of the family who emigrated to New York with the help of Arturo Toscanini, her "other father."[29] She only reconciled with the mother after the war. The elder son, Wieland (1917-66), succeeded his mother as director after the war. Upon his death, the brother Wolfgang took charge. Two of his children, Eva and Gottfried, became instrumental in the making of the film, but, as Syberberg points out with regrets, they too broke with him when the film became a sensation.

Many families have a skeleton or two in their closets, and it was predictable that the friendship between Hitler and "Bayreuth" would receive some attention. But the Wagners were probably unprepared for Syberberg's objective, if they recognized it, and for his ability to make Winifred Wagner reveal more than the family wanted the public to know. It certainly did not help that the German television showed the five-hour film in a scaled-down version of 104 minutes. The abridged version naturally retains the sensational revelations at the expense of the less spectacular recollections. But in either version, Winifred Wagner's comments must be viewed against a long tradition reaching back to the composer himself. The problem starts with him.

One thing is Wagner's musical genius and achievement (as well as luck) in the form of the festival. Something else altogether are his prose writings and the image of himself that he cultivated and tinkered with throughout his life. This persona expressed on numerous occasions opinions that earned him the reputation of an anti-Semite. Nonetheless, both in his lifetime and later, Wagner was revered as an icon of German culture. Consequently, his books and articles also became tremendously influential. Hitler greatly admired Wagner. He claimed to draw inspiration from the composer's work, and his actions confirmed his professed devotion to Wagner, as this film makes abundantly clear. But just as he expanded his love for the composer to include the Wagner clan, who so-to-speak became his substitute family, so he also shared Wagner's bias and transformed this prejudice into state policy, with mind-numbing consequences. As have many others before him, Syberberg does not tire of emphasizing the unbroken line of intolerance that escalated into genocide in the twentieth century. Of course Wagner died in the nineteenth century. Furthermore, his life and pronouncements also present many inconsistencies. Therefore, Syberberg does not accuse him of the horrors of the Third Reich, but places him in the line of tradition that led to the disaster. And in that line of tradition, much closer to the present, stands "Bayreuth" with its guardians. During the Third Reich, Winifred Wagner ruled as the Queen of Bayreuth. Her initial meeting with Hitler took place in 1923 when she was twenty-six and he thirty-five. It developed into a genuine and, for her, profitable friendship. The Wagner children knew him as "Uncle Wolf." This friend became a promoter and protector of both the festival and the family, much as King Ludwig's patronage had saved Wagner and his great dream. This is an important link in Syberberg's Trilogy. Of course Winifred Wagner paid for this Faustian pact with the Devil after the war when she, like Leni Riefenstahl, faced trial for aiding and abetting the Nazi cause. Her property and assets, including the car, were confiscated, and she was banned from Bayreuth for many years.

Now Syberberg induced her to talk about her life. Eschewing the artistic dimension of her involvement, she focuses on private affairs. As she had in court, she again claims to have been a non-political person, a citizen never engaged in political activities. Even the most uninformed viewer soon discovers contradictions and distortions in her recollections. The scandal was caused by her insistence on separating the Hitler she knew from the monster by that name who did not exist for her. Hitler came to the festival annually from 1933 to '40, stayed as a guest at Wahnfried, exempted her sons from military service (Wolfgang only after his first war injury), and even advised her in artistic matters related to the festival. He also enjoyed these visits in Bayreuth. Albert Speer described the atmosphere during Hitler's visits: "He was gay, paternal to the children, friendly and solicitous toward Winifred Wagner. . . . As patron of the festival and as a friend of the Wagner family, Hitler was no doubt realizing a dream which even in his youth he perhaps never quite dared to dream."[30] The film shows how Mrs. Wagner is unwilling and unable to revise her views of him even when confronted with the facts of history. More than once does she mention the loyalty, *Treue*, that a friendship entails. With similar steadfastness or stubbornness, she cannot confess any feelings of guilt. She does not con-fess, but pro-fesses allegiance to a friend and an era when she and her festival flourished: Hitler's patronage assured her a prominent profile, generous subsidies, a guaranteed full house for all performances, capped wages for the artists, and an easy pick of the best artists in the Reich. Apart from Leni Riefenstahl, very few other women could rival her position in the male-dominated Third Reich.

Clearly, Winifred Wagner is an eminent representative of her time and country. Then, like Brünnhilde, she was hurled from her exalted status into exile. But does she seek the redemptive return of the Ring? Does she perceive the effort needed to restore a just order of things? Obviously not. She serves Syberberg mostly as a negative example. But with the help of her children and grandchildren, the film interview might still have constituted a collective attempt towards a reckoning with the past, a recognition of responsibility, an admission, a resolve. That would have meant a move towards a redemption for "Bayreuth" and a function as a role model in the work of mourning, the *Trauerarbeit*. The family did not see it that way. While recognizing that they had preserved the artistic legacy of the master, Syberberg deplores their missed opportunity: "And not only they [the Wagner family], all of us have this work to do: the work of mourning,. . . . Where is the redeeming word from Bayreuth, for instance, this little 'Yes, we too are guilty'" (*Filmbuch*, 289). Syberberg published these words in 1976. His own *Trauerarbeit* was to conclude with *Parsifal* in 1982. But many years had to pass before vaguely similar words came from the Wagner family. Finally, in 1997, the composer's great-grandson Gottfried Wagner published his history of "Bayreuth," *Wer nicht mit dem Wolf heult* (He Who Does Not Howl with the Wolf).[31] Not *wolves*, but *Wolf*, Hitler's nickname. And here, at long last, a family member *confesses* or airs many hushed-up family secrets. Some skeptics wonder if this compilation of revelations would qualify as a first step toward an exonerating admission. At least one reviewer considers it to be merely a salvo in the war of succession within the Wagner dynasty.[32] On the other hand, a note on the Internet in November 1997 quoted the Israeli newspaper *Haaretz* as reporting that Dr. Gottfried Wagner was teaching a seminar on music and anti-Semitism at the Ben Gurion University in Beersheva, starting in December 1995.[33] Considering the location, topic, and speaker, Dr. Wagner's preoccupation with his family's past may just be that belated first move towards a redemptive reckoning. His involvement in Jewish-German dialogue and numerous lectures on similar topics around the world appear to confirm this concern. Unfortunately, his book of 1997 still contains accusations against Syberberg. The reservations remained during his visit at the University of North Texas in Denton in late March 2004. Nonetheless, Dr. Wagner stated repeatedly on that occasion that he was glad that Syberberg's documentary had been made.

In 1975, when *Winifred Wagner* caused an instant sensation, Gottfried Wagner did not yet have enough independence to defy the family. He eventually withdrew his name from the film credits and ended his friendship with the Syberbergs. The filmmaker's reaction to this rejection is palpable in the long essay "Meine Trauerarbeit für Bayreuth" (My Work of Mourning for Bayreuth) in his *Filmbuch* (245–96). This text in thirty-four mini-chapters replaces the book intended to accompany the film, a project that had to be abandoned when Gottfried Wagner withdrew his co-authorship. In spite of the wealth of articles published about this documentary, Syberberg's own report remains the most informative. The public almost expects anything from his pen to be polemical, and so is this piece. But one can also detect the writer's pain of loss, uneasiness over his own role, and anger. In part revenge, in part defense, in part lamentation, it still is an indispensable companion to the film.

Of particular interest are the passages about details that do not appear in the film. One learns, for instance, that a tape recorder supplemented the camera, and that it delivered the only documentation of the more relaxed conversations between takes. One of them concerned the phrasing of Mrs. Wagner's concluding sentence. After some deliberation, she accepted Syberberg's suggestion, which was really a question. And thus she ends her reminiscing with these words: "The public seems to be surprised that I was silent for so-to-speak thirty years, and asks why I suddenly have decided to talk now. And I return the question: Well, why not?" (*Filmbuch*, 284–85). According to the sound recording, Mrs. Wagner laughingly characterized the question-as-answer phrase as a Jewish formulation. Coming on the heels of her professed fond memories of Hitler, this conclusion adds a twist to her presentation that did not go unnoticed by the public who shared her loyalties. Some even inquired later if Syberberg was Jewish, since he planted these words in her mouth (*Filmbuch*, 292). The readers, who have by now become alert to the director's principle of composition, will recognize this detail in the film as typical of counterpoint: one hears two or more versions of the same basic "subject" simultaneously. They sound very unlike each other, rather like contrasts. They really represent different stages of transformation. One version manifests itself brashly in the content of the words, the other subtly in the syntax.

This kind of musically inspired verbal overlay develops also in another statement made by Winifred Wagner. She confides that the old Nazis resorted to a new code word for Hitler's name after the war, since one could no longer speak openly about him without getting into trouble. Therefore, she continues, they referred to him as *U.S.A.*, an acronym for *unser seliger Adolf* (our late Adolf). That entails both the U.S.A. that fought a world war to crush the enemy Hitler, and a Hitler alias *U.S.A.* Besides, popular parlance uses the name U.S.A. interchangeably with America. What does her remark mean for Syberberg's use of these names? His books and films refer frequently to America as a motif. Since he delights in ambiguities, one may suspect that Winifred Wagner's example of doublespeak from now on informs also his choice of vocabulary whenever he mentions the dictator or anything pertaining to the United States. They may not cancel each other out as opposing political forces. Rather, they could possess a chord-like doubling in counterpoint, enabling each to evoke the other, in addition to retaining their own identity. For, of course, during a fugue, one hears the "voices" or subjects simultaneously. In *Winifred Wagner*, the play on semantic ambiguity involving U.S.A. and *U.S.A.* is explained in prosaic words that give the impression of silencing any musical overtones. But the speaker nonetheless introduces a musically related mode of expression in spite of herself. As Mrs. Wagner's memory reveals, her mind has blocked out big sections of the past from her consciousness. In both meanings of the fugue, this old woman does not display any capacity for movement and transformation. She presents a schoolbook example of an arrested psychological fugue. Of course real music is absent in this film. In section 12 of his essay, Syberberg alludes faintly to such lacking ability by describing her and her years of glory as *unmusisch*, not just "unmusical," but "lacking devotion to the Muses" (253). He contrasts her with several respected admirers of Wagner, such as Hans Mayer, Ernst Bloch, Thomas Mann, and Theodor W. Adorno. The same passage also introduces Hannah Arendt's phrase "the banality of evil," to which he adds the inverse, "the evil of banality," in reference to Mrs. Wagner's way of thinking. With this turning-around he carries out in words the musical motion of crab (retrograde, *Umkehrung*) and claims that it provided him with the needed "key" to approach his task. His quasi-musical handling of the language imitates, then, a capacity for change and development. At the same time, it describes her place as a counterpoint movement in crab (retrograde). For in spite of the *unmusisch* Mrs. Wagner, the film continues the principle of composition. This dimension emerges best in the pattern of editing and prompting of topics. For instance, screens of script occasionally interrupt the visuals, sometimes as black text on white background, sometimes white on black. The text may repeat or elaborate on the spoken narration, or even correct it. It may block out the soundtrack, or only the image, or be accompanied by Syberberg's voice-over, etc. The pattern of variations of this editorial interference conveys the composition so subtly that most viewers would consider the work to be nothing but a primitive, filmed monologue, devoid of artistic merit.

Although not a part of the Trilogy, the film of Winifred Wagner's memoirs nonetheless claims its place in Syberberg's series on "German" topics. A strong, but unchanging, rigid representative of her generation, this woman serves as a foil for Karl May and his inner transformation. More importantly, for Richard Wagner, whose legacy she guarded and preserved; and for Hitler, who emerges as the invisible protagonist of the film, and to whom she remains unflinchingly loyal. It is this fondness for her friend Wolf that caused the sensation wherever the documentary was released. Understandably, the public debate focused on the political dimension of her remarks. This focus is reflected in the title of an article Syberberg published in France, "Je n'ai jamais fait de politique."[34] It quotes Mrs. Wagner's remark that she had never been active in politics. Besides reporting on the interview with her and the break with the Wagner family, Syberberg mentions a longer version first published in *Die Zeit* as "Winifred, Wahnfried und wir." The interest in the topic was enormous, also beyond Germany's borders. Gradually, other aspects of the film began to be examined, such as the role of memory.[35] This film is probably the most successful part of Syberberg's German series in achieving its intended effect. Two reasons may be the deceptive simplicity of the composition and the non-threatening protagonist. In other words, the artistic component remains almost undetectable and does not divert attention from the narrative. And it is easy to accept the old woman as a relative or neighbor, someone close enough to provoke the shock of recognition, at least easier than would be the case with Hitler a few years later.

Mrs. Wagner's death in 1980 provided an opportunity for Syberberg to publish his commentary-cum-obituary in *Der Spiegel*.[36] Starting by characterizing her as a great woman, he could rest assured that his article would arouse indignation and provoke protests. Of course, readers did respond, e.g. in the issue of March 24. He outlines her position and accomplishments as a list of paradoxes, always careful to balance negative with positive. That also extends to his personal impression of her. While he sometimes felt like her "adopted son" during the filming, he also reports looking down into abysses and saw her covered with blood as she laughed about the fate of the Jews (235). This "Shakespearean figure in the myth of the twentieth century" will now survive as a monument in his film, he states. Perhaps Syberberg's comments would have caused less ire if he had not repeatedly referred to this documentary, and thus preserving, function of his *Winifred Wagner*. Also the centennial of her birth in 1997 produced numerous media commentaries. Quite a few of them reveal the impact of Syberberg's film by quoting from it.[37]

Winifred Wagner premiered in Paris in August 1975 and in Germany at the Filmforum in Düsseldorf in November of the same year. The television versions are drastically abridged, with various filmographies citing running times of ninety and 104 minutes. The video version released in 1993 restored the original length.

Syberbergs Filmbuch

In 1976 Syberberg published the *Filmbuch* that includes a section on the *Winifred Wagner* documentary. It takes stock of his cinematic and printed work up to and including this film. It contains seven chapters of unequal length, his filmography, and numerous illustrations not reproduced elsewhere. The chapters are:

[1]. "Film als Musik der Zukunft. Eine Ästhetik" (Film as Music of the Future: an Aesthetics). The thirteen sections covering eighty pages discuss primarily his films. The original publication, *Le Film, musique de l'avenir*, appeared as a special issue of *Cinémathèque* in 1975. The occasion was the first retrospective of Syberberg's work in Paris. The texts contain a wealth of information mixed with the filmmaker's thoughts on aesthetics.

[2]. "Film-Alltag" (Everyday Life with Film). The second chapter adds more of the same, gradually interspersed with autobiographical data and comments on contemporary conditions. Syberberg's independence develops into the role of critic and challenger as the animosity between him and the movie establishment intensifies. The second half of the chapter consists of reprinted, unkind reviews of his work in the German media and his comments on these reviews.

[3]. "Wörterbuch des deutschen Filmkritikers" (Dictionary of the German Film Critic). These thirty-seven pages of brief paragraphs with cue-words in dictionary format continue to illustrate German reviews of Syberberg's movies. The selection includes only negative statements, giving the impression of total rejection in Germany. Of course his films also met with some appreciation, as a survey of printed

reviews would easily prove. Otherwise the films would not have been distinguished with a long list of German prizes and awards. However, the increasingly inimical reception of his work is conveyed clearly and serves as a contrast to the following unit.

[4]. "Französische Kritik" (French Reviews). The forty pages of French reviews of *Ludwig*, *Hierneis*, and *Karl May* were all translated into German by Helga Elisabeth Syberberg. These essays are without exception informed and informative, analytical as well as sensitive to the aesthetic intentions, and, of course, they are positive.

[5]. "10 Jahre Film in Deutschland. Aktuelle Filmtexte" (Ten Years of Cinema in Germany: Currently Relevant Texts about Film). The six essays by Syberberg appeared originally between 1970 and '76 in newspapers and journals. The first is "An die Kinobesitzer und die Presse" ([Open Letter] to Owners of Movie Theaters and the Press). It announces his independent distribution of *San Domingo*. The text justifies this course of action and explains the circumstances prompting it. The second text, "Warum Ufa-Stars?" (Why UFA Stars?) responds to criticism against *Karl May*. It defends the use of actors who had been professionally active during the Third Reich. They represent German film history, and it did not begin with UFA or Hitler, the writer maintains. Seen in retrospect, these actors underscore the continuity in Syberberg's program and are indispensable as carriers of motifs and themes in his work. The third unit reprints "Die Zukunft des Kinofilms aus deutscher Sicht" (The Future of Cinema from a German Perspective). Problems, challenges, and opportunities relating to German cinema are outlined in five sections. Then follows "Drei Tage in Hollywood" (Three Days in Hollywood) describing the filmmaker's experiences and impressions during the Filmex 1976, where he showed *Karl May*. The next text is "Karl Valentin." This entertainer (1882–1948) was a Bavarian Chaplin who also tried his hand at film. The memory of him informs both *Ludwig* and *Hitler*. The text elaborates on that connection. The concluding essay is "Nach zehn Jahren" (After Ten Years). This attack on the German movie business and film journalism introduces most of the issues and arguments found in Syberberg's subsequent publications. It is clear that the gulf separating him and his opponents has become too wide to be bridged. And he is too passionate to stop his crusade.

[6]. "Meine Trauerarbeit für Bayreuth" (My Work of Mourning for Bayreuth) of fifty pages contain much informative material on *Winifred Wagner*. In addition to excerpted transcripts, the chapter also discusses the genesis and the reception of the film, as well as Syberberg's reflections on the Wagner family. As mentioned, he also published summaries or excerpts of this material in several articles.

[7]. "Film als Fortsetzung des Lebens mit anderen Mitteln" (Film as the Continuation of Life by other Means). The postscript recapitulates the mains points while adding elaborations and anecdotes. Already here one finds a reference to Plato's cave. More than thirty years later, this idea matured into a project for the international art exhibit "documenta." Only in passing does the text touch on film as a projection inwards. It serves as a transition to the announcement of the next film, *Hitler*.

Chapter 4

Hitler: Ein Film aus Deutschland

Syberberg's *Filmbuch* of 1976 announces *Hitler* as being in preparation, arousing anticipation and speculation. For the filmmaker, 1976 was a busy year that included some travel, for example a trip to London in November in connection with the film about Winifred Wagner. Then, between February and October 1977 he completed the shooting and editing of *Hitler*. Syberberg was involved as scriptwriter, director, and main producer. Besides his own company, financial support came from two other German sources, from France and from Great Britain.

Syberberg refers to his film as *Hitler: Ein Film aus Deutschland*. In the English-speaking world it is known as *Our Hitler*, a title suggested by Francis Ford Coppola. The screenplay of the film appeared as a book in French, English, and German versions.[1] All three editions retained the original title. The German book edition differs from the English version in that it includes a fifty-page essay by Syberberg, which in the translation was abridged to twenty pages and supplemented with an eight-page preface by Susan Sontag. Her text is also a condensation of a chapter in her book *Under the Sign of Saturn*.[2] The following discussion will draw on both the movie and the book with quotations taken mainly from the English version of the printed script.

Seven hours long, the movie lacks a main title at the beginning, at least in the consulted video version. As the numeral one makes room for the German, French, and English words for the *Grail* on the screen, it is not clear if this word identifies the whole film or perhaps the first part. Most filmographies apply it to the first part, including Syberberg's own listing on his home page (www.syberberg.de). According to his book of 1981, *Die freudlose Gesellschaft*, his friend Coppola thought at first that "The Grail" was the intended title of the whole movie (109). Indeed, the author leads the reader to assume that "Der Gral" was the intended title. But further on in the same book, he justifies the change with his concerns for the next film project, *Parsifal* (274). The book to the film, however, identifies both the movie and its first part as *Hitler: Ein Film aus Deutschland*. That is also the title given in the printed announcement of the plans for the movie in the *Filmbuch* (305). In subsequent publications, Syberberg refers to it only as "the *Hitler* film." The finished version does, however, leave the viewer uncertain about the main title. The confusion may have been intended for several reasons. First, the act of naming has a revered precedence in Genesis. Syberberg may underscore the difference to that text by denying his creation a proper name. Also, the topic is not so much the title figure as the spectator, the "Hitler in us." This Hitler is the abyss in every person and therefore has innumerable names. Or, when repressed, remains nameless.

After a second, short visual segment, the film officially "begins" by listing the credits, including Syberberg's name. But not until the end of the fourth episode does the main title appear. The German script includes it while the English version omits it. But both mention it when it reappears at the end of part 1, this time with its own subtitle: "Hitler: Ein Film aus Deutschland: Von der Weltesche bis zur Goethe-Eiche von Buchenwald" (Hitler: A Film from Germany: From the World Ash Tree to the Goethe Oak of Buchenwald). A reader who has not seen the film version cannot tell where this identification occurs for the first time. It may be an insignificant detail, but interesting when exploring the composition.

Confusion has also surrounded the classification of the movie. The public expected a documentary on Hitler. After all, Syberberg had established himself with some notable films using interviews, research, reporting, and analysis. All of that is present and noticeable in this film, too, but the result defies labeling. A semi-fictional work, then. A voice-over early on even claims, "Everything is purely fictitious." The problem with that is the constant intrusion of authentic historical sound and visuals. Reality informs the fiction mercilessly, leading on, prodding, illustrating, correcting, confronting, and disturbing. Clearly, the filmmaker disregards the usual format of either the documentary or mass entertainment, although some early sections possess the potential for the latter. Rather, he intends the work to serve as a therapist's tool to heal a patient suffering from fugue.

The public's confusion continues with the structure. The four main parts consist of many smaller sections, but unlike the segments in *Ludwig*, they lack individual titles. As these units contain various numbers of episodes and camera takes, the viewer cannot always tell where the divisions come. The English edition of the script identifies them with a little blackened sun disk. The eclipsed sun is an apt symbol for dealing with the repressed Hitler phenomenon, since the dictator had chosen for his emblem the swastika, an ancient design of a swirling sun with bent or broken rays. But are there really 36 separate mini-chapters as suggested by these black disks? Since the German original does not contain them, one cannot be sure of the total. The author even increases the confusion by adding a unit in the book that was presumably planned but not filmed. By drawing attention to this "invisible" episode, he can still include references to a ballad by Heinrich Heine, "Die Grenadiere." Richard Wagner composed the music to it during their contacts in Paris. Much as Wagner repressed the memory of Heine and his friendship with him in his autobiography, so Syberberg, too, has "repressed" an episode involving a Jew by not filming it. It would appear that Syberberg carries the exercise of identification to a considerable length. He includes himself among the afflicted Germans.

The film places great emphasis on the concept of identification. Both the voice-over and many of the characters express time after time uncertainty about their own separate identity. The consciousness of being someone unique is gradually undermined while the collective, communal response to Hitler gains power through soundtrack and visuals. The first step in Syberberg's program aims at weakening the defenses against identification with the nation that supported Hitler so enthusiastically. With these barriers removed, the viewers should gradually discover that Hitler is a projection of their own inner self. Regardless of age and nationality, they are nudged on to recognize in their own human nature the capacity for the evil that Hitler represents. To make this possible, Hitler has to be shown as an ordinary fellow human being with whom one could possibly identify, at least in some minor way. Hence the emphasis on both the "harmless" man and the celebrated leader in documentary photos and the trivia of his daily routine from the myopic perspective of his valet.

Before the film presents the political Hitler visually, it prepares the viewer through a number of projections, most notably a series of Hitlers as various people envisioned him, such as a clown, a house painter, a Jack-in-the-box, an imitation of Chaplin's dictator playing with the globe, and others, all seen in the flickering light of the early moving pictures. As the film continues with photos of Hitler's parents and baby Adolf, the voice-over borrows Thomas Mann's expression "brother Hitler." Eventually, André Heller's voice reminds the audience, "It was the defeat of arms that brought us away from him, not understanding" (58).

Gradually, the photographic projections that fill the background begin to show more variety, including glimpses of the victims of the Third Reich. These brief, almost subliminal, images include a famous photo of the Nobel Prize winner Ossietzky as a prisoner and that of an anonymous young female inmate at Auschwitz. Eventually the focus shifts to an SA officer, representing the ranks of Hitler's most dedicated followers. The actor is Peter Kern in uniform, much as he had appeared in the rhumba episode in *Ludwig*. He is recreating the confession of the mass murderer in Fritz Lang's movie *M* of 1931. That psychopath was played by Peter Lorre (Laszlo Löwenstein), who had to flee into exile during the Third Reich. As the child murderer M, his most famous role, he was captured by members of the underworld and faced a tribunal presided over by the gangster boss (Gustav Gründgens). Manipulating the constellations of roles and actors, the director now "updates" the situation by presenting the criminal in Nazi attire. This twist preserves the memory of the 1931 model, while also creating an effect resembling counterpoint. Writhing on the floor, whining and stammering, Kern claims that he cannot remember what he is being accused of and that he really "can't help it" (Engl. ed., 61). These words reverberate in the minds of most Germans, para-phrasing as they do the famous statement of Martin Luther to the emperor at the Diet of Worms, as well as the popular refrain of Lola-Lola's song in the *Blue Angel*. These icons in the history of religion and cinematic art respectively are now joined by a murderous madman who cannot admit guilt, to say nothing of responsibility. He is a shattering display of denial, coming so soon after the subversive approach to Hitler.

This approach has been slow and gradual. It begins with a space voyage into a dark, starry universe, which is our innermost self according to the subtitles. This idea repeats the ancient view about the correspondence between the macrocosm and the microcosm. The travel inwards ends in a poorly defined area illuminated by spotlights and surrounded by darkness or projected images. This space is strewn with a jumble of objects relevant to the episode. Sometimes much of it hides behind billowing fog blurring memories and distinctions. Somehow, as the credits disappear from view, the notion of a beginning mingles with that of an end when the background shows a detail from the grotto in Wagner's *Rheingold*. That opera is the first in the tetralogy named after the magic ring of the Nibelungen. But simultaneously we hear the concluding music from *Götterdämmerung*, the last of the four operas. Of course, a ring does not have a beginning or an end. The thought is disturbing in view of the topic to be explored. Hitler and no end? A second jolt follows immediately. The first live person to appear in the film, and who will reappear on numerous occasions, embodies here the allegory of democracy. The concept is a cherished notion, especially to people in the West. Syberberg is no exception, to judge from his choice of actress: His own little daughter Amelie. But there is something alienating about the figure. Democracy appears and dresses as a grey-haired old woman in a long black cloak while playing with dolls. An ancient idea forever young? Or a youthful idea grown senile before its time? As with the visual and acoustic hints of overlapping beginning and end, so youth and old age converge in the allegory blurring distinctions of time. The viewer's surprise soon turns to alarm as a narrator (Harry Baer's voice) relates a fairy tale in which democracy is identified as the cause of all misery in the twentieth century (36). This may be one of the scandalons to which one actor alerts the viewers. Not only do Syberberg's writings and this film refer critically to the debased versions of democracy, that is, a political system with unfettered market-driven economy, materialism, manipulation, abuse of and by media, lack of spirituality and ideals, etc. But they also reiterate that it was democracy that paved the way to power for Hitler. Children learn in school that Hitler "took" or "assumed" power. Repressed is the fact that he was elected democratically with broad support, and, taking advantage of weaknesses in the constitution, could consolidate his power legally. Only then did he change the system from a constitutional democracy to a people-supported dictatorship. Syberberg emphasizes repeatedly that the majority of voters supported the new system and saw in their leader of humble origins a projection of their own aspirations. Hence the variations on *projection* throughout the film.

The prostitution of the law under Hitler continues, the film implies, in both East and West Germany, but in new disguises. Stark visuals, some involving nudity, supplement three lists of vocabulary taken from a "Dictionary of the Inhuman." On the first list, Nazi terms aim at the elimination of the unwanted (76–77 in the book). The second list with East German expressions pertains to political conformism and suppression of dissident art (78). And finally, the West German equivalent concentrates on film critics' jargon (79). The two post-war lists include names of writers and critics who, in Syberberg's view, embody the corruption of democracy. Much of the accompanying soundtrack documents the bookburning by students in 1933, giving their voices as they solemnly throw individual volumes on the pyre. This emphasis on words is a prominent feature of the film. Except for some occasional music and "static" from outer space, the viewers are bombarded with voices and verbal expression without relief. Much as thoughts drift through the mind, these voices continue incessantly, with numerous interruptions and non-sequiturs. For example, the old radio roll call of party martyrs interrupts the voices of the book burning, which in turn had cut off the ruminations of the invisible narrator. The interruptions function like the stretto (*Engführung*) in a fugue. Sometimes several soundtracks run simultaneously. After an hour, exhaustion sets in. Words, words, words. One is surrounded by relentless talk, even when one expects silence. For example, the circus director, seen in one of the first episodes and later called circus announcer, wears the make-up of a mime and should, then, really be a mute performance artist. But while in the arena, he, entices the audience with promises of upcoming events, and when reminiscing, is unable to stop soliloquizing. Words have lost their magic and have become cheap. Parallel with the development of such sciences as philology and linguistics, the word has been deprived of its mystical dimensions, has been reduced, debased, and abused like the Law. The film demonstrates it at great length, both in the language of National Socialism and in modern usage.

There is a method behind this verbal barrage: a weakening of mental defenses, a preparation for self-scrutiny, and a search for repressed memories. At the same time, the emphasis on words hints at a quasi-spiritual dimension in various stages of transformation. It is supported visually by back projections, such as Doré's illustrations to the *Divine Comedy*. Several religions revere the divine *Logos*, usually translated as the Word. To Christians, the Word or *Logos* refers to Christ, with the Latin *ratio* and other synonyms being of less importance. By contrast, Hitler is often viewed as an Anti-Christ. He, too, professed to lead his believers into a new and better world like a redeemer. He even selected a title, *Führer* (leader), to include such a nuance. The term evokes the ancient Egyptian Thoth and Greek Hermes, both divinities known as *Logos* and guide or leader of souls into the Otherworld. The torrent of words in the film functions at times like the current of Lethean propaganda, threatening to carry along and overwhelm the viewers' critical faculties. Unlike the Word of the Bible, this *Führer* leads his uncritical followers to hell. Several sections of the film actually play in hell and limbo. Once there, the viewers can no longer escape the dictator's charisma and the followers' élan. Trapped in the Otherworld of the film, the viewers encounter the dead awakening to haunt them. In part 1, some of these specters assume the shape of dolls. As small-scale portrait puppets they arise from their coffins. Here Hitler, Göring, and others, held by their human "supporters" and ventriloquists, think aloud or reminisce. They put on a chilling revue of old-time mentality, while being visible projections of the supporters' thoughts. Scariest is perhaps Fitzliputzli, the devil-clown and staple merrymaker on German puppet stages. This figure links up with several features found in Syberberg's work, for instance Richard Wagner. Enchanted with puppet theater, the composer was familiar with the names of the stock characters, including Fitzliputzli. His wife mentions the name and discussions about puppet theater on several occasions in her diary, while the composer uses the names in one of his letters to King Ludwig II.[3] Furthermore, Karl May wrote a story named *Professor Vitzliputzli*. The destructiveness associated with the carrier of the name has here been transferred to the narrator, while the professor himself is good-natured. Most important is probably Heine's poem in four parts, "Vitzliputzli," in *Romanzero*. His Moloch-like Mexican deity displays more clearly than the other figures the relationship with the Aztec divine pantheon. There he is known as the blue Huitzilopochtli.[4] This god of the poem decides to move to Europe after the arrival of the Spanish conquerors to take revenge on the Europeans. Being immortal, he will simply assume a new manifestation ("change the plumage"), become a devil, and work as an enemy of his enemies. This force begins to resemble the Hegelian "World Spirit." As a stock character of German puppet theater, Fitzliputzli has retained a sulfuric and threatening connotation, even as entertainment for children. In Syberberg's film, the Fitzliputzli puppet makes some startling remarks. He suggests that Hitler's place is not in hell, that he might be great, and that this greatness would cause hell to burst in the seams if he should be placed there. Presumably from the throng of followers filling up the space. The translator chose *big* for the original *groß*, making Hell burst because of Hitler's physical size. That option deprives the statement of its diabolical insinuation. Fitzliputzli confides that he is looking for a new place on earth again an wonders in what guise he should appear. The puppet reminds us, the viewers that he has been made immortal by us and is in us. Knowing Heine's version, one is prepared for a bloodthirsty, divine power of changing apparition seeking retribution. Not surprisingly, the next puppet to "speak" is Hitler as the beloved children's clown Kasperl, as if produced or projected as the devil puppet's new guise. The ventriloquist for the Kasperl doll is Rainer von Artenfels, the same actor who portrayed the young Hitler in *Karl May*. Both Fitzliputzli and Kasperl can claim connections to Syberberg's documentary on Konrad Pocci of 1967. In the nineteenth century, one of Pocci's ancestors had introduced these characters at the Bavarian royal court in his numerous puppet plays and skits for children. And finally, not to be overlooked is the only female doll in this line-up: a little Eva Braun who holds a Hitler doll in her arms. The serial miniaturization identifies the *mise en abyme* function of this episode. At the bottom of the *abyme* (*abîme*, abyss), these specters remain alive.

The *Hitler* film includes several characters and actors from Syberberg's earlier movies. Among them is Harry Baer, who reappears repeatedly, sometimes talking to a doll looking like Ludwig II. The disjointed ruminations of Baer-Ludwig continue the theme of melancholy and helplessness, now accented with such visual reminders as the polyhedron and Jupiter square from Dürer's *Melencolia I*. Speaking as Ludwig, Baer repeats the prophetic warnings the king had made concerning his impending sacrificial death. Politics, art, his death, everything worthy has become mass entertainment for profit. The various aspects of this theme borrowed from Benjamin and Adorno had already been quite pronounced in *Ludwig*. Now they keep reappearing like chunks in a murky soup of the unconscious, with other ingredients also surfacing with every new stirring of the pot.

In the Baer-Ludwig scenes one can recognize how the mentioning of the victims of the Third Reich triggers awareness of guilt. Here for the first time the *felix culpa* is heard, "happy guilt." A blasphemous, painful term when heard in context, since Baer-Ludwig refers to the national preoccupation with guilt without sympathy for the subject, calling it a sadly beautiful business for art (45). Guilt is, then, considered a premise for artistic endeavor, being the result of sinful action in the recent past. Syberberg borrows the Latin term from the Catholic mass. Without the sin or Fall in paradise, there would be no redemption through Christ. The term *felix culpa* occurs in a prayer during the consecration of the Easter candle in the old Latin mass on Saturday preceding Easter Sunday. Of course, the Fall from innocence and the subsequent longing for a return to paradise have inspired artists throughout the Christian era. Without sin, no guilt; without guilt, no redemption. But what does Baer-Ludwig mean by "subject" in the missing "sympathy for the subject?" The victims or Hitler, or us, the viewers? And who is the Redeemer? Syberberg leaves room for divergent interpretations. Incidentally, the *felix culpa* returns towards the end of part 1 in an enigmatic figure. The two Latin words appear on a sign attached to a standing mummy wrapped in plastic strips. To the introductory music of *Parsifal* the camera shifts repeatedly from the little girl in a black cloak playing with the Ludwig doll to the mummy and back. Each time one sees the mummy, more of the wrapping has been stripped away, revealing more of the body inside. Early in this process, only one eerie eye stares out of the wraps, maybe a visual reminder of the film classic *Die Augen der Mumie Ma* (*The Eyes of the Mummy*) by Ernst Lubitsch. Gradually, Syberberg's mummy reveals itself as a nude, female mannequin, another doll continuing the theme of projection and *mise en abyme*. But this mute figure only appears as layer after layer of wraps have been stripped away, still lifeless and unrecognized. The circling strips of plastic wrap find their counterpart in the strips of celluloid film that surround the little girl's cloak. Apparently she also personifies film. All such details tend to reappear in a kaleidoscope of shifting combinations.

The image of the child surrounded by strips of film both ends part 1 and introduces part 2. Again the title appears in German and English: "Ein deutscher Traum . . . bis ans Ende der Welt: A German Dream . . . Until the End of the World." The repeat at the end of part 2 omits the subtitle but adds Syberberg's name. By now the viewer knows what to expect: More of the same. That means no cinematic action, a series of static tableaux, narrator's voice-over, soliloquies by actors, a bewildering montage of visual impressions in a studio, and an additional soundtrack or two with historic recordings (speeches, news broadcasts) or music. As before, the imagery abounds in quotations from the arts: cinema, literature, painting, the dramatic genres, architecture, and sculpture. Early on, one notices, for example, self quotations from *Ludwig* and *Karl May*, both shown in an episode where Harry Baer as himself philosophizes in front of a gigantic eye. The pupil of this eye serves as a screen for the film quotations. However, without the script on hand as a reference, the viewer could not make sense of the dark visual narrative. It shows Karl May paying homage to the image of Death shortly before his own death and King Ludwig in grieving solitude upon learning about Wagner's death. Nor are the viewers likely to recognize the expression from *Karl May*, "the vast domain of our soul" (96), or the visual quotation of Baer sprinkling confetti snow over a miniature village, using a tin box showing a little girl as ornamentation, or the prophetic worry about the wrong man coming. As Baer's ruminations jump from one topic to another, much like a stressed mind struggling in vain to concentrate, the images also include glimpses of Amelie Syberg with the Ludwig doll. At one point one sees her against the projection of Wagner's death mask to the accompaniment of music from *Parsifal*. The components will reappear in Syberberg's next film. In spite of the apparent incoherence, the emphasis on death and gloom, and refracting mythologizing of the mind's world, the theme of the little girl begins to assert itself against the other topics. In this section, Amelie is again situated in a *mise en abyme*: A very small person, a living child, playing with a doll in the likeness of an adult. On the tin box one sees the image of a still smaller girl. Even the pupil of the eye relates to the child in a Hermetic string of semantic links. The Latin *pupa* (girl) and its diminutive *pupilla* (little girl, pupil) connect the girl as her parents' "apple of the eye" to the "pupil" of the eye. A further development is the German word for doll, *Puppe*, which refers to the miniature version. The viewers are finally faced with their reflection in the eyes of a facing Other, so to speak as the miniature in the pupil. The little actress, then, does no longer represent only democracy or film. She is also the viewers' reflection in the eye of the camera. She is the miniature version of ourselves. But sometimes we do not see ourselves reflected in the eye of the other as a beautiful child, but as a distortion or even Death. The reflection can assume shifting manifestations. Since the *pupa* also refers to the chrysalis of butterflies, the same word offers a link to the cycle of metamorphosis as well. The sequence of different manifestations in the life cycle of one insect informs the film's various "reflections" of the human countenance. The visual and verbal play on identity in changeable forms echoes the musical fugue with its modulations and interplay of the subject, also called tonic, leader, or *dux*, with its variations in counterpoint.

Harry Baer's concluding remarks in this episode offer a modulating transition to the next unit. Another mythic fairytale, these remarks focus eventually on the leader elected to guide humanity back to their lost paradise. He is a man from the midst of the people. They wanted him and they created him (97).

The circus arena of the first part has now changed to a carnival fair, where a magician takes the place of the circus director. The character, played by Rainer von Artenfels, is modeled on Dr. Caligari in the classic movie of that name. Another source of inspiration is the Tarot trump card called "Magician." While the stars of the inner universe fill the upper background in this scene, the lower half shows the magician's wall of pictures, not unlike a hall of distorting mirrors. Before describing them and his other curiosities to us, the spectators, he presents a freak show. This sequence of descriptive, respectively self-descriptive, introductions constitutes a variation of the flickering revue of Hitler projections in part 1. The men in this revue are at first immobile and blend in with the background of photographic panels. One by one they come alive and step forward. They represent five "small" men in the entourage of the Nazi leadership: First Himmler's masseur, then a cosmologist, an astrologer, Hitler's valet, and an unidentified man, possibly Hitler's projectionist. The astrologer may have been inspired by Erik Jan Hanussen (born Herschel Steinschneider, 1889–1933), one of Hitler's teachers about occult matters.[5] The cosmologist is undoubtedly Hanns Hörbiger (1860–1931), an Austrian engineer who developed the cosmic ice theory, which he "received" in a vision.[6] Incidentally, his granddaughter, Christiane Hörbiger, plays Luise in the first film Syberberg made with Kortner. Himmler actively supported the cosmic ice theory, and Hitler expressed interest in it. Dismissed by scientists, this mythically inspired corpus of thought informs Syberberg's imagery of the Third Reich mentality. The reader may remember the expression in the *Filmbuch*, "the tip of an ice age society" (113). Both in *Ludwig* and *Karl May*, snowy landscapes do not only represent coldness, but also hostile and ideologically poisoned environments in contrast to an exotic dream world. There is no winter in paradise. The contrast between lush landscapes and wintry coldness takes on contrapuntal qualities in Syberberg's collection of visual signs.

In this episode, the German book edition garbles the lines of text preceding the cosmologist's first words (138). The English version has sorted it out (100). Someone who reads only the German edition without seeing the movie could not tell which character the actor Peter Lühr portrays. This might very well be one of the obligatory glitches in metaphysical works of art. However, the absence of an identification of the cosmologist in the German text varies the suppression of Heine in the first part and anticipates another and similar suppression of information later in the same episode. While the valet, played by Hellmut Lange, testifies as the embodiment of the "banality of evil," here also of the humanity of the banal, an unidentified character quietly interrupts him by taking his place.[7] The viewer now sees Peter Kern continuing in this role talking about the "man who cremated Hitler." Neither the viewer nor the reader can be sure which of the two characters carried out the task.

In the few minutes Kern commands the viewer's attention, he succeeds in hauling in a fisherman's net full of Syberbergian references and self-quotations. One is not sure whether to shout "Bravo!" or shake one's head in amazement. Then, a mentioning of Wagner's Bayreuth prompts his call to Wagner, asking if he can hear him (102). Perhaps the character assumes that Wagner's ghost still lurks around in this existence as the other apparitions we have seen. When the man then begins to yodel so as to elicit an echo, one is of course reminded of the yodeling King Ludwig in his resurrection scene as well as Theodor Hierneis' attempt, which resulted in eagles' cries. This time the yodeling actually yields an echo. One is not sure if it comes from Wagner's ghost or the surrounding soul mates in the freak show. But the sound has clearly caused some sympathetic reverberations. Warming to the topic of Wagner, Kern's character explains how Wagner's music " was written in blood, and blood, as we all know, is a very special potion; it attracts the devil unless it is drawn from the heart" (102). This statement, which refers to Faust's written pact with Mephistopheles, must hold a special attraction for Syberberg, since he has used it in several publications.[8] Whether or not Wagner wrote his music with blood from his heart remains unanswered, but one suspects that the mysterious speaker has been attracted by the blood. After all, the actor's name is Kern, and the German noun *Kern* means "kernel" or "core." That is the word used by Goethe's Faust as he watches the transformation of a black dog into Mephistopheles: "Das also war des Pudels Kern!" (So that was the poodle's core!). The pact between the two is signed with Faust's blood. These two characters entered Syberberg's oeuvre already with the filming of the Brecht productions, one of them being Goethe's early version of the theme, his *Urfaust*.

Whether a mephistophelian or a fitzliputzlian character, Kern's anonymous character in hat and dark leather coat is also an utterly devoted follower of Hitler. When his narrative jumps from Wagner's music to "I was involved from beginning to end," stressing the "I," he seems to revert to the man who cremated Hitler's body. He ends his "number" with: "The only chance for the greatest mass murderer in world history" (102). One presumes that he means suicide was Hitler's only chance to escape capture, and by destroying the body this little man is claiming a place in history for himself. A negative heroism, then, consisting in obliteration of evidence, the very opposite of historic fame. What sets Kern's appearance apart from the rest of this revue is the suppression of his identity in the printed script. This again "corresponds" to the planned but not filmed episode based on Heine's poem in part 1, but with the twist that this time the film includes the unit while the printed version suppresses the information. The two segments display many other similarities and correspondences: the theme of love and loyalty, references to death, grave, resurrection, and soldiers. In the Heine episode they were grenadiers still expressing faith in Napoleon after his unsuccessful campaign in Russia, in the second episode devotés of Hitler who survived the defeat of World War II. And, of course, there are Richard Wagner and Peter Kern's character. One recognizes the works of contrapuntal progression. On the narrative level, it would seem, then, that the film and the book carry on something like a tense relationship full of lies, but with unintended glimpses of truth on occasion, much like a mind unable or unwilling to recognize its own nature. Usually, the voices and printed words represent memories of the conscious mind, whereas the silent or semi-suppressed dimensions resemble the submerged parts of the iceberg. They appear to some extent in the visuals.

Sometimes these presences are visible, but it takes a narrator to make the viewer recognize them. However, the new Dr. Caligari is not a reliable narrator. He mixes and distorts history, myth, new inventions, and Third-Reich-style propaganda, sometimes with an audible touche between numbers. The curiosities surrounding him constitute a strange collection. The stuffed eagle and wolfhound, for example, carry emblematic significance among the political symbols. Among the "negative" objects the magician displays a rat as a representative of the "adversary" and a cat without eyes. The latter, so he informs us, illustrates how the boys in Hitler's elite academies learned to become tough by picking out eyes on live cats, which, one hears, was OK, because Hitler did not like cats.

Only in retrospect does one realize that the long list of curiosities makes a 180 degree turn, with equivalents or correspondences on each side. At the division or turning point one finds the eagle and its American cousin, the tasteless chicken, or "rubber eagle." Then follow the insects, possibly Kafka's bug, Gregor Samsa, and the monkeys for "breeding-down purposes." The cat without eyes finds a counterpart in the dish of blue eyes of SS men, poked out by soldiers in Stalin's Red Army as it "liberated" German-held territories. The exterminating power of rat semen "corresponds" to the bottle of Hitler's semen and its regeneration story. A hyena balances the wolfhound, and so on. For the magician's tale of the Grail and Holy Lance one recognizes a counterpart in a panel of two allegorical figures, presented in his version as Faith and the Agnostic.

Not until the magician comments on these two figures can one see them clearly. They had been in plain view much of the time, but in the dark background along with all the other panels of Sascha Schneider's paintings, Hitler's portrait, the caricature ears from a Valentin-Brecht photo, the female guard at Auschwitz, a pyramid, and much more. All the while, the background soundtrack periodically decreases and increases in volume, adding another layer of impressions. Intermittently, it cuts in with snippets of radio broadcasts from the war years. And imperceptibly, the magician's role approaches that of a radio announcer. The German script ,but not the English version, alerts the reader to this gradual shift. Early in the episode, the magician's lines are identified by the actor's name followed by "magician" in parenthesis: "Rainer von Artenfels: (Zauberer)." Soon the title in parenthesis disappears. But on two occasions at the end of the freak show, as he prepares to introduce the two allegorical figures, the descriptive narrative refers to him as the *Ansager* (announcer). This change parallels the transformation earlier of the circus director into a circus announcer or barker. In other words, while the character retains the trappings and function of an entertainer, he also assumes the radio announcer's role of dispensing politically correct information as it would have been approved by the Propaganda Ministry. This added dimension informs his introduction of the two female figures.

The photographic panel shows two medieval sculptures in relief. Artenfels presents them along with several other types of performers at a *Markt*, including such unexpected categories as cannibals, prophets, and conjurers (104). Actually, he does not say *Kannibalen* but *Menschfresser* (people eaters), a construct patterned on "fire eaters," which one might anticipate at a carnival fair. However, his "prophets" somehow refuse to integrate themselves among muscle men and modern-day magicians. One would have expected fortune tellers. And what market is he talking about? Does he mean the fairgrounds (*Jahrmarkt*) or the stockmarket? A naïve viewer assumes that the frame of reference is restricted to the carnival fair, but soon encounters difficulty with the continuation of the presentation. For the two girls are supposed to "belong" to the company just described. Artenfels identifies them as Faith and Agnostic. The sad and blind one represents the past and hails from the ghetto of life (104). The passage sounds as enigmatic and incoherent as many other statements in the film. But the observant reader or viewer will have noticed a second word that does not fit the language of the speaker: "ghetto." One wonders if the prophets and the ghetto somehow reveal more than intended about the magician himself. His model in *The Cabinet of Dr. Caligari* was able to read Kabbalistic literature and lead an (imagined) double life as carnival magician and the director of a psychiatric hospital. One suspects that the unexpected choice of words from Syberberg's entertainer also indicate a dual nature of the speaker. The "prophets" and the "ghetto" combine with the contrastive treatment of the two figures to identify one of them as representing Judaism. Still, a viewer who depends on English subtitles will remain uncertain, since the figures are named Faith and the Agnostic. Here the scripts help remove at least that uncertainty as a descriptive passage identifies the figures as statues of Church and Synagogue in the Cathedral of Strasbourg. The film attempts to equate that bit of printed information with the intermittent sound from a mass. The recording renders a Russian Orthodox mass. One may wonder why the director did not choose excerpts from a service in the Cathedral of Strasbourg? The most likely answer is that the Orthodox liturgy has retained more of the older music derived from Jewish rituals. The soundtrack is therefore closer to both Christian and Jewish traditions than the spoken commentary.

At this point, the "announcer's" identification of the two figures remains misleading, or at best unclear. For example, the Agnostic's predicament has been made to sound harmless by the reference to enhancement in art and mythification. One might hear what one wants to perceive. One should also be aware that the English translation of the names loses an important nuance. *Glaube* is rendered correctly as "faith," but *Unglaube* does not mean "agnostic." An agnostic professes uncertainty, lack of knowledge, about the teachings of a religion. To a Gnostic, of course, faith and knowledge about divine matters may be close to synonyms. In everyday parlance one would prefer "non-belief," "skepticism," or "heresy" as a better contrast to "belief" or "faith." Or "belief" would need a modifier, such as "Christian." The German text gives the contrast of *Glaube* as *Unglaube*. An *Ungläubiger* in church history usually reers to a heathen or infidel. But like so many other words, it, too, assumed a new meaning in the Third Reich. The positive term, *gläubig* (faithful), came to denote the committed follower of Hitlerism, an individual who pledged allegiance to the *Führer* and his gospel. The borrowing of religious terminology is no coincidence. A well-known example of such coloring of traditional vocabulary occurs in Hannah Arendt's *Eichmann in Jerusalem*. As the condemned Eichmann faced the gallows, he uttered some final words: "He began by stating emphatically that he was a *Gottgläubiger*, to express in common Nazi fashion that he was no Christian and did not believe in life after death" (252). *Glaube*, then, would not necessarily indicate belief or faith in Christianity. This noun and the cluster of related words add a meaning reflecting a political and quasi-religious ideology. By this token, the statue called Church and here renamed *Glaube* allegorizes the faithful of the Third Reich, while the Synagogue, now named *Unglaube*, represents the opponent of, or contrast to, this system. The original statues flanking a portal in the sanctuary could be viewed as complementary representations, but were more often interpreted as contrasts. Now they are presented as irreconcilable contrasts. The entertaining pratter of the magician reveals itself as a subversive distortion and indoctrination, but with unintended overtones conveyed by the semantic ambiguities. Through them, one can perceive several meanings simultaneously.

If one persists in scratching through additional layers of semantic veils, one uncovers finally something hidden. The clue is the syntax in the German descriptions of the sad figure. The non-German word order in these statements attracts attention. First, when talking about her as the past or old times that "always" looks sad, one would expect "always" to precede the expression "die *immer* traurig aussehende alte Zeit." But contrary to German usage, the speaker inserts *immer* between *traurig* and *aussehende* (104). Then he continues by again combining *always* with the symbols of the old and the new systems. The result does not sound German. Either the adverb *immer* (always) should precede *traurig*, or be replaced with an adjective modifying the first noun, e.g. *die ewigen Symbole*, or it needs to be moved so as to modify the verb, which turns out to be missing. As a native German, Syberberg has no excuse for using such a peculiar syntax. Unless, of course, the irregularity signals something. The speaker may, for example, not be quite as "German" as first assumed. And in both examples with *immer*, the adverb seems to refer to, or at least be closer to, the Synagogue than to the other figure. The language associated with a synagogue is Hebrew. Could Hebrew possibly influence the sentences and cause the strange German? Webster's two-way Hebrew dictionary gives the transliterated equivalent "always" as *tameed*. The *Brown Hebrew and English Lexicon* offers six definitions for that entry, all of them being nouns and adverbs relating to continuity or repetition. The last one reads "daily (morning and evening) burnt-offering." With one more detour via Greek one can glimpse the connection. The Greek word for this kind of biblical sacrifice is *holocaust*. Although the two statements with the peculiar syntax would not form meaningful sentences if one simply replaced *immer* with *holocaust*, the invisible connection of *immer-tameed-holocaust* nonetheless imbues the references with a new dimension. Hidden somewhere under layers of words lies the painful fact of genocide. This part of the submerged iceberg does not reach the surface, but it affects the color and movement of the water above it. Hence the irregular German syntax. Similarly, many other clumsy or garbled sentences merit an analysis with a Hebrew dictionary at hand. The Hebrew or Jewish presence is submerged or suppressed, but reveals itself somehow. A composer might express this through counterpoint and overtones. Syberberg resorts to visual, semantic, or acoustic means.

Enriching the semantic layering is the rotation of actors in several roles. Some of them appeared in earlier films by Syberberg. As already mentioned, Rainer von Artenfels played Hitler in *Karl May*. In the fairground episode he dons the habit of Dr. Caligari, evoking all the associations surrounding that character. His language reveals a multiple personality speaking German mixed with both Nazi and Hebrew characteristics. The distinctions of individuality are being blurred or suffused with characteristics of apparently incompatible figures. One is again tempted to think of fugal movements with variations playing simultaneously. Not only do several actors reappear in this film, but they also take on a series of roles. For example Harry Baer, who continuously questions who he is, tries on the role of Ellerkamp, Hitler's film projectionist. When describing the dictator's passion for cinema, Baer-Ellerkamp calls Hitler the greatest filmmaker of all time (109). While provoking questions about that from the viewers, this unit also illustrates the difficulty with classifying the dialogue in much of the film. As with the handling of speech in the Brecht film, so one here also wonders if it is a monologue or a dialogue when the character is thinking aloud or addressing the camera, that is, the viewers. The I and the Thou remain elusive. Several times in the course of the film a character will emphasize "ich und du" and "du und ich," pulling in the spectators. A variation of the hard-to-define soliloquy occurs, for instance, when a socialite, played by Johannes Buzalski, talks to a group of party guests. Most of them turn out to be store mannequins and cardboard cut-outs of photos. And these mannequins conjure up Walter Benjamin's *Passagen-Werk*. Not only do the store dummies of the 1920s seem to belong in his Parisian arcades, but also his numerous references to modernity as hell fit the film's atmosphere. And in this strangely talkative cinematic hell, actors and roles become interchangeable. Rainer von Artenfels in black leather coat soon reminisces as young Goebbels about his born-again experience, while a loud rhumba-tune and the background projection establish a link to the dance episode of Hitler and Röhm in *Ludwig*. And when the enraptured Artenfels-Goebbels exclaims, "That is a prophet!" about Hitler, one remembers only too well the earlier reference to prophets in the magician's remarks. In this closed universe of the mind, one continuously stumbles over such cross-references. Everything relates to everything else.

Two more episodes stand out in the long part 2, the first one very short, the other extremely long. The former has supplied the most widely reproduced still from the film: A toga-clad Hitler rising from the grave of Richard Wagner. No longer the circus announcer, Heinz Schubert gives a haunting performance of Hitler's ghost or corpse emerging from hell. The scene is modeled on an illustration by Gustave Doré for "Inferno Canto X" of Dante's *Divine Comedy*. There one sees Dante and his guide Virgil staring at a ghoulish resurrection.[9] According to the book, little Amelie Syberberg and a life-size mannequin in Wagner's cloak recreate the onlookers, but one cannot distinguish them against the dark background in the film, at least in a video version viewed on a television set. What initially looks like a resurrection proves to be a brief apparition to give a speech. Among the introductory remarks, the spectators as Hitler's audience hear him state that he gave them what they put into him, and what they wanted to hear and do (128). The film already presented similar statements, declaring Hitler to be a projection of the people's wishes. Another of his utterances here is again heard three scenes later, now from the lips of a disciple of the ice cosmogony (128). Yet another statement will be repeated by Syberberg himself in reference to his own struggle years later. It should come as no surprise, then, that this fictional Hitler speech hits the limits of referentiality, also in hidden quotations and name dropping. Those viewers who are not asleep by now have been busy attempting to identify visual and audible quotations. Now they must be startled at what they hear. One such reference conjures up Wagner and Heine, again together. Hitler says that he is the bad conscience of the democratic systems, (129). The first part of this statement paraphrases a sentence in Cosima Wagner's diary. Her husband had been reading to her from a volume of Heine's posthumous works and commented on the author, who had been his friend in Paris and a baptized Jew: "'He is the bad conscience of our whole era,' R.[ichard] says, 'the most unedifying and demoralizing matters [*sic*] one can possibly imagine, and yet one feels closer to him than to the whole clique he is so naïvely exposing.'"[10] One remembers from part 1 how Syberberg half-suppressed an episode with an echo of Wagner and Heine from their friendship period, and how Wagner minimized their friendship in his published memoirs. But privately, he still paid attention to Heine, even years after the latter's death. This discrepancy between the public and the private memory of the composer finds a correlate in the Hitler ghost's references to "the Jews." At first his words sound rather similar to what Wagner might have said. That would not surprise anyone, since this figure wrapped in a toga-like shroud emerges from the composer's grave. And Wagner was known as an anti-Semite. Hitler, then, as a reincarnation and intensification of Wagner? The image is persuasive. Chronologically, Wagner preceded the dictator, dying six years before Hitler was born. The latter's admiration for Wagner the man, his art, and his legacy is well known. One could therefore, with considerable justification, see in this cinematic episode Hitler's spirit or ghost (*Geist*) emerge from Wagnerian soil. In other words, a direct line leading from Wagner's intolerance to the Holocaust. That is how much of the world views the composer today: Wagner, the proto-Nazi.

Wagner had also issued another statement with a similar choice of words. It appeared in 1869 in the republication of his article "Judaism in Music."[11] Referring again to Heine, the composer wrote: "He was the conscience of Judaism, just as Judaism is the evil conscience of our modern Civilisation" (100). Now the Hitler apparition calls himself the bad conscience of the democratic systems. In assembling a list of these cases of "bad conscience," one becomes aware of similarities and contrasts. Regardless of nuances, the doubling of Hitler and Judaism for the same designation comes as a shock until one remembers the workings of counterpoint.

However, this interpretation does not exhaust the readings of the tomb episode. For one thing, this Hitler identifies himself as an artist (128). On a naïve level, one might therefore attempt to restrict the connection between Wagner and Hitler to the emulation of an admired role model who achieved his artistic objectives against great odds. But Hitler as an historical phenomenon does not allow such a harmless version to stand alone. It is through the association with Wagner that Hitler returns to haunt the viewers here, and similarly, much of the world remembers Wagner's name as linked with Hitlerism. Like Heine, both have something to do with a bad conscience. Syberberg applies the phrase to himself as well. In 1975 he discussed his plans for this film and stated: "I know that Hitler as the topic of a movie won't work. But that does not prevent me from playing the [role of the] conscience of the nation" (*Filmbuch*, 138). One is reminded of the *bad* conscience, as in Wagner's comments about Heine. When comparing Wagner's statement with that put in Hitler's mouth, a significant shift in the subject has taken place. Wagner had spoken about Heine in the third person; the Hitler ghost refers to himself. The grammatical subject and "other" is no longer Jewish. But the speaker undermines this distinction by continuing to speak in the first person while tacitly quoting from another famous source: "I am a man, with two eyes and ears like you, and when you prick me, do I not bleed?" And he concludes the statement with "I too, I too am one of you." Yes, Adolf Shylock. By appropriating the plea from *The Merchant of Venice* (3.1), the speaker merges with the unseen other. The intended effect of this scandalon is, of course, to provoke a strong reaction in the audience. But strangely enough, the critical discussions consulted for this study pass over the passage without voicing shock or surprise. Perhaps most viewers are so overwhelmed by the length and intensity of the film that they become incapable of recognizing and distinguishing allusions, even when they are quite obvious. Unaware of the fugal principle at play, viewers are unprepared for the double-speak or even fourfold barrage of impressions. In this episode, Hitler, that is the musical "dominant," has moved into the place of the tonic or *dux* (leader, *Führer*). On occasion, the audience can recognize other versions of the tonic as they play in counterpoint. One has the impression that they intrude into the flow, or interrupt somehow. The musical term for such overlapping is *stretto* or *Engführung* (narrow passage). The visual equivalent of the narrow passage is the grave.

More obvious than the quasi-musical parallels is the reflexivity involving Syberberg's other works. The allusion to Shylock revives the memory of Fritz Kortner's Shylock. The second documentary about the actor recorded him reciting this very passage. Thus, joining the Jewish character is a Jewish actor, both unseen, but thanks to the medium, distinctly audible.

Hitler concludes his address with a salutation more suitable to a letter than to a speech, identifying himself as the viewers' "brother Hitler" (129, Gm. ed., 164). The phrase "brother Hitler" is borrowed from Thomas Mann.[12] While in American exile, Mann wrote an essay with that title in March 1939, well before World War II and the Holocaust. This essay calls the dictator a catastrophe and many other strong epithets. And still, Mann is able to coin the term "brother Hitler." It is a necessary task, he asserts, to put aside hatred and grapple with this demonizing phenomenon, to recognize oneself in him, even at the risk of forgetting to say no. Although he does not say so, one wonders if he has the Gorgon in mind. An encounter with Medusa was deadly unless one could view her through a mirror. The importance of this essay for Syberberg's cinematic mirror merits a book of its own. Let it suffice here to mention just a few other related thoughts from Mann's text recurring in the film: The degradation of Wagner's art for political purposes; "the bad conscience" in connection with Hitler's need to assert himself; the recognition of Hitler as an artist; the "child of hell," a term encountered later in the film; "projection of the unconscious;" and throughout the essay, the need to acknowledge and recognize the shared human drive empowering Hitler so as to overcome him.

Syberberg's affinity for, or indebtedness to, Mann's thoughts on this subject has gone unnoticed in the critical literature.

The concluding salutation of the Hitler ghost reverberates faintly with the horrors that the speaker does not identify in his speech. He clearly identifies his perceived adversaries, but not their fate. For example, he boasts of having liberated the intellectuals of the "Jewish Mafia," of harboring hatred of the Jews, and of having given his people "the persecution of the Jews." But the reality of those words might still be distorted and minimized by admiring listeners. His final words, however, conceal the truth that unmasks the brother as a Cain of unprecedented proportions. The farewell phrase begins with *forever*, and that word contains the clue. As used in "Our Father," Luther translated it as *in Ewigkeit* (Matt. 6.9). The Hitler apparition, however, uses the less common expression *auf ewig*. It now presumably suggests lasting love and loyalty. It contains an adverbial use of the adjective *ewig*. One of the most common adverbs to match this adjective is *immer* (always). One remembers the peculiar use of that adverb in the magician's comments on the Synagogue. His presentation revealed the semantic chain of *immer-tameed-holocaust*. The ghost uses a word from the same cluster of concepts. Although the syntax now is typically German, the chosen expression is not so common, letting the memory of semantic echoes cling to the adverb.

The English script compares the Hitler resurrection scene with a black mass (127). That term conjures up notions of magic, secret rituals, and alchemy. Syberberg makes some use of alchemical symbolism, appropriately enough in view of the Nazis' fascination with the occult. Especially the color changes denoting the stages in alchemical transmutation appear frequently. It was no coincidence that Hitler chose the three most prominent of these colors for his flag. Black represents a stage in the process in which the substance to be purified disintegrates (*nigredo*); white (*albedo*) is a stage of rebirth, and the final one is red (*rubedo*).[13] This three-part symbolism occurs, for instance, in the scene with young Goebbels. He is wearing a black leather coat. While he reminisces aloud, the tune and lyrics of a rhumba keep drifting in and out of our attention. Since the rhumba is an Afro-Cuban rhythm, the black African element inhabits the soundtrack as well. Goebbels' recollections end with the euphoria of his born-again experience (*albedo*), while the background songs now emphasize vocabulary such as bright, shine, sun, and light. Soon after, the speakers load their texts with references to the color red, as with blood, against a red background. Another round begins with the "black mass" and dark clothing, followed by Hitler's "resurrection" and white shroud, and ends with Shylock's words about bleeding. The division between two such color sequences and quasi-musical movements falls right in Hitler-Shylock's words as he claims to be "one of you." He begins the sentence by repeating "I too." In German, the second occurrence requires a reversed word order, resulting in something like "also I": ("Ich auch. Auch ich . . ."). At the period where the retrograde begins, the dark stage suddenly teems with black American occupation soldiers dancing with German girls around the closed grave of Wagner and Hitler. They dance to a tune with lyrics by Brecht about the dead waking up and coming up black (130).[14] This continues with frosty scenes illustrating the ice cosmogony and then more talk about blood. Other sections of the film do not emphasize the alchemical sequence so transparently, but practically all elements recur and mingle in various stages of comparable change all the time.

The Hitler tomb scene is by far the most frequently reproduced image of the film. But to judge from the literature about it, it is recognized more so for its visual impact than for its complexity and reflexivity. Number two in attracting critical attention is the long presentation by Hitler's valet, played by Hellmut Lange. In this unit, the main carriers of counterpoint are the spoken narrative and the photographic backdrops, both conveying their separate stories. The most conspicuous contrapuntal divergence occurs in such scenes where the valet's myopic recollection contrasts with sweeping vistas of the Bavarian Alps in the background. This little man from the bottom of the social hierarchy was placed so close to his master that his view became, and remains, microscopic. With an amazingly clear memory he focuses on details and minutiae of the *Führer*'s daily routine as he witnessed it all, such as how many biscuits Hitler ate for breakfast or what kind of shaving cream he liked. Valet Krause is unable, or unwilling, to consider broader issues. As with Theodor Hierneis before him, he represents the perspective from below. And like Hierneis, he gives the viewers a tour of his ruler's environment, but much of the time does not relate to what they see. In some instances one perceives the narrator's frame of mind through the distortion of proportions. The photographic projections, which as usual fill the entire background, sometimes show details of the interior of the chancellery vastly enlarged, with a diminutive narrator in front. In his mind these places still loom large. Only after the glimpse of the bombed ruins of some of these interiors does one realize that the valet himself is moving around in an intact world of memories. So vivid is this imagined reality that one hears footsteps on the stone floors and saluting with heels clacking. This man was privy to much sensitive information, but what he shares with the viewers is trivial, and the Hitler he presents is an almost ordinary man with distinctly human idiosyncrasies. However, Mr. Krause does not divulge any details about Hitler near the end of his life. Somehow that period did not exist. One remembers how Theodor Hierneis regaled his audience with equally trivial insider information, and somehow he revealed that he knew more than he wanted to discuss. He had obviously been paid to keep silent about the king's death, as his rubbing fingers of a money-money-money gesture confirm. What about Hitler's valet? One first sees the actor in the freak show at the carnival fair. He was the one who had his remarks interrupted by the anonymous man for a short while. When the valet continued his talk, he was still focusing on Hitler, as if there had been no interruption. Why had the magician not introduced the interrupting fellow as he had the other four? Did the reference to the man who had cremated Hitler's body really, or also, apply to the valet? Being so devoted and close to the dictator, he would have been a logical person to carry out the task. But visually, he has been disengaged from that identity and has been replaced with someone nameless. Returning to the valet's long presentation, one realizes that he does not address the traumatic last phase of his years with Hitler. Unlike Hierneis, who also keeps quiet about something, Krause might suffer from fugue.

The concluding episode of part 2 shifts abruptly to André Heller playing a nameless character. He supposedly portrays the "contrasting mirror image" of the filmmaker. The credits in the German script list him only as a "guest." To the faint strains of Beethoven's Ninth Symphony he ruminates on the vastness of the universe, eventually arriving at the cosmos as a molecule, the molecule as a cosmos, as well as human destiny and guilt. The background projections and surrounding objects continue the referentiality to Syberberg's other work and the themes of the movie. Part 2 ends almost as it begins to the music of Mozart's Piano Concerto in D Minor, the head of little Amelie with closed eyes, and the title in German and English, *A German Dream*. This time the subtitle is missing and Syberberg's name added.

The third part of the film has received relatively little critical attention. One reason may be the length of the work. By the time one arrives at the second half, the mind is saturated with impressions. And since the film lacks dramatic action in the traditional sense, one is hard pressed to remember and assess what is going on. Another reason might be the subject matter. By now the movie has reached the most painful topic of the Third Reich history, the Holocaust. While the spoken words, for long stretches at a time, present the official, semi-documentary views of, and reports by, uniformed SS men, the viewers are either squirming over so much revived hate propaganda, or, and that is a danger, relive with nostalgia a period long suppressed and condemned.

This part begins with the familiar frame: the little girl's face with closed eyes, the numeral three, and after some introductory visual and acoustic preparations, the title. The background snippets of music have now changed from Mozart to Wagner with strains from "Siegfried's Death" in *Götterdämmerung*. The title appears in full, but without the director's name: "Das Ende eines Wintermärchens und der Endsieg des Fortschritts. The End of a Winter's Tale and the Final Victory of Progress."

In the rondo of interchanging actors and roles, Heinz Schubert has dropped his Hitler shroud and reappears as Himmler, second in command in the Nazi hierarchy and the mastermind behind the Holocaust. In a therapist's exercise he would be as difficult a target for identification as Hitler. Not surprisingly, then, he is shown from his soft side, stripped down physically and psychologically to display a person with numerous weaknesses. He dominates four successive episodes of unequal length. The first one is by far the longest and most complex. The visible situation is a massage session in which the masseur, played by Martin Sperr, gives Himmler a treatment. This time the masseur's skills seem to be based on esoteric principles, to judge from periodic hand gestures. They appear to shake off unwanted collected charges. His hands may also dislodge psychic forces in the process. For a moment one is reminded of the scene in *Ludwig* where the king gets a facial massage. While his flabby belly is being kneaded, Himmler's perspiring face displays discomfort and increasing anguish at the vision he experiences. In double exposures we observe the projections of his official, ruthless persona in a sequence of several uniformed

SS officers emerging from the background. Their speech-like inner monologues first elaborate on the "subhumans" and the danger these pose to their adversaries. Then a disembodied voice produces a modulating shift in focus. This voice, belonging to Harry Baer, describes an invisible scene in an extermination camp where prisoners are being forced into the gas chambers. Somehow his voice restores their visibility, as a series of historical photos of concentration camp inmates from now on fills the background. In the foreground, the SS men reappear, each in turn narrating from his observations and involvement. Like automatons these figures remain unaffected by their gruesome reports. Time after time one notices that their lips remain closed while we hear their voices. Even in their immobile state they have disengaged themselves from their image in uniform. One officer, played by Peter Kern, presents an exception by undergoing a perceptible change. Unlike the stony faces of the others, his features betray emotion, and eventually, he begins to lip-synch with his separate voice. It is nothing like his whimpering recreation of the murderer in *M*, but there is a trace of life and humanity in this character. The background offers a visual correlate. The projection focuses on a young woman on the way to the gas chamber. Looking directly into the camera, she tries to cover her nudity with her arms. As the SS officer (Kern) relates his memories, several camera takes move her closer. Finally her face fills the background, transforming her gaze into the Eye of God. This eye continues to haunt the viewer for a long time. One may wonder why the director did not use a zooming camera for this step-by-step approach to the face. Only in his next book of 1981, *Die freudlose Gesellschaft,* does he discuss his aesthetic principles in the Hitler film. By refraining from employing sophisticated camera work, he supposedly refuses to emulate Leni Riefenstahl's techniques. Especially her films made at Hitler's request (*Triumph of the Will* and *Olympia*) display pioneering photography. Her technical accomplishments served Hitler's cause. Syberberg's simple use of the camera reveals a different loyalty. He deliberately avoids the techniques and tricks she made famous, such as mobile cameras, zooming, and clever cuts, for a reason: "But once having confronted Riefenstahl and her system and her master standing behind all this [=Hitler], one would have to defeat her master and his system on her territory, if possible."[15] He apparently succeeded in this. His contrapuntal handling of images, sounds, and motifs more than compensate for lack of technical bravura. In the scene with the officer and the victim's face, the division between a live character in the foreground and the still in the background lends a certain subliminal effect to the diminishing distance to the face. The viewer's focus rests on the man in the foreground. And still, one wonders about the use of double exposure of Himmler and his SS men. The technique was used to great effect in numerous movies of the Third Reich, e.g. *Jew Süß*. Is this exception to Syberberg's stated principles a gesture of identification or of a shared burden? Again, counterpoint adds at least one answer.

Peter Kern's SS officer introduces the motif of *sympatheia* when he describes the executioners' psychological stress from their reactions. Adopting as his own the words by Himmler (177), he tries to make himself and the viewers as jurors believe that the conflict between carrying out the atrocities and remaining "decent" made him and the other officers hard (168). While this officer's toughness proves questionable, one of his alter egos carries the hardness to its inhuman extreme. With no more emotion in his face than the puppets in part 1, he advocates the extermination of this "corroding plague" (174). This phrase may also be a veiled reference to Richard Wagner, who opposed intermarriage between Jews and Gentiles due to the "corrosive" effect of Jewish blood.[16] Ironically, the same character also introduces the motif of intercession when he comments on the number of petitions by Gentile Germans trying to help a "decent" Jewish friend. The speaker remains oblivious to the cruel irony of his words: so many decent Jews, and so much trouble for the SS men to remain *anständig* (decent) in their murderous work. The semantic shift presents yet another example of quasi-musical transformation. This character is portrayed by the same actor who plays the valet. By interrupting Kern's soliloquy, he reverses the sequence of the last speakers in the freak show, where Kern had interrupted Lange. Obviously, these two revues relate to each other. In the first one, the magician continues the show by "discussing" the two allegorical statues. The continuation of the second line-up brings on a concentration camp trusty in his striped uniform (Johannes Buzalski). Cowed and timid, this character conforms with the prejudicial view of his oppressors. Trying to survive by mimicry and adaptive behavior, he mouths one of Himmler's statements that extols the demand for personal integrity, and on the other hand the Germans' moral duty to the nation to kill the nation which wanted to kill them (163, 175). A sadly ambiguous pronouncement, coming from the lips of one of the victims.

The rest of the episode with only Himmler and the masseur resembles a dialogue except on two occasions when the masseur addresses the spectators with voice-over, as if thinking aloud. In one of these instances he quotes a passage from the Bhagavad-Gita which Himmler found significant, because in it a voice announces its rebirth whenever injustice has taken over the world. Himmler associates this statement with his Führer (178). Referring to a divine power, this attribution makes Hitler look very much like a returning vengeful deity. But in Himmler's eyes, more like a redeemer and a Parsifal figure.

In a twist of the power constellation, the masseur suddenly emerges as the stronger of the two. In his distorted mind, Himmler justifies his destructive mission as duty. But believing in reincarnation, he hopes to expiate his sins in another lifetime or two through "positive" tasks. The masseur convinces him of the need to begin with these positive actions right away to help his soul. And so Himmler quietly pardons the list of condemned prisoners for whom the masseur intercedes, for a hefty payment from them, of course. This Schindler-like character later comments on living in a time in which business is humane compared with the ideas and when corruption can save lives (181). In the system of that time, "corruption" became a life-supporting virtue, and the "decency" of the SS a deadly ideal. The episode brings back the coexistence of the semantic variations of these concepts. Although official ideology imbued the words with new meanings, their traditional definitions continue to sound along, much as the melodic variations of a fugue.

Within the film, the masseur experiences some success in manipulating Himmler. He also hypnotizes an astrologer into supporting his efforts. The subsequent meeting between Himmler and the astrologer, which begins with a reading of horoscopes, ends as a confession of a confused sinner clinging to the illusion of being misunderstood. His ideas of the human and humaneness no longer coincide with those of the biblical or Western definitions. Sadly, these concepts also confuse the translator of the English book version. One needs to read both versions or see the movie itself. At issue is Himmler's helpless grappling with such ideas as *menschlich* (human), *unmenschlich* (inhuman), *Menschheit* (humanity), *Menschlichkeit* (humaneness), and *Humanismus* (humanism). To say nothing of the *Untermensch* (subhuman). Himmler, the nail-biting wreck of a man, is contemplating betrayal of the Reich, not because he wants to save the prisoners, but because, with imminent defeat, his own judgment is approaching. He presents a pathetic contrast to his flinty SS men, figments of the warrior he wants to be.

The next episode takes place at Hitler's Alpine retreat, Obersalzberg. Here Peter Kern portrays Ellerkamp, Hitler's former projectionist. Harry Baer had tried on that role briefly before. Ellerkamp leads the viewers on a tour of the ruins in a format that appears familiar. Theodor Hierneis had played the guide of King Ludwig's castles, and valet Krause had as a cicerone of sorts also revisited Obersalzberg. Now another surviving, low-ranking insider shares his memoirs with the viewers. At first glance he seems harmless, being a sentimental and jovial man. But he does have a nasty habit of playing with his pocket knife. One cannot help thinking of the gangster Mack-the-Knife of the *Threepenny Opera*. Ellerkamp, too, tests the echo of the mountains with his yodeling. This time the echo is, or is drowned out by, a military march coming from his transistor radio. It is equipped with a cassette player that allows Ellerkamp to play authentic recordings dating from the Third Reich. The boombox provides a second soundtrack for the scene. So, as before, the lecture or reminiscing monologue of the tour guide is occasionally interrupted or accompanied by historical sound bites. Notable among them is a speech by Hitler which ends with a praise of his healthy nation: It is *kerngesund* (sound as a bell, or thoroughly sound to the core). The German version offers a pun on Kern's name. Ironically, Heinrich Heine made a similar statement a hundred years earlier. In his "Nachtgedanken" (Night Thoughts) he writes about the Germany from which he fled that it is a thoroughly healthy country: "Es ist ein kerngesundes Land." Even when reduced to the component of a word, *Kern* reverberates with contrapuntal effects. And again, Peter Kern embodies an everyman-character whose mental and moral condition is anything but *kerngesund*.

The speech mentioning the healthy nation also alludes to religion. Many details in the movie contain direct as well as barely noticeable religious overtones, some being mock-religious and even blasphemous. For example, sound snippets from the grave scene in *Aïda* in Hitler's record collection contrast with the "reawakening" of life in late morning (194–95). And the Alpine compound, Ellerkamp informs the viewers, had been expanded by building around the old core, the way one used to build a cathedral around a chapel. The former projectionist is suffering from

Heimweh and is apparently making a pilgrimage to a sanctuary of his past. Although the tune of a Christmas carol also evokes a religious celebration, the strongest reference occurs at the picknick table where Ellerkamp's pun perhaps serves as a disguise to distract the spectators' recognition from another modulating allusion. While unpacking his lunch and talking nostalgically about Hitler's afternoon teas, he drops the word *Schnitzer* in the sense of "blunder" or "error." The word is derived from the verb *schnitzen*, meaning to cut or carve. No sooner has the word fallen than he nicks his finger while cutting off a piece of sausage and begins to bleed. The sight of his blood reminds him of a remark the dictator made to him. Hitler had his blood drawn periodically for his high blood pressure. Seeing his men enjoy a meal with meat, he quipped that he would have them make blood sausage from his superfluous blood, since they liked meat so much. And Ellerkamp adds with his mouth full, that he loves like blood sausage (198). A shared meal, blood, a redeemer-leader—if this alludes to a black mass, then the spectators are here witnessing an unholy communion. In view of Syberberg's play on words, one might also wonder if he includes the metaphoric meaning of "finger" in this episode. If so, he may weave in an allusion to circumcision, another ritual of participation and belonging to a religious community. The *Schnitzer* would in that case supply a barely recognizable counterpoint to the Nazi surface narrative. The Christian parallel is easier to detect.

The mock-Christian quasi-transubstantiation assumes a more mundane but not less blasphemous continuation as the disciple relates one of his master's childhood experiences telling it in the first person singular. The textual narrator merges with the storyteller. That is, the former projection-ist with the vivid imag(e)ination is still projecting images of the mind, blurring the usual notions of frame and content, as well as identity and past and present. So carried away is he by his nostalgia that he calls for Hitler's dog to share the leftovers of the meal. He breaks down crying at the end of the Deutschland-anthem when reality takes over. Like the valet, so also the projectionist shares intimate, innocuous details devoid of political or ethical issues. But unlike Krause, he reveals the stress of living in a fantasy of selective memories. His *pathos* is, in spite of the inappropriate comparison, related on a semantic level to the Passion of Christ, thus carrying on the theme of a mock-religious frame of reference. But as the knife and his tears reveal, Kern-Ellerkamp does not represent a *kerngesunde* nation.

An abrupt switch to Harry Baer and a ventriloquist's dummy of Hitler introduces the last segment of part 3. At this time one associates Baer's face primarily with the melancholy, pensive man probing his identity. Hiding in his shadow, however, are his earlier portrayals of King Ludwig and Ellerkamp. From the viewer's perspective, he represents a cluster of identities in one manifestation. The new impersonation of Ellerkamp by Kern functions as a fulcrum, letting Baer try on a different role. Now, with the Hitler dummy, he assumes two additional roles. For it is, of course, the ventriloquist's words one hears from the dummy's mouth. Their conversation is a split monologue. To accentuate this divided self, Baer adds yet another nuance by presenting himself as a sad Jew, who in the course of this scene strips away the many layers of clothing worn by the doll. Besides providing the diabolical and cynical miniature an opportunity to vent his outrageous opinions, the scene mainly serves to emphasize the fragmented personalities, or if one prefers, multiple identities of the actor.

The setting for this monologue is again the dark chamber, a replica of the first movie studio built by Edison and called by him the Black Mary. Surrounded by props from this and other Syberberg films, Harry Baer continues the exploration of his inner world. The first statement of this episode establishes a nexus between Germany and Hitler that resembles a hidden identity. The puppet complains to Baer that he is being treated like an unwelcome incubus disturbing the sleep (201). The nightmare that disturbs the sleeper had been identified in the very first words spoken in the film: "Denk' ich an Deutschland in der Nacht, dann bin ich um den Schlaf gebracht" (Whenever I think of Germany at night I am robbed of sleep). This is the beginning of Heinrich Heine's "Nachtgedanken" (Night Thoughts) and his most famous lines besides the "Lorelei." One hears them initially as the camera focuses on the Black Mary for the first time. Now the Hitler dummy evokes Heine's statement. One may ask what the musical effect of the voices would sound like. Also if this brings Heine back into the picture. Some viewers might question the recurring references to Heine and to equating his exile from Germany with that of the emigrés under Hitler. His life was not endangered for having been born Jewish. Rather, he had jeopardized his freedom through sustained, deliberate provocation of authority in a country with very limited civil liberties. Nonetheless, his yearning to return home to see his old mother is the reason for the poem. Baer's *Heimweh*, on the other hand, is a pain, *Weh*, inflicted on him by his homeland, *Heim*. A similar polyvalence occurs in the prayer towards the end of *Ludwig*. Now the Hitler dummy imbues Heine's words with his own incubus, modulating the textual melody to a different key. Besides the Heine paraphrase, numerous visual and acoustic details establish links to part 1. Several of the elements from the beginning of part 3 also recur at the end. The little girl with closed eyes accompanies the credits as they scroll over the screen with both Syberberg's and the actors' names. However, only the main title, "The End of a Winter's Tale," is given, not the subtitle.

The inspiration for this title was probably not so much the *Winter's Tale* by Shakespeare as *Deutschland: Ein Wintermärchen* by Heine.[17] The latter is an epic poem in twenty-seven "capita" of various lengths describing with sarcastic humor the poet's first trip home from exile in 1843. One passage relevant to the film occurs in caput 26. The narrator examines Hammonia's prophetic throne, but faithful to his promise, he does not relate the oracle. To judge from the surrounding text, the revealed future of Germany could only instill pessimism. The "progress" praised in the ventriloquist's episode confirms the atmosphere of the poem.

Part 4 begins with the German title and subtitle: "Wir Kinder der Hölle erinnern uns an das Zeitalter des Grals" (We Children of Hell Recall the Age of the Grail). The *Children of Hell* is a phrase borrowed from Thomas Mann's "Bruder Hitler" (54). This time the initial static from space that surrounds the child's head resembles a stormy wind. The section consists of three long and several short connecting episodes with varying degrees of complexity. When the image is simple, the spoken language demands full attention. When visual impressions crowd the field, the text lightens up on occasion or recedes into background sound.

André Heller's very long first presentation is fairly easy to follow. Disregarding cinematic conventions and possibilities, he entertains the viewers with a lecture, much of it read aloud from a script. The talk weaves together documentary episodes from the lives of Hitler and other Germans during the Third Reich, with an occasional rumination approaching assessment and opinion. All earlier themes and motifs return at some point: love and hate, guilt, sacrifice, art, prediction, and not the least, the merger of projection and identification. When Heller relates the dictator's identification with the nation, the pseudo-religious Hitler worship of the masses assumes visibility in the endless background projections of public ceremonies, such as rallies, parades, speeches, cheering crowds, all of it authentic footage or stills. After a brief transition about the culmination in a Dionysian frenzy of a nightmare, which turned into a "battlefield of the self" (217), Heller suddenly quotes two famous poems about peace by Goethe, "Des Wanderers Nachtlied" (Wanderer's Night Song) and "Über allen Gipfeln" (Over All Peaks). The effect is a shock. For, as Heller points out, Goethe penned these poems under an oak tree in an area that became the concentration camp Buchenwald. In a similarly jarring fashion, the comments move between Hitler's followers and the victims. Although the latter remain invisible in this section, they are present in the text. One memorable quotation is the curse from *Jew Süß*. It turns into yet another occurrence of a suppressed element somehow recognizable in the film. Goebbels censored these words in what otherwise became a propaganda film. For example, Süß called for the townspeople's days to be filled with grief and their sleep disturbed by pain (219). He also wished that their memory should be cursed, their town destroyed by fire from heaven, and that they should blaspheme God. And so it came to be. The sleep-robbing grief and pain has haunted many, fugue crippled the memory of others, and the fire from heaven consisted of blanket bombardments in World War II. To make sure the curse is being fulfilled in all details, perhaps so as to divest it of its malignant power, Syberberg adds some blasphemy, such as his version of the Lord's Prayer in *Ludwig* and a hymn later in part 4 in *Hitler*. Clearly, the *Götterdämmerung* did not end with World War II. The aftermath became a new phase in the agony of our era, with ecological disasters, questionable political and economic trends, as well as a cultural and spiritual decay that the Hitler dummy labels "his victory."

The following short unit reintroduces the dummy to let him elaborate on his intentions. Not surprisingly, the goal was world rule by a "chosen racial elite." He mentions three models: the Roman empire as a Western system of world domination; the British empire for its national feeling and genius enabling it to subjugate a fifth of the world; and the Jewish people, for the practice of religious racial purity and a sense of mission by a chosen people (225). And he refers to himself as the Anti-Christ (226). Not until late in the episode can one feel confident that these statements are meant to come from the Hitler doll. The temporary confusion turns first to indignation and anger, because the voice belongs to Harry Baer, who is the only live person in sight. But he does not speak. One is reminded of the sequence of SS officers in Himmler's hallucination. Their monologues were audible, but their lips did not move. It takes a while to recognize the Hitler dummy lying on the floor. Supposedly then, the ventriloquist's dummy does the talking through a disembodied voice, and his statements are as provocative as before. The scene marks the end of the war in the accompanying radio broadcasts, such as the English report on the liberation of Auschwitz or another on Hitler's death. Throughout the film, these documentary sound samples have introduced, besides music and German broadcasts, statements in English, French, Russian, and Japanese. The actors' lines represent standard modern German, dialect, and Old High German in the quotations from the ninth century apocalyptic poem "Muspilli." It deals with the souls of the deceased, the Last Judgment and the end of the world about the time when the Anti-Christ was overcome. The narrator mentions that Hitler read this poem while in prison and writing *Mein Kampf.* The idea of an Anti-Christ stays with humanity until the end. Hitler as the Anti-Christ and as an immortal, negative force such as Vitzliputzli and a Hegelian *Weltgeist* is a frequently varied theme in the film. The refusal of many to grant him the status of an exalted, albeit diabolical, figure can perhaps be seen in his diminutive size whenever the allusions occur. And similarly, the unresolved problem of memory, identification, and insight prolongs the melancholy that Harry Baer displays.

André Heller introduces the next long unit. Although other characters intermittently steal the scene, it is really Heller and Baer who lend their voices to the inner dialogue cum monologue. The setting has shifted to Obersalzberg today, at the opening of a Hitler museum.[18] Interrupting the inner dialog are the mayor of the town (Martin Sperr) and the director of tourism (Peter Kern), who represent the worst of the modern spirit, eager to cash in on the Hitler nostalgia while indulging their own fondness for the past. The transition from Heller's probing seriousness to the two entertaining entrepreneurs offers a glimpse of the mechanics of Syberberg's quasi-musical mode of composition. For, as usual, the film continues to emulate in image, sound, and words the structural characteristics of a musical composition. The following comments examine this equivalency as if it were played on an organ.

The organ has long been the preferred instrument for fugues. It can be quite complex with many pipes, several keyboards, and a variety of stops and levers that affect the sound. Some of these devices are called couplers. They allow the player to combine or activate several keyboards simultaneously. With the help of a coupler, the organist may press just one key and produce the sound from several keyboards for a richer or different effect. Syberberg lets André Heller pull such a coupler in his introductory remarks. The cue is semantic. The coupler is in German called *Koppel.* This polyvalent word possesses the unrelated meaning of "pack," as in a pack of dogs or wolves. Listing some of the memorabilia at the new museum, Heller names Hitler's eight dogs, now stuffed for display. Eight canines are definitely a pack or *Koppel.* With their introduction, the mayor and the director of tourism change the tone to that of up-beat entertainment. Like Heller and Baer, they also speak in turn, but break on occasion into a song-and-dance number with a doubling of voices. In a variation on the theme, they both begin, as Heller had before, by giving a speech, manuscript in hand, extolling the popularity of the new museum. The episode is obviously a parallel to the scene with tourist hordes in King Ludwig's castle. Dreaming of a Bavarian Disneyland, the director of tourism openly and with pride praises the lowest common denominator for the enterprise with culture wiped out and genuine popular taste prevailing (229). The museum offers a little bit of everything for everybody, ranging from the pistol used in Hitler's suicide to a mini-Dachau. With his sunglasses on, the director looks like a gangster when holding this weapon. A listing of coming special events contains the cue that disengages the coupler that had consisted of multiple canines. For on the anniversary of the dictator's death, the director promises a memorial celebration for the lone "wolf." Add to that a stuffed German shepherd in plain view. The lone Wolf (= Hitler) and the dog become the *Koppel* that affects the sound again. The two garrulous men turn their backs to the camera, still discussing with each other, but with their voices inaudible. The tonal effect has changed noticeably. One can now again hear André Heller give his sarcastic description of the "greatest show of the century" to be played again and again. Syberberg may have been inspired to this equivalent of the effect of couplers by Paul Celan's poem "Todesfuge" (Death Fugue). It is the most famous literary text in German on a Holocaust topic written by a Jewish survivor. It is also a textual fugue of unsurpassed artistry that includes "dogs" for the same purpose, although with a more lethal effect, as discussed in Olsen's study.[19] One finds an additional indication of the influence of the "Todesfuge" in the film's complete title, *Hitler: Ein Film aus Deutschland.* Recurring four times in Celan's poem is the description of Death as a master from Germany. Not only would many equate the historical Hitler with Death personified or Death's deputy, but also the subject in Celan's sentence, the *Tod*, points to such an identification. With its *d* hardened to a *t*, it is pronounced like the name Thoth in German. Thoth was the Egyptian deity corresponding to Hermes and Mercury, who conducted the souls of the deceased to the underworld. And "conduct" and "conductor" are polyvalent words. "Conductor" translates, a.o., to *Führer*. The next noun in Celan's refrain, *Meister* (master), is emphasized overtly and covertly in Syberberg's books. And the concluding words of the film's title, *aus Deutschland,* also occur in the refrain of the poem. The title of Celan's text identifies it as a fugue. That and many other similarities between the two works corroborate the quasi-musical composition of the film. And as the "Todesfuge" is a double fugue with two subjects, so also the film presents a split or divided subject (Olsen, 194). At this point in the film it manifests itself as the mayor and the director of tourism. They constitute variations of the two nameless characters portrayed by Baer and Heller. So, when the two promoters regain their voices and sing together, Heller may have pulled an organ stop such as the celestina, for their song number has changed from a lascivious pop tune to an old folk hymn to the Virgin Mary. Maybe the hymn points to the origin of a genuine or unadulterated "popular taste." But the effect is close to blasphemy, because these panders to the public taste do not seem to connect their questionable enterprise with a need for divine intercession. The hymn deplores the Virgin for release from their affliction (233). It is, however, part of the entertainment in a show. Are the two performers aware of their most debilitating affliction? At least they have not forgotten the words of the hymn yet.

The main attraction of the museum is an underground hall with pylons and the soldier's tomb, as planned for the victory celebration that did not take place. The hall is crowded with architectural models by Albert Speer, Hitler's architect. These miniature buildings represent the dream of a new Germany as envisioned by Hitler. The little girl reappears here, now dressed in black again. The sound alternates between radio broadcasts from the days of the war and the voice of Heller who speaks as Hitler in the first person singular. Also echoing Dr. Martin Luther King, this voice tells us about having had a dream, but concluding with the death of light and all life (234). The alchemical element of blackness is both visible in the cloak and evoked audibly as well as indirectly with Dr. King being a black American. Soon after, the voice wonders who will be next, hinting at a force in a new manifestation (237). This voice from the tomb continues with amoral cynicism. In spite of the confused logic and incoherence of the rambling text, the main idea emerges clearly. This Hitler is a libidinal force, a dynamic power inherent in the turning wheel of time. Such "greatness" can only unfold with the sacrifice of millions, either as destroyed enemies or as the heroic deaths of supporters. The force itself, of course, is too preoccupied with creating the dream to worry about such petty human concepts as morality and love.

The voice changes as Harry Baer takes over. The shift in voice and perspective is triggered primarily by a visual pun on *Koppel*. Among the props scattered throughout the hall, the camera catches the architectural model of a cupola. The German word for a dome or cupola is *Kuppel*, which, according to the Grimm dictionary, can also function as a spelling variant of *Koppel*. Bad pun, some will groan, but it does the trick. The manipulation of a coupler on the organ alters the way the instrument sounds. And in the film the new tone comes from Baer. He introduces the people affected by the Hitler phenomenon, both victims and supporters, in a parade of names. As this human mass passes by the tribune of the leadership, Baer refers to that group as "bloodhounds." Not only is blood the preferred signifier for alchemical *rubedo*, but the bloodhounds also function as a pack or *Koppel*. Immediately, female names join the list and change the imagined sound of the chorus.

All the while the little girl remains the only live figure in the picture. She moves around restlessly in this hell populated by photographic cut-outs and dolls hanging from gallows. The gallows continue the chain of variations on the theme of *tree*. As in Christianity the crucifix of Christ's Passion correlates with the tree of knowledge in paradise, so these gallows correlate with the Yggdrasil, the Germanic, pagan tree of life that appears in many of the film's episodes as well as in *Ludwig* and *Parsifal*. Syberberg may also have had in mind Heinrich Heine's trees. In numerous poems with German themes Heine mentions trees as the foremost characteristic of the country, almost in a synecdochical function. In one of his books the director quotes a statement by Heine that he found in English during a visit to San Francisco: "Mine is a most peaceable disposition. My wishes are: a humble cottage . . . and a few fine trees before my door; and if God wants to make my happiness complete, he will grant me the joy of seeing some six or seven of my enemies hanging from those trees."[20] And here they hang. Apart from a possible esoteric reference to the "Hanged Man" card of the Tarot deck, the association with Heine's words would mostly serve as a reminder of the "other" subject in counterpoint. The dolls dangling from Syberberg's gallows represent the convicted at the trial in Nuremberg. At one of these gallows one again encounters a coupler of sorts. Two figures hang together in a tight embrace. One is a small model of Goebbels' charred corpse, the other the sex-doll of Eva Braun with its open mouth. How could this grisly sight function as the visual equivalent of a musical component? Again the connection is both visual and semantic. The two are a coupling couple. Their copulation hints at similar vocabulary in French and German: *coupler, kuppeln*, etc. Actually the camera performs an additional act of sexual coupling by moving shamelessly towards the open mouth, producing a change in sound. Earlier the film included an Eva Braun doll with a tiny Hitler doll in her arms. Also at that time she was the only female among the puppets rising from their coffins. Her words were few and silly, debasing her even further. Cooing, she called the doll her baby. A visual reminder of this detail appears as a projection of this tiny Hitler doll in the open mouth. The director leaves no room for doubt: this Eva corresponds to the Virgin Mary holding her Redeemer Child. Maybe this is how the Virgin looked to the singers of the hymn in the previous scene? The blasphemy is consistent with the reference to Hitler as the Anti-Christ.

The semantic coupler results in Heller reappearing with the ventriloquist's dummy of Hitler. Heller vents his indignation over everything that is wrong with the present world and attributes this predicament to Hitler as his legacy. With increasing bitterness he congratulates the Hitler figure on his eventual victory. What is missing in this litany of accusations is a *mea culpa*. The speaker offers no admission of inherited responsibility or of understanding human nature. While he displaces all guilt for the past on Hitler, the dummy remains silent. The modern man has not only projected his inner Wolf, he also rejects any link to him. They remain unconnected as the camera dwells on the dummy and Heller, like Amfortas, focuses on a crystal globe, now with a snowy landscape inside. This snow globe with its tiny Black Mary inside is one of the most complex symbols in the film. Easiest to recognize is its relation to the precursor in *Citizen Kane*. But it also assumes some qualities of the Grail, pointing ahead to Syberberg's next film.

The following scene is accompanied by choral music from the finale of Gustav Mahler's Resurrection Symphony (Symphony No. 2 in C Minor). These sections anticipate the choral excerpt of Beethoven's Ninth that will be heard later. The choice of a Jewish composer marks a deviation from the previous music selections. It identifies the soundtrack quite clearly as carrier of one of the contrapuntal variations, with Harry Baer embodying another. The scene takes place in a dark setting, as if inside the crystal ball or the mind. Drifting clouds of vapor underscore the "mental" nature of the environment. A large eye on canvas continues the theme of reflexivity, while the prismatic stone from Dürer's *Melencolia I* rests in front of the chair in which Harry Baer reclines. Sitting on a blond blanket, he has also draped Wagner's cloak around him. This time his melancholy seems directed at the stone. It is not clear if he contemplates it or projects it. One hopes at least that he has acknowledged its existence. The environment increases in complexity as suddenly an old man's face appears projected onto the starry background. The features are those of Karl May, who had preached the striving spirit and the victory of good forces. Since Syberberg's film about him concentrates on his last years during which May approached the goal of his spiritual aspirations, his presence in this scene might represent an antidote to Baer's melancholy.

Addressing the viewers, Baer continues Heller's and the dummy's thoughts. People will think of him as being crazy, he admits. "Crazy" or "deranged" is in German *verrückt*. Syberberg plays on both the literal and the transferred meaning of the word. Derangement is a central concept in the Kabbalah, resulting from the "breaking of the vessels" and announcing the need for restoration, *tikkun*.[21] The choice of words might hint at a Kabbalistic or Jewish dimension. Perhaps Baer's character is deranged, but he cannot praise the world he lives in. Without transition, he asks rhetorically if "we" have scolded or insulted anyone (243). Who is speaking now? Whom else does he include besides himself? And if he speaks as the "inner Heller" or his alter ego, what happened to the Hitler dummy? One cannot see it in the picture. However, through an analogy with a detail in another Syberberg film one might suspect its presence. The path of this association leads from the underground nightmarish hall at the museum displaying the anticipated victory celebration. In *Ludwig*, a similar victory celebration in 1871 in a cave-like setting turns into a nightmarish revue. During that dream, the Richard Wagner midget had been hiding in the folds of a long garment. The path of association continues to Wagner's tomb which appears in both films. In *Hitler*, the dictator's ghost rises up from this grave, draped in a toga-like shroud. The blond blanket covering Baer's chair could easily be the toga-shroud, suggesting the presence of the ghost. One wonders if the dummy might be hidden under the Wagner cloak. A still in the book shows what might be two little feet sticking out from under the cloak, but one cannot be sure, and the film is too dark to allow any conclusion. The assumption that the doll is concealed on Baer's lap under the cloak would explain the strange pronouncements made by him. Coming from the Hitler figure in Baer's voice with only the man being visible, these statements would suggest a possible acknowl-edgment of a dual nature in him. Baer's sadness tempers the effect of the Hitlerian insolence and cynicism.

Admittedly, the scene with Baer in the chair lends itself to conflicting interpretations. This character is still melancholy, perhaps even aware of his dualism. A not quite convincing reading might identify him as one of the "new men" that Heller abhors, similar in spirit to the mayor and director of tourism. But they are not afflicted with melancholy and reflection. Baer does not fit their profile. Another view might recognize only Hitler's voice in him, pointing to the dialectical trading of roles between Heller and Baer in the preceding episodes. But Baer's self-contradictions refute that interpretation. His words betray two divergent minds. Since the Hitler projection is no longer visible in the room with him, he may have recognized himself in the puppet projection and can say with Goethe's Faust, "Two souls, alas, are dwelling in my breast." With Mephistopheles materializing soon after Faust pronounces these words, it is clear that the "other" soul is a diabolical element in Faust's nature. Assuming that Baer's dual soul also harbors such a force, one does not have to look far for confirmation. His initial statement quotes the Hitler puppet remark to him earlier in part 3 about who is closer to God than the guilty man (207, 242). And then he quotes himself commenting on that statement, identifying the speaker as the devil (207, 243). But Syberberg does not call him Mephistopheles. Most references to the devil take the shape of Fitzliputzli, or Vitzliputzli, as Heine spelled the name. And Heine, incidentally, refers to himself as howling with the German wolves in caput 12 of *Deutschland: Ein Wintermärchen*. If Heine informs the nameless character portrayed by Harry Baer, then he is capable of sounding like the Wolf. The presence of such a wolf could, of course, account for the plural *we* as subject. Heine also knew the dark side of human nature, including his own. He concealed his melancholy under the disguise of parody and irony. Forever the cynic and provocateur, this "bad conscience" of his era remained *zerrissen* (torn) between his exile and Germany and his Jewish and Gentile German legacies. The poet grew up as Harry Heine but changed his name to Heinrich Heine when he was baptized in 1825.[22] Harry Baer shares the same first name. Furthermore, as Baer in this scene, so Heine also looked weak and sickly towards the end of his life, being confined to bed much of the time. A blanket and a cloak would have been natural for his bedside chair. One might be tempted to call the melancholy, nameless character Harry Baer Heine.

This tentative identification also points to another instance in which the movie might suppress Heine's name. That, of course, demonstrates how political correctness treated Heine during the Third Reich: with silence. It was as if he had never existed. Even his "Lorelei," which had become a cherished folk song, was printed in those years with the notation "Poet unknown." The film version without Heine's name continues the "afflicted" way of thinking. Serving as a voice for the Hitler ghost and dummy, the Baer-Heine character still possesses the power to alienate, even when the association has been made. That Syberberg intended the association of this character with Heine is suggested by many cues in the text. Not only did Heine supply Vitzliputzli and poetic fragments, but he also published a book with a topic that permeates Syberberg's work. In 1847 Heine wrote the prose libretto for a Faust ballet in five acts, *Der Doktor Faust: Ein Tanzpoem*.[23] In this version the devil is female and named Mephistophela. Syberberg may have avoided that name because it would have been too recognizable. Heine's preface and appended explanations introduce many topics related to the theme, such as puppet theater and Faust's assistant, but also some not found in other discussions of Faust. Heine points out repeatedly that the devil is an artist, using both *Künstler* (artist) and *Artist* (performer), perhaps inspiring Syberberg to his references of Hitler as an artist. Heine also reports that witches complained about the icy coldness of the devils' embraces. One usually thinks of hell and its rulers as being hot. The association of coldness with devils adds a diabolical and contrapuntal dimension to Syberberg's frequent references to wintry coldness. Besides, Heine also compares the witches' celebration on Blocksberg with a *Reichstag*. The traditional Mephistopheles was by no means an unimportant little devil, he claims, but "high-ranking in the hierarchy of the underworld, in the government of hell, where he is one of those statesmen that one can make into a chancellor" (44). *Reichskanzler* was precisely the title Hitler held before he became president and changed both office and title. These prophetic words come true in the film when Hitler identifies himself as the devil or Anti-Christ. Syberberg saved a few other phrases from this book by Heine for later use.

The change in subject from *we* to the third person pronoun *man* (one) modulates to the next episode. Here Heller returns with his surroundings unchanged: A dark film studio strewn with dead leaves and crowded with familiar objects, including Baer's Wagner-cloak and chair, the stone, and the Hitler dummy in plain view. The compulsively talkative Heller lets his mind wander from the black chamber of human imagination to the numerous variants of the Grail. Instead of the chalice of Chrétien de Troyes he emphasizes Wolfram von Eschenbach's stone Grail that fell from heaven. And, referring to that version, Heller claims it reminds the banished angels of their heavenly paradise and keeps alive the yearning to return. He blames this paradise for bringing sin into the world. Talking incoherently and with the agitation of a manic depressive, he finally disappears into the background projection of the crystal ball with the Edison's Black Mary inside. Seeing the nothingness of human life on a cosmic scale and no longer accusing the Hitler dummy of all wrongs, he does not yet grapple with questions of his own nature or responsibility. But he does appear to find some solace in the projections of human imagination, the legacy of stories and art coming from the interior. He obviously portrays a troubled but probing mind with notable deficiencies. Comparing him with the two souls in Faust, he does not measure up to either Faust or Mephistopheles. But Goethe's old magus has an assistant who shares some similarities with Heller's character. This *famulus* succeeds later in creating a *homunculus* in a test tube. The miniature being is not quite a full person yet, but represents on a small scale a significant result of creativity. The assistant's name is Wagner. The Heller character's behavior and fascination with art and the Grail make him look like Wagner's descendant, perhaps Richard Wagner. The choice of name is not as arbitrary as it appears at first glance. Syberberg himself offers a hint that the name possesses special connotations. While observing that several of his films are self portraits of their maker, he states it would be so much more pleasant to have chosen Goethe, Bach, or Beethoven than Ludwig II, May, Hitler, and the Wagners. And what a fitting joke of history, he muses in this context, that the assistant of Goethe's Faust is called Wagner (*Die freudl. Ges.*, 360). The composer who shared that name became known as an anti-Semite. His one-time friend Heine came from a Jewish background. Both of them experienced exile, in Wagner's case, repeatedly. Both were creative artists with a passionate and ambivalent interest in things German. In this film, they, or the nameless figures exhibiting their characteristics, represent facets of the "German" soul under scrutiny. By equipping the two nameless characters in part 4, played by Baer and Heller, with features of Heine and Wagner, Syberberg has assigned them complementary roles with Faustian shadows. But in some scenes with voice-off, both of them lend their voices to Hitler's statements. The dummy in turn paraphrases lines of Heine's poetry as his own words, while on other occasions Wagner's music provides the sound. In brief, the identities are fleeting and overlapping, more like counterpoint or double and multiple exposures in photography. Still, the bundles of associations evoke the presence of Heine and Wagner.

At the end of the episode, Heller-Wagner joins Baer-Heine in the crystal ball. Although no mutual recognition or interaction occurs in the film (one does not see them together), their shared site of contemplation allows for a coexistence in creative complementarity. They both bring a separate awareness to the task, and with their differences they might inspire each other to new insights. As two manifestations of the human mind, and with their pronounced human shortcomings, they contribute the potential for the catastrophe that the film displays. However, they also represent the diversity needed for personal growth and healing. They have not yet taken note of each other, but they have both found the way into the black chamber.

Syberberg attaches almost mystical significance to the Black Mary or *camera obscura*, letting Heller refer to it as the black mother of imagination (246). This symbol lets him connect the imagery of the film camera with the Grail legends, religion, and psychology. The camera needs both light and darkness as well as internal and external forces to produce and project an image. The interdependency parallels the binary code of dynamics as a built-in dual aspect of unity. Edison, the inventor of artificial light, called his his darkroom study the Black Mary. Syberberg retains Edison's term for its links to mysticism. Both Christianity and many pagan religions have revered black mother figures, such as Ma-Kali in India, Diana in Ephesus, and Isis in Egypt.[24] Christianity may have continued the memory of a black *Prima Mater* in its numerous sanctuaries with a Black Madonna, e.g. in Montserrat (Spain), Chartres (France), Guadeloupe (Mexico), and many more.[25] Also as dark Earth, this maternal origin represents the womb and tomb of human life. The Gospel of John, which does not refer to the Virgin by name, calls her Divine Child the Word and the Light. Light issuing from darkness? One is also reminded of the beginning of Genesis. Whether viewed as goddess, person, or earth's matter, a body becomes the temple of something luminous and divine, a process in which darkness gives birth to light, or inversely, light evolves from darkness. This view of blackness does, of course, not coincide with the notion of darkness as a sinful or satanic contrast to a divine light. But early in part 2 of the film, Baer refers to the crystal ball with the Black Mary as the Grail (93). This evokes Wolfram von Eschenbach's version of the mystery as a precious stone from heaven. Wolfram does not specify whether the stone was sent as a gift or fell from

Lucifer's crown during the revolt of the angels. This introduces an element of uncertainty or ambiguity. The poet could just as well have had in mind the scattering of the Divine sparks, a different version known in Gnosticism and Jewish mysticism. The Grail variants mentioned by Heller in the film have fallen from the stars (246). Especially his reference to Lucifer's crown is intriguing. Lucifer changed in the Bible from an exalted angel to a diabolical adversary of God. But pagan lore still places him in a starry heaven, albeit under different names. Lucifer, or the Bringer-of-Light, is also known as the Morning Star and Phosphorus. At least some ancient astronomers knew that the Morning Star is identical with the Evening Star, also called Hesperus, Venus, and Isis.[26] How can one explain the two different genders for the deity or spirit of the same luminary? Ptolemy comments on this dualism without specifying the planets by name: "They say too that the stars become masculine or feminine according to their aspects to the sun, for when they are morning stars and precede the sun they become masculine, and feminine when they are evening stars and follow the sun."[27] This cluster of diverse, even contrasting, mythical identities may account for some of the Grail variants, since the Grail has many functions and is, above all, an attribute of something celestial. The feminine association with this origin appears to have been lost in Western literature. But Seltman points to one instance where the maternal source of an important child (Horus and Amor) made the transition from pagan to Christian tradition. In Cypros, for example, he reports about Venus/Aphrodite that " she still lives on, at least in name. In more than one Cypriot village church the Paphian [i.e. Venus] has been merged in the Virgin Mary, who is supplicated there under the title Panghia Aphroditessa."[28]

Although hinting at the numerous refractions of the Great Mother symbol, this digression has not yet thrown any light on the riddle of the Black Mary as the black mother of imagination (246). It presumably refers to a chamber of our inner creative Self, a chamber teeming with images. The similarity to a film camera is easy to recognize, but is Heller's black mother related to the Great Mother? Here one needs to keep in mind the Neoplatonic concepts of correspondences and proportions. The microcosm reflects imperfectly the macrocosm, "as above, so below," in a chain of miniaturizations. Thus the crystal globe turns into a primitive version of our site of creation through transformation and projection. The link would be the ability to emit, as a black chamber, or reflect, as a crystal or mirror, or give birth to, a form of light. But what about the snow in the crystal ball? It only swirls around when the globe is shaken. A snowy, immobile ground suggests that no life is stirring. That would be life-threatening, as one sees it in Caspar David Friedrich's painting of a shipwreck being ground under by masses of ice. One also remembers that the lowest regions of Dante's Inferno are icy and frozen. By comparison, falling snow still depicts a frosty world, but the sphere has been shaken by an external force. This affects the human soul, the little black chamber of transformation where reaction becomes action. The merging of several frames of reference including the Black Mother, the Black Mary, the Grail, and the crystal sphere, results in a complex grid of imagery and correspondences. Elements of it recur in all of Syberberg's work.

One of these related elements is the eye, which, of course, also is spherical. It is most conspicuous in the canvas with a large painted eye reproduced from Ledoux's *Eye Reflecting the Interior of the Theater of Besançon* of 1804. Americans are also familiar with the concept of the "Eye of God" as it appears on the one-dollar bill. The all-seeing Divine Eye becomes connected to the Last Judgment in part 3 of the film when the face of a female prisoner at Auschwitz gazes from the background screen behind an SS officer. A similar effect emanates from the piercing eyes of King Frederick II, whose features fill the background a few times. The painting on which this projection is based hung in Hitler's bunker. The dictator supposedly shot himself in front of it. But the eye is also a mirror reflecting the viewer. What one perceives in the eye of the other, or a mirror, is a reflection of oneself. The viewer is reminded of the Eva Braun sex doll and how the camera moved towards her open mouth. Incidentally, the eyes of the Braun doll do not reflect anything, but her substitute vagina turns into a projection mirror reflecting a little Hitler. In this game of reflexivity and degradation, the mirror image is only a tiny doll, but still it presents a continuation on a sliding scale of the Hitler mentality in a visualized form. Some of the anatomical concepts associated with the eye, such as lens and iris, also belong to the realm of photography. With the history of photography and of cinema integrated in the grid-like frame of reference, Syberberg draws on semantic branching and a large body of implicit narrative. Clearly, this kind of aesthetics calls for meditative, repeated viewings.

When Heller disappears into the wall projection of the crystal ball, the scene shifts abruptly to the little girl. She had been out of sight while the "inner action" alternated between Heller and Baer. She is standing with closed eyes in front of the large eye in the Ledoux painting. Little Miss Democracy is also Miss Film. Surrounding her black cape, strips of film hang down from the shawl that covers her head. This *pupilla* is now "reflected" as a projection visible in the big pupil. Waking up of her dreams or memories, she turns to look into it. Its center is transformed into the wintry landscape from *Ludwig*, complete with the accompanying music. But as she again closes her eyes, something triggers a sudden change. She becomes as restless as Heller had been earlier. As she begins to move, she carries with her a strange-looking reddish-brown plush dog. This floppy toy has the face and mustache of Hitler. Is this the "lap dog" that may have been hiding on Baer's lap under his robe? Both a lap dog and a toy dog might indicate a transformation of the original Wolf. Simultaneously, one is suddenly overwhelmed by the chorus singing Schiller's "Ode to Joy" in Beethoven's Ninth Symphony, at full strength.[29] The text praises Joy, *Freude*, as the "daughter of Elysium." If the black-robed child embodies also this Joy, then she descends on our world from a realm accessible only through death. Heller and Baer desperately long for joy and release from their condition, but its arrival seems premature. They are still incapable of feeling joy. One must conclude that the jubilant music constitutes the contrapuntal contrast to the situation evoked in the film. And yet, several other words in Schiller's poem inform the visual narrative. It celebrates Joy also as a *Himmlische* (celestial apparition) and *Götterfunken* (divine spark). These words establish a connection with the mystical tradition and help explain some of Syber-berg's visual vocabulary. Heller's character referred to the Grail and Lucifer's crown as having fallen from heaven. The crystal globe with the Black Mary inside is called a Grail. When the sphere is transformed into a tear, the girl is in it. These are obviously shifting manifestations of something hailing from the Beyond. At long last Schiller supplies the word *Götterfunken* (divine spark). The concept is known in the Kabbalah and Gnosticism in connection with the emanation story. It makes it the mission of each individual to complete the work and restore the divine sparks to their rightful place. By focusing on the little girl while the music overwhelms the viewers, the film creates a link between her and the mystical imagery. It is not an identification, but rather a suggestion of close association. The child may be the "daughter of Elysium," but she is still heir to an unwelcome legacy. As she walks energetically, she throws down the canine toy and tramples it. This outburst of rage may express a child's helpless attempt to cope with incapacitating stress. But it also visualizes a process of inner conflict and its resolution by overcoming (kicking) the source of distress. Her gesture corresponds in a musical fugue to the pedal point, a strong surge of sound in the pedal register of an organ. It decreases gradually in volume. The strong sound surrounds the girl in the form of Beethoven's music. The musical pedal point takes its name from the Latin word for foot, *pes*, plural *pedes*. Thus music from the "pedal" register of the organ is produced with the feet. Visually, the child resorts to vigorous footwork to release her feelings. Then, as she drops her black cloak, revealing a white gown, she picks up the reddish dog again with some hesitation and sits down to contemplate it. This grappling with a pommeled and weakened canine toy appears to be the director's hope for a transfiguration of the latent Wolf or Hitler potential in human nature. The process starts in the Baer-Heine scene and continues when Heller-Wagner joins him in the Black Mary. The child, as a synthesis and innocent beginning, must learn to accept this part of the psyche (and her legacy) and overcome it. Her acceptance of this burden helps her complete the task as she walks towards the camera and disappears in a black cloud.

Why is the cloud black? Syberberg loves his fog machine. Most of the time the vapors of a mental landscape are white, obliterating the contours of reality. Already Wagner had used red steam to surround his sleeping Brünnhilde with a wall of "flames." Syberberg imitates the effect once in the underground hall where the "fires" on the pylons throw off reddish, cascading smoke. There exists, then, a precedent in the film for a water-based fog to simulate fire-induced smoke. The alchemical implication of such a transformation is strengthened by the color changing to black. The child and her toy undergo a transmuting process in smoky fire. An additional indicator is the toy dog. Not only does the color combination suggest alchemical imagery, but also the Hitler face points in that direction. This dog is a Wolf. The alchemical wolf symbolizes antimony and all its saturnine correspondences. As such it is often depicted as devouring the king, as in C. G. Jung's *Psychology and Alchemy* (338). The next stage in the process of trans-

tation takes place on a pyre where the flames break down the physical entity, allowing a rejuvenated king to separate from the remains of the wolf. The resurrected figure represents the purified result of the process. As lethal as the wolfish antimony may be, it can itself undergo distillations and transformations, alchemists thought. In its most purified stage, the fifth essence, it gains beneficial qualities: "For it takes away pain from wounds and heals marvelously."[30] The Hitler-Wolf element has been in plain view through the ventriloquist's dummy and the toy dog. One assumes, then, that the little girl represents the result of the transmutation process when the wound has healed. But as Syberberg uses more than one frame of reference, one should also keep in mind the psychological and quasi-musical dimensions of his imagery and other possibilities. For example, although this sequence supposedly takes place in the hellish underground hall of the museum, or the subconscious, this could as well be Auschwitz. If so, then the black smoke rises in a crematorium through an invisible chimney. The musician playing this fugue would have activated an organ stop known as *flûte à cheminée*. It is called so because of the chimney-like tubes sticking out of the lid on the organ pipe.[31]

The transformation process continues in the following sequence as the child again moves towards the big eye. Its center shows, or "reflects," the crystal Grail sphere with the little black studio. From the background of this mirror of herself several figures step out: the chtonic maternal dragon and the weeping little King Ludwig, followed by *Requiescat in pace*. She may have released them, allowing them to rest in peace.

As the picture changes, the sphere gives way to a suspended crystal tear against the background of a sundered projection of King Ludwig's artificial paradise. The outward sign of inner contrition, the tear is a potent agent of change. Both the sphere and the tear-shaped bottle with its flue or chimney are glass vessels used in the alchemical refining of human nature. At different times one sees these chambers of transmutation contain a little Black Mary. The impure human ore, the *prima materia*, has suffered through a series of processes, some of which one recognizes in the film, e.g. the girl's trampling of the toy. Other components with alchemical connotations are colors, death, tomb, disintegration, resurrection, copulation, snow, wolf, eagle, other birds, projection, and more. The film contains enough of this imagery for a doctoral dissertation. Of special interest is the conclusion with the little girl in the glass tear. Her pious pose before she closes her eyes is modeled both on a photo of young Mary [!] Pickford and a French postage stamp issued during World War I in which a little girl is praying for peace.[32] The innocent child in a tear-shaped vessel represents the end of a long process. Frequently this stage was depicted in alchemy as Mercury in a glass bottle (Any popular book on alchemy contains such pictures). But, the reader will object, the film shows a little girl in the alembic, and Mercury is a male deity. Yes, but Mercury is also the spirit of a planet with a dual gender attribution, like Venus, depending on whether it appears in the sky in the morning or in the evening. The already quoted words by Ptolemy apply equally to Venus and to Mercury. The latter's feminine counterpart appears most often as a virgin in alchemy, occasionally as a hermaphrodite. In Syberberg's film, this figure is a little girl, the black pupil or apple of the eye, and Black Mary. Amelie Syberberg's name even shares the syllable *mel* with the Greek word for "black," *melas*.

It would seem that the film ends on an ambiguous, but faintly hopeful note. The historical disaster called Hitler functions mainly as the reason for guilt and a crippled psyche. Once an individual faces the similar abyss of bottomless hatred and negative potential in his or her own heart, the process of transmutation or healing can begin. A Christian might in this situation appeal to the Virgin Mary for help. She remains the most eminent intercessor for sinners. Perhaps Syberberg also draws on associations with the Kabbalistic Divine Presence on earth, the Shekhinah, as a guiding force for believers. This mystical aspect of the Divine is usually expressed in female terms. But whether Jewish, Christian, or pagan, the Western tradition has found solace in the faith in a merciful power intervening for believers. In the film, the child in the glass tear, with her hands gathered in prayer, and with her attributes of the Black Mary, could be praying for her forebears or someone dear who needs intercession. Her pious gesture might also relate to the end of Heine's *Deutschland: Ein Wintermärchen*, which refers to hell and the final judgment. One remembers that already part 3 of the film carries the title "The End of a Winter's Tale." In stanza 18 of caput 27 Heine reminds the reader of the "saints" who through prayer achieve salvation for some fortunate souls in hell on Judgment Day. But, the poet warns in stanzas 21–22, there are also hells from where no soul escapes and where even the Redeemer cannot show mercy, namely Dante's kind. Whomever poets condemn to hell in their art is forever beyond redemption. This association imbues the tomb scene in the film with an added dimension, since it took its inspiration from Dante's "Inferno." Like the *Divine Comedy*, the film operates with terms like paradise, limbo, and hell, and even the ancient Elysium. Its Germanic equivalent, Valhalla, actually has a branch in Bavaria. The hall of fame of that name has long been a tourist attraction. The museum in the film imitates the Valhalla or Elysium in its underground hall of fame for Nazi heroes. To remove any doubt about the nature of this environment, the soundtrack first conjures up a parallel to the Elysium in Book 6 of Virgil's *Aeneid*, where ghosts form a parade of martial heroes. They do that also in Harry Baer's narrative. A bit later, the soundtrack celebrates Joy, the Daughter of Elysium. So both above and below ground, the film shows abodes of the dead. The spiritually and morally dead walk and dance above ground in modern hell, and the killed and executed dead reside below. If Heine is right, many of the characters have been condemned forever by the artist. The two nameless ones who are grappling with their legacy and their identity are therefore the most likely candidates for intercession. They have entered a process of transformation in which the child plays a role. The poet and his words about intercession and condemnation inform both the surface and the subtext of the film. The concept of faith, in all its manifestations, remains the core of the creative irrationalism that Syberberg defends throughout his work. Rationalism, then, is fraught with human limitations. Irrationalism, on the other hand, leaves room for some hope, such as for intercession for divine mercy, and for creativity. The little girl, the film director's own child, represents that hope and faith.

The conclusion of the fourth part with the child in the tear continues the pattern of a musical accompaniment. The music ends to the sounds of Mozart's Piano Concerto in D Minor. Perhaps Syberberg insists on this concerto because the Hitler ghost had remarked about Mozart that he was not his man (129). With Mozart's help, Syberberg's composition both begins and ends in D Minor. Beethoven's symphony with the choral "Ode to Joy" is also in D Minor, although the Ode itself is in G. The musical dimension and the dark, starry sky of the concluding images evoke a famous passage in Thomas Mann's *Doktor Faustus*. The ending of the protagonist's final composition, the symphonic cantata "Lamentation of Doctor Faustus," is described in very similar terms. The narrator reflects on the paradox that hope seems to emerge from deepest hopelessness as the transcendence of despair. About the final sound from a lone cello he muses, "But the tone that hangs reverberating in the silence, that no longer exists, that only the soul is still listening for, and that was the final stage of mourning, [it] is not that anymore, [it] changes its meaning, standing like a light in the darkness."[33] These words could also apply to Syberberg's film.

The title of the fourth part appears at the end, "Wir Kinder der Hölle" (We Children of Hell), but not the subtitle. In the coda, between the credits and the three repeated words for the Grail, several segments of text appear, of which three especially inform our understanding of the film. One repeats the first stanza of Heine's "Night Thoughts," ("Whenever I think of Germany at night"). The quotation underscores the nexus Germany-Heine-anguish. Written in the first person singular, the lines speak both for the poet and for the filmmaker. One assumes that the given quotation expresses the thought Syberberg wants to convey. But the possibility exists that also the omitted stanzas color the statement, such as the longing for the mother. The second text of interest is a Bible quotation that "corrects" a pronouncement by Goebbels quite revealingly. In the movie, the voice of Goebbels states twice what could be taken for a paraphrase of 1 Cor. 13.2, namely that faith can move mountains. He wanted this mountain-moving faith to fill all believers (92, 210). The King James version reads: "[A]nd though I have all faith, so that I could remove mountains, and have not charity, I am nothing." The capacity for, and presence of, love is, then, the quality that makes a person human and strong; the lack of love identifies the believer as "nothing." The third text on the screen mentions a projection into the "black hole of the future," followed by *Der Gral, Le Graal*, and *The Grail* in capitals scrolling and disappearing, leaving only the starry black sky. Whatever hope is kindled by the "Ode to Joy" and the little girl's innocence is tempered by the long-term cosmic outlook dwarfing everything in our lives. But on the human scale, the ability to ignore this amounts to a productive madness, a creative irrationalism that Syberberg regards as indispensable. Faith and love are his cardinal virtues, whereas hope appears to belong to a different category called *Wahnsinn*. Or at best an effort to effect change. For the black hole in the sky sucks in all stars within its gravitational field, meaning that even heavenly bodies undergo cycles of luminosity and dark stages of change.

The images one sees in the firmament have traveled untold light years to reach Earth. In other words, one sees the past, not the present, and the future may already have happened in the next galaxy. While the mind goes dizzy pondering the mysteries of time and space, and while searching for ways to change the past in the present, hope is reduced to the resolve to change the "future," as we understand it. With the child's changing appearance as old, ageless, and young, as well as her multiple allegorical roles, she seems to represent the dynamics of continuity, akin to the norns, and the irrational synthesis of the cardinal virtues. If one should resort to dialectical terminology in the context of the film, then the thesis, Hitler and his way of thinking, interacted with its perceived antithesis in such unprecedented, destructive ways that very little was left with which to construe a synthesis. Syberberg implies that much of both parts perished in the process, one physically, the other spiritually and morally. But he replaces the historical Hitler with the "Hitler in us," selecting Heller and Baer as the main representatives of thesis and antithesis. Their convergence in the Black Mary appears to attract or produce the child as the synthesis. Her allegorical functions suggest a connection between her and the healing qualities of the Grail, Black Mary, and creativity. The prospect for a synthesis depends on the restoration of the shattered remains. Whatever one wants to read into the child, she represents that prospect.

In the concluding scenes the viewers have lost sight of the historical Hitler and the cinematic recreations of him. The real topic is someone else: we, you, I, everybody. Viewed in artistic refraction, the capacity for good and evil is shown as present and as the interplay of dynamic forces in all humans. The abyss of hate, pain, and destruction known as Hitler is latent in the human psyche. The medium used to convey the message is film, and the child is also the carrier or allegory of this medium. As Syberberg reminds his readers repeatedly, film is the principal art form of the twentieth century, and this art is his chosen medium in the attempt to open eyes and minds for the needed insight and transformation. His films are works of art drawing on imagery from all fields of cultural and political history. He demands a lot of the viewers. Actually, the *Hitler* film is sufficiently complex to prevent many viewers from comprehending all of it or appreciating it as art. The visual and auditory frames of reference presume familiarity with German history, art, film, literature, and music. Those who do not recognize the allusions and quotations fail to see coherence and correspondences or hear resonances. In such cases, the myriad details remain unconnected, arbitrary, even meaningless. Just one detail can serve as an example. In the underground hall of the museum, numerous photographic cardboard cutouts "populate" the set. One that is not made from a photo looks like a human caricature. It consists of two males wearing uniforms. They are placed close to the gallows, as if taking a walk in the grisly landscape. They are actually details from Otto Dix's painting *Kriegskrüppel* (War Cripples) of 1920. Accompanying them, Harry Baer's voice describes a parade of victimized masses passing the tribune where Hitler is standing. These include "subhumans," Jews, gypsies, and crippled war veterans (237). The cost of survival, then, the viewers assume, spells physical helplessness and life-long pain. But why did not

Syberberg use a photo of a real handicapped veteran? Perhaps he did not want to condemn the real surviving sufferers to this hell. He based this detail on a painting that was included in the exhibit on "Degenerate Art" in 1937.[34] Here the authorities displayed 650 confiscated or impounded works of art as a contrast to the simultaneous exhibit on "German Art." George Grosz, played by Peter Kern in *Karl May*, also had the honor of being included among the "degenerate" artists. The painting by Dix from which Syberberg borrowed the details may have inspired the text one hears. The distorted features of these crippled veterans reflect the dehumanization they suffered, first by those in power during the war when they were forced to fight (as experienced by the artist), and later by the Nazis by being declared degenerate. As such they enter the play of reflexivity as well as the frame of reference for art and history. Similarly, every other visual and acoustic detail also functions on several levels.

Anticipating that his film would be misunderstood, Syberberg added a long essay to the printed screenplay. The abridged English version consists of a preface and excerpts of the first and second and all of the third sections of the "Introduction." Missing are segments four to seven. As interesting as the introduction is, it does not offer an elucidation or explanation of the film. Admittedly, some of the author's remarks help reduce the number of misunderstandings and point the reader in the intended direction. Some of the sections are preceded by quotations of other writers, for example Michel de Montaigne, who states that he himself is the subject of the book (3). Accepting this pronouncement as a premise also for the reader and viewer, one searches for characters in the movie with whom one could identify. The child is a safe bet, Baer and Heller might qualify in some of their scenes. But the list of acceptable possibilities is soon exhausted. This is where the film becomes uncomfortable and the viewer uneasy.

The author begins by comparing modern (West) Germany's political and economic success with its ethical and creative condition, which he declares to be bankrupt. He quickly states his concern: "Can and should a film about Hitler and his Germany explain anything in this respect, rediscover identities, heal and save [*erlösen*]?" And he continues musing if the Germans can ever free themselves of the oppressive curse of guilt if they do not get at the center of it (3) This is the first time he mentions guilt. He does not identify the cause of this guilt, assuming that the reader acknowledges its existence. He describes the thrust of his efforts as overcoming the "Hitler within us." Not surprisingly, this phrase became a stumbling block for viewers and readers on both extremes of the political spectrum. The "brownish" public, those with old and neo-Nazi sympathies, chose to recognize different things in the movie. And many among the victims of the Third Reich refused to accept the premise of guilt at all, and by extension, the notion of a latent capacity for a Hitler-like behavior. Henry Pachter, for example, rejects the film's view of human nature: "Is Syberberg trying to suggest that, after all, Hitler was human, too?"[35] But the introduction makes clear that Syberberg addresses primarily a German audience. His observations on contemporary (West) German society and

its ills (*Misere*) turn into admonitions to overcome and conquer the Hitler potential
in the psyche and to build up a new identity through recognizing and separating,
sublimating and working on the tragic past (3). This alchemical process in mind and
heart constitutes a work of mourning (*Trauerarbeit*), which Syberberg compares
with the tragedy of the ancients.One must learn to recognize the sinister potential
and accept it in the therapeutic process of art, as a method of overcoming and
acknowledging the guilt. He calls it a sad model. The important task is to mourn
through art (4). The last sentence does not convey the whole meaning of the
original, illustrating the difficult task of translating Syberberg's prose.The German
text reads: "Es geht um die Kunst zu trauern." Another rendering would be: "The
issue is (or: It is a matter of) the art of mourning." The German allows a shift of
stress, yielding two possible interpretations: First, "to mourn through art." The act
of mourning receives the emphasis. The second possibility stresses the art that
facilitates the mourning process. The focus is on art. The German word for art,
Kunst, is related to the verb *können* (can, be able to). The etymology surrounds it
with a faint aura of additional meanings, such as ability, knowledge, a subject to
study and master. The author offers an aid in learning how to cope with mourning.
He offers therapy, in other words. The two possibilities are not mutually exclusive.
At the same time, Syberberg's statement also serves as a coded declaration, a
banner of sorts. It evokes a much quoted rallying call by Richard Wagner to his
supporters: "Hier geht's um die Kunst!" (Art is what it's all about; or: The
important thing here is art!). It was often heard again after World War II in
Bayreuth and in the media, but then with a slightly different nuance. The
admonition now seemed to imply: Forget about the Nazi history of the Bayreuth
festival, forget about the composer's offensive bias, forget about the Wagner
family's loyalties to the past; forget all this and concentrate on Wagner's art!
Syberberg's declaration amounts to a counter rally: The important thing is the art
of mourning. And he borrows Wagner's words to formulate it, anticipating a
statement he makes later on: "Hitler is to be fought, not with the statistics of
Auschwitz or with sociological analyses of the Nazi economy, but with Richard
Wagner and Mozart" (9). His intended treatment appears to be a combination of
homeopathy and allopathy.

The introduction of the German screenplay consists of a 51-page essay, "Die
Kunst als Rettung aus der deutschen Misere" (Art as Salvation from the Miserable
German Situation). It is subdivided into seven sections concentrating on film and
its mission. The emphasis on cinema as the most important art form of the twentieth
century accounts for the prominent cinematic frame of reference in the essay and
in the film itself. It assumes a representative function. In that capacity, it illustrates
a positive irrational creativity contrasted with totalitarian art, Hitler's fascination
with film, the suppression of free film before and after 1945, and its prostitution in
a market-driven system. It now becomes the main emblem and agent for change.
This thought winds like a red thread through all sections of the essay. The author
transfers to the cinema as a *Gesamtkunstwerk* the same ambitious mission that
Richard Wagner propounded for his festival dream in Bayreuth. And Wagner's

intention, as it surfaces repeatedly throughout his volumes, was to harness the power and potential of his art as a quasi-religious substitute in a secularized society, which, in his opinion, was decaying in all respects. The ideal was the ancient Greek theater that still retained a memory of communal spiritual rites. The Nazis understood this only too well when they in turn harnessed film and the Bayreuth enterprise to serve their objectives. Syberberg willingly chooses the role of Don Quixote when he again raises the banner of Idealism, rallying against a corrupt and corrupting establishment, and seeing in film a force for constructive change. With the spread of new technologies, especially the cyber world, his attention has since changed direction. But in 1977–78, he fought eagerly for film as a redeeming agent or medium in a sick society. At least that is how he viewed his own works.

As film is hailed as the art form of the twentieth century, so psychology can claim that position among the medical sciences. It was inevitable that Syberberg would resort to psychology for his *Hitler* film. But, one may wonder, where does he include representatives of this science, such as Freud, Jung, or Adler, among the characters? Where does he quote them? He doesn't. The entire film is an application and demonstration of their insights. Of course most branches of psychological inquiry were dismissed as "Jewish science" during the Third Reich. Syberberg therefore treats this suppressed field as he does the victims. With few exceptions, they remain unrecognized, voiceless, or in the background. Still, through the contrapuntal composition, they are more or less perceptively present. As mentioned before, the composition is built around a concept shared by both music and psychology: fugue. The fugue is the problem and the treatment. Syberberg is also cognizant of the limits to healing through therapy. Thus some of the characters in the film and prospective viewers are beyond help. But the children of that generation inherited the guilt without carrying personal blame. Among them one finds the sufferers struggling with melancholy because they are still sick of *Heimweh*. Their children in turn may be able to approach Hitler and German history in a more constructive way. Hence the juxtaposition of melancholy and joy, reflecting the simultaneity of several generations.

The state of affairs in West Germany provoked Syberberg to many critical remarks. His observations induced him to make the film. Most of these remarks were omitted in the English version of the screenplay. The issues and opinions are familiar from the *Filmbuch*, but are updated to include comments on the early reception of the *Hitler* film. The German indifference to this work nourishes the author's zeal in his condemnation of the box-office yardstick used to distribute financial support to filmmakers. In his view, the main criterion for support rests on such maxims as "Eat shit — ten million flies can't be wrong" (Gm. ed. 58). He consoles himself on the rejection by the German movie establishment with the proud statement, "No, I am not their man," paraphrasing the remark that he let his Hitler ghost make about Mozart: "But he is not my man." He also prophesies on a change he thinks may take place one day in the movie distribution business, namely that people may prefer to view their movies at home. And this came to happen in the years since he penned his essay. He anticipates this possible change with optimism. For, when the public is able to study segments of a film analytically through repeated viewings, much like a book or score, a new aesthetics will evolve, he hopes. In the meantime he is being ostracized and accepts his pariah status as a new freedom. He has even "died of Germany," as others may of infection or hunger (49). Syberberg should not have been surprised at the rejection. A seven-hour long film containing, among many topics, blunt attacks on the modern German movie industry and society was bound to be received as a provocation. The filmmaker's written and spoken elaborations did not ingratiate him either.

One of the fairly neutral topics in Syberberg's essay is his "aesthetic scandal" to combine Wagner with Brecht to an anti-Aristotelian system. This statement has received much attention in the reviews, although most readers will remain confused about what it entails. The third part of the essay discusses the dramatic legacy stretching as a continuum from antiquity to Brecht. Syberberg treats this artistic heritage as if he were discussing the Kabbalah. He describes himself as an heir to occidental culture and therefore wants to cultivate its tradition. Some of the characteristics he adopts for his films belong to the "epic" dramaturgy practiced by Brecht. This includes, for example, extensive narration instead of action, a frame using a narrator, monologues, breaking of illusion, alienation, rotation of actors and roles, episodic structure, etc. Syberberg has appropriated the entire array of "epic theater" praxis, including a never-ending system of quotations, text, subdued colors, and the occasional "return" of modern film to the jerky sequences of the first motion pictures. For example, one technique with multiple objectives consists in slowing down a strip of film, such as Hitler petting a subservient dog. Each frame is shown just long enough to make the viewer aware that the "moving" picture is really an illusion consisting of individual stills. Also, that this authentic historical sequence is merely a representation on film. Only a passing reference to the *Gesamtkunstwerk* alludes to the Wagnerian part of the "scandal," which should be read as "scandalon." This might suffice, since the numerous snippets of Wagner's music illustrate the concept of several arts combining into one composite. Syberberg does not, however, betray how much he has learned from Wagner's handling of musical structure, ranging from leitmotif to counterpoint. Nor does he allude to the presence of Wagner as a representative figure in Heller's unnamed character. His aesthetic program has evolved since its beginnings, but has remained surprisingly consistent.

The continuity in Syberberg's cinematic work is underscored in part by the reappearance of several cast members. Most notably, Harry Baer and Peter Kern, but also André Heller, Heinz Schubert, Peter Moland, and Rainer von Artenfels among the actors, and behind the camera, Gerhard von Halem and Dietrich Lohmann. Heller is perhaps the most colorful of the actors. He joined the cast coming from Circus Roncalli, an "alternative" circus with artistic pretensions. This Austrian multi-media talent is known as a poet, painter, playwright, singer, filmmaker, fireworks designer, and landscape artist. When in early 2000 the rightist Austrian politician Joerg Haider caused consternation abroad and waves of protests at home, Heller took to the streets with the crowds. His anti-Haider addresses at rallies were quoted worldwide.[36] In 2002 he and Othmar Schmiderer made a documentary about Hitler's secretary, then an old woman. *Hitler's Secretary (Im toten Winkel: Hitlers Sekretärin)* takes an approach similar to Syberberg's *Winifred Wagner* and *Theodor Hierneis*, since the interviewed person was a low-ranking employee. The fact that Heller's father was Jewish adds a nuance to his Wagnerian role, something akin to a counterpoint. His compatriot Kern has also reacted to the same issues, to judge from a recent film comedy of his, *Haider lebt* (Haider Lives).[37] Syberberg complains in the essay that neither the actors nor the film had received any prizes in Germany. In 1977 the British Film Institute selected *Hitler: a Film from Germany* as the best foreign film of the year. But later in 1978, Peter Kern received the German Film Award in gold for his acting. And in January 1980 the work received the Bavarian Film Award.

As a result of careful planning, cinematic aesthetics, and budget constraints, Syberberg completed the shooting in twenty days and edited the film between February and October 1977. In May that year he showed a one-hour excerpt of it at the International Film Festival in Cannes. It created quite a stir in the press and resulted in an interview on French television.[38] Syberberg stated on that occasion that he had originally intended to call the film "Hitler in Us: A Film from Germany, the Land of Progress" (14). On November 21 and 22, 1977 the premiere took place in London during the International Film Festival there. The film was received with great acclaim and much public debate. Abroad, that is. Apparently few German critics had attended the screenings in Cannes. Of course Syberberg wanted as much public attention as possible. Claiming that the German media ignored the work, he did the unheard-of: He withheld the film from the International Film Festival in Berlin, the most important media event in Germany. He also withheld it for some time from distribution in Germany. To explain this move, he penned an open statement, "Wir leben in einem toten Land" (We Live in a Dead Country), which appeared in *Die Zeit* on June 20, 1977.[39] It vents his anger with some of the same points made in his essay in the *Hitler* book. He laments that his country is not only dead, but "it is not even a country any longer. Centerless. Without a spiritual identity. . . . The Jews left, the mafia remained" (17). And the mafia is, of course, the German movie and press establishment. The phrase that Germany is a dead country recurs frequently in his publications throughout the 1980s. With that kind of obituary, his film does not seem so much to strive for healing as to put the dead and the living dead to rest. Although much in the statement repeats the essay in the script book, it offers some nuggets of information. For example, both *Karl May* and *Winifred Wagner* received top ranking at the British Film Festival in the years they were presented (18). Of course Syberberg's statement did not endear him to the organizers of the Berlin Festival or the German movie establishment. Wolf Donner, the director of the "Berlinade," printed an open letter to Syberberg in *Die Zeit* that summarizes the situation and adds some nuances. Besides pleading with the filmmaker to change his mind and show the work at the festival in Berlin, Donner accuses Syberberg of nourishing an unending feud with the German film critics so that he can present himself as a persecuted Jesus.[40] Syberberg's response appeared in the same weekly newspaper in January 1978, "*Hitler*—noch nicht für

Deutschland (*Hitler*: Not Yet for Germany).[41] The editor's introduction confirms the filmmaker's complaints that he needed lawyers to force various magazines and newspapers, including the *Süddeutsche Zeitung*, to retract defamation and lies about him. Not surprisingly, Syberberg places the blame for the standoff on the German media. But, he concludes, he made the film for Germany and hopes to show it there later. His defiance cemented his image as a difficult, arrogant, and paranoid provocateur. The filmmaker may also have harbored fears about more malicious attacks. At least one article claims that concern for his daughter prompted his decision: Sereny, for example, states, "In fact, Amelie is the main reason that he doesn't want to run *Hitler* in Germany. 'That is where they will really try to get at me—through her—because I used my child in that film.' The tension in his voice was almost tangible. Syberberg is a very angry man."[42] Two additional reasons may also have compelled him to withhold the film for a while. First, *Hitler* may not have been completed in time for the Berlin event. Although years of planning enabled Syberberg to finish the shooting in an unbelievably short time, the editing process lasted considerably longer. In Berlin, he would have had to present the final seven-hour version, not excerpts of a work in progress, as he had done in Cannes. And second, 1977 proved to be a Hitler-year of German cinema. Among the entries at the Berlin Festival was *Hitler: a Career* by Joachim C. Fest and numerous other films dealing with the same period. If Syberberg had presented his film in Berlin in 1977, he would not have attracted the undivided attention to his topic, and the media would have subjected his work to predictably harsh comparisons with the competing entries. He may in particular have resented a juxtaposition with Fest's *Hitler*, on which he comments disparagingly in his reply to Donner and in the essay of his book. Whatever the motive for withholding the film, his action did not improve his image at home.

First shown in Great Britain, the movie then started its French run in Paris. It was scheduled to be shown in the Latin Quarter at the Studio des Ursulines, but bomb threats caused some unwanted publicity. It eventually opened at the Pagode in the Rue du Babylone, according to one of the German critics who traveled to Paris to cover the event.[43] His review is one of the better Syberberg earned in Germany, but even it does not express enthusiasm or admiration. The writer, Hans Blumenberg, admits to being confused, and while attempting to describe the film to his readers, claims, "Syberberg's aesthetics is aimed at overwhelming, not at comprehension" (46). But he does acknowledge Syberberg's "unique" and "ingenious" background projection technique, calling it an ideal medium for his polyvalent chains of associations. Discussing with mild sarcasm the unusual "soul landscape," he reveals his problems with understanding when he erroneously attributes Heine's poem "Night Thoughts," which is recited at the beginning and appears printed at the end of the film, to *Deutschland: Ein Wintermärchen.* He did not bother to doublecheck. Nor did he perceive how Heine informs the content throughout. Blumenberg's difficulty with the film signals that it may indeed be too Hermetic to reach its intended audience.

The German premiere followed in Aschaffenburg on July 2 and 3, 1978 for a select audience. The setting was a symposium on Hitler ("Streitfragen zur Zeitgeschichte"). The organizers had invited internationally renowned researchers on Hitler, among whom many disagreed with each other and even avoided each other, ranging from the extreme right to the extreme left. Syberberg was the only moviemaker among the discussants, since Joachim Fest, whose film on Hitler Syberberg had criticized, declined to participate. Among other no-shows was Robert Kempner, prosecutor at the trial in Nuremberg. Again bomb threats were issued, in particular against Syberberg's film. The most notorious panelist was the British author David Irving, who was balanced at the other end by the British Germanist J. P. Stern and the German political scientist Iring Fetscher. To judge from Janßen's printed review, this academic conference became quite a circus, complete with television crews, masses of armed police, demonstrators, and throngs of people who could not be admitted. About the debate with and against Irving, Syberberg remarked: "I see through Irving's game—it is a crazy one."[44] After the speakers agreed on their failure to come to grips with Hitler through rational, analytical means, he offered as his alternative the irrational language of cinematic art. The reviewer reports how Syberberg repeatedly earned applause for his comments. Janßen's praise of the film is possibly the most appreciative assessment to come from a German source: "After Thomas Mann's epic work about the composer Adrian Leverkühn, Syberberg's *Film from Germany* is the second magnificent artistic transformation of the horrible past, a *Doktor Faustus* in celluloid" (3). He goes on to characterize the seven hours' performance as a catharsis. During the symposium, one session was devoted to a discussion with Syberberg about his film, this time with an audience that had actually seen it. In October 1978 the first screening in Vienna was accompanied by a public debate between Syberberg and the author Rolf Hochhuth. The German run began in Frankfurt am Main, timed to coincide with the annual book fair.

In the following years, *Hitler* was, and continues to be, shown worldwide. As is the case with many of Syberberg's films, the screenings often take place at universities and cultural centers during special events, such as film festivals, special film series, various commemorative events, discussion seminars, or retrospectives. It has also become part of the curriculum in numerous university courses in a wide range of disciplines. In the United States, Francis Ford Coppola's company Zoetrope handled the American distribution initially. Due to its length, the film was usually presented as a special event with full day runs, only interrupted by a lunch break. Syberberg was present when it was shown several times at the Palace of Fine Arts in San Francisco. On one of these occasions passions flaired again. The American Nazi Party demonstrated outside with participants in combat gear. Inside, leftists were also protesting, taking over the stage for a while. Neither group had seen the movie. The audience got testy with so much disturbance, but the program proceeded as soon as peace had been restored.[45] The Californian public was impressed with the film. Di Matteo wrote that it "restores credibility to the word 'masterpiece.' (It's also the ultimate horror movie)."[46] A few lines further he describes it as an "act of cinematic hubris if ever there was one—this dense, verbose, incantatory, purging film" (72). In New York, it was presented on four occasions in the Avery Fisher Hall of the Lincoln Center in January 1980, with an audience of 9,000 ("Syberberg," 88). By comparison, only a total of 150 people saw it during a six-day run in Frankfurt am Main, and the combined audience in Frankfurt, Hamburg, and Munich did not match that in San Francisco, where it ran as a special event for three days ("Syberberg," 78). Coppola had suggested the title under which Americans became acquainted with the film, *Our Hitler*. Wistfully, Syberberg ponders this change in a short essay, first published in 1980.[47] The pronoun "our" reflects the understanding that he had wished to encounter in Germany. He did not meet with much support in television circles there either. When the film eventually did appear on German television, it was without the media efforts surrounding the American series *Holocaust*, such as commentary and discussions, while across the border, both the screening on Austrian television and in movie theaters were followed by two-hour discussions ("Syberberg," 78).

Syberberg's own essay on the film set the tone for much of the critical literature that followed. This literature has swelled to a considerable library, not including short reviews and polemical pieces. An early collection of articles appeared in February 1980 in a special issue of *Cahiers du Cinéma* simply called "Syberberg." After four chapters by Syberberg follows one chapter consisting of three articles by Susan Sontag, Alberto Moravia, and Heiner Müller, and three interviews with Francis Ford Coppola, Douglas Sirk, and Michel Foucault. They all express appreciation of the film. Foucault's interview is one of the earliest texts that Syberberg collected and distributed in fifty copies, *Pressedokumente 1973-78*. The French philosopher emphasizes the relationship between horror and banality, or in his words, the four Horsemen of the Apocalypse and the little maggots of everyday life.[48] Moravia, who describes the film as an oratorio, concentrates on Himmler's masseur, who in real life managed to reduce the genocide in Holland.[49] Perhaps best known is Susan Sontag's essay, "Aventures dans la tête," expanded to "Syberbergs Hitler" in the German version published soon after, as "Eye of the Storm" elsewhere, and later as a chapter in her book *Under the Sign of Saturn*.[50] This appreciative essay remained for several years the most substantial study on the film. Unfortunately for Sontag, it also earned her lasting animosity from Syberberg's enemies in the German press, unabated as late as 1990. Especially her conclusion provoked much scorn: "Syberberg's film belongs in the category of noble masterpieces which ask for fielty and can compel it. After seeing *Hitler: A Film from Germany*, there is Syberberg's film—and then there are the other films one admires."[51] "Compel fielty" is the expression that the critics could not swallow.[52] And she concludes: "As was said ruefully of Wagner, he spoils our tolerance for the others" (165). To many Germans, Richard Wagner's name possesses an incendiary power. Without the last paragraph, Sontag might have remained unscathed, but her essay would probably also have been overlooked by Syberberg's detractors.

Four of the French articles in *Syberberg* were included in a German collection of essays that appeared later in 1980 with the title *Syberbergs Hitler-Film*.[53] The contributions by Coppola and Sirk were omitted, while articles by Jean-Pierre Faye,

Jean-Pierre Oudart, Christian Zimmer, and Vito Zagarrio were added. All the texts had appeared elsewhere before. Strangely enough, Syberberg expressed no satisfaction at seeing such positive comments by respected artists and intellectuals, and that even in his own country where he felt like an outcast. In his next book he took issue with the translation (*Die freudl. Ges.* 239–42). Especially Faye's article suffered in the process. Numerous examples illustrate how the translation teems with a cliché-ridden and ideological vocabulary. It reveals precisely the kind of thoughtless conformist attitude Syberberg attacks untiringly. What especially peeved him was the fact that all the examples were "improvements" imposed by the editorial board on the translation prepared by Mrs. Syberberg (239). The preface by the editor confirms that the *Hitler* film had met with cynical and unfriendly treatment in the German media. In time most German newspapers and magazines carried reviews of *Hitler* or interviews with Syberberg about the film. It unleashed an unprecedented debate. The reception in Germany ranged from mixed to negative. Syberberg added to the fuel by adopting an accusing and aggressive tone in numerous published statements. In contrast, critics in other countries praised the film as a highly significant masterpiece. The factual but inimical preface by the German editor of *Syberbergs Hitler-Film* illustrates this dichotomy, since it is frosty, while the chapters were all contributed by foreigners and express admiration.

Most scholarly studies of Syberberg's *Hitler* film have appeared outside Germany. To the few exceptions count individual chapters by Hans Rudolf Vaget and Anton Kaes, as well as John Sandford's entry on Syberberg in *Cinegraph*.[54] Written in English are, e.g., chapters on Syberberg in books about German film by John Sandford (1980), Timothy Corrigan (1983), James Franklin (1983), Russell A. Berman (1984), Anton Kaes (1989), Eric Santner (1990), and others.[55] Thomas Elsaesser's study of 1981 remains one of the more important journal articles on the film.[56] Syberberg has himself commented on numerous occasions on his film and its reception in various countries. Much of this appeared in his book of 1981, *Die freudlose Gesellschaft*, but one also finds short items scattered in magazines and journals. An excerpt of the essay in his printed film script appeared together with reviews by Susan Sontag and Barbara Rose in *Vogue*.[57] This issue of the magazine devotes the entire page 257 to a portrait photo of Syberberg. One sees only his head above a fur collar. Does that suggest he is shivering in a frosty climate? The ice cosmogony has become reality? A fur coat is a strange choice of attire for a photo session, unless, of course, the collar is made of wolf's fur. With his insistence on rotating actors and roles in *Hitler*, one may assume that he, too, would play the Wolf sooner or later. He had first presented this nickname of Hitler's in *Winifred Wagner*. But in Syberberg's oeuvre things are not always what they look like at first glance, and besides, he is an inveterate punster who plays with similes, metaphors, symbols, and allegories, and everything in between. Looking at a man in wolf's clothing conjures up a related expression, "wolf in sheep's clothing." Heine had borrowed this biblical expression for a false prophet when referring to himself in caput 12 of *Deutschland: Ein Wintermärchen*. Syberberg uses the term in his book of 1981, referring to his teachers in East Germany after the war. To display their political correctness, they were wearing a new political pin on their lapel where they had formerly worn the pin of the Nazi party: "Our leading dogs as wolves in sheep's clothing" (*Die freudl. Ges.*, 144). Syberberg may also be playing with the inversion of that phrase, which he borrows from a film critic in his *Filmbuch*. The critic had coined the term "sheep in wolf's clothing" in reference to Ingmar Bergman (119). There was no love lost between Syberberg and this critic, whose scathing review of *San Domingo* he reprints in his *Filmbuch* (124–25). By playing with this expression, Syberberg can pay his tribute to Bergman and tease the critic with, "See, I'm as great as Ingmar Bergman." At the same time he presents himself as the unrecognized innocent lamb that so many of his compatriots consider a dangerous Nazi seducer and Hitler admirer. And then there is the Lamb of God. He does play the role of the Crucified One in all his writings. But to the casual reader, the picture only shows a man in a fur-collared coat.

Chapter 5

A Chilly Climate

In 1977, the same year *Hitler* was released abroad, Syberberg edited and published a book on photography, *Fotografie der 30er Jahre: Eine Anthologie.*[1] This collection comprises 166 photos that had appeared between 1930 and 1940 in the French yearbook *Arts et Métiers Graphiques*. The photographers whose works are reproduced include such international notables as Berenice Abbot, Cecil Beaton, Henri Cartier-Bresson, Horst, Germaine Krull, Man Ray, and Steicher. Many of these photos are portraits, which comes as no surprise in view of Syberberg's fascination with faces as landscapes. His introduction provides the analytical anchoring for the selection. Since the pictures had originally been included in yearbooks, he notes, they represented the best of the year in the eyes of the editors. That makes them representative of the prevailing aesthetics and elevates them to the status of documentation of an era. Examining the characteristics of the selection, and one assumes, of the original yearbooks from which they were culled, Syberberg points out what is missing: many names that became famous later, social issues, political reportage, daily life. It is photography as art and as timeless representation. And, he asks rhetorically, does it, because of the missing dimensions, reveal more about itself and its time than it intended? (5). He goes on to list some of the developments and events that rocked the Western world in that decade. It was a period eliciting nostalgia or horror in the survivors, and in art it was a time of "degenerate art" as well as "art for the people." "A bad time for a minority, and it [the minority] represented often the best ones," he reminds the readers (5). Emphasizing the sporty eroticism in fashions and the ornamental elegance in photography, he establishes a parallel between the nonpolitical pictures and the aesthetics of photography in the service of politics. Therefore, he adds, he also includes work by Willi Zielke, one of Riefenstahl's camera men for her *Olympia*. He concludes that, indeed, one can recognize the same *Formwillen* of societal "progress" in the photo selections. This is so in spite of their deliberate avoidance of the "real" world. This kind of photography constitutes an attempted counterworld to reality, with high aesthetic pretensions and detachment from politics and social problems. In the experimentation with forms, light, and shadow, Syberberg discerns abstractions that parallel those of the other arts, but in the portraits he sees only the last imitations of portrait painting. He calls these photos "pictures without meditation. Without aura, but with magic" (6). Finding them empty and devoid of any moral aspect, he calls them "dangerously beautiful." And as a counterworld, this photography was powerless to prevent the coming disaster. Syberberg continues, sneaking in a long list of undeclared references and self-quotations from his *Hitler* film. His conclusion advocates the need of our age for its own photographic documentation that reflects truthfully the new consciousness.

The anthology supplements Syberberg's cinematic and written work. It illustrates through contrast how his own aesthetics deviates from that of the Third Reich and prevailing trends. He refers repeatedly to the *Modernität* (modernity) of the thirties, and while eschewing the terms "modernism" and "postmodernism," he establishes himself as an outsider and non-conformist in his creative work. This critique of modernism/modernity and its pictorial aesthetics has gone largely unnoticed by the critics, among whom many prefer to see his work as strictly modernist. That labeling would, of course, make it easier to classify him, especially since "modernism" has remained a slippery term and has been tainted with fascism in a growing body of literature. But Syberberg cherishes being *unzeitgemäß* (untimely) in all meanings of that word. In his own film aesthetics, he draws inspiration from the German expressionists, often in the form of visual quotations. Dr. Caligari, for example, reappears in *Hitler*. On a superficial level, this use of the past might seem to support Siegfried Kracauer's thesis that there is a direct connection leading from German expressionist film to Hitler, as expounded in his *From Dr. Caligari to Hitler*. Syberberg disagrees with that view. In an interview, a reporter brought up Kracauer's claim and its refutation by Fritz Lang and requested Syberberg's opinion. He thought that Lang was right and called Kracauer's theory a beautiful intellectual game. Reality was more complex.[2] By severing expressionism from modernism in this interview, and himself from the implied modernism of the thirties in his photo book ("the aesthetics of modernity"), Syberberg may have attempted to shield himself against accusations he knew would come. They were based mainly on his *Hitler* film. To be sure, he had unambiguously excoriated the mentality of marketing the commodity called Hitler in his film, but ironically, many Germans perceived him as being in a league with these marketeers when so many movies about the Nazi years were released almost simultaneously. More serious was the doubt left in the mind by the topic and the nature of his film. It is not a traditional documentary. It does not explain or tell the viewers what conclusions to draw. And, Syberberg had gone on record in his *Filmbuch* that he had to care deeply about his subject to make a film about it (60). His *Hitler* presents enough unfiltered Nazi material to mislead a sympathetic or gullible mind. Since most Germans did not see the film themselves, they depended on the not-so-friendly critics for an opinion. From now on, Syberberg was suspected of being a Nazi sympathizer or worse. The photo book had no effect on his image.

The film critics and reporters are not the only ones to blame for this image. Syberberg has supplied them with statements useful for that purpose. Most of his published articles and books could be distorted to suit any attack. Beginning with the *Hitler* film and the photo of him in a fur coat (wolf's fur?), an increasingly ambiguous Syberberg emerges in public. More and more often he appears to be speaking with a forked tongue. Keeping in mind the principles of counterpoint and fugal progression, one can recognize what is happening: The musical "subject" or tonic proceeds into a new movement where it changes its function in a melody that is transformed into a variation (inversion, crab, inversion of crab), while the tone that had been the dominant becomes the new tonic. Its version of the melody sounds different because it occurs in a new register or variation. The simultaneous presentation of both versions creates a composite too complex to allow easy identification of its parts to an untrained ear. An illustration of Syberberg's Modulation or transition into the next quasi-musical stage is his article "Form is morality."[3] The American series *Holocaust* elicited these comments when it ran on German television after a hard sell by the producers. The four installments and reruns became a media event with massive support by the press and high viewer participation. Syberberg does not criticize the acting or photography. But he does take issue with just about everything else. His major argument against the series is its primitive soap opera format. As film, it is an unworthy monument for the victims. The German movie critics found nothing wrong with that. Obviously, many must have felt uneasy on that account, but lacked the courage to point out any deficiencies. Syberberg paraphrases the editor of *Die Zeit*, for example, who supposedly wrote that in this case, "reservations about the low level of its artistic achievement should be set aside, since the question here was one of morality" (11). Not so, counters Syberberg, referring to the program as an Auschwitz show from Hollywood and Auschwitz as a consumer product. He quotes morbid comments about the series overheard on his tour with his *Hitler* film in Israel, such as "a soap opera with soap supplied by Ilse Koch" (11).[4] And he is offended that this program was made for profit. He remarks that to the best of his knowledge the producers have not donated any of the proceeds to a fund for the victims or a related worthy cause (13). "Isn't it a victory for Hitler when the ashes of Auschwitz are turned into gold for Hollywood?" he laments. The greed does not stop with that: "People see in front of them every ten minutes advertising spots for Coca-Cola and Ford cars, for detergents in amongst the dead of Auschwitz and Frau Weiss' walk into the gas chamber and the uprising in the Warshaw ghetto" (12). The commercial interests impress themselves on the viewers so blatantly that the marketing effort merges with the for-profit motive of the producers and becomes symptomatic of much in society that Syberberg abhors.

A third point concerns the media manipulation of the television audience, resulting in the desired mass reaction. The episodes on German television were followed by phone-in discussions. This broad participation combined with the absence of critical voices reminds Syberberg of Goebbels' propaganda methods. And furthermore, he deplores that the program tells at best a part of the truth. By concentrating on one family, it ignores the larger context. A minor objection concerns the television format, which makes it too easy on the viewer to watch with no personal effort involved, not even that of going to a movie theater.

In brief, Syberberg fails to acknowledge any redeeming qualities in the series. One can easily point out weaknesses in his argumentation. The objection to watching the program in the comfort of one's home is contradicted by his own prophetic statements about video versus movie theater in the essay in his German script book to *Hitler*. Since a television program can be taped for repeated viewing, and since most movies soon find their way to the video stores, the viewers have the opportunity to examine a film the way Syberberg wants it done: repeatedly, critically, analytically, with reflexion and discussion. Also untenable is his rejection of the narrow focus on one family. Syberberg claims that every honest film about Hitler can only be about "ourselves" (14). But this film is not about Hitler; it concerns the family Weiss. If the title had reflected that, the issue might not have been raised, and the family would still have functioned on the screen as representatives of millions. The fact that the characters are Jewish did not prevent the viewers from empathizing. The simple narrative actually made it easier for the public to identify with them and share their anguish. Of course that approach is un-Brechtian, but nonetheless effective in pulling on the heartstrings. Syberberg also wants to achieve that, as he states in his book to *Hitler*: "Hitler and all the idealism of his misled followers can be conquered only with the heart" (13). But while his road to the viewers' heart passes through their brain, that of the *Holocaust* producers leads through the guts to the heart.

Syberberg's objection to the media promotion of the series could be dismissed as envy if it were not for some justification in his criticism. This kind of publicity success may seem innocent to Americans used to aggressive public relations in all commerce, including the marketing of the arts. But the event illustrated precisely the manipulation of public opinion and calculated emotional response that Goebbels and his ministry of propaganda perfected. Syberberg sees it as a repeat of the national, communal surge orchestrated by those brown masters. And in Germany the critics kept silent. Hypocracy, cowardice, maybe intimidation prevailed. This was different in other European countries, where the public debate was much more diverse. Thus, the critical observations about the handling of this media event are not unfounded.

The two main objections are presented with weightier moral authority. They discuss the two sides of the same coin. The commercials during the program revealed its true nature as clearly as the primitive format: the series is a soap opera for entertainment and profit. "Our most sacred grief turned into money," Syberberg complains, " Auschwitz as a consumer product" (15). The magnitude of the traumatic topic requires a different vehicle than a trite formula: "I believe that the dead of Auschwitz and Treblinka and Buchenwald, the maimed, the sufferings of this world, deserve the passions of Bach and not the operettas of Franz Lehar or soap operas from Hollywood" (15). This opinion was shared by many, also in the United States. To Syberberg, the soap opera does not possess artistic merit, and for him morality resides in the artistic form: "[I]t is totally unthinkable that a bad film can have a good moral effect" (13). This kind of thinking reveals an indebtedness or affinity to the theories of Adorno and the Frankfurt School, especially on the relationship between ideological forces and artistic form.[5] The shared premise is the political significance of aesthetic structure, since it reflects the artist's response to the political implications of societal codes. Syberberg protests against a code seen in the handling of the series that he recognizes as potentially fascist, or at least reminiscent of the Nazi system. It would also identify him as solidly with the thinkers of the Frankfurt School, who were forced to emigrate during the Third Reich. Since he does not explicitly identify his allegiance, it went mostly undetected by readers. Many of them also remained unconvinced by his arguments. What if the movie was not intended to be a memorial to the victims of the Holocaust? What if no loftier objective than box office success motivated the producers? These issues seemed inconsequential. To Syberberg that would be incompatible with the topic. By comparison, *Schindler's List* and *Shoah* might have elicited a different reaction from him. Nonetheless, *Holocaust* was adopted into the curriculum in many German schools. And Syberberg's undifferentiated negativism amid a nation-wide, semi-official endorsement of the film raised eyebrows. The article discredited him in Germany. The media establishment found it easy to present this article and other statements as proof of a rightist mind. In Germany, *rightist* does not mean merely conservative, but also close to neo-Nazi. It did not matter that Syberberg repeatedly tried to clarify his position. In the interview with Erkkila he even described himself as a leftist of a special kind because he took a position of opposition (211). This position had become necessary, he continued, because in those years the majority was leaning left, both in politics, media, and cultural life. Whenever a big block assumes power and imposes itself on society, opposition is called for. And his opposition aimed at the fatness of power. This distinction was of no interest to his enemies.

Whenever Syberberg's fellow Germans gave him a cold shoulder, he would always find solace in France. That is where his next publication appeared. It is simply called "Syberberg." It is a special issue of *Cahiers du Cinéma*, dated February 1980. He contributed chapters 1 through 4, while the fifth consists of the interviews and essays already mentioned in the previous chapter (Sontag, Moravia, H.Müller, Coppola, Sirk, Foucault).

Chapter 1 is dedicated to Francis Ford and Eleanor Coppola, with whom the family Syberberg spent several weeks as their house guests in '79. Actually, Syberberg traveled to San Francisco repeatedly that year. This time the Coppolas had invited several European filmmakers, turning the stay in California into a retreat of stimulating discussions on film theory, plans, and hopes. Coppola offered to handle the distribution of the *Hitler* film in the United States. Abundantly illustrated with snapshots, this part consists mostly of fond memories of friendships and new impressions.

Chapter 2 is subdivided into six segments with separate titles. The first is "Vidéo-mémoires (projet)" (Project for Video Memoir-Portraits). The text outlines tentative plans for a series of documentaries, for the most part biographies and memoirs of, resp. interviews with, important Germans. This would continue the author's earlier work on Kortner, Schneider, Pocci, and Winifred Wagner. He deplores the lost opportunities for such recordings of many already deceased, for example Freud, Bloch, and Brecht. Such a national film library would be a recording of history using the medium of our age. The second section, "J'accuse" (I Accuse), continues the argumentation, identifying Goebbels as the originator of the idea. He had employed twenty-four camera men for such projects during World War II. Some thirty of their documentaries still exist in the film archives in Koblenz. Placing the infamous propaganda minister in a constructive frame of reference was a deliberate scandalon. Syberberg knew well enough that this would elicit mixed reactions. Goebbels' present-day successors at the funding sources are neglecting their duty to erect their own monument to our era, Syberberg maintains, attacking with arguments familiar from previous texts. The main thrust is directed against the prevailing materialism, the so-called progress, and consumer mentality. The target shifts from government via opinion makers to the population. The title of this section forms the beginning of the first sentence. With it, Syberberg evokes Émile Zola's open letter of 1898 during the Dreyfus Affair.[6] One is hard pressed to find overt parallels between Zola's "J'accuse" and Syberberg's text. But both are passionate protests against the government's (mis)handling of its duties. Zola's resulting exile might compare with Syberberg's ostracism. And in both cases, the public institutions suppress or disregard the truth. A classic case of intertextuality is the bundle of unstated issues surrounding the two accusers, for example anti-Semitism targeting Dreyfus. By borrowing the words of a famous defender of a Jewish victim in a flawed system, Syberberg echoes the voice of a champion of justice, while he himself champions a project inspired by an anti-Semite, but also the remembrance of the whole past. The faint reference to the French protest preserves the "other" strand of text and reveals the counterpoint as still continuing. This composition has two subjects or themes, as evidenced by two additional variants that come to mind. They, too, belong on opposite sides (Nazi film and Jewish exile) and affect Germany and France. One could serve as a pseudo-musical "answer" to Goebbels' project of documentaries. Not intended to preserve the memory of outstanding lives, but to promote the eradication of lives, the German movie *Ich klage an* (I Accuse) was released in August 1941. The Nazi government planned to use it to prepare the population for the legalization of euthanasia. Such measures had already exterminated more than 50,000 mentally handicapped and incurably sick, but were discontinued in 1941 due to public reaction.[7] The movie presents assisted dying by choice as a merciful alternative to a slow and painful death. The other quasi-musical variant is the introduction to Heinrich Heine's *Französische Zustände*, also known as his *Vorrede* and *J'accuse*.[8] Protesting measures in Germany, especially in Prussia, to suppress modest gains in civil rights, Heine attacks the authorities: "I accuse them of abusing the confidence of the people, I accuse them of offending the majesty of the people, I accuse them of high treason against the German people, I accuse them!" (377). This passionate attack sealed Heine's fate and doomed him to exile for the rest of his life. Syberberg's "J'accuse" is, by comparison, directed against a contemporary system. Its democratic modus operandi shifts the censorship decisions to critics and committees composed of Syberberg's enemies in the press. This forces his work into exile.

The third segment of this chapter, "A propos du Festival de Munich," continues with five suggestions for transforming the annual film festival in Munich. The author envisions more diversity, flexibility, and rotation of sites. He is apparently drawing on his experience from participating in numerous film festivals abroad. The next unit reprints a letter to the University of Marburg ("Lettre à l'Université de Marburg"). It outlines ideas for a degree program in film studies at the university.

At the time of writing, such studies were offered at academies, but not as part of a more prestigious university program in Germany. This is followed by a letter to the Austrian television company ORF ("Lettre à la Télévision autrichienne"), in which Syberberg suggests in seven points a monthly program, "Syberberg Presents." He has in mind an interview format with introduction and commentary, primarily but not exclusively, of intellectuals and creative people from all branches of the arts. The final section is called "*Parsifal*: Éléments pour un projet de film" (*Parsifal*: Elements for a Film Project). Already occupied with research for his next film, he lets these pages evolve around illustrations that would be incorporated in his concept. One such element is the Parsi-phallic dimension of Wagner's plans. Syberberg also draws attention to the cupola of the Grail sanctuary, playing on the visual nexus in the *Hitler* film between *Koppel*-couple-copulation-*Kuppel*-cupola, and perhaps also in a more creative sense, a reference to Coppola. Another page discusses his heterodox interpretation of Kundry. Some of these tidbits were later superceded by the book on the *Parsifal* film.

Chapter 3 is called "Le métier de cinéaste" (The Profession of a Movieman). The word *cinéaste* can refer both to a film afficionado and to a creative filmmaker. It started as an unedited interview with Serge Daney and Bernard Sobel, but reads like an essay. Studded with illustrations and movie stills, it treats three topics. The first is a technical explanation and assessment of the frontal projection which produces the background in many of Syberberg's films. The reader gains an appreciation of the artistic possibilities of this old device, which Syberberg rediscovered and perfected. The second topic is marionettes or puppets. Inspired by the famous essay on marionettes by Heinrich von Kleist, the filmmaker elaborates on his use of dolls in *Hitler*.[9] While Kleist's essay discusses only the suspended marionettes, Syberberg uses all kinds of dolls in his film. He is fascinated by the shared characteristic in the small imitations of humans and animals: they can only move when manipulated by external forces. "And for me," Syberberg states about the human controlling agent, "that's the spiritual background for this technique, because my idea is that the Hitlers [the puppets] were manipulated by others. And in this particular case, by us" (61). Two of the accompanying illustrations show the development from inspiration to application in the film. Gustave Doré's etching includes numerous corpses in lidless stacked coffins. Similar figures appear in part 1 of *Hitler* as little Nazi dolls "resurrected" with the help of the actors holding them. Other remarks deal with the importance of light in Syberberg's work. In the documentary on Winifred Wagner, for example, only natural daylight illuminated the room. It would seem, then, that Mrs. Wagner was no luminary in her own right, since she received her light from an outside source. The third subdivision is "Les Citations" (The Quotations). Among the examples one notices the snow-filled glass ball from *Citizen Kane* and the famous phrase of the philosopher Kant, "Above us the starry vault, and the moral law within me." The text also links together the child and Kleist's puppets, presumably because of their function as miniatures in a *mise en abyme* setting, as well as their unconscious innocence. The child is not only the beginning and end of the *Hitler* film, the text concludes, but also its center.

The fourth chapter, "Du pays mort d'une société sans joie," consists of eighteen pages of aphoristic passages. They contain many excerpts and formulations that were included in Syberberg's next book of 1981. In addition to the critical observations of modern Germany, one also finds scattered snippets of autobiographical information. The accompanying photographs constitute a family album of the author's childhood and youth, with the last four illustrating the political climate of post-war East Germany. These four snapshots depict parades during an international youth festival in East Germany. Had not the portraits of Stalin replaced the swastikas, one could easily have mistaken the disciplined rows of uniformed people for participants in Nazi-era public festivities. Without commentary on these illustrations, Syberberg conveys that a similar spirit ruled East Germany and Hitler's Germany: political streamlining and conformity were imposed on everything. These city photos from the years in Rostock imply a contrast to the other pictures of a happier childhood environment in the country. Apparently, this lost paradise functions as a counterworld to the contemporary society criticized in the text.

For a while some aspects of the Third Reich continued to preoccupy Syberberg. In an essay published in France he returns to Hitler and his aesthetics.[10] Reminding the reader that the dictator had aspired to a life as an artist, Syberberg examines the consequences of an authoritarian system under Hitler with him as the ultimate state artist. Following seven "theses" outlining his premises, Syberberg declares Hitler's aesthetic impact to be the mephistophelian avant-garde of art in the twentieth century. Of course military plans dictated many developments, but the dictator's own concern with the socialist ideals gave the impetus to the development of the Volkswagen (car of the people) and the scenic layout of the *Autobahn*. His involvement in Albert Speer's preparations for postwar building projects did not proceed far beyond models and plans, while his influence on the visual arts and film was profound. Movies for the masses became carriers of state intent, especially as entertaining escapism and indoctrination; Leni Riefenstahl's commissioned mass spectacles probably benefited from events organized for the purpose of being filmed; the weekly newsreels were not only shown to Hitler first, but he frequently contributed the commentary himself (no sources given, 380). And finally, about 80 documentaries of prominent Germans were made. The goal was to create what Syberberg calls "Germany: A Film by Hitler." In all facets of government involvement, the aesthetic considerations harnessed technology, appealed to the masses, emphasized efficiency, and soon resembled a total work of art in the service of state propaganda. Syberberg does not fail to mention Richard Wagner's significance for Hitler. He even wonders if there would have been a Hitler without Wagner. One also learns that the dictator had chosen *Parsifal*, under the direction of Wieland Wagner, to be played at the peace celebration ending World War II. The analysis of Hitler's aesthetics imposed on the Reich concludes with a glance at the present. The grand schemes have been transformed, but are equally pervasive and manipulative, the writer concludes. Consumption, leisure time pursuits, and economic interests have replaced the concern with art. Propaganda has been renamed public relations. In brief, modern society has only refined, but by no means abolished the use of aesthetics to serve state purposes. Hence the views and measures imposed by Hitler functioned as an avant-garde both to the current art scene and to society. Since this was a mephistophelian avant-garde, the development has brought hell, one must conclude. The pessimistic view is only softened by the chance that still exists to transform today's society. By that the author means primarily Western Germany, one assumes, and by extension, the Western world.

Die freudlose Gesellschaft

The ills of German society became one of the three major topics in Syberberg's publications, the others being himself and his films. He continued working with unrelenting energy, writing, traveling, preparing *Parsifal*, and attempting to acquire funding for it. His main publication from this period is a collection of prose pieces in book form, *Die freudlose Gesellschaft*.[11] The volume is dedicated to Mrs. Syberberg and begins with an introduction in seven parts. The bulk of the volume consists of two "Books" connected by a shorter section called "Parenthesis." The material is further arranged into 381 numbered sections varying in length from two-line aphorisms to small chapters. The longest of these are subdivided into passages preceded by asterisks.

Syberberg had already used the expression "joyless society" in earlier publications. Now it appears as the title of a book. Again and again he returns to the psychological problem of not being able to experience joy after a trauma for which the grieving process has been stunted. Without proper grief, then, no healing occurs and no joy later, he contends. This happened to so many Germans that he transfers the result to society as a whole. The word "joyless" may also refer obliquely to the title of the film classic *Die freudlose Gasse* (*Joyless Street*) of 1925 by Pabst. Here, too, stress is on an exasperating situation following a world war with inflation, political instability, and unemployment, as well as its disintegrating effect on social norms and individual integrity. The joyless street eventually turns into a street of the corrupt. Finally, the title of the book also plays on *freudlos* and *Freud-los* (without Freud). Sigmund Freud himself died in British exile just as World War II broke out. The medical specialty he pioneered, psychoanalysis, was suppressed by the Nazis as a "Jewish science." Since Freud was Jewish, Syberberg uses *freudlos* and *Freudlos* synecdochically, characterizing modern Germany as a country without Jews. Of course that is not statistically exact, since the Jewish population in Germany tops 60,000 and is increasing with a steady influx of immigrants from the former East Block. Still, their numbers are too modest to match the influence the Jewish Germans exerted on their environment before the Third Reich. In the professions, in the world of business, and most importantly, in cultural life, their contributions exceeded their statistical share. Without the biblical salt, the German bread does not taste right, Syberberg seems to imply. The society he presents in his book is heavily flawed and becomes the main target of his critical observations. The author does not refer to the past. But as a result of its horrors, the Jewish Germans disappeared. All tensions and conflicts among the Germans are now among Gentile Germans, Syberberg reminds the reader (8). His compatriots can only blame themselves for the frustrations of daily life. And cinema reflects best how raw the climate has turned: "[E]verything has become unspeakably malicious, rigid in humor or thinking and debating, . . . and ruthless" (8). Without mentioning Freud by name, but pointing to a Germany without Jews, the author repeatedly calls it a country of the dead and a *freudlose* society. Here Syberberg equips the modern German variant of democracy with a negative prefix. In quick succession he piles up such descriptive expressions as technocrats, progress, democrats of consumption, enlightenment of the people, democratic pharisees, materialists, leftist establishment, intellectual chauvinism, progressive culture conformists, the mediocre and the followers, and consumption pluralism. With a Brechtian twist on the Thirty-Years' War (1618–48) he presents his notes as "partisan texts from the thirty-years' peace of corruption of total democracy." This "totalitarian" society has become sad, he states, aching, a country without Jews, without wit, and colder than ever before (9). Symptomatic of the prevailing mentality is the rebuilding of the country in an international style. Not only do the Germans reveal their abandonment of time-honored traditions, but also a denial of their identity, Syberberg charges (47). Worse, this turning-away from historical roots has escalated into a hatred of their own origin. Of course, the unstated contrast to this rejection of roots is the identity through shared tradition among practicing Jews. Syberberg cherishes tradition in both forms, the Kabbalah and the worthy aspects of the German legacy. This vocabulary and concomitant ideas are familiar from his earlier works. With or without examples, he presents a general condemnation of the weaknesses in his society. The undifferentiated, critical attitude continues to identify his adoption of the philosophy of Adorno and the Frankfurt School. However, considering his position as a self-proclaimed prophet and outsider, the tone might have been the same in any era or place where he would have been able to express his views. The reference to the cold climate echoes the comments encountered in his *Filmbuch* and several movies, where they allude to the ice cosmogony. Besides signaling elements of intertextuality, the coldness metaphor links the Nazi quasi-science and mentality with its successor society.

Two details in the introductory notes indicate a shift in focus. First, a statement identifies Syberberg's activity as a "work of mourning for a democracy after Hitler" (9). One would assume, then, that the *Hitler* film meant a working-through of the painful past, at least for its maker. Now the work continues, but the grief is caused by present-day Germany. The future of the movie has become the present of the book, and his new country, a democracy in name, causes the author *Leiden an Deutschland* (suffering caused by Germany). The other detail is the word *Trauerarbeit* (work of mourning). This word undergoes a transformation, ending as *Trauerkunst* (art of mourning). The link serving as a fulcrum is *Werk* (work), a synonym of *Arbeit*. With its related verb *werken*, *Werk* covers the same semantic range as the English "work" and the Greek *techne*, reaching from "work" and "craft" to "art." Thus an artisan's and an artist's crowning achievement is a *Meisterwerk;* a piece of art is a *Kunstwerk*; and Wagner's total work of art is a *Gesamtkunstwerk*. In the sense of art, *Werk* becomes a synonym of *Kunst*. Moving on the scale of *Arbeit-Werk-Kunst*, Syberberg skips the middle link by jumping from *Trauerarbeit* to *Trauerkunst*. No longer is his preoccupation, and the product of this effort, only a work prompted by grief, but also an effort to transform the grief into art. This grief or mourning is born of his suffering, caused by his modern country, *Leiden an Deutschland*, a special form of *Heim-Weh*.

Of course the text refers frequently to the *Hitler* film for comparison, illustration, or documentation of Syberberg's positions. On his travels to special events with the film, he feels like a priest and healer (15). Through this vocabulary he assumes a liturgical role in the book, intoning oracular statements full of paradoxes. Readers familiar with *Hitler* will recognize some of them, e.g. gaining joy from the highest degree of joylessness, or light being born out of darkness. In a similar vein, Syberberg's joy, *Freude*, only emerges on the other side of death and grief. His envisioned mission of art born of mourning has nothing to do with entertainment and escapism. To Western ears, his declaration sounds as if coming from a different age: "Let's put an end to the domestication of art as the handmaiden of politics. Art as the spark of mercy of the Divine projection in each of us" (21). The first sentence uses the language of scholasticism in the struggle for supremacy between philosophy and theology, now seen as the struggle between art and politics. The second sentence introduces concepts familiar from the Kabbalah and Neoplatonism (spark, projection or emanation). This is not what one expects in a contemporary discourse on art and politics. And the statement continues: "The yearning for the transcendental, the infinite, the higher, at least as [a] way. [A] way in the direction of truth, wisdom, immortality and that which we call love" (21). This is an untimely, *unzeitgemäßes*, program for art in an age that too often considers art as an investment or entertainment. With his art declared a counterworld to the state of modern society, Syberberg sets out as a self-appointed heretic and gadfly, lamenting prophet, and outcast. His books express his opinions and artistic program more explicitly than the movies. *Die freudlose Gesellschaft* is no exception.

To some extent, the subtitles of this volume point to major topics in the subdivisions. As expected, discussions on *Hitler* and its reception fill much of the "First Book." The shorter mid section, "Parenthesis," introduces a less corrupt, rural antidote and a different perspective. The "Second Book" includes the preparation for the next film project. But with a few exceptions, topics and subtopics turn up repeatedly in all sections. They are not treated in major blocks of coherent discussion. The first impression is therefore that of an unsystematic jumble of notes. Occasional passages refer to dated, current events. Since some of these scattered references occur in a chronological sequence, they lend the text a semblance of a diary. In several of his films, Syberberg uses the ambiguous format of monologues that actually address the viewers, but without becoming true dialogues. The blurring of genres continues in his printed work. In this book, he borrows features from the diary, but without relinquishing the quasi-dialogue with the reader, as indicated by the numerous question marks, especially at the end of paragraphs.

In spite of the division into numbered and short chunks of text, the book does not lend itself to browsing. Only upon sustained reading does one discover the inner structure of an apparently incoherent, accusatory, and repetitive jeremiad. As the recent films, so also this book is constructed on musical principles. The topics are really themes and motifs. They keep resurfacing and recombining in patterns of transformation resembling variations in a composition. It is not necessary that a lengthy discussion of an issue be repeated in its full extension; a name or brief reference suffices. Since Syberberg himself is one of the topics, one frequently encounters passages about his aesthetic views, the reception of his latest film and preparations for the next, and his feud with the media establishment. And this establishment encompasses the movie industry, all forms of German media, the credit-granting commissions, and the incestuous relationship among all of them. His interactions with these sectors reappear regularly with shifting emphasis. When not an ostracized outsider, then Syberberg the private individual recurs. Therefore this volume also contains numerous autobiographical nuggets. Sometimes only an oblique self-quotation returns Syberberg as an unidentified allusion. It possesses the flexibility of a musical chord in which the individual notes bring together the "tunes" of the author, the topic(s) associated with the original occurrence of the phrase, cinema in general, and the meaning in a new context. The following example paraphrases a statement made in *Karl May*. After describing how avarice, power games, and conformism create a need for opposition, Syberberg points out the dangers of indifference and complacency, concluding with: "And wait for the wrong man to come, again" (72). This paraphrases an oracular comment made just before Karl May's lecture attended by young Hitler. Like this statement, most of the "hidden" self-quotations function as junctions in a grid of associations and references. They are of course related to the leitmotif, but retain the complexity and flexibility of counterpoint.

Whereas most movies communicate primarily through visual means, printed texts depend on words. Defying this distinction, Syberberg relies heavily on semantic power in both genres. A few examples suffice to illustrate his technique in *Die freudlose Gesellschaft*. Beginning the book by describing himself as a representative of opposition and exclusion, Syberberg suddenly comments on the lack of Jews in the country (8). The abrupt change of topic makes the reader aware of the missing transition. The gap calls for a link in the readers' mind between the outsider and the missing minority. The association is strengthened by a caustic reference to the culture industry and politics as having been "cleansed," *rein geworden*. However, a few lines further one reads, "Wir sind unter uns. Und wie" (We are among ourselves. And how). The grammatical subject appears to identify with the majority through the plural *we*. But the style prevents the reader from assuming that the writer belongs to the majority after all. The preceding passage declares the book to be a mirror and seismograph of conditions, "in the authenticity of an extreme existence." The revealing word is *Authentizität*. It is an uncommon loan word in German made famous by Adorno's defense of it. In the essay "Wörter aus der Fremde" (Words from afar) Adorno responds to criticism against his use of foreign words in a radio series on Proust. *Authenticity* is one of them. Adorno devotes a page and a half to his justification and elucidation of this lexis.[12] Actually, the profusion of foreign words is a hallmark of his style. Syberberg's sentence that includes *authenticity* also uses several other foreign words. He could easily have replaced some of them with more typically German equivalents. By his choice of words, Syberberg achieves several objectives: The unusual word alludes to a Jewish giant of German culture without revealing his name; the link to the unnamed Adorno creates a subtle transition to the following comments on a Germany without Jews; and through emulation of Adorno's style Syberberg tacitly aligns himself with the persecuted minority. In other contexts he hints explicitly at the chosen identification through such conditional phrases as "What would they say if I at least were the illegitimate child of a Jewish mother?" (153) and "If I were Jewish, everything would be clear and explanatory" (323). In the same vein are defiant statements like "Yes, I am degenerate" (192, 242). These repeated declarations usually occur at the conclusion of an heretical statement. The term *degenerate*, of course, alludes to the art exhibit of 1937 on "degenerate art" meant to illustrate politically unacceptable art. Syberberg's adoption of the label *entartet* means more than just being different or not up to the accepted standard. It also signals solidarity with the repressed artists of 1937, exclusion through discrimination, art criticizing current conditions, and the implicit accusation that his opponents harbor a Nazi mentality. During a visit to San Francisco in '79, Syberberg said to an American interviewer who had seen his *Hitler* that he was free to make the film this way because he is not Jewish or the son of a Nazi father.[13] Not being Jewish, he still considers himself related by choice, a *Wahlverwandter*. Apart from solidarity, he also shares in a discrimination strong enough to send his films into exile abroad.

The topic of the missing Jews surfaces already in the title of the book. It also indicates that one can read the book on more than one level, with the described society being both *freudlos* and *Freud-los*. Of course, Freud's name is a variant of *Freude* (joy). It recurs several times, as well as many other names of prominent Jewish writers, musicians, and painters. But just as often, a name or reference appears imbedded in a related word, such a *freudlos*, or as a trace in a cluster of synonyms and antonyms, such as *traurig, Trauer, trauern, heiter, froh,* etc. One recognizes the workings of tonal themes or fragments in a chain of contrapuntal transformation. Alienating elements join in as variations of other themes presented simultaneously. Sometimes the *Freud(e)* theme only reverberates very faintly as *Spaß* (fun), while other melodic topics dominate the field. When the series of metamorphoses requires the inversion, the carrier words may assume a negative or pejorative meaning. Syberberg reserves that function for the *Holocaust*, the Hollywood soap opera also discussed in an article, and *Judas-Kuss* (Judas kiss). More versatile are the recurrences through phrases or quotations. Thus headlines of concepts borrowed from Adorno, general psychology and Freud's theories, such as "contrasting imitation" and "mirrorlike identity," apply to the criticized target. So do "the banality of evil" and Syberberg's variation, "the evil of banality." The phrase does not need Hannah Arendt's name for identification.

Another example of reverberating words occurs in the passage directed at the "masters of progress." Syberberg concludes: "Denn der Meister des Fortschritts ist ein Meister aus Deutschland, wir kennen ihn gut" (For the master of progress is a master from Germany, we know him well, 354). Not only does he again appropriate the phrase *ein Meister aus Deutschland* from Celan's "Todesfuge," but also the meter.[14] The concept of *Meister* enjoys great prestige in German traditions. Ironically, it was not stressed by the Nazis, perhaps due to its Masonic connotations. The *master race* was therefore usually *Herrenvolk. Herr* and *Meister* are synonyms in many cases, but with *Herr* (lord) being preferred for religious uses and *Meister* denoting the person of an earned position of accomplishment. However, *Meister* in the sense of "rabbi" and "teacher" is also the address form to Jesus in the German Bible. The reference to Celan's *Meister* makes one aware of the role this word plays in Syberberg's oeuvre. The use stretches from his dispossessed father's efforts to acquire a master's license in photography to the description of Syberberg's early work in television as years of apprenticeship, with clear echoes of Goethe's books on Wilhelm Meister. And one remembers Karl May's nickname, the "Mayster." In many cases, Syberberg's use of this term retains its revered meaning, but in this book, it includes also Celan's meaning. With all its possible associations, the *Meister* as used in this book constitutes the most powerful evocation of both the missing minority and the Hitler mentality without identifying the issue explicitly.

A closely related term is "clean" as in the mentioned description of a Germany "cleansed" or *rein geworden* of its unwanted minority (8). Syberberg uses the two most common words for clean and pure, *sauber* and *rein*, as well as numerous derivatives, such as *Reinwaschung der Schuldigen* and *Frau Saubermann*. This obsession with cleanliness applies to the modern Germans, while Syberberg fouls up the nest in contrast (177). However, in the section written in the mountains, he describes the simple pleasure of a hot tub bath. He too can be clean, but not once does he mention words for cleanliness in this passage. Nor does he apply any words for dirt to the Jews he refers to. But thanks to the structural principle, he can heap such terms on topics relating to his compatriot and current society. This vocabulary includes *Gestank* (stench), *Müll* (garbage), *Abfall* (trash), *Scheiße* (shit), *Schmutz* (dirt, smut), *Kloake* (sewer), and dozens more. When the counterpoint calls for a simultaneous appearance of the "cleansed" Germans and the unwanted group, one reads, for example: "The democratic Pharisees, that means: they wash their hands, [but] the dirt is inside" (25). The biblical *Pharisee* points back to its origin while also applying to the Gentile Germans who cannot wash off their impurity. A similar convergence occurs in the characterization of Rainer Werner Fassbinder. He functions as Syberberg's antipode among German moviemakers. Until his premature death, he was celebrated as the anti-establishment *enfant terrible* by all the media. Syberberg presents them as hypocrites who think: "We are no Hitlers.

We love that, [we] allow people like that to live" (279). In Syberberg's work, names often carry a meaning. Fassbinder's first name, Rainer, is a variant of Reiner and René and is pronounced like *reiner* (pure). But Syberberg also describes him as being *schmuddelig* (grimy). Since Fassbinder was not Jewish, "only" bisexual, and in spite of all provocations and posturing, was still accepted in his homeland, he does not quite fit the pattern. Rainer is not quite a *reiner* German, but being only *schmuddelig* did not call for drastic measures. The reason for the muted contrast is the counterpoint of several themes, one of them Syberberg himself. Another example lets two sentences express similar ideas, but with vocabulary from separate spheres of culture. The current form of "enlightenment" has become a holy cow, *eine heilige Kuh*, the author maintains, conjuring up the dance around the golden calf: "Bis zum Tanz ums goldene Kalb" (144). In other words, the idolatry of technology in modern society is juxtaposed with a comparable form of aberration in the Bible. The contrast suggests that the criticized enlightenment really stands for a blind faith in a false kind of progress.

"Progress," or *Fortschritt,* is a frequent word that catches the reader's attention. Syberberg usually attributes a negative meaning to it. Already in *Hitler* the term characterizes Hitler's success. The association between progress and Hitlerism continues in the book while also being linked to a modern, ruthlessly dominating and unthinking mind. The continuation of this kind of attitude is about to destroy our earth, Syberberg reiterates. By occasionally using the related verb, *fortschreiten*, the author makes clear that belief in *Fortschritt* as advancement towards something better is dangerously naïve. Unlike the English verb "to progress," the German combination of *fort* and *schreiten* can also simply refer to moving away. One does not necessarily move upwards towards loftier, nobler goals. One hidden reason for the emphasis on *Fortschritt* is its central position in Syberberg's complex of words describing motion. They also provide cues for the tonal subtext. Other terms found for movement in general include *Bewegung* (movement) and *Massenbewegung* (mass movement), *Entwicklung* (development), and *strampeln* (kick around). Add to that the illusion of movement in motion pictures. The libidinal urge to move, *Trieb*, is harnessed into many combinations. Among the opposite concepts belong references to frozen conditions and obstacles to movement, such as *Mauer* (wall, esp. the Berlin Wall), *Getto* (ghetto), *Gefängnis* (prison), and *Grenze* (border). The last word spawns, a.o., *Grenzüberschreitung* (transgression), a cherished notion in Syberberg's challenge to conformism. Directional hints are provided in *Rückzug* (retreat), *Auferstehung* (resurrection), *Himmelfahrt* (ascension), *Fallgrube* (pitfall), *Untergang* (downfall, demise), and *übersetzen* (translate, set across). Syberberg revitalizes words by restoring an echo of their original or less common meaning. Therefore *Revolution* is not only an uprising, but also a circular movement, similar to *Weltzyklus* (world cycle). And *Untergang,* as well as the verb *untergehen*, occur both in the sense of "demise" or "destruction," as in the somber oxymoron "Bessere Zukunft und Untergang" ([a] better future and ruin, 184), and as sinking or going under: "daß das Schiff untergeht" (that the ship is about to sink, 184). Syberberg also manages to combine this directional verb with an upward movement. This happens in the description of a restaurant in New York. Its decor was salvaged from a third class diningroom of a sunken steamer. Today it is a luxury restaurant for the affluent. Third class has moved up to become upscale and first class (188).

On occasion, the author avoids a noun by only describing the activity, such as the moves of several well known journalists among German publishing houses (249). Their job changes resemble a round of musical chairs, coming full circle. Or a mention of Titian in Venice suffices to allude to his painting *The Ascension of the Virgin*. Still, *Fortschritt* remains the most prominent word in the group of directional nouns. The prefix explains the peculiar negativity burdening the word. The reality of *fort* (forth, away) relates to *Exil, Emigration,* and *Flucht* (flight, escape), even to escapism. A synonym of *Fortschritt* is *Fortgang* (progress, departure). Strangely enough, Syberberg avoids this word, perhaps because it would have made his play on semantics too transparent. The threatening kind of progress, *Fortschritt*, stands for everything that caused the emigration during the Hitler years. Also, the author does not tire of lamenting that his works survive in *Exil*, while he himself had to seek refuge, *Zuflucht*, behind the leafy walls, *Mauern*, of his private *Getto*. Thus the theme of "progress" links up regularly with those of the missing minority and Syberberg. Occasionally the themes of Jews and Gentiles overlap or intersect, depending on the forms of counterpoint. Then one encounters such terms as the chosen ones, *die Auserwählten*, referring to the Gentile Germans (152), and those related through affinity, *die Wahlverwandten*, applying to Jews (152).

Connected to these themes are numerous explicit and implicit references to Heine. While the name occurs sparingly, the text reawakens the memory of him through such frequent vocabulary as *Traum* (dream), *Alptraum* (nightmare), and *schlechtes Gewissen* (bad conscience). They relate to quotations from Heine's poetry and statements about him in the *Hitler* film. The referential selection of judicially chosen expressions does not begin and end abruptly within one film or book. Both genres operate with the same concepts. Moreover, each individual work functions as a part of a larger whole. From that follows that topics also point forward to the next major work. And sure enough, the *Parsifal* theme enters as an explicit topic in the last third of the book. As expected, it also figures logically and semantically in more subtle ways throughout. Parsifal the pure fool must err and suffer before being worthy of finding the Grail. Recurring words related to "erring" are *irren, Irre,* and *Irrtum*. The motif of foolishness finds perhaps its most up-to-date equivalency in *Blödmann* and its worst pun in *Tor* (fool) in the unrelated meaning of "gate." The concept of purity occurs already in the introduction with Germany having been "cleansed" (*rein*) of its Jews. Other frequently occurring anticipatory expressions include *Bahre* (bier), *Wunde* (wound), *Ödnis* (wasteland), *Mitleid* (compassion), and *erlösen* (to redeem). The society depicted in the book is spiritually, morally, and artistically bankrupt. It is already a country of the dead, much as the Grail Kingdom at Parsifal's return.

Important but less obvious are the allusions to the medieval *Parzival* by Wolfram von Eschenbach. The passage about Syberberg enjoying his bath (232) finds its equivalent at the end of Wolfram's "insert" between books 2 and 3. Similarly Syberberg's description of the bath occurs towards the end of the "Parenthesis," which follows the second major chapter. And the author repeatedly uses an expression with which Wolfram defines the hero's name, "rehte enmitten durch" (right through the middle). This effort to find the way or penetrate to the core of the matter echoes for example in such expressions as "durch alle Exaltationen der Melancholie hindurch" (right through all manic stages of depression, 16) and "durch diesen Hitler mitten hindurch" (12). However, he does not quote Wolfram extensively in Middle High German. Such close quotation is reserved for Wolfram's contemporary, Walther von der Vogelweide (275). By weaving in references to them, Syberberg tacitly includes allusions to Richard Wagner and his *Parsifal,* as well as to *Tannhäuser,* in which Walther and Wolfram both figure as characters, and *Lohengrin,* who is Parzival's son. Naturally, many barely recognizable hints aim at Wagner. One example is the prohibition against applauding mentioned in connection with unionized American musicians (84). Wagner wanted no applause after the first act of *Parsifal.* A second example is the scribe Beckmesser of the *Meistersinger.* Anonymously, he enters the field of associations with the mentioning of the spreading practice of establishing an honorary office of *Stadtschreiber,* or municipal scribe (254), as an honorary position for a local writer. Regardless of apparent issue, person, or country, usually more than one topic is buried in the text. The cue can be structural, thematic, or semantic. The Middle High German quotation continues the practice from *Hitler* of including elements from several languages and periods. This time one again notes many French and English words, a few Spanish and Latin expressions, Hebrew with *Mene Tekel* (169), and Greek with *Panta rhei* (249). Through such fragments Syberberg demonstrates his love of transgression, *Grenzüberschreitung.* He constantly crosses linguistic barriers.

This penchant for overstepping boundaries also surfaces in his praise of heresy (e.g. 89) and increasing disregard for standard syntax. Syberberg is capable of writing elegant German when he wants to. His syntactical idiosyncracies are deliberate. They will be examined at a later point. Not so easy to classify are the statements with incendiary effect. Syberberg knows how to provoke indignation. Sometimes he may declare a matter to be a scandal. In doing so passionately, he often comes across as unpleasantly blunt, but factual at best and opinionated at worst. On other occasions he plants a real scandalon without identifying it as such. This happens when he e.g. holds up old Nazis with political conviction and ideals against modern anti-Nazis with no higher aspirations than instant gratification. He calls the latter category *Konjunkturdemokraten* (weather vane democrats, 264). Could the old Nazis possibly have had more strength of character? He juxtaposes the two groups, poses provocative questions, and refrains from answering. Of course most readers would consider themselves anti-Nazi. In view of Syberberg's criticism of society, many of them would apply the comparison to themselves and be offended. Worse, many would suspect the author of sympathizing with the brown past. He invites this kind of hasty inference. In this case he raises the question of merit for hypothetical representatives of a group covered by blanket condemnation. He does not try to induce readers to recognize the Hitler in themselves as an abyss of negativity. This time the image might display more positive qualities. The author also refrains from specifying names, circumstances and the kind of ideals he has in mind. One could imagine a conscripted soldier of World War II professing patriotism and loyalty to the required oath. The thoughtful reader might probe the possibilities and hesitate to draw conclusions. Most, though, would take exception to the very question. It violates a taboo. To the compatriots Syberberg criticizes, a meritorious Nazi is an oxymoron. Keeping in mind the compositional principles of the book, one perceives that the themes of old time and today's mainstream Germans are brought together so as to converge in the text. And again, one recognizes transgression as an important device in Syberberg's discourse. Other cases of converging themes also frequently result in oxymorons. Some examples are *Starker Zwerg, schwacher Riese* (strong dwarf, weak giant, 224), *rettende Katastrophe* (disaster that saves, 316), and *irrationale Vernunft* (irrational reason, 366). Unusual as they are, the paradoxes grab the attention, reveal themes or motifs emerging in them, and activate the associative grid by prodding memory. The components recur in constantly altered manifestations through changing combinations. They come close to being verbal leitmotifs. As these, a theme and its transformations recur throughout a work. They help remember something previously introduced but presently absent. From a temporal perspective, they possess the power of transgression. But unlike the usual literary leitmotif, they often contain the topic itself.

Neither Syberberg's previous publications nor *Die freudlose Gesellschaft* discuss the principles that underlie their literary structure. However, they all comment on the author's theory of film aesthetics. He refers to several of these texts on page 195, but two of them were unavailable for this study. One is an essay on cinema as the music of the future in the *Cahiers* of the Cinémathèque française in 1975 or '76. However, most, if not all, of this publication is included in the *Filmbuch*. The other text also appeared in France probably in 1975. It supposedly discusses Syberberg's use of dolls in *Ludwig*. Most of his thoughts on the subject seem to have found expression in his later publications, such as the special issue "Syberberg" of *Cahiers du Cinéma* in 1980 (60-65). In *Die freudlose Gesellschaft* he also devotes a page to this topic. As did Heine in the introduction to his *Faust*, so also Syberberg mentions the puppet play as inspiration for Goethe's *Faust*. He also discusses briefly the role of marionettes in Kleist's already mentioned essay "Über das Marionettentheater" and his own use of dolls in *Hitler*. Without revealing the esoteric significance of the concept, he points to the alienating effect of dolls on a modern mind, especially when the doll represents Hitler. The Nazi dolls in the film are, after all, held and manipulated by us, he reiterates.

Syberberg's book declares that Hitler was a diabolical master of the cinematic medium (103). And not only of film. Because of him, nobody dares talk about state art any more: "It [state art] was incriminated by the Third Reich, the highest perversion of the total work of art of state and community" (21). Syberberg intimates in scattered comments that Hitler viewed his own life and death as a work of art. With Germany as his avowed alter ego, the country would be an extension of this work. But what would make Hitler the diabolical master of film? Syberberg suggests two answers. Apart from the fact that the dictator loved movies and included a projectionist in his staff, he took a lively interest in the weekly newsreels, as he already mentioned in an article. These used to precede the main feature in movie theaters. Especially after World War II started, the newsreels, or *Wochenschauen*, became the most significant visual documentation of the events. Hitler supposedly referred to them as his great epic (147). They are still considered important enough to be included in the State Archive, Syberberg notes. Hitler's other cinematic masterworks are the two "documentaries" Leni Riefenstahl produced for him, the two-part *Olympia* and *Triumph of the Will*. They are also kept in the State Archive. Syberberg does not explicitly deny their merit as extraordinary works of art and as politically involved art. But his lack of praise relates to their function: They support and help glorify an authoritarian system. For Syberberg art must be opposition (21). He even asks if Hitler did not really organize the rally in Nuremberg to suit Riefenstahl's cameras (74). Thus the dictator who commissioned the work and the filmmaker who executed the order become closely related in this argumentation. For the author, Riefenstahl represents the same kind of progress in cinematography that he abhors in his "so-called democracy." For example, she pioneered the moving hand-held camera. She also achieved impressive effects through such innovative techniques as zooming, panning, "riding" cameras, and clever cuts. All this mobility served seduction, Syberberg charges (70–71). It resulted in "intoxication without head and heart." Forgotten in this development was the origin of film, namely projection of something with the aid of light. Film depends on projection, both as its mechanism and its soul. It also developed concurrently with psychoanalysis, which refined the understanding of psychological projection. Hitler, the author states, projected his own dreams of a master race onto the crowds cheering him. They, in turn, projected their hopes and aspirations on their charismatic leader. This reciprocal system of projection must also function in film. That is, the movie activates the viewers whose projections come alive. This, Syberberg admits, is a similarity between his art and Hitler's technique (79). But their results and objectives differ. The meticulously achieved euphoria at Hitler's rallies and speeches are reflected in Riefenstahl's cinematic effect. The author calls this a perverted form of the Dionysian frenzy (80). He, too, aims at stirring the projections of his viewers, but not to make them bounce directly back at him. It is rather a matter of inducing the viewers to gather these loosened powers, examine them, meditate on them, while activating both mind and heart. Syberberg's counter principle is the Apollinian "Know Thyself." He formulates his distancing from Riefenstahl's techniques with Nietzsche's Apollinian-Dionysian dichotomy as frame of reference, characterizing her films as follows: "This is the perverted form of the Dionysian frenzy according to the old principle *Panta rhei*, 'everything is in flux,' everything is moving" (80). He opposes her technique based on mobility and aiming at euphoria to his own ideal: "Against that stands here that other old principle of

Gnothi s'auton, the Apollinian 'Know Thyself' through the light of reason in music" (80). Syberberg declares himself clearly on the side of the Apollinian principle. The reference to music confirms his compositional preference. To this comes his guiding thought on "Light of understanding as [the] center of projection of our meditation" (80). Such terms as meditation, light, and understanding (= insight) would be out of place in discussing Riefenstahl's films for Hitler. Not surprisingly, Syberberg found these ideas in an area not associated with cinema. His concept of light and projection takes its inspiration from the Kabbalistic and Gnostic idea of divine emanation. It symbolizes creation as a flow of light from a divine source. The worthy "vessel" receives this precious influx and, when overflowing, lets it continue its circulation. Weaker vessels may break and disrupt the flow. It becomes the spiritual mission of each person to restore the circulation and return the "light" to its divine origin. This imagery connects Syberberg's ruminations on projection as light with the viewer as the receiving vessel of this lesser light. Still, this modest "illumination" might help restore the intended course on a greater scale. The adjectives used to describe his projection as light reveal the frame of reference: *meditativ*, *geistig* (spiritual), *moralisch*, and *seelisch* (psychological). His own cinematic program is therefore incompatible with Riefenstahl's methods, which are enhanced through mobility and aiming at seduction: "But once I had declared my opposition to a Riefenstahl and her system and her master behind it all, I had to overcome her master and his system in her [own] field, if possible" (70). With the conviction of fighting for the good cause, Syberberg summarizes his program: "The last exertion had to be to step into the arena against this master of cinema [and] beat him not only morally and spiritually, but also aesthetically and technically. For form is morality" (70–71). Syberberg's films adhere to this declaration. They make only sparing use of technical innovations and possibilities. The most telling landscape remains the human face. The narrative techniques draw on Brecht's episodic drama with epic and alienating characteristics as well as Wagner's, and especially Bach's, compositional principles. In brief, he is an unusual phenomenon in our days. Syberberg has often described film as the aging child of the twentieth century (referring to the black-robed, grey-haired child in *Hitler*), but also as a seismograph and a product for the masses. As Walter Benjamin points out repeatedly in *The Work of Art in the Age of its Technical Reproducibility*, cinema is not the product of one artist for one viewer. If this is correct, Syberberg claims, then it assumes the function of an event for the masses and might be compared to the cathedrals of the Middle Ages. It should express something of the spirit and the values of its age (11). The experience of art, including film, would be comparable to walking through a cathedral. For this kind of art, Syberberg relies on tradition and old ideas. And yet, they often look revolutionary new. This is not only so because they are so different from the average movie for entertainment. But they are also imbued with imagination and a creative recombination of familiar elements. They are the product of a revolutionary traditionalist.

Syberberg concludes *Die freudlose Gesellschaft* with thanks to a list of people

who have been important to him. In the paragraph naming André Heller occurs what
appears to be an error (383). The author states he got to know Heller at their first
private get-together on the evening *Winifred Wagner* appeared on television for the
first time in Austria. This documentary was first shown publicly in 1975. Heller had
a small role in *Karl May* in 1974. The timing of their meeting must therefore be
incorrect, unless the implication is that their contact during the filming of *Karl May*
was strictly professional and superficial, and that the two men really did not get to
know each other while they worked together. More likely, this peculiar slip is the
obligatory defect in a Hermetic work. Actually, much of the conversation from
Syberberg's and Heller's get-to-gether was included in one of Heller's books, *Es
werde Zirkus*.[15] The chapter is dated August 13 and 14. The date refers to 1976,
shortly "before the end of the Roncalli Circus" (157). Four of the accompanying
photos show the two men talking. In one of them they are seated at a table with wine
glasses between them plus the tape recorder, all on a raft in Lake Wolfgang. The
text is an interview with Syberberg posing the questions. One may wonder if not
Heller with his circus inspired the beginning of the *Hitler* film, which shows a circus
arena against a background of the planets in space. Heller's book mentions that his
play *Die größte Poesie des Universums* (The Greatest Poetry of the Universe) was
performed with (his?) music in the Roncalli Circus during the summer of 1976
(160). Also Heller's role at the end of *Karl May* underscores the continuity in
Syberberg's cinematic cycle. Dressed in a white suit Heller appears as an announcer
addressing us, the spectators. Early in *Hitler*, the circus announcer varies and
continues the role while also wearing white. Considering Heller's many talents, one
suspects counterpoint to be the reason for the undramatic action allowed him in the
early sections of *Hitler*. In Brechtian fashion, he reads much of his part from a
manuscript. In 1979 Syberberg wrote about Heller that he never memorizes any
text.[16] Nonetheless, in later sections he displays an animated Wagner figure who at
least knows how to act. Syberberg's thank you passage in *Die freudlose
Gesellschaft* indicates that he felt indebted to Heller. Their meeting at Lake
Wolfgang inspired him to use Heller as a "contrasting mirror" to himself (383). He
does not mention where to put the stress, on the contrasting or the mirroring. But
this half-Jewish, non-conformist Austrian lets Syberberg reintroduce the notion
from the beginning of the book, "Germany without Jews." This motif in the book
and subtext in the *Hitler* film also continues in his work.

As Syberberg's movies, so also *Die freudlose Gesellschaft* was received with
kinder reviews abroad than in Germany. In his book *Der Wald steht schwarz und
schweiget* the author quotes from appreciative articles and reviews in *Libération,
Le Monde, Les Nouvelles Littéraires,* and *Télérama* (498–99). In contrast, the
review in *Der Spiegel* starts out with "Welch ein aberwitziges Buch" (What a Crazy
Book).[17] Deceptively, the first column follows in a friendlier tone. It even describes
the book as impossible to put down. The reviewer also admits that Syberberg is
right in his criticism of many flaws in German society. But from then on everything
is negative, with most comments being *ad hominem*. The author is ridiculed as
being a fuzzy-headed, self-righteous egomaniac and wanna-be Christ. Susan Sontag,

who had committed the crime of writing the first significant and appreciative study of the *Hitler* film, is labeled his John the Baptist. The reviewer finds the author's accusations that hit too close for comfort to be infamous and rejects the "mystic smoke." Then, deftly and systematically, he distorts references so as to present Syberberg as an admirer of Hitler. This begins with phrases like "the subliminal tendency to exculpate and whitewash Hitler" (169). He equates Syberberg's views with an alleged Nietschean polarization of a glorified Dionysian principle and an ossified, decrepit form of the Apollinian. This does not only misrepresent Syberberg's use of these terms, it turns it around 180 degrees (168). And the central theme of joy, *Freude*, is likened to the Nazi slogan and social program *Kraft durch Freude* (Strength through Joy). Although the reviewer finds that society needs such gadflies as Syberberg, he recommends that the author, who had professed pleasure in the old-fashioned, simple life experienced during his vacation, should act on it. In stead of filming and writing incomprehensible things, he should earn a living by scrubbing old-fashioned, genuine wood floors. Understood is: and stop attacking the journalists. A second German review treats the book and its author in a similarly malicious manner.[18] It admits that the criticism is justified and summarizes several of the points made in the book. The rest of the article ridicules the author. One reads, for example, "Syberberg would like to be a *rechter* (real or rightist) intellectual, but he has neither a thought-through position nor precise concepts" (96). The writer asks rhetorically why a respected publishing house would publish this book. He is also greatly surprised that Syberberg "was allowed to" publish his book to *Hitler* with Rowohlt. He is even shocked that Syberberg "was permitted" to quote from Schiller's "An die Freude" incorrectly. The reviewer seems unaware that Syberberg is quoting from Beethoven's much revised and abridged version of the poem. His access to publishing outlets is declared a scandal. It would appear, then, that Syberberg was only too right in his assessment of the leading German reviewers and critics. The tone is noticeably different in a Swiss review by Iso Camartin.[19] It places the book in the context of Syberberg's films and publications, summarizes some of the issues, and views the polemics from a neutral vantage point. The reviewer predicts that the German critics will not like this book any better than the films, especially *Hitler*. Much in it is bound to irritate. One of the examples of incendiary statements in the book is, "Never was Germany more Germany than with and under this Hitler." As before, Syberberg's work was received with interest abroad and with spite at home. And still, the book reappeared in a paperback edition at Ullstein two years later.

One topic that surfaced in *Die freudlose Gesellschaft* continued to preoccupy Syberberg for some time to come: Rainer Werner Fassbinder. Syberberg and his moviemaker friends began to assist the young Fassbinder in 1970 by making their Arri theater available to his films. As the years passed, the others and Fassbinder accommodated themselves to the modus operandi of the media world, made peace with the money-lending forces, and profited in return. Syberberg became the outsider. The initial solidarity and mutual recognition of talent between him and Fassbinder eventually gave way to a strained coexistence at a distance. Fassbinder must have recognized himself as one of the unnamed, spineless weather vanes criticized in Syberberg's publications. Realizing that Syberberg had become a persona non grata with his German Trilogy, Fassbinder joined the attackers in several articles and interviews, berating and accusing him of plagiarism: "And a quite resourceful [Werner] Schroeter-imitator has come forward, who, while Schroeter was waiting helplessly, skillfully marketed what he had pilfered from Schroeter. In Paris people for a good while actually believed this trafficker in matters of plagiarism, Hans Jürgen Syberberg."[20] He does not specify what had been purloined or in which movies these imitations were discovered, but continues, "It was pretty exhausting to tell people in France that it wasn't we who were the epigon[e]s of the more slippery Syberberg, but that we had been the victims of a brutal ripoff, in part of our most personal wares" (198). The choice of pronoun *we* suggests that Fassbinder accuses Syberberg of plagiarizing both Schroeter and himself. Then, again without substantiations or explanations, he steps back and concludes, "But even Syberberg, independent of the great desire to be able finally to let things surface, represents the great opportunity to make 'great films' with Werner Schroeter's own personal discoveries, an opportunity denied the original talent" (198). If Fassbinder had bothered to read Syberberg's publications, he would have found ample discussions and explanations of the latter's aesthetics and techniques. Perhaps he had but took his chances that the German public and film journalists were not familiar with Syberberg's writings. Syberberg's scattered comments on these accusations make it clear that Fassbinder aims especially at the frontal projection technique. Syberberg does not claim to have invented this versatile technique. Actually, in the special issue of *Cahiers du Cinéma* called "Syberberg" he devotes two pages of text and illustrations to the technology, history, and his own improvement of this tool. This kind of projection had been developed in Hollywood more than fifty years earlier, but eventually fell into disuse. Fassbinder's friend Harry Baer had played the title role in *Ludwig*, where Syberberg introduced the technique in his work. Baer had also starred in Fassbinder's *Katzelmacher*, a movie that Syberberg "quotes" in *Ludwig*. However, he only used a tiny fragment of dialogue in an ironic and alienating function.[21] At that time Fassbinder did not recognize Syberberg's contrapuntal use of montage. In any case, he did not feel flattered. One can only speculate that personal resentment played a part in his numerous attacks.

Fassbinder could easily serve as Syberberg's foil and antipode among the German filmmakers. They were contemporaries, emerging into public view in the sixties, both gaining acclaim and notoriety with their films and views. They even both created clusters of movies that became known as German trilogies. However, the list of similarities also brings out their differences. First, where Syberberg transgresses boundaries in aesthetic technique founded on ethical resolve, Fassbinder assaults the sensibilities of the public apparently for the sake of sensation. For example, in *Germany in Autumn* he appears nude and masturbating in front of the camera. And his fifteen hours long *Berlin Alexanderplatz* abounds in brutality and violence, especially against women. Furthermore, where Syberberg declares a programmatic solidarity with the persecuted Jews, Fassbinder flaunts his lack of sensitivity, especially in his play *The Garbage, the City, and Death*. The protagonist is a ruthless Jewish real estate speculator during the rebuilding of Frankfurt am Main after World War II. When in 1975 both the Jewish community and the population at large took to the streets in mass protests against the announced offensive play, authorities stopped the rehearsals at the Theater am Turm, where Fassbinder enjoyed a short-lived stint as artistic director. The same fall, his script was turned into a movie, *Shadow of Angels*, directed by Daniel Schmid. Fassbinder appears as one of the actors. The public controversy dragged on for several years.[22] During this time Fassbinder spoke about going abroad into "exile," but stayed on. To judge from his continued production of movies, the scandal did not hurt his ability to secure funding for his projects.

This does by no means exhaust the list of differences between the two filmmakers. But what irked Syberberg most must have been Fassbinder's success with the media establishment. Syberberg describes the two of them as the "outcast" and the "incast."[23] In spite of Fassbinder's cynical and aggressive posturing, he had been bought by the controlling powers and was now being manipulated by them, Syberberg contends, predicting that " this cannot end well."[24] This "suicidal pact" made him into a symbol of contemporary Germany, literally representing everything Syberberg abhors. He was right in that Fassbinder would self-destruct. After the latter's death in 1982, Syberberg noted, "If I should have to present Germany's ruined condition, it would be like him, with this face, this figure, these films and their errors, sensitive, wounded, lonely, destroyed."[25] And he adds, "He was a master of film in Germany, as a sign of our destruction at the time of his [own] biggest bankruptcy" (35). One notes the use of *Meister* in this connection. The memory of that word in Celan's poem and Syberberg's use of it in *Die freudlose Gesellschaft* establish beyond doubt the frame of stated and tacit references. And with the mention of a suicidal pact, Syberberg also alludes to a modern-day Faust.

One more circumstance added to Syberberg's acrimonious view of Fassbinder. The accuser was really the plagiarizer. Not only did he quote liberally from Syberberg's films, but he also received widespread praise for precisely these features. In *Die freudlose Gesellschaft* Syberberg lists some of these borrowings from *Ludwig* and *Hitler*, especially in the epilogue of Fassbinder's *Berlin Alexanderplatz*. They include the resurrection of the title hero, music changing into yodeling, Isolde's love death as in *Ludwig*, the "madonna" with swastika-wearing doll, the black mother, switches in accompanying music, and the list goes on (284–85). Perhaps Fassbinder meant this as a tribute to Syberberg. But the irony is that the German critics celebrated him for "his" innovative aesthetics, and ignored the originator. Whether the German journalists honestly did not know Syberberg's films and thus could not recognize Fassbinder's indebtedness, or suppressed Syberberg's name deliberately is difficult to ascertain. In any case, Fassbinder harvested the accolades for many of Syberberg's cinematic accomplishments.

Part 2

Chapter 6

Introduction and First Prelude to *Parsifal*

The plans for *Parsifal* had been maturing for years. At long last, in 1980, Syberberg began to apply for funding, matching grants, and loans. He describes this process in *Die freudlose Gesellschaft*. He tried all German federal, state, and private sources that normally support the arts. The disappointing results were not only a matter of competition for funds. Two factors in particular contributed to the situation: First, Syberberg himself. In most cases, the members of the various committees evaluating applications included his enemies. They were the same journalists and reviewers who had treated his films with venom and whom he, in turn, had exposed in his *Filmbuch* and attacked in *Hitler*. Moreover, his most recent films ripped open wounds that would not heal. If Syberberg had caused such discomfort at home and "discredited" his country abroad with his focus on Nazi-related themes, what could one expect of his next projects dealing with similar topics? After all, he himself had placed Hitler's corpse in Wagner's grave. Now he wanted to make a film of Wagner's *Parsifal* that Hitler had admired so much. Not only that. He also applied for funding for a documentary on the composer. The latter project is described variously as "Richard Wagner" and "Wie ein Bühnenweihfestspiel entsteht" (How a stage consecration festival play comes about). In the final round, Syberberg did secure sufficient support, much of it from abroad.

Then came the problem with the music. A film of *Parsifal* would need the same resources as a performance on stage, for example singers, musicians, and a conductor. The simplest solution would have been to use recorded performances, preferably from Bayreuth. But Wolfgang Wagner in Bayreuth declined to support the man who had exposed his mother on film. Syberberg was apparently not able to use any recording made by a Bayreuth festival ensemble. It did not help that Pierre Boulez, the festival conductor at the time, was willing to assist. Mysteriously, all other German outlets for recordings were unavailable. As a result, also the music for the film came from abroad. In retrospect, one might wonder if Syberberg had not really wanted that outcome, considering his solutions to the dilemma.

Part of the work started in the summer of 1981 with Armin Jordan conducting the Philharmonic Orchestra of Monte Carlo and the Prague Philharmonic Choir. The musical recordings were made in Monte Carlo by the French company Erato. The singers of the major parts represented an international mixture. Incidentally, except for the roles of Gurnemanz and Klingsor, the leading actors appearing on screen are not identical with the singers whose voices one hears. A special case is the conductor of the unseen orchestra, Armin Jordan, who also plays Amfortas on screen, while the voice comes from the invisible Wolfgang Schöne.

Those familiar with the history of *Parsifal* will see the significance in choosing this particular orchestra and this chorus. Monte Carlo and Prague play their roles in the early history of the work. Angelo Neumann, the director of the German Theater in Prague, tried to secure Wagner's consent to present *Parsifal* on his stage. He had already sufficient experience with the other music dramas that the composer could refer to Neumann's ensemble as a "Wagner theater."[1] Although the composer's response was evasive, he agreed that Neumann "might" be allowed to present the work on special occasions after his death.[2] But of course, *Parsifal* was the one work Wagner wanted to secure for his own festival stage in Bayreuth. This was the purpose of the *lex Parsifal*, which was supposed to protect Bayreuth's monopoly on *Parsifal* for thirty years beyond the composer's death. But already in December 1903 the Metropolitan Opera defied this ruling by staging the work in New York. Concert excerpts were presented in other locations even earlier. One of the first comments on such a concert comes from Nietzsche. The philosopher, who had broken off his friendship with Wagner during the progress of the composition of *Parsifal* and who had only scorn for the libretto, was enraptured by the prelude. He heard it played in Monte Carlo in 1887. Syberberg reprints a lengthy quotation of his praise in a letter to Peter Gast of January 21, 1887, including such expressions as a "sublime and extraordinary feeling, experience, event of the soul in the ground of music."[3] Monte Carlo was also the location of one of the earliest initiatives to appropriate *Parsifal* for other European theaters. Not only did this event disregard the composer's wishes, but the environment of the gambling resort was felt to defile a semi-sacred work. Lichtenberg referred to the setting of the event in 1913 as this *Spielhöllentheater in Monte Carlo* (theater of the gambling hell of Monte Carlo).[4] Syberberg's selection of artists associated with Prague and Monte Carlo reveals his nonconformism and spirit of opposition to "Bayreuth's" claim on a quasi-religious leadership role.

In this context one also recognizes another referential function of the Black Mary from the *Hitler* film. The Black Mary, the reader may recall, was modeled on Edison's workshop. Not only does Edison's preoccupation with artificial light enter the frame of reference, but also an early film of *Parsifal* marketed by the London branch of the Edison Manufacturing Company Ltd. Produced shortly after 1900, this silent *Parsifal*, Edison Film no. 6845, was about one hour long. (Lichtenberg, 42). In Germany, Max Reinhardt produced another *Parsifal* on film in 1912. By joining the company of such illustrious rebels against the *lex Parsifal*, Syberberg declares his independence of and distance from the Bayreuth establishment.

After the completion of the recordings in 1981, work continued in Munich with filming in the Bavaria Studios. This phase lasted thirty-five days.[5] It so happened that the first production of *Parsifal* under Wagner's direction also ran over that many days in Bayreuth. Its sixteen performances were shown between July 26 and August 29, 1882, just half a year before the composer's death. Syberberg's film aimed at the centennial celebration of *Parsifal* and would, of course, also be ready for the centennial commemoration of Wagner's death in 1883. Since the director was unable to make two related films as he had planned, the resulting project supposedly incorporates visual elements from the proposal for "Richard Wagner." The companion book appeared simultaneously in 1982, with the French edition being practically identical.[6]

The following discussion of the film serves as a running commentary, interspersed with information that one hopes will facilitate the understanding of the work. Since not all readers will be familiar with this version of *Parsifal*, a partially descriptive approach was chosen. For, of course, Syberberg's accomplishment rests on the visual treatment of the material, as Wagner provided both the score and the libretto. Every new production of a dramatic work amounts to a new interpretation. That applies also to an opera film. It must convey its rendering primarily through visual means, secondarily through non-disturbing other means. Syberberg has employed both methods. He kept every note of the score and every word of the libretto. However, he took liberties with the stage instructions. And acoustically, on a few occasions, other sounds invade the sound track when the music is silent. Structurally, he expanded the narrative in two ways. First, he framed the work with two shots at either end of the film. Second, he added silent visuals to accompany all three preludes.

Filmed entirely in a studio, this *Parsifal* does not imitate the theatrical setting so noticeable in, e.g., *Ludwig*. The director dismissed the traditional shooting of an opera production on a stage. Nor did he select a realistic environment as in Losey's *Don Giovanni*, not even the refraction between fiction on stage and reality in the audience as seen in Bergman's *Magic Flute*. Instead, Syberberg found a solution of his own device: an unabashedly artificial setting in a studio. The action unfolds in, on, and around the huge concrete model of Richard Wagner's death mask. This stony landscape has been divided into fourteen sections, much like the body of the dead Osiris. Their arrangement can change the environment as needed into passages, chambers, or a large hall. Besides combining flexibility with unity of location, this environment is also an unsurpassed solution to the problem of finding a setting for a utopian story. Even Wagner's literary sources from the Middle Ages failed to provide an identifiable location for the Grail. The Grail Kingdom remains inaccessible to so many because it is not so much a geographic site as a state of mind, a phase in an individual's spiritual development. As a spiritual goal or paradise, it has no location (*topos*) and remains a u-top-ia. What better place, then, than the head of the creator of this story. That is where his ideas developed into the *Parsifal* he bequeathed to the world, or as he envisioned it, to a select community. But, one might object, the environment is the copy of a dead man's mask. It is as lifeless as the man's body. Yes, but the art work keeps on living nonetheless. Even other life forms may continue in a dead body, as Syberberg showed with the maggots in *Scarabea*. One remembers the repeated reference to *Wurm* as "worm." In the first act of *Siegfried*, Wagner uses the word with two additional meanings, first referring to the dragon, "Fafner, der wilde Wurm," and soon after to Siegfried when he was a baby, "den kleinen Wurm." Through punning, Syberberg may create a semantic link between worms and his chosen setting. The most common German word for a mask is *Maske*. But for a carnival mask one also encounters *Larve*

(Wagner died at the conclusion of carnival in Venice). And *Larve* is a polyvalent lexis that can also designate the larva of an insect. It would seem, then, that the landscape shaped like a death mask is intended to evoke both *Maske* and *Larve*. Several visual details later in the film reinforce this ambiguity. Although one prefers not to associate the characters moving around in the head with larvae or maggots, the fact remains that a dead person's ideas can live on for a long time after the originator's demise. And this is the work that Wagner struggled with for so long, only completing it shortly before his death. It was his artistic testament. More so than Wagner's earlier work, *Parsifal* represents the old man's insight. The landscape recalls the peaceful features of the mask, linking the story of Parsifal with the story of his/her maker.

The film begins with the shorter of two framing units. A sibyl or fortune-teller with long, flowing hair stares into the camera. Since the camera lens is also the viewer's eye, her gaze appears to probe our soul. Her features do not reveal what she sees. Nor can one recognize either the content of or the reflection in her crystal ball. As a prophetess she knows the future, but while she slowly closes her eyes, this knowledge remains undisclosed to the viewers. Since her features stay tired and serious, it appears that she does not foresee anything uplifting. This face that almost fills the screen belongs to the mysterious Kundry, played by Edith Clever. Accompanying the mute image is Yvonne Minton's voice singing Kundry's lament early in the second act as Klingsor awakens her, and the sound of the bell or gong following the conclusion of that act. The two sound excerpts belong to the opposite ends of this middle act. The effect repeats the impression of merging contrasts encountered early in *Hitler*: the child playing with dolls while looking like a grey-haired old woman. The montage blurs the concept of time as well as of beginning and end. And now, the two sound tracks and the image combine as entwined carriers of a story.

The darkness of the surrounding yields to the second part of the frame. This longer unit also consists of three strands of information: one sound track and two visual narratives. The sound presents fragments of the composition as recorded during rehearsals of the orchestra. Throughout, one distinguishes the voice of the conductor giving instructions in French to the orchestra, for example mentioning the kiss, *boucher*. Another voice briefly renders a fragment of the prophesy. But most of the time, the audience is listening to the orchestra trying out various themes and motifs. This preparatory musical and vocal accompaniment ignores the sequence of these fragments, but presents, in the reduced form of themes, several musical and narrative elements supplementing those in the prelude.

While the orchestra rehearses, the credits scroll over a background of various images. Already before the list reaches the technical contributors, several details catch the viewer's attention. First the title screen. Divided over four lines, it reads: "RICHARD WAGNER | PARSIFAL | von | Hans Jürgen Syberberg." Lacking any punctuation, the text is ambiguous. One is inclined to read it as "Richard Wagner's *Parsifal* by Hans Jürgen Syberberg." That may be the expected interpretation. But since the capital letters appear to establish a hierarchy, one could also view the first and second lines as one continuous title consisting of a three-part name. That would present the composer as a Parsifal, establishing an identity between him and the title hero. It could also suggest that the film has two topics, namely the composer and his composition. Both readings gain plausibility in view of Syberberg's thwarted efforts to gain funding for one film of *Parsifal* and one about Wagner. The two possibilities are not mutually exclusive. But while one can easily recognize Wagner's presence in the visual narrative, one is hard pressed to perceive an overlapping identity between the composer and the quester.

The next noteworthy detail is the omission of the subtitle. While Wagner referred to all his dramatic works for Bayreuth as *Festspiele*, only *Parsifal* was burdened with the clumsy subtitle *Bühnenweihfestspiel*, "stage consecration festival play." Wagner stated on several occasions that he wanted *Parsifal* to consecrate or inaugurate (*weihen*) his stage in Bayreuth. Although it had opened in 1876 with the first festival, financial setbacks caused it to remain closed between 1876 and *Parsifal*'s premiere in 1882.[7] One could, however, also read a different meaning into the subtitle. The first component, *Bühne*, establishes an undisputable link to a stage. The last component, *Spiel*, can be any kind of drama, play or game, and even music. The third element, *Fest*, points to a festival, celebration, or any festive occasion. A *Festspiel* or *Bühnenfestspiel* translates then as a "(stage) work for a festive occasion." That leaves *Weihe*, which, besides "consecration" and "inauguration," also denotes "initiation." Linked to *Bühne*, it could mean "inauguration of a stage," but in an apparently less mundane sense than just "grand opening." *Weih(e)fest* might be an initiation festivity, a *Weih(e)festspiel* an initiation celebration play, and a *Bühnenweihfestspiel* an initiation celebration to be played on a stage. The whole four-part compound might aspire to loftier, perhaps more exclusive, connotations. That is undoubtedly how the term was and still is interpreted by many Wagnerians. They see Wagner's theater as the center of periodic gatherings in the spirit of ancient Greek mystery festivals. The members of the Greek community (nation, congregation) would undertake a pilgrimage to a sanctuary and not only attend, but partake in the ritual being presented. In this sense, the initiation, *Weihe*, applies to each participant. In view of the emphasis on ritual and religious borrowings in *Parsifal*, this function of the work becomes apparent. When one also considers Wagner's other books and articles in the *Bayreuther Blätter*, it is easy to recognize the spirit of a loyal community. Hitler was quick to capitalize on this special status of the Bayreuth festival by patronizing the enterprise. In this respect his measures exceeded the support of King Ludwig.

But if *Weihe* can also be the initiation of an individual, what about Wagner himself? Apart from presiding over the event, did he include himself in the consecration or ritual? Was the *Weihefest* perhaps a celebration for himself? Considering Richard Wagner's penchant for devious behavior, this Tricky Dick may very well have had an esoteric purpose for his final work. His long association with Masonic circles comes to mind, especially in Bayreuth, in spite of his demonstratively written declaration that he had changed his mind about joining the local lodge.[8] Whatever was Wagner's intention and regardless how one chooses to interpret *Bühnenweihfestspiel,* Syberberg omitted the word from the title frame. By separating the action from a stage, he eliminated part of the ambiguity of the subtitle. Logically, he refers to *Parsifal* in the book as a *Weihfestspiel,* giving the viewers a (filmed) play for a festive initiation (34). The omission of the subtitle also signals a departure from "Bayreuth," the festival theater, and its role during the Third Reich.

A third surprise provided in the credits of the film concerns Parsifal. The role of the title hero is divided on several individuals. That is, of course, common when a movie presents a character in different stages of life. Although Wagner let two singers alternate in the role on separate evenings in 1882, he did not specify that the role should be shared during a performance. One might wish he had. The foolish teenager of the first act must develop into a mature and worthy redeemer in the third act. The addition of a beard may, of course, create the illusion of elapsed time. But usually the singer is too mature for the role in the first act. Strangely enough, Syberberg shows little concern for a quasi-realistic handling of the role. He does, however, let a child play the youngster Parsifal in the prelude, that is, before the curtain would part in the stage version. Later, the film introduces a male Parsifal I and a female Parsifal II, portrayed by the amateurs Michael Kutter and Karin Krick. The voice belongs to Rainer Goldberg of the Dresden Opera. At this point, the viewers are only aware that Parsifal's appearance will change several times.

The fourth surprise is the last role mentioned in the credits, the "alto voice from above." Not all printed versions of the score and the libretto include a separate entry for this unnamed character in the list of *dramatis personae.* In stage versions the singer even remains invisible. Syberberg adds three epithets to the entry: Grail Carrier, Synagogue, and Faith, none of them specified by the composer. The increased importance of the Grail Carrier is underscored by the reappearance of Amelie Syberberg in the role, with the words being sung by Gertrud Oertel. Usually, one thinks of Wagner's Grail society as being exclusively male. The sopranos and altos in the chorus are hidden upstairs in the rotunda of the Grail Hall, and they supposedly represent the boys and young novices in an otherwise monastic environment. The young boys' taunting of Kundry in the first act clearly marks her as a female outsider, who, in spite of the balm she brings for Amfortas, is barely tolerated. Wagner's medieval sources differ markedly in this respect. Although chastity is expected of the inhabitants in Wolfram von Eschenbach's Grail Kingdom, the king is granted a normal, loving marriage. The Grail society is modeled on life at a royal court in the age of chivalry, and hence consists of both men and women. Wolfram's Grail Carrier is King Amfortas' sister. Although Wagner's text weaves in references to Gahmuret and Gawan, it remains silent on the topic of the Grail Carrier. One notes therefore with some interest that for Wagner's own production in 1882 a female singer, a Miss Kramer, carried the Grail.[9] A photograph of her in stage costume shows her as a definitely feminine character.[10] More importantly, Cosima Wagner's diaries confirm the gender of the Grail Carrier in her list of lunch guests on July 17, 1882.[11] Syberberg could therefore point to a significant precedent for his choice of a woman for this role.

When he also enhances the figure with the names of Synagogue and Faith, a subtext surfaces. One remembers these words as related to the names of two religious statues from the Cathedral of Strasbourg, Church and Synagogue. They appear in the *Hitler* film as Faith (*Glaube*) and Non-Faith (*Unglaube*). Faith tacitly represented the quasi-religious ideology of the Third Reich, clearly contrasted with the other sculpture. Now both concepts share the same manifestation, and also with the "alto voice from above," and the Grail Carrier. The presence of the Synagogue reveals a new dimension of this *Parsifal*. An additional frame of reference may be the terminology used about Wagner's most devoted supporters. Many members of the Bayreuth circle revered him and his ideas with an ardor resembling religious conviction. As Mary Cicora reports, they divided the audience at Bayreuth festivals into believers (*Gläubige*) and nonbelievers (*Ungläubige*).[12] This distinction between sectarian adherence and critical appreciation uses words that highlight the connection between the Wagnerites' way of thinking and the political ideology of the Third Reich. The Grail Carrier represents quite divergent concepts.

While the list of credits scrolls over the screen, the camera tells its own story. A collection of photo postcards is spread haphazardly, apparently floating on brown, polluted water or an oil spill. A similar jumble of photos had been lying on a table in *Karl May*. This time, the pictures have landed in an unprotected and dirty environment where an occasional wisp of fog drifts over the surface. Most of the photos show ruins of buildings. Such sights would be familiar to elderly Germans who remember the devastation of World War II. However, not all of these pictures come from Germany, although they defy easy identification due to montage. One shows a large church with a cupola amid a stony desert. One is hard pressed to discern if this is the Vatican or the Italian church that supposedly inspired Wagner to the design of his Grail Hall. Most startling to Americans is the montage photo of New York. Against a virile skyline, a close-up shows a leaning or supine Statue of Liberty. The strange shape to her right is Chéreau's Bayreuth stage prop of the wall surrounding Brünnhilde in *Siegfried*. What does the picture convey? Does the Statue of Liberty signify, like Brünnhilde, a goddess exiled from her heavenly abode to an existence of degradation? Is it a reminder that Wagner had considered emigrating to the U.S.? A reference to Winifred Wagner's *U.S.A.*? A symbol of betrayed or defiled ideals? Or an image of crumbled power? The cumulative effect of the photos suggests the aftermath of a cataclysm, perhaps the end stage following the *Götterdämmerung*. Similarly apocalyptic language occurs frequently in Syberberg's publications, usually in reference to contemporary Germany, which he calls a "country of the dead." But also the old Wagner talked constantly about the decline and demise, *Untergang*, of Germany, as recorded in his wife's diaries, for example on March 20, 1881. In chronology, *Parsifal* followed *Götterdämmerung*, which ends with the conflagration and collapse of the world. Logically, then, these initial images present an end stage, both continuing where the *Nibelungenring* left off, and perhaps starting another cyclic development.

Consistent in keeping with this concept, the photos show only immobile architectural remains devoid of living nature or people. The only thing moving is the camera, which pans repeatedly over the pictures. The restlessness of the camera contrasts with its static use in Syberberg's previous films. One remembers how, in *Die freudlose Gesellschaft*, Syberberg declared war on Riefenstahl's techniques, especially her use of mobile cameras, both for their seductive effect and, most importantly, for carrying out Hitler's aesthetics. One also remembers the cynical Hitler puppet bragging about a final victory while pointing to the ruthless and destructive forces completing the task. Now, for the first time, Syberberg appears to appropriate some of Riefenstahl's tricks. While this should not surprise the reader already alerted to his use of counterpoint, the survival of the abhorred aesthetics suggests, if not a victory, at least a continued existence of the mentality it represents.

As the camera pans away from the floating photos, darkness fills the screen. This dark frame marks the transition to the prelude. More ruins rise into view, this time a three-dimensional model suggesting Wagner's Grail Hall of 1882. Or more precisely, of what is left of it. Touching the base of this rubble, the brownish liquid flows by slowly. The color raises the question if the poisonous-looking fluid represents the thinking of Hitlerism. Syberberg does not tire of attacking the lingering legacy of a brownish (read: Nazi) past. A spear and a chalice are stuck in the brown muck. These relics of the Grail Temple indicate that the utopia where the Grail was revered has suffered the same fate as shown on the photos, some of which become visible again. It is a world in shambles. The last element in this desolate environment to come into view is a dead swan, its feathers soiled with the dark liquid. The swan motif will reappear several times, but here it seems to suggest that also animals and nature have succumbed to the destruction.

Imperceptibly, the camera continues to pan, until it suddenly is stopped by a movement coming from the photographed world. An unseen force has stirred in what looks like a lifeless environment. The brown surface has given way to an accumulation of brown, dead leaves, and into this pile an arrow lands. The surprise caused by the indirect sign of life diverts the spectator's attention from all the leaves. While they appear in many of Syberberg's films, their symbolic value has escaped the critics' attempts to understand their use. To most viewers and reviewers, the dead leaves only clutter up the studio floor as Syberberg's meaningless "signature" prop. But of course he imbues them with meaning, as their repeated appearance in *Parsifal* will indicate. At this point in the prelude, the leaves blend in with the world of debris and remains. One cannot tell if they only signal the coming of winter or the death of the trees or both. But the thought of winter brings back the memory of the coldness metaphor and its consistent use in several films preceding *Parsifal*.

The arrow landing in the leaves signals a transition to live acting. It belongs to little Parsifal, who plays with his bow under the watchful eyes of his mother, Herzeleide. This and the following episodes anticipate dramatically events narrated epically in acts 1 and 2. Of course, since the orchestral prelude does not call for any singers, the actors are mute. The silent episodes convey much information as well as illustrating the music. In view of all the publications on the *Parsifal* music, this study will concentrate mainly on the visual exegesis. But, as for example Alfred Lorenz points out, three major themes dominate the prelude, the love, Grail, and faith themes, all comprised of several motifs.[13] A comparison of such components with the visual narrative confirms a close correlation, sometimes in unexpected ways. Similar correlations exist also in the rest of the film.

Some viewers may not recognize the title hero and his mother right away. But obviously, the swan and the child's play with bow and arrow point logically to the shooting of the swan in the first act. And the mother's devotion illustrates what Kundry tells about her in the second act. In addition to this, Syberberg also introduces details with leitmotivic function. For example, the boy is wearing a crown of goldpaper. Child's play, one might think. Actually, the prelude presents a child's world and all the attractions of which memories are made. But the boy is not just play-acting the role of a prince. He is of royal birth, wearing the visible symbol of his special status. Although the audience learns the names of his parents in the first act, Wagner omits the information about royal status and family ties to King Amfortas. Syberberg restores this detail found in Wolfram von Eschenbach's medieval version. In addition to the alchemical significance of the golden material and royal symbolism, the director introduces with the crown the first of several objects having a serrated edge. The jagged shape looks torn, *zerrissen*. The term is known in German romanticism and psychology. It is especially associated with the poet Heinrich Heine. In the European Grail literature, Perceval/Parzival is a troubled quester embodying this term par excellence. In Syberberg's version, a child's toy-like attribute assumes multiple signifying powers, thanks to the grid of such associations.

Although short in duration, the scene with mother and child abounds in cues with several functions. They present visually themes and motifs conveyed in the music. As such, they introduce visual elements with a leitmotivic power comparable to melodic fragments. They anticipate, or establish, a sequence of related motifs later on. Some of these details also relate to other films by the director. The apparent self-quotations constitute the net of references that identify this *Parsifal* as a part belonging to a larger body, in Syberberg's oeuvre as well as that of Wagner. And here, as throughout the film, he weaves in references to the medieval version, as if offering corrective reminders of what Wagner interpreters ignored.

Beginning with the environment, one sees first a snow-covered forest background. It continues the impression of a lifeless and chilly nature. In a quasi-tonal fashion it varies the motifs of death and Hitlerism. This background soon shares the field with an artists's rendering of Hunding's cabin from the *Walküre*, recalling its recreation by King Ludwig in the Bavarian forest and its return in *Theodor Hierneis*. The tree around which the cabin was built was in Wagner's version the Germanic Tree of Life, the Yggdrasil. Stripped of its leaves and surrounding structure, it appears in miniature several times in *Hitler*. The operatic backdrop thus triggers a multitude of associations. But apparently its function does not yet relate to the end of the world. Only at the end of the *Ring* cycle does its dead wood nourish the fire of the *Götterdämmerung*. The view in the prelude shows the tree still surrounded by the cabin, whereas the snow-covered trees present a frozen world devoid of life. The split background thus repeats the cyclic transition between end and beginning, again blurring the sense of time.

Wagner's art revived the mythic tree. When King Ludwig imitated this art for real life, his servant, Theodor Hierneis, did not know what kind of tree it really was. In the royal cabin it was just known as the World Ash Tree. But as Hierneis informs the viewers, the ash was really a linden tree. Syberberg's correction in the book on Hierneis that it was a beech brings into relief the difficulty in interpreting myth.[14] Even minor features are subject to ignorance, misunderstanding, or downright ideological manipulation. What might, then, not happen to myths such as the Parsifal story? Another reason for reintroducing the tree is the attempt to link the Tree of Life to the destruction of life during the Third Reich. Syberberg lists one of the subtitles of *Hitler* as "From the World Ash Tree . . . to Buchenwald." The name of this concentration camp means "beech forest." Whenever Syberberg equips his cinematic settings with layers of dead leaves, Buchenwald and the horrors it represents inform the scene. He may, of course, also have been inspired by Gustav Klimt's painting *Buchenwald*, which, thanks to its early date, shows an innocent beech forest, its ground covered with dead leaves. Even more likely is a metonymic link to Richard Wagner. As usual, semantic polyvalence creates a grid, a *Sprachgitter*, allowing the flow of associations. The German word for a leaf, *Blatt*, also means a "sheet of paper" and a "journal." In the plural, *Blätter* might evoke Wagner's journal, *Die Bayreuther Blätter*. Many of his essays and shorter prose pieces appeared there. Since some of the composer's articles included anti-Semitic slurs, and since his closest collaborators expressed the same bias, one might consider the journal "brownish" or proto-Nazi years before the Nazi party saw the light. These brown *Blätter* may, then, have found their place in the film, along with the concentration camp. By extension, they may also point to the journals and newspapers containing the poison-pen reviews by Syberberg's enemies.

Whether beech or ash, the leaves evoke a cluster of associations. Some of these pertain to Wagner's use of the World Ash Tree. It was in Hunding's cabin Sieglinde met Siegmund. The incestuous fruit of their love was Siegfried. Surreptitiously, the movie setting showing mother and child against the backdrop of this tree therefore also evokes incest. At this point in the prelude, one might dismiss that thought as totally inappropriate. After all, Sieglinde is not Herzeleide, and besides, Sieglinde dies giving birth to her son. Still, the connection is strengthened by two other details. When Herzeleide tries to take away the primitive bow and gives her son a larger, beautifully made replacement, she presses a kiss on his cheek as he wiggles out of her arms. The kiss is an important theme in Wagner's music. As innocent as the maternal kiss is, it becomes associated with her in her son's memory, contributing to his reaction to Kundry's attempted seduction in the second act. The other factor is less transparent at this point. But even the most naïve viewer must wonder why the sibyl of the initial scene is played by the same actress as Herzeleide. This actress, Edith Clever, will reappear as Kundry later. Even before Kundry's appearance, the mother's identity raises questions. Unlike Parsifal, who is identified in the credits as being portrayed by several individuals, the sibyl and Herzeleide share the same manifestation. This alerts the viewer to something unusual about the mother. Supporting this possibility is the star-studded, navy cloth that covers Herzeleide's chair and the ground around it. This chair has the contour of a throne. Is she the Queen of the Night? The mythic Great Mother? Considering how stylized the setting is, a mythic connection gains plausibility.

As little Parsifal struggles loose from his mother's embrace, he absentmindedly grabs the offered bow while holding on to his own self-made one. Something has caught his attention. Now follows his encounter with the "knights in shining armor." Parsifal mentions the episode during the interrogation in act 1. The episode with them in the film is almost equally brief. As the narrative indicates, the encounter causes the boy to leave his mother. This reference, as also the others relating to Parsifal's childhood, was inspired by the medieval sources.[15] But unlike Wolfram's dialogue over six long stanzas, the knights in the film move into view only long enough to be observed by the child, and then glide away again while seated on a carrousel-like scaffolding. The consequence is the same as in Wolfram's and Wagner's texts: A grief-stricken Herzeleide watches her son depart. Only in retrospect can one recognize the three young people in armor. They are the two adult Parsifals flanking the Grail Carrier. Although wearing a shiny scale-covered garment, she holds a book in her hands, not a weapon or shield as expected of a knight in armor. Again, Syberberg has opted for an artificial, strictly stylized tableau in lieu of a realistic episode.

It may not be readily apparent that the adaptation fits only partially the reference in Wagner's libretto and not at all Wolfram's episode. Syberberg replaced the meeting involving the four knights in shining armor with a sight that the medieval Parzival had not witnessed personally, namely that of two knights abducting a young lady. They are being pursued by the four knights who stop to ask questions of Parzival. Two details reveal the substitution: The number of people in each group, and the Grail Carrier. In the credits her other epithets include "alto voice from on high," Synagogue, and Faith. The last name points to a probable identity with the kidnapped damsel, Imane of Beafontane. *Imane* means "faith" in Semitic languages.[16] In both Syberberg's and Wagner's versions, the child sees the ideal to which he aspires, but only Syberberg presents the apparition of the future Parsifal as a divided (*zerrissen*) individual, plus (the) Faith that will sustain him/them. The predicament of Faith as Imane, Wolfram's damsel in distress, might signal a loss of faith in the world that lures the child. Assuming an identity between Imane and the cinematic Faith, one might expect other Semitic characteristics as well. And indeed, she is also the personified Synagogue. The paired allegories of a triumphant female Church holding a chalice and a sorrowful Synagogue with a lance recur frequently in iconography during the years when Chrétien and Wolfram composed their Grail stories. Numerous examples of these allegorical figures from the age of the crusades abound in literature, paintings, altars, and church windows.[17] Of particular interest might be a medallion window in Abbot Suger's choir in the abbey church of Saint-Denis, since a visual reference to this sanctuary appears later in the film.[18] If the sad-looking Faith in Syberberg's episode evokes the abducted Imane, does she also represent the members of the synagogues abducted to concentration camps? Even if the film should only intend to conjure up the medieval events that preceded the modern persecution, why does Faith hold a book in her hands? Is it a volume of sacred scripture? Perhaps the Grail story? Held in the hands of this character, the volume might signal a partially Hermetic origin with an Arabic or Jewish transmission of the subject matter.[19] Wolfram von Eschenbach himself claims a non-Christian source for at least part of his story, a "pagan" book by Flegetanis, found by Kyot the Provençal in "Dolet" (Toledo or Tudela) in Spain.[20] This Flegetanis was descended from King Solomon on his mother's side. Of course Syberberg's book to the film does not elaborate on any of these possibilities.

The presence of Faith at Parsifal's side raises questions with no clear answers. If Parsifal as knight plays the role of abductor, he repeats the act of the Arthurian hero who did the same to Queen Guinevere or the God of Hades who abducted Demeter's daughter. In either case, archetypal violence triggers a period of loss, mourning, and cyclic events, as suggested in the carrousel-like structure carrying the trio. If, on the other hand, all three "knights" only embody the lures of worldly chivalry, then the middle figure may have retained more than just the name of Faith from the *Hitler* film. The shadow of a brown past from that film might then fall on all three figures and what they represent. And finally, since Wagner's Parsifal has not yet appeared as one sees him in the first act, might the two actors sharing the role also assume other parts? If so, they would share an important characteristic with the sibyl/Herzeleide/Kundry figure. The little episode invites interpretations not usually associated with Wagner's music drama. At this point the observations will view it only as an appearance of the shining knights inspiring little Parsifal's departure. The character appearing as Faith grants visual presence to the motif of faith in the music. At the same time, she faintly recalls the medieval sources.

As Parsifal emerges from the dark path that led him away from his mother, he arrives at a puppet stage. On this stage the boy watches scenes of the Parsifal story with puppets, costumes, and backdrop modeled on the performance of 1882. The stage action repeats select dramatic and narrated events of act 1, including a falling swan felled by a youthful Parsifal and one of the flower maidens, called *teuflisch holde Frauen* (women of infernal charms) in Gurnemanz' description of Klingsor's magic garden. She is probably Carrie Pringle, the British soloist who enchanted Wagner. His shouts of "bravo!" during the flower maidens' performance suggest he was as susceptible as King Amfortas to Klingsor's kind of magic.[21] Not only is the king's seduction presented visually, but the flower maiden's presence underscores the parallels in Wagner's life and the legend. The mythic nature of the narrative accounts for some unusual details, such as the reappearance of the star-studded blue cloth and the bleeding wound in a slab of flesh seen as a separate entity. Also another detail raises questions: Is the temptress laughing or crying after the wounding of King Amfortas? Kundry does both in the course of the play, but her laughter does not express amusement; on the contrary, it camouflages her distress.

The puppets display a surprising feature. With the exception of the swan and a white dove, which are suspended from above like true marionettes, the figures are controlled with rods from below. The forces animating them obviously belong in the invisible lower regions. But unlike the puppets in *Hitler*, no human intervention can be seen. The fact that the dolls are supported and not suspended eliminates the fleeting moment of balance in grace, an important point in Kleist's thoughts on marionettes.[22] Syberberg nonetheless refers to this text in his book to the film as he summarizes the first chapter: "Action scenes, then, in the form of dolls for the prelude, comic strips for children, made naïve. Richard Wagner for some and for the others who know about Kleist and his seriousness" (69). The author assumes the same pose as Wolfram von Eschenbach in his *Parzival*. Choosing the bow and arrow as his symbol, Wolfram announces his story as being on two levels, one for the wise and one for the simple-minded.[23] Like Wolfram, Syberberg only hints at less accessible dimensions in his work. Wolfram's name is usually suppressed. He appears mainly in visual references and, in the book to the film, in paraphrases. Nevertheless, Wolfram's and Wagner's roles in relation to Syberberg resemble those of Flegetanis and Kyot in relation to Wolfram: the distant source, the modifying transmitter, and the presenting artist-interpreter.

As mentioned in the previous chapter, Syberberg introduced dolls and puppets in *Hitler*, and discussed them and puppet theater in various texts. All this seems to point to their extensive and final use in *Parsifal*. The puppet theater constitutes an easily accessible component of the Wagner story within the film. Not only does this episode recreate faithfully segments of Wagner's 1882 staging, but it is also an art form for which the composer expressed both interest and fondness. He described the "Kasperl theater" as the last remaining " sphere of life of the original spirit of German folk theater," adding that this gave him the hope that this "folk spirit" might be rekindled.[24] But the use of puppets also links several themes in Syberberg's oeuvre, such as dolls and Faust, especially in Goethe and Heine, the former being inspired to his work by fairground puppet versions, the latter commenting on this. While the puppet theater traditionally kept alive ancient themes long abandoned in literature, it was often the last phase before oblivion. Thus the puppet episode echoes ever so faintly the initial visual emphasis on decay and demise. Underscoring this bleak view is the selection of details played on the puppet stage. While Parsifal hunts the swan, King Amfortas is suffering and Titurel prays. Redemption is only a hope.

The king's predicament shows him lying at the front edge of the puppet stage. His position is literally a positioning at the abyss, a *mise en abyme*. This term applies to several artistic devices or techniques, in which *abyme* (*abîme*) no longer refers only to an abyss or the center detail in some heraldic designs. Syberberg introduces all the variants outlined by Dällenbach. The most common form is the component that is an incomplete or miniature version of the larger work in which it is embedded. For this form Dällenbach offers the following definition: "A *mise en abyme* is any internal mirror that reflects the whole of the narrative by simple, repeated or 'specious' (or paradoxical) duplication" (36). The puppet episode comprises a chain of miniaturizing "mirrors." First, the child Parsifal watches a puppet Parsifal. Second, the flower maiden tempts the invisible Wagner while Kundry seduces Amfortas. And third, the puppet play within the play presents segments of the whole narrative. A similar constellation had occurred when the child Parsifal observed the adult Parsifal(s) in shining armor. Both that encounter and the puppet play serve as "generic shifters," adding more examples to those discussed by Dällenbach (71–74). The encounter of live actors in a mime or mute scene is followed by another genre of art, the puppet play. It, in turn, shifts abruptly to a different genre in disguise, a "paradoxical" duplication, depicting Herzeleide. The mother who had first appeared as a live actress is now presented dead. The actress looking like a sleeping Herzeleide imitates the stone effigy on a sarcophagus. More precisely, it or she recreates the tomb sculpture of Eleanor of Aquitaine in Fontevrault. The identifying detail is the open book in her hands. A visible full-page illustration in that book shows King Arthur and his knights at the round table with the Grail in the center. One assumes, then, that the volume includes the Perceval/Percyval/Parzival story. Thus the Grail narrative in book form constitutes yet another case of mirroring *mise en abyme* that also includes a shift in genre. One wonders if this is the same book that the Grail Carrier held while seated between the two knights. Far from being merely a sequence of Parsifal-related illustrations to the music, the prelude observes old and intricate artistic techniques.

The evocation of Eleanor of Aquitaine conjures up some medieval dimensions that the usual stage version of *Parsifal* ignores. Eleanor of Aquitaine (1122-1205) became the queen of France through her first marriage and the queen of England through the second.[25] Her daughter, Marie de Champagne, was the patron of Chrétien de Troyes, making it possible that Eleanor also knew him, and hence his *Perceval*. Marie's son Henry later claimed the title King of Jerusalem. Eleanor's son Richard Lionheart became a legend during his lifetime. Her second husband, Henry II of England, was also a count of Anjou. His grandfather, Fulk, Count of Anjou, was King of Jerusalem and although married, also a Knight Templar. This dynasty provided the fictional paternal line of Parzival's ancestry in Wolfram's text. Strangely enough, Chrétien omits any real-life aristocratic ties for his Perceval. Of special interest to Wolfram von Eschenbach was Eleanor's ancestor Count William, born in 752. He was a commander in Charlemagne's army who fought the Saracens in Spain. He later withdrew to a monastory he built near Montpellier, Saint Guilhem-le-Désert.[26] This canonized ancestor of Eleanor's is the title hero of Wolfram's *Willehalm*. He may also have inspired the pious character Kyot of Katelangen in *Parzival*. The name Kyot is thought to be derived from Catalan-Aragone Guillot, a diminutive form of Guillem/Guilhem, or William in English.[27] Since Eleanor and her prominent family not only belonged to Wolfram's world, but even inspired his work, it seems appropriate to include an allusion to her in this version of the story, be it only as an unidentified image in death.

Syberberg adds a surrealistic detail to his image of the queen on a draped bier: her hands close the book. Even in death, Herzeleide is only slumbering. The movement identifies the "paradoxical" element in Dällenbach's examples of the *mise en abyme*. As the camera pans over her outstretched body and crown, the Wagner death mask comes into view for the first time. It functions as the background and another *mise en abyme*: in front lies the dead character as a sculptured portrait, behind her the profile of the deceased Wagner's three-dimensional portrait mask.

After this genre shifter the camera turns slowly to the next unit, which returns to the theme of puppets. Five dolls of Wagner dominate this scene. Thanks to select close-ups and slow panning, the viewer is kept in a state of confusion until the camera "moves away" to a long shot and again pans over some of the scene at a distance. This tableau does not tell a story as the sequence on the puppet stage does. Rather, it presents simultaneous situations, or facets, with all five dolls portraying Wagner as a mature man. The reader may remember the early references to the doll as a miniature *pupa* and, linked semantically, as the little "other" reflected in the eye, *pupilla*. Dällenbach's various definitions of mirrors and reflections also continue to apply. For example, as the large concrete death mask is paired with the first doll in the foreground, both faces are seen in profile. At this point one only sees enough to conclude that the doll is lying face up. Another doll standing next to this figure is a puppet of Kundry. While she had appeared as a beautiful temptress on the stage, she now wears the costume and hair of the wild and ugly Kundry from act 1 of the 1882 performance. Again, one cannot tell if she is laughing or crying at the sight of the supine Wagner replacing Amfortas. This variation on a theme from the puppet play provides the link to the Wagner revue. Another Wagner puppet is using a sledge hammer and a note-shaped chisel against the eardrum of an oversized human ear, making the blood squirt. This view of Wagner as composer is based on a famous caricature by André Gill in *L'Éclipse*.[28] As the camera pans, a tree-like form appears, momentarily evoking the Tree of Life in Hunding's cabin. The crown of the tree widens into a partially covered crystal ball or round goblet. One assumes it is the sibyl's attribute, but it could also present a variant of the Grail as chalice. A third Wagner doll continues the ambiguity. The figure is tied to a column or pillory modeled on a detail in Jan van Eyck's polyptych altar piece known as the *Ghent Altar*. On the largest of its inside panels, surrounding the Lamb of God, angels hold two objects associated with the Passion, a cross and a pillar for the whipping. The column to which the Wagner doll is tied may therefore establish a tacit connection to a Christ-like suffering. Of what nature would that suffering be in Wagner's case? Since the doll also gestures with one free arm to the spectators to come closer, is it inviting attacks or viewers for the spectacle? The doll does not wear any resemblance to Christ. Dressed in a feminine, pink robe blurring gender distinctions, the puppet recalls the sybaritic lover of precious fabrics and aromatherapy, to say nothing of lovely women. One of these was Judith Gautier, who supplied the pink silk for Wagner's robe and a long list of other indulgences (Gutman, 394–96). Maybe this Wagner in pink is gesturing for Judith to come to him. Soon another robe of Wagner's enters the field, this time in dark blue, lined in a glittering star-studded sky. The star motif had already appeared on Herzeleide's throne cover and again on the stage floor. Stars also adorned her shroud on the bier.

Perhaps a Star of David enters the association with Judith Gautier, since she was Jewish. And then, of course, there is the question of Wagner's ancestry. Was his biological father his mother's first husband or her second, Ludwig Geyer? And was Geyer Jewish or not? He was the only father the composer knew and loved. Incidentally, Wagner grew up as Richard Geyer. The world may never know the truth. Already the composer burned the correspondence between his mother and Geyer; later the widowed Cosima Wagner and her helpers collected and selected the documentation for the Wagner Archive.[29] If any objectionable evidence still existed in public registers and religious records, Nazi investigators would have destroyed it. After all, Hitler admired Wagner, patronized the Bayreuth Festival, and practically elevated Wagner to the rank of *the* national composer. This composer had to be a pure "Aryan." Still, questions about the composer's family background crop up in every Wagner biography. Perhaps Syberberg is hinting at hidden Stars of David seen only on the lining, but not on the outside of the robe. Wagner's obsession with anything Jewish often assumed hateful and provocative forms, also in his private life, as Cosima Wagner's diaries attest. Still, inconsistencies abound, supporting the star motif as a sign of Wagner's ambivalent feelings. A more obvious frame of reference for the star-lined robe is, of course, the Hermetic notion of microcosm and macrocosm. As a microcosm, each person reflects, however imperfectly, the universe. Another *mise en abyme,* then, but set apart from the surrounding puppets. Two more Wagner dolls appear, almost as a couple. One depicts Wagner as a conductor, baton in hand, the other as a poet and writer, wearing the famous beret and holding a notebook. Only in the long shot at the end of the Wagner revue can one recognize that the first puppet lying on the ground is attached to a crucifix. It looks like the cross from van Eyck's painting. A crown of thorns lies on the floor nearby. An additional item in this revue with associative ties to the *Ghent Altar* would be the tree-footed, covered crystal globe. Like Wagner's Grail, it finds its counterpart in the painted chalice into which blood streams from the wounded Lamb of God. The clash of revered religious symbols and the Wagner poses as a Christ-like martyr crucified or waiving for his lady-love to come to him smacks of blasphemy. But as mentioned in the chapter on *Hitler,* Syberberg makes sure the curse in *Jew Süß* comes true, and it included destruction and blasphemy. At the end of this revue, many viewers have expressed confusion about it. Certain is only that by focusing on Wagner, it "belongs" to the Wagner component of the combined film project. It addresses Wagner as artist and as a man of highly conflicting qualities. Above all, it presents Wagner as the world sees him, as a caricature and hedonist, crucified by many but divine in the eyes of devotees. As representations of a complex personality, these roles or poses resemble facets of a prismatic stone.

This resemblance triggers the apparition of precisely such a stone as the camera keeps moving. It is a copy of Albrecht Dürer's polyhedron in *Melencolia I.* It was featured already in *Hitler.* Of course it does not only function as a self-quotation, as Syberberg wants the reader to believe (*Parsifal,* 69). With its apparently reflexive surface, it is a "mirror in the text," as Dällenbach calls the *mise en abyme.*

Its presence points both backwards in Syberberg's oeuvre, suggesting a connection with melancholy and mourning, and forward to its reappearance as a revered object. As mirrors, the surfaces should reflect the environment, including the camera. But, befitting Dällenbach's paradox, instead one sees a lake with a huge tear drop hanging over it. Is it the lake in which King Ludwig's body was found? And who shed the tear? Syberberg? Or Wagner, perhaps? Syberberg's book refers only to Cosima's diaries as the inspiration. She had dreamed about Parsifal and had seen a large tear drop over the world (*Parsifal*, 69). This might be the only faint reference to Cosima in the Wagner revue. The tear is also another detail familiar from the *Hitler* film. But already there it might include a reference to Nietzsche, whose thoughts were widely appropriated and abused during the Third Reich. And since Nietzsche had admired Wagner before their break, he belongs to the Wagner narrative in *Parsifal*, where references to him appear in oblique as well as easily recognizable forms. The tear drop hails from his *Thus Spake Zarathustra*. In part 4 of the prologue, Zarathustra states: "I love all who are like heavy drops falling one by one out of the dark cloud that lowereth over man: they herald the coming of the lightning, and succumb as heralds."[30] The proximity of the five Wagner dolls establish a connection between the multi-faceted Wagner and Nietzsche's heralds. Especially the caricature doll hammering on the ear supports such a notion. Of course it ridicules Wagner primarily as a composer. But in that capacity he viewed himself as a pioneer and herald of the "music of the future." Less obvious may be a possible revisionist interpretation of the caricature: instead of attacking the listeners' sensibilities, the figure might be trying to open the ear, or catch the attention of an indifferent public. The choice of target, an ear, evokes biblical echoes. Among numerous admonitions to pay attention one finds, e.g., recurring verses in Revelation beginning with "He that hath an ear, let him hear." Nietzsche also made use of that statement, putting it in the mouth of his Zarathustra (173). And Wagner did consider himself the bearer of a message, as his essays in *Die Bayreuther Blätter* attest. He was undoubtedly thinking of himself when he stated, "The Thinker is the backward-looking poet; but the true poet is the foretelling Prophet."[31] Whatever the message, gospel, or mission, many may view Wagner as a prophet or forerunner. But of what or whom? A return to Nietzsche's first quotation deepens the ambiguity, as Zarathustra continues: "Lo, I am a herald of the lightning, and a heavy drop out of the cloud: the lightning, however, is the *Superman*" (10). Unfortunately, Nietzsche's concept of superman, *Übermensch*, lent itself too easily to ideological abuse as *Herrenmensch* and *Herrenvolk*, while others not included in that designation were declared suitable for elimination. The lethal power of lightning invites the association with Hitler and the race he wanted to promote. In view of Wagner's numerous anti-Semitic pronouncements, he fits handily into the pattern as a forerunner and preparer of Hitlerism and the mindset leading to the Holocaust. With Richard Wagner being one of the two subjects of the film, possibly a Parsifal variant himself, the political implications throw a shadow over the prelude. One wonders if it will be possible to separate the traditional title hero and his quest for the Grail from this web of associations.

The tableau that triggered these reflections consists of nothing but dolls and a few other objects. The last object to come into view, the apparently reflective polyhedron, functions as a genre-shifting *mise en abyme*. Not until the camera pans away from the stone does one become aware of yet another part of the tableau that had been hidden behind the puppets. It consists of two people sitting on the ground and huddling together in front of a draped box. The cover complicates its identification. With the shape of a double cube it looks too short for a coffin, but might function as an altar. That assumption gains support from the *Ghent Altar*, making it a transformed version of it. The dimension reminds one of Albrecht Dürer's discussion of the "Delic Problem" and the doubling of a cube.[32] Wagner studied Dürer's work while he was composing *Parsifal* and still intended to join the Masonic lodge in Bayreuth. Also of interest is the versatility of this geometric shape. If one imagines the double cube as constructed of flat squares, it can be "unfolded" into a flat, four-armed cross. And the crucifix appears in many versions in the film, beginning with the first prelude. The veiled altar lends a sacral note to the setting. Its proximity to the two huddling people suggests a connection between them. These two are the adult Parsifals, sleeping and immobile. Their combined silhouettes look like an embryonic clump. Only as the young man stirs and gets up, bow in hand, can one distinguish them as two figures. While one part of this pupa-like shape unfolds into a young man who slowly walks towards the rocky landscape in the background, the female Parsifal continues slumbering. As the death mask is the location for the action in all three acts, Parsifal's approach marks the end of the prelude.

In retrospect it becomes clear that Syberberg has added a substantial unit to the three acts of the music drama, changing its visual composition to four major parts. The addition consists of four distinct sections: visuals accompanying the "rehearsal music," a pantomime, a puppet play, and a Wagner revue. To this come the introductory frame and several transitional segments comparable to preludes and a coda. Overall, this new portion reflects the composition of the whole work. The expansion is shorter than any of the acts. Its length and relationship to the three acts parallel the status of *Rheingold* within the *Ring des Nibelungen*. Just as the Rhinemaidens reappear at the end of *Götterdämmerung*, so also the sibyl of the first part of the frame concludes the film. The treasure taken from the bottom of the Rhine finds its counterpart in Grail and spear, while later Siegfried's mission is revised for Parsifal. More intriguingly, the gold that everybody wants is brought up from the depths. This core action of the *Rheingold* appears to serve as the guiding thought behind the film's first part. The depths and lower regions have always symbolized the unconscious parts of the mind. The idea of the unconscious was by no means alien to Wagner. For example, he considered the "driving life-force" to be unconscious and instinctual (*Wagner-Lexikon*, 841), and he claimed that this also applies to the creative urge of the artist (842). If one equates the new segment of the film with the realm of the unconscious, it would be logical to consult Freud and Jung, the best known pioneers of psychoanalysis, resp. analytical psychology. The fact that Syberberg entitled his book preceding this film *Die freudlose Gesellschaft*, might lead one to assume that *Parsifal* would also be *freud*/Freud-less and possibly leaning only on Jung's insights. But thanks to the director's consistent use of counterpoint, one can rest assured that Freud is also present.

Both Freud and Jung subdivided the unconscious parts of the psyche into two areas. Freud describes them as the unconscious that is incapable of consciousness, and the pre-conscious that can reach consciousness under certain conditions; it functions like a screen between consciousness and unconsciousness.[33] This second area contains also personal memories that have been forgotten but can usually be recalled with some help. Jung operates with similar concepts, but calls them the collective and the personal unconscious.[34] The latter contains, besides forgotten memories, also repressed material and components that are close to the "threshold" of consciousness. The part of the mind that lies furthest beyond consciousness is called the "unconscious" by Freud and the "collective unconscious" by Jung. It is shared by everybody, due to the structure of the human brain. Its content exceeds that of one individual's life experience. In *Faust II* Goethe calls it the "realm of the Mothers." Always active, the forces inhabiting this realm manifest themselves, e.g., in religions, myths, art, and dreams. Being in part instincts and undifferentiated forms, they assume a shape compatible with the individual's experience or society, although the important ones are recognizable across all cultures. Freud calls them imagoes, Jung archetypes. The most important of these psychic figures is the Mother, a few others being the Child, the Shadow, and the Anima/Animus. In addition to personal forms, the unconscious forces can also assume other shapes, for example symbols. Some of this imagery appears in the first part of the film in a simple form.

Returning to the beginning of the film, one realizes that the sibyl is not an ordinary fortune-teller or even a prophetess, but also a force from the unconscious. She is the Great Mother who, in Jung's words, "as the first incarnation of the anima archetype, personifies in fact the whole unconscious [. . . and is] the gateway into the unconscious, into the 'realm of the Mothers.'"[35] With the encounter of this Mother, the viewer enters a world of which one is normally unaware. After the miniature prelude consisting of visuals accompanying the credits and "rehearsal music" follows the first section or mini-act with live characters. Here Edith Clever returns as a mother, with her throne over a starry, blue ground confirming her as the mother imago or archetype. She appears here in her loving and protective manifestation. But she, as well as all the archetypes, possesses several, often contrasting natures. Her son with the golden crown is the holy child, the potential for fulfillment and redemption. The crown serves as a solar symbol revealing his divine nature. In this realm of the "Eternal Feminine," to use Jung's words, "slumbers the 'divine child,' patiently awaiting his conscious realization. This son is the germ of wholeness, and he is characterized as such by his specific symbols."[36] This suggests that all the objects may function as symbols, as can other visual details and musical themes. The difficulty in narrowing down the identity of the knights in shining armor confirms their archetypal function. The hero appears split in two manifestations, one male, one female. In alchemical imagery they represent the components of the stone (*lapis*) or *prima materia*, to be perfected. Often depicted as a hermaphrodite, king and queen, or a virgin, they also appear in symbolic guise, e.g. as the sun and moon, or gold and silver. They represent here two halves of the symbol of wholeness, a state which Freud calls the super-ego and Jung the Self. Jung describes the often antinomial Self as a *complexio oppositorum* and paradoxical, " in that it represents in every respect thesis and antithesis, and at the same time synthesis."[37] In the film's context, the couple appears as the potential manifestations of the conscious and the unconscious of the Self. Between them sits the Grail Carrier with the many names as the synthesis and uniting archetype that brings the sought-after treasure. She represents the virginal form of the alchemical Mercurius. This numinous imago, also known as the Kore, the daughter, or the maiden, is one of the variants of the Great Mother. The book in their hands constitutes a shared attribute. These five figures are imagoes or archetypes and the only characters in the first part to be played by live actors.

The puppet theater represents another content of the unconscious. More dependent on cultural input than the personified archetypes, it nonetheless contains myths and legends known over a long time and a wide area, in brief, it is an extensively shared legacy. It too presents archetypal figures, e.g. Gurnemanz as the Wise Old Man and symbols such as the dove and the Grail. By comparison, the Wagner revue fits the definition of Freud's pre-conscious and Jung's personal unconscious. Closer in time, Wagner is primarily a German phenomenon, and a problematic one to many. His five manifestations embody the persona that the world came to know. Having become forces of his own unconscious, they appear beyond the confines of the Wagner head. But they also function as part of his compatriots' cultural legacy, justifying their inclusion in the collective unconscious. The other persona, the death mask, looms in the background, creating one of numerous occurrences of *mise en abyme*. Not by coincidence do the parts of the prelude take place outside the mask landscape. Only to a small extent personal, the unconscious lies beyond the grasp of conscious control. What happens in the mask landscape, on the other hand, relates more closely to Wagner's more or less conscious world. And the ruler of that world is in dire need of a redeeming agent. Responding to that need, this force arises from the unconscious and approaches the mind landscape.

Chapter 7

Act One

The scenery of the opening of act 1 conforms reasonably well to Wagner's stage instruction. A rocky landscape with an open area in the middle fills the view. Dead leaves and drifting fog cover the ground. Although this place lies within the Grail Kingdom, it is located at some distance from the castle, that is, the center of the mind landscape. Through the opening framed by tall rocks one catches a glimpse of the Wagner mask profile serving as the horizon. This is only one in a long list of projections used to vary the background. The chin section of the mask has been pulled away from the remaining face, creating an alienating gap. This gap mirrors, and thus identifies, the open area of the foreground where the action is about to begin. Imperceptibly, the camera has zoomed closer, revealing three sleeping persons. But before Gurnemanz and the two squires wake up, the background changes into a different landscape: the tip of a rocky outcropping with spruce trees blocking a low sun, its rays dividing the clouds into bands of color. As the camera continues to zoom, one soon looses sight of the sky. The book to the film, *Parsifal: Ein Filmessay*, identifies the painting serving as background as *The Cross in the Mountains* (*The Tetschen Altar*) by Caspar David Friedrich (40). As only its center section is visible, one may not recognize the painting, especially since the crucifix with the gilded Christ sculpture disappears from view so quickly. The director could have selected many other views for this projection, both photographs and paintings. The setting for this episode is supposed to be in the Pyrenées somewhere in "Montsalvat" near the Grail Castle. Syberberg, however, selected a view from Bohemia by a German romantic artist. This provides a link to Wagner's biography, since the composer visited the area repeatedly. As interesting as the included portion of the painting are the other parts that are omitted in the film and not mentioned in the book. For example, the frame with its Masonic symbolism adds a dimension of ecumenism unacceptable in orthodox circles. Wagner was close to Freemasonry during his years in Bayreuth, but that activity was kept discreet. Perhaps the silver star at the apex of the gilded frame inspired Syberberg to choose this picture. It is the Evening Star that also appears as the Morning Star.[1] Its ambiguity seems to transform the landscape into a view at sunrise, accompanying the awakening of the sleeping characters. However, Friedrich had an evening scene in mind. The controversy surrounding the painting upon its completion in 1808 prompted him to describe his interpretation: "Jesus Christ, nailed to the tree, is turned here towards the sinking sun, the image of the eternal life-giving father."[2] Clearly, Syberberg's references to this painting as depicting morning are erroneous. But the statement and the painting include several elements that also recur in the film, such as cross, gold, and the crucified Redeemer. With his death an old world died, the painter maintained: "This sun [God the Father] sank and the earth was not able to grasp the departing light any longer. There shines forth in the gold of the evening light the purest, noblest metal of the Saviour's figure on the cross, which thus reflects on earth in a softened glow" (78). This obviously puts the Christ figure in the role of transmitter and mediator. Here one is reminded of Syberberg's preoccupation with light in *Die freudlose Gesellschaft*. He too uses light as the image of divine emanation and its reflection and multiple refractions down toward the human level. But perhaps most intriguing in the new context is the use of the sunset as a sunrise. The end of the day converges with the beginning. Incidentally, the German *Dämmerung* (twilight), as chosen by Wagner for his *Götterdämmerung*, applies to both dawn and dusk.

As Gurnemanz rises and wakes the boys, Wagnerians experience the first shock. This Gurnemanz is a vigorous man in his best years, not the old, white-haired knight of stage tradition. But unlike some other surprises in the film, the deviation from tradition has a precedent: Wieland Wagner's staging of *Parsifal* in 1937 also included a beardless, dark-haired Gurnemanz.[3] Sung and acted by Robert Lloyd, the character possesses a wealth of knowledge and memories appropriate for an old man.[4] But given his role as hermit and possibly educator of the squires, age becomes irrelevant. This character is also the first example of Syberberg's twist that lets all the major male roles except Parsifal be portrayed by men of similar age. In the opening scene, Gurnemanz and the two boys or squires (*Knappen*) are taking turns in guarding the forest around the Grail Castle. For this task one would expect not only alert, but also armed and strong guards. Wagner, however, incongruously entrusted the duty to two children and an old man. He molded the Gurnemanz character from four figures in the *Parzival*. One is Liaze's father who provided the name for Wagner's character. This knight, who does not live near the Grail Castle, wants Parzival for his son-in-law and teaches the young boy the skills of chivalry. The second inspiration is the hermit, King Amfortas' brother, who teaches Parzival about religious matters. The third is the Grail guard who confronts Parzival the second time he trespasses onto Grail territory. The fourth is the penitent who rebukes Parzival for bearing arms on a Good Friday. None of these men would be as old as Wagner made his Gurnemanz, but they all contributed to the character. Beardless and with his hair still brown, the cinematic Gurnemanz restores the youthfulness of the medieval characters. With that change follows his ability to bear arms, suggested by his leather outfit under the caftan. Black leather appears repeatedly on protective garments of knights. But his tattered blue caftan sets him apart from the other knights, identifying him as the hermit.

This Gurnemanz is young enough to hope for the impossible against his better judgment. He knows the prophesy that only a "fool made wise through compassion" can heal the king's wound. Nevertheless, he asks two approaching knights if the herb obtained by Gawan had brought any relief. Hearing the answer, he refers to himself as a fool, a *Tor*, for harboring such a hope. In Chrétien's and Wolfram's versions, Gawan does not set foot in the Grail Kingdom. As Parzival's alter ego, he belongs to King Arthur's court and its secular pursuits. However, he does possess medical skills, as shown in his treatment of Urjanz' wound. Wagner restricts the parallel exploits of Parzival and Gawan to this one attempt by the latter to help cure Amfortas. Just as Gawan's herb fails, so will Parsifal's visit soon after. Gawan does not appear on stage at any time.

The conversation is interrupted by Kundry's approach. Wagner resorted to teichoscopy, making the characters comment on what they are watching off-stage. Until now, one long camera take sufficed. But suddenly, the view cuts to the approach of a doll-sized Kundry on horseback riding through the air. This is how the characters see her, and their imagination allows the return of puppetry. One sees the puppet Kundry, not the actress, against a fairytale night sky with round stars and riding a carrousel horse manipulated from below. She is known to the group watching her. The squires describe her in terms of *die Wilde* (the wild woman) and *die wilde Reiterin* (the wild horsewoman). As her unusual mode of travel, so also these epithets prepare the audience for the arrival of an extraordinary outsider. German folklore abounds in stories about "wild people" often associated with witchcraft.[5] And the "wild horsewoman" evokes the Wild Chase, the horde of pagan gods and ghosts of the dead riding through the air at midnight.[6] Heine, for example, drew on these myths in *Atta Troll*. From the comments of the children, the audience cannot guess what the woman's role is. However, they use her name and wonder if she brings any important message. That establishes her as a messenger. The Grail Kingdom is inaccessible to ordinary people, according to the fairytale level of the narrative. Its center is a mysterious object with magical powers. It is therefore not so strange that Kundry too is endowed with mysterious characteristics. But she is obviously not welcomed as a member of the Grail society. This character was treated quite differently in the medieval sources. As the Ugly Damsel and Wolfram's Cundrie la surziere she wears both dress and emblem identifying her as belonging to the Grail society she serves. Cundrie is learned and familiar with courtly behavior. Among other activities she brings the weekly wafer that sustains the anchorite Sigune and the medications that cure Gawan of his injuries inflicted by the lion. Strangely enough, she does not attempt to help King Amfortas, knowing it is futile. Wagner modified her role of messenger, her striking appearance, and exotic origin for his Kundry. In addition, he borrowed Cunneware's laughter and Sigune's information about Parzival's identity. But these inspirations merely contributed to his Kundry. In his narrative she becomes a much more central figure with numerous additional characteristics.

When Kundry lands, the film deviates briefly from the stage instructions. She does not stagger into view looking wild and deranged. The actress emerges from water. One assumes it is the same lake where the king will bathe, seeking solace for his pain. Although only one lake is mentioned in the text, the mask landscape could provide two, namely the eye sockets filled with Wagner's tears. Since the king's bath takes place out of view, there is no need to present both bodies of water on the screen. Not only is water the chtonic element of origin, but the location also identifies the water as tears. The viewer may remember the image of a tear in the prelude. It appeared there as the reflection on a facet of the polyhedron. Now the motif returns as part of the mask landscape. It raises many questions to which the context does not yet grant an answer.

As Kundry floats to the rocky edge, a blond cloak surrounds her body. It looks like the same wrap that enveloped Gurnemanz in his sleep and, in *Hitler*, Harry Baer in his Heine pose. Climbing on land, Kundry frees herself from this cover, much as an insect emerging from its cocoon. While floating in the water she had been immobile, giving the impression of being drowned. "Beautiful as Ophelia," Syberberg comments in the book (72). Maybe so, but two other inspirations from Wagner's oeuvre also come to mind. First Senta after she threw herself into the sea to redeem the Flying Dutchman from his curse. Also Kundry is subject to a potentially everlasting curse, making her function as the Dutchman's and Ahasuerus' female counterpart. But is she also a redeemer like Senta? The other inspiration might be the Rhine maidens from *Rheingold* and the *Götterdämmerung*. On the evening before he died, Wagner had been reading about the water sprite in *Undine* by Friedrich de la Motte-Fouqué, played the mournful theme "Rhinegold, Rhinegold" from his own music drama, and said in bed before he fell asleep, "I feel loving toward them, these subservient creatures of the deep, with all their yearning."[7] *Der Fliegende Holländer* was the earliest of his works that Wagner chose for his canon in Bayreuth, and the *Götterdämmerung* the last one before *Parsifal*. The two associations would therefore again combine beginning and end, just as the Rhine maidens do within the *Ring* cycle itself. And another detail may not be coincidental. While photographs of the first Rhine maidens show flowers adorning their hair, Kundry also wears a wreath around her head.[8] However, having lost its roses, it has turned into a crown of thorns. Whoever Kundry may be, this "subservient creature of the deep" wears the attribute of a suffering Redeemer. In the prelude the Kundry puppet had been standing next to the Wagner doll stretched out on a crucifix, a crown of thorns lying near them. Now she shares the role and theme of the sufferer, as the music soon confirms. The shifting parallels and similarities give the impression of a fleeting identity revealing at any time one or several of her many facets.

The crown of thorns as Kundry's attribute invites to a digression. It serves as another reminder of Heinrich Heine. He claimed in *Deutschland: Ein Wintermärchen* to have worn more than one thorny wreath in his youth. Writing in exile about his homesickness, he confides: "I even longed for the places, for those Stations of the Cross, where I carried the cross of youth and my crowns of thorns" (660). A few lines further he modifies this homesickness so as to join the suffering "fools" of the film: "I believe one calls this foolish yearning 'love of fatherland.' I do not like to speak about it; it is basically only an illness. Being bashful, I always hide my wound before the public" (660). These lines contain several motifs central to *Parsifal* and Syberberg's work: Appropriation of imagery from Christ's Passion, *Heimweh* for an elusive paradise, Germany, foolishness (*Torheit*), and the wound. Heine's hidden wound and Heine as the wound are the most famous ones in German literary history. Hiding his feelings behind wit and mockery, he transgresses into blasphemy in another stanza of the same work: " In the reddish morning light [I saw at the roadside] the image of the man who was nailed to the cross. The sight of you fills me with sadness every time, my poor cousin, who wanted to redeem the world, you fool, you savior of humanity!" (635). With both Heine and Wagner resorting to identifications with Christ and other unorthodox allusions to him, and in view of their friendship in Paris, it comes as no surprise that Heine begins to emerge as more than a Wagner reference in the film. Already in the fourth part of *Hitler*, Heine and Wagner figured as two unnamed but complementary aspects of the German soul. If one may indulge in establishing equivalencies in the Wagner and Parsifal narratives, one realizes, of course, that all the characters inhabited Wagner's mind. But it seems that Wagner would claim most parallels with Amfortas. His detested rival Meyerbeer then moves close to Klingsor, and Heine comes to resemble Kundry. As a former Herodias she also shares a Jewish history with him. Yet, somehow, Wagner shares some qualities with all of them.

Reborn from the wet element and still wearing a crown of thorns, Kundry directs only a few words to Gurnemanz as she gives him a small flask of balm from Arabia. Considering the setting, this Arabia may be any part of Spain under Moorish rule as well as more distant lands where Arabic was spoken. Medical science in this culture had gained high esteem, which might reflect on the potency of her balm. But more important is the fact that Kundry can mysteriously procure aid from and interact with non-Christians viewed as enemies north of the Pyrenées. She moves between the worlds but does not appear to belong anywhere.

Remembering that Kundry shares her face with the sibyl and the mother in the prelude, the viewer soon realizes that this figure has now emerged from the (collective) unconscious. As Jung points out, the mother imago or archetype can assume many forms, but she functions most importantly as the soul image of a male subject.[9] She is the Anima or inner feminine counterpart to a man's persona or public mask. While this façade represents a consciously adopted ideal, the man's feminine hidden nature usually remains unidentified in the unconscious, containing the characteristics missing in the persona. But whose Anima is Kundry? One must assume that the portrait landscape points to Wagner himself. His death mask is a persona. Also Amfortas functions as the composer's acknowledged face. Already in 1859 Wagner described the Grail king as the "center and main subject" of the plot.[10] Amfortas' longing for release from his misery finds a correlate in Kundry's curse, from which she too yearns to be relieved. And just as Amfortas rules his community, so also Wagner addressed a public of like-minded adherents in his articles. They both function as centers and representatives of their respective communities. Within the fictional narrative, all the characters reside around, on, or in the head landscape. One might view it as a representative setting relevant to many Germans. Such a widened scope does not, however, prevent Kundry from functioning as an autonomous character who, within the plot, is fixated on the Grail society.

As if the mystery surrounding Kundry did not suffice, Syberberg adds more confusing detail to the environment. Before Kundry sinks to the ground in exhaustion, the background turns into a projection of a montage. Unrelated to the libretto, the gigantic door in the projection belongs to the Italian palace where Wagner jotted down some of his earliest thoughts on *Parsifal*. So the director informs the readers in the book to the film, attempting to connect the Wagner story with the plot (72). Imbedded in this background is a Clytaemnestra figure as Edith Clever had portrayed her on stage. The actress separates momentarily from her character as Kundry and becomes a motif in her own right. And of course, the murder of Clytaemnestra resulted in a curse on Orestes. But significantly, the affliction suffered by the royal Greek family was terminated by Iphigenia. In other words, through human intervention within the same family. Thus the *Oresteia* with its theme of guilt and redemption echoes faintly through an otherwise questionable device. And finally, it is possible that the projected door hints at the path called "door" in the Kabbalistic Labyrinth or Sefirotic Tree of Life (the Hebrew letter and word *daleth*).[11] That would define and locate the scene as a stage in a quest leading through numerous turns and paths.

A similar function may be the reason for the large window near the spot where Kundry collapses. The Sefirotic Tree also contains a path called "window," namely the Hebrew *he*. But more obvious is the link to Wagner's biography. The window is modeled on one in the room where Wagner died, and the water trickling down over it suggests perennial tears, *unendliche Tränen*, Syberberg explains. But he does not reveal whose tears they are. His own, perhaps? Or Kundry's? Wagner's? Cosima's tears mourning Wagner? Tears caused by Wagner? The circulating water works as a fountain, and its proximity to the lake of tears appears to join Kundry's contrition with Wagner's weeping. They are both trying to atone for some form of guilt. The base of the fountain is a rectangular basin of surprising darkness. It looks like an open grave. This was exactly the dimension of Wagner's tomb in *Hitler*, but neither the composer nor Hitler's ghost emerges from it this time. Since the surrealism of the background projection and the window fountain distract and confuse most viewers, one might question their incorporation. In their defense, however, one should point out that also Wagner's plot abounds in magic and strange psychological transformations. Furthermore, the incongruity of the cinematic additions finds its justification in the location, the landscape of the mind, where everything is possible.

So far the audience has not been aware of any vegetation in this landscape. True, the ground is still littered with dead leaves, but the only trees were part of the early background projections. That changes as the king arrives. The background is suddenly the lower part of a huge tree. What had previously looked like stones and rocky walls turns into gigantic roots of the Tree of Life. The leaf-strewn ground reveals again that either the tree is dead or fall has robbed it of its crown. As the attendants set down the stretcher carrying Amfortas, one cannot help thinking about the temperature in the lake where he wants to bathe. The medieval versions make the king seek the lake for the purpose of fishing. Wagner opted for an ablution. The viewer may wonder if the castle does not provide bathing facilities for a king. The ablution points toward an alchemical process, suggesting that the composer viewed the plot as a symbolic narrative. Actually, this episode is missing in the medieval sources.

The king's attendants are surprisingly young people. Although the four carrying the stretcher wear black leather breast plates over their white garments, the group looks too young to be arm-bearing knights. They are obviously squires. One may ask why not adults carry the heavy litter. The choice does not stem from insufficient funds to pay adult extras, as dozens of bearded monks will prove a bit later. Jung's theories may offer an explanation. In his discussion of the child archetype, Jung distinguishes between the unity and the plurality of its manifestation. The presence of many children, he observes, can suggest an incomplete synthesis of the personality, which is still in the "plural stage": "[A]n ego may be present, but it cannot experience its wholeness within the framework of its own personality, only within the community of the family, tribe, or nation; it is still in the stage of unconscious identification with the plurality of the group."[12] Not only does the observation fit Amfortas, it might also help identify this stage of the narrative as still playing partially in the unconscious, more precisely, the personal unconscious. For this undeveloped part of the personality Freud coined the term *Id*. It is ruled primarily by passions and instincts.[13] Thus Amfortas, who is far from being healed and whole (*heil*), surrounds himself with a retinue of children and young teenagers.

Two of the young attendants in the procession display the king's attributes by wearing his foot-long cloaks, one red, the other blue. This detail was added by Syberberg. Especially the magnificent royal blue cape attracts attention. The fabric is adorned with stars embroidered with gold. The inspiration for this work of art is a cloak made for Henry II (†1024), a king of Bavaria who later became emperor. The garment is cut as a semicircle with the pattern imitating the firmament above, complete with named constellations.[14] The wearer becomes the axis or spindle of the universe. The head of this person takes the place of the pole star. The thought was familiar to the Hermetists and Gnostics of antiquity, as Jung points out.[15] His discussion shows how closely it is connected with psychic facts. Quoting Hippolytus, he first identifies the "Original Man" with the father of the *perfectus* and with the *Papa* and "mummy," equating him with the microcosm in mortal man (213–14). This would correspond to Titurel in Wagner's narrative. Jung continues, "The Original Man in his *latent state* . . . is named *Aipolos*, . . . because he is the Pole that turns the Cosmos round" (216). Clearly, this status was intended for Amfortas, who succeeded Titurel on the throne. Due to his wound, however, he is no longer the "perfect" man. This mythical "explanation" obscures the fact that, while the real stars surrounding the celestial North Pole circle it slowly, the pole star also changes over time due to the precessional motion.[16] King Amfortas, the owner of the splendid symbol, is no longer fit to wear it. He no longer can, or should, function as the support and center of the firmament. But his successor has not appeared yet. The circular symbol of an otherworldly center was anticipated in the illustration of the book held by the dead Herzeleide. There the Grail sat in the center of King Arthur's round table. In analogy with the Hermetic adage "As above, so below," it appears that no brilliant star is currently marking the celestial North Pole, reflected in the injured king unable and reluctant to serve as the upholder of the inherited order. Instead of the royal cape he wraps his reclining body in a blond blanket. It had covered Gurnemanz during his sleep and the floating Kundry in the water. In contrast to them, Amfortas cannot emerge from this cocoon-like wrap due to his injury.

Despite his condition, Amfortas addresses his entourage with the authority of a king. Somewhat enigmatic is his reaction upon learning that Gawan had left the court: "Ohn' Urlaub?" (Without permission?). This may sound despotic to modern ears, but expresses also the king's fear of losing an esteemed supporter. Without a retinue, Gawan would be extremely vulnerable to Klingsor's magic. His departure without a proper farewell also indicates a breakdown of order, echoing Amfortas' own wish to escape his duties. Furthermore, it anticipates Parsifal's unceremonious exit and subsequent arrival in Klingsor's realm. The king forbids his men to follow Gawan's example, assuring them that he has resigned himself to await the fulfillment of the prophesy. And now, for the first time in Wagner's version, but for the second time in the film, one hears part of the prophesy, as the king repeats it to himself: "Durch Mitleid wissend, der reine Tor" (knowing through compassion, the pure fool), who will arrive to liberate the king from his suffering. Promising redemption, the prophesy creates hope. However, the king realizes the futility of hope, remarking, "Der reine Tor, mich dünkt ihn zu erkennen, dürft' ich den Tod ihn nennen" (The pure fool, I think I recognize him if I might call him Death). The idea that life is wrought with misery that only ends at death is generally viewed as a sign of Schopenhauer's influence on Wagner. The interpretation is justifiable enough, considering Wagner's familiarity with the philosopher's thoughts. But not until Syberberg's film version have Wagner interpreters drawn the conclusion of that philosophical outlook. If Amfortas is not freed from his misery until he dies, and death is identical with the pure fool, what does that make Parsifal?

No sooner does the king receive the flask of Kundry's balm than he proves that he, too, is a fool. Thanking Kundry, he assures her he will try it, if only as a sign of gratitude for her loyalty. Hope has been rekindled. Her response, "Was wird es helfen?" (What good will it do?) reveals a sudden insight that was not available to her when she procured the balm. It may bring relief for a while, she knows, but no cure.

As the king's procession continues toward the lake, the squires' attention returns to Kundry. Their remarks reveal suspicion and hostility. Only Gurnemanz' gentle rebuttals prevent an escalation that might have turned into physical aggression. Meanwhile, Kundry plays with the leaves on the ground. No longer merely part of the scenery, they assume the role of signifying attributes. The verbal aggression accompanies Kundry's act of covering herself with leaves, creating the semblance of counterpoint. One remembers the possible association of leaves, *Blätter*, with Wagner's journal, *Die Bayreuther Blätter*, and their frequent anti-Semitic comments. The boys' hostility towards the *Heidin*, (the pagan woman), finds a visual equivalent in the leaves falling on her. Wagner's wife recorded that he remarked about Kundry's appearance, "Everything about Kundry is costume—her ugliness, her beauty—all of it [is] a mask" (Sept. 2, 1881). Since a mask serves to change the appearance of the wearer, it follows that Kundry shares at least two characteristics with some insects known for their camouflage, namely butterflies. They undergo metamorphosis with each stage producing an apparently different animal. As the text reveals later, Kundry has undergone a comparable series of distinct existences, often under different names. And, if her appearance functions as a mask or camouflage, she resembles such butterflies as the European commas and the Oriental leaf butterflies. When resting, these insects look like a dead leaf. The protective look can even develop into mimicry. In that case a defenseless butterfly imitates the appearance of another poisonous species that predators leave alone. One wonders if Kundry covers herself with leaves in an attempt to be indistinguishable from Wagner's *Blätter*. Another German word for the plural of "leaves" or "leafage" is *Laub*. Via Hölderlin's use of *Laub*, Syberberg imbues his visual trope with an additional dimension. In the middle of Hölderlin's late poem "Der Kirchhof" (The Cemetery) occurs the phrase *Laub voll Trauer*, or "leaves full of mourning."[17] Since the director has frequently commented on his films as being works of mourning, and subsequently, art of mourning, the apparent echo from Hölderlin assumes significance. Leaves as images of grief continue to accompany the theme of melancholy, as they had already in *Hitler*. But as with the tear symbol, the leaves defy easy deciphering. One may guess at Syberberg's grief over present-day Germany, as expressed in *Die freudlose Gesellschaft*. Or his grief over Wagner for acting like Wagner. Temporally linking these two causes is the genocide occurring midway between them. Pointing in that direction was the earlier rumination over leaves from the uncertain Tree of Life that might relate to Buchenwald. The corroboration of this connection emerges from the semantic underpinning of the imagery. Again Hebrew offers the bridge. Brown's dictionary lists the equivalent of "leaf" or "leafage" as a three-letter noun consisting of *'ayin, lamed,* and *he*. Next to this entry stands another word made up of the same three letters, but with different meaning and pronunciation. Its definition reads "whole burnt offering." Transgressing language barriers again, one turns to Greek, where the burnt offering is rendered as *holocaust*. The biblical Hebrew word for Holocaust and leaves share, in other words, the same spelling. This contiguity adds the last contrapuntal variation on the piles of leaves littering the ground. Again, the theme of the Holocaust is part of the semantic and visual counterpoint, present but undetectible to many. Without knowing anything else about Kundry at this time, one discovers a connection between her and the Holocaust.

During this scene a visual detail added by Syberberg deserves mentioning. One of the squires remarks scornfully that Kundry's balm is probably a magic potion that will only bring destruction to their master (*Meister*). Her face expresses distress, but on hearing these words, she sticks out her tongue for a moment. That gesture could mean several things. Either she is mocking the squires silently, or she is acting like an imbecile or also someone lacking control over facial muscles. Most viewers will assume that she either does lack control or is faking it. Such pretense might accompany her self-protective play with leaves. But Syberberg probably had in mind such behavior by a goddess in Hindu mythology. This might serve as a reference to Wagner's extensive studies of Eastern religions and myths from all cultures. This knowledge is evidenced by a prose-sketch for a music drama he never composed, "Die Sieger" (The Victors). The Indian goddess recalled by Kundry's behavior is Kali, one of the manifestations of the Great Mother. Like Kundry, she too has several names and many different appearances (Grimal, 223). As Ma Kali, or Black Mother, she dances the cosmic dance. However, her dance supposedly takes place in the human soul at the level of the microcosm (Grimal, 224). In this role she looks terrifying, wild-eyed, with a "lolling tongue," clutching a human head, and wearing a necklace of other human heads. As Kali, she appears to dance on Siva, her husband, who lies outstretched as if dead. The destructive phase is followed by regrets during which she lets her tongue hang out. In the film, Kundry shares several of Kali's characteristics. As a sibyl she knows the future; as the mother she loves and protects little Parsifal; and as Kundry, she acts as a "wild," destructive, and then remorseful manifestation, with the tongue suggesting their identity. The decapitated heads, the peculiar necklace, and the dynamic between her as Kali and Amfortas as Siva return as motifs later. It is quite likely that Eastern myth, especially the Indian Great Mother, contributed to Wagner's Kundry. Needless to add, also this Great Mother inhabits the collective unconscious.

During most of the following scene, the camera dwells on Gurnemanz and the squires. Prompted by the aggressive remark that Kundry is a pagan and a sorcerer, Gurnemanz admits that she may indeed be cursed, living again to atone for guilt from an earlier existence. These lines reveal the belief in some sort of serial lives, conflicting with Church doctrine. As Prakriti in "Die Sieger" shows, the idea had been familiar to Wagner for a long time. Also the Dutchman was subject to a curse that deprived him of death. It does not appear that he had undergone reincarnation. His redemption comes only from the self-sacrificing death of another person, not through his own atonement for previous wrongdoing. In Prakriti's case, she must atone for wrongdoing in a previous life by overcoming her passion through renunciation and thus reach a higher level of human perfection. Her kind of redemption seems closer to Gurnemanz' words. However, his following reminiscences cause some confusion. One learns that Titurel, Amfortas' father, had first found Kundry in the forest close to where he was building the Grail Castle. She was "asleep, stiff, lifeless, like dead." And in that condition Gurnemanz himself had found her shortly after Amfortas had been injured. Since most readers already know that she is identical with the temptress who seduced Amfortas, it would appear that she slips in and out of her roles or manifestations in less time than usual life spans. She does not have to be reborn as a baby to start another existence. Of course, a psychological interpretation of the plot recognizes her as the mother imago or archetype from the realm of the collective unconscious. It would account for her variable periods of manifestation. Another source for this peculiarity may have been Indian myth where divine forces coexist, but manifest themselves as separate entities. A third source appears to be Jewish mysticism. The Kabbalah developed doctrines on transmigration of souls quite early.[18] Such ideas found literary expression during the twelfth century, and metempsychosic doctrine was known among Kabbalists and Cathars in southern France at the time when Wolfram von Eschenbach worked on his *Parzival*. He repeatedly refers to his immediate source as Kyot the Provençal, probably meaning Kyot from Provence in southern France. Although Wagner borrowed only select features from Wolfram's narrative, he was certainly aware of the heterodox atmosphere surrounding the earliest texts about Parzival. Of interest for our understanding of Kundry are especially some characteristics of Kabbalistic teachings on metempsychosis: Transmigration of souls was connected mainly with sexual transgression; the punishment consisted of repeated reincarnations (*gilgul*) in order to atone for acts committed previously and repair the damage; and, in *ibbur*, the soul of the departed might enter the soul of a living adult for a limited period of time to carry out specific commandments.[19] These points apply in Wagner's handling of Kundry's existences. He lets each reincarnation period end with a state resembling death, followed by an awakening to a new life. It is not yet clear what Kundry's guilt in her previous lives may have been, but her repeated reawakening from a death-like stupor supports Gurnemanz' unorthodox assumption of repeated lives. Even without such a mysterious personality, Kundry's ability to transcend borders as a messenger marks her as a liminal figure in the Grail society. It is worth noting that she wakes up to life within the Grail Kingdom and somehow relates to characters near the Grail. She is obviously drawn to them as much as to the Grail itself. Wagner downplays her previous existence as Herzeleide, although the music hints at their identity. And in Wolfram's version Herzeloyde was one of Amfortas' sisters.

As Gurnemanz' narrative continues, he reveals for a brief moment the sleeves of a red garment worn under his caftan. Up to this point, red attire distinguished the Grail kings in the film. The color may identify Gurnemanz as a member of the royal family. If so, then the color restores the family ties between Wolfram's hermit and his brother, the king. This relationship plays a prominent role in Wolfram's text, but is abandoned by Wagner. He made Gurnemanz one of Titurel's generation. He was supposed to be eighty years old in the first act and ninety in the third act.[20] Wagner also eliminated Frimutel, Amfortas' father, and changed the grandfather, Titurel, into Amfortas' father. In the puppet play of the prelude, the puppets of Gurnemanz and Titurel show two bearded, old men, faithfully modeled on photos of the singers in 1882. While their presence in the film pays tribute to Wagner's version, Syberberg also restores the family ties in Wolfram's text.

More important is Wagner's deviation from another, much debated detail in Wolfram's romance. In both texts, the Grail has been brought to earth from the heavens, but Wolfram does not lift the veil of mystery surrounding its origin. His hermit talks about the acquisition of the Grail on two occasions. In book 9 he tells Parzival it was left on earth by a "host" that returned high above the stars. This version, which purports to quote the sage and astronomer Flegetanis, is closer to the Hermetic *krater*.[21] Possibly, if the "host" should refer to the fallen angels in Genesis 6.2, Wolfram might share with Philo of Alexandria the assumption that at least some of these angels "soared upwards back to the place from whence they came."[22] The hermit's second version in book 16 corrects the earlier story, referring to these angels as exiled spirits who are condemned forever. This correction or negation, which occurs towards the end of the narrative, belongs to the pattern of transformations in the text, but it could also be an attempt to bring the work in compliance with the teachings of the Church. It refers unequivocally to the fallen and condemned angels who begot the giants on earth. The latter were "men of renown" (Gen 6.4). The Enochian literature, which informs Wolfram's description of the Ugly Damsel and her brother, includes some names of these "Watchers," e.g. Asael, Azazel, Baraquel, Gadriel, Kokabel, Samiel, and Sahriel.[23] It is intriguing that the first human guardian of the Grail, Titurel, and his son, Frimutel, have equally angelic-sounding names.[24] Are they descended from the Watchers and giants? Wagner avoids questions about these possible sources. Although he too lets the Grail derive from above, he ridicules Wolfram's tale about the Grail's origin. In a letter to Mathilde Wesendonck of May 30, 1859, he dismisses Wolfram's version in favor of the pre-Islamic holy stone of Kaa'ba in Mecca, which is a meteor.[25] Unable to use this or Wolfram's version, he appropriated a significant change from the French Christianizing adaptations of Chrétien's story: Wagner's Grail is the chalice used first by Jesus during the last supper, and subsequently by Joseph of Arimathea to catch the blood and water flowing from the spear wound in the Savior's side when he hung on the cross. To this he added the spear, or lance, of the Roman centurion Longinus, who inflicted the wound. This revered relic was supposedly acquired later by Charlemagne and was in the following centuries kept with the imperial crown jewels. By comparison, neither Wolfram's Grail nor his bleeding lance have any relation to Christ's Passion. By adopting the two religious symbols and increasing their importance in the narrative, Wagner threw a mantle of acceptability over an otherwise heterodox subject matter. He also treated it in a way reminiscent of medieval Christian legends: he added the fanciful twist of having both of the sacred relics first removed from earth and then delivered by descending angels to the pious Titurel. This mantle of Christianizing might have been necessary in a predominantly Catholic Bavaria that already had reason to distrust Wagner.

In keeping with the Christian symbols, Wagner also had to move the location of Amfortas' injury. Since Longinus' spear supposedly wounded Christ in the side, it had to inflict the same kind of laceration in the same location on Amfortas' body. This was, of course, intended to strengthen the similarity between the suffering king and the suffering Savior. One is therefore surprised to read in an earlier prose version that Longinus pierced Jesus in the thighs. Wagner made that statement in 1865 in a summary of the plot requested by King Ludwig.[26] There he also placed a wound in Amfortas' side.[27] But he still made the title hero heal the king by letting the spear touch his thighs. Obviously, the break with biblical tradition was intended to draw the monarch's attention to the probable location of both injuries. Of course the plot summary was not intended for the general public, of whom many would not be familiar with the details in the medieval versions of the Grail stories. Wolfram had let the king be wounded in the genitals. This may have been a mythically powerful form of incapacitation, but not suitable for Wagner's needs. As the letter to Mathilde Wesendonck proves, Wagner's early plans included a hint of two wounds: "With the spear wound and probably another one as well,—in his heart [!]—the poor and horribly suffering man knows no other desire than to die.[28] Although the final version kept only the wound in the side, the lower injury keeps festering under the cloak of invisibility.

Through such maneuvers, Wagner's Gurnemanz can tell the boys a story worthy of fairy tales and pious legends. But every once in a while a detail lifts the veil. One example is Gurnemanz' comment that those serving the Grail move "on paths that no sinner can find." Although not close enough to be a paraphrase, it evokes an echo of the Book of Baruch 3.20 and especially 3.31: "No one knows the ways or can find the paths to it," with the context referring to wisdom. This Apocryphal text is included in the Septuagint and the Vulgate, but has been excluded from the Protestant Bibles. Already Martin Luther separated it from the rest of his Bible translation. Few Protestants would therefore recognize the echo, whereas Catholics might. According to a pre-Vatican II missal, the passage occurs as a reading in the Catholic mass for Saturday of Easter week. This use of the text would thus hallow the borrowing. Besides, belonging to the rites of Easter week, Baruch's words seem appropriate in a drama with such emphasis on Good Friday. A glance at the context in the Baruch passage informs the reader that people of many countries and eras, including the giants, had perished because they did not walk the paths of wisdom and insight; instead they perished through their foolishness, *Torheit*. The exceptions were Israel and Jacob, God's servant. In other words, salvation depended on recognizing and choosing the paths leading to wisdom. Gurnemanz is talking about the paths leading to the Grail. Especially a fool, a *Tor*, made wise through compassion, must find these paths to heal Amfortas. This appears to establish a connection between wisdom and the Grail. If Wagner associated Baruch's wisdom with the wisdom tradition, however, the Catholic Church might have been alarmed. That tradition has repeatedly been at odds with both religious and secular authorities. Already at this point in our examination one must therefore wonder about the religious substance of the work. Pious, yes. Orthodox, no.

The long epic scene in which Gurnemanz teaches the squires about the past shifts the action to the verbal and musical narrative. Devoid of drama in the usual sense, it concentrates on Gurnemanz. While the boys settle in as listeners, he moves around occasionally, responding to their questions. At one point he stretches out his arms as if he too were crucified. The viewers already know most of his tales from the puppet play in the film's prelude. It seems, then, that not only has Syberberg retained the undramatic scene faithfully; he has even added to its epic nature by presenting the material twice. Here one recognizes the genre-shifting function of the *mise en abyme*. The small-scale mute puppet version anticipates an opera version with human actors and one real singer. Since the puppet play and the entire prelude also mirror the action of the following scenes, a pattern of visual music begins to emerge. The parts are variations of each other in what resembles the subject or basic melody and its inversion.

Other filmmakers might have chosen to insert flashbacks to enliven Gurnemanz' interrupted narratives. Resisting that cinematic possibility, Syberberg restricts his visual articulation to the scenery. On two occasions he changes the background, which is visible between huge roots. These projections reflect Gurnemanz' narrative literally. When he mentions the arrival of the angels at night, the background also displays a star-studded darkness. Defying realism, this night sky is an enlargement of Wagner's star-lined robe from the prelude. And when the topic moves on to the paths leading to the Grail Castle, the background lights up in shades of red showing the Grail Castle. The prelude had presented the interior of its hall and photos of other sanctuaries as ruins. Now the backdrop combines and varies the theme of sanctuaries. Dominating the composition is a walled castle on a hilltop. This motif is based on Christian Jank's sketch for a backdrop of Valhalla in *Rheingold*.[29] Although the abode of the gods lacks a sacral connotation, it helps return the composer's biography as a subject. On January 17, 1883 Cosima recorded in her diary Wagner's mixed reaction to a pamphlet he was reading. Its author was Nietzsche's brother-in-law, Dr. Bernhard Förster. This pamphlet, *Parsifal-Nachklänge* (Echoes of *Parsifal*), had just been published in Leipzig. In it the author observed that the fortress of Valhalla had been transformed into the Grail Temple. At least this remark earned Wagner's approval. But it was not good enough for Syberberg. He revised the design by adding other buildings to the surrounding hillside. Most conspicuous among them are a pyramid, a Greek temple, and a mosque with cupola and minarets. The mosque makes one think of the most famous ones, the Hagia Sophia and the Dome of the Rock. Clearly, when Gurnemanz mentions the paths to the sanctuary, its exterior should include a spiritual component as well. This also reflects the multi-cultural nature of the Grail story. Perhaps equally important is the semantic implication of the cupola. One remembers that in the fourth section of *Hitler*, the cupola joined a cluster of words relating to copulation, be it linguistically or associatively. In *Parsifal*, interior and exterior views of cupolas occur repeatedly, beginning in the prelude. And now, right after the backdrop lights up with fortress and sanctuaries, Gurnemanz relates how Klingsor castrated himself, thus confirming the sexual nimbus of the cupola. The two motifs appear clustered, as one expects it in a contrapuntal composition. Syberberg did publish some ruminations on the phallic and vaginal associations of cupola and Grail, but only in French.[30] As a consequence, German reviewers are largely unaware of them. Curiously enough, he does not mention the spear in this context.

At long last Gurnemanz' narrative reaches the prophesy, which the audience now hears in its entirety for the first time: "Durch Mitleid wissend, der reine Tor, harre sein', den ich erkor" (Wise through compassion, the pure fool, wait for him whom I chose). Actually, *wissend* does not mean "wise" but "knowing," a substitution probably guided by the need for a two-syllable word. In the medieval source, similar words appeared miraculously and briefly on the Grail. Wagner blurred the miracle by making the prophesy appear in a dream-like vision, *ein heilig Traumgesicht*, using the archaic meaning of *Gesicht*.

The pages' prayer-like repetition of the prophesy marks the transition from this long scene to the next. It is being interrupted by startling off-stage shouting and commotion provoked by Parsifal's shooting of the swan. In Wagner's staging, the bird fluttered across the stage, as Syberberg's version recreates in the puppet play.[31] The abrupt switch in events creates a dramatic moment. The pious pose of Gurnemanz and the boys accompanying the repeated prophesy transforms the words into a prayer which is being fulfilled. Surely Amfortas must have prayed for relief a number of times, but one does not know how and in what frame of mind. But when pure-hearted Gurnemanz and his young charges pray for him, their ardent wish appears to conjure up the hoped-for redeemer. This power of prayer becomes plausible even from a secular point of view when one considers the event a psychological development. With the activity taking place in Wagner's head, all the characters are forces of one person's mind. The healthy and constructive forces now rally to overcome the paralyzing debility of other areas. The fact that the healing energy cannot accomplish the task yet shows that other steps are needed to prepare the decisive action. The newcomer may be the right fool, but his thrill of killing for sport already indicates a lack of compassion.

Reflecting the excitement over the killed swan, the camera abandons the long takes in favor of a couple of short ones. It cuts abruptly to Kundry, who is still playing with dead leaves at the edge of a "creek," really a flow of white vapor. In gradually intensifying red light that possibly echoes the bloodshed involving the swan, she crawls away. In view of the periodic references to Wolfram von Eschenbach, one may wonder if the juxtaposition of creek and leaves entails a hidden pun on Wolfram's name. If the leaves hail from the Tree of Life, an ashtree, they would indicate the proximity of such a tree, an *Esche*. The German word for "brook" or "creek" is *Bach*. A creek surrounded by ashtrees would be an *Eschenbach*, which is one reading of the poet's name. Now the image of creek and leaves coincides with the uproar over the shooting. Early in Wolfram's narrative, the boy Parzival also kills a bird. Inspired by this detail, Wagner adapted it for Parsifal's entry in Grail territory, changing the trespassing into a crime. It is not an obvious quotation, but more than a reminiscence, worthy of an equally subtle evocation of the medieval poet and his text. The quasi-musical antecedent of the killing appears earlier in the prelude when the camera pans from the dead swan directly to the arrow landing in the leaves. In retrospect one recognizes a reference to Wolfram's text in that detail as well.

At this point the camera cuts to a knight who reports the incident to Gurnemanz. Finally, the title hero makes his entry through a passage in the boulders. The ground is suddenly covered in billowing snow-like vapor. One remembers the function of coldness, ice, and snow in Syberberg's grid of associations. As a carrier of meaning this visual symbol might refer to Wagner's chilling statements, to Hitlerism, and to its legacy in current German society. Parsifal's arrival triggers a similar, visible coldness that may relate him to that legacy. Later on this imagery assumes additional nuances. And of course, one should not forget the prominence of white in the sequence of alchemical transmutation. Besides, the "snow" could also function as another link to Wolfram's Parzival. His arrival is preceded by acute coldness caused by the planet Saturn. This coldness affects King Amfortas by intensifying his pain. The same phenomenon happens five years later when Parzival's second visit at the Grail Castle again coincides with coldness and Saturn's return from one of its "little loops" (Hoyle, 75). Syberberg may even be trying to establish a semantic link between Saturn and the young actor's name, Michael Kutter. This name resembles the English noun *cutter*, which has been adopted into German as a loan word for a film lab technician who edits strips of film. Many Germans would pronounce this loan word as the name Kutter. The activity of cutting gains a mythic dimension in connection with the planetary deity Saturn. First inflicting and later suffering the "unkind cut," Saturn is in Greek Cronos, who in popular transmission merges with Chronos, or Time. Still in our days, on New Year's Eve, old Father Time appears with his attribute, a sickle. This figure went into folklore in his skeletal reduction as the Grim Reaper. His attribute was modified to the related scythe. With this tool the Grim Reaper would harvest the dying. Thus Saturn/Cronos/Chronos has long been associated with a cutting activity, both as it relates to a power-toppling emasculation and to the image of Death. Both of these associations are relevant to the plot. Klingsor and Amfortas both suffer from sexual mutilation (although Wagner veiled the parallel), and Amfortas thinks the prophesy promises liberation only through death. Perhaps, then, his redeemer will not only replace him on the throne, but also usher in the end of an era, or at least Amfortas' demise.

The association of the name with Cronos/Time/Grim Reaper includes the other ancient deities Thoth and Hermes/Mercury. Especially the latter is known for his function as guide of souls to the world of the dead. With the caduceus as his attribute, Hermes as guide also translates as "conductor" and *Führer*. One remembers the questions prompted by Syberberg's title of the film: Wagner a Parsifal? And what about the Hitler ghost arising from Wagner's grave? The caduceus also returns Celan's "Todesfuge" to the cluster of literary "correspondences," where the officer holding an "iron" in his hand is about to shoot his prisoners. These associations grow out of the similarity between *Kutter* and *cutter*. But one can also find other German meanings of *Kutter* that endow the name with pertinent significance. Grimm's dictionary lists four entries for the noun *Kutter*. The first one gives the meaning "vessel with a narrow neck." Whether imagined as a jug or an amphora, the *vessel* points to two areas of significance in our context. The first hails from the Kabbalah. A central event in Jewish mysticism is known as "the breaking of the vessels" (Scholem, *Kabbalah*, 135–40). It necessitates human intervention in the restoration process. This task describes Parsifal and his mission. The other application for a "vessel with a narrow neck" can be found in alchemy. Many of the procedures in an alchemist's laboratory would take place in containers of various materials and shapes. This meaning of the name identifies Kutter as the living vessel in which or whom the transformation occurs. Actually, this Parsifal is not only the vessel, but also its content. Another entry under the noun *Kutter* is a Swabian dialect word for "trash" or "garbage." At first glance this looks like a totally irrelevant, or at least inappropriate, association. After all, the hero fulfills all hopes miraculously in the end. But alchemy suggests that the director selected his actor in part due to his name. As Parsifal he represents the raw material that must be transmuted to its purest form. The designations for this stone, *lapis*, or *prima materia*, span a long list of terms, ranging from the most despicable substances for the early stages to the sublime and semi-divine for its most accomplished forms. The concept of garbage would not even be the basest element in this imagery. For the despised forms of the potentially precious material one finds, for example, children's urine, loose stool, and muck, according to Herbert Silberer.[32] It is vile and worthless and thrown on the dung pile: "It can be had for the asking and can be found anywhere, even in the most loathsome filth," Jung claims (*Psych. and Alch.*, 313, 358). Both Silberer and Jung maintain repeatedly that the arcane language of alchemy really describes the characteristics and workings of the human personality, predating modern psychology by hundreds, if not thousands, of years. The center of its concern, the gold-making endeavor, outlines mechanisms and stages in the development of the psyche. The potential for human perfection, respectively the healing force within a troubled mind, must be cultivated and brought through many processes before it attains its potential or heals the affliction. Thus the young boy appearing in the first act incorporates one important quality of the title hero, a significant name, but he is not yet ready to be the redeemer of the prophesy.

Also the "snow" surrounding Parsifal on his entry would conform to the alchemical subtext. Red and white signify stages in alchemical transmutation. The film joins the surprise of white with an equally unexpected red sky. Again, this background is only visible above the boulders. An unnaturally red band of sky is punctuated by a strange stone outcropping that had not been visible before. As difficult to recognize as the crucifix in Friedrich's painting, it represents the monument of an erect penis. Not too subtly, this attribute accompanies Parsifal on his arrival, underscoring the Parsi-phallic qualities of the title hero. He brings to the action the libidinal élan, in Jung's and the later Freud's broader sense, which Amfortas and Klingsor are lacking due to their mutilation. Syberberg had hinted at this in his comments on cupolas, most obviously in the included sketch by Heinrich Zille, "The Rising Sun."[33] The drawing shows women with lifted skirts welcoming a solar phallus rising over the horizon. Several ramifications of the phallus spring to mind. It appears to be modeled on the ancient monuments on the Greek island of Delos. A whole series of such large sculptures once adorned a walk in the temple precinct dedicated to the Hyperborean Apollo. This was considered one of the holiest shrines in the ancient world, where the deity supposedly became incarnate at certain times, probably as at Stonehenge every nineteen years.[34] This provenance of Parsifal's attribute links Mediterranean antiquity with the Celtic world, as behooves a hero at home in Arthurian literature. More importantly, it establishes a connection between the hero and the sun god, who, as the Hyperborean Apollo, is identified with the Child Horus.[35] This one can also recognize early in book 3 of Wolfram's version. In Delphi, at another famous Apollo shrine, one finds the upright stone known as the "navel of the world," the Omphalos. It is generally seen as a crude equivalent of the Delos sculptures. Not surprisingly, its name is often spelled with a double *l*. As a solar god, Apollo represented a complex aggregate of divine powers. Only at a late point did he become the god of moderation and such admonitions as "Know thyself." Through Apollo's attribute the film reintroduces the ancient inspirations visible in Parsifal's development into the wise Guardian of the Grail. However, equally powerful is another association provoked by the same image and the sun god, namely the old sun sign called swastika. The picture of the swirling sun with four broken rays does not only function as a correspondence to the phallic monument. The twentieth century also saw it revived as a prime political and ideological symbol. Associatively inseparable from the Third Reich, it eclipses all other sun images by its notoriety. Due to this power, any sun sign evokes it through association. Through such correspondences, Parsifal appears endowed with strength and virility, and although the swastika is absent, also with this symbol tainted by history. Thus the title hero seems related to a problematic solar imagery just as the Wagner narrative to withered *Blätter*. Their shared ties to the brown past might be compared to notes shared by related keys.

As Parsifal enters through the passage in the rocks, a crowd of squires and knights gathers around him. One glimpses Kundry on the periphery. For a moment she had been sitting in the "melancholy pose," resting her elbow on a knee, with the hand supporting her chin. One of the squires had taken the same position while listening to Gurnemanz. Most Germans relate it to the fallen angel in Dürer's *Melencolia I*. Thus this position can serve as a correlate to the prismatic stone in the same picture: They both express melancholy, the subject of the composition. The periodic return of these correspondences confirms the quasi-musical handling of the visual component. In *Die freudlose Gesellschaft* one encounters its textual antecedent in a strongly altered variant: as jubilation. The book quotes from Walther von der Vogelweide's poem "Ich hân mîn lêhen" (I have my fief, 275). Absent, and therefore practically unidentifiable in the interplay of counterpoints, is one of Walther's most famous poems, "Ich sâz ûf eime steine" (I sat on a stone), in which he describes his melancholy pose and frame of mind, musing on the political situation of his time. Since Walther von der Vogelweide figures along with Wolfram von Eschenbach as a character in Wagner's *Tannhäuser*, the pose also allows their and the composer's names to reverberate ever so faintly. Also worth noting is that melancholy, and thus the "melancholy pose," equates the stage of *nigredo* in the alchemical process of transmutation.[36]

Kundry abandons her melancholy pose as the crowd surrounds Parsifal. The young actor appears now for the third time, the first being the "shining knights" episode and the second the conclusion of the prelude when he left his female alter ego. He still wears the brown tunic and bow, but has also acquired a white horse with red reins. Contrary to expectation, he does not ride into view, but walks, leading his horse by the reins. The visual arrangement of the title hero with a white horse at his side being surrounded by strangers is reminiscent of a scene in Josef von Sternberg's *Scarlet Empress*. There the title heroine, Catherine II, played by Marlene Dietrich, is also holding her white horse while a crowd is closing in. Since Syberberg has been "quoting" from numerous movies in his earlier works, this reference should not surprise. Sternberg and Syberberg share a similar aesthetic program. And just as Sternberg made a series of movies starring Dietrich, beginning with *The Blue Angel*, so Syberberg and Edith Clever, his Kundry, also collaborated on a series of films, beginning with *Parsifal*. The environment in the *Scarlet Empress* is wildly expressionistic, perhaps inspiring Syberberg to abandon realism in *Parsifal*. One is even tempted to see a related use of names. Dietrich's character is renamed Catherine in her new Russian homeland.[37] The name contains the Greek word for "pure," as one also recognizes it in "catharsis" and "Cathar." As the "pure one," she parallels Parsifal, the pure fool. Karin Krick, who plays the female manifestation of Parsifal, has not emerged yet, but her first name, Karin, is a variant of Catherine. It may also inform the scene.

And then there is the white horse with red reins echoing the white snow and red sky. It recalls the Tarot card showing Horus on a white horse. This connotation might help in locating the action in the Sefirotic Tree or Labyrinth, where it denotes a path leading to Yesod. In Revelation 6.2–3, one of the four horsemen heralding the end of the world rides a white mount. This association would strengthen the notion of another imminent *Götterdämmerung*. Also adding to that idea is another passage in Revelation 19. 11–13 in which the Word of God appears on a white horse. This parallel underscores the Christ-like qualities of the title hero later on. But the animal triggers several other associations as well. For example, Fritz Lang's Siegfried rode a white horse in the first part of his *Nibelungen* of 1924. In addition to the alchemical color combination, the animal allows Wagner's work to reenter the narrative. Brünnhilde's mount, Grane, appears in *Walküre* and again in *Götterdämmerung* when she gives it to Siegfried in the prologue. Later, as she prepares to ride it into the funeral pyre, Brünnhilde gazes on the dead Siegfried and mourns the man who was pure like the sun. The presence of the horse suggests that the luminously pure, innocent, and stupid Siegfried has been resurrected as the pure and foolish Parsifal.

The hero is at first portrayed by a young photographer and amateur actor named Michael Kutter. Syberberg refers repeatedly to his two adult Parsifals as "lay people" *(Laien)*, as if suggesting that other professionals of his ensemble belonged to an order of initiates. It seems the director wanted the real-life status of non-actors to echo the predicament of Parsifal, who remained an outsider until becoming "wise through compassion." Since both Parsifal and the squires wear knee-length tunics, there is little in their appearance to identify the newcomer as different, except that Parsifal's clothing is brown. His tunic is closer to the Bayreuth tradition than the medieval sources. Its unisex cut conceals a slender but muscular body, while revealing the strong legs worthy of an avid bicyclist or mountain climber. Parsifal's brown wig conforms to Wolfram's description of his hero. Overall, the first impression of the young man makes it look as if the Parsifal statue by Zumbusch had come alive. Caspar Clemens Zumbusch created marble statues of all major characters in Wagner's operas for King Ludwig. The king in turn gave Wagner copies or adaptations of them to adorn his home. Syberberg introduces the recreation of one of these Parsifal statues later in the film.[38] However, on closer inspection one wonders if the Führer would have approved of Syberberg's Parsifal. To be sure, Kutter is as handsome as the role demands. But his features do not conform to the "Nordic" ideal of the Nazi eugenics program promoting the blond and blue-eyed "Aryans." Too many people, both past and present, have wanted to see in Parsifal the politically ideal redeemer. Hitler's admiration became the strongest indictment of the work resulting in, e.g., Gutman's statement: "On the darkest level,—and one easily accessible to many of these disciples [i.e. subscribers to the *Bayreuther Blätter*]—*Parsifal* is an allegory of the Aryan's fall and redemption" (427). One assumes, then, that the redeemer must be a fellow "Aryan" and not a Galilean at home in the Bible. Contrary to such expectations, Syberberg's actor displays dark eyes and pronounced cheek bones and, when not wearing the wig, black, straight hair. He could easily portray more exotic roles, such as a Gypsy or a real-life Parsi. A digression on these associations may be in order here.

At one time numerous, the Parsis, or Parsees, are followers of Zoroaster (Zarathustra). Wagner was familiar with their faith, as he refers to them twice in his "Religion and Art" of 1880. When Islam displaced the old religion in their Persian homeland, part of which was known as Aria or Areia in Hellenistic times, many of them fled to India.[39] Most of their descendants still live there and practice their religion.[40] They are known for their silent towers of the dead and emphasis on purification. The Gypsies, on the other hand, moved in the opposite direction a few hundred years later, leaving the Punjab region in the Indus valley. Many settled in Persia for several hundred years until new, probably religious, reasons again triggered a mass exodus. It brought some of them all the way to Europe around 1400.[41] Several details are of interest here: the claim made by some gypsiologists that the Sigynnes, an Oriental people that used to inhabit Iran, are identical with the Gypsies; furthermore, that Gypsy tradition contains Zoroastrian elements, and finally, that the Prakrit dialect of Sanskrit is almost identical to the dialect of the Gypsies.[42] Sanskrit and Gypsy language belong to the Indo-Iranian branch of the Indo-European family of languages. Another word for this branch is Indo-Aryan.[43] In other words, the Gypsy language, Romani, is Indo-Aryan. Usually referred to as Sinti or Roma, the Gypsies might, then, have stronger claims to Aryan roots than many Europeans, at least through their language. That leads us back to the slippery term "Aryan." In Wagner's days, the word began to change from a linguistic term to a racial concept. The Nazis wanted to be, or at least promote, the purest "Aryans" of all. They persecuted the Gypsies as ruthlessly as Jews and other unwanted minorities. Also entering the field of associations is Nietzsche, whose break with Wagner occurred during the work on *Parsifal*. His *Also spake Zarathustra* takes its inspiration from the same roots that Gypsies claim for their traditions.

This digression was prompted by the appearance of Syberberg's Parsifal. Knowing the director's penchant for contrapuntal composition, one may assume a quasi-polyphonic treatment of the title hero. To the Christianizing interpretation he adds, e.g., the Wagner narrative, heterodox elements from Wolfram's story, and psychological touches. And one wonders what elements might serve as a counterpoint to a Wagner heralding Hitler. One might suggest a Jew, a Parsi, or a Gypsy, or at least someone incompatible with the Nazi ideal. Although Syberberg does not divulge much information about his Parsifal actor, one suspects that some personal qualities secretly inform the character. Supposedly a Swiss, Kutter as Parsifal would be a non-German redeemer of the stricken Amfortas. The help would come from abroad, not from within Germany. As a professional photographer, he would work with light and darkness, sharing the medium with Syberberg who also started as an amateur photographer. But nothing else is revealed about him. The only visible hint of counterpoint is the discrepancy in appearance between the handsome young man and the Nazi ideal "Aryan."

This Parsifal looks confident as he approaches, leading his horse. As Gurnemanz begins to cross-examine him, his first answer still expresses confidence: *Gewiss*, certainly, he is the one who felled the swan. But as Gurnemanz laments its death, the young boy's cockiness melts into contrition and, one assumes, compassion for the animal he killed so thoughtlessly. Among the pages and squires surrounding the swan one notices the blond boy next to Parsifal. He resembles the little blue-eyed Parsifal from the prelude. This is how many would have expected the hero to look. The dead bird is eventually covered with a black cloth and carried away on a litter. When the cloth slides off momentarily, one discovers that the bird has been transformed into a porcelain swan. Suffering and grief have been converted into art, *Trauerkunst*. Needless to say, the sculpture evokes the swan in *Lohengrin*, the heraldic use of the swan motif at King Ludwig's court, and the birds the king gave to Wagner for his pond in the garden. The transformation is, of course, Syberberg's addition.

The inner change in Parsifal progresses into confusion and humility when he cannot answer five consecutive questions about himself. He cannot even give his name. Each answer contains a negated form of to know, *wissen*. The first of these displays an unusual choice of words. Responding to how he could commit such guilt, *Schuld*, Parsifal responds that he did not know *it*, "Ich wusste sie nicht." One would have expected a different verb, *kennen*, or a that-clause instead of the pronoun object. This draws the attention to the verb. A participle of it, *wissend*, occurs in the prophesy, "Durch Mitleid wissend." The motif of knowledge or wisdom and its opposite or negated form are making a clustered appearance as if in counterpoint. A variation soon follows when Gurnemanz comments that the only one he knows who is equally stupid, *dumm*, is Kundry.

Increasingly insecure, Parsifal's eyes search helplessly for answers around him. For a brief moment they gaze directly into the camera. But, of course, no help comes from that lens, that is, the viewers. The reflection of light in his eyes makes them glitter in a way seen at least once before in Syberberg's films. Towards the end of *Karl May* an enthusiastic young Hitler with equally shiny eyes leaves the men's hostel to attend May's final lecture. The light reflected in eyes relates to the reflection and refraction of light in the Kabbalistic and Gnostic emanation stories. But unlike the golden sculpture of Christ on the crucifix in Friedrich's painting, the light gleaming in Hitler's eyes would be transmitted by an Anti-Christ.

Not knowing his name, Parsifal displays sufficient ignorance about himself to qualify as a *Tor*. Still in the same interrogation another question about his bow could easily have resulted in a contradiction. Wagner's hero tells Gurnemanz that he himself had fashioned the weapon. Syberberg, however, equips his character with an exquisitely made bow with the soft curves resembling the contours of a viola d'amore or violin. It will soon assume symbolic significance in the film. Obviously, this is not Parsifal's self-made weapon, but the one his mother gave him. The boy had grabbed it while his attention was captivated by the approaching knights. Thus he may think of it as his own old bow. The spectator knows better. It is the gift from his mother. On the semantic level the bow, *Bogen*, refers both to the stringed weapon and to the arrow-shaped stringed staff playing on a stringed instrument. The historical relationship between the two parts of the weapon and those of the viola or violin are reinforced visibly through the contour of Parsifal's bow. Being his attribute, the bow had accompanied him since the departure from his mother. In this scene he throws it away along with the arrows.

Although Parsifal does not remember that Herzeleide had given him the bow, he does remember her name. The bow and her name are mentioned in quick succession, strengthening the connection between them. By introducing Herzeleide's name, Wagner prepared the ground for Kundry's recognition of the intruder. Whether or not he intended Gurnemanz to recognize him remains unclear. Therefore the next question posed by Gurnemanz has been viewed as a sign of racism: "But you yourself look noble [*adelig*] and of high birth; why did not your mother let you be trained in better weapons?" Ignoring Wagner's pun involving noble (*adelig*) and the eagle (*Adler*) mentioned in the preceding line, critics have interpreted the boy's noble appearance as an expression of Wagner's racial bias. Gutman, for example, claims: "Not by accident did Gurnemanz almost immediately remark upon Parsifal's noble, highborn appearance. He knew what signs to read. Racial heredity and strict breeding, not natural selection, formed the new mechanism of salvation. Wagnerian eugenics had come into being"(423). Such ideological readings abound in the Wagner literature, encouraged by the composer's own essays in the *Bayreuther Blätter*.[44] They all operate with such expressions as "Aryan redemption." For this scene, the notion may or may not apply depending on whether or not Gurnemanz recognizes Herzeleide's name. In Wolfram's version, Parzival tells the hermit who his father is, and this enables the recognition of the "dear sister's son," (228). Syberberg strengthens the likelihood of such a recognition by making Gurnemanz wear the royal color on his almost hidden clothing. Thus he restores the family ties from Wolfram's text, hints at Wolfram as co-author, defuses the racial interpretation, and manages to infuriate both pro- and anti-Wagnerian ideologues.

Having heard Parsifal mention Herzeleide, Kundry joins the exchange by answering Gurnemanz' question. She concludes by referring to both mother and son as fools. Obviously, she knows surprisingly much about them, but nobody asks how she acquired this knowledge, *Wissen*. For the first time in Wagner's text she laughs mockingly. The film introduced Kundry as a puppet twice in the prelude, but at that time the viewer could not determine if she was laughing or crying. But her laughter now appears to recur in a series of variations, the most changed version presenting her crying.

Parsifal is not at all offended by being called a fool. He listens to her enraptured. Subsequently he continues by relating the encounter with the men in shining armor, the party of *glänzende Männer*, who lured him into running away. But new and surprising is the mention of giants. Parsifal tells how the bow helped him protect himself against big men, *große Männer*, while Kundry confirms his narrative by referring to his attackers as giants, *Riesen*. A spectator may assume that grown, armed, and hostile strangers would look like giants to a boy, or that he does not know the word. But it is Kundry who uses the term. Wagner may again place the action in a mythic past when giants roamed the earth. He had already introduced giants in the *Ring*, but finding them in the medieval sources, he did not invent them. However, considering how much he deviates from Wolfram's text, one is still surprised that he reintroduces the giants. After all, Wolfram's angels who brought the Grail were the fallen angels from Genesis 6.2 who later begot the giants. Wagner's angels bring the chalice and the spear after Christ's Passion. No giants fit into that frame of reference. Apparently, Wagner's giants are intended to recall the mystical literature drawing on the Book of Enoch and on the Book of Baruch. But the fact that they are now also evil, *böse*, labels them as adversaries and establishes a link to the giant transformed into a dragon that Siegfried overcame.

As Parsifal begins to ponder the difference between good and evil, the dialogue again brings up his mother. Kundry's comment that she had seen Herzeleide die results in Parsifal's sudden aggression. This episode contains several silent but visual deviations from Wagner's stage instructions. As the text requires, Parsifal first attacks Kundry with a choke hold while Gurnemanz intervenes and calms him down. However, the gradual change in Parsifal's reaction results primarily from Kundry's hold on him. She finally presses his head against her as if to console him in a motherly embrace. Or is it an embrace with sexual overtones? The gesture revives memories of Herzeleide's hug in the prelude and prefigures the temptation scene in act 2. Syberberg develops the motif of the kiss/embrace into a series of contrapuntal variations.

Another change concerns the drinking horn with which Kundry is supposed to fetch water for Parsifal. She brings the water in her cupped hands. And instead of giving him to drink, she gently strokes his hands and face with her wet hands, clearly caressing him. Gurnemanz praises her for overcoming evil with kindness. Her action, however, leaves enough ambiguity to justify her retort, "Nie tu' ich Gutes," (I never do good deeds). In Wagner's text her response looks like a meaningless contradiction. In the film one is not so sure of her motive.

A third detail is the move away from the rocky surroundings towards an otherwise empty, but conspicuously red background. Perhaps suggesting passion and violence, it changes a few minutes later to black. Thus Parsifal's grip, weakness, embrace, and wet massage are all seen against black. As observed before, the alchemical color change denotes a transformation. The stage of blackness, *nigredo*, breaks down the substance to be transmuted. Often depicted as death and decomposition, it is a necessary phase. Shattered by the news of his mother's death, Parsifal engages in a physical altercation followed by a *coniunctio*-like exchange, experiences a numbness resembling paralysis, suffers a physical collapse, and undergoes a wet treatment similar to a bath. In brief, the scene demonstrates a sequence of alchemical processes. The result is a change preparing Parsifal to be taken to the Grail Castle. Wagner's text only hints at this action, relying on the music to convey its transforming nature. Syberberg translates the process of change into visual alchemical steps.

Separating the action in the foreground from the black background is a surrealistic, large wooden frame. It supports an oversized bow and arrow. Most of the time only a section of the feathered arrow and the string are visible. The red feather identifies it as representing part of Parsifal's equipment that he had tossed away in the swan scene. Kundry had picked up one of these arrows and was holding it when Parsifal attacked her. Both the dimension of the arrow-and-string combination and the artificiality of its presentation alert the viewer to a change in its function. This change illustrates the invisible transformation in Parsifal: only a portion of his old nature is left. But faithful to medieval tradition, Syberberg includes more than one meaning of a symbol. Besides, the musical nature of the images lets several possibilities be perceived simultaneously. The most obvious symbolic function hails from Wolfram's *Parzival*. While describing the glimpse Parzival catches of Titurel after the Grail ceremony in book 5, the narrator intrudes into his story, informing the reader or audience that he is withholding some explanations for later. He begins his digression with "I shall give you the bowstring without the bow. This bowstring is a figure of speech." And true enough, Syberberg does not emphasize the bow either, only the part of the arrow that touches the drawn string. Since Wolfram couches the stanza about his famous metaphor in unclear language, numerous studies have tried to elucidate its meaning. Clear is only that the string represents the story, that it must be drawn to launch the arrow, and that the narrator does not shoot it yet because his message would bore some and be lost on many.[45] But it deserves mentioning that bow metaphors were common in Wolfram's days. Numerous religious treatises equated the string and the bow with the New and the Old Testament, which must function together to activate the human arrow.[46] For now, Wolfram deemphasizes the bow, which would have some connection to Titurel and, so his literate audience would conclude, also to the Hebrew part of the Bible. Instead he presents the string as his story. It would be associated with the New Testament. In that part of the Bible Christ figures prominently. In view of the "partial" treatment of the bow image one is also tempted to think of the teachings about the three eras formulated by Joachim de Fiori (ca. 1130–1202). His widespread thoughts about the Trinity were condemned by the Church in 1215. Joachim divided human history into three ages, the first being that of the Father (Old Testament), the second that of the Son (New Testament), and the third that of the Holy Spirit. Joachim had prophesied the beginning of this eschatological, third kingdom, in German *Reich*, to start with the 42nd generation after Christ's birth, ca. 1260, preceded in the 41st generation by the advent of the Anti-Christ.[47] And this figure can be found in Revelation at the end of the New Testament. It would appear, then, that the symbol on the wooden frame does not only serve to recall Wolfram's text, but also the spiritual echoes reverberating in his metaphor. Another "meaning" of Syberberg's symbol reveals itself in the shape of the bow fragment. Its contour echoes that of a violin bringing to mind the historical relationship between the weapon and the instrument. The bow of the instrument developed from the hunting bow, being originally just a curved stick with a string, or a *Sehne* in German.[48] It would resemble the self-made weapon that the child used in the prelude. The Latin word for the string, *fides*, also applies to the earliest form of the string instrument. *Fides* has, however, several other meanings, e.g. "integrity," "loyalty" (*Treue*), "confidence," and "faith." Especially *fides* as "faith" attracts attention. It returns the character Faith as an object symbol. When she first appeared between the adult Parsifals, the child was holding his two bows, looking at the group. In retrospect one recognizes a double *mise-en-abyme* in that constellation. Faith is, then, a force from the collective unconscious who can assume several forms. As a numinous figure she appears in the prelude both as a maiden and as an object symbol. Jung describes this archetype as an aspect of the Mother, who, when observed in a man, belongs to the Anima type (*Archetypes*, 182–83). Not only can such psychic figures assume a variety of manifestations, he continues, but they also possess quite conflicting characteristics, functioning in positive or negative roles (183). Just as the Great Mother can turn into a Terrible Mother, so also her aspect as a maiden or daughter possesses the potential for converting into her own opposite. In *Hitler* the figure lost her name of Church and became Faith, clearly functioning as a contrast to *Un-Glaube*, previously known as Synagogue. Syberberg may have had in mind Jung's definition of *enantiodromia*, which means "running counter to." With reference to Heraclitus, Jung defines it as a "play of opposites in the course of events," or also as the principle of destruction and contruction governing all cycles of life (*Psychological Types*, 426). In this context he quotes Heraclitus: "The bow (biós) is called life (bíos), but its work is death" (426). It is not clear if Wolfram and Wagner had this in mind, but the bow plays a role in their texts as well as in the film. When Wolfram says he is presenting the string without the bow, his most probable frame of reference is the religious associations of these images. It could be a case of double-speak as well, with the Latin equivalent of "string,," *fides*, also referring to "faith." Syberberg's Grail Carrier named Faith, Synagogue, and Voice from on high is obviously endowed with a spiritual function related to Parsifal's mission. Like Wolfram's bow with its symbolic ties to the Old Testament, the Synagogue can recede in favor of the string image and still remain present as Faith/*fides*.

Wagner used the arrow as a symbol for Lohengrin. He described his hero as "the lost arrow which I shot after the surmised but not yet known noble find

[Elsa]."[49] Lohengrin first had to become aware of the "truly feminine that will bring redemption to me and the whole world" (898). Wagner's transfer of an object symbol to a human character leads back to the religious implication of the bow-and-string image. With the bow and string equating the eras of the Father and the Son, then the arrow begins to look like a symbol of the third era, the Third Kingdom or *Reich*. Again the association with the Third Reich clings to Parsifal as the human arrow. Jung also considers the arrow a masculine symbol, like the lance, and as a libido-symbol. In Wagner's version, Parsifal had killed the swan with the arrow. Since the bird inhabited the head landscape like everything else in act 1, it appears that Parsifal attacked a part of his own organism. Jung observes about such a constellation: "Being wounded by one's own arrow signifies . . . a state of introversion: . . . the libido sinks 'into its own depths' . . . and discovers in the darkness a substitute for the upper world it has abandoned—the world of memories" (*Symbols of Transf.*, 292). In this descent lurks a danger of becoming stuck and moribund.

Even when seen only partially, the objects on the scaffolding call forth a host of associations. Nietzsche too made use of a similar image. Despising ordinary men with their limited aspirations, his Zarathustra laments: "Alas! there cometh the time when man will no longer launch the arrow of his longing beyond man— and the string of his bow will have unlearned to whizz!" (11).The individuals whose drive propel them beyond mediocrity are related to the rain drops heralding the lightning. Such prophets and precursors of the *Übermensch* would of course need a bowstring drawn to an angle in order to advance far enough. And the bowstring seen behind Parsifal is pulled and ready to shoot.

Another man who studied Nietzsche and wrote extensively about him was Martin Heidegger. He apparently contributed the concept *Gestell* concretized in the film as the support for the bow and arrow. In his "Question Concerning Technology," *Gestell* becomes a central term which it is impossible to translate satisfactorily. Usually rendered as "enframing" or simply as *Gestell*, it combines in its components multiple definitions. Besides the tangible "stand," "support," "frame," "scaffolding," etc., it can also denote, via the polyvalent root-verb *stellen*, "position," "location," "situation," and much more. Heidegger elucidates some of these possibilities over several pages as he imbues the word with a new meaning.[50] He considers it the essence of the modern age, the challenging predicament that could help bring about the revelation or uncovering (*Entbergen*) of Being (*Sein*). But it is also a great danger. Applying this term to the visible contraption near Parsifal, one may discern in it the externalized, unconscious quest for the Grail. Unconscious because the image is incomplete, but as part of a weapon it still possesses the power to kill. Any launch will be fraught with danger. This reading was prefigured in the previous scene by Kundry holding the arrow. Pushing Parsifal to the edge of an emotional abyss, she functioned as a human *Gestell* for the arrow as well as a genre shifter. She will encounter Parsifal again in act 2, and for the second time represent a threatening danger. But for now she lets go of Parsifal and withdraws to a hollow in the barren landscape. One recognizes the area as a dry eye socket of the concrete mask. Overcome with the urge to sleep, she knows her current "life" is over: "Die Zeit ist da" (time has come), she comments. As a new stage in life unfolds for Parsifal, she rolls up in a fetal position and exits hers. This is the second time a character appears in such a position. It first occurred at the end of the prelude involving the two Parsifal actors.

In view of the black background and alchemical process that Parsifal has suffered, he too might as well be entering a different existence resembling death. Seen from this perspective, Gurnemanz, who is about to accompany Parsifal to the Grail Castle, might then function much as a Valkyrie, or also as Parsifal's Ka. The Ka was in ancient Egypt the spiritual double of a person, an entity that survived physical death and in whom the soul, Ba, dwelt.[51] One might also be tempted to think of Hermes or Thoth, the ancient deities guiding the souls of the deceased to the world of the dead. Their alchemical equivalent is Mercurius. Among the Jungian archetypes one also finds the Wise Old Man, who, like Gurnemanz, functions as a teacher and psychopomp (*Archetypes*, 35–37). Wolfram did not equip his Parzival with such a guide to the Grail Castle. This scene is Wagner's invention.

And an awkward scene it is on stage. A visible change in scenery must substitute for an inner transformation. Wagner resorted to a scrolling backdrop that eventually showed the interior of the Grail Castle at the end of the accompanying "transformation music." One visitor to Bayreuth during the first *Parsifal* season was impressed with the achieved illusion, but noted: "When Gurnemanz began to accompany Parsifal to the Grail castle, I became slightly dizzy. What happened? It appeared as if the house with the entire audience started to move."[52] On the occasion described here, everything worked well, and the interior of the hall was in place when the light increased to the effect of the desired C-Major chord. But while Gurnemanz and Parsifal would pace back and forth to the accompaniment of repetitive bell music, Wagner experienced enough problems with synchronization and mechanical malfunctioning to discourage imitation in other theaters. Most stage versions just draw the curtains during the transformation music while the two men can be seen walking by. The cinematic treatment allows other options, and Syberberg takes advantage of them. He retains the changing environment, but with a twist.

The transformation episode sees the two men move through several locations in the mask landscape. The beginning of this peregrination starts slowly with their brief dialogue marking the transition from stationary to moving action. "If you are pure, the Grail will refresh and feed you," Gurnemanz sings, thinking of the prophesy. Having proved himself to be a fool, the young boy must also be a pure soul, *rein*. One remembers Syberberg's frequent play on purity and its opposite in *Die freudlose Gesellschaft*, clearly developing this theme in preparation of *Parsifal*. One conspicuous carrier of meaning was the name Reiner/Rainer. Although it does not relate to 'pure' semantically, the shared pronunciation suffices. As early as in *Karl May* Rainer von Artenfels had portrayed Hitler, returning in the *Hitler* film as a ventriloquist holding a Hitler puppet. Other links to *rein* are two names, Karin Krick as Parsifal II (Karin = Katherine, the pure) and Rainer Goldberg, the invisible tenor singing the role of Parsifal throughout (Rainer = *reiner*, "pure"; Gold = alchemically pure substance). Thus Parsifal should possess plenty of purity, but whether all of it is of the "Aryan" kind remains to be seen.

Hearing that the Grail will feed and refresh him, Parsifal asks naïvely, "Wer ist der Gral?" (Who is the Grail). Strangely, most translators insist on rendering this line as "What is the Grail?" The subtitles in the film read correctly *who*. Gurnemanz' answer does not refute a personal referent. This might suggest that Wagner interpreted the Grail as a symbol with a more flexible meaning than the chalice from the Last Supper later holding Christ's blood. Then Gurnemanz adds: "I think I recognized you correctly." In view of the context he obviously refers to the potential redeemer of King Amfortas. But the statement could also reinforce Syberberg's additional interpretation borrowed from Wolfram, namely the recognition of Parsifal as a member of the royal family. Gurnemanz repeats now what he had expressed in different words before, making the text assume contrapuntal variations. A similar occurrence follows shortly when he informs Parsifal that only a person guided by the Grail can find the way since there are no paths to follow. He had previously told the squires that no sinner could find them. In this scene he also pronounces the most frequently quoted words of the libretto, "zum Raum wird hier die Zeit" (here time turns into space). It should be clear, then, that the interchangeability of the dimensions, and hence altered perceptions, indicates a different kind of existence and/or consciousness.

In accordance with Wagner's stage instructions, Gurnemanz puts his arm protectively around the young boy's shoulders in what almost looks like an embrace. They are apparently embarking upon a dangerous passage. But as they proceed, Parsifal soon walks ahead of him with Gurnemanz trailing and only holding on to one shoulder as if avoiding to get separated. At first Parsifal moves as if sleepwalking or in a trance, leaving the audience to observe the changing environment. Accompanied by the transformation music, the two men move through the maze in the mask landscape. Early on, a cleft in the rock reveals a background projection of Brünnhilde riding on Grane. This glimpse returns a bundle of motifs. First, the Valkyrie's mission of collecting the souls of heroes dying in battle, suggesting that she is accompanying Parsifal; or that mortal danger is lurking ahead, since she also functions as harbinger of imminent death for a hero who sees her. But Parsifal pays no attention to her. Other echoing motifs are the magical ring from the Nibelungen treasure now replaced with the Grail; Siegfried; and, finally, the horse. Soon the image of Brünnhilde's mother, Erda, appears through other crevices in the rocks. The Madonna-like sketch of Erda belonged to Wagner's plans for *Rheingold*.[53] In addition to recalling Wagner's story in the combined plot, these feminine apparitions also surround Parsifal in a surreal new world. Erda's name means Eartha. The hero is regressing into the unconscious with its primeval archetypal forces, or the "Mothers," as Goethe called them in *Faust II*. Here Freud's *Interpretation of Dreams* confirms that Parsifal is indeed entering a dream-like state (485–97). The walk through the passages of the head takes him back beyond the preconscious to the remoter unconscious with its memory sections, according to

Freud's charts (489–91). In the waking state, Freud explains, thought processes move through the apparatus of the mind from the "sensory operational end" to the "motor end" (488). In dreams and hallucinations, however, the movement goes in the opposite direction: "If we call the direction which the psychic process follows from the unconscious into the waking state *progressive*, we may then speak of the dream as having a *regressive* character" (492). A similar backwards or inwards move accompanies intentional recollection, since the memories it tries to reach lie forgotten and hidden in the unconscious. When such memory-traces are activated and become conscious, they show less "sensory quality" than the original perceptions (490). But: "We call it regression if the idea in the dream is changed back into the visual image from which it originated" (493). The regression characteristic of visions and dreams, Freud notes, corresponds "to thoughts transformed into images; and [I] would assert that only such thoughts undergo this transformation as are in intimate connection with suppressed memories, or with memories which have remained unconscious" (494). With the puppet play showing the action in the Grail Kingdom and the prelude viewed as the realm of the unconscious, one now concludes that Parsifal will witness events that either have become suppressed memories or are plain unconscious. The path to this realm should lead him away from his preconscious or barely conscious state of mind.

The path winds through the head landscape like a labyrinth. Its most colorful section is the time tunnel. Here Syberberg combines the statement about time turning into space with Freud's concept of regression. With the projection of Erda visible at the beginning of the tunnel, she appears to preside over the passage of which the walls are covered with flags. The recent ones are placed close to her, most conspicuous among them a swastika. One searches in vain for the current German flag, since Germany was still divided when the movie was made. Although both Germanies used the same colors in their national symbols, black-red-gold, the East German flag included the communist emblem in the center. However, rows of small banners flutter overhead, and some of them have one or another of the colors. Thus the modern German symbol is present, but divided into separate units. Moreover, some of these have pointed tips, repeating the pattern of a serrated edge. The fragmented image is *zerrissen*. As the walkers proceed through this passage towards the camera, the flags on the walls become increasingly older. The easiest one to recognize towards the end of the passage is the flag of the Holy Roman Empire of the German Nation, or First Reich. Founded by Charlemagne in 800, but without this flag and its long title, that empire lasted roughly 1,000 years, until the Napoleonic Wars. Therefore the presence of this and other historical flags makes the walkers appear to move backwards in history, or time. But since they are simultaneously proceeding forwards in space, one may suspect that Syberberg's visual counterpoint is at work again.

Parsifal paces quickly through this corridor of flags, with Gurnemanz still following and holding on to him. Only at a bend in the tunnel close to the camera does Parsifal stop. The walls of this section are covered with narrow, tall banners in combinations of red, white, and black. They all wear a cross or cross-like emblem: a white Christian cross on black, the Templar *croix pattée* on white, and a white dove on red, reminiscent of the emblem of Wolfram's *templeise*. These banners differ from the political flags in the time-tunnel in that they represent religious societies or institutions. Here Parsifal becomes aware of the environment. Numerous dark corpses line the passage and floor. Parsifal had passed some earlier in the maze, but paid no attention, either because their color blended in with the rocky background making them less conspicuous, or because he walked in a trance. Now corpses surround him and block his way. With his big eyes taking in the grisly sight, he stops but without comprehending what he sees. Who are the dead surrounding him? The first thought springing to mind is the Holocaust and its victims. This interpretation is based on a forward-moving, or spatial, reading of the quasi-musical progression through the time tunnel. The swastika at the beginning of the corridor leads to the victims at the end of that stretch. Besides, surrounding the dead, the three colors of the tall banners echo the tricolor swastika further back. Parsifal's sudden stop and stare also express the incomprehensible nature of the Holocaust. A second interpretation might take its cue from the colors: another alchemical stage of transformation overwhelming or affecting the hero. A third reading observing the regressive move in time would find a footing in the medieval religious conflicts. The Christian cross refers then to the crusades as well as the Inquisition and their victims. The Templar cross represents the order of monastic warriors who were very much a part of the crusades until secular and Church cooperation transformed them into martyrs. And the dove symbolizing the Holy Spirit points to Wolfram's Grail society and, one may assume, untold heretics, such as the Cathars, who were persecuted ferociously. It may be no coincidence that Wagner placed his Montsalvat on the northern slopes of the Pyrenées, where also the Cathar fortress of Monségur fell to crusaders in 1244. The emblems fluttering over this segment of the passage clearly point to a period of religious fervor and persecution with large numbers of casualties. This third interpretation develops into a related but separate fourth reading. It appears that Parsifal has reached a particularly dangerous location on his itinerary. One might say he stopped at the edge of a precipice where many have perished before him. The dangers behind him, such as the sight of the Valkyrie, and the dead around him indicate a series of tribulations to be overcome, a ritual ordeal similar to the trials in *The Magic Flute*. There the hero must prove himself worthy of initiation or admission to an esoteric society inspired by Freemasonry. Now Parsifal must overcome fear and dangers lest he too perish, physically or metaphorically. Gurnemanz, who had continued alone when Parsifal stopped, beckons him to follow. Hesitantly, the son of a widow proceeds, stepping gingerly over the corpses.

At last the two have reached the end of the passage. Addressing the young boy again, Gurnemanz makes clear that one more test awaits Parsifal: "Let me see if you are a fool and pure," he sings, thinking of the prophesy which Parsifal has not heard, continuing with "and what knowledge may have been bestowed on you." Wagner replaced *Weisheit* (wisdom) with *Wissen* (knowledge), perhaps hoping to blur the indebtedness of his text to the wisdom tradition. More important is what

Gurnemanz omits. The pure fool must also feel compassion in order to gain his insight or wisdom, "durch Mitleid wissend." This is the two-part test ahead. Not only must Parsifal react with compassion to the suffering he is about to witness, but he must also understand what it is all about. Both here and later, when Gurnemanz addresses Parsifal after the Grail ceremony, Wagner's text does not mention *Mitleid*. The emphasis is on understanding or knowledge resulting from the unstated compassion. To this the film adds an ever so subtle visual nuance concerning the definition of compassion. The word is often given as "pity" in English translations. This misses the semantic composition of *Mit-Leid*, "com-passion," and *sym-patheia*. Being composites, all three words entail shared suffering. Wagner sometimes referred to *Mitleid* as *Mitleiden*, using the infinitive as a noun. This would stress the experiential involvement of the subject who both shares in the suffering and perhaps witnesses someone else's suffering. But not embedded in the composite lexis is the wish to help the sufferer unselfishly. That shade of loving kindness has grown up around the word without being expressed explicitly in the compound itself. This is the shade Syberberg adds tacitly. It shows up in the rocky wall blocking the way for Gurnemanz and Parsifal. Apparently a dead end, it splits just enough to create a gap leading into the Grail Castle. This brings to mind a passage in the Bible. In the King James version, 1 Cor. 13. 2 reads: "[A]nd though I have all faith, so that I could remove mountains, and have not charity, I am nothing." Parsifal may possess sufficient faith to move mountains, but his enabling quality as redeemer depends on his insight from experience as well as love for others. That redefines *Mitleid* as "loving compassion." In other words, the film adds a biblical nuance where Wagner's text does not express it. Of course the quotation also invites other interpretations and associations. The reader may remember this reference to the Bible from the chapter on *Hitler*. The German quotation appears at the end of that movie as white script against a black, starry sky. As a literal quotation it corrects a paraphrase by Goebbels heard twice on the soundtrack. His version sounds,"Faith can move mountains." He then appeals to the listeners to let this mountain-moving faith fill them all. Goebbels had no use for love, only the blind faith of the believers in his gospel. Thus both in Wagner's passage and in the ideology of the Third Reich love or charity is missing. In the first and last moments of *Hitler* one sees a split mountain against a starry backdrop. The landscape is borrowed from King Ludwig's artificial paradise. In addition to that visual antecedent, the dividing mountain in *Parsifal* has, then, been prefigured several times. Through these antecedents the quotation alludes both to the Bible and to its antithesis, Nazi ideology. Those not believing in their mutually exclusive contrast should remember that Hitler intended to annihilate both the Hebrew and the Christian legacies of the Bible, as revealed in Rauschning's memoirs of his conversations with Hitler.[54] The chapter called "Anti-Christ" quotes Hitler as stating, "That will not prevent me from eradicating Christianity in Germany with unfailing thoroughness" (50). Further down on the same page he continues, "But it is decisive for our people whether it has the Jewish-Christian faith and its weakly morality of compassion or a strong, heroic faith in God in nature, in God in one's own people, in God in one's own destiny, in one's own blood." In the same paragraph Hitler also claims, "One is either a Christian or a German. One cannot be both" (50). Compassion, then, belongs in Hitler's view to the "weakly" morality of Bible-based Christianity and is scheduled for eradication. It is clear that at least in this context Hitler's definition imbued compassion with a meaning that did not fit into his program. His ideal heroes should be cruel and strong. Through Gurnemanz' omission of compassion in the references to Parsifal's test, the meaning of the prophesy becomes ambiguous. Its *Mitleid,* as in *Mitleiden*, might refer to experienced suffering along with others, for example in a battle, or it could be loving kindness spurred by others' pain. However, the contrapuntal effect of the moving mountain also activates other allusions. One amounts to a self-quotation. After all, Syberberg does refer to details from his *Hitler* and *Ludwig*. Furthermore, the inclusion of faith, *Glaube*, in the quotations from the Bible and Goebbels reveals another melody playing in counterpoint, namely the young female character with the many names. Another association provoked by the opening crack leads to Wagner's report on the *Parsifal* performances in 1882 to the king. There he announced the decision to change the future entry to the Grail Castle into a gate in the cliff that splits open (Strobel, 3:249). Syberberg carries out that intention. His gate *is* the splitting cliff. And finally, the dividing mountain creates a rift, a *Riss*, in the rock wall. *Riss* is related to the verb with the past participle *zerrissen* (torn asunder). That word also functions as an adjective which has already occurred repeatedly as a motif. And now, as the wall splits, this *Riss* reveals a world from a different dimension.

The first impression of the view beyond is dominated by the background of a ruined cupola. In accordance with Wagner's stage instructions, the two men have now entered the Grail Hall, and the perspective is therefore from the floor and up. Remembering Syberberg's imagery associated with a cupola and seeing the ruined condition, the viewer can easily guess the nature of Amfortas' affliction. The *Riss* of the entrance points in the same direction. The design for the original 1882 cupola and the octagonal space it tops was inspired by the cathedral in Siena, which Wagner visited repeatedly in August and September 1880.[55] He may have been equally intrigued by the stone artwork in the pavement of that edifice, although Cosima's diary does not mention it. Another sanctuary that could and should have inspired the composer is the Dome of the Rock in Jerusalem. Standing on the Temple Mount, the octagonal base of the golden cupola surrounds the sacred rock that has a long history of veneration. This Temple Mount and its structures were the headquarters and raison d'être for the Knights Templar. Their cross emblem reappears in the film as the Grail society gathers for the ceremony. And so does the dove emblem adapted from Wolfram's *templeise*. Although the poet does not specify the location of their temple, one may assume that at one level it functioned as the center of a spiritual Jerusalem. One is encouraged to note that in spite of all the liberties Wagner took with his subject matter, he retained the historically significant design for his Grail Hall. But its ruined condition in the film indicates also the fate suffered, not only by Amfortas, but also by the Grail community at the hands of Wagner and his successors.

Parsifal and Gurnemanz disappear from sight for a while as the inhabitants of Montsalvat file in to fill the hall. But since this hall is still situated in the head landscape, Syberberg dispenses with the tables set for a love feast in a large room under the cupola. In the shots preceding the dialogue between Amfortas and his father, most of the residents move through and to relatively narrow spaces surrounded by rock walls. Some of them carry torches as if they had emerged from dark recesses of Wagner's head. The series of shots with men on the move brings to mind an observation by Jung: "I have often noticed that the symbol of the crowd, and particularly of a streaming mass of people in motion, expresses violent motions of the unconscious. Such symbols always indicate an activation of the unconscious and an incipient dissociation between it and the ego" (*Symbols of Transf.*, 207). With this stirring of the unconscious taking place in Wagner's head, one may assume that it affects all the forces inhabiting these depths, including Parsifal, who has arrived from the collective unconscious of the prelude. What he experiences in the next section of the film differs markedly from the stage instructions and the viewers' expectations, adding to a confusion in the viewer that must resemble what he feels. Perhaps some of the huge boulders represent building elements from the crumbled hall. But just as the music drama takes place in a landscape of the mind, so also this new environment disregards reality. A series of shots captures the gathering of the Grail society, beginning with knights in armor facing each other in a passage closest to the rift. Their mature voices belong to the Prague Philharmonic Choir. Leaning against the rock while singing, they appear at first to be part of the walls. One by one, as they begin to move away in procession, the figures disengage from the rock and take on the contours of individuals. Other shots depict people arriving from various sides while white vapor billows down the rock sides. Some men wear monastic robes with a few displaying the dove emblem of the *templeise*. The "younger voices" called for in the music belong to novices. One of them shows a remarkable resemblance to the Parsifal actor without the wig. One realizes that probably all the non-singing actors also assume several roles, as already observed in the prelude. Furthermore, the division of most roles in visible actor and unseen singer creates composite portrayals of fleeting identities, reminiscent of Kortner in *Kabale und Liebe*.

Wagner's text calls for successive choruses of knights at ground level and young men and boys heard from two levels in the cupola. Hence the visual sequence presents the gathering of the Grail community in the same order of voices. However, since the camera divides the episode into more takes than one expects for the three stanzas of eight, eight, and six lines, the visual movement helps distract the viewer from the hopelessly convoluted text. No existing translations come close to it, most being by necessity very free approximations. The knights announce that whoever rejoices in doing good deeds ("wer guter Tat sich freut"), is granted the comfort of the love feast. Then the novices declare themselves willing to shed their blood for the "sinful worlds" in imitation of the Redeemer, whose body or flesh, *Leib*, they hope will live on in them. Subsequently, the ethereal boys' choir describes how faith is alive and the dove is hovering, ending with the admonition to partake of the wine and bread of life. Hearing these words and, on opera stages, seeing the monastic celebrants line up at the refectory tables, the viewer expects a liturgy similar to communion in mass. It was not the first time Wagner relocated a religious rite to the stage. In the *Meistersinger* the opening chorus represents a congregation singing a hymn that concludes the church service. This time both the situation in the Grail Hall and the text remind one of an early choral composition by Wagner, "Das Liebesmahl der Apostel" (The Love Feast of the Apostles) of 1843.[56] This "biblical scene" was performed in the Church of Our Lady in Dresden with a chorus of 1,200 male voices and a 100-member orchestra. Like the Grail Hall, so also the sanctuary for the concert accommodated singers in the cupola. These are marked in the printed version as "Stimmen aus der Höhe" (voices from on high). They express some comforting words by Jesus in the first person singular. In other words, they represent a pronouncement coming from a divine source, accompanied by the rushing music of the Holy Spirit descending on the apostles and disciples. A single alto voice from on high returns in *Parsifal* on a very similar occasion, a love feast of pious believers. One wonders if also this singer represents a divine presence at the ceremony. Other similarities between the two gatherings occur in the form of a miracle and, less dramatically, in the language. The text of 1843 anticipated many words and phrases inspired by the last supper that recur in the first act of *Parsifal*. The Grail congregants seem to expect their priest-king to conduct a communion. Of course such a ritual on an opera stage, even on Wagner's own stage, would be considered sacrilegious in nineteenth century Catholic Bavaria. Anticipating the protests, Wagner changed the liturgy into a love feast with a ritual that only resembles the communion. For example, in the libretto published in 1877 the novices sing that "the Redeemer, whom you praise" transforms his blood and flesh into the wine and bread offered to the worshipers.[57] The libretto in the score of 1882 renders the same passage with a different subject, namely the "loving spirit [spirit of love] of blessed comfort."[58] This did not suffice to silence objections. Numerous critics have seen the ritual as a black mass and nothing but blasphemy. But the motif has been prepared in Syberberg's earlier films: the requiem with beheading and distorted Lord's Prayer in *Ludwig*, the prayer in the crypt and death scene in *Karl May*, and the prayer tune to the Virgin recited in the museum in *Hitler*. The pattern of counterpoint should have carried the visual melody into a predominantly non-blasphemous movement in *Parsifal*. Although Wagner's words form one strand of the narrative which still offends many critics, the visual counterpart has weakened the potential for sacrilege. On the other hand, Wagnerites probably level similar accusations against Syberberg's treatment of Wagner's revered work. The knights in armor, monks, and novices gather to kneel in prayer-like meditation; the mentioning of faith and dove produces the already familiar emblems on banners and garments; nowhere does one see tables set for a love feast; and no sooner do the younger voices introduce the "sinful worlds" than the camera cuts to the approach of Amfortas, the sinner at this court.

The king's procession crosses an open space with a crumbled rotunda as background, moving from left to right towards the camera. The movement away from this hall suggests a different location for, and hence perspective on, the action to follow. Leading the procession are two young girls carrying objects, one being the bleeding wound on a cushion, the other fragments of stucco. Actually, the viewer cannot tell what she is carrying, but page 10 of the book identifies the items as stucco fragments from bombed-out Wahnfried and a stucco rose from King Ludwig's grotto at Linderhof. It appears that the stucco relics somehow demand the same veneration as the gash surrounded by a slab of flesh. Since the Wagner story is interwoven with the Parsifal plot, one assumes that the function of the fragments must at least partially belong to the biographical narrative. What connotations might they evoke? Well, Wahnfried and "Bayreuth" still fill the hearts of many Wagnerites with enough devotion to warrant an annual pilgrimage rivaling believers' travels to Lourdes and Santiago de Compostela. And Wahnfried, being a present from King Ludwig, was destroyed by bombardment during World War II. This physical destruction might be seen as a visible correlate to "Bayreuth's" moral status during the Third Reich. But at the same time the Wahnfried fragments are treasured as relics of a past to be remembered. The rose fragment from Linderhof relates both to Syberberg's *Ludwig* and to Wagner's friendship with the king. Near the unfinished palace at Linderhof King Ludwig had constructed a "Venus grotto." The inspiration came from *Tannhäuser*, where the title hero rests in the lap of Venus. After the victory of Christianity the pagan goddess of love was demonized into a queen of the underworld and temptress of carnal pleasures. This image makes Venus a twin of the temptress Kundry. The latter had also appeared as a puppet in the prelude and had been mentioned earlier in Gurnemanz' narrative. The theme is present again, but barely perceptively in the stucco rose. In the second act Kundry is called Rose of Hell. That brings also up the contrapuntal echo of the Virgin Mary as the Rose of Heaven and Holy Mother. And on a more mundane level, the rose serves as a reminder of Wagner's love of rose water, especially as a fragrance for his bath water provided by Judith Gautier. He also had a sister named Rosalie, but there is no indication that she figures in this work. But clearly, the stucco fragments carried before the king are treated with sorrow and reverence. Syberberg compares them with relics of saints venerated in medieval sanctuaries (*Parsifal*, 102). He may have been inspired to include them by several French Grail stories that influenced Wagner's narrative. For example, de Boron's version describes the Grail procession as comprising also "des dignes reliques avec" (worthy relics with it).[59] And similarly, Wolfram's procession includes both the Grail and other items. The reintroduction of such paraphernalia serves to make the narrative themes and motifs appear visibly.

The king himself sits in a reclining position on a throne carried by knights and squires. That is, one assumes this is the king, for one cannot see him. The human shape is entirely covered in a blond blanket, with only some dark hair sticking out. The blanket looks like those that had enveloped Gurnemanz and Kundry earlier. With the hidden body stiff and immobile, the wrap creates the impression of a worm or chrysalis from which a new life could soon emerge. The throne is modeled on that of Charlemagne in Aachen (Aix-la-Chapelle). In the prelude Herzeleide was sitting on it, but since it was then covered with the star-studded blue cloth, one could not recognize its shape. The throne recalls the establishment of Charlemagne's First Reich. It relates to Wagner's biography as well. In 1845 when he staged *Tannhäuser* in Dresden, the stage decorations ordered from Paris did not arrive in time, forcing Wagner to substitute old sets from other operas. For the singers' hall he had to resort to Charlemagne's throne room from *Oberon*, which the audience remembered only too well.[60] The composer would certainly have objected to another reminder of Charlemagne's throne room for his *Parsifal*, but Syberberg forces the throne on him. At the same time, the sight triggers the memory of a "correspondence" found in Heine's *Deutschland: Ein Wintermärchen*. In this verse epos, Hammonia, the patron goddess of Hamburg, tells the narrator about two thrones in her family (664). One is the throne in Aachen on which her father, Charlemagne, sat on the day of his coronation. The other is the one she inherited from him. It is a more modest throne for use at night. The first throne has, then, a not so dignified companion piece. But while the historical seat functions as a symbolic representation of Charlemagne's Reich, Heine's second facility possesses the power of an oracle foretelling Germany's future when the seat is raised. The revelation is so horrible it knocks the narrator unconscious. Not only does the throne in the film awaken two conflicting bundles of associations, but it also conjures up the author of that tale. The presence of Heine may not reverberate as noticeably in this context as in *Hitler*, but the associations crop up regularly. Amfortas' throne carried in the procession even brings to mind a second Heine passage, this time from *Atta Troll*. It describes how four men carry the killed bear sitting on a carrying chaise, "as a sick guest at the spa," a thinly veiled reference to the composer Meyerbeer.[61] Somehow, the throne elicits overtones of unexpected diversity. Even more so in view of Wagner's resentment of Meyerbeer and Heine's play on the latter's name. He reads the last syllable of the composer's name as *Bär*, or "bear."[62] Atta Troll, a run-away circus bear, pronounces proudly his identity in caput 9, claiming as his heritage several German words for bear: *Zottelbär, Brummbär*, and *Petz*. "I am not ashamed of my origin," he declares, "I am as proud of it as if I were descended from Moses Mendelssohn" (558). How ironic, then, that the maiden name of Wagner's mother was Petz.[63] Presumably poking fun at Meyerbeer, who had added Meyer to his name, the barb could also apply to Wagner, since Petz means "bear." And since the bears in *Atta Troll* are despised and persecuted, one can easily recognize the allusion to discrimination of Jews in a Gentile society. The hint of a suppressed similarity between Wagner and Meyerbeer adds an ironic touch to the biographical narrative. It also revives the memory of Wagner's pathological lack of gratitude that turned into aggression against his former benefactor. And since the film covers the body carried on the throne, one cannot be entirely sure who occupies the seat.

Immediately behind the king follow the attendants wearing the red and the celestial cloaks, this time carrying a litter with the sculpture of the killed swan with the red-tipped arrow still sticking out. The rear guard is composed of four knights with shields. Being white with black crosses, the shields display the inverse of the crosses on black banners seen earlier. The transformation might be compared to a musical inversion.

In the final stage of the entry scene the sopranos and altos are heard from the cupola. Supposedly these voices belong to boys who do not themselves participate in the ceremony at floor level, but who nonetheless imbue the liturgy with an angelic air. Of course on any stage women sing this part, but they remain invisible. This is also how men and women would be segregated in a traditional Jewish synagogue. But of course, the subscribers to the *Bayreuther Blätter* as well as more contemporary critics view the Grail Temple as a sanctuary inspired by Christian tradition. Syberberg reintroduces women at the highest level under the cupola. Seated on top of the concrete cliffs and surrounded by *rising* vapor, three of the women personify Cosima Wagner, Judith Gautier, and Mathilde Wesendonck. The four young girls and the boy represent Cosima's children. In other words, these figures belong to Wagner's life more than Parsifal's. However, little Siegfried looks like the child Parsifal in the prelude. They all surrounded Wagner, helped and inspired him, and surpassed the role of muses during the genesis of *Parsifal*.

With the conclusion of the stanza for sopranos and altos, the arrival scene comes to an end. A stage version would now show Amfortas resting on an elevated dais, the covered chalice on a table in front of him, and a large number of monks at long tables around him. The film, on the other hand, lets the congregants kneel, stand, or sit in various locations in the head, all focusing on their meditative devotions. Contrary to the stage directions, one has not yet seen the Grail under cover nor witnessed the actual arrival of the king at the table on which the Grail should rest. The traditional gathering has become a dispersed exercise of piety. Faith may be present, but each group of participants experiences the ceremony differently. For some, a Grail held aloft by the king could only be imagined. This fragmentation or dispersal of participants in what should be a spiritual in-gathering correlates with the ruined condition of the sanctuary. Wagner's vision of the Grail mystery has not survived intact in the death mask landscape.

At this point the stage directions call for Titurel's voice to be heard from a niche in the wall behind Amfortas. Wolfram placed him in an adjoining room. Syberberg places him underground, which is logical enough, since the voice is supposed to sound "as if coming from a grave." The abrupt cut to Titurel offers another surprise. If this were really a grave, one would expect the chamber to be finished as a mausoleum or crypt worthy of a king. Instead one sees an excavated cave supported by rough beams, water dripping audibly from above into a puddle on the ground, and the killed swan thrown down near the wall. In some close-ups the dark rear wall becomes visible as a surface of corrugated tin, a hint at the fire curtain on the Bayreuth stage (Spotts, 200). Leading up, solid stone steps reach to the rectangular opening overhead. This rectangle has the same dimension as the basin of the window fountain mentioned earlier and as Wagner's grave from which Hitler's corpse rose. This time Titurel inhabits the grave. The role is played by Martin Sperr and sung by Hans Tschammer.[64] The relocation of the father's voice to a subterranean realm identifies the psychological function of this force. Although buried and out of sight, the paternal archetype emerges as a voice from the collective, and here also personal, subconscious. Anticipating Jung's distinction between the mother and the father archetypes, Wagner's Titurel represents the dynamism of the paternal archetype (Jung, *Archetypes*, 101–02). After all, to him belongs the voice that urges his unwilling son to conduct the Grail ritual. One of the mystical properties of the Grail is to strengthen and prolong the life of those who view it regularly. In the case of Wagner's Titurel, this renewal depends on his son's willingness to honor the Grail tradition and to remember everything his father's legacy entails. Since Amfortas is a mature man, but still dark-haired and presumably in his best years, one expects his father to look like the white-haired monarch shown in the puppet play. But as Gurnemanz, so also Syberberg's Titurel appears to be of the same age as his son. Thanks to the regular exposure to the Grail, or so one assumes, the old king still looks young. In Wolfram's version, members of the Grail society can turn grey-haired, but they do not die. The psychological function of this character explains the surprising youthfulness: Amfortas is really carrying on an inner dialogue with himself. Here the Wagner story intrudes into the Parsifal narrative again. This Titurel looks like King Ludwig. More exactly, like the last painting of him by G. Schachinger. But unlike the Bavarian king, Titurel is blessed with a superb set of teeth. Of course the repeated allusions to King Ludwig also recall Syberberg's *Ludwig*. Actually, the same actor, Martin Sperr, had been scheduled to portray the older Ludwig in the second half of that movie. But when an accident on the first day of shooting prevented his participation, Harry Baer took over both parts of the title role (*Parsifal*, 99). Not only did this planned division of a role anticipate the divided Parsifal by ten years, but *Ludwig* also included a resurrection of the king after his execution. That is what Wagner had planned for his Titurel as late as in the 1877 publication of the drama. Even modern editions of the score include a note towards the end of the third act indicating, "In the first edition of the text it said here: Titurel is rising in the casket while giving blessings. This episode was not carried out on the master's instruction."[65] In 1972 Syberberg modified the "master's instruction" by letting Wagner's *Landesvater* pop up like a Jack-in-the-box. Since Wagner had suppressed the detail in *Parsifal* in 1882, Syberberg relocated a parody of it to *Ludwig*, where the dead king actually sits up in the coffin, his face expressing shock and dismay at the hordes of tourists desecrating his royal hideaways. He and his world still intrigue the present generations, so on even the most prosaic level one could say he still lives on. Now he returns much like Kundry in her metempsychosis in a different role. The Ludwig theme has undergone a contrapuntal transformation. Wearing a royal blue cloak adorned with ermine, Titurel is as insistent that his son carry out his duties as King Ludwig was in spurring Wagner on in his work on *Parsifal*. Already in August 1865 the composer had to comply with the king's request for a prose outline. A full twenty-seven printed pages, the version is very close to the final libretto.[66] Not only did King Ludwig admire Wagner's art and support him with astounding generosity, he was also his *Landesvater*. This feudal role of a sovereign towards his subjects is now repeated on a different level between Titurel-Ludwig and his son. That relationship establishes a parallel between Amfortas and Wagner as sons of demanding fathers. Both resent, and suffer under, the fathers' expectations. However, this comparison soon hits a limit due to other "roles" played by the composer and the king, especially in their correspondence with each other. For example, Wagner referred to himself as a fool, while he and Cosima adopted the nickname Parzival for the king (Strobel, 3:149). The king wrote to Wagner, "You are my world, my savior!" (Strobel, 2:20). Wagner responded by calling his benefactor "my gracious savior who preserves me and my works for the world" (Strobel, 2:27). And like Amfortas, so also Wagner sighed over his tribulations, begging for the cup to pass him by (Strobel, 2:307). He actually referred to himself in Christ-evoking terms more than once. In 1873, for example, he wrote to Eduard Schuré that the political situation made him suffer: "I am, as it were, hanging on the cross of the German idea" (Gregor-Dellin, 771). Such overlapping connotations inform also the characters in the film, quite visibly in the crucified Wagner of the first prelude, as faint hints in other contexts.

For some time, both before and after Amfortas withholds the Grail from his congregants, the Grail society has been undergoing a deterioration similar to the decline Wagner described as applying to his contemporary Germany. This religious, physical, and moral decline was supposedly spreading in spite of the country's political rise as the new (second) Reich established by Bismarck. Wagner made it his mission to combat the so-called degeneration with art to show the way toward spiritual and general revitalization. He published most of his thoughts on this topic in a series of essays in the *Bayreuther Blätter*, among them "Religion and Art" (1880), "Of What Use is This Insight?" (1880), "Know Thyself" (1881), and "Herodom and Christianity" (1881). Known as his "regeneration" texts, they were written between the publication of *Parsifal* as a drama in 1877 and the conclusion of the score in 1882. Due to the time frame of their genesis, *Parsifal* is generally seen as the music drama that more so than the preceding ones expresses Wagner's idea on "regeneration." Many also consider it his most anti-Semitic work, with the "Aryan" program as a hidden agenda disguised in the pseudo-religious content. This widespread interpretation of *Parsifal* views Amfortas' sin as sexual defilement through intercourse with a Jewish temptress, not as a transgression against the code of chastity implicit in the text. According to the same thinking, Amfortas and his Grail society are Gentiles, while Klingsor and Kundry are Jewish and therefore "must" die by the end of the play. Wagner provoked such readings through his writings, actions, and private comments. One can therefore not dismiss the view as distorted or exaggerated. It would have been a relief if Wagner had lived and worked in a pattern of contrapuntal composition, making the Jew and the Gentile simply two voices of the human subject. But although his music dramas do not contain explicit anti-Semitism, they suffer from being surrounded by prose writings that express such bias clearly enough, starting with "Judaism in Music." Much of contemporary scholarship on Wagner has therefore consisted in reinterpreting the music dramas as veiled carriers of prejudice and subversion.[67] Seen against this trend, Syberberg's treatment of Amfortas and Titurel assumes new nuances.

Titurel's appearance provides several clues. First of all, his resemblance to Ludwig II brings to mind another paternal Ludwig, namely Wagner's father or stepfather, Ludwig Geyer. Although Mr. Geyer died at a young age, the composer still mentioned him frequently in private while he was working on *Parsifal*. Geyer was not forgotten, then, but due to the uncertain "heritage," suppressed both by Wagner, his descendants, and by Nazi authorities (Spotts, 174–75). The memory of this Ludwig was so-to-speak relegated to a mental storage closet (*Rumpelkammer*), much like a skeleton in a closet. Or in this case, a mummy in a closet. This closet lies under the Bayreuth stage. When the composer's grandson, Wieland Wagner, assumed the leadership of the festival in 1951, his motto was *Entrümpeln,* "cleaning house" or "clearing out the closets"; in other words, discarding the contents of the *Rumpelkammer.* Although this is usually understood as a resolve to a fresh start without the ballast of the "Bayreuth" tradition, it also resulted in turning the back on the history of "Bayreuth's" role before 1945. One suppressed the past without dealing with it. But just as Amfortas' father, the past still continues to haunt the king.

As Titurel sits pleading with his son to conduct the Grail ceremony, one leg is seen sticking out from under the cloak. It is totally bandaged, as is also the only visible arm. Most of his body appears to be as wrapped as a mummy. The mummy is familiar to the reader from the chapter on *Hitler*. In spite of the bandaging he is able to hold up a spear and remain seated. This pose was inspired by Ingres' painting *Jupiter and Thetis*, as the book to the film notes (99). The brief reference establishes a connection between Jupiter and Titurel. Jupiter, as well as his father before him, ascended to the position of ruling god by emasculating and forcefully dethroning the father. Later times relegated Jupiter to the same kind of underground "grave" that his forefathers and Titurel inhabit, dead as gods but still alive as mythic and psychological powers. The revolution, or circular progression of time, has now almost reached the end of the Amfortas era, and the advent of the new leader will dispatch him to join his father. His injury indicates that the process has started. Furthermore, Jupiter had transformed himself repeatedly into a swan in his amorous pursuits, and a dead swan is lying next to Titurel. Jupiter as a "correspondence" can, moreover, be found in the Sefirotic Tree of Life (or Labyrinth) where it "belongs" to the *sefira* Chesed. Among the other attributes associated with this position one finds water (yes, the puddle is there), the color blue (yes, Titurel's cloak is blue), and the swan (Regardie, 52–54). Since Jupiter is also a planetary deity, one wonders if other celestial correspondences from the Tree of Life will appear as correlates to other characters. Amfortas' splendid starry cloak, which he is unable to wear, might fit into such a pattern. The imagery of the Tree of Life was borrowed from Jewish mysticism and has been appropriated and/or adapted by many esoteric movements. The names of the connecting paths of the Tree of Life are the same as those of the trump cards in the Tarot pack, supplemented by the Hebrew letters that also form words when pronounced. The reader may remember the references to "Door" (*daleth*) and "Window" (*he*). Another might be the "Back of the Head" (*qoph*), applying to the scene when the head of a boy blocks the view of the dead swan.

Among the trump cards one recognizes the "Fool" and "Death." The imagery associated with the twenty-two paths and ten *sefirot* describes the progression of the soul. Jupiter appears in this system merely as a correspondence to a *sefira*. Similarly, Syberberg's book mentions his name only in passing when describing Titurel as sitting "in the pose of Ingres' Jupiter." A comparison of the painted god and the film's character confirms the pose as being similar. In addition, Jupiter is holding a spear in his right hand, and so is Titurel. The latter's spear is partially wrapped in black fabric, and the angled top section suggests that the shaft is broken. A broken spear is an attribute of the personified Synagogue in numerous medieval artworks, for example in the Cathedral of Strasbourg. Implying defeat and impotence, the attribute expresses polarity and, obviously, antagonism toward Judaism. Now the film equips Amfortas' father with this symbol. One might be tempted to downplay its function to merely a sign of weakness. After all, Titurel refers to himself as being too weak to conduct the ritual. Since a spear is commonly seen as a masculine symbol, Titurel evokes not only Jupiter, but also the latter's emasculated forefathers. The unkind cut as a mythic rite of passage still haunts his grave chamber. But the broken spear retains its significance as a religious attribute in a subtle way towards the end of the Grail ceremony. Having seen the Grail, Titurel rejoices. The film does not actually show him witness it. Contrary to expectation, he lies down as if returning to the slumber of the dead. This gesture makes his dialogue with Amfortas resemble the appearance of a ghost or mummy-wrapped corpse. The apparition of Hitler's corpse from Wagner's grave comes to mind, especially since the opening above has the same dimension in both graves. But unlike the Hitler episode, Titurel's corpse stays underground. His body quickly turns grey as if icing over or becoming a cocoon or stone. Suddenly the rear wall of the grave chamber opens up to a mausoleum full of sarcophagi. Of course this view is one of Syberberg's projections onto a frame-filling screen. That means that Titurel's supine figure joins other effigies in a crypt. The book to the film informs the reader that this crypt can be found in the Royal Abbey of Saint Denis: "— the royal graves of France, the country where the Parsifal legend originated and the Holy Land of Ludwig II of Bavaria" (99). True enough, although Eleanor of Aquitaine, who prefigured Titurel as an effigy in the film, is not buried there. As usual, Syberberg's comment omits other important reasons for a visual reference to Saint Denis. The reasons are hidden mainly in the architecture of that sanctuary. One is a stained glass window that includes a personified Synagogue.[68] Another is a series of statue columns removed from the building in 1771. They represented " Old Testament figures showing the royal ancestry of Christ and the concordance between the Old and New Testaments" (Crosby, 284). A third reason is the shape of the original crypt, its ambulatory, and radiating chapels. They served as foundations and supports for the choir, ambulatory, and radiating chapels exactly overhead on ground level (Crosby, 243). Viewed vertically, the two designs looked the same with one resting on top of the other. Viewed horizontally, the figure columns flanking three portals presented a continuity that started with outstanding men and women in the Hebrew Bible, continuing into the Christian era. Thus, although being a Christian sanctuary, the Abbey Church of Saint Denis incorporated, preserved, and displayed the Judaic foundation of the Christian faith. The saint after whom it was named is in popular tradition identified with Dionysius the Areopagite. The mystical writings attributed to him, or a Pseudo-Dionysius, have long been revered in esoteric schools (Querido, 104). When the film places Titurel in the crypt of Saint Denis, he becomes a part of this tradition. Moreover, his inclusion in this crypt identifies him as a 'foundation" for the Grail Hall above. Since the rites there are presumably inspired by a Christian liturgy, one assumes that the spirit from the supporting level below is closer to Judaism. Titurel's spear identifies him as belonging to the older stratum. It is, after all, the Synagogue's attribute. One is again reminded of the bow-and-string symbol with its religious implications. Father and son represent two religious traditions as well as two eras. A corroborating allusion is the transformation of Titurel into an apparent stone effigy. One is reminded of Fritz Lang's *Siegfried*, where the title hero kills Alberich, upon which the latter and all the Nibelungen dwarfs turn into stone before the spectators' eyes. Most recent literature on both Lang and Wagner interprets Alberich and the Nibelungs as barely veiled Jewish caricatures.[69] Like Titurel and the pre-Celtic fairy-like Tuatha de Danann, the Nibelungen had also been relegated to an underground realm.[70] Furthermore, Titurel's underground location (in the film) evokes Wolfram's story. He lets Parzival's father trace his ancestry back to fairies. The father, Gahmuret, subsequently dies in the service of a geographically and historically remote but still powerful potentate called a *baruc*. Perhaps Wagner read that title creatively and reinterpreted his Alberich not only as an *albe rîche* (rich elf) but also as *al baruch*. However, for his Titurel he invented a Christianized setting replete with two relics from Christ's Passion. Even if one dismisses all these associations, Syberberg obviously reinvests Titurel with an Old Testament connotation. This he achieves primarily through the broken spear and the crypt in the Abbey Church of Saint Denis. Another hint is the star pattern on the cloth draped over the bier or sarcophagus on which his transformation occurs. All these stars have six points, like the Star of David. Perhaps also the similarity with King Ludwig could be viewed in this light, due to the monarch's disdain for Wagner's anti-Semitism. Wagner could not afford to reject the king's offer to use his orchestra and conductor free of charge for *Parsifal*. When Wagner objected to the conductor, Hermann Levi, on the grounds that he was Jewish, the king showed no sympathy for his prejudice. From Wagner's perspective, the king must have appeared as a champion for those the composer abhorred. The monarch's fondness for the Jewish actor Josef Kainz would support that view, as well as his visit to the synagogue in Fürth in 1866 (Gutman, 414). That might place the "imposing" King Ludwig in the same category as Hermann Levi, who "was imposed" on Wagner against his will. In this respect, Wagner's reluctance to obey his king resembles Amfortas' refusal to serve. The latter actually persists in his unwillingness quite vigor-ously. But blurring these associations is the nickname Wagner gave the king. In the early years of the patronage, he was referred to as Parzival in Wagner's family circle. He was literally Wagner's savior. As already mentioned, the composer also addressed the monarch as his redeemer in their correspondence, e.g. his letter to the king of April 29, 1866.

Towards the end of the long monologue, Amfortas prays, "Nimm mir mein Erbe" (remove my legacy/heritage from me). Even if one reads *Erbe* only as "inherited duty," the plea to be released from it activates a double echo. One comes from *Ludwig*, the other from the Bible. The cinematic King Ludwig, who wants to be released from his monarchic duties and the conspirators, utters a plea similar to that of Jesus' "Remove this cup from me." The film about Ludwig also abounds in quasi-biblical references, including the foot-washing, the pose of the beloved disciple, the statement "It is finished," an execution, and finally, a resurrection. These Christ-like allusions do not really fit Ludwig, since he appears unworthy. But whether blasphemous or just contrived, the similarities are obvious. The confusion stemming from the pleas for release by King Ludwig in the earlier film and King Amfortas on the one hand and the apparent merging of Titurel and King Ludwig on the other dissolves in the daring religious referent. Both Christ as the Divine Son and the Father are aspects of a triune but one Divinity, the Church teaches. Syberberg may also have been inspired to his quasi-mystical multiplication of avatars and the distribution of eras by Emma Jung. She observes in *The Grail Legend* that the medieval Amfortas " corresponds to an *imago Dei* that is suspended, suffering, . . . he is thus essentially the image of the Christian age and more especially of its second half" (298). About Titurel she states, "[T]he apparently living Grail King must have personified a still older god-image; actually, the pre-Christian, Old Testament or pagan *imago Dei*, a father figure" (298). Emma Jung's observations, which were first published posthumously in 1960, coincide with the film's treatment in numerous details. As her book does in its scholarly fashion, so also Syberberg's artistic handling of the religious, mythical, and historical dimensions serves to elucidate psychological complexities. As one discovers, he had his reasons for locating the action within Wagner's head.

An even more important source of inspiration may have been the studies by Emma Jung's husband, Carl Gustav Jung. Especially his *Aion* discusses several symbols of the psyche that also happen to occur in Wolfram's, Wagner's, and most visibly, in Syberberg's versions of the Grail story. Drawing on copious ancient and medieval literature, Jung identifies, for example, the Gnostic father-image as the unconscious in terms applying remarkably well to the film's Titurel. He is eternally young, both male and female, and represents the "latent possibility of consciousness" (191). By giving Titurel the appearance of Ludwig II, Syberberg rejuvenated the father. "Male and female" fits him after the mythical, unkind cut. The film about King Ludwig also has the subtitle "Requiem for a Virginal King." This adjective, *jungfräulich*, is rarely used about a man today. Besides, not only is Titurel-Ludwig underground, the ideal location for the unconscious, but he also returns to slumber, signaling the latency, or intermittent activity, of consciousness. Jung describes this "original man" as a symbol of wholeness and a cosmic Anthropos as evidenced by his royal insignia (198). Especially in his latent state he

is named *Aipolos*, "the Pole that turns the Cosmos round" (216). One remembers
the starry mantle that Amfortas has inherited but cannot wear. Furthermore, while
quoting from such diverse sources as Hippolytus and Paracelsus, Jung also adds
such terms as "Papa," "cadaver," and "mummy in a tomb" to the list of names and
epithets of the unconscious (213). Since Titurel-Ludwig speaks from the grave and
is wrapped like a mummy, there can no longer be any doubt that Titurel represents
an archetype of great complexity.

This father symbol undergoes further differentiation as a God-image in Jung's
Aion (189, 192). In this context, so Jung explains repeatedly, it is related to Christ
as the "inner man" and "second Adam" (201). The Christ theme is prevalent in the
chapter named "Gnostic Symbols of the Self." Most, but not all, of the quoted
literature deals with concepts from ancient and medieval Christian Gnosticism.
Wolfram incorporated a significant number of neo-Manichaean and Gnostic
elements in his version, and Wagner added others, e.g. Kundry's reincarnations. It
comes as no surprise, then, that the film resorts to imagery borrowed from that
tradition. Jung's discussion of this symbolism can only be considered serendipitous
for Syberberg.

As the God-image of unconsciousness, Titurel is also the begetter and
organizing principle of consciousness. The creation or result is Amfortas, whose
sin, in Jung's line of thought, is a fall or relapse into unconsciousness through
"union of opposites" (*Aion*, 193). Gustav Klimt's painting *The Kiss* may serve as
a variant of this theme. As a result of his fall, or injury, Amfortas is no longer the
"perfect man." In Jung's symbolism of the perfect man, the Greek concept of *teleios*
is central (212-13). The word means primarily "whole" and "complete," but
possesses many nuances, such as "initiated," "perfect," "pure," "having received
nous" (spirit), "having *gnosis*," and "being without spot or blemish." Clearly,
Amfortas is not intact and therefore not *teleios*.

While Amfortas exhausts himself in his lamentations, he remains seated on the
throne, still wrapped in the toga-like blanket. The throne is placed at the edge of
Titurel's open grave, creating an abyss for Amfortas. This positioning at the abyss
varies the pose of the Amfortas marionette in the prelude, where it was placed at the
front edge of the stage. As expected, the king is seated in a spacious "hall" with the
rearranged concrete segments of the Wagner mask serving as walls. Visible above
them is a still taller mountain wall with a few architectural details, not the domed
interior called for in this scene. Nowhere can one see the numerous men kneeling
and anticipating the liturgy. Actually, only the king's attendants surround him,
replete with the wounded swan of porcelain and the bleeding wound on a cushion.
In stead of the pseudo-realism of a miraculous ritual, the film opts for a symbolic
and psychological enactment. Throughout this scene the camera pans or adjusts
from close-ups to long shots, concentrating, for example, on the wound when
Amfortas mentions it. Practically all reviewers of the film have commented on this
alienating object. Most of them refer to its similarity with the female anatomy.
Strangely enough, one searches in vain among these articles for any recognition of
its psychological dimension. Separated from Amfortas' body, the bleeding gash is

clearly a projection of something or someone rejected. Both Freud and Jung define this concept in similar terms. For Freud's use of the word one encounters this definition: "Projection is the process by virtue of which internal perceptions of feelings which are unacceptable to the individual are projected to an outsider or to some outside force" (Fine, 127). Jungians choose different words for the same idea: "The situation in which one unconsciously invests another person (or object) with notions or characteristics of one's own . . . One also projects negative feelings."[71] Amfortas' condition is not just a physical affliction; the division in projected wound and body indicates a psychological denial and rejection. A rejection of whom or what? Klingsor and the temptress, it appears. Without them there would not have been a wound. But the father-son constellation also points to Amfortas' heritage, which he probably shares with the temptress. Perhaps one may formulate his rejection as applying both to the temptress and everything she represents as well as his heritage and everyone reminding him of it. Wagner's obsession with everything Jewish would justify that interpretation.

Amfortas' concluding appeal following "Remove my heritage [or legacy] from me" deserves a comment. He continues with "schließe die Wunde" (close the wound), "daß heilig ich sterbe" (that I may die holy), and "rein Dir gesunde!" (regain health and purity for you). He is praying for three things: relief from inherited duties, healing, and death. Why would he want to die if he might gain relief from both his legacy and his affliction? This death wish defies explanation unless one remembers his earlier statement on the way to the lake. Amfortas says there, "[T]he pure fool, I think I recognize him if I might call him Death." He knows at heart that only death can relieve him from his misery. He welcomes death. But he does not want to die a maimed man. If Jesus could die with spear- and nail-wounds in his body, why cannot Amfortas make peace with his injury? And what does his wound have to do with purity? He seems to believe that an intact body is the only worthy vessel for a holy or forgiven soul. Amfortas' thinking is not unique. The attitude can be found in, e.g., the practice and philosophy of alchemists. A condition for completion of their work is the wholeness or oneness in themselves, as outlined in the "Tabula smaragdina" and Geber's *Summa perfectionis*, Jung explains in *Psychology and Alchemy* (255). Writers on spagyric work presuppose a similarity between the practitioner and the secret of matter. Quoting from several old sources Jung continues by stating that the alchemist must be worthy of his task: "He must accomplish in his own self the same process that he attributes to matter, 'for things are perfected by their like'" (*Psych. and Alch.*, 267). In other words, an operator with a physical, intellectual, or emotional handicap is not likely to succeed in an effort aiming at alchemical perfection. Wagner touches upon the same issue in the article "Herodom and Christendom": "It was a weighty feature of the Christian Church, that none but sound and healthy persons were admitted to the vow of total world-renunciation; any bodily defect, not to say mutilation, unfitted them."[72] The need for having an unblemished body may also relate to requirements practiced by some esoteric societies, more recently by Freemasons. For example, at least until 1875 candidates for admission to Masonry had to be fit mentally, morally, and physically, with the last prerequisite specified as "a perfect youth, having no maim or defect in his body."[73] Another source of inspiration might be the Kabbalistic and Gnostic teaching of the broken vessels. The *sefirot* that fractured under the stress of the divine flow caused sparks to get lost. The human mission consists in repairing the damage and restoring the transmission. It is worth noting that Wolfram von Eschenbach, who usually refers to the ailing king as Anfortas (without strength?) also occasionally writes Amfortas. That form of the name includes, or embraces, the German *Amfora*, which of course means "vessel." And this amphora is broken up by the embedded letter *t*. Amfortas is literally a broken vessel in need of restoration. With *t* read as the Hebrew *tau*, mystics would think of the *tau*-cross, a crucified Amfortas. But as Scholem points out, the Kabbalah also indicates that the restoration process (*tikkun*) results in a reconfiguration of the four *sefirot* that had not been shattered, supplemented by a fifth combined from those that had broken (*Kabbalah*, 140). Each of these new forms represents a phase in the process of catharsis. As a broken vessel, Amfortas would be "reborn" as a component of the fifth new *parzuf*, Ze'eir Anpin. Amfortas has not accepted that predicament of transformation. He associates an intact body with holiness and wholeness. That might indicate an indebtedness both to the Kabbalah and to Catharism, which shared some Gnostic roots with Jewish mysticism, such as the belief in reincarnation. Both Wolfram and Wagner may have had in mind the Cathars in connection with Amfortas' predicament. Neo-Manichaean-Gnostic Catharism was so widespread in Southern France in Wolfram's days that, according to Ignaz von Döllinger, certain geographic designations, such as a "Provençal," meant both a man from Provence and a Cathar, an "Albigensian," both a man from Albi and a Cathar.[74] Wolfram's alleged source, Kyot the Provençal, may, then, have been a Cathar. "Cathar" (pure) provided the root for the German *Ketzer*, or "heretic" (Döllinger, 127). Other terms for Cathars included Arrians, Arians, and Paterins. For example, the Roman tribune Cola di Rienzo was accused of being a Paterin (Döllinger, 129). He became the title hero of Wagner's *Rienzi*. It appears that Wagner was attracted to characters with an unorthodox belief already early in his career. Despite numerous dogmatic differences among them, the Cathars disputed the dogma of Christ's divine nature and shared a dualistic belief, in which the fall of Lucifer and the angels plays a central role (Döllinger, 54–55). These angels are trapped in living bodies and must undergo a series of reincarnations until they are reborn in the soul of a perfect one. The perfect or pure ones are the "real" Cathars, a small number within the community of followers. They have undergone the baptism of the Holy Spirit, *consolamentum*. They must, in contrast to the supporters and "believers" (*credentes*), lead a severely ascetic life. These saints or perfect ones had to complete a probationary period of at least fifteen years before receiving the *consolamentum*. Besides severe fasting, they must refrain from taking a life, eating meat, owning property, or touch a person of the opposite sex (Döllinger, 204–6). Upon their death, the souls of the perfect ones, and the angels trapped in their persons, return directly to heaven (Döllinger, 205). By Cathar standards, Amfortas as the highest ranking member of the Grail society should have received the baptism of the Holy Spirit and lead a saintly, ascetic life. But he had jeopardized this state of holiness by transgressing two of the rules: through *minne* service to a lady in Wolfram's version and explicit sexual indulgence in Wagner's text, and through the use of arms. In the medieval text he even killed the knight who inflicted his wound. Unlike the *templeise*, Amfortas should have refrained from fighting to avoid killing anyone. In his fallen condition Amfortas' only hope for redemption is healing and a repeated rite of the *consolamentum* by another pure one. After that, an early death would be the best protection against renewed sinning. If the character of Amfortas was really modeled on a Cathar spiritual leader, one may wonder why not the hermit could assume his position as priest and leader of the believers, since he appears to be a holy man in several versions. One reason not mentioned in Wolfram's text could be that the hermit had not yet completed his probationary period; another could have been the need for dissimulation to avoid suspicion of heresy. The fact that he changed the story about the fallen angels might be read as such a protective strategy. Wagner, on the other hand, refashioned the subject matter thoroughly and incorporated elements from several religious traditions. This syncretism has received a Christian veneer through the treatment of Grail and lance, but has not strengthened the inherent logic of the narrative. But both the medieval and Wagner's texts are convincing parables of psychological development.

Another possible source of inspiration is Jewish mysticism. As unlikely as this connection appears in view of Wagner's prejudice, it emerges as a strong probability also in his version of the story. According to his text, the Grail holds the blood collected from Christ's wound. But only during the ceremony does the Grail begin to glow and does Amfortas feel its effect. An "indwelling" is taking place. As in the Roman-Catholic Eucharist and Neoplatonic syncretic ritual, something divine is being drawn down to the ceremony. In Hebrew tradition, Moshe Idel explains, the Divine Presence, or Shekhinah, had retreated from the Temple to heaven as a consequence of ongoing human sin. Human intervention is required to induce it to descend again.[75] During Amfortas' meditation it first makes its presence perceptible through a ray of light from above and through the luminosity of the Grail. Only subsequently does it continue into Amfortas, occupying his body. His own sinful blood flees, leaving his body through the wound, which now bleeds profusely. This magical occurrence echoes Idel's analysis of several Kabbalistic descriptions: "On the ground of these parallels, we can seriously consider the possibility that the Temple service was conceived as inducing the presence of the Shekhinah in the Holy of Holies; thus the service can be seen as a theurgical activity" (168). The author emphasizes the priest's function as the vessel for this indwelling: "According to some texts, the structure is not a building, but the human body, which is the living statue on whom the indwelling of the Shekhinah takes place" (168). Idel corroborates this with several textual examples from Hebrew sources and concludes: "Therefore, beside the theurgical 'reparation' of the Sefirot, man is able to cause the descent of the divine influx upon himself" (169). This is later varied: "[T]he person is viewed as a vessel collecting the divine efflux" (170). Amfortas' problem is of course the imperfect condition of his "vessel." According to the Kabbalah, his affliction should also affect the Divine, since Jewish mysticism shares with Hermetism the belief in a correlation between everything above and below. Idel quotes from the *Sefer he-Yihud*: "For when the lower man blemishes one of his limbs, as that limb is blemished below, it is as if he cuts the corresponding supernal limb. . . . For when the human form is perfect below, it brings about perfection above" (184). According to the libretto, Amfortas appears able to perform the ritual without any diminished effect or indication that the Divine Presence suffers with him during the ritual. Wagner may have weakened the Kabbalistic effect by emphasizing a Christianized ceremony. However, one might interpret the non-comprehending Parsifal, and hence the delayed redemption through him, as a sign that the divine transmission struggles through a flawed passage. Another sign appears later outside the death mask.

As with so many events in Wagner's dramas, the action can also be viewed as an externalized presentation of an internal experience or process. The film has already prepared the viewer for a non-traditional handling of the Grail rite. It therefore comes as no surprise that the visual action deviates from the printed stage instructions.

The music dictates the length of the Grail ceremony, which actually fills the second half of act 1. Before Amfortas sinks back in exhaustion, the camera had dwelled for a while on the separated wound. Nearby, resting precariously on a tiny shelf in the mountain wall, stands a small statue of Parsifal. Like Titurel and the swan, this character has also been transformed into a work of art in stone, but no larger than a Nibelung. Although it had not been seen in the procession, this copy of the Zumbusch statue apparently takes its place in the ritual as a revered visualization of the promised redeemer. Propped against the rock, the figure faces a precipice, much like Amfortas, who is situated at the edge of the tomb-abyss, much like Kleist's Prince of Homburg. The appearance of the statue precedes the division between two contrapuntal movements, since the chorus soon mentions the prophesy about the promised fool. But as a *mise en abyme* it also functions as a genre shifter. As the image changes to a large open book surrounded by children and young girls, one hears only men's voices. The discrepancy between sound and image marks the first instance of a shift in genre based on manipulation of the word *genre*. This loan word reverts to French, where it also means "gender." Of course one soon discovers that the book contains music, probably the score of the music being played. Thus the *mise en abyme* still functions as a genre shifter in the prevailing sense as well: the readable version as compared to the audible version. The surreal book, resting on a ten-step staircase or Jacob's Ladder, is surrounded by angelic-looking young "singers" and cloud-like vapors. It disappears suddenly for a glimpse of Titurel below. For the last time, he calls for the uncovering of the Grail, "Enthüllet den Gral!"

According to the libretto, Amfortas now proceeds with the ceremony. The film avoids the reenactment as outlined in print. The viewers find themselves abruptly outside the mask landscape to the accompaniment of orchestral music only. The profile of Wagner's death mask forms the horizon of a flat, empty expanse strewn with dead leaves. Crossing this space from the left side of the camera toward the background, a young girl walks slowly with the train of her dress trailing. As she approaches the mask, two children in her wake come into view. They carry a stretcher with a large object covered with cloth. The arrangement combines several familiar motifs, each functioning as a visual leitmotif: the litter or stretcher, which previously had transported the king and the swan, the carriers' struggling with the weight of their burden, and an object concealed under a cloth. The two youngsters follow the young girl, making the progression look like a procession. They disappear into the mask landscape. Of course the mask is again a projection onto a huge screen, and an invisible smaller screen a few feet in front of it hides the passage into which the group disappears. Syberberg had introduced a similar effect in the fourth part of *Hitler*. At this point one can only guess that the three approach the Grail Hall to participate in the ceremony, which is now in progress.

A cut to the large book surrounded by "singers" restores the harmony between voices and image, at least at first glance. This time the accompanying voices are sopranos heard "from on high." The reader is reminded of Wagner's "Liebesmahl der Apostel." There the voices "from on high" are singing words by Jesus in the first person singular (268). The parallel of voices "from on high" in the early composition and the Grail ceremony suffers a notable transformation that also functions contrapuntally within the film. Not until this scene can one discern the contents of the open pages of the book. One page contains music. As the book to the film points out, it consists of an excerpt of the *Parsifal* score that Wagner mailed to Judith Gautier as thanks for the silks and fragrances she sent him from Paris (98). This returns the memory of Wagner's love-life and sybaritic taste during a supposedly sublime ritual. Conflicting with the words resembling those of Jesus from on high are Wagner's carnal passions. The other page of the open book shows a sketch of Wagner. It is the portrait sketch made of him the day before he died. The visibility of his features coincides with the paraphrase of Jesus' words during the Last Supper. Presumably celebrating a ritual modeled on that event on Maundy Thursday, Wagner as the author of the statement intrudes into our consciousness. Of course he does not repeat verbatim the wordings from any of the biblical gospels, but lets the voices sing, "Take my body, take my blood, for the sake of our love." This is soon varied as, "Take my blood, take my body, in remembrance of me." The last phrase was clearly inspired by Luke 22.19. As the film presents it, Wagner seems to pronounce these words, imitating the action of Christ while addressing Judith. Again one remembers the crucified Wagner doll in the prelude. And did not Wagner try to adapt the biblical Jesus to his own image in the draft and notes to "Jesus of Nazareth"?[76] Does he function as a Christ to his believers? Does the juxtaposition aim at blasphemy? The visual reminder of Wagner and his foibles introduces a jarring counterpoint.

During the ceremony numerous brief scenes provide some visual variation in the slow and static plot. The group with the book appears several times. Some changes in the constellation of the "singers" raise questions. Why, for example, are

Cosima's five children missing the next time one glimpses the three women sitting on the highest boulders, and later, when the children are restored, why is Mathilde Wesendonck missing? One suspects a pattern resembling moves back and forth in time, an effect similar to the progression through the time tunnel. Another cut to the young girl from outside reveals her to be the mournful Grail Carrier. She now appears with a crown resembling that of Herzeleide's. In her right hand she holds a staff wrapped in black fabric and topped by a cross. The wrapped shaft revives the memory of Titurel's spear that is also wrapped in black gauze. But her staff is not broken. In her left hand the young girl holds a shiny chalice. Unlike Wagner's crystal vessel and Wolfram's stone container, this goblet is of reflective metal. It was probably inspired by Chrétien's golden cup. Her attributes identify her as the Ecclesia, or Church, allegory from the Cathedral of Strasbourg. Named Faith in *Hitler*, that figure displays a triumphant pose at odds with the black gauze and dejected demeanor. They suggest mourning more in line with the complementary statue named Synagogue, now also named Faith. As Grail Carrier, this character appears to have undergone a partial metamorphosis. She embodies several related identities. The composite nature of this figure may suggest the attempt by Christian authors to adapt an older, non-Christian idea for their purposes. From a compositional point of view, the roles converge in this figure. But as the counterpoint imbues the melodic components with new functions, e.g. when the dominant becomes the tonic, and they are heard together with several other transformations of themselves, they sound differently and are difficult to recognize. Syberberg's Grail Carrier inspires as many different interpretations as the Grail itself. As the bearer of the precious symbol she becomes a vessel in her own right. The Synagogue statue from Strasbourg carries in her left hand the tablets of the Law (or what looks like them). This symbol expresses the Law in a way reminiscent of Wolfram's oracle appearing on the Grail that dictates the action of its believers. He refers to the Grail Carrier, the king's sister, as the queen, *diu künegîn,* and maiden with the crown, *diu maget mit der krône.* But more importantly, he calls her Repanse de schoy. This name deserves a closer look.

At first glance Repanse de schoy looks like a clumsy attempt to transliterate a French-sounding name into German spelling. The *de* reveals the supposedly French origin. And *schoy* apparently corresponds to the French *joie* meaning "joy." *Repanse* looks like an amputated adaptation of *récompense.* This line of reasoning allows the name to read as "recompense of joy," an interpretation undoubtedly intended by the poet. But Wolfram was a wily and learned bard, not the illiterate entertainer many take him to be.[77] Repanse de schoy's name may not only evoke the reward awaiting the quester after a life of tribulations. The disfigured "recompense" has an interesting equivalent in Brown's dictionary of biblical Hebrew. One entry (*gimel, vau, resh, lamed*), or *gural,* lists under its fourth definition "portion = recompense, retribution." Several biblical examples illustrate the use as "implying divine agency." One of these passages is in Isaiah 17.14: "This is the portion of them that spoil us, and the lot of them that rob us." The other definitions offer nuances such as one's portion, allotted share, boundary, lot, apportion of lot, and fortune. Most importantly, the lot cast for decisions concerning assignment of property, punishment, or reward is carried out with small stones. The lot stones are spelled either with four letters, as the Hebrew word above, or with only three letters (*gimel, resh, lamed*), or *grl*, for which no vocalization is indicated. Both words look suspiciously similar to *graal, Gral,* and *grail*. And Wolfram's Grail is also a stone. The preceding entry in the dictionary, which may or may not be related etymologically, includes a *t* in it (*gimel, resh, teth, lamed*). It refers to vessels or basins used in the Temple. With this cluster of Hebrew words in mind one might be tempted to read the Grail Carrier's name as containing the Grail in it, and also as having something to do with divine agency.[78] A medieval name often expresses a quality of its bearer. Repanse de schoy might therefore be expected to share properties of the Grail. As for the divine agency, one is again reminded of the comments by Idel about the ancient service in the Temple being theurgic. The priest would call down the Divine Presence, or Shekhinah. This presence also accompanied the Israelites after the exodus from Egypt as a pillar of fire at night (Exodus 13.22). Wagner may have adapted this expression in his stage instructions when calling for "a blinding ray of light" to descend on the Grail and activate its luminosity. Syberberg's Grail Carrier does not "descend" visually, but she is obviously called from afar to be present during the ritual, hinting at the notion of a divine presence.

The Grail Carrier in Wolfram's story has also *schoy* in her name. If the poet adapted the French *j* to *sch* in German, why was he not consistent with the rest of the word? The French vowels in *joie* should be rendered as *oa* in German. Did he actually pronounce *schoy* to rhyme with "boy"? This is less likely than his using the inconsistent spelling as a scandalon. It catches the attention of the educated reader who wonders why. A consistent transliteration would have yielded *schoa*. And that sounds like the Hebrew word that is usually rendered in English letters as *shoah*. It means "destruction" and "ruin." With the Grail Kingdom often viewed as the abode of the blessed dead, the Grail Carrier's name now reverberates as "peace in death" or "reward after death." Of course Wagner does not give the carrier of his Grail a name. He only specifies that four "boys" carry in the covered ark or shrine containing the Grail, and that they assist in the unveiling. The already quoted passage in Cosima Wagner's diary mentions a Miss Kramer as *the* Grail carrier during the 1882 season. One can therefore not be sure if the production under Wagner's direction followed, or deviated from, his instructions in the libretto on this point. But the fact remains that he deemphasized the role in the printed version. Syberberg moves to the opposite extreme, endowing his character with multiple roles. They are of course all related. Given the Semitic Imane in Wolfram's story, one suspects that a Hebrew, or at least non-Christian, origin serves as the common denominator. This element surfaces again in the Grail Carrier's name. Of course Syberberg does not spell out her name, it suffices that Wolfram did. If one pronounces the last part of Repanse de schoy's name as *Shoah*, the Holocaust returns to the narrative. It already informed Kundry's play with brown leaves, and they again cover the ground that the Grail Carrier must cross to reach the landscape of the mind. This hidden dimension may explain in part the mournful look of the young girl. She is not only grieving over Amfortas' predicament, the sinfulness of the world, and the passing of Old Testament hegemony in matters of faith. She also mourns the millions murdered during the Shoah. Since the character is played by the director's daughter, one may assume that she functions as a visible extension of himself in this expression of grief.

The libretto states that darkness sets in during Amfortas' prayer, that a ray of light falls from above on the Grail, which now turns luminous radiating a red glow. The film observes some of these instructions while focusing on the Grail Carrier. As the environment darkens, the mirror scales on her dress begin to emit or reflect reddish light. This reflective surface of her garment had previously established a vague resemblance of her outfit with the armor of the two knights flanking her in the shining-knights episode. Wolfram's Parzival had at first held these knights for celestial beings. A parallel occurs in one of Gustav Klimt's paintings of Athena, who wears a golden armor with scaled breastplate. Thus not only the chalice but also the person holding it emanates intensifying light. One is hard pressed to distinguish if the surface is the source of the light or only transmits it. Eventually, as a concession to Wagner's idea of the Grail ritual, a drawing of it by Paul Joukowsky is reflected on the shiny surfaces of dress and goblet.[79] Thus Amfortas, sketched in black and white and holding up a wide, radiating vessel, appears only as a reflection. The fractured and fragmented image reintroduces the genesis of the first production, but not its actual presentation on stage or screen. Nonetheless, the superimposed, mirrored image conveys the diversity of interpretations of the Grail and its ritual.

During the scenes that show the Grail Carrier with her attributes and mirrored effects, she is standing outside the mask landscape. The viewer saw her enter this landscape upon her arrival. Now she has emerged alone, presumably from this same background. She left behind her helpers with the covered object, but acquired a crown, cross, and goblet while inside the Wagner head. Her scale-covered dress, however, did not change. It would appear that she arrived when called, but then removed herself to a position outside the sanctuary. Did she leave at her own initiative? Did Amfortas' injury cause an obstacle? Or was she turned away due to her unwelcome "legacy"? In the book to the film Syberberg only hints at technical difficulties as the reason for placing the projections during the Grail ceremony outside the head (111). Maybe so. But one is entitled to suspect that he again omits the real reason. For example, on p.106 he describes the Grail Carrier as coming from the eye where Kundry had lain down to sleep. This might suggest a connection between Kundry and the young girl. The director also wants to present the reflection on her dress as being "like memories of old times" (107). Kundry as the Great Mother and remotest archetypal Anima of diverse manifestations cannot be integrated into a conscious mind. If the Grail Carrier is one of her avatars, she cannot be integrated either. That might explain her position outside the head. Jung's theory of the Great Mother and her younger version displays great similarity with the ancient Demeter-Persephone constellation and with the Kabbalistic imagery surrounding the Holy Name. From a Kabbalistic perspective the Grail Carrier functions remarkably like the Shekhinah. This Divine Presence on earth is one of four anthropomorphic symbols corresponding to the four letters of the Name. The fourth letter, the second *he*, represents the "lower" Shekhinah.[80] But the reflection of Amfortas in the mirrored dress suggests that a second, different ritual is taking place simultaneously. His Grail may be the only mystery the assembly contemplates. Perhaps the congregants can see her as clearly as the viewers can, but since the film disperses them in meditating groups, one cannot be sure what they perceive. If this figure is related to the Divine Presence of the Hebrew Temple, it is worth noting that Wagner does not make Titurel build a church, but a "sanctuary," a *Heiligtum*. And the stage instructions make it clear that the Grail ceremony takes place in a hall (*Saal*), also called diningroom or refectory (*Speisesaal*), not the sanctuary. In Wolfram's version, the Grail is kept in its temple, except when the Grail Carrier brings it to the banquet hall for the duration of the feast. The film restores several temples on the hillside surrounding the castle. Thus the Grail Carrier could bring her covered and unidentified object from one of them to the castle. The film leaves the viewer free to identify her with a divine power or with just a member of the Grail society arriving from outside. Still, her presence appears to activate the transformation celebrated by the community, or, at least, her luminosity coincides with the activity.

The ritual suggested by the visible treatment is restricted to the revelation of a luminous Grail. The film omits the meal resembling a love feast or communion. With Amfortas out of view throughout a series of camera takes, the viewer is left bewildered about the ceremony. Again, this confusion parallels Parsifal's perplexity. Only the diminishing reflective illumination of the Grail Carrier and her chalice and Titurel's transformation into stone indicate the conclusion of the ritual. The subsequent six or seven short scenes show the dispersal and return of the participants. As they again form processions or file by individually, several new details come into view.

As in the arrival stage many of the celebrants carry objects. In addition to those already seen one notices another large chalice, probably representing the Bayreuth productions of *Parsifal*. Also, a magnificent crown has joined the parade of relics. It is a replica of the crown of the Holy Roman Empire of the German Nation. Although that crown was not made as early as in Charlemagne's lifetime, Albrecht Dürer painted a famous "portrait" of the empire's founder wearing it. Wagner admired Dürer's work and was probably familiar with this depiction. The crown is an object of legend and lore, not the least due to its large "orphan" gem, *der Waise*. It is viewed by some as a sun symbol.[81] That, as well as the crown itself, returns history and sun symbolism to the narrative. The tips of little Parsifal's crown introduced the sun imagery in the prelude. But also the name of the gem stone, *orphanus* and *Waise*, might have contributed to its inclusion. Of course Parsifal is an orphan. Besides, it has been claimed that *orphanus* evolved in popular language from *ophthalmus lapis,* and that word, "stone of the eye," brings us, via *pupillus/pupilla*, to "apple of the eye," "pupil," as well as "a small child" and "orphan" (Kampers, 455). Syberberg played with these semantic links in *Hitler* where his little daughter played an important role. Now grown to a teenager, she returns to the screen, and with her, the *pupilla* reference. Another reason for including the imperial crown among the relics had been prepared by Charlemagne's throne. Viewed nostalgically, both it and the crown bear testimony to a bygone era of unity and vigor. They are revered like religious relics. At the same time they also accentuate the current lack of such unity and vigor, much as the serrated edges in earlier imagery hint at *Zerrissenheit*. This symbolism could apply both to the age of Wagner, who bemoaned his country's need for "regeneration," and to Syberberg's Germany of 1982, still divided and also in need of spiritual regeneration, as he has stated repeatedly in writing.

The camera cuts unexpectedly to the exterior of a ruined Greek temple. One assumes that this is one of the sanctuaries around the castle. Actually, this ruin is the projection of a painting, *The Temple of Juno at Agrigentum*, by Caspar David Friedrich from ca. 1830.[82] Its condition resembles the dilapidated state of the various Grail halls that had appeared previously. Perhaps the choice of Mediterranean architecture from antiquity illustrates Wagner's enthusiasm for Greek religious rites. His idea for the Bayreuth festival took its inspiration from Greek theater. Equally pertinent may be the temple's dedication to Juno. A mere shadow of the older Great Mother, this goddess had also suffered a decline in status. If the ruin suggests the temple from which the Grail was brought, it hails from a distant era that has gone down in ruins. In the foreground stands a flat-bed cart with a covered object. One wonders if this is a transformed version of the stretcher seen earlier with the Grail Carrier. Four young people arrive and unveil the object before hauling the cart away. It is a replica of the polyhedron in Albrecht Dürer's *Melencolia I* of 1514. Another version of it appeared toward the end of the prelude. As a *pars pro toto*, this symbol of melancholy seems to be all that is left of former glory. One also wonders if the stone is related to the orphan-stone of the imperial crown. With its surface of polished facets it resembles human nature, which is also composed of so many aspects or qualities. While one side turns toward heaven, another reflects the earth. Wolfram described the Grail as a stone, so maybe it counts as a variant of the impossible-to-define goal of the quest. A few scenes later a monk carries away a smaller version of this stone, while another bears a covered spherical object that may be the globe-shaped Grail from the prelude. As if this proliferation did not suffice, a Christ-like participant also carries away a veiled chalice, evoking other stage Parsifals. Obviously, the Grail is not one defined object, perhaps not even an object at all. After all, Parsifal had asked *who* the Grail is. The sequence seems to offer all variants but no clear answers.

Amid a series of scenes with movement one static episode stands out. While men's voices sing the last stanzas of the knights, we see these warriors in full armor in a tight formation. Their faces are mostly hidden behind helmets and tall shields. Only the camera moves backwards, away from the knights, until Parsifal comes into view outside a rocky portal. Modeled on the *templeise*, the men present a dichotomy of pious words and martial appearance. They are apparently addressing the immobile Parsifal, hoping that he will reveal himself as the promised redeemer. In Wolfram's version this hope was shared tacitly by the assembled company. Wagner lets only Gurnemanz express this hope, while the others pay no attention to the half-hidden guest. Syberberg changes that while introducing an element of ambiguity through the formation of the group. He takes his cue from the stage instructions. They specify that the knights embrace each other solemnly before departing. We do not see them embrace or even move in this instance. But as they sing of love, fiery blood, happy companionship, and brotherly loyalty, one realizes that their formation leaves a path through the group. Obviously they hope to entice Parsifal to penetrate through this passage to join them. Their effort amounts to an attempted seduction. The sexual overtone seems at first incongruous with the sanctity of the occasion. However, the words allow such an interpretation, the formation suggests it visually, the moving camera imitates Riefenstahl's "seductive" technique, and the film's contrapuntal composition confirms it. The arduous knights prefigure the flower maidens.

In most of the episodes centered on the Grail ceremony, walking individuals and groups in procession provide movement. On a few occasions, billowing vapor, rising or falling, adds to the movement. These directional flows indicate the pseudo-musical stages in the visual composition. Eventually, the assembly has almost dispersed. One the last novices carries away the Parsifal statue. This is Michael Kutter without the wig. Portraying a different aspect of a seeking person, he nonetheless activates the memory of the Parsifal the spectators have come to know in the film. One sees Parsifal in several facets or manifestations, and now in another *mise en abyme* constellation of man and statue. At long last the focus rests on Michael Kutter as Parsifal still standing in the same spot as before. Now the king's procession passes directly by him. The wound on the cushion bleeds profusely, the celestial cloak worn by an attendant is as splendid as before, but the king is resting outstretched on his litter. Again one can only catch a glimpse of his hair. The rest of him is hidden under his blanket and behind the surrounding attendants. Parsifal may see even less of him than the viewers do. Throughout this take he presses a hand against his heart, but otherwise appears lost in a trance or state of confusion. When Gurnemanz asks if he understands what he has seen, he can only shake his head. This does not surprise the viewers, since they are likely to be equally confused. Gurnemanz loses his patience and sends him out through the rocky portal. Resembling the opening crack through which Parsifal had entered, it now closes behind him. Gurnemanz' dispatching words refer back to the swan Parsifal had killed as he entered Grail territory: "[I]n the future leave the swans alone and look for a goose, you gander!" These words also bring to mind Wolfram's text where an unseen page mocks Parzival as he leaves the castle, shouting, "You are a goose" ("ir sît ein gans"). One day later Parzival encounters the three drops of blood in the unseasonal snow in book 6. The drops have come from a wounded goose. The pattern of white and red reminds him of his wife whom he had left to visit his mother. Syberberg adapts part of this episode by letting Parsifal ponder three spots in a patch of "snow" outside the mask landscape. Confused by what he had observed in the Grail castle, the fool's thoughts may now seek refuge with the memory of the female companion he left behind as he set out on his adventures. Be it for only a short while, he may remember his alter ego who was still asleep as he walked away. This detail revives the motif of remembering versus forgetting and reintroduces the feminine aspect that does not appear in Wagner's text. It is, however, important in Syberberg's version of the story. Perhaps Parsifal's thoughts and the intensity of his feelings produce a result similar to what the prayer-like words of Gurnemanz and the squires had called forth earlier. It produces the presence of the Voice from on high.

During these last moments of act 1, an alto voice "from on high" sings the first two lines of the prophesy. The film moves this usually unseen character from the inner cupola to the outside, where she looks down on Parsifal from the top of the head landscape. Sharing with him the cold and now dark external world, she repeats the messianic promise, as if to console him and remind him of his mission. This alto voice is also portrayed by Amelie Syberberg. When she appeared with him in the shining knights episode, she was seated between him and his female alter ego. This constellation invites more associations than mentioned earlier. From a psychological perspective the three might represent the male and female complementary halves and the virginal Mercurius of the Self. Or from a spiritual point of view they might represent the body, soul, and spirit of the personality. Wolfram's text hints at such a tripartite nature repeatedly. Somehow, this mysterious figure "from on high" might be closely related to both Parsifal and to his female counterpart. Still wearing her reflective dress, the Voice from on high has now added the Synagogue's broken lance wrapped in black, but has shed the attributes of the Church. Since the mask background during her appearance at the Grail ceremony threw doubt on the character's physical position, one assumes at first that she has been lingering outside. But it is more likely that the intensity of Parsifal's feelings has drawn her to him. With Titurel turned to stone in his grave and no other link to a religious past, neither the despairing king and his followers inside the castle nor the young fool outside seems prepared for the task of the promised redeemer. Maybe the reminder of the figure with the many names helps him realize that the prophesy means him. He knows that he is ignorant and foolish. He may have sensed the temptation of the knights' plea. And he has discovered compassion, both for the swan and for the king. But how will he go about acquiring "wisdom"?

Chapter 8

Second Prelude and Act Two

The end of the first act and beginning of the second are clearly marked in script on the screen, paralleling the drawn curtain in an opera theater. This continues Syberberg's fondness for chapter divisions that remind the viewer of the silent motion pictures.

Neither the libretto nor the film indicates the lapse of fictional time between the acts. But for the second time the director takes advantage of a prelude to add a visual story that fills in some of the gap. One recognizes the mimetic treatment as a variant of the silent scenes in *Ludwig* and *Karl May*. Without dialogues they show moving or transported actors to the accompaniment of music. This contrasts with the circus director in *Hitler* who wears the make-up of a mime, but talks compulsively. The preludes of *Parsifal* resort to mute acting accompanied by Wagner's music. Also the second prelude functions as a transition. It provides a link in the content, illustrates motifs and themes in the music, and weaves in references to Wagner's life and works. Parsifal is the only live person in these three scenes. To judge from his attire, he has been in contact with the world of chivalry. Wearing a red cloak, he is armed with sword and shield. The color serves ever so faintly as a connection to Wolfram's Parzival, who for a while was known as the Red Knight. More importantly, the red cloak revives the association with the royal family and alchemical transformations. Now it may also signal passion, potential for carnal desire, and secular pursuits.

Parsifal's buckler displays a Medusa head on the boss. This ornament looks like another link to Wagner's biography. In 1869 the composer republished his *Judaism in Music*, which had first appeared as an article in 1850. In the appendix to the republication he blames Eduard Hanslick's polemics against his later works, especially *Music of the Future* of 1861, for the oblivion suffered by the earlier publication of 1850. Twice he refers to Hanslick's criticism as a Medusa head (106, 107). For example, Hanslick's most influential text became a "Medusa's head which was promptly held before everyone who evinced a heedless leaning toward me" (106). Now Wagner wanted to redirect the public's attention to his early text, where he for instance states about Heinrich Heine: "He was the conscience of Judaism, just as Judaism is the evil conscience of our modern Civilisation" (100). The author concludes the pamphlet with an admonition to his Jewish readers: "But bethink ye, that only one thing can redeem Ahasuerus: *Going under!*" [*untergehen*] (100). These words have sealed Wagner's reputation in much of the world. He intended to outmaneuver the effect of Hanslick's socalled Medusa head. Instead, he confirmed it by changing it into a reminder of his most notorious essay. As the

Medusa head returns on Parsifal's shield, he appears to have grappled with her successfully.

Although reduced to an ornament, Medusa's once lethal stare may still act as an evil eye to deter or kill enemies. One wonders how Parsifal acquired this piece of protective gear. In Greek myth Athena used the head of Medusa, whom Perseus had killed on her instructions, as her aegis. Now, somehow, she, or a similar divine power, may have equipped Parsifal with the same protection. Freud commented more than once on Medusa's head as sexual imagery. He equated both her decapitation and the snakes replacing her hair with castration.[1] With her gaping mouth, Medusa's face also became a threatening representation of the female genitals. Threatening because the mouth might still bite, thus again implying castration. The Greek legend makes young men petrify in terror at the sight of her. Considering Athena's own powerful glance and the effect of Brünnhilde's apparition on Siegmund, the deadly eye enters the permutations of the "gaze." This word is featured prominently in the book to the film. At its beginning stands a quotation from Nietzsche's comment on the music of *Parsifal*. It includes the phrase "the melancholy gaze of love" (9). And during Amfortas' first appearance in act 1, Kundry displays a sad glance that illustrates that remark. Then Nietzsche's phrase returns as the title of the chapter on act 2. This suggests that the gaze functions as a visual motif with one of the variants being the deadly glance.

Parsifal moves slowly through the landscape as a pensive observer, revealing neither feelings nor comprehension. Actually, he resembles the marionettes of the first prelude. Remembering Gurnemanz' remark about time and space, one concludes that the "stations" of the hero's wandering refer to stages in time that affect or express his inner development. As expected, the environment in these scenes is no more realistic than the landscape of Wagner's head. It includes visual challenges that gradually tax the viewer's sense of orientation. In the first unit Parsifal is walking towards a distant mountain range. Since he will soon arrive at Klingsor's castle in the second act, the background should show the Pyrenées, as the libretto indicates. But distorting this view is the humanoid shape of the foothills. The rocky formation of a supine, nude woman continues the motif of petrification, but also of seduction. The suggestive pose reminds a German viewer of the Hörselberg, or Venus Mountain, well known from the Tannhäuser legend. Since Wagner's Tannhäuser dallied with Venus in her mountain, the allusion to the composer's early opera does not require much guesswork. The winding staircases leading up between the "legs" of the formation indicate clearly the direction and nature of Parsifal's adventures ahead.

The sexual imagery soon becomes more explicit. Adapted from the work of the Belgian artist Félicien Rops, a metal monument dominates the next scene. Here a bar transforms an upright penis into a cross. Situated in the mountains, this cross makes a travesty of the roadside crucifixes depicted so often in the paintings of Caspar David Friedrich. The projection of one of them formed the background when the first act began with prayer. Also in the first act, the phallic monument visible for a moment as Parsifal arrived saw its erotic connotations muted through the connection with the Apollo temple on Delos and sun symbolism. Thanks to its anatomic component, the new monument can still support such associations while remaining a cross. However, its proximity to the stony feet of the Venus-like formation accentuates a sexual dynamic. And finally, a cross built with the erect member transforms the image of virility. It now includes a dimension of restraint or suffering or even mutilation, as in the case of Amfortas and Klingsor. The message conveyed by this monument is polyvalent, identifying it as a symbol. It clearly marks the entry to a world with challenges of a sexual nature.

The third scene continues this theme while adding complexity. Now the upright penis returns as a restored plaster version of the Delos temple monument. It stands next to the sculpture of a young woman, as if following her. She is based on an allegorical figure in Eugène Delacroix's painting *La Liberté sur les barricades*. One reason for including a reference to this work may have been Nietzsche's aphorism, "Delacroix eine Art Wagner" (Delacroix [is] a kind of Wagner).[2] In the painting the figure appears as the force inspiring her followers to storm the barricades while holding a rifle in one hand and waving the tricolor with the other. Created just after the July Revolution, the painting became known to Germans through Heine's review of it.[3] Besides reintroducing Heine, the visual quotation provides a link to the theme of seduction. It does so through reviving the memory of the typical breaking of mood or style in Heine's text: In a less respectful reference to the scantily dressed figure he calls her a *Gassenvenus* (alley Venus, 309). Seen in Syberberg's altered constellation, she might be beckoning the male follower. This would continue the theme of seduction already seen in the knights' appeal to Parsifal and prefigure his experience in Klingsor's garden. But of course, both the painting and Heine's text (most of the time) present the allegory as an inspiration. Even her adaptation in the film could still function as a positive force. One cannot help remembering the now shopworn words in Goethe's *Faust II* about the uplifting and inspiring feminine principle, "das ewig Weibliche zieht uns hinan." This view would interpret the Parsiphallic symbol as an image of human striving, Goethe's *Streben* as well as Freud's and Jung's libido in its broadest sense. On the other hand, Syberberg removed Liberté from the context of the painting, covered her cap with a veil and even omitted what she holds in her hands; in other words, the details that help identify her are missing. The amputation suffered by the male symbol has been transferred to the female form. One sees only a fragment of a woman with her arms raised. She could actually also represent the opposite idea: a victim fleeing her assailant. In that role she would relate to the Statue of Liberty seen while the credits scrolled over the screen. The Liberty was lying flat against a background of virile skyscrapers. Both of these figures might, then, express helplessness and victimization. Their predicament brings to mind Brünnhilde's debasement: a goddess reduced to a human pawn of male aggression. The theme of a divine power exiled from heaven and banned to humiliation among humans is central both in the Kabbalah and in Gnosticism. One begins to recognize the outline of Kundry's fall. Syberberg could have found numerous works of art to express his symbolic fragment, but obviously, Heine's review of *La Liberté* provides the optimal network of links to the rest of the plot. Heine's text even mentions a symbolic wedding, a *hieros gamos*, involving a loving sun (311). Thus Syberberg could still establish a connection between Heine's sun in the review and his own male image, which retains its power as a sun symbol. In addition, his allusion to the painting introduces obliquely the topic of revolution, an idea dear to Wagner as well.

While Parsifal's encounters with these symbols activate associations leading in several directions, a certain unity prevails through the simple format and the nature of the symbols. Nothing really happens in the dramatic sense, since the protagonist merely passes through the landscape. Works of art inspired the symbols, which are only representations of human forms, not live characters. They have developed from archetypes of the unconscious mind, but they were given shape by ideas at home in the conscious mind. As Jung explains, archetypes are structural elements of the psyche that possess a great deal of autonomy and energy: "The symbols act as *transformers*, their function being to convert libido from a 'lower' to a 'higher' form." (*Symbols of Transf.*, 232). By exposing Parsifal to a series of such objects, the sequence indicates that some inner development is taking place, all related to sexual energy. The Medusa head also suggests success in a previous conflict or temptation of a similar nature.

As Parsifal looks around, observing the environment, snowy vapor billows in and fills up the lower part of the screen. While the viewer wonders what this wintery apparition has to do with the constellation, another image glides into view in the foreground. A bas-relief of a saintly head touches the "snow," its halo broken by a hammer. Curiously, Syberberg's book, which primarily discusses the technical aspects, identifies the head as belonging to Christ in a sketch for the *Last Supper* by Leonardo da Vinci (116). Not mentioned is the resemblance of the head with that of John, the beloved disciple, in the finished fresco. Likewise not mentioned is a third possible attribution. The head might belong to Mary Magdalene. Long before Dan Brown's bestseller *The Da Vinci Code*, starting at least with the Gospel of Philip, she has figured in uncanonical literature as an important member of Jesus' inner group.[4] The image could serve, then, as a reminder of Christ, John, or Mary Magdalene, as well as the Grail love feast with its biblical overtones. The snow vapor covers the lower face, making the head look uni-sex. The halo turns out to be the sickle in the communist emblem. Through the alienating treatment of details it takes a while for the viewer to connect hammer and sickle as belonging together. The composition repeats the theme of possible violence in the background, creating a *mise en abyme*, with several potential victims. But what does the communist emblem do in the Parsifal narrative, one may wonder. Here the Wagner strand comes into play. The composer's admirer and one-time friend Nietzsche coined the expression of "philosophizing with a hammer." And already during his years in Paris, Wagner embraced socialist ideals. The creator of *Rienzi* and *Art and Revolution* participated in the revolution in Dresden. Even his prose outline for "Jesus of Nazareth" presents the protagonist against a revolutionary background. And according to Cosima Wagner's diaries, as late as on June 17,1881 her husband still remarked that he was always in favor of the rebels. More often than not, revolutionary forces turn against religion, as was the case with communism, explaining the juxtaposition of halo and hammer. But undoubtedly, the philosophy expressed in the communist emblem represents a revolution against tradition and authority. When Klingsor was rejected by Titurel, he turned against the laws of the Grail society. His domain represents the result of a revolution, a counterpart and threat to the Grail world. And now the environment forms the threshold to Klingsor's world. Not surprisingly, it too is located in the death mask. However, Syberberg avoids showing how Parsifal enters this domain. The naïve viewer assumes it lies just beyond the mountains. Others remember the staircases and conclude that Parsifal will ascend from the huge stony toes and continue into the Venus mountain, following in Tannhäuser's footsteps.

As the second act begins, one sees Klingsor seated on the forehead of the mask landscape. This location corresponds to the tower in Wagner's stage instructions. The viewer already knows what Klingsor looked like in Wagner's staging of 1882. The puppet of him in the first prelude was, like the other marionettes, modeled on photos of the original singers. Neither Wagner's final version of the libretto nor the early prose outlines specify Klingsor's religion or nationality. Rejected by Titurel for his self-castration, he has become a magician and necromancer on the non-Christian south side of the Pyrenées, presumably somewhere in Islamic-ruled Spain. It was a multi-cultural society that usually tolerated Christian and Jewish minorities. Wagner, who put a Christian veneer on his Grail society, does not divulge if Klingsor is a renegade Christian or a scorned convert. Suffice it that he has become a powerful enemy and counter force to the Grail community. Encouraged by Wagner's other writings, such as "Modern," both Nazis and anti-Wagnerians read Klingsor's "Oriental" affinity as meaning "Jewish." Wagner himself hinted at this privately. Gutman's biography, for example, states about Klingsor: "He stands outside the mystical processes of Wagnerian redemption–the Jew as the composer had finally come to see him, the figure he described as 'the incarnation of the characteristic evil that brought Christianity into the world.' Klingsor represented not only the Jew, Wagner told Cosima, but the Jesuit, too" (429). However, the main criterion for viewing Klingsor as Jewish seems to have been his adversarial role. With Wagner's publications on Germany's need for regeneration in mind, one can easily equate the Grail society with Germany in need of a savior. Hence, the adversary had to be the force Wagner abhorred. This view is perhaps expressed most passionately by Gutman, who sees *Parsifal* as Wagner's moral collapse. Using "Aryan" in practically every other sentence, he remarks about Klingsor's action: "He has already possessed himself of another fateful token of Aryan superiority, the shaft of Wotan, now baptized as the sacred spear that once pierced Christ's flesh, provoking the flow of super-blood. The Grail and spear, in Westernhagen's phrase, 'ancient Aryan symbols of life-renewal,' are the fetishes worshiped in *Parsifal*" (428). This spear Gutman describes as "that holy apparatus of Aryanism outrageously appropriated by Jewry" (430). In contrast to the ideological reading of Klingsor and the plot, most stage versions of *Parsifal* present the story on its naïve level of fairytale. Since Syberberg does not support that kind of simplicity, one may wonder what he has in mind for Klingsor's role. The director offers several other interpretations discernable through the character's attributes.

First, Klingsor as the Jewish villain is one reading that takes into account the view shared by Gutman as well as the Nazis. It reveals itself in the Oriental rug surrounding the throne. Wagner repeatedly used *Oriental* as a synonym for "Jewish." The most obvious connection between the words occurs in his article "Shall We Hope?": "Opposite the statue of Hans Sachs in Nuremberg there rose a sumptuous synagogue of purest Oriental style."[5] And in "What is German?" the word serves as one of several synonyms familiar to Wagner's readers. While pointing out disparities in Bismarck's new Reich, Wagner mentions the widespread poverty amid a robust "free trade," languishing industry despite a flourishing "business," etc. And in this wedding festivity of old (*originaldeutsch*) and new, the most recent politicians lead the dance "with Oriental decorum."[6] Already in *Hitler* Syberberg resorted to an Oriental rug as an image for a Jewish element. In a series of deliberately old-looking, flickering film snippets of Hitler caricatures, reflecting how different people thought of him, one such unit shows him as a snarling Hitler-dog biting and tearing at a small Oriental rug. Now a larger one covers the ground around Klingsor's seat.

Second, Klingsor as the pagan adversary threatening a Christian brotherhood can be recognized through his seat. It is the pagan counterpart to Amfortas' and Charlemagne's throne. The founder of the first Reich introduced Christianity in his realm with fire and sword. In one famous victory over the Saxon chieftain Wittekind (Widukind) and his army, Charlemagne destroyed a sanctuary renowned for its *Irminsul*, a wooden column topped by a carved image of a deity. Klingsor's throne is fashioned after this Irminsul. Its most famous depiction appears in a bas-relief on a mountain-wall in the vicinity of the battle field. Located in the Exsternsteine in the Teutoburger Forest near Detmold in Westphalia, this relief shows several disciples taking the dead Christ down from the cross. One of them is standing on a bent or broken stylized tree identified in folklore as the Irminsul. This monument serves, then, as an allegory of paganism bending in defeat to Christ, who is victorious even in death. Numerous other associations surrounding this image allow Syberberg to create additional links to his work. As a column of wood, the Irminsul joins the rank of hallowed trees in mythology. Charles Walker calls it "the mystical German 'Tree of Life,'" connected with the great Nordic Yggdrasil tree (116). This is the very tree of which the wood is used to start the world conflagration of Ragnarokk, or as Wagner called it, *Götterdämmerung*. It returns in the first prelude of Syberberg's film when seen behind Herzeleide and more subtly, in the Kabbalistic variant called the Sefirotic Labyrinth or Tree of Life. Another connection to the film shows up in the name of the pillar. In popular transmission the Irminsul is associated with Hermann the Cheruskan, or Arminius in Latin. Philologists, e.g. Jacob Grimm, dispute the links of Irmin-Armin-Hermann, but contributing to this association is the victory the Cheruskan chieftain gained over a Roman army led by Varus in 9 A.D.[7] This battle also took place in the Teutoburger Forest. The names Arminius and Hermann inform the film subtly.

Armin Jordan conducts the unseen orchestra besides portraying Amfortas. Hermann Levi conducted *Parsifal* in 1882 and again after the composer's death. In some people's view, this son of a rabbi would be closer to Klingsor, although he bore the name of the Cheruskan hero. The two conductors named Armin and Hermann suggest a hidden complementarity in the film. Furthermore, the Irminsul was presumably dedicated to the highest god of the Germanic tribes, Wotan. He corresponds to Hermes/Mercury, a less exalted deity in the Mediterranean pantheon (Grimm, 98). Many Greek monuments to Hermes took the form of "herms," ithyphallic columns topped by a Hermes head. With the Irminsul as a possible herm, imagery of vanquished power and sexuality is suggested by the broken monument. The phallic cross monument in the second prelude could be viewed as a variant of this symbol of subdued power. Finally, the Irminsul is often translated as *universalis columna* (e.g. Grimm, 97). This refers to the spindle of the universe. Here one is reminded of Plato's spindle of Necessity in the story of Er, son of Armenius (!), in *The Republic* (614–619). It looks like a column of light stretching through heaven and earth, "holding the revolution together" and having parts made of adamant (616c). This last word embraces the name of Adam, which in Hebrew means both "man" and the "soil" from which the Creator made the first man. Read hermetically that means, then, that Plato's pillar of the universe contains elements of human nature. One version of this concept already appeared in the film: the celestial mantle that Amfortas is unable to wear. The attendant wearing this garment functions as a human upholder and spindle of the embroidered universe. One even perceives a muted echo of it in Wolfram's text. There a mirrored column tops the tower of Clinschor's magic castle. Since Gawan, Parzival's alter ego, becomes the master of this castle, it functions as a variant of the Grail castle. Also, in book 9, the hermit asks Parzival if he saw the spear "on" the Grail castle, "saehe du daz sper ze Munsalvaesche ûf dem hûs?" (234–35). The only spear Parzival notices there is the bleeding lance. This establishes a link between a lance and the pillar in Wolfram's *Parzival*. Jacob Grimm also refers to a manuscript of *Titurel*, parts of which are attributed to Wolfram, where one of the center pillars of the Grail castle is called Irmensul (96). One may, then, assume a correlation between the protruding top or center of the Grail castle, its human lord, the lance, and the celestial spindle.

Third, Arminius' or Hermann's victory over the Romans gained a cherished place in nationalistic lore. It was fired by dreams of German reunification in the nineteenth century. Kleist's play *Die Hermannsschlacht* is one famous literary example. Such nationalistic impulses, combined with a revival of neopaganism in the early twentieth century, made the Externsteine into a mystical cult center under the Nazis. Contributing to occult lore are numerous caves and an ancient chapel high up in one of these rock formations. Renowned for its solstitial light effects, it supposedly sheltered the prophetess Veleda (Walker, 166). Whatever the facts may have been, the Externsteine gained notoriety as a Nazi cult center. This provides an additional link to Syberberg's incorporation of the Irminsul. Now burdened with associations linking it with Nazi ideology, Klingsor is seated on the bent or broken upper part of the Irminsul, clutching the lance. As specified by Wagner, this weapon is fashioned after Longinus' spear used on Golgotha. His pose imitates that of Titurel in his grave and Jupiter in the painting. The shaft of his spear or lance is neither broken nor surrounded with black gauze. If the man holding this lance were *teleios*, he should be the upholder and lord of the universe. Only the broken throne reveals a lack of needed perfection. Another hint of this twist in associations comes with the singer's name: Aage Haugland. A native of Copenhagen, he is one of only two actors in the film who also sing their roles, the other being Robert Lloyd as Gurnemanz. To be sure, Haugland portrays Klingsor superbly, as he also did at the Metropolitan Opera. For this role the director selected a Scandinavian, a typical "Nordic" man. One needs to remember how the Nazis emulated the blond and blue-eyed "Nordic" type as their ideal "Aryan." At this point the reader may object that many viewers will not even be aware of who sings Klingsor's part, so why read so much into a name? But is it just a coincidence that his name has the same initials, A. H., as the object of widespread and problematical cathexis? Perhaps one also should consider his black leather clothing. The *Totenkopfverbände* of the SS wore black uniforms. The director introduced the black leather coat for Goebbels and Kern's Ellerkamp in *Hitler*. And apart from the useful alchemical color designation, leather also carries esoteric significance. When Wolfram's Herzeloyde equips her son with an outfit of cow-hide for his departure, she supplies him with a protective, coarser second skin needed in a world of less spiritual beings. By analogy, Syberberg's characters in black leather clothing are not only warriors; they are also part of a coarse and spiritually weakened environment. But if Klingsor is associated with Nazi ideology, the targets of his aggression turn into the opponents, resp. victims, of Nazism. Titurel had already displayed some attributes pointing in that direction. This constellation would suggest that the Grail society might (also) be less Gentile than generally assumed.

Fourth, the allusions provoked by Klingsor's clothing do not stop with 1945. Syberberg is at odds with much in contemporary Germany as well. He may easily have had in mind two other kinds of post-World War II groups. One of them is inseparable from the rebellious youth movements surfacing in the late sixties. The German equivalents of Hell's Angels were known as the *Halbstarken*, (semi-strong) and *Rocker*. As in the US, they appeared as gangs dressed in black leather and riding motor cycles. Seen as an anti-establishment phenomenon often prone to violence and lawlessness, they might serve as a proto-type for the film's Klingsor. Syberberg's films even provide some predecessors for this affiliation, e.g. the gangs and rebels in *San Domingo* and the motor cyclist in the crowd at the guillotine in *Ludwig*. But more threatening is Klingsor as an unacknowledged and resistant strain of fascism encapsulated in the body of democracy. Besides, many so-called democratic views and procedures only amount to a different kind of coercive system, the director has maintained repeatedly. His Klingsor also represents this threat as seen in the trophies surrounding his throne: dismembered body parts, including the penis-Liberté group, a hand, and five or six heads. They belong to King Ludwig II, Nietzsche, Karl Marx, Aeschylus, and Wagner. The king's head appeared already in the guillotine scene of *Ludwig*. He has again succumbed to and been appropriated by the revolutionary and plebeian forces that danced in his nightmare scene. And they are still strong, earning a handy profit from his dreams of paradise. Also Nietzsche became harnessed for use by twentieth century ideologues. Having declared God dead and praising the superman of the future, he had reason to recoil in horror at the interpreters of his gospel. Karl Marx' dreams of social reform turned mostly into dictatorships worse than the systems he fought. And Aeschylus let Apollo plead in Orestes' favor towards the end of the *Oresteia*. Matricide is not as onerous as patricide, the god pronounced, extolling the father as a parent while reducing the mother to a mere incubator. Maybe Aeschylus too realized the error of the argument and that the gods might reimpose the curse on the Atrides. The portrait head belonging to Aeschylus actually consists of two parts. One is a barely visible Greek theater persona of tragedy, the other a human face above the mask. The small theater mask resting on the surface of Wagner's death mask creates another *mise en abyme*. And the head of Wagner, of course, who succumbed to Klingsor's power in several ways, adds another one. All the faces stare with wide open eyes, as if brought down by Medusa. The five heads plus a mask echo the five Wagner dolls with the Kundry marionette in the first prelude. And, as Cosima recorded, Wagner remarked about Kundry that everything about her is a mask (Sept. 12, 1881). Syberberg translates that statement literally.

The most arresting characteristic of Syberberg's Klingsor derives as much from Wagner as from Germany throughout the twentieth century. Klingsor is an archetypal shadow. One can turn to both Freud and Jung for clarification of this concept. In *Totem and Taboo* Freud explains a psychological defense mechanism that sometimes evolves from ambiguous feelings in a mourner against the dead person. Grief and love are mixed with feelings of guilt and unconscious hostility against the deceased. This situation often develops, Freud claims, among family members: "Such hostility, hidden in the unconscious behind tender love, exists in almost all cases of intensive emotional allegiance to a particular person, indeed it represents the classic case, the prototype of the ambivalence of human emotions."[8] This sounds like a fitting description of Amfortas' feelings towards his father. One automatically assumes that he harbors love and devotion, but one searches the text in vain for expression of either. However, the unwelcome legacy entails obligations he loathes. His emphatic *Nein*! eventually gives way to feelings of duty as he carries out the ritual. The father is buried but not dead in Amfortas' mind. As mentioned previously, some of Titurel's attributes indicate a Jewish heritage. With Wagner sharing Amfortas' predicament of obeying a demanding king, especially as relates to his artistic work, one is inclined to view Wagner as a parallel to Amfortas. The composer possibly also believed he had Jewish ancestry and rejected the idea of such a legacy in the extreme. His, and Amfortas', reactions go a step further, as Freud's text suggests: "But this hostility, which is painfully felt in the unconscious in the form of satisfaction with the demise, experiences a different fate in primitive man: the defense against it is accomplished by displacement upon the object of hostility, namely, the dead" (854). This psychological defense results in a projection, with the hostile feeling that one is unable or unwilling to acknowledge in oneself being attributed to the target of the resentment. In Freud's view, such displacement would make Klingsor a distorted version of Titurel animated by Amfortas' resentment. Jungians call such a negative projection a Shadow, "an unconscious aspect of the personality characterized by traits and attitudes which the conscious ego does not recognize in him- or herself ."[9] According to Jung's theories, Klingsor seems to embody the same kind of hostility outlined by Freud, and he represents the negative feelings harbored by Amfortas/Wagner. About the Shadow Jung states in *Aion*: "Projections change the world into the replica of one's own unknown face" (9). Such projections also lead to an autistic condition that changes the world into a dream, and the resulting feeling of sterility is explained by projection as a "malevolence of the environment" (9). Klingsor might, then, embody anti-Semitic feelings projected not only from Amfortas and Wagner, but also from many of the director's contemporary compatriots. The Nazi-related associations encourage the assumption that Klingsor's hate is at least to some extent anti-Semitic. Syberberg's *Hitler* and publications have overtly and covertly accused his countrymen of harboring a fascist way of thinking disturbingly like the era that many do not have the courage to face. This legacy lives on at the unconscious level. Now it has gained a name: Klingsor. If Amfortas and those he represents could muster the courage to scrutinize their feelings, they might have discovered an inner mirror. Jung claims: "True, whoever looks into the mirror . . . risks a confrontation with himself , . . . the face we never show to the world because we cover it with the *persona*, the mask of the actor. But the mirror lies behind the mask and shows the true face" (*Archetypes*, 20). This confrontation with the Shadow, he continues, "belongs to the more unpleasant things that can be avoided so long as we can project everything negative into the environment" (20). Obviously, Amfortas has not confronted Klingsor successfully. But as mentioned, Klingsor elicits numerous and conflicting associations. The reason for that, of course, rests on the continuation of visual counterpoint.

When Klingsor first appears, the background is dark. As the perspective changes, a building surrounded by flames comes into view. It is one of the German bunkers from World War II on the Atlantic coast. This shelter for Hitler's forces strengthens the link to the Nazi association. But the fiery walls also bring to mind the flames surrounding the sleeping Brünnhilde before Siegfried awakens her. "Time is at hand," Klingsor sings, "Die Zeit ist da." He has seen Parsifal approach his castle and knows that special forces are needed to stop him. Kundry had pronounced the same words in act 1, indicating the need to "sleep." In English this looks like the biblical phrase, e.g., in Revelation 1.3. Luther's translation has "Die Zeit ist nah." It sounds close enough to be mistaken for the other. Now parodying Siegfried awakening Brünnhilde, Klingsor repeats the phrase to force Kundry out of her sleep-like condition to a new role. As he begins to apply his magic, a widening crack opens up in the ground in front of him. This crack splits the forehead of Wagner's persona, where deep down in his mind Kundry is buried. The action varies the moving mountain entryway of the first act, as well as the literal *mise en abyme* of a position at the edge of an abyss. While smoke rises from the cleft, Klingsor awakens Kundry who is at the bottom of this *Riss*. Calling and naming her, he repeatedly reminds her, "Dein Meister ruft," (Your master is calling you). Like the *Meister* in Celan's "Todesfuge," Klingsor holds the power of life and death, but presumably through magic. Although he begins to address Kundry as the Nameless one, *Namenlose*, he also conjures her up by some names from her previous existences: *Urteufelin* (primeval she-Devil), suggesting Lilith, Adam's first partner; *Höllenrose* (Rose of Hell) as a contrast to the Virgin Mary, the Rose of Heaven; and Gundryggia, a construct with pre-Christian Germanic roots. *Gund-* is an Old High German prefix signifying "battle" or "war," making Gundryggia fit for a war goddess perhaps related to the Valkyries. And most interestingly, he calls her Herodias. As the wife of Herod, Herodias belongs in a biblical setting. This name contributed the most to Kundry being labeled as Jewish.

When the viewer is allowed a peek down into the crevice, one sees Kundry seated in a pose borrowed from the Swiss artist Johann H. Füssli's (Fusely's) *Silence and Melancholy*. She had previously appeared in the "melancholy pose" of Dürer's *Melencolia I*. Syberberg is again presenting the concept of melancholy, contrasting it with mourning, *Trauer*, as an affliction still not healed. Contributing to this emphasis on a psychological condition may have been both Freud's essay "Mourning and Melancholia," which discusses the clinical aspects of the topic, and Alexander and Margarete Mitscherlich's *The Inability to Mourn*.[10] Their book emphasizes the predicament of many Germans after the Holocaust and after much personal suffering during World War II. Syberberg's frequent references to his previous works as *Trauerarbeit* show that both melancholy and mourning still play a role in *Parsifal*. And Kundry suffers from the former, as her pose reveals. A third source of inspiration may have been Jung's *Psychology and Alchemy*. Discussing the descent to the depths, he mentions that the first stage of the alchemical process, *nigredo*, "was felt as 'melancholia' in alchemy and corresponds to the encounter with the shadow in psychology" (36). Klingsor fits the descriptions of the Shadow.

In this scene Kundry is called back to life from a location that resembles a tomb. The fact that she does not wake up on the surface of the eye socket in the head landscape where she curled up to sleep, underscores the psychological dimension of the character. But at the same time the film obeys the libretto. Wagner had sent Kundry to sleep in the underbrush of the forest, only to have her rise from this condition in the depths below Klingsor's tower. And as the composer did in *Rheingold* when Wotan conjures Erda to appear from a cleft in the ground, he again specified that also Kundry emerge surrounded by bluish vapor. Not only does Syberberg retain the vapor, but he also emphasizes the similarities in the two appearances. He reintroduces the ascension from a crack in the ground and includes Erda's image in the first act. Both Kundry and Erda represent the same Great Mother and psychological archetype.

Before Kundry stirs, one notices a collection of objects surrounding her. Not all forces of the unconscious assume personal form. Parsifal's bow and arrow have stayed with her, as does the hair-covered, translucent garment from her previous appearance. At that time her long "hair" seemed to provide a modesty cover for her upper torso. This time she wears a loose-fitting caftan and emerges with only her own somewhat shorter hair. The presence of the hair-like camouflage item draws attention to its symbolic meaning. One remembers Wagner's remark that everything about Kundry is a mask; in other words, she is not what she appears to be. And since the Grail story has always exuded mystery full of esoteric symbolism, one should remember the prominence of Hebrew in esoteric imagery. One Hebrew equivalent of *hair* is spelled with the letters *daleth, lamed,* and *he.* It shares this spelling with an unrelated noun meaning "door" or "gate." A variant spelling of this door is *daleth, lamed,* and *tau.* Among the definitions of that lexis one finds figurative uses, such as "aperture of womb" and "easily accessible woman." This hints not only at the role Kundry will play in the second act, but also at the Venus mountain in the preceding prelude. The spelling meaning primarily "door" also coincides with the pronunciation of the letter *d, daleth.* One of the paths of the Sefirotic Tree or Labyrinth is labeled *daleth,* suggesting a location in the hero's quest and serving as a landmark, as it were. Thanks to the centrality of Hebrew in Western (not only Jewish) mysticism, and the spelling conventions of this language, it invites to associative movements on a grid of semantic links, sometimes even skipping from one language to another. In this case the "hair" lying next to Kundry emits multiple signals.

More difficult to recognize is a pile of strange blocks near Kundry. They are miniatures of the Wehrmacht bunkers used along the front lines in World War II. Since a large model had appeared briefly behind Klingsor, its return in a small format but large number attaches this "correspondence" to Kundry, as if she were already allied with, or fighting, Klingsor in warfare. As the Shadow and *Meister,* he possesses the power to subject the deepest forces of the psyche to serve his objectives. Uttering the first of her famous screams, Kundry reacts slowly and begins climbing up an iron ladder (another potent noun!), while struggling with a gradual awakening. A second groaning scream attests to her aversion for her newest subservience to Klingsor and his plan. During the ensuing dialogue, or verbal duel, she remains standing on the ladder so that she is visible only from the waist and up, while Klingsor remains seated on his Irminsul throne. Considering that both antagonists are restricted in their movements, one can only marvel at the dynamics of the scene. This results partially from admirable acting, in part from impressive directing. Of course Wagner provided text and sound, but the image can also convey the tension and its nuances. While Kundry bemoans her curse, the camera dwells on her. The curse is her longing (*Sehnen*) for redemption. Redemption is only attainable through the man who resists her seduction, Klingsor reminds her. When she turns towards him, one sees both of them. But during their sparring, the camera cuts back to her, making the dialogue sound like a soliloquy of inner turmoil. This "conflict" is again followed by a view of both when she bends backwards, facing him across the chasm. She laughs mockingly at Klingsor's strength against seduction. He has not acquired it through chastity but through self-castration. Her scorn triggers his tormented monologue. During this soliloquy the camera shows alternately Klingsor and Kundry in a series of short takes. Each ends in a dissolve with transitional double exposure. Clearly, Klingsor and Kundry are two aspects of the same mind. They are similar aspects in that both are powerless against their urge, understood in the context as the sexual drive, and suffer under this feebleness; but they are conflicting aspects in that Klingsor seems to lack the compassion Kundry exhibits for him at one point during this scene. The view of Kundry and Klingsor as related forces of the mind comes close to the prevailing interpretation of them in Wagner literature. They are usually lumped together as the Jewish characters. The film both suggests and contradicts this view. Especially one ambiguous gesture by Kundry in this scene could be seen as pointing in several directions. During the sequence with dissolves she bends forwards as if closing the gap separating her from Klingsor. Seen in profile, she appears for a moment to lower her face to kiss Wagner's head lying at Klingsor's feet. The book to the film even implies a kiss here (121). In reality she bends over next to the head until her forehead touches the Oriental rug. It and not Wagner is apparently the object or aim of her gesture. And the "Oriental" rug hints at a Jewish element. Remembering the brown leaves and their semantic connection to the Holocaust, one may assume that Kundry here mourns its victims. In contrast, Klingsor in his black leather outfit on the Irmensul seat has also gained connotations of a different kind. This is underscored by the camera technique. Syberberg resorts to dissolves very sparingly. It is a sophisticated technique compared to the simple camera work prevailing in his films. He had expressed opposition to Riefenstahl's camera innovations of this sort in *Die freudlose Gesellschaft* on the grounds that they carried out Hitler's aesthetics (70–71). Above all, dissolves became an ideologically potent technique in several movies of the Third Reich. Especially *Jew Süß*, which is notorious for its propaganda, uses dissolves to reveal the "true nature" of its Jewish characters. For example, a dissolve transforms the head of the elegantly dressed protagonist at court into his ghetto head.[11] As in that movie, Syberberg's two characters provide a matched or paired couple that simultaneously suggests differences and identities. But the use of dissolves leaves one undecided: does the technique reveal the "Aryan" to be a Semite, or does the technique add the Nazi connotation to both characters? Does it do both? As with most of the muted and ambiguous elements, counterpoint accounts for transformations and simultaneous variations blurring the original contours.

At different times during this scene both Kundry and Klingsor bemoan their urge or longing, *Sehnen*. The text remains vague about its meaning. Klingsor covets the Grail and presumably, since he is the villain, also the control over or destruction of the Grail society. Kundry wants to "sleep" without degrading revivals. Each recurrence of the word might also refer to sexual urges as well as to a yearning for other goals. This brings Wagner's version of *Sehnsucht* into close proximity to *libido*. It retains the meaning of the sexual drive, as in the early works of Freud, as well as that of the life-force or general energy, as in Jung's texts. Wagner's infinitive used as a noun, *Sehnen*, allows Syberberg several Hermetic links to another German word, *Sehne*, or "sinew." Sinews were once used for strings on musical instruments. That concept was introduced in the comments on the bow and its string in act 1. The medieval bow metaphor equated the bow with the Old Testament (Father, Judaism, early times) and the string with the New Testament (Son, Christianity, later or contemporary times). Both the stringed bow and its arrow lay beside Kundry as she woke up to Klingsor's summons. On a semantic level, these objects anticipate the utterance made soon after. And it could even be read as a longing for redemption. Both Kundry and Klingsor suffer from it. The imagery also revives the semantic connections of the bowstring with *fides* and its synonym meaning "faith." That returns Faith/Grail Carrier/Synagogue, etc. to the picture. Again reduced to an object symbol at Kundry's side, she apparently "belongs" to Kundry, like an attribute or potential variant of the maternal archetype. One remembers also the comments on *enantiodromia*. Jung discusses the concept that everything also encompasses, or can become, its opposite (*Psychological Types*, 426). Thus Kundry as the chtonic Mother can also appear transformed as the divine Daughter (Kore), as a seductress and as a virgin, as a destructive power and as a saving angel, all these being personifications of psychic forces found in, e.g., myths, dreams, and fantasies. In this instance, Kundry wakes up with the symbol of her contrasting potential at her side.

Lying near her were both bow and arrow. The arrow points to Parsifal, who is mentioned several times by Klingsor and also echoed in the music. And now, for the second time, Parsifal's arrival causes alarm and commotion. Contrary to Wagner's instructions, the film shows the defenders of Klingsor's castle who try to block the hero's entry. Not only does their master summon them up from the same fissure from which Kundry rose, but he also addresses them as knights and guards, *Wächter*. The word has almost the same meaning as *Hüter*, with which Gurnemanz aroused the sleeping squires in act 1. The dormant warriors had been invisible when the spectator looked into the abyss. Now they swarm up like insects, wearing the miniature bunkers as helmets. This demonstrates that object symbols can assume human form. Their fight against Parsifal takes place out of view, while Klingsor's comment on it constitutes a second and more dramatic teichoscopy than the squires' description of Kundry's ride in act 1. The battle itself differs from Parsifal's reception on Grail territory, but at first it seems rather pointless. After all, Klingsor summons Kundry for the sole purpose of seducing Parsifal. But perhaps Kundry and the flower maidens also belong to his armed forces. The skirmish allowed Wagner to display Klingsor's sadistic reactions to the fighting as well as to provide more narrative information. One also assumes that some kind of psychological defense mechanism is called for. Furthermore, it allows Syberberg to draw attention to his symbolic objects and to introduce several projections onto the background. For example, the phallic monument from Delos becomes visible again, this time unmistakably damaged. And two images projected into the darkness acquire an unreal quality: a female head and a tower-like scaffolding. It reminds the viewer of the contraption that supported the gigantic bow and arrow in the first act. The *Gestell* is now seen from the narrow side as an upright structure with a platform in the top section. It invites comparisons with the towers along the death strip that formed the German-German border while the country was divided. Even more insistent is the association with the watchtowers in concentration camps. That again paints Klingsor in two conflicting roles. As a Jewish antagonist he would have been a prisoner in such a camp. But he is armed and dressed in black like the SS guards of the concentration camps. And he has power. This all points to Klingsor as a Nazi. The other projection, the female head, appears for the first time when the camera interrupts this sequence briefly for a shot of the victorious Parsifal, accompanied by Klingsor's voice describing him.

Parsifal has now entered the magician's castle. Still holding a blood-stained sword, he lets the red cloak slip off his shoulders. Kundry has disappeared from view, but is obviously related to the projected apparition in the dark sky. She is busy preparing for his seduction somewhere else. The last take of the lengthy episode again shows Klingsor rejoicing in anticipation of Parsifal's imminent fall. Here Wagner's stage instructions call for a transformation of scenery. Klingsor and his tower should sink out of view while his magic garden rises to fill the stage. The film changes that to a transformation according to psychological processes. As Klingsor raises his arm, the surface of his cape smoothens into a mirror "reflecting" a jungle. This is his magic garden teeming with palm trees, huge blooms, and tropical vegetation.[12] The image is based on Wagner's version of 1882 and serves as a transition to the next major segment involving Parsifal and the flower maidens. But again one is faced with a mirror that does not reflect what should logically appear in it. One sees neither the movie camera nor the viewer's face, but the untamed jungle of the unconscious. In retrospect, this insight helps "explain" the similarly unexpected reflections in the prismatic, mirrored stone seen in act 1.

As expected, Syberberg's magic garden does not resemble that of 1882. He does, however, include a glimpse of it as Wagner wanted it to look. This enables him to establish visual links on several levels of narrative which otherwise would be enigmatic, e.g. between Kundry and Wagner's Venus. Syberberg is not the first Wagner interpreter to discover a relationship between Kundry in the garden with Parsifal and Venus in the Hörselberg with Tannhäuser. Carl Dahlhaus, for example, concluded in 1971: "In Wagner's oeuvre, as he understood it, there is a tendency toward a mythological system, to a leitmotif technique in his poetry which reaches beyond the individual drama."[13] Dahlhaus continues by pointing out a number of details in *Parsifal* that were prefigured in Wagner's earlier music dramas. Similarly, Syberberg weaves in visual connections to the other works whenever such instances occur. But the "mirrored" image of the original garden constitutes mainly a reminder of the voluptuous setting that even Wagner's audience found too colorful.

In its own way the film modifies a detail that had impressed the audience in 1882: the change of scenery by raising and lowering the settings. Instead of Klingsor sinking out of view, the camera moves down, and the spectators with it. The "reflection" in Klingsor's cape soon widens to fill the screen on a lower level. From a psychological point of view, this move is logical since Klingsor, the Shadow, hails from the personal unconscious that is closer to the surface of consciousness. He does not move while the action is shifting to a deeper realm of the unconscious. Even within the framework of the fiction, Syberberg's choice makes more sense than Wagner's. In 1882 Klingsor appeared high up in a tower, whereas the flower maidens embellished the garden on ground level. The camera descends now to their level. A second modification concerns the colors of the garden. Instead of imitating the garish blooms of 1882, the director subdues them to a monochromatic landscape in blue-grey. It is animated by marionettes modeled on the original singers in their flower-like costumes. As in the first prelude, also these dolls appear to be controlled from below like puppets. But unlike the earlier puppet episode, they move to the sound of still invisible singers. As the words dictate, both voices and movements express fear and confusion. And again, Klingsor's *mise en abyme* functions as a genre shifter resulting in a puppet performance.

The transitional stage with marionettes ends with Parsifal's arrival. Rising into view from below he soon dominates the picture. His sword, shield, and red cape lie scattered on a rock that also moves up with him. Bathed in a contrasting reddish light, he has thrown an open, dark mail coat around his shoulders. It suggests that he remains on guard against attacks. But alchemically, the color change indicates a beginning transition to *nigredo*. Another dissolve changes the image again. With this technique now associated with Third Reich practice, one assumes that the redeemer hero and the seductive girls are more related than appearance indicates. A Jungian would concur since they all are forces of the same mind. Parsifal, however, ascends from a deeper layer of the unconscious.

As Parsifal's face dissolves into the nearest flower maiden, his adventure in the garden begins. The discrepancies between the cinematic scene and the Wagner tradition amount to both a refutation of Wagner's version and a reinterpretation. According to Wagner's directions, Parsifal first appears on the wall surrounding the garden before jumping down into it. This allows time for the flower maidens to flutter around in confusion before they surround him. For most of the episode the girls are supposed to move to and fro and eventually dance around him. Only when he tries to free himself does Kundry's call interrupt the dancing and caressing. The garments of the girls should suggest petals and leaves, with hats imitating bluebells and veils adding to their allure. Only the veils have remained in the film. Reminders of the girls' identity are now flowers and leaves painted on a few faces. Scantily dressed or veiled, many reveal considerable nudity. A few exceptions attract attention. One girl wearing a helmet underscores the similarity in function with the Grail knights attempting to lure Parsifal into joining them. Another girl resembles a fully dressed Judith Gautier, a third the female Parsifal, and yet another resembles the Grail Carrier. With her head covered in a black veil, she is contemplating a human skull. The cranium is a common symbol in art associated with death. It is no coincidence that Jesus was crucified on Golgotha, a hill named after the death's head. It also appeared as an emblem on black SS uniforms. And since Jung's thought informs much of the film, one must also consider the significance of the skull in alchemical imagery. Jung explains that there exists an unconscious identity between the psyche of the alchemist and the "arcane substance" or spirit imprisoned in the matter on which he is working. Its symbol is the skull signifying a vessel of transformation, "because it is the container of thought and intellect" (*Psych. and Alch.*, 267). Jung continues by describing the skull as a symbol of the *mortificatio* of Eve, the feminine aspect of the (masculine) *prima materia* (268). The goal of the process is to attain the Philosopher's Stone or *lapis*. "But again, the stone is man," Jung states, pointing to an "identity of something in man with something concealed in matter" (269). The "vessel of transformation" hinting at a feminine aspect of Parsifal is another reminder similar to the blood drops in the snow.

This feminine element is now surrounding Parsifal in multiples. But contrary to Wagner's instructions, the girls remain immobile, placed along the walls of the labyrinth through which Parsifal moves. When they ask plaintively who will play with them, he assures them with a smile that he will be glad to do it. As if such a diversion would mean a regression in his quest, Syberberg makes him take a few steps backwards while making the statement. This might also signal a crab (retrograde) movement in his contrapuntal composition. And when Parsifal passes the girl contemplating the skull, he takes hold of an upright post near her and swings himself partially around it. One is inclined to view the wooden pole as a variant of the Irminsul or celestial pillar. The proximity of the cranial "vessel of transformation" suggests the potential of Parsifal's development: he may become the upholder of his universe.

As Parsifal walks through the winding passages, he sometimes drops out of sight. His brief absences permit the picture to conform to the text. For example, early on when the flower maidens comment that the sword is still dripping with blood from his fight on the ramparts, one does not simultaneously see the hero with sword in hand. He soon after walks among the girls empty handed. They, on the other hand, mostly sit or lean against the rock walls of the passages. This echoes the position of the knights seen soon after Gurnemanz and Parsifal entered the Grail Castle. In both instances the hero faces temptations, witnesses suffering, and undergoes a shattering experience. Just as he remained resistant to the knights' appeal, he now gets impatient with all the female wooing. But these girls do not pursue him physically as Wagner specified they should. Some are clearly captive. One is caught in a fishnet; another is tied with rope. A third is only partially visible, as if trying to emerge from the rocky surface. A surrealistic twist, one might think at first. But if these figures represent unconscious forces, then Syberberg treats the situation logically. He may have been inspired by the mentioned phrase in Jung's study, namely "spirit imprisoned in matter" (*Psych. and Alch.*, 267). When Parsifal notices the girls' fragrance and asks if they are flowers, their answers support both the notion of a stationary organic existence ("We grow here") and of belonging to a psychological realm ("[we are] fragrant spirits"). Obviously, the encounter affects Parsifal's understanding of himself. Wagner's text hints at it as one of the flower maidens teases Parsifal, "Do you let the flowers woo the butterfly?" The butterfly has always been a favorite symbol of metamorphosis. That word now applies to Parsifal. But on the visual level, the butterfly passes the flowers without showing much interest in them. Toward the end of the wooing, when some voices accuse him of being cold and timid with women, Parsifal appears to suffer dizziness or weakness, as he had done in act 1. Leaning against the rock and closing his eyes for a moment, he also assumes the same pose as some of the girls. He could easily blend in. This might visualize the danger of yielding and regressing deeper into the unconscious, or also of "trying on" their role, exploring what the feminine element experiences. However, he soon recovers and escapes into open space. All the while, the narrow passages had suggested the crowding and inhibiting circle of girls in the text. In view of the Venus mountain, the passage also assumes a vaginal dimension.

When Parsifal arrived in the garden, he left his weapons, cape, and mail coat behind. He no longer wears the brown tunic, but clothes worthy of a fairytale prince. Especially the brocade bolero is arresting. Its bottom hem has been cropped into a zigzag edge. That returns the memories of serrated or torn elements in the film, including Heine's *Zerrissenheit*. But also Nietzsche comes to mind. From about the time when Wagner sent him a copy of the printed *Parsifal* drama, Nietzsche withdrew and became increasingly critical of him. In *Der Fall Wagner* (*The Case of Wagner*) of 1888 he praises Bizet's *Carmen* as also being a work of redemption (96–97). He finds this work infinitely more inspiring than *Parsifal*. The male protagonist, Don José, is a bullfighter. When dressed for the arena, he wears an outfit with a bolero. The target of his passion represents an untameable force of nature similar in some ways to Kundry. Now dressed like a bullfighter, Parsifal enters a different arena. When he eventually reaches its center, he too will meet and battle a monstrous force, as Theseus did in Daedalus' labyrinth. No, Kundry does not look like a Minotaur. Still, as a chtonic power, she is related to the Egyptian celestial cow goddess making her the female equivalent to the bull monster.[14] More important is Nietzsche's reference to Wagner as the Minotaur: "Oh, this old robber! He robs us of the young men . . . Oh, this old Minotaur! What he already has cost us!" (*Der Fall Wagner*, 123). Now Parsifal enters the labyrinth dressed like Don José, the bullfighter, headed for an encounter as dangerous as that facing Theseus. Since it takes place in the innermost of Wagner's head, one may assume that Kundry shares more than a few attributes with her maker.

Wagner knew *Carmen*. According to his wife's diaries, they attended a performance of the opera on Nov. 3, 1875, in Vienna. For the composer, a bolero would probably not so much signify a garment as the Spanish dance of that name. Cosima's diaries report that such a dance occurred to him in a dream. On Aug. 14, 1878, he dreamed that he composed a ballet with a bolero for the garden scene of *Parsifal*. It is unlikely that he entertained the idea while awake. But since the film reveals the unconscious recesses of the composer's head, Syberberg feels free to reintroduce a bolero, however, not the kind using castañettes.

Actually, the film eliminates the dance of the flower maidens altogether. Perhaps the director tries to "correct" Wagner in this scene. The film already hinted at parallels with *Tannhäuser*. That was the work that was booed out in Paris presumably because it lacked a ballet in the second act. Wagner paid dearly for his refusal to adjust to popular taste. But in *Parsifal* he did place a ballet in the second act. Rarely, perhaps nowhere else, does one find a ballet with such seductive music. Maybe the holiness of the Grail subject required the ultimate in sensual

Parsifal. Wagner wrote the fragment to "Komm, komm holder Knabe!" while working on the *American March* in 1876 (Gregor-Dellin, 692). "Wanting to be American," he added on the note paper. This symbiosis of America and seduction finds its visual equivalent in the film's first prelude in the ambiguity involving the reclining Statue of Liberty. A similar degradation of a feminine allegory befell Delacroix's Liberté in Heine's review, when he calls her an alley Venus. And Wagner did not think any more highly of his flower maidens, as Cosima's diaries indicate. On March 28, 1878, he referred to them as his alley girls. His enthusiasm for this sensual element assumed demonstrative expression in 1882 during the first *Parsifal* season. Wagner attended all performances in his theater box. But, according to the diaries, he did not arrive until the second act on several occasions. That is what the Jockey Club members in Paris used to do, arriving mainly to enjoy the ballet in the second act. As if imitating the very spectators who ruined his performance of *Tannhäuser* were not enough, Wagner also expressed his delight in the flower maidens (probably not only Carrie Pringle) with repeated, loud shouts of "bravo!" provoking hisses from his audience. This emulation of the Jockey Club members may fit into a contrapuntal pattern of life and work, as intended to be recorded for posterity. Otherwise his behavior could only be called pathetic. Syberberg wants none of the seductive ballet. Admittedly, the young girls sound more alluring than the Rhine maidens and Venus' entourage, and their varying degrees of nudity may add a sensual note. But their captive immobility, sadness, and alienating appearance create a contrast to Wagner's intended effect. Thus Syberberg tries to achieve what Wagner only pretended to want. For in his written opinions Wagner wanted the flower maidens to appear naïve and innocent. At least that is what he claims in his article "*Parsifal* at Bayreuth, 1882."[15] The coaxing strains of the thirty singing dancers and especially the six soloists, "took on an air of childlike naïveté that, touching through a matchless intonation, was utterly opposed to that idea of sensual seduction which certain people had presupposed as the composer's aim" (304). A similar tone prevails in Wagner's report to King Ludwig, who, much to the composer's chagrin, did not attend any of the *Parsifal* performances in Bayreuth. The letter rejoices in the creation of complete naïveté, the maidens being truly flowers and the entire scene being the most perfect staging he could imagine (Strobel, 3:248). Neither the king nor any reader of the libretto would have been fooled. As Gurnemanz explains in act 1, the defenders of Klingsor's castle are former Grail knights who had succumbed to the seduction of these diabolically beautiful women. Wagner's only rationale for including them is the temptation of Parsifal. By comparison, the film presents the theme contrapuntally throughout, first with the mention of a kiss, then a maternal kiss and embrace, the seduction of Amfortas on the puppet stage, and the come-hither gesture, all of this in the first prelude alone. The first act includes Gurnemanz' narrative and protective gesture, Kundry's gesture, and the ardent knights. Now the maidens will soon be succeeded by Kundry's illuminating kiss. And still, the strongest reason for the film's different treatment of the flower maiden scene is its psychological significance. Oblivious to the helmet-wearing Valkyries among the girls, Parsifal moves restlessly through the passages as if exploring an unknown terrain of the mind. Some of the female forms have not yet emerged from the rocks into three-dimensional figures, and most of them touch the background like bas-reliefs. Even the "maternal" ones cradling puppets of flower maidens in their arms are seated and thus still part of the rocky ground. These figures have not yet developed into rounded individuals. As forces of the imagination they may be alluring in some ways, but unfinished and hence powerless to snare Parsifal.

While the camera sometimes zooms and rides through the passages, Parsifal keeps wandering through changing locations. At one spot the window fountain reappears with an accumulation of small objects seen earlier. Another fountain visible between the rocks (a background projection) is more difficult to recognize. It shows a detail from the middle panel of Hieronymus Bosch's triptych *The Garden of Delights*. Enigmatic and fantastic as much of Bosch's art is, this image is soon after replaced with another projection from the same work, this time the right panel depicting warfare as hell on earth. Syberberg has focused on the pair of oversized human ears, pierced and held together by an arrow, and with a knife blade protruding between them. The blade displays an embossed letter, either a *B*, perhaps signifying the artists's initial, or the Hebrew letter *shin*, suggesting a location in the labyrinth. As pronounced, the letter is often translated as the word "tooth." One is reminded of Freud's interpretation of Medusa's castrating mouth. Belonging to a nightmarish vision, the ears-and-knife shape consists of a metal weapon and an injured organic component. The combination has the outline of the male genitals. Simultaneously an entity inflicting and suffering pain, it illustrates the conflicting urges or potential inhabiting the recesses of the mind. The pierced ears bring back the Wagner caricature from the first prelude. The combination as a whole also echoes the phallic crucifix of the second prelude. Whatever associations the Bosch images may evoke, *The Garden of Delights* includes extremes of excess, both in the pursuit of pleasure and in despair and suffering. Klingsor's garden offers the same desolate outlook, the film implies.

To the extent the flower maidens belong to Klingsor's realm, they also personify melancholy, as Jung explains in *Psychology and Alchemy* (36). This stage of *nigredo* in alchemy finds its parallel in the multiplicity of female forms. It is as if the anima had split into many figures, her state resembling a dissolution (88–89). The force possessing the potential to relieve the suffering has regressed and is making contact with previously unknown layers of the personality. Parsifal passes through this "Garden of Delights" easily, since the film has diminished the carnal temptations. The female forms have been reduced to sculptures in various degrees of completion. Parsifal is no Pygmalion. As envisioned by Wagner, beguiling dance, embraces, and caresses should supplement the sensual music with more than suggestive lyrics, creating a highly charged scene rivaling the bacchanal in *Tannhäuser*. Syberberg deprives the viewer of such a sensual interlude. Maybe he was partially inspired to this treatment of the episode by Ernst Bloch's "Rescuing Wagner through Surrealistic Colportage (1929)" in *Heritage of Our Times*

(338–45). Since the author belonged to the emigrés who had to flee the Third Reich, he constitutes a counterpart to Jung, who, as a Swiss Gentile, did not share that fate. Bloch groups Wagner's operas, especially the *Ring* cycle, with the imitative, stuffy, and insufferably boring world of the Victorian parlor. He contrasts them with Karl May's unpretentious, exotic, and captivating adventure stories, praising the latter as pure and unadulterated colportage. Colportage fires the imagination much as fairytales do. Bloch relegates colportage to the world of dreams, fairytales, and folksy fairgrounds. The magic of such child-like fantasy worlds is, Bloch suggests, the antidote needed to save Wagner's work from himself (338). His operas contain too much phony myth; his symbols, such as the dragon guarding the Nibelungen treasure, fail as symbolizations of abstractions, and the theatricality does not proceed beyond kitsch and the *Gartenlaube,* or "arbor." The latter concept characterizes nineteenth-century German sentimentality in literature, art, and aesthetics, according to Bloch (340). Lo and behold, Parsifal is supposed to meet the temptress Kundry in an arbor of the magic garden. Wagner poeticizes the term into *Blumenhag,* a "flowery enclosure." Only later does he change it to a grotto. Syberberg seems to apply Bloch's recipe for saving Wagner from himself by having the "fair," or carnival, break down the world of the parlor. Inseparable from the fairgrounds are colportage and fairytales, Bloch maintains: "*Colportage* is therefore the most authentic rescue of Wagner" (341). His discussion of colportage includes such characteristics as dream, excitement, action, triumph at the end, a fairytale-like hero, and the surrealism of a dream-bazaar. Another chapter of the same book describing this kind of world mentions the Oriental touch, asking, "Does it not begin immediately spiced, for nose, ear and eye at the same time? (158). He mentions puppets, Gypsies, "the mystery of dangerous depths," and offered attractions piled high. The intoxicating lures through an Oriental maze even include a devil (Samiel) hovering as a face in a black room, and an exotic princess or queen. All this popular magic is only a front that hides terrors. All the lustre is beset with pitfalls, it is "activated 'entertainment' directed against mythical powers, and above all as their overthrow" (102). Wagner's version already includes some of the fair's characteristics. The film adds the maze, the devil's face in a black room (Wagner's death mask as a moon in a dark sky); objects piled high, a carrousel horse, puppets and a glimpse of a marionette stage, a queen, and even the fairytale look of the hero with the raised collar framing his face. Most conspicuous may be the surrealistic treatment of the whole episode. By contradicting Wagner's instructions so drastically, the cinematic version of this episode achieves what Wagner only pretended to want. In view of his enthusiasm for Carrie Pringle and imitation of the Jockey Club members, the change may indeed amount to a rescue. In the process, it also evokes Syberberg's *Karl May,* since Bloch considers May a healthy counterpart to Wagner. But while the director's treatment of the flower maiden section of the film suggests new accents for the hero's adventures, it forms only the first half of Parsifal's experiences in Klingsor's world.

When Parsifal escapes from the labyrinth into open terrain, he finds himself up on the belly of the mountain resembling a woman. The background is again a projection showing a pattern reminiscent of barbed wire. Although surrealistic, it awakens associations of captivity. Perhaps Klingsor's garden of delights is a prison camp with the watchtower glimpsed behind him earlier. One assumes that Parsifal stands outside the barbed wire fence. A drawn detail behind the fence suggests a creature on the other side. One can only see its hand or claw. Since the frame of reference for the labyrinth and the bullfighter includes a monster with both animal and human features, one accepts that the apparition may look human while possessing nonhuman characteristics.

Kundry's voice calling on Parsifal by name interrupts this speculation. The young fool who does not know his name now remembers that his mother once called him Parsifal. The magic that Klingsor had applied to produce Kundry's emergence and compliance is again invoked with this call: The knowledge of someone's name confers power over that person. Parsifal obeys by reentering the Venus Mountain. In Wagner's version he is still in the garden. The first glimpse of Kundry shows her in a splendid fur-trimmed garment and a headband of glittering stones. She sits on the elevated throne already seen in the first prelude with Herzeleide and in act 1 serving Amfortas. With steps leading up to it and a starry, dark background (the lining of Wagner's navy robe), Kundry has become the Queen of the Night or the Queen of Heaven from the Kabbalah. After a brief cut to Parsifal who still ponders the name, the camera returns to Kundry who is slowly descending the steps while carrying a crystal ball. The stars have now moved underfoot. Herzeleide's starry, blue cloth covers the ground around the throne. The change confuses the viewers' sense of direction, is she really descending to the stars? From a compositional perspective the episode may mark an inversion. But while the heavens have changed location, a different background surrounds the throne. It looks like a wall of brocade with an intricate pattern and embroidery that includes a large pearl. Syberberg describes it as splendor borrowed from or inspired by King Ludwig's interiors: "The second projection to Kundry's second call is a detail of Oriental fabric from the world of Ludwig II with peacock ornaments and pearls" (*Parsifal*, 137). One wonders why he mentions it at all. The film contains so many visual surprises not identified in the book. One assumes the reference does not only intend to emphasize another deviation from Wagner's stage instructions. Just as likely is the link to Syberberg's own *Ludwig*. Also pertinent might be a reminder of the role King Ludwig played in Wagner's life and the genesis of *Parsifal*. Nor should one overlook the hint hidden in "Oriental fabric." And consistent with the alchemical subtext of the film, both peacocks and pearls function as symbols. The peacock colors indicate an advanced stage in the transmutation process.[16] The pearl is one of the manifestations of the precious stone. Jung, for example, elucidates a quotation from the *Pirkê de Rabbi Elieser* thus: "In the darkness of the unconscious a treasure lies hidden, the same 'treasure hard to attain' which in our text, and in many other places too, is described as the shining pearl, or, to quote Paracelsus, as the 'mystery,' by which is meant a *fascinosum* par excellence" (*Symbols of Transf.*, 330). And finally, this comment on a Jewish text might point to imagery of the Kabbalah and related esoteric systems. They consider the pearl as an attribute or "correspondence" of Binah, the Divine Mother and Queen of Heaven (e.g. Regardie, 50).

It would seem, then, that Parsifal has advanced, or regressed, as Freud would say, in a dreamlike state beyond the multiplicity of female forms denoting splitting and dissolution. He is now approaching the maternal archetype described by Jung as the "gateway into the unconscious." Wagner envisioned the transition between the two stages as the reluctant withdrawal of the flower maidens. Laughingly they should let go of Parsifal while calling him a fool. The film suppresses the laughter. Syberberg resorts to the crystal ball that Kundry holds. It was with her in the very opening scene of the film. But now a close-up shows the still immobile girls in the globe as a "reflection" surrounded by vapors. Kundry commands the apparitions in it to recede. Syberberg's book explains the use of the sphere as an attempt to camouflage a lack of synchronicity in the last scene of the flower maidens (136). As usual the director emphasizes the technical aspects in the book. But in view of the significance and usefulness of this round object, one cannot help surmising that he planned to use the crystal globe for this purpose from the beginning. Jung points out, "In Neoplatonic philosophy the soul has definite affinities with the sphere. The soul substance is laid round the concentric spheres of the four elements above the fiery heaven" (*Psych. and Alch.*, 83-84). Within the visual narrative this would apply to Parsifal's soul, although he himself is also one of the forces in this world of the mind. With the disappearance of the splintered manifestations of the feminine the sphere proves itself as a symbol of transformation. Actually, Syberberg could not have devised a better way to depict the psychological process.

Wagner himself suggested the dreamlike nature of the flower maiden episode. Before Parsifal discovers Kundry, he wonders aloud if he had been dreaming all of this, "Dies alles—hab ich nur geträumt?" The dream continues with a cut to Parsifal showing him at the end of the passage and without the bolero. He has shed the attribute of fairytale prince, bullfighter, and "torn" personality. He is also surrounded by dead leaves. With his sleeveless shirt and breeches he looks younger and more vulnerable. He has apparently penetrated the narrow passage behind him and is reaching an inner chamber or the womb of the Venus Mountain.[17] Visible through a crack in the rock walls of the chamber is a projection of a drawn face and a claw-like hand, both glimpsed separately earlier in the same act. One assumes the face and the hand belong to the same person. In the process of identifying the head, several possibilities pass review. It might belong to Heinrich von Kleist whose work informs both *Parsifal* and other Syberberg films. The tousled hair falling over the forehead resembles his hairdo in several portraits. Another possibility is Heinrich Heine, who sported the same hairstyle in his youth. Actually, the eyes of the projection look remarkably like those of Heine in an 1831 portrait by M. Oppenheim. And of course, Heine belongs to the subtext of *Parsifal* as well. But the eyes also resemble those of Edith Clever who portrays Kundry. Although the coiffure differs, the temptress Kundry appears to be the more likely choice for a female power observing Parsifal. She may be viewing him through the crystal sphere as he materializes in front of her. But why did not Syberberg use a photo of

Clever for this projection? He has again resorted to a work of art. However, instead of rendering the painted details, he copied them in an alienating black-and-white drawing that permits a series of tentative identifications. The source of the two body parts is Titian's *Venus of Urbino* of 1538. The choice is consistent with the film's associative links to Tannhäuser in the Venus Mountain. Syberberg probably took his inspiration from Wagner's comments. Cosima's diary entry for Jan. 4, 1881 includes: "A sketch of Kundry, brought along by Jouk.[owsky], pleases us a lot. 'Actually,' says R.[ichard], 'she ought to be lying there naked, like a Titian Venus.' Now this has to be replaced by finery." Of course the composer could not present the seductress in the buff on his or any other respectable stage, and certainly not in what he called the holiest of his works (Dahlhaus, 201). Syberberg plays with the nudity, in part by shifting it onto some of the flower maidens, in part by his Brechtian alienation technique. He does not show the whole Venus in her nude splendor. But the hand chosen for the projection rests on her pudenda. Thanks to the cropping of the fragment, the viewer does not recognize the context. Were it not for a ring on one of the fingers, the drawing could even be mistaken for a claw. These two tricks, fragments out of context and their altered presentation, preserve some of the polyvalence that characterizes the painting as a whole.

The other detail, the face, also preserves a feature for which the painting is famous. Venus gazes directly at the beholder. The erotic nature of her smile and the setting could easily produce the death of innocent thoughts or peace of mind in a male viewer. Thus the power of her gaze bears a faint resemblance to the lethal glance of the Valkyries, Athena, and Medusa. More importantly, the direct gaze of the goddess functions like the representations of the all-seeing Eye of God. Regardless from which angle the viewers observe this Venus, her eyes meet theirs. They seem to follow the beholder. Her "omnivoyance" and effect on the viewer is akin to the "animated" objects of veneration in ancient theurgic rites, such as statues containing the power of the deities they represented. It would appear that the miraculous glow and effect of the Grail during the ceremony belongs to the same tradition of theurgic immanence. Parsifal has now "called forth" the power of the goddess, the Anima herself. The second act has seen him repel Klingsor's knights and resist the flower maidens. Now comes the third and decisive test. Since he is no longer wearing the bolero, the association of a fight fades in favor of a rite of passage. Several of the ancient mysteries come to mind.

Kundry does not look dressed for seduction. Under her fur-trimmed garment a long-sleeved dress displays a monochrome pattern of butterflies, the symbol of metamorphosis. Since Wagner let the flower maidens reverse the role of butterfly and flowers in their text, it comes as no surprise that also Syberberg plays with the concept. One remembers an occurrence in the first act when Kundry covers herself with dead leaves. She might be using them as camouflage to blend in, just as a leaf butterfly is indistinguishable from the foliage on which it sits. The big family of butterflies includes a cousin by the name of Psyche, the same Greek word that also means "soul." The pattern on Kundry's dress suggests, then, that she and Parsifal are indeed closely related. They are both forces of the collective unconscious, or the human psyche. But for a while one cannot recognize the pattern on Kundry's dress due to the fur-trimmed cover garment. As the book points out, her attire resembles those of the figures in Van Eyck's paintings (138). Especially his depictions of the Virgin lavish such splendor on the reveered mother of a holy child. Such connotations lead away from thoughts of seduction. Syberberg had already created associative links to one painting by Van Eyck in the first prelude. There he grouped the pillory, crucifix, and chalice with the Wagner doll. The attributes of Christ jarred with their new context, as if the counterpoint produced a disharmonious combination. And a seductress dressed like the Holy Virgin promises another occurrence. The clash of seemingly incompatible elements or associations points to a counterpoint under the guise of blasphemy. Her clothes may, however, also point to a hidden quality in the temptress. She possesses many qualities, some of them quite in contrast to each other. Not only might this seductress be Jewish, as Mary was, but she might also have given birth to a redeemer child. After all, Parsifal is a redeemer, and Herzeleide shares the face with Kundry. The psychological subtext would even require the saving force to emerge from the maternal Anima. As such she is the Goddess.

Having heard the voice calling out to Parsifal before bidding the girls to recede, the hero is not yet sure if the name he heard is his. With his eyes bashfully fixed on the ground, he speaks up: "Riefest du mich Namenlosen?" (Did you call me, the nameless one?). The following camera take concentrates on Kundry endowing Parsifal with a name. This amounts to an empowering of the hero. Knowing and using the name of someone else is one thing. Klingsor could conjure up Kundry, forcing her to obey the call. And in the first act Parsifal's ignorance of his name allows Gurnemanz to retain his authority. But Kundry's call leads to something else. When Parsifal refers to himself as the nameless one, she informs him of his name and even mentions his parents in quick succession. This is the famous passage that has been ridiculed in many Wagner studies. The target of derision is the presumed translation of Fal Parsi as "the foolish pure one." Kundry uses these appellations before adding "Parsi Fal, the pure fool." It is generally assumed that Wagner took his information from the introduction in Josef Görres' modern German translation of *Lohengrin*. Görres claims "that even the name of the hero Parcifal can be derived easily from Arabic: Parsi or Parseh Fal, i.e., the pure or poor fool, or dumb [*thumbe*] in the language of the poem" (Introd., vi). In a letter to Judith Gautier of Nov. 22, 1877, Wagner lectures her on the meaning of the name: "This is an Arabian name. The old troubadours no longer understood what it meant. 'Parsi fal' means: 'parsi'—think of the fire-loving Parsees—'pure'; 'fal' means 'mad' in a higher sense, in other words a man without erudition, but one of genius."[18] Gautier, who was an author and scholar in her own right and translator of Chinese and Japanese poetry, disagreed. He might have done better had he investigated the Persian language, also called Farsi, since the Parsis or Parsees came from Persia.[19] His remark that the troubadours did not know the meaning of the name refers to the conflicting explanations surrounding the names of Chrétien's Perceval and Wolfram's Parzival.[20] Hans von Wolzogen, a long-time editor of the *Bayreuther*

Blätter, wrote a philological study of Parsifal's name.[21] Although he could confirm that *parsâ* is Persian for "pure," "chaste," and "pious," that *parsî* means "Persian," and that *fájal/fajjil* in Arabic means "imbecile," he could not document a compound noun or noun-adjective combination resembling Parsifal's name (164–65). But interestingly, he points to Goethe's *West-östlicher Divan* as a likely contributing inspiration (165–66). One of the sections of this work is the "Book of the Parsee," and the nine lines quoted from this unit contain "pure" and "impure" six times. But Goethe uses the term *Fal* in the sense of "oracle." Wagner admired Goethe and knew his writings well. Not mentioned in the consulted literature on *Parsifal* is still another possible source to be discussed later. If it played a role in Wagner's scheme, he concealed it well. The semantics of the name may have been of minor importance to him. But he did eventually, in 1877, decide on an idiosyncratic spelling of the name that identifies the work as his. And since he also mentioned the Parsis, one may assume that their preoccupation with personal and ritual purity contributed to his choice of spelling. The major reason for the play on Fal Parsi and Parsi Fal may have nothing to do with semantics. The transposition offers a convenient mechanism to mark a quasi-musical caesura in the text, similar to the fugal transformation of a basic subject to its crab form. Syberberg did the same in the ghost scene of *Hitler*. Wagner may have been inspired to this metathesis by Gottfried of Strasbourg and his Tristan alias Tantris. More importantly, it helps Parsifal learn or acquire his identity.

The following scene, which begins with vapors tumbling down the rock walls, employs subtle camera work resulting in dramatic intimacy while retaining visual interest. The camera cuts occasionally from one character to the other, letting the viewer focus on the "speaker." In the mid section, when Parsifal kneels at Kundry's side, one sees both of them simultaneously. Panning and zooming enliven each stage. Remembering the director's statement on the seductive camera work of Riefenstahl, one suspects that the power of seduction to some extent has been relegated to the camera. Kundry has some help. But visually, the image does not abide by the libretto. There is, for example, no bower with a bed of flowers, nor is Kundry scantily veiled. Instead the environment appears to be similar to the space where Amfortas "conducted" the Grail ceremony. In addition to dead leaves on the ground one also discovers Parsifal's shield propped up against the wall, making the Medusa head face the hero. No longer part of his own protective armor, this element spells danger to the beholder. But apart from signaling danger it may also function as a *mise en abyme* miniature variant of Kundry. She too presents a danger to Parsifal at this time.

After explaining the meaning of Parsifal's name, Kundry identifies her mission as relaying this name to him. After all, she asks, was not the desire for this knowledge what had brought him there? One would read this as his desire to know himself. To the viewers' surprise and contrary to the libretto, Parsifal does not seem to look at her. When he addresses her, he is really talking to himself. At first his glance is even directed at the ground, as if too bashful to face her. Later he looks into empty space, struggling with emerging memories, emotions, and confusing thoughts. At one point one sees both characters in profile turned towards each other, but Parsifal's unruly hair covers part of his face, leaving the viewer to guess. Obviously, the Medusa head has no effect; that means, then, that he does not gaze into Kundry's eyes.

Kundry's long narrative aims at reviving Parsifal's earliest memories. It focuses on Herzeleide's love, grief, and death. Through the play on Herzeleide's name Wagner weaves in another case of metathesis. Inspired by Wolfram's manipulation of names and nouns, Wagner changed the mother's name from Herzeloyde to Herzeleide (heartache).[22] This allows the separation of the name into two nouns, *Herz* and *Leid*, and an exchange of their sequence ("ihr brach das Leid das Herz, und—Herzeleide—starb").

Kundry's words evoking the devoted mother achieve their intended result. They direct Parsifal's thoughts to his early memories, produce the insight that his departure caused her death, and awaken his guilt over this outcome. No longer kneeling, he crouches in remorse at Kundry's side. At least at this point the viewer can no longer overlook the fact that she is sending out mixed signals. Her emotionally laden narrative conflicts with the occasional glances observing Parsifal. She is clearly probing the effect of her words. She has again several objects lying at her side. One is Parsifal's arrow. It keeps reappearing periodically, each time enriched with new associations. Thanks to this web of memory-triggers, the film introduces a parallel to the visible situation. In the first act Syberberg had placed an oversized replica of the bow and arrow on a scaffolding and had also let Kundry hold an arrow soon after, making her imitate the function of the *Gestell*. This contraption and its human equivalent brought to mind Heidegger's comments on *Gestell* as a dangerous predicament. One can easily recognize that Kundry as the temptress represents a threat to Parsifal. The memory triggered by the arrow recognizes it as a small-scale version of the larger situation, a *mise en abyme*, where *abyme* still possesses the dangers of an abyss. But to many German viewers, the same association will also activate yet another reference from literature. Much like the strings of a viola d'amore, Hölderlin's famous lines from his hymn "Patmos" begin to reverberate, "Wo auch Gefahr ist, wächst das Rettende auch" (Wherever there is danger, the saving [force] also grows).[23] Not only does the quotation support the notion of danger, but also of the *enantiodromia* of the temptress. Presently she still appears to be a helper. Parsifal needs every aspect of this experience to fathom the depths of his own nature. Only with this insight will he be able to carry out his mission. And Kundry is the force that offers him the opportunity to acquire the necessary wisdom. Empowering him with his name, she endows him with strength for the ordeals ahead.

Another object at Kundry's side emits the same kind of conflicting signal as the arrow. It is a doll of Parsifal fully armed and dressed in a mail coat. The mail coat appeared in the first puppet play, but not on Parsifal. And as one of the "shining knights" he wore an armor, but not until his arrival in Klingsor's garden did he wear a mail coat. Thus the doll that the temptress kisses so lovingly during her narrative is not a miniature of the child, but of the young man in front of her.

Oblivious to the warnings of so many "mirrors in the text," Parsifal is gradually drawn closer to the seated Kundry. During the early part of the scene she reveals a different aspect of the situation. Before caressing the doll she keeps the palms of her hands facing Parsifal. This position with arms raised from the elbows and palms facing forwards occurs on many ancient Egyptian murals. The pose, probably symbolizing a gesture of calling, even serves as the hieroglyph of *ka*. This concept has no exact equivalent in Western thought, but is believed to represent an immortal aspect of a person related to vitality or energy.[24] Then, as Parsifal bends down in remorse, his forehead touching the ground, she holds her hand outstretched over his head as if blessing him. Her palms appear to emanate some kind of power or "vibrations." They contradict the calculating glances that seem to duplicate the deadliness of the Medusa gaze. Kundry's hands also attract attention through the position of her fingers. She groups together the index finger with the long finger and the ring finger with the little finger, leaving a V-shaped gap in the middle. This unusual posture expresses a Kabbalistic message. It presumably renders the numerical total of the ten *sefirot* and the 22 paths of the Sefirotic Tree (Holroyd, 57). That total points towards the last *sefira*, Malkhut, and the completion of the "downward" movement through the labyrinth. The location identifies the feminine apparition as related to the Shekhinah, or Divine Presence on earth. As will be discussed later, Parsifal has reached the only portal that will lead to an ascent.

The Kabbalistic element suggests, then, an additional dimension of an already polyvalent situation. Alerted to the language of hands, the viewer recognizes an earlier gesture as also being meaningful. While describing Herzeleide's worries, Kundry makes a brief gesture during which her index finger appears to cross her lips. It is the Harpocratic admonition to remain silent. The demand for secrecy characterized all ancient mystery rites, as R. E. Witt points out.[25] Hence this gesture identifies Parsifal's experience as part of an initiation. Since such events often consisted of a series of tests and rituals years apart, one might read Parsifal's story as a veiled representation of a candidate's pursuit in what resembles the ancient mystery rites. The quest appeared dressed in imagery that varied according to time and culture. Central to most was a loss followed by seeking and finding. Orpheus searched for Euridice, Demeter mourned Persephone, the soul longs for a lost paradise, Isis searched for Osiris, resp. for the lost part of him, and Parzival sought his mother and later the Grail. Several circumstances strengthen the association between Parsifal's experience in the film and the ancient mysteries. Since Edith Clever lends her features to the "gate-keeping" prophetess, Herzeleide, Kundry, and the temptress, they all merge into one figure of mythic proportion related to religion and psychological symbolism. This describes the position of, e.g., Demeter, and even more so, of Isis in the age of syncretism: the Great Mother of infinite names and wisdom (Witt, 22–23). Especially the position of Isis in the trinity of divine father, mother, and son gave rise to several parallel versions of her quest to restore and resurrect Osiris after he had been killed and later dismembered by Seth. Most versions present both the miraculous conception and the birth of her son Horus as a resurrection of her spouse, who lives on in the son. A description of Osiris/Sarapis by the Neoplatonist Porphyry concludes with these words: "And this is why tradition has made Osiris her husband, her brother and her son" (Witt, 44). Both Osiris and Horus were sun gods. Solar imagery also surrounds the cinematic Parsifal, who, like Horus, was born after his father's death. The parallel lets him emerge as the masculine counterpart to the Goddess. She, incidentally, was associated with the moon. Supporting the association of the hero with the solar deity is his Parsi-phallic dimension, since he possesses or represents the one part of the father's body that could not be restored. Isis collected fourteen parts of Osiris' body. It is probably no coincidence, then, that Syberberg divided the head landscape into fourteen sections. As Witt elaborated in *Isis in the Ancient World*, this goddess eventually borrowed features from, or merged with, most important female deities of the known religions, including the entirely anthropomorphic goddesses of the Graeco-Roman pantheon. During the era of Hellenism she became simply *the* goddess of many names with shrines and mystery rites in numerous locations. The acquired features account for her diverse characteristics. She was, for example, the personification of Wisdom (*sophia*) as well as of virginal, spousal, and maternal qualities. She fused with Athena as Neith in the temple at Sais, and with the many-breasted Diana/Artemis in Ephesus (Witt, 67). She was also frequently depicted holding Horus like a Madonna with the Holy Child while wearing a headdress showing the horns of the moon embracing a sun. Thus Syberberg's references to Jan van Eyck's sumptuously dressed Madonnas gain an added nuance. Suffice it that he equips the temptress with an aura of the Queen of Heaven, especially in her manifestations as the goddess of Eleusinian and Isiac mysteries. Her Harpocratic gesture confirms that the meeting with Parsifal belongs to such a ritual.

Although the admonition to secrecy accounts for the paucity of surviving information about the mysteries, bits and pieces of descriptions and allusions have allowed scholars to outline some characteristics of initiation rites. The film consists of a series of steps resembling such rites, with especially the first prelude and the second act incorporating elements celebrating the Goddess. So far in act 2 the hero has persevered and overcome several ordeals. While Wagner envisioned the latest trial to resemble sensual temptation in the form of music, dance, and female allure, all parts of ancient ordeals, Syberberg postpones the carnal temptation in favor of a progression through subterranean passages full of "statues." Statues also featured in the rituals as well as degrees of nudity (Witt, 160–61). Sexual abstinence was very important in the ritual, and so was a private encounter with the deity in some ceremonies. The *unio mystica* would take place in an inner chamber between the applicant and the appearing deity. Whether the experience was a sexual union, a *hieros gamos*, or another form of intimate revelation probably varied with the rites in question. Nor can one ascertain how the experience was produced. It may have resulted from convincing apparitions and technical display, from a dreamlike trance, from visions ensuing from meditations and ascetic preparations, or from drug-induced hallucinations. In any case, the experiences convinced the participants. Like them, Parsifal has now been admonished to secrecy. The goddess appearing before him displays several aspects of the Great Mother of a myriad names, including Herzeleide. But where Wagner's stage version at first glance appears to restrict itself to a test of seduction, the film expands on the initiation experience. The emphasis on the initiatory circumstances is justified by Kundry's use of Parsifal's name. It was, of course, Wagner's idea to let the temptress empower the hero. This would parallel Isis' role as a supportive and saving maternal force, also in her mysteries. The effect of Kundry's long narrative promotes remorse and insight about guilt in Parsifal. The followers of the Goddess practiced penitence as preparation for the ceremonies. Isis was also the goddess of compassion, a quality Parsifal must learn. She shares with the temptress the identity of sorrowing spouse and mother. Syberberg shows this side of her for the second time here. The first prelude had presented her passion as a silent drama, imitating the related pantomime of the Isiac rites.[26] Actually, most nuances presented in the film are suggested in Wagner's text. One example appears in the dichotomy of the temptress' last statement before the kiss.

Kundry's lines leading up to the kiss present her from contrasting perspectives. The first third of this text belongs to the Goddess as teacher encouraging insight: "Bekenntnis wird Schuld in Reue enden, Erkenntnis in Sinn die Torheit wenden" (Confession will end guilt in remorse, insight will turn folly into conscious mind). While she pronounces this, the camera moves just enough to reveal the Medusa head in the background. What sounds like an absolution from sin introduces a very different admonishment in the following words: "Die Liebe lerne kennen, die Gamuret umschloß, als Herzeleids Entbrennen ihn sengend überfloß!" (Get to know the love that embraced Gamuret, when Herzeleide's passion covered him searingly). This sudden switch to the ardor of Parsifal's parents marks a departure from the extended description of Herzeleide's sorrows, but it was prepared in the gestures illustrating the love for her son. As the son is being prepared for the role of the father, one recognizes the succession from Osiris to Horus and back to Osiris. What may offend as incest in myth becomes more acceptable as psychological growth and understanding.

Unfortunately, the details of Wagner's own direction of this scene remain unknown, but the film adds a touch from the composer's life. Only now does one become aware that the "stone" on which Kundry sits is a miniature of Wagner's death mask. As Dällenbach points out, the *mise en abyme* can also function as a genre shifter, in this case, a shift that includes the Wagner narrative. While Kundry demonstrates Herzeleide's rapture in Gamuret's embrace, she leans backwards on her perch as if it were a canapé. In view of the facial features of the stone, it must be an uncomfortable surface! Nevertheless, it functions as a piece of furniture recognizable as "Judith." This was the name Wagner gave to a chaise longue in his study. Enamored with Judith Gautier, he conducted a passionate correspondence with her while composing *Parsifal*. In the same letter of Nov. 22, 1877, in which he expounds on the name of Parsifal he also asks her to buy for him six meters of yellow silk, "a very beautiful and exceptional cover—for my chaise longue—which I shall call 'Judith!' . . . All this for mornings well spent on *Parsifal*" (*Selected*

Letters, 877). And he concludes the letter with "Adieu! my dearest, my 'dolcissima anima.' Your R. W." A cluster of motifs converge in this letter: Judith Gautier, Wagner's amorous fantasies on "Judith," *Parsifal*, and even the Anima. In the film, of course, Judith Gautier figures as a splintered version among many other fragments of the Anima.

The book to the film includes several stills from this scene. However, at least some of them show shots from rehearsals with Parsifal looking at the temptress. The film itself avoids the direct gaze with eye contact. Also when Kundry proceeds to bare a breast, one cannot see Parsifal's face. Her words accompanying this gesture identify her as the mother: "Die Leib und Leben einst dir gegeben, der Tod und Torheit weichen muß, sie beut dir heut—als Muttersegens letzten Gruß der Liebe—ersten Kuß" (She who once gave you body and life, she against whom death and folly must yield, she offers you today—as the last greeting of maternal blessing the first kiss—of love). Describing herself as one against whom death has no power, she is obviously no ordinary mortal mother. Even "folly" must yield to her. One might at first read *Torheit* as "naïveté" or "lack of carnal experience." But death and folly belong together here. The maternal blessing seems to imply the gift of the opposite: not death, but wisdom and insight. Her kiss will confer the blessing. This cluster of concepts identifies the situation as more than an attempt at seduction.

As the temptress kisses Parsifal, the film at first conforms to the instructions in the libretto. She takes the initiative and showers him with passion worthy of a seduction. A passive recipient, he lets himself be overwhelmed, keeping his eyes closed. So far the encounter points to a sexual initiation with the added dimension of incest. But in the course of the embrace Parsifal ends by having his face pressed against her exposed breast. This detail suggests a different nature of the situation. Rather than kissing a lover's body he may be imbibing the milk of the mother. How would any woman try to seduce a young boy by making him assume the role of her infant? It would appear, then, that Kundry as the mother is really guiding the emotional development of Parsifal here: exciting him sexually before reminding him of the mother-son relationship. He now experiences arousal, but cannot yield to his urges because of the taboo. He learns enough to realize what sexual union entails but without committing the act. Technically he remains a virgin. The pose involving a baby at his mother's breast also endows the situation with mythical echoes. Again one remembers the statues of Horus suckling Isis. That nourishment would impart divine status. Parsifal has become Horus. The kiss and the milk of the divine mother have conferred a new insight (*gnosis*).

Parsifal's sudden insight causes his withdrawal with the outburst "Amfortas!" As he tears himself away from Kundry, the camera dwells on him alone for a while. His ensuing soliloquy consists of several distinct sections, the first being a description of arousal and confusion. His initial reaction is an identification with the king through his wound, which Parsifal now feels burning in his own "heart." Then he recognizes it as a different kind of fire, namely a yearning, *Sehnen*, that overpowers his senses. On one level of narrative, Parsifal has realized the origin and nature of Amfortas' affliction, experiencing the same sensual rapture. Thanks to this shared feeling, he also understands Amfortas' predicament. Parsifal experiences *Mit-Leiden.* The reader will also have recognized *Sehnen* as a power word in Syberberg's and Wagner's semantic grids. It evokes the other dimensions involving the string of the violin, *fides*, and Faith.

A transition to the next segment presents itself as a quick glimpse of Kundry, who observes the emotional attempt at self-analysis intently. As the camera pans slowly from her back to Parsifal, the screen fills with the darkness of the rock wall between them. This blackness lasts several seconds and forms a visual abyss. When the camera reaches Parsifal, he stares right into the lens, spellbound by his vision and feelings. For a moment the spectator may wonder what he sees. It is not likely to be the temptress, although she induced this look into the pit. As Siegfried learned fear at Brünnhilde's side, so Parsifal appears to be experiencing a similar epiphany. Since his gaze meets the spectators' eyes, we, the viewers, turn out to be the abyss. Human nature is what overwhelms him, a bottomless pit of potential for good and evil. Like a divine revelation, Parsifal is experiencing *gnosis*, a knowledge of himself and all human nature. This reaction, as well as his role in the drama, reminds one of Walter Benjamin's "Angelus Novus," an angel who sees only disaster upon disaster in the past while the storm of progress forces him to back away towards the future.[27] Parsifal, whose task is to repair the damage of the past, recognizes the challenge of his mission. Another possible link on the grid of associations leads back to the Wagner narrative. In 1865 the composer sent a poem to King Ludwig called "Am Abgrund" (At the Abyss). It begins with these words: "Am Abgrund steh' ich; Grausen hemmt die Schritte; der mich geführt, verloren ist der Pfad" (I am standing at the abyss; terror inhibits my steps; the path that led me is lost).[28] If feeling lost, Parsifal may need both time and help to find his way again. His new insight seems to stun him.

While Parsifal describes his feelings, he gradually backs away from the camera. Obviously the abyss he stares into is also the reflection of himself in the mirror of the camera lens. His experience resulting from the *unio mystica* has imparted a shattering insight into his own nature as well. The identification with Amfortas, recognition of Kundry's predicament and role, and the consequences for himself produce a perceptible reaction in him. Jungians might describe it both as an introjection or assimilation, since he feels empathy towards the objects, and as an introversion, that is, a withdrawal and an inward-turning of the libido. It regresses to the collective unconscious when the situation calls for a change in orientation and a new adaptation. Jung explains in *Symbols of Transformation*: "When therefore a distressing situation arises, the corresponding archetype will be constellated in the unconscious. . . . Its passing over into consciousness is felt as an illumination, a revelation, or a 'saving idea'" (294). The film translates this visually. As Parsifal slowly recedes into the dark rocky passage, his feminine counterpart appears behind him and moves towards the camera. Under the face of Wagner's death mask on a black background, much like a full moon of Isis, he finally disappears into the darkness, leaving the young woman to take his place. This time the *mise en abyme* has produced not only a shift in genre affecting the content of the text, but also a shift in gender. The French *genre* can also mean "grammatical gender." But since the voice singing Parsifal's lines continues to come from Rainer Goldberg, the discrepancy between appearance and voice creates an alienating effect. Brecht would have applauded.

If one accepts the equivalency of Parsifal's name suggested by Wagner, then Michael Kutter plays the Fal part and Karin Krick the Parsi half. As already mentioned, the name Karin is a form of Catherine, which contains the Greek word for "pure." The surprise of a new Parsifal, and to boot a female one, is softened by two preparatory circumstances. First, she appears twice in the first prelude as Kutter's companion in shared situations. And when he leaves her still slumbering, his departure indicates that he leaves behind a part of himself. Second, Wagner's text makes such a remarkable turn in content at this point that a change in the subject becomes less alienating. The experience has thoroughly rattled and transformed the hero. He has become a new person. Jung would consider the feminine half of Parsifal as the indispensable opposite that together with the masculine half forms a bisexual whole, a balance of complementary qualities of the psyche. She represents a latent unconscious content that is activated by a violent affect. Jung describes such a predicament as a " condition in which the ego-consciousness is thrust aside by autonomous contents that were unconscious before. So long as the unconscious is in a dormant condition, it seems as if there were absolutely nothing in the hidden region. Hence we are continually surprised when something unknown suddenly appears "from nowhere"' (*Archetypes*, 279). Now this helpful feminine power that had remained slumbering in the depths of Parsifal's nature comes to the fore. Not only does she intervene in his behalf, but for some time even becomes the only manifestation of the hero.

The second Parsifal shares with her male counterpart a slender figure, but otherwise displays many complementary characteristics, such as big blue eyes and an oval face. She reminds one of a delicate doll, but as the situation soon proves, a doll tough as if made of porcelain. Presumably a puppeteer by profession, Karin Krick as Parsifal II encourages associations of puppets, *pupa*, and *pupilla*. Considering Parsifal I's fixation on the camera lens, she might even have emerged as his reflection in the eye of the camera. Their complementarity goes even further. While Amfortas had been maimed for his sexual indulgence, and Klingsor resorted to self-mutilation, Parsifal I resisted this indulgence and emerged as a transformed person who is not only chaste and wise, but also lacks the problematic organ. This feature of their complementarity helps create a balance that encourages sublimation.

The metamorphosis of the hero is also reflected in what the female Parsifal envisions. She continues the soliloquy, but soon shifts her glance from the lens to the side of the camera. She does not see the abyss, but the Grail. More precisely, she relives the Grail ceremony from the first act. The completed exchange of the two Parsifals coincides with the abrupt jump in the libretto from "sinful desire" to the "holy blood" in the Grail. This shift in orientation also conforms to Jung's description of a psychological transformation. When a crisis precipitates introversion, he claims, its mechanism functions "by means of ritual actions which bring about a spiritual preparation, e.g., magical ceremonies, sacrifices, invocations, prayers, and suchlike" (*Symbols of Transf.*, 294). And Parsifal's reaction, which started as an identification with Amfortas, continues with a reliving of the Grail ceremony.

Perhaps the intensity of Parsifal's *Sehnen* has contributed to the miracle of a divine presence, much like the incident in the first act when Gurnemanz' prayer-like description of the prophesy seemed to induce the hero's arrival. Thus in words and music, but not visually, the Grail ritual is celebrated again in the second act in Kundry's presence. In words compatible with Christian usage Parsifal II describes a religious experience. While the holy blood glows in the Grail, she imagines hearing the Savior's lament over the unworthy priest: "'Erlöse, rette mich aus schuldbefleckten Händen!' So rief die Gottesklage furchtbar laut mir in die Seel ('Redeem me, save me from hands defiled by guilt!' Thus called the divine lament frightfully loud into my soul). Undoubtedly the deity, presumably the Christian Savior, needs human intervention. But in most religions the relationship is the other way around: humans pray to God for help. The uncertainty about how to interpret this grows to confusion when one realizes that the text is ambiguous. The divine message may or may not come from the chalice containing the holy blood. Parsifal states, "[N]ur hier, im Herzen, will die Qual nicht weichen. Des Heilands Klage da vernehm ich" ([O]nly here, in my heart, the pain will not subside. I perceive the Savior's voice there). *Da* can mean both "then" and "there." Read as "there" it might point to the Grail with its luminous content, but more likely to Parsifal's heart, which is mentioned immediately before the Savior's lament. In the latter case, the divine voice speaks from Parsifal's heart to her/his soul. This would imply an immanent trace of divinity embedded in human nature. The thought is familiar in Christianity: a pious woman like the Virgin Mary can be pregnant with a divine child. Most male mystics, for lack of a womb, strive to make their heart a temple worthy of sheltering God, imitating a Catholic sanctuary with its consecrated host in the ciborium. But the thought is also at home in Gnosticism as divine sparks imprisoned in human bodies. Even the Kabbalah operates with related imagery, as does Heinrich Heine. In the introduction to *Deutschland: Ein Wintermärchen*, he includes a similar statement. In a series of conditions for reaching his ideal of Germanness and patriotism he includes: "[W]hen we save the God who lives on earth in man from his debasement, when we become God's redeemers . . ." (608). It appears that Wagner was familiar with the idea of divine immanence. He was possibly inspired by the medieval mystic Meister Eckhart, whose works he admired. If one views the lament as originating in Parsifal II's own heart, then she hears the plea to redeem the divine force in herself. The other reading views Amfortas' person as the "desecrated sanctuary" or Grail temple. As parallels to Osiris and Horus, Amfortas and Parsifal become two divine aspects of human nature in different stages of unfolding. But psychologically, their constellation, as well as the sanctuary and the head landscape, all point to forces within the same personality. Parsifal's vision of the Grail ceremony culminates in a painful insight. She has committed the sin of ignoring this divine plea for help.

Kundry, who has been observing Parsifal at a distance, interrupts the soliloquy at this point. Her words cause another abrupt change in Parsifal. Switching from her own sin of omission to an imagined memory, the new hero/heroine envisions the seduction of Amfortas by Kundry. Much of the vision could also apply to the embrace experienced a few moments ago. She ends by rejecting the temptress in strong words: "Weiche von mir! Ewig—ewig—von mir!" (Go away from me! Forever—always—away from me!). One remembers the hidden meanings of *ewig* in the ghost scene in *Hitler* and shudders at this possible dimension of the wanted separation. But "Weiche von mir" are also the words of Jesus rebuffing Satan and his temptation. These words influence Kundry's conflicting forms of address as she begins to plead with Parsifal. The object of her desire is both a *Grausamer* (cruel one) and a *Böser* (evil one) as well as *Erlöser* (redeemer) and *Heiland* (savior). Two pages further the target of her passion becomes a *Göttlicher* (divine man) and *Gott* (god). One needs to read Wagner's text carefully here. Only in this scene is Parsifal addressed as a redeemer and god. However, the character using the terms is raving in fits of madness. Parsifal talks (sings) about bringing redemption, also to Kundry, but does not claim to be a redeemer. Later, in the Good Friday scene, Gurnemanz explicitly distinguishes the Redeemer on the cross from the redeemed person who is visible to all creation. A close reading reveals that Parsifal is indeed not to be confused with the Christian Redeemer, but functions as a human tool in the process of redemption. Nowhere does the text identify Parsifal as the biblical Christ. However, Wagner blurred the issue by adding New Testament echoes, beginning with Kundry's rantings and culminating in the Good Friday scene. The first implicit parallel occurs in the words of rejection that evoke Jesus rebuffing Satan. This triggers Kundry's memories of an earlier existence that resulted in her curse. During a confession-like narration of these memories, the sexual nature of her appeal mingles with an ambiguous frame of reference. It is generally assumed that Kundry refers to Jesus of Nazareth when she reminisces with a sad glance into the camera: "Ich sah—ihn—ihn— und—lachte . . . da traf mich sein Blick" (I saw him—him—and—laughed . . . then his gaze hit me). Wagner prepared and supported the assumption through his choice of religious terminology (*Erlöser*, *Heiland*) and the accompanying "Jerusalem music." Some editions of the text also capitalize the object, *Ihn* (Him). Klingsor had referred to Herodias as being one of her identities in the past, and that name makes her a contemporary of Jesus. Of course Wagner merges two legends here. It was Ahasuerus who was punished for refusing to help Jesus on his way to the crucifixion. Wagner had already alluded to the Ahasuerus myth for his Dutchman and also considered himself a similarly restless spirit.[29] Thus his Herodias is a Wagner double and female Ahasuerus, a detail that may have contributed to including a female Parsifal. The other myth concerns Herodias as the mother of Salome. When Herodias was rebuffed by John the Baptist, she demanded his decapitation. As she kissed his severed head, his eyes opened and looked at her and his breath hit her face. She was immediately struck with madness, laughing uncontrollably, and found herself condemned, like Ahasuerus, to await a redeemer.[30] Following Wagner's ambiguous hint that

Kundry's victim might be Jesus and her redeemer a returning Savior, numerous Parsifals have been made to look like Jesus on stage, also in Bayreuth. The film shows one such look-alike carrying a chalice in the first act. But the film adds new dimensions to such connotations. Some of this widening of perspective occurs through associations with John the Baptist. Being a cousin and forerunner of Christ, the figure allows interpretative links to biblical references and piety while remaining only close to the Christ idea. Besides, John the Baptist is the patron of Freemasonry, which played a role in Wagner's life while he was working on *Parsifal*. Visually, both Christ and John the Baptist inform the quester. One might, of course, easily ascribe the gaze that punished Kundry to a divine source. That would agree with such imagery as the all-seeing Eye of God and the lethal aspect of deities like Medusa and Athena. However, the Herodias myth links the head with the powerful gaze only to John the Baptist. Instead of excluding one, the director includes in the film visual references to both the human and the divine cousin since the Christ idea figures in alchemy and analytical psychology. A minor hint may be the shrub next to Kundry as she recapitulates the moment of her curse. Very little greenery has appeared in the landscape of the death mask. Therefore the clump of vegetation attracts attention. It is difficult to identify the plant, but a strong possibility is a form of acacia. It presumably provided the material, shittim-wood, for the biblical ark and altar of the Tabernacle, the crown of thorns, and even the cross on Golgotha, according to Arthur Edward Waite.[31] It is known in Freemasonry as a symbol of resurrection and immortality, and as Waite claims, it signifies "simplicity, innocence and the mind turning from evil, as if with instinctive horror" (3). The simple and innocent mind describes the medieval Parzival well enough, fits just as well John the Baptist who rejected Herodias' advances, while also suggesting the resurrection and immortality of Christ. Wagner's and Syberberg's Parsifal borrows features from all three.

But Kundry's past as Herodias points more unmistakably to the Baptist. One cannot help wondering if Heine's treatment of Herodias also inspired Wagner to include that name among Kundry's avatars. She appears in *Atta Troll*, which Heine wrote in 1841 during Wagner's friendship with him. The work is set in the Pyrénées, as is *Parsifal*. During midsummer night, under a full moon, the narrator witnesses the Wild Chase. Riding in the sky with other gods and ghosts is Herodias, who plays with the head of the Baptist. Of course midsummer day is his feast day in the Church calendar. And as Wagner's *Meistersinger* and Shakespeare's *Midsummer-Night's Dream* tell us, all kinds of spook and mischief can be expected during midsummer night. Heine's narrator imagines grieving at Herodias' grave near Jerusalem during the day. At night she has to join the Wild Chase, for that is her punishment. Heine's story does not mention any redemption for Herodias or consequences for the narrator, but he retains her obsession with the Baptist, madness, curse, and emotional impact on the viewer. Whether his Herodias informs Wagner's character or not, it returns Heine to the subtext of the film. Incidentally, midsummer night would be the perfect timing for Parsifal's encounter with Klingsor's magic and its potential havoc for the future.

Of the three adventures facing Parsifal in Klingsor's world, Kundry poses the most serious threat. Stage tradition presents her behavior as an attempt at seduction fueled by increasing madness. Taking his cues from the text, primarily Kundry's empowerment of Parsifal, Syberberg accentuates the initiatory nature of the scene in the first half. Thus her change from benevolent goddess to temptress and danger follows a pattern characteristic of many ancient mysteries. Especially the syncretist understanding of an aspirant's ordeals, as preserved in Freemasonry, appears to inform the scene. The difficulty in distinguishing specific Isiac or Eleusinian steps throughout the event may be assumed to lie with Wagner's as well as Syberberg's source of inspiration. Waite, for instance, refers to Orphic, Thracian, Isiac, Bacchic, Kabiric, Eleusinian, Adonic, Mithriac, Venusian, Vulcanic, and Osirian mysteries as informing Masonic rites and lore. He states about Masonic initiation ceremonies that "the reader should understand that one and the same series of Sacred Ceremonies is intended, one and the same initiatory process and revelation; and that what is true of one applies with equal certainty to all the others" (24). Parsifal's experiences in Klingsor's world conform to some step or other in various initiatory rites, including those of Freemasonry, it seems.

In the end Kundry is rejected by Parsifal as Herodias was by the Baptist. The fact that two women portray these roles in the film adds a contemporary note to the situation. After all, an hour's tryst between two heterosexual partners would hardly make modern viewers blink, regardless of any mythic and symbolic overtones. The new Parsifal has acquired a prophet's conviction and an almost superhuman insight. Thus she can refer to Kundry's redemption as being part of her mission. The premise for redemption is for Kundry to relinquish her *Sehnen* (longing). Now burdened with the connotation of uncontrollable sensual yearnings, the word and its visual equivalents have evolved into another contrapuntal transformation. In this long scene it has become the curse itself.

When Kundry's repeated pleading earns her only a rough rebuttal, she finally loses all control and slips into a deranged fury. This episode stands out as one of Clever's most impressive performances. Accompanying her madness are a renewed apparition of the Delos monument as background and the Medusa head on Parsifal's shield. Kundry's eruption escalates in three stages. First she calls for help to prevent Parsifal II from leaving. This appeal goes presumably to Klingsor and his knights. The second section addresses Parsifal with a curse on all paths she may seek that lead away from Kundry. Significantly enough, the only roads and paths mentioned in the libretto so far are those leading to the Grail and which no sinner can find. The third part of Kundry's outburst invokes erring, *Irre*, for Parsifal. This noun can refer to both a labyrinth and to a state of confusion. The first meaning suggests that Parsifal will continue the quest within the confines of the labyrinthine passages of the head landscape. The second one hints that psychologically, the affect displayed by the anima figure is too powerful to permit an integration of the conscious with the unconscious that the new Parsifal represents. According to Jung, also the female manifestation of Parsifal represents a chtonic Anima-nature of the syzygy, as frequently observed in male-female pairs of deities (*Archetypes*, 59). Such pairs he recognizes in, e.g., mythology and Gnosticism, also singling out the *yang* and the *yin* of classical Chinese thought as an example (59). But the film offers a visual hint that also Kundry and Parsifal II are indeed closely related components of the mind. For a brief moment they appear standing, one partially behind the other, their faces forming a double profile. That pose is well known from commemorative coins and medallions. Such depictions usually show a royal ruler with the spouse or the heir. It would seem, then, that the Anima, at the time of her most dangerous influence, helps release the redeeming *Kore*. The double profile presents not the maternal archetype and the son, but the same Great Mother and her daughter, resp. a younger version of herself. Discussing the Anima and the syzygy, Jung points out that the projection-making factor is identical with the mother-imago, and it could be mistaken for the real mother. "The projection can only be dissolved when the son sees that in the realm of his psyche there is an imago not only of the mother but of the daughter, the sister, the beloved, the heavenly goddess, and the chtonic Baubo" (*Aion*, 12–13). This younger archetype has now awakened and become the active redeeming force replacing the hero and overcoming the destructive mother. Parsifal's transformation and the nature of the conflict find a close parallel in Jung's *Symbols of Transformation*. As the result of the inhibition of sexuality, he explains there, "[A] regression will eventually occur in which the sexual energy flowing back from this sphere activates a function in some other sphere. In this way the energy changes its form" (158). In the hero's case, his form becomes female. Consistent with this observation, the phallic attribute does not appear with the new Parsifal. Sexuality seems almost alien to her nature. Continuing his analysis of libido in regression, Jung observes that "the incestuous energy-component becomes as it were desexualized, is led back to an infantile level where, if the operation is successful, it attains another form, which is equivalent to another function" (*Symbols of Transf.*, 158). This process occurs with difficulty, he states, since "the primary instinct is composed of an endogamous ('incestuous') tendency and an exogamous one, and must therefore be split in two. This splitting is connected with consciousness and the process of becoming conscious" (158). True to this statement, not only does the film let Parsifal assume a female manifestation, but it also retains the male hero, as one discovers later. One cannot help assuming that Syberberg's division of Parsifal was at least partially inspired by Jung's insights, and furthermore, that Jung's analysis was influenced by Wagner's text, to which he often refers in his books.

Faithful to the typology of medieval art, Syberberg also evokes a complementary contrast to Jung's theories, namely Freud's ideas. Especially Freud's thoughts on the Oedipus complex proved fertile for the film. Considering Freud's familiarity with ancient myth, one recognizes impulses emanating from the Osiris-Isis-Horus constellation and their variants and parallels in other myths. At the center of the Oedipus story is incest. Also important in Freud's theories is the symbol of the phallus representing the paternal imago or archetype. It fills a central place in the ego of the son, whose challenge becomes to distinguish between his own identity and that of the father. He must restrain his libidinal instincts and refrain from taking his father's place vis-à-vis his mother. With the Delos monument as Parsifal I's attribute, the film equips him with a bundle of qualities supported by and supporting Freud's observations. Shown sometimes only partially visible, sometimes as a variant, the sculpture may appear maimed or intact as needed. Parsifal only learns about his father through Kundry, who, as the temptress, reminisces demonstratively about the conjugal union of Parsifal's parents. These reminders of his father and the paternal role as lover fail to achieve the desired effect in the hero, especially when he ends the embrace in the position of an infant at his mother's breast. The film, but not the libretto, displays the conflicting forces animating the devouring and still protective maternal imago.

This brief mentioning of Freud will suffice, since Peter Zagermann's *Eros und Thanatos* discusses several psychoanalytical concepts central to *Parsifal*, e.g. the phallus symbol and the Oedipus complex.[32] The study culminates with a chapter on the seduction scene (299–355). Touching upon, among other topics, the threat of castration, the immanent divine, and sublimation, the author does not elaborate on the transformation of the hero. He had apparently not seen Syberberg's film. As alienating as the hero's transformation has been to many reviewers, and probably viewers, the film's handling of Parsifal's encounter with Kundry in Klingsor's garden is the first and successful attempt to integrate the insights of both Freud and Jung. They actually inform this section of the film quite noticeably.

Returning to the plot, one finds the rejected temptress raging and cursing Parsifal II. She literally pulls down the power of the curse with her arms. Having heard her cry for help, Klingsor now appears against a reddish background. The following camera takes introduce some welcome deviations from Wagner's stage instructions. He wanted Klingsor to hurl the lance at Parsifal, only to have it stop and float in the air above the hero's head. Parsifal is then supposed to grab the lance and make the sign of the cross with it, a magic gesture that causes the collapse of Klingsor's world. Instead, Klingsor is too weakened to throw his weapon. He collapses and drops the lance. Psychologically, it makes sense to let him expire from his own weakness, as also Kundry experiences a similar demise, although off-screen. In the scene where Klingsor conjures Kundry up from her "grave," the series of double exposures had revealed them to be, among other possibilities, two manifestations of the same entity. The major danger posed by these forces has been conquered, and both of them look lifeless. There is no need for a sign of the cross, as the libretto specifies. The sign alluded to by Parsifal II's statement is now the cross formed by her own upright body carrying Kundry, who rests horizontally in her arms. Their cross-like constellation functions as another visual quotation from film history, namely Erich von Stroheim's *Wedding March* of 1928. His "Iron Man" in armor carrying a girl made a brief appearance already in part 4 of *Hitler*. The evocation of this not so pious character plays in counterpoint to the religious idea of the cross and its magic power. Just as strong, though, is the effect of Parsifal's gaze. For with Kundry's collapse, she has acquired some of Kundry's powers. This manifests in her glittering eyes as she refers to the "sign" that overcomes Klingsor and his magic. As if to illustrate the nature of this transfer of divine power, Parsifal

II has suddenly gained Athena's helmet. Like that goddess, Parsifal the blue-eyed fells her adversary with her glance. Instead of Medusa's head on her aegis she carries Kundry in her arms. This imperious-looking warrior maiden makes one think of one of Gustav Klimt's paintings of Athena. Depicted from the waist and up, the goddess looks down on the viewer, whose head would presumably reach up to her chest. Her breastplate consists of reflective, golden scales. If this were a real statue or apparition, the viewer's face should be reflected in the shiny surface of the armor. In that case the viewer would have seen his or her own features where the Medusa head should be. The artist used only paint on his canvas, avoiding the mirroring effect. So does Syberberg with many of his "mirrors in the text." But when the male Parsifal looks into the abyss before backing away, one assumes that the image may very well be his own reflection, functioning more or less as a quasi-Gorgon of some potential. Now that his female counterpart walks away victoriously, she clutches in her arms another and no longer active Medusa. Kundry's body covers the breastplate where the Medusa head would have been affixed. Besides, her eyes are closed. Incidentally, it appears that Riefenstahl's rolling camera inspired the invisible cart supporting the two actresses. One sees Parsifal II only from the waist and up, making it possible for her to "carry" Kundry. And one remembers that she shares her glittering eyes not only with her male alter ego after he shot the swan, but also with the young Hitler in *Karl May*. These characters possess the power to kill.

The lower part of the Delos monument again appears in the background while the music describes the collapse of Klingsor's world. The sculpture is still there when a sudden cut to the male Parsifal reminds the viewer that the title character now possesses both manifestations, even if only one of them is visible at times. But obviously, Parsifal I has receded, at least temporarily, to the role of a passive companion. This reduced role conforms to Jung's description of what can happen in an emotional upheaval. The loss of balance relegates the conscious part of the ego (Parsifal I) to continued exploration of the collective unconscious as a stage in adapting to external realities. Meanwhile, unconscious influences (Parsifal II) predominate. Their activity at restoring the equilibrium will, states Jung, " achieve this aim provided the conscious mind is capable of assimilating the contents produced by the unconscious, i.e., of understanding and digesting them."[33] The film creates a visible equivalent of such assimilation in progress by entrusting the spear to Parsifal I at the end of act 2. The weapon corresponds to the "contents produced by the unconscious" that now will be returned or restored to the Grail community. This stage with the female Parsifal in the active, leading role lasts until the reunion in the Grail Hall. The split can, of course, also be seen as the effect of Kundry's curse on Parsifal. But the division into a predominant female and a secondary male Parsifal follows the pattern outlined by Jung for a transformation process in the ego. Following the violent confrontation with unconscious contents, all parts of the ego must strive to integrate and assimilate them. "In that event," he writes, "there is an alteration of the ego as well as of the unconscious contents. . . .[T]he ego is ousted from its central and dominating position and thus finds itself in the role of a passive observer."[34] Jung adds that the afflux of unconscious contents has created a new figure that eclipses the former ego in scope and intensity. The division can develop into a composite that Jung calls the Self. Freud views such development as the refinement of the ego to super-ego. But at this point in the film, it is not yet clear that Parsifal I will play a subordinate role in much of act 3.

When the camera cuts to the young man, one does not see him immediately. He has been leaning against the rock wall, much like the flower maidens earlier and the knights in act 1 when Gurnemanz and Parsifal arrive at the Grail Castle. Now he steps forward, clutching the holy lance. This symbol of virility and restraint is joined by the shield with the Medusa head in Parsifal's other hand. Armed and protected, he sets out to follow his female counterpart, reminding Kundry, who is off-screen, "You know where you can find me again!" Accompanied by the last strains of the music of act 2, the background changes in quick succession to red and white, illustrating several alchemical steps. A brief close-up of the anima confirms her presence, but she has abandoned her role as temptress and Kundry. Appearing as the oracle with the globe, she raises her head while closing both eyes. This "portal" to the collective unconscious has returned to a latent or dormant state and is barely able to acknowledge Parsifal.

The last shot of the second act succeeds the end of the music. Parsifal II, carrying what looks like a lifeless Kundry, strides towards a portal in the background. Klingsor has been left behind, but what remains of Kundry is brought along, as if to be put to rest in a safer environment elsewhere. Parsifal II could easily have abandoned her here, as the libretto suggests. Parsifal I follows a few yards behind them. While they cross the open space one hears bells tolling. Since the background is now black, one assumes they announce midnight. Just as audible signals mark time and events at the Grail Castle, so the film introduces a similar indicator. Syberberg's book reports that the sound is borrowed from the first act (167). Due to the timing, it triggers an avalanche of associations. Foremost among them is the bell at midnight in the penultimate section of *Also Spake Zarathustra*. This bell begins to chime after the "higher men's" adoration of the donkey. That animal brings to mind both the protagonist in Apuleius' *Metamorphoses* and his transformation in the Isis mysteries and the ass in Shakespeare's *Midsummer-Night's Dream*. Besides, Shakespeare lets Theseus remark towards the end of act 5, "The iron tongue of midnight hath told twelve." Apparently the marking of time concerns both the daily cycle, here midnight, and the summer solstice. And in *Parsifal* the emphasis on the seasons moves backwards, from snow-covered trees in the first prelude, to dead leaves of autumn dominating act 1 and midsummer in act 2, and on to the vernal equinox with Good Friday in act 3. Syberberg observes the cardinal points of the calendar. The reminder of the ass, on the other hand, relates to the theme of stupidity. The animal is still considered the epitome of foolishness in German, where *Esel* also means "fool." But in both of the mentioned works the donkey spell is lifted for a transformation back to human appearance. A similar metamorphosis has taken place in Wagner's text: Parsifal is no longer a fool, but a future bringer of redemption. The film's division of Parsifal into two manifestations makes the change even more dramatic. One also remembers that the bell sound Zarathustra hears is coming from below ("from the depth"). It hints at things that cannot be heard by day.The midnight bell beckons Zarathustra, who announces, "Let us now wander! It is the hour: let us wander into the night!" (358). It appears that the bells and midnight belong to the nether regions of the psyche, a hidden, dark world of the unconscious to be traversed. And then there is Heidegger's "peal of stillness," *Geläut der Stille*. . .

One may wonder if the added detail of the bells in the film also might relate to the Wagner strand of the narrative. If so, then the link is probably Franz Liszt's *The Bells of Strasbourg Cathedral*, a composition based on a poem by Henry Wadsworth Longfellow. In the prologue to the second part of Longfellow's *Christus: A Mystery*, Lucifer struggles to tear down the cross on the spire of the Cathedral of Strasbourg.[35] The bells join the voices of the Archangel Michael and his hosts preventing this in what takes the form of a battle of voices, bells, and orchestra. In the following pages Walther von der Vogelweide appears, and later some of the characters find themselves in a portal of the cathedral while the bells chime. One of the portals of this sanctuary houses the statues of the Ecclesia and the Synagogue. Clearly, the Strasbourg Cathedral belongs to the subtext of Syberberg's work. And Wagner knew Liszt's composition well. The first impression left him less than enthused, to judge from Cosima's diary: "Arrival of my father's *Die Glocken von Strassburg*, a curious work; done with great effect, but so alien to us" (Jan. 28, 1875). On March 10 of that year the composition was performed in a concert in Pest together with Beethoven's Piano Concerto No.5 and excerpts from *Die Walküre, Siegfried*, and *Götterdämmerung*. This was the only concert at which Liszt and Wagner appeared together.[36] Over time Liszt's composition must have left a deeper impression, for on Dec. 28, 1877, Cosima recorded: "R.[ichard] works on the 'Holy Grail March,' he has cut out the crystal bells; he looked again at my father's *Die [Glocken] von Strassburg* to make sure he has not committed a *plagiarism*." While Wagner opted for tam-tams, Syberberg includes the bell as a contrapuntal correlate to the sound introducing the transformation music of acts 1 and 3.

One more detail attracts attention at the end of the second act: the portal in the background. Separating the lit foreground from the darkness beyond, the posts of this gate look like two feet belonging to a gigantic standing statue. Could they belong to Goya's *Giant*? That picture does not show the feet of the monstrous apparition, but conveys clearly the disturbance it causes among humans and animals. Or do they derive from the Book of Daniel 3.31–45? Here Daniel interprets the king's dream of a huge idol made of various materials. Its feet are built of iron and clay, elements of uneven strength that herald the future shattering of the kingdom. One notices that Syberberg's portal of feet shows cracks in the ankles. That makes it likely that the material is fragile. Another possibility is the golem's clay feet. This figure is well known in folklore, literature, and early German film. Like the temptress, the golem also displayed destructive power before being destroyed. The possible referentiality to German film history strengthens the probability that a golem informs the scene. This turns into certainty when one remembers the meaning of this Hebrew word. Webster's dictionary translates it as "boor" and "dummy" in modern Hebrew, whereas Brown's biblical dictionary gives "embryo" (*gimel, lamed, mem*). The former fits Parsifal as a fool, the latter finds at least two visual equivalents in the film. In the first prelude the two Parsifals sit huddled together as one clump. Even after Parsifal I gets up and leaves, Parsifal II remains in her fetal position. In the first act, Kundry withdraws to "sleep" and lies down in the same embryonic pose. The association triggered by the Hebrew word suggests something unfinished, developing, or dormant. As forces of the psyche the characters do wake up eventually and become active. Or, if one prefers, they are born. At this point in the story, "reborn" might be a better term. With the maternal Anima already introduced as a sibyl ("portal to the unconscious") and as the Venus Mountain, it would be natural to associate the stony or clay feet with Kundry. Parsifal I had passed the stone feet of the supine female-looking mountain before he entered into the passages with the flower maidens. But if one considers the story about the golem, it becomes apparent that Klingsor might also be a good fit. In the legend about the golem the rabbi overcomes it by erasing the first letter, an *'alef*, from the word chiseled into his forehead. The action changes the word from meaning "truth" to "death" (*'emeth > meth*). This causes the destructive, man-made Adam of clay to collapse. Klingsor, being a threatening Shadow, collapses in a similar way when the temptress fails. Another golem also likely to inform this image appears in Paul Celan's "Einem, der vor der Tür stand" (To one who was standing before the door).[37] This golem is the brother of the narrator who is also silenced in mid-sentence by a rabbi. As in *Parsifal*, two related forces existing in the human mind are brought down together. And one of them is standing at the "door." The detour via Hebrew serves as a reminder that a portal or gate is *daleth* in Hebrew. This concept is important in the Kabbalah, where it applies to the tenth *sefira*. It is usually viewed as a female principle. Scholem notes, "[T]he last *Sefirah* is for man the door or gate through which he can begin the ascent up the ladder of perception of the Divine Mystery" (*Kabbalah*, 112). The portal of feet forms the exit of Klingsor's world. But the darkness beyond suggests that the "ascent up the ladder" will encounter many obstacles. Kundry's curse is about to take effect. The malediction she called down on Parsifal was *Irre* (confusion). Grimm's dictionary gives the Greek "labyrinth" as one equivalent. Cosima Wagner's diary indicates that also the composer used the term in that sense: "Parsifal's wanderings in the labyrinth" (Nov. 2, 1878). "Labyrinth" happens to be another term for the Sefirotic Tree as well. That makes it look as if the labyrinthine paths and stations of the plot in the film could serve as such a Kabbalistic paradigm. Of course, Scholem and other writers on Jewish mysticism point out repeatedly that the Kabbalah is really a blueprint for the psyche. Again one is reminded of the versatility of Syberberg's choice of setting for his *Parsifal*.

Chapter 9

Third Prelude and Act Three

The first image accompanying the prelude reveals a closer view of the crystal ball that Kundry as the sibyl had held near the end of act 2. Like children's snow globes, this sphere also contains a flat landscape. It is a circular labyrinth with a leafless tree in the center. The lower half of the ball is dark, just as the world in the globe on the backside of Hieronymus Bosch's triptych *The Garden of Delights*. The labyrinth continues the theme of Parsifal's curse, *Irre*, which translates as "erring" and "labyrinth." Both its shape and the tree evoke the Kabbalistic paradigm of the Sefirotic Tree. The labyrinth obviously illustrates Parsifal's inner and outer world of wandering, searching, and toils. But both symbols offer a potential and attainable goal. Perseverance can lead the quester to the center of the labyrinth, which allows a climb up the tree. Parsifal had already visited the lowest point of the Sefirotic Tree.

As the camera turns away from the globe, the view beyond shows a barren, dark, and chaotic wilderness. The boulders of the death mask provide only winding paths through narrow cracks. It is an environment made for getting lost. While Parsifal II gropes through this wasteland, one glimpses shifting projections beyond the openings between rocks. Some depict Edith Clever, others scenes from Wagner productions in Bayreuth. Most conspicuous is the reddish walls and "flames" surrounding sleeping Brünnhilde, famous from Pierre Boulez' and Patrice Chéreau's productions of the *Ring*. These projections expand the scope of Clever's roles. Not only does she lend her face to several figures with various names in *Parsifal*. She also represents, or at least echoes, Brünnhilde. The pagan daughter of the highest god, Brünnhilde was exiled from her abode to earth. Surrounded by a wall of flames, this mythic model for Sleeping Beauty would return to life among humans if the right hero could overcome the obstacles and liberate her to a new existence. Siegfried did, but did not complete his mission. The flaming walls indicate that the next awakening has not occurred yet, and that Kundry's sleep parallels that of Brünnhilde.

During this stage of Parsifal's erring the landscape remains bleak and dark with falling snow and wind. Untold seasons have passed. Parsifal II eventually stops on a narrow bridge of planks and puts down her burden. The big bundle is wrapped in the navy star cloth seen earlier with Herzeleide and Kundry. That is the only hint that the bundle contains Kundry. When Parsifal II walks off, it looks as if she finally is letting go of her load. But she only disappears momentarily to retrieve the spear. This object must now serve as a reminder of Parsifal I, who seems to have lingered behind. Carrying the spear, Parsifal II picks up her burden again and continues until she reaches a small clearing. Here she again puts down the bundle, which now reveals some long hair at one end. She also covers this big clump with an additional blue cloth so as to conceal the star pattern underneath. Kundry is now abandoned in a dormant or dead-like condition just as Brünnhilde in her sleep. The latter's wall of flames is visible in the background. But the shape of the bundle indicates that Kundry is curled up in a fetal position. With the Hebrew word for "fetus" being *golem*, one recognizes the return of a theme. Kundry is waiting for another rebirth. As Parsifal II prepares to continue her journey, she picks up the spear and the shield with the Medusa head, which mysteriously has found its way to her. One assumes she must have arrived back at a spot where Parsifal I had left the shield behind. While Parsifal II hesitates for a moment, one becomes more aware of the surrounding. To her left stands the scaffolding seen in act 1, now with the bow prominently displayed along with the arrow and the string. This awakens all the associations related to the *Gestell*, Wolfram's and the medieval use of bow-and-arrow imagery, as well as the individual bow, string, and arrow. Like visual leitmotifs, they recall themes, situations, and characters. For example, Kundry had functioned as a *Gestell* when she held the arrow in act 1. Whereas the scaffolding then emphasized the string and the arrow in accordance with Wolfram's comment (120), it now includes the entire bow. Echoing the contour of the bow is the outline of a large object in the foreground. It looks alien among the rough boulders, but cannot be identified yet.

Taken as a whole the scaffolding becomes a major leitmotif encompassing a cluster of smaller themes and motifs. Could it possibly possess additional symbolic powers not recognized so far? Of course it is a convenient vehicle for translating melodic elements recurring in the music. But the setting in this prelude, perhaps also its appearance behind Klingsor early in act 2, reveals a dimension of a different nature. It would apply to each appearance of the apparatus in the film, but this setting shows it clearly. The scaffolding represents also the *organon* of the ancient Hermetic scriptures. This Greek word for "instrument" can actually mean many things, but three definitions pertain to Syberberg's film. The word, and thus its visual equivalent, functions variously as a "musical instrument," as an "organ" of the body, or as a "tool, instrument, or engine." The third definition applies broadly to any implement used for making or doing something, including an engine of war. The scaffolding is an engine of war. It supports the bow and arrow and should function as a catapult to launch the arrow. In the sense of *organon* the scaffolding evokes the use of this word in the "Kore Kosmu" text, where Hermes agrees to devise a contraption that will serve as an impediment to human striving.[1] To curtail the powers of a humankind that does not know or respect any limits, Hermes announces, " I will devise a secret engine, linked to unerring and inevitable fate, by which all things in men's lives, from their birth to their final destruction, shall of necessity be brought into subjection; and all other things on earth likewise shall be controlled by the working of this engine" (Scott, 1:485). According to this reading, Parsifal is still subject to the power of a divinely imposed impediment. In Wagner's version, this is the curse Kundry calls down late in act 2. Kundry is closely associated with the *organon* as the power that imposes it, as a *Gestell*, and as the power that helps Parsifal overcome the temptations. Incidentally, Wagner knew the Hermetic texts well, as evidenced by Cosima's diary entry of, e.g., April 5, 1873.

Parsifal II pays no attention to the scaffolding. Before she moves on, the dim background changes into another projection: the drawing by Joukowsky of Amfortas lifting the Grail. This image had appeared as a reflection on the Grail Carrier's dress in act 1. It returns the Grail ceremony to the visual narrative. As a projected memory, this apparition seems to give Parsifal the strength to resume her wanderings. It actually reveals a great deal about Parsifal's inner state and maturation. S/he no longer needs a trauma to bring back forgotten memories. They have become part of his/her consciousness. Of course the manifestation of the hero shown here is the half that does remember. Not being able to remember is precisely what characterizes the fool in act 1. Not knowing his name or where he comes from displays his lack of identity. In act 2 the temptress not only gives him his name, but she also prods him into realizing what he has forgotten. First this process returns vague memories of a name, then of his mother, finally of the divine lament perceived during the Grail ceremony. This stage brings on the transformation in him. The viewers do not hear the divine lament during the first act. But Syberberg introduces its equivalent: the mournful Grail Carrier with the reflective gown. It now becomes clear that she really does represent a divine presence, since the lament is perceived during the ritual. And Joukowsky's sketch of the ceremony identifies the moment. The Grail Carrier's presence coincides with the lament. Now the image reflected on her dress returns as a memory. Parsifal remembers the divine lament. The projection of an inner process also suggests that the Grail Castle may be close. Since Parsifal had carried Kundry with her as a visible and psychological baggage, the paths cursed by Kundry had not led Parsifal to stray far from her. It seems that Parsifal has found the way back to the vicinity of the Grail, also enabling Kundry to awaken in that environment again. As forces of the same mind, they inhabit the same landscape.

The prelude comprises 40 bars of music. Forty is a significant numeral in Wolfram's story, the Bible, and alchemy. Wagner subjects Parsifal to a similar span of tribulations and "processing," but makes it equate about ten years. Gurnemanz is supposed to look quite old at the onset of the third act. But the film presents him as youthful as before. It needs only a gentle turn of the camera for a transition from the prelude to a focus on Gurnemanz as he comes out of his hermit's cabin. Contrary to the stage instructions, he still wraps himself in his blond blanket as protection against the morning chill. As in the first act, he soon drops this cocoon. A dripping icicle on his cabin contributes its share of information: spring is coming, the ice and water metaphors are still operative, and the falling direction of the drops might indicate a quasi-musical inversion. Gurnemanz has heard groaning and soon finds Kundry hidden among leaves and huge roots (boulders covered with "bark"). No longer curled up in a fetal position, but outstretched, she is cold and stiff, making Gurnemanz wonder if she is really dead. But he had heard her groan and hopes she will return to life again. Holding her in an embrace, rubbing and stroking her, he breathes on her stiff hands to warm her. This revival attempt ends with his putting her fingers to his mouth, as if kissing them. Inobtrusively Gurnemanz varies the theme of embrace and kiss, now devoid of any sexual overtones. Kundry finally opens her eyes. Realizing that her curse has forced her into yet another existence, she emits a loud scream, just as she did upon awakening in the second act. In his book to the film Syberberg compares her scream with that of a baby upon birth (192). But of course, Kundry has been reborn as an adult. Her screams upon awakening also resemble those of a mother in childbirth. Each time coincides with Parsifal's approach. Her non-verbal utterance produces the arrival of the saving agent. From a psychological perspective, the Anima archetype has undergone another metamorphosis. She now appears as a penitent. The scream is her loudest statement, followed soon after by a contrite "Dienen . . . Dienen!" (To serve . . . serve!). These are Kundry's only words in act 3, although she is present and visible much of the time. The nature of her transformation suggests that the confrontation with Parsifal caused the change in her. Parsifal had admonished her to relinquish her yearnings, *Sehnen*, understood as sexual passion. But this drive had also been identified in part as a longing for redemption during her reminiscences of the Jerusalem experience. That shift in emphasis has worked its effect on the new Kundry.

Suddenly Gurnemanz and Kundry become aware of an approaching stranger in armor. The figure advances slowly from a background projection that illustrates the spiritual condition of Parsifal. The image shows Caspar David Friedrich's painting *Abbey in the Oakwood* (*Abtei im Eichwald*, 1809–10). Again a picture is cropped. It concentrates on the chapel in ruins among dead oaks. Not visible are the cemetery stones and the monks' funeral procession. Of course they too inform Parsifal's and the Grail community's condition as well as reintroducing the motifs of death and processions. As the members of the convent put to rest one of their dwindling number, so the trees have lost most of their branches, and the sanctuary has crumbled leaving only one wall standing. Parsifal's inner temple sheltering the divine spark exhibits an advanced degree of decay. But at least the structure still represents a sanctuary. Gurnemanz recognizes that this stranger does not belong to the Grail community. Except for the helmet, the short armor and the greaves are made of black leather. Parsifal II also wears a white cloak and tunic and carries the spear and shield. The vest-like leather armor appears to be modeled on that of the Valkyries in Chéreau's productions.

Apparently oblivious to Gurnemanz' words, Parsifal II eventually reacts when chided for wearing armor on Good Friday. Gurnemanz had mentioned the "holiest" of days several times, but only now does he identify it as Good Friday. The timing of the meeting between Parsifal and the hermit and Amfortas' healing at the end are two of only a few borrowings from the medieval sources in this act. Wagner has by now made the story distinctly his own. Parsifal II sets down her weapons, takes off the helmet, and kneels in prayer. Watching her, Gurnemanz recognizes her as the fool who had killed the swan years ago. This is one of the occurrences where the visual presentation causes an awkward discrepancy with Wagner's libretto. The viewer has gotten used to Parsifal's deep voice and acknowledges that a quester can be male as well as female. But Gurnemanz recognizes Parsifal based on the hero's appearance. Here Brecht's alienation theories must kick in, forcing the viewer to disengage from the plot and view the situation critically. Analytical psychology comes to the rescue. The characters are archetypal forces interacting in the process of integrating and restoring a balance between conscious and unconscious components of the psyche. Even on the level of fairytale one could find extenuating circumstances to explain the illogical words. Gurnemanz may suffer from poor eyesight. And obviously no other armed outsider has advanced so close to the Grail Castle on paths that no sinner can find, so this stranger has got to be the fool. Besides, stage tradition requires a different-looking Parsifal in the third act, usually a more mature, bearded singer. The cinematic Parsifal II does look remarkably different from the young fool of the first half of the drama.

Gurnemanz' excitement turns to jubilation when he recognizes the spear. Syberberg follows tradition here and presents it as Longinus' spear that pierced the side of Jesus on the cross. Wolfram von Eschenbach did not link the weapon wounding Amfortas with the Bible. Wagner lifted this detail from the French versions. The assumed original spear became a revered relic of the German emperors in the Middle Ages and is still kept with the imperial insignia and some choice relics in the Vienna *Schatzkammer*. An object of such historical and legendary fame rivals the Grail in significance in Wagner's story. For Gurnemanz it is a holy object bringing him to his knees in pious adoration.

With Gurnemanz kneeling, Parsifal II rises and starts communicating. The ensuing exchange is kept visually interesting with the help of camera moves, background images, the actors' contributions, and, eventually, one added surprise not included in the libretto. While Parsifal describes the difficulties in finding the way back to Amfortas, the camera has moved around to allow the scaffolding into view in the background. The *Gestell*, still supporting bow, drawn string, and arrow, illustrates the words symbolically on several levels. Not only does the combination display tension in anticipation of a goal or target, but also the semantic reverberations caused by "string" and the violin outline of the bow are becoming perceptible. One also remembers the *Gestell* as a dangerous predicament according to Heidegger, and as an *organon* or "secret engine." Later, as Parsifal II blames herself for Titurel's death, a blurred landscape of flames surrounds her head in close-up. It shows a section from the right panel of Bosch's *The Garden of Delights*, where warfare leaves a burning world in ruins. When this panel appeared as a background projection in Klingsor's garden, another *organon* constituted its center of attention: the cannon-like war engine consisting of two human ears with a knife blade protruding between them. Obviously, Parsifal experiences this hell on earth. If she had only paid attention to the divine inner voice pleading for help while he/she witnessed the Grail ceremony, Amfortas would have been healed sooner, and he would not have caused his father's death by withholding the Grail from him. One must remember that periodic contemplation of the Grail keeps the congregants nourished and alive, whereas Amfortas wants to end his pain through death. To achieve that he deprives the entire Grail community from contemplating the magic object, resulting in his father's death. Hearing how much the Grail community needs healing, Parsifal II looks for a moment into the camera. This intercourse between viewer and actress belongs to the most intense forms of communication in the film, and, as described earlier, to the polyvalent means of conveying ideas. Just a few moments before the direct gaze the miracle takes place. It identifies Parsifal as the promised bringer of relief. The holy lance is transformed into a cross-tipped shaft. While Gurnemanz jubilates "O Wunder!" in reference to the spear, the film replaces it with the cross that the statue named Church holds in the Cathedral of Strasbourg and that the Grail Carrier has during the ceremony in act 1. The miraculous return of the spear turns now into a visible miracle. The transformation changes the weapon into a symbol of faith. And Faith is one of the names of the character Amelie Syberberg portrays. The cross is her attribute as Grail Carrier, a lance when appearing as Synagogue. All her manifestations center on a symbol of religious belief and human striving. Now Parsifal II comes equipped with both attributes in succession. Psychologically, this suggests a close relationship between these characters. Parsifal II has acquired the qualities that the symbolic figure illustrates. And from a compositional perspective, another transformation imitating stages in music may be in order. One of the earliest examples in the film is the transformation of the dead swan into a work of art. This time the miracle illustrates, one assumes, the inner change from confusion to confidence and faith, from blind struggle to clear mission. But it also fits in with a medieval tale of wondrous events. Wagner had presented such events in several music dramas. For example Senta's self-sacrifice redeems the Flying Dutchman, and Elisabeth's prayer redeems Tannhäuser, whose pilgrim's staff suddenly comes alive and sprouts leaves. Maybe the word *pilgrim*, which Gurnemanz uses to refer to Parsifal, inspires this repeated miracle involving a staff or shaft. It appears that the other Wagner music dramas continue to inform *Parsifal*.

During Gurnemanz' narrative following the transformation, both Parsifal and Kundry listen intently. Kundry, however, also moves around in this scene, fetching a small bundle wrapped in blue cloth. It looks like a miniature of the one that contained her earlier. As she sits down, she begins to unwrap its contents. The first object she uncovers is the puppet of Amfortas from the first prelude. Its appearance coincides with Gurnemanz' description of him. Then emerge the Klingsor puppet and a string of tiny dolls identified in the book to the film as devils and Nibelungs. Although that would support Klingsor's realm as being related to diabolical and "underground" forces, as much current Wagner literature claims, one is hard pressed to recognize the small figures. Klingsor's knights might fit here, but some of them could just as well be the skulls on Kali's necklace. The last item Kundry unwraps is the puppet of Titurel, just as Gurnemanz reports on the latter's death. Her "unburdening" herself returns these figures visually to the action while functioning as a cleansing rite akin to confession.

As in the first act, Parsifal is again about to faint. The film cuts to her next position as she sits surrounded by Gurnemanz and Kundry. They have helped her to a spot near a spring. This place is located under the nose on a flatter and wider version of the mask landscape. The large nostrils behind the group suggest that they might inhale and exhale, thus moving air. This reminder of *pneuma*, or spirit, hints at the resemblance of a divine presence. The first prelude included a dove in the puppet play, another symbol conveying the same idea. The use of objects as symbols continues with the jars and jugs lined up close by. Just as a fractured amphora is embedded in Amfortas' name, so one also expects the earthen vessels to relate to human carriers of divine contents. After all, Adam was made of earth or clay. Parsifal I comes to mind, since Michael Kutter's name means "vessel." And the "breaking of the vessels" is a central event in the Kabbalah already familiar to Wolfram, as his narrative implies. One broken, prostate amphora is visible behind Parsifal to the left. Another jug is now used for water to wash Parsifal's feet. During a sequence of pious rites, Parsifal proves to be or become an intact vessel strengthened by the others surrounding her. Not only Kundry and Gurnemanz, but also Amfortas, Klingsor, the knights, and Titurel contribute with their presence to prepare the redeeming force. The Kabbalistic inspiration for this visual arrangement will be discussed later. Let it suffice here that several religious traditions converge in this scene. Western viewers can easily recognize the adaptations from Catholic rituals, especially as found in the masses between Palm Sunday and Easter.

The borrowings begin with the ablution. Gurnemanz and Kundry remove the armor, upon which Kundry washes Parsifal's feet, anoints them with oil, and dries them with her long hair. During this scene she displays humility and a penitent's demeanor. When she lifts her head and meets Parsifal's glance, their gaze is mutually comforting. Maybe the Gorgon's power has been reduced to the decoration on the shield, which is no longer in view. The gesture of washing another person's feet is a detail contained in Wagner's libretto. It is based in part on Luke 7. 37–38, where an unnamed "sinner" kneels to wash Jesus' feet with her tears, dries them with her hair and finally anoints them with precious ointment. In John 12. 1–9, Mary, sister of Martha and Lazarus, does something similar. Popular tradition has merged these women into Mary Magdalene. This Mary Magdalene is the most important female character in Wagner's "Jesus of Nazareth," where act 4 includes a variant of this scene (279–80). The mass for Monday before Easter contains a gospel reading that includes the passage in John 12. 1–9. Of interest is also that on Maundy Thursday, many churches celebrate the foot-washing narrated in John 13. 1–15. The celebrants commemorate that Jesus washed the feet of his disciples. Now Kundry carries out the activity. This ritual was included in *Ludwig*. Wagner alters the activity to let Gurnemanz repeat the first and the third steps, sprinkling water and subsequently oil on Parsifal's head at her request. That exceeds the simple act of ablution. The pouring of water over Parsifal's head resembles a baptism. That rite has its place in the mass of Saturday before Easter, as does the sprinkling of blessed baptismal water on the celebrants. But Gurnemanz' blessing continues with "May thus the sorrow of any guilt recede from you!" This sounds like an absolution following confession. It may also have been inspired by Wolfram's Good Friday segment, where Parzival confesses to the hermit. In reference to sin, remorse, atonement, and forgiveness, Parsifal has now been ritually cleansed of any imperfection and is declared pure ("du Reiner"). And Parsifal's request that Gurnemanz anoint her head as well reminds everyone in no uncertain terms that this amounts to the Old Testament equivalent of a coronation. The anointed head does not need a visible crown. Twice in quick succession one hears the word *king*. First Parsifal asks Gurnemanz for the anointment, "so that still today he may greet me as king." Gurnemanz responds while receiving the flask from Kundry (from where did she obtain it?), "So it was promised us, thus I bless your head to greet you as king." On these two occasions the orchestra underscores the joyful solemnity with a flourish. Also worth noting is the fact that both the Hebrew *Messiah* and the Greek *Christos* mean "the Anointed One." This episode includes Wagner's two most obvious references to a biblically inspired redeemer, but he does not identify the hero as Jesus.

The following camera take coincides with a noticeable contrast in the volume of the music. Soft strains accompany Parsifal and Kundry in this brief scene. They both seem to be standing in the eye socket of the mask landscape. It has now become the sacred spring nourished by streaming tears. This is the water from which Kundry emerged in act 1, and where now her baptism takes place. While contemplating the associations of tears and blessed baptismal water, one also recognizes that the ritual does not resemble a Christian baptism. Parsifal pours water over Kundry's head, pronouncing, "[A]ccept the baptism and believe in the redeemer!" Who is the redeemer, and what does the baptism signify? Numerous statements by Wagner point demonstratively to a belief in the Christian Redeemer. However, the interpreters who see Kundry as a Jewish character and Parsifal as an "Aryan" figure view the rite as a step toward elimination. For example Hartmut Zelinsky, one of the most widely read Wagner critics in Germany, attributes that intention to Kundry's baptism. In "Rettung ins Ungenaue" he builds his case on the use of the kettledrum in the score and an entry in Cosima Wagner's diary.[2] A closer look at his discussion can serve as an example of a widespread interpretation of the scene and the assumed ideology of *Parsifal*. The premise and condition for the "redemption of the redeemer" is, according to Zelinsky, "the baptism and with it the demise of Kundry, the representative of all that Wagner associates with Judaism" (102). Cosima's diary entry of Feb. 3, 1879 reports how pleased her husband was with the composition of the baptism, telling her, "[T]he entry of the kettledrum in G is the finest thing I have ever done!" Her next sentence continues: "I accompany him downstairs and he plays to me the anointment of Parsifal by Gurnemanz, with its wonderful canon, and the baptism of Kundry with the annihilating sound of the kettledrum: 'Obliteration of the whole being, of all earthly desire,' says R.[ichard]." Zelinsky quotes jumbled parts of this passage, although carelessly ("the anointment of Parsifal by Titurel"[!]), and adds, "here one gains an impression of to what extent Wagner's music is, and is intended to be, a carrier of *Weltanschauung*" (102). This conclusion sounds ominous indeed. Too bad it does not fit the music. The kettledrum enters for the first time to accompany Parsifal's last words to Gurnemanz, " to greet me as king!" It adds to the first flourish at this point. Then it sets in again six bars later to accompany Gurnemanz' words "to greet you as king!" This time the motif is inversed to a falling interval of G to D sharp, and again the instrument adds import to the atmosphere of solemnity. After resting a while, the kettledrum kicks in again with the same interval two more times during and right after Gurnemanz' concluding words, "[N]ow remove the last burden from his head." The head referred to here is presumably that of Amfortas, whose unwelcome Grail duties Parsifal will now assume. Zelinsky had no use for these words by Gurnemanz. But if one insists on reading the text from his perspective, one might imagine that the "redeemed one" is really Wagner, and Parsifal is now admonished to "remove the last burden from his head" by making a Christian of Kundry. After Gurnemanz' words the kettledrum is silent. The score does not even include it during the following baptism scene. There can be no doubt that the kettledrum underscores twice Parsifal's new status as king and then his relief for Amfortas. Rereading Cosima's lines one is not sure whose "whole being" and "earthly desire" have been obliterated. Kundry's? Parsifal's? Amfortas'? Even if Wagner should have meant Kundry, the words might have a more spiritual meaning than assumed by Zelinsky. One might also wonder about the discrepancy between Cosima's description and the final form of the music. If she recorded the details in their proper order, Wagner must have revised the music several times. As late as on July 18, 1882, she wrote, "He adds a drum roll to the crowning of Parsifal ." Or she may have been too tired when writing (always before going to bed) and confused about the timing of the kettledrum and to whom her husband's words referred. Her memory may also have played a trick on her to support her own bias. And finally, Wagner may have fed her misleading statements about the musical draft, knowing that she would record everything for posterity. He obviously did want to be remembered as an anti-Semite. Or was the discrepancy intended to serve as a scandalon? The fact remains: the music of Kundry's baptism scene does not conform to Cosima's diary entry.

After the anointment scene with the kettledrum, the camera cuts suddenly to the spring where Kundry's baptism takes place. The accompanying music is slow and gentle. Unlike the libretto, where this episode fills only a few lines of text, the music reveals it to be a scene in its own right. The shift in the music and the change of location suggest that some time must have passed since the anointment. This is confirmed a bit later when distant bells announce midday. Parsifal and Kundry are both standing in the water. Parsifal bends down, scoops up water in her hand and pours it over Kundry's head. As they slowly step back on dry ground, Kundry leans on Parsifal while crying. Thus she adds her tears to those streaming from the mask filling the eye socket. Parsifal has apparently brought her redemption and, psychologically, strengthened the saving force in her own nature. Most viewers will, however, interpret Parsifal as a redeeming Christ figure and the baptism as a ritual inspired by Church tradition. But the words differ enough from the Christian rite to allow other views. Judaism, Parsism, and other religions also know ritual ablutions. The emphasis on physical and spiritual purification suggests a new stage of increased holiness and some form of a new beginning. Syberberg adds a surrealistic detail here that, at least briefly, gives a biblical as well as heretical touch to the situation. Beyond the rocky horizon darkness rules until suddenly a projection of Armin Jordan (conductor and Amfortas) fills the sky. He seems to be conducting the unseen orchestra playing the music to the action unfolding visibly. The apparition lasts until the camera is brought around to focus on Parsifal and Kundry stepping out of the water. Why does Armin Jordan intrude into this scene? Of course the book to the film does not elucidate anything beyond the technical challenge of the camera move. Again possibilities based on associations soon crowd the scene. One intention may have been to hint at Wagner's conductor, Hermann Levi. As Cosima recorded for posterity, the composer pressured Levi repeatedly to be baptized, but to no avail. Thanks to King Ludwig's conditions, Wagner could not replace him with a Christian conductor. Syberberg may also allude to Wagner as conductor, since Jordan portrays Amfortas as well. And that character is generally viewed as being a cover for Wagner himself. On August 29, 1882, the last performance, Wagner sneaked away from his box, joined the orchestra in the pit, and took the baton from Levi at some point during the third act. While sources agree that he conducted the third act to the end, they differ on the beginning of this surprise move. Gregor-Dellin sets it at the 23rd bar of the transformation music (825); Levi's letter to his father describes it as happening "during," and Cosima in the diary that it happened ""after," the transformation music.[3] So although Wagner apparently did not conduct the orchestra during Kundry's baptism, he did so soon after. The conductor in the sky would be the most immediate connection for an association with Wagner. Many interpreters consider Amfortas and the Grail society to be a thinly veiled allegory of a suffering Wagner and Germany in need of regeneration. Others see Wagner as a prophet heralding a "redeemer" to come. In either case, one could associate the apparition in the sky with Wagner's presence, either as overseeing the baptism according to Zelinsky's thinking, or functioning as the redeemer himself. But of course Syberberg's system of counterpoint presents more than one version of the subject. True enough, the director had introduced a Wagner puppet as a crucified figure in the first prelude, suggesting also a link between the composer and a Christ-like role. But might not also the two characters in the water relate to Wagner's view of himself? If he equated Kundry's baptism with "obliteration of the whole being" and that was the wanted outcome for a representative of Judaism, then he would have to play the role of Parsifal. And Parsifal is assuming Christ-like characteristics through the anointment. But why did Kundry wear a crown of thorns upon her arrival in act 1? Does not that attribute mark her as another Christ? The Bible tells us that Jesus was baptized by John the Baptist. That might allow a different constellation with Kundry as a Christ parallel. And, remembering the apparition in the sky, one realizes that the actor-conductor's name is Jordan. Jesus was baptized in the Jordan river. Thus, within this grid of associations Jordan informs the scene, and the other characters assume the functions of the Baptist and Christ. If Wagner could be compared to a prophet pointing the way, he might also be identified with the Baptist. Although Wagner as the puppet suffered on the cross, he might equally well be hiding behind Kundry, the Ahasuerus figure with whom he did identify and who also wears a crown of thorns.

These attributions do not exhaust the director's use of counterpoint. One actually perceives several transformations of the subject playing simultaneously. Wagner the prophet as a modern John the Baptist or forerunner had already been evoked in the ghost scene of *Hitler*. And Hitler as *Führer* (leader, conductor) apparently viewed himself as a redeemer "conducting" his people to a new world. This association endows Parsifal the redeemer with the nimbus of National Socialism that so many, for example Zelinsky and Gutman, see in him and the text. The nimbus remains even if the view shifts to Parsifal as Wagner's ideal of himself as a forerunner. Another version introduces other Jewish-inspired counterpoints besides the Levi connection. Armin Jordan appears beyond the contours of the landscape, or "over the mountains." That happens to be the title of an aphoristic essay by Theodor W. Adorno, "Über den Bergen."[4] The text uses Snow-White and her mother as the starting point for a discussion on melancholy, hope, and illusion. The queen mother who dies giving birth to a child with beautiful white, black, and red characteristics constitutes the awareness that the end means death for the individual. Hope is futile, as truth cannot be distinguished from illusion, *Wahn*. And yet, Adorno claims, hope is what enables us to go on living (157). Many related ideas converge in his text, such as the alchemically significant color combination, melancholy, hope, illusion, and salvation. It puts a damper on Parsifal's jubilant ascension to the Grail guardianship. Adorno joins a group of other Jewish writers including Walter Benjamin, Ernst Bloch, Paul Celan, Heinrich Heine, Sigmund Freud, and for the Kabbalistic dimension, Gershom Scholem, who all inform the film. Celan may actually provide an additional association for Jordan's appearance. The director may be referring to his poem "La Contrescarpe."[5] Through its choice of words it evokes both Adorno and Heine. Especially the identification of the country "behind" the mountain as the Winter Fairytale expresses the disillusionment of Adorno's text and the location in Heine's *Deutschland: Ein Wintermärchen* (285). The film appears to suggest equally somber allusions for someone facing death in Germany. It looms as another stage in the process of change. Last but not least, Nietzsche, who repeatedly declared himself spiritually close to Wagner, used a similar term, *jenseits der Berge*, "beyond the mountains," in *Der Fall Wagner*, referring to lost illusions (406). Whatever one chooses to see in the apparition over the mountains, it may also connect the narrative with the Wagner strand again. The composer himself had envisioned a similarly ghost-like apparition in the sky in another text: an army led by Emperor Frederick II in the second act of "Die Sarazenin" of 1843.[6] Syberberg probably could not resist introducing a detail with so many echoes.

As a footnote to Jordan's appearance in the sky one might wonder if the director also wanted to use the conductor's name as a reference to the *Meistersinger*. That too would reintroduce Wagner's biography. This opera takes place on the day before and on the feast day of John the Baptist. It begins with an end as a congregation in church concludes the service by singing the last words of a hymn: "Edler Täufer, Christs Vorläufer, nimm uns freundlich an dort am Fluss Jordan" (Noble Baptist, Christ's forerunner, accept us kindly at the Jordan). Also early in act 3, the topic of David's entry for the singing contest combines the feast day of St. John, the name day of the protagonist Hans Sachs (Hans = Johannes = John), and a renewed reference to baptism in the Jordan. Maybe Syberberg wants to draw attention to the *Meistersinger* as a forerunner or work anticipating parts of *Parsifal*.

The more closely one contemplates the baptism in *Parsifal*, the more features become apparent that exceed the familiar Christian sacrament. First, one witnesses two "baptisms," one of Parsifal by Gurnemanz, the other of Kundry by Parsifal. Neither uses the terminology of the Church for this ritual, but both wet the believer's head with water from a sanctified source. Gurnemanz accompanies the sprinkling with a blessing and absolution; Parsifal pours water while saying, "Accept (take) the baptism and believe in the redeemer." One could easily interpret both actions as equivalents to the Christian ritual, which admits an individual into the membership of the Church, and equates a rebirth in Christ. In this case, it might secure Kundry's acceptance into the Grail society. Somehow that does not sound compatible with Cosima's diary entry. Rather, Wagner may have merged the ritual ablutions and baptism in Wolfram's text and in Cathar sources. While Cathars dismissed baptism in water, they practiced a baptism of the Holy Spirit called *consolamentum* (Döllinger, 1:204). This rite appears to be closer to the plot. Both Kundry and Parsifal are approaching the goal of their journey. If they were Cathars, they would hope for the *consolamentum* as the last and indispensable rite of redemption. The status it conferred entailed purity and strictest asceticism, but also made the *perfecti* dependent on others for help with most mundane chores, including earning a livelihood. Due to its demands for a holy lifestyle, most Cathars postponed the ritual, spending much of their lives as "believers" and "servants" of their *perfecti*, or saints (Döllinger, 1:237). This might explain Kundry's wish to "serve," her only words in act 3. Therefore, if her baptism corresponds to the Cathars' baptism of the Holy Spirit, she would probably want to die soon while pure. Her curse, one remembers, is a series of reincarnations without the peace of death. But with the *consolamentum* and in a state of perfection, her death would bring release and her soul, that is, the fallen angel trapped in her person, could return to heaven immediately. However, any infraction of the prohibitions would nullify the *consolamentum*, as appears to have been the case with Amfortas. Thus for younger receivers of this rite, an imminent death might have been the only practical assurance of the promised redemption. This may relate to Wagner's comment emphasized by Zelinsky, assuming it refers to Kundry's frame of mind. But that does not yet fully account for Jordan's presence in the sky. It was noted during Parsifal's baptism that the nostrils of the Wagner mask could be imagined to emanate breath or *pneuma* on the rite. That would equate some form of spirit. Not the Holy Spirit, to be sure, but at least the spirit of the maker of this drama. Döllinger adds a pertinent explanation of the Holy Spirit as understood by the Cathars. During the fall of the angels, only their souls were exiled to earth, trapped in human bodies, and doomed to metempsychosis until released in the death of a saintly "pure" Cathar who had received the *consolamentum*. The angelic soul would then return to heaven and be reunited with its spirit. This spirit was known as the "holy spirit" (Döllinger, 1:219). The dualists among the Cathars taught that the soul was united with its holy spirit during the *consolamentum*. It looks as if this holy spirit coming to Kundry has the appearance of Jordan/Wagner as conductor. If the apparition assumes this function, then the film presents a "spiritual" presence also for the second baptism.

Just as the Catholic Church blesses baptismal water before its liturgical use, so also alchemy views water as a potent substance for transformation. Every popular volume on alchemy contains illustrations showing characters in a bath, baptismal font, lake, spring, fountain, or other basin. They invariably undergo a change intended to lead to the perfect material in the end. One may safely assume that the rituals involving water in act 3 produce similar transmutations. The film emphasizes the importance of the water even more than the libretto. In addition to the spring, the film introduces the jugs, a birdbath, the rectangular basin of the window fountain from act 1 and 2, one of Bosch's fountains, the lake, and an octagonal fountain. To that come Kundry's tears, ice, dew, vapor, polluted water, and Wagner's tears feeding the spring. Water functions as a symbol. Since a symbol derives from both the conscious and the unconscious, it possesses the power to reconcile opposites, heal, and transform (Jung, *Aion*, 180). Significantly, only in this scene can one recognize that the basin of the eye socket is fed by tears from Wagner's head. Are they tears of contrition? Does he also undergo some form of transmutation? He should, if Kundry functions as his inner mirror. In any case, water continues a consistent pattern of symbolic significance. Water, and not so much the ritual, produces the transmutation. And concerning the water of Jordan, Jung claims that alchemists equated it with the Logos, "thus bringing up the analogy with the Chalice" and the cup in 4 Ezra 14.39–40 (*Psych. and Alch.*, 468–69). This water gives life, heals, and serves as a uniting symbol (471). Throughout the film some form of water recurs in various stages of circulation. This links the imagery to the tradition of "living waters" in Christian, Jewish, and ancient symbolism. For example, the divine efflux of the Kabbalah, which is often presented as an emanation of light, can also be seen as life-giving water that strives to circulate back to its holy source of origin. The typology of regeneration through circulation includes water springing from the rock, the *silex*.[7] Syberberg grants this trope a significant function with the lake or spring of tears from the stony head landscape.

Not only water, but also the vegetation and the landscape assume importance in this segment. To music renowned for its beauty, Parsifal, Kundry, and Gurnemanz experience the "Good Friday magic." It is contrasted repeatedly in word and image with the magic of Klingsor's garden. Fresh green and clumps of flowers, probably primrose, cover the meadow. Although it is surrounded by the wilderness seen in the prelude, it is a partially cultivated landscape. One recognizes that on scattered crates with flowers and herbs waiting to be planted. Actually, the landscape borrows the glass roof of a greenhouse, namely the glass ceiling of the film studio. Just as the wasteland before, so the verdure around the spring reflects a new state of mind. In the second act Klingsor's cape "mirrored" his 1882 garden, and it looked like a jungle. When Parsifal arrived, that environment turned into a barren, rocky landscape. The Good Friday meadow constitutes a contrast. Wagner's text refers to it four times as an *Aue* and once as a *Wiese*. Also the book to the film discusses the meadow scenes using the same nouns. The *Wiese* in the book hints possibly at a famous allusion in Thomas Mann's *Doktor Faustus*. The seventh chapter of the novel weaves in the word *Wiesengrund* (greensleeve) three times in a lecture on Beethoven's sonata opus 111 (75–76). It has long been recognized as the author's homage to Theodor Wiesengrund Adorno, whom he had consulted about music throughout the writing of the novel. Adorno belongs also to the subtext of the film. However, Syberberg does not repeat Mann's use of *Wiesengrund*, although he incorporates it visually. His garden reminds one of the garden of Eden, especially since the text of this segment includes several references to religious concepts. First Gurnemanz identifies the day as Good Friday, then a few lines later mentions the Redeemer, prayer, and "Himself on the cross." If this religious frame of reference revives an echo of a restored garden of Eden, then paradise may have been regained. It even features an angel. This is not the *Angelus Novus* suggested when Parsifal I backed away from the camera. This time the central column of the octagonal fountain is topped by a sculpture of the archangel Michael standing above two layers of water-spewing dragons. St. Michael overcomes the dragon called Anti-Christ in Revelation, but here one sees ten or twelve of them. They are obviously personal forces that individuals must conquer. They have been transformed so as to send out streams of healing water. Of course the name of the archangel also recalls Michael Kutter. More importantly, the octagonal fountain points to its source of inspiration, Jan van Eyck's polyptych known as *The Ghent Altarpiece*. Van Eyck's artwork informs the film repeatedly. The fountain appears in the lower center of the panel known as "The Adoration of the Lamb." This is again a religious piece of art rooted in medieval iconography, where every detail is imbued with symbolism. Syberberg's *Parsifal* reads the same way. Both the painted fountain and its functional recreation in the film are fed by water coming from Jordan, that is, Jordan in the Holy Land and the Jordan/Wagner spring. One remembers Jung's statement that the water of Jordan also serves as a uniting symbol (*Psych. and Alch.*, 471). In the painting one recognizes its uniting power in the two groups of men flanking the fountain. The right side shows kneeling apostles and standing dignitaries of the Church, the left side, kneeling prophets and standing patriarchs representing the Synagogue. Both groups are peacefully united in contemplation of the fountain. This differs strongly from an earlier painting by the same artist, *The Fountain of Life*, where the members of the Church and the Synagogue react in disturbing contrast to the water symbol between them. Not only are the composition and the fountain in *The Ghent Altarpiece* conciliatory, but the inside panels are set in a new or heavenly Jerusalem. That equates a regained paradise, as underscored by the blooming landscape. The cinematic fountain serves as the setting for Parsifal's kiss on Kundry's forehead, which absolves her from the guilt confessed in the second act.

The entire long Good Friday segment centers on rebirth and renewal, as the text proves. Gurnemanz points out that Good Friday is not at all an occasion for bemoaning the Savior's passion and crucifixion, but for rejoicing in regained innocence and redemption. For Kundry that spells the final cycle of life on this earth, read on one level of interpretation. Her tears join those of the "sinner's [Wagner's] tears of remorse." They form the "holy dew" that restores life to nature, that is, Wagner's features. Of course, in alchemy tears are the most potent agent of transmutation. If the tears produce a transformation and the water of Jordan serves as a unifying symbol, does that affect Kundry as the penitent Mary Magdalene? Maybe the unifying power could unify or merge the two natures suggested by her double name, namely a holy person and a sinner. If the names are united into one, it might become a restored virginal symbol. The book to the film hints at something of that sort: "The change to the more serene areas of the meadow is accompanied by a virginal Kundry, who is coming to herself here, finally"(196). Several details support the transformation as resulting in a new Virgin. Some of her attributes in the second act echo paintings of Virgin Mary by van Eyck. In view of her role as temptress, the association appeared blasphemous then. That is, until one remembers how counterpoint works. Now the Virgin Mary "melody" can be perceived without the other, alienating transformations of the theme that usually play simultaneously. Medieval iconography confirms the link between the symbol of a fountain and the Virgin. For example, Rupert of Deutz, a thirteenth-century influential commentator on the Song of Songs, lets Virgin Mary state, according to Carol Purtle, "I am the fountain of gardens, . . . I, by his grace, am a well of living waters."[8] Just as van Eyck did, so also Syberberg sets this fountain in a garden-like clearing. It is framed by tall elements (concrete mask segments and props), making it look like an enclosed garden. That was a common epithet of the Virgin Mary in the Middle Ages. The same passage of Rupert of Deutz includes these words by the Virgin: "I am the garden, . . . I am a garden sealed, . . . and my shoots are a paradise of apple trees" (Purtle, 106). Of course nowhere does Syberberg state unequivocally that the new Kundry has been transformed into another Virgin Mary. But this mother imago with a savior child wears clothes inspired by Marian paintings in the second act and has now been reborn as an adult virginal woman. Klingsor referred to her as the Rose of Hell. Virgin Mary is known as the Rose of Heaven. Furthermore, on several occasions the film includes Kundry's hair as a conspicuous attribute. One remembers the semantic links in Hebrew between "hair" and "gate" or "door" (*daleth*). Also the gate joins the list of the Virgin's attributes: "In his commentary, Rupert [of Deutz] follows traditional teaching in equating the closed gate of the temple with the Virgin. . . . 'The gate of the sanctuary, what is it if not the Virgin, through which for the first time there opened for us the door of the outer sanctuary, the heavenly sanctuary'" (Purtle, 109). Mariology also praises the Virgin as the Womb of Salvation, Church (Ecclesia), Bride, and the human soul.[9] The list of Mary's attributions would have only limited interest were it not for two ramifications: the status of her child and the indebtedness to Jewish mysticism. Both in the words of the libretto, the prevailing interpretation of the work, alchemical symbolism, and analytical psychology, Parsifal has developed into a redeemer figure. This Christ-like savior encourages the association of the mother imago or anima with the Virgin. A Kabbalistic parallel is also consistent with the work, and Syberberg's interpretation accentuates it. And so does Jan van Eyck's altarpiece. The inner panels that constitute the central axis reveal a Kabbalistic composition as adapted by a Christian artist. Suffice it here that the symbols of Virgin Mary quoted from Rupert also apply to the Shekhinah as the tenth *sefira*. In his book *Von der mystischen Gestalt,* Scholem discusses a number of these symbols. One learns that the Shekhinah is, for example, identical with the heavenly mother (the "supernal" Shekhinah, 169), she is the sphere of redemption (170), the gate, garden, fountain, moon, shrine (171), rose (179, 184), and water (181–82). But unlike the Virgin she can fall under the control of the "other" or evil forces. Then the Shekhinah can also assume chtonic, destructive, and demonic qualities (183–85). Besides, she suffers the exile shared with the Jewish people (162). One can discern the characteristics and lot of Kundry, both in these and other attributions. As a generally assumed Jewish character, she unites in her person a number of symbols and functions at home both in medieval Christianity and Jewish mysticism. One could, then, read both the garden and the fountain with its healing waters as projected extensions of Kundry. Actually, the director may have sneaked in one more allusion to the Shekhinah in the Good Friday segment. On her circumambulation in the garden, Kundry passes a draped, huge object mentioned in the book to the film as a "female violin" (199). The contour of the instrument was glimpsed in the prelude, and now it has a violin bow stuck in it. Anything related to a violin or a bow will by now elicit a chain of associations: early violin, in German *Fidel*, which is the Latin *fides* alias Faith, Church, and Synagogue; and the string of the bow is *Sehne*, base for *Sehnen* = yearning. Incidentally, Cosima Wagner's diary occasionally also refers to her son as Fidel (e.g. Jan. 11, 1881). The violin is draped in Kundry's blue cover and therefore not recognizable. The visible lower part looks thoroughly organic, more like a giant human heart. That word recalls the *organon*, which can also mean an "organ of the body." And the heart belongs in Scholem's list of symbols of the Shekhinah (157). It would appear, then, that the imagery unites both Christian and Jewish interpretations. This imbues Kundry with more significance than usually recognized. At this point her humility veils her status and makes her look devoid, or purified, of any human personality. The chtonic dragon mother (Tiamat, Python) has been transformed into a source of healing, pure water. And the fountain in this segment is octagonal, like many baptismal fonts. Siegfried and the archangel kill a dragon, Kundry is a transformed one.

The scene at the fountain ends when Gurnemanz notices the bells tolling the noon hour. This time the music marks high noon. As before, Parsifal leads, now with both Gurnemanz and Kundry following. The libretto specifies that Gurnemanz walks first, but the director uses the opportunity to repeat the embrace. He lets Gurnemanz protectively put his arm around Kundry's shoulder during their first steps. Later, when she stops, he beckons her to come along, as he did with Parsifal in the first act. This time the transformation music accompanies a different approach to the castle. Commensurate with Parsifal's anointment, a projection of a Christ icon fills the background several times. The image is cropped so as to include only the face. A bend in the path soon conceals the icon and attracts the viewer's attention. The turn is made necessary by a pile of objects. They include the heads seen earlier around Klingsor's throne and Parsifal's bow and arrow, all covered with a sheet of clear plastic. Their leitmotivic power reminds the viewer that these forces have now been reduced to memories. Actually, they form a pile reminiscent of Bloch's description of attractions at a fairground. But their accumulation also resembles a heap of junk awaiting the garbage collectors. This effect emits two semantic reverberations. As noted earlier, Michael Kutter's last name is also a German noun with several meanings, one of them being a dialect word for "garbage" or "junk." Although visually still absent, the male Parsifal is again evoked through an object symbol, as he was before with the statue of the archangel. The second link on the *Sprachgitter* relates to another German word for trash, *Kehricht*. All the discarded items have been swept into a pile. To sweep or clean up is *kehren*, which can also mean "to turn around" or "reverse." The heap does cause a turn achieved primarily through a panning camera. Such a turn or shift in direction is *Kehre*. That lexis is a central concept in Heidegger's thought and the title of one of his essays.[10] Remembering the director's comments on Riefenstahl's camera work, one wonders if the timing of the moving camera and the evocation of Heidegger's *Kehre* is just a coincidence. At the time when Syberberg planned and filmed *Parsifal*, many critical books and articles appeared about Heidegger. They concentrated on the philosopher's accommodation to Nazism and self-incriminating refusal to discuss the topic after World War II. One might therefore view the visual reminder of Riefenstahl and Heidegger as a faint brown shadow. The counterpoint is still at work. The concept of *Kehre* suits the plot perfectly. One remembers Kundry's association with *Gestell*. And it entails danger, most explicitly associated with forgetfulness about the nature of Being. Kundry induces Parsifal repeatedly to remember his mother, and in the second act he even bemoans his forgetfulness. But forgetfulness can be overcome. The nature of the danger inherent in the *Gestell* harbors the possibility of such a turnaround or *Kehre*.[11] Syberberg juxtaposes the *Gestell* with the pile of objects at the turn in the path. For Gurnemanz this means only the re*turn* home to the Grail Castle. For Parsifal it entails also an introv*ersion* with insight, and for Kundry both a return and a conv*ersion* with liberation from previous desires and restraints. To underscore the transformation resulting from the *Kehre*, the scaffolding has changed. On one side of the passage stands the remnant of the familiar structure with arrow, bow, and string. On the other side stands the tall covered shape with the violin contour constructed from parts of the scaffolding. It displays Kundry's attributes of starry cloth cover, wig, flowers, and a violin bow. The cloth covers its "organic" surface that was visible during Kundry's circum-ambulation. This concealed resemblance with a heart restores its identity as an *organon*. The engine of war has been partially dismantled and transformed into a heart, a physical organ that is also a musical instrument, *fides*, and Faith. The bow, of course, finds its equivalent in the violin bow. The tension of the string, the *Sehne*, is balanced by the loosely draped cloth, hanging hair, and flowers. One symbol suggests longing and impediments, the other the release from these constraints. Again the physical transformation of an object mirrors an invisible, internal process.

The three pilgrims pass between these two structures with the Christ icon visible in the background. This *eidos* of the divine in human form now presides over the uncovering or disclosure (*Entbergen*) of the technical machinery used on the set. For example, the backside of the window fountain reveals a fan moving air (*pneuma*), perhaps as part of a pump moving water. These mechanical parts and contraptions belong to the "challenge" that the *Gestell* or *organon* poses.[12] At first sight baffling, deconstructionist, and disillusioning in an already unrealistic environment, such details still pose challenges to the viewers. One tries as best one can to identify intended associations. Not surprisingly, the consistency in compositional procedure helps one recognize some of the transformations.

At one point Parsifal II stops to let Gurnemanz and Kundry catch up with her. She stands in front of the projected icon so that the cross tip of her staff fills the pupil of one eye in the Christ face. The cross in a circle is a mandala. Not only does the cross represent the Christ idea as the Self, but the combination of the circle and the four-armed cross is a prominent symbol of wholeness in Jung's books. The Self, or archetype of wholeness, often assumes symbolic form. Among the most important ones are, so Jung states, " geometrical structures containing elements of the circle and quaternity; namely, circular and spherical forms on the one hand, which can be represented either purely geometrically or as objects; and, on the other hand, quadratic figures divided into four or in the form of a cross" (*Aion*, 224). Such symbols of wholeness represent the goal of human development and ethical achievement, variously referred to as, e.g., the stone (*lapis*), Christ, Anthropos, or the Self. Jung summarizes one section on these symbols by calling them "the greater, more comprehensive Man, that indescribable whole consisting of the sum of conscious and unconscious processes. This objective whole, the antithesis of the subjective ego-psyche, is what I have called the self, and this corresponds exactly to the idea of the [Gnostic] Anthropos" (*Aion*, 189). The film makes it clear that this goal is close to being reached, and with it the inner God activated. Since Wagner's text becomes strongly religious in the third act, the countenance of Christ supports the prevailing interpretation of "Redeemer." The face is typical of medieval depictions of Christ, especially on icons and church windows, with the eyes of Christ meeting those of the beholder. The deity represents the Christian Trinity, and the film echoes the emphasis on three by presenting a triad of pilgrims. But the cross has four points, and the anthropomorphic symbolism of the Kabbalah operates with a divine quaternity (heavenly father, mother, son, and daughter). As the Kabbalah informs the film, one suspects that the development of the Self has not been entirely completed yet. Even as disparate writers informing the work as Jung and Heidegger agree on the significance of the quaternity. Heidegger, for example, refers to the "fourfold of heaven and earth, mortals and gods."[13] And Jung states: "The well-known significance of the 'fourth' helps to explain its connection with the 'whole' man, for the fourth always makes a triad into a totality" (*Aion*, 184). His

Aion includes several reproductions of medieval art showing the Christian Trinity crowning the Virgin Mary. This might be viewed as meeting a psychological need for "completion" of a quaternity. Van Eyck's *Ghent Altarpiece* includes a crowned Virgin Mary seated at the Deity's right hand. Unless the Christ icon is intended to constitute the fourth element evoked by the cross in the circle, then the fourth member is still missing.

The transformation music accompanies the slow peregrination. About midway a different background projection demands attention. It shows the dying Tristan with Isolde at his side. Besides returning another Wagner work to the subtext, it also hints at the suffering hero as a self portrait of the composer. But more to the point, it reminds the viewer of an early plan that Wagner abandoned. He had intended to introduce Parsifal as a character in *Tristan and Isolde*, where he was supposed to visit Tristan shortly before the latter's death (Gregor-Dellin, 393). Syberberg restores the detail. Of course he also remains faithful to the medieval custom of offering multiple meanings of imagery. The projection may depict Tristan and Isolde, point to the composer's early plan, hint at a suffering Wagner, and, not the least, prefigure Amfortas in agony, who will soon return to the screen. The last link is hidden in a letter from Wagner to Mathilde Wesendonck of May 30, 1859. He still spells Amfortas' name with an *n*: "Looked at closely, it is *Anfortas* who is the centre of attention and principal subject. Of course, it is not at all a bad story. Consider, in heaven's name, all that goes on there! It suddenly became dreadfully clear to me: it is my third-act Tristan inconceivably intensified" (*Selected Letters*, 457). Thus Tristan who longs for death both prefigures, and substitutes for, Amfortas. The Grail king may not appear in person yet, but the "visual music" evokes him.

At long last Parsifal, Kundry, and Gurnemanz enter open terrain, or a *Lichtung*, as Heidegger would call it. They head for the background projection of the night sky. It is a close-up of Wagner's navy dressing gown with starry lining. As seen before, a second, unnoticeable screen allows the characters to enter into the background, as it were. The entry of the group suggests an acceptance into the composer's innermost world. Perhaps his private world resembles that of Heine, since the star-studded view can also serve as another reference to the poet. Among the notes to *Atta Troll* that Heine did not include in the published version one finds several stanzas with related imagery. One of them describes the night as sparkling with stars and covering the mountains like a mantle.[14] Since Syberberg already referred to Heine's "Grenadiere" with music by Wagner in his book to *Hitler*, one almost expects additional links, especially in view of the Herodias passages in *Atta Troll*. Like the friendship with Heine, the stars on the lining belong to the composer's unpublished private life. This hidden universe reveals itself as the microcosm called Richard Wagner. Once inside the starry robe, Parsifal and the other two pilgrims approach a staircase and begin to ascend it to the first strains of a male chorus. This approach to the Grail Castle differs even more from Wagner's instructions than the first "transformation" walk in act 1. This is where the composer wanted the mountain walls to open. Syberberg internalizes the action and

lets his characters find the opening in the robe projection. The staircase stands
alone and leads straight up to the stars. The lower section had already served
Herzeleide, Amfortas, and Kundry as steps to a throne. Now it forms the first few
steps of Jacob's Ladder. Meanwhile, the invisible chorus reveals the proximity of
the Grail Castle while also repeating the discrepancy between image and sound
experienced in the first Grail ceremony. There the men's voices and the sopranos
did not always materialize on screen as expected. This quasi-musical dissonance
recurs here.

While the group of three ascends the staircase, the camera cuts to the Grail
company. The next six camera takes focus on men moving in single file. Initially
they walk through narrow passages, then mount steps leading to the surface. Some
carry torches, reminding the viewer of how dark the interior of the "castle" must be.
Having arrived on a higher level, some are seen walking on a road framed by tall
boulders, while others cross a bridge over the road. Being perhaps just a plank, the
bridge is practically invisible. It brings to mind another pronouncement of
Nietzsche's Zarathustra: "Man is a rope stretched between the animal and the
Superman—a rope over an abyss. . . . What is great in man is that he is a bridge and
not a goal: what is lovable in man is that he is an *over-going* [*Übergang*] and a
down-going [*Untergang*]" (8–9). The polyvalence of these two concepts, usually
translated as "transition" and "demise, decline, sinking, end" reverberates as a
visual part of the music. The men on the move have not reached the stage of
Superman or a Catharist *perfectus*. Lamenting Titurel's death and experiencing the
decline of their Grail society, they represent and express the condition of a
moribund organism. As in the first act, the constant movement of people suggests
strong motions of the unconscious (Jung, *Symbols of Transf.*, 207). The abundance
of vapor confirms the psychological dimension. Sometimes the vapors cascade
down the rocks, at other times they billow on the ground. According to the libretto,
the viewers are witnessing the entry of the knights in the Grail Hall, one chorus
group carrying the coffin with Titurel, the other carrying the covered shrine with the
Grail and the bier with Amfortas. The refectory tables have been removed, making
room for the funeral, *Totenfeier*, with a black baldachin and coffin. Amfortas has
promised to conduct the Grail ceremony for one additional and last time. The
responsorial parts of the two choruses express both grief over Titurel's death and
resentment against Amfortas, now called "the sinful guardian." He has apparently
not inherited his father's strength. The "holy strength" would have been his *teleios*,
spiritual, and physical perfection. But what happened to God, who, according to
Wagner's words, gave himself into Titurel's care? God's presence should be the
blood collected and mysteriously preserved in the chalice. That provides the text
with a tangible divine presence. But one cannot help wondering why such a magical
setting would need the external signs of luminosity of the Grail and light from
above. Wagner obviously thought the "inner God" needed such signs of
manifestation on stage. What would happen to the divine content in the Grail if
Amfortas should succeed in getting himself killed, as he pleads with the knights to
do? Why would God be so totally dependent on this one sinner? It appears that this

sinner is really Wagner and the others only minor fragments of his psyche. His inner God needs all possible support to receive and give redemption. Wagner tried to adapt his medieval sources but could not weld them to a convincing story on this point. Only when remembering the Gnostic, Manichaean, and Catharist belief in the angelic souls trapped in human bodies or the divine sparks fallen into unclean matter, can one read coherence into Wagner's version. He also appears to have borrowed elements from the Kabbalah. The composer actually was familiar with literature about Jewish mysticism well before he started on the score of *Parsifal*. For example, beginning with Dec. 17, 1874, Cosima Wagner's diary records that the composer was reading "by himself" the *Geschichte des Urchristentums* (History of Earliest Christianity) by Aug. Fr. Gfrörer, and "liking it very much."[15] The first volume discusses early Jewish theology and the Kabbalah. The diary mentions this work fourteen times over the next few months, nine times referring to the first volume of the set. This suggests that Wagner studied the contents thoroughly. Since volume 1 appeared in 1831, and other books on the topic were published in subsequent years, Wagner may have been acquainted with Jewish mysticism for a long time. Numerous aspects of *Parsifal* (and *Parzival*) appear to have been been inspired by the Kabbalah rather than derived from other spiritual traditions. The composer could rest assured that exceedingly few admirers would recognize such leanings in his music dramas. Even his wife does not elaborate on his knowledge of such topics in her diary, referring to Gfrörer's work as a "book on Christian mythology." Contemporary admirers might be more inclined to recognize the psychological dimensions in *Parsifal*. But also the Kabbalistic lore is heavily psychological in nature, as Scholem and Idel assure their readers repeatedly. The predicament of Amfortas and his society supports that claim, with the king representing most visibly a broken vessel unable to repair itself.

Amfortas' condition should have deteriorated since the first act, but Wagner's only indication of a decline is Titurel's death and the listlessness of the knights. The film translates the decline of the Grail Kingdom into a psychological Wasteland. Again a few corpses lie around on the ground. But the moving crowds display the new condition more plainly. At first glance they consist of knights, monks, and men in the secular clothes of earlier centuries. One is reminded of the male inhabitants in Wolfram's Schastel Merveil. Those who had been young at the beginning of the spell could not advance to knighthood. Perhaps the novices and aspirants from the first act have met a similar barrier blocking admission to the order. Or are they renegades contemplating a return to secular life? Some of them even remain silent as they file by, as if bitter and disillusioned. At least one of them resembles Parsifal I. Spiritually dead and without hope, they all look downcast. At second glance some of the congregants even reveal themselves to be corpses. A few look like walking mummies covered in billowing plastic. Others are walking dead displaying skulls. The *Parsifal* book mentions that the dressed corpses are modeled on the dead in the catacombs of Palermo, which Wagner visited while on Sicily (219). The biographical detail is less important than the fact that some of the assembling inhabitants are dead or dying. As Amfortas' entourage, they represent an extension of him. Since he is unable to function as the spindle or upholder of his universe, as shown with the celestial mantle, the impending ceremony assumes a new dimension. Syberberg's book refers to this gathering as an "eschatological rite" (219). But as usual the book does not elaborate, leaving the comment as a hint. The rocky environment represents Wagner's mindscape, which Parsifal is approaching. From one perspective, his group is ascending to the starry inner universe which is in need of a pole star. A new era is about to replace the existing one.

The transition from the gathering scenes to Amfortas consists of two quick takes. A cut to the trio on the staircase confirms that Parsifal is approaching, and the following black frame leads to the dead swan in oily or murky water. This is the bird that Parsifal killed and that was transformed into a piece of art. While it may be a visual reference to Wolfram's text, Syberberg lets the dead swan also join Titurel in the grave. Furthermore, a swan belongs in the sky as the constellation Cygnus. Actually, one finds many elements of Wolfram's version in the firmament, including a Grail. One is tempted to assume that Syberberg is trying to restore part of the medieval astrological-astronomical frame of reference. Most importantly at this stage, the glimpse of the swan again connects Parsifal's approach with the Grail society now assembled around Amfortas.

The swan fades into the Grail society as Amfortas begins his lamentations. This time he is surrounded by a large, mostly seated, crowd that includes the youngsters and the two attendants in the red and the celestial robes. Amfortas is reclining on a draped bier, weakened from profuse bleeding. His blood fills several buckets and discolors the ground between him and the wound on a cushion. The throne, on which he is no longer able to sit, stands off-screen, with only the steps leading up to it in full view. The blood and the distance to the throne suggest the imminent demise of the king. The projected wound also indicates that he has not succeeded in internalizing it or accepting what it represents. As in Wolfram's version, Amfortas begs for death as release. This is expressed in a three-step crescendo of intensity. During the first of these phases the knights are supposed to open Titurel's casket accompanied by general lamentations. The film omits this detail, but cuts to another screen-filling projection of a sketch for the 1882 production. It shows Titurel's casket under a pair of black baldachins in a black-and-white tiled hall. A luminous Grail stands in the background. The image possesses referential power: to Wagner's plans and first production, to a Masonic funeral rite, and to its brief appearances in Syberberg's *Ludwig* and *Hitler*. The former shows the king lamenting his predicament in front of the same backdrop. In other words, the director's King Ludwig prefigures Amfortas as well as Titurel. The detail suggests that Syberberg was planning his *Parsifal* quite early, just as Wagner nurtured his version over many years. And finally, the visual inclusion of a casket conforms to the libretto. The Grail ceremony is combined with an unorthodox requiem. And *requiem* occurs in the subtitle of *Ludwig*. It links up with *Parsifal* as the beginning and conclusion of a cycle.

The projection of Titurel's catafalque accompanies the second section of Amfortas' lines. While the camera keeps zooming away from or closer to the king, the gathered crowd becomes invisible at times. As in the first act, his soliloquy is an inner dialogue with his dead father imago. He addresses him in a prayer asking for two things: that the Redeemer's blood (in the Grail) may again bless and strengthen the "brothers." That part indicates Amfortas' willingness to conduct the Grail rite. And second, that he may be blessed with death. For both of these supplications he prays that his father shall intercede for him with the Redeemer. In the first act, Amfortas directed his prayer to God; this time he prays indirectly through his pious father's soul. As he loses himself in his appeal to his father, the gathered crowd has good reason to think he will renege on his promise to display the Grail and conduct the ritual.

The knights begin to protest loudly, urging him to proceed with the ceremony. The camera cuts to the knights in armor as they rise to their feet. This hint of insurrection introduces the third and most passionate stage in Amfortas' agony. This man is too consumed with his own anguish to consider the needs of his entourage. As he sinks back on the bier, Amfortas appears to have spent all his strength. Not only does he not want to, he may not be able to conduct the ceremony. He is a dying man. Syberberg obviously agrees with Adorno on this point. The latter wrote in his essay "Zur Partitur des *Parsifal*": "[É]*lan vital* and affirmative gesture are so absent that one believes no more in the redemption at the end than sometimes in fairytales. . . .[I]n the end Wagner kept his loyalty to his Schopenhauer better than those who want to degrade him to the apostle of regeneration."[16]

At this point the camera shifts to Parsifal II, who has arrived unnoticed. Standing with the cross-tipped staff on high ground, she is seen against a black background, not the ruined Grail Hall. Thanks to the slow music, the camera can tell a long story while Parsifal begins to sing "her" 17 lines of text. This helps distract from the words, some of which, when taken literally, describe how "holy blood" oozes from the tip of the "lance" longing for its related source in the Grail. In the meantime the camera zooms, pans, and rolls, allowing views of the assembly surrounding Amfortas, of Kundry, and of Gurnemanz. Kundry stands in thought near the throne, now wrapped in a voluminous cape resembling Gurnemanz' blanket. While Gurnemanz approaches Amfortas and kneels at the bier, she slowly turns towards Amfortas and Parsifal II, who is standing on an elevated cliff in the background. According to the printed text, Parsifal addresses Amfortas at this point. The words that make Kundry lift her head and turn are, "Be whole, released from sin, and expiated, for I now hold your office." This amounts to a healing, absolution, and release from duties. The words should have the same ritual effect as the *consolamentum* of the Cathars. The following blessing adds the appearance of an unorthodox final rite for the dying in addition to the requiem for Titurel. This is the moment Amfortas has been hoping for. But contrary to expectation he remains silent. He who can lament and wail for 20 minutes on end has no words of thanks for either Parsifal or Titurel. Neither he nor the assembly expresses relief or joy over Parsifal's pronouncement. Syberberg draws the logical conclusion from this surprising silence. Amfortas and his society have already expired. In the first act the king had remarked about the prophesy that he thought he would recognize the pure fool if he might call him Death. He may have been right. And death is what he prayed for.

But also Kundry hears Parsifal's pronouncement about being "whole." The statement clearly elicits memories in her. To be "whole" means a reunion with Amfortas, and be it only in death. As she observes him from a distance, her wrap and posture echo a famous German statue, that of Lady Uta in the Cathedral of Naumburg (1250–60). Uta, with her husband at her side, and several other aristocratic donor couples adorn the sanctuary as statues of saints do in other Gothic churches. As in the *Ghent Altarpiece*, so also here the donors are depicted as part of the sacred space, reminding worshipers at each mass to include them in their prayers. Similarly Syberberg surrounds Amfortas, as he appeals to his dead father for intercession, with quotations from these two religious works of art donated for the sake of intercessional masses and prayers. The film becomes, as it were, the centerpiece of a triptych.

The viewers' contemplation of Kundry as Uta is interrupted briefly. Parsifal had blessed Amfortas' suffering as the cause producing compassion and understanding in the fool. When the word for "fool," *Tor*, sounds, the orchestra repeats Parsifal's motif. With this dual introduction, Parsifal I makes his entry into the assembly, followed by his female counterpart who has left her perch on the cliff. He wears his brown tunic, she her white one. He carries the lance, she the transformed one. They share, then, two of the attributes belonging to the Synagogue and Church statues in the Cathedral of Strasbourg. Only now does the male Parsifal announce that he is returning the "holy spear" to the Grail community. The delayed introduction of the original lance is one of several deviations from the composer's stage instructions. According to Wagner, Parsifal's action accompanying his first words is to heal Amfortas by letting the spear tip touch the wound. Amfortas is later supposed to adore the Grail on his knees along with the others. Syberberg changes the ritual, which is independent of the words.

The two Parsifals stand side by side, delivering the happy news to an immobile crowd. Again the expected reaction, joy and relief, remains absent. This assembly looks as dead as Amfortas with the exception of Kundry. The camera has backed sufficiently to include her again. Still in the same pose she now wears also a golden crown. It is more splendid than that worn by Uta. Suddenly she moves towards Amfortas, whose bier has been joined by an identical second, draped bier where the wound had been. As she lies down on it, she and Amfortas resemble two stone effigies on royal tombs, like those in the crypt of St. Denis. They have at long last been united, and she has been restored to her original status. Unlike the dim crowns of the Grail Carrier and Herzeleide on her sarcophagus, Kundry's crown glitters. Its golden hue indicates the alchemical stage of *rubedo*, the final phase in the transmutation process. As two complementary halves, she and her king have been united as a "whole" couple. The libretto instructs her to collapse and die during the Grail ceremony, leaving the others alive. The film restores her to dignity first before letting her expire at Amfortas' side. Their stone-like presence changes the Grail Hall to a sanctuary, as similar royal tombs also adorn many medieval churches.

As anticipated, the Grail ceremony differs from traditional stage versions. The entire Grail society, including Gurnemanz, has become as immobile as figures in a painting. While the two Parsifals conclude their lines with "Uncover the Grail, open the shrine," the camera cuts to a view devoid of people. A rocky wall is surrounded by rising vapor. Suddenly a crack opens in the rock and slowly widens into a lit passage. Is the rocky landscape the shrine, one wonders. Wagner's instructions indicate that mountain walls open up to reveal the Grail Hall at the end of the transformation music. Syberberg relocates this detail to the end of the act. The film had included a similar effect in the first act. But the characters are now supposed to already be in the hall. Now as then, the moving rock evokes the same association with the biblical statement "and though I have all faith, so that I could remove mountains " (1 Cor. 13.2). Faith is again present, both as the faith theme in the music and as a visual evocation, although not seen as the character of that name. As the Voice from on high she may, however, have joined the unseen singers in the cupola.

The following sequences play out while voices "from on high" sing the last words of act 3. These are the most enigmatic words of the libretto, "Erlösung dem Erlöser!" (Redemption for the redeemer!). If the fool is the redeemer, then Parsifal, as well as everyone else who had been referred to as a fool, has achieved what was also attempted for Amfortas. The act of intercession has brought the coveted boon also to the intercessor. But in the second act Parsifal II remembers hearing a voice calling for help during the Grail ceremony, "The Savior's lament I hear there, . . . Redeem me, save me from hands defiled with guilt." Forgetting about this *Gottesklage* became one of Parsifal's sins. That means, then, that the redeemer is a divine force present in the human body. Such belief resembles the Catharist teaching about angelic souls trapped in human bodies. Similarly the Gnostic and Kabbalistic versions of the fallen sparks express belief in divine elements awaiting human intervention for their return or redemption. The "immanent God" was also familiar to Christian mystics, e.g. Meister Eckhart, whom Wagner admired.[17] Much has been written about these lines in *Parsifal*.[18] Let it suffice here that the syzygy named Parsifal has reached the Christ-stage in personal development that Jung describes as the Self. Easily confused with the biblical Christ, this level of psychological wholeness is an *imago Dei*. The process of advancement and structure of the Self (the stone or *lapis*) are the main topics in Jung's *Aion*. He elaborates most succinctly on the development of the Self towards a Christ-like perfection ("individuation") in the chapter called "Christ, a Symbol of the Self" (36–71). The book does not only present a wealth of imagery for the individuation process gleaned from a variety of ancient sources, but also discusses at length the male-female complementarity and the four-fold structure of unity. While distinguishing between perfection and completeness, Jung states: "The Christ-image is as good as perfect (at least it is meant to be so), while the archetype (so far as known) denotes completeness but is far from being perfect. It is a paradox, a statement about something indescribable and transcendental" (68–69). Jung continues by referring to this paradox as a "fundamental conflict," a predicament propelling the best in human nature to yearn for wholeness with perfection: "To strive after teleiosis in the sense of perfection is not only legitimate but is inborn in man as a peculiarity which provides civilization with one of its strongest roots" (69). This striving for a union of the Christ-image with the archetype, or of perfection with completeness, can also be expressed as a move towards conjunction of opposites (70). To this Jung adds, "Naturally, the conjunction can only be understood as a paradox, since the union of opposites can be thought of only as their annihilation" (70). Syberberg renders the opposites as male and female, thus illustrating Jung's tenets. Actually, the film translates the quaternio into the (re)union of two couples: Amfortas and Kundry, Parsifal I and Parsifal II.

Only a few times have the adult Parsifals appeared together before. On none of these occasions does Parsifal I seem to pay attention to Parsifal II. Even when they join the gathering in the third act, they enter a few seconds apart and do not look at each other. Only now, in the opening formed by the cracked mountain, do they come face to face. She approaches him affectionately, ready for an embrace, while snowy vapors billow around their feet. He, however, hesitates. Only very slowly does he enclose her in his arms while looking quite serious. Why the reluctance? One little detail explains the reason. She appears to be wearing her greaves. They formed part of her armor when she arrived at Gurnemanz' cabin. Although her tunic and flowing, long hair give her a soft, feminine appearance, the greaves reveal the warrior maiden. Like Brünnhilde, the other Valkyries, Athena, and the Gorgon, her gaze has consequences for mortals. Parsifal I's reluctance shows that he can only gradually accept his mortality. This insight marks the final phase of psychological maturation. In alchemical terms, the embrace marks *coniunctio* in the transmutation process. Parsifal II's white tunic identifies her as the white (silvery, lunar) feminine part, Parsifal I's brown tunic qualifies him as the reddish, masculine (solar, golden) element. Their union completes the cycle. But, like a ring, a cycle or circle has no real end. The process continues while starting over.

According to the instructions in the libretto, Parsifal takes the Grail from its shrine, prays, and holds it up for the assembly to contemplate. While the light dims, the Grail becomes luminous, a beam of light falls on the ceremony "from on high," a white dove (the Holy Ghost) hovers over Parsifal's head, and Kundry dies, whereupon the curtain falls. The singers on stage act out their roles mutely as in a pantomime, to the ethereal strains of the invisible singers in the cupola and the Grail music. In the published libretto of 1877 Titurel was supposed to revive at this time, sit up in his casket and bless the assembly. Wagner suppressed the detail in 1882. Only a footnote in the score remains as a reminder. Syberberg adapted the revival for the king's pop-up appearance in *Ludwig*. And of course, his Titurel looks like Ludwig II. Somehow, then, the detail has been preserved but relocated to an overlapping beginning of the German Cycle. Also Titurel's casket, or *tumba*, appears in *Ludwig*, replete with King Ludwig's lament and prayer. The *tumba* prayer is transformed to a *rhumba* with Hitler dancing in the nightmare segment. The bier as *tumba* returns when the crowd prays at the king's corpse. A bier reappears in Karl May's death scene. Then, in *Hitler*, American occupation soldiers dance on Wagner's grave. Therefore the flower maidens cannot dance, as it is time for the *tumba* to return. The *tumba* prayer belongs in a mass for the dead. While the crowd's prayer in *Ludwig, Requiem for a Virginal King* distorts the Lord's Prayer, the requiem at Titurel's coffin and the two biers is sufficiently removed from the Church mass to avoid blasphemy. At least that was Wagner's intention. Cosima recorded that "R.[ichard] is pleased that in *Parsifal* he has not depicted the action of the service in the Temple, but has concentrated everything into the blessing of the Grail" (June 17, 1878). Nonetheless, many voices have accused Wagner's ceremony of being a black mass. With the *rhumba* again giving way to the *tumba*, Syberberg's ring is closing. The end joins the beginning of his German Cycle.

In some respects *Parsifal* also marks the closing of a cycle in Wagner's oeuvre. The composer excluded his early operas from being performed on his stage in Bayreuth. Thus *Der fliegende Holländer* became the earliest and oldest work in the "canon." It centers on a cursed man longing for redemption. His redeemer, Senta, reappears as Kundry floating in the water in the film. The opera was first presented in 1843, the same year that saw the performance of "Das Liebesmahl der Apostel" in the Church of Our Lady in Dresden. This composition anticipates many features recurring in *Parsifal*. They include unseen singers in the cupola called "voices from on high," a religious celebration as the commemorative occasion, the perceptible effect of the Holy Ghost descending, and the voice of the Redeemer. The text includes phrases strongly reminiscent of the Eucharistic expressions in *Parsifal*. And already in this early work some singers admonish, "May everyone carry the Redeemer in his heart" (267). The composition was performed in a sanctuary. *Parsifal* transforms an opera house into a sanctuary and even includes references to a redeemer. During his years in Dresden Wagner became familiar with the "Dresden Amen," which characterized the liturgy in the Church of Our Lady. This old bit of melody returns to form the basis of the Grail motif.

As the orchestra weaves the Grail and Faith motifs into an ethereal coda, the embracing Parsifals fade into a tableau of double exposure. They appear superimposed on a wide, footed vessel, a *krater*, behind them. The director alerted the viewer to the significance of double exposure early in act 2, when the image kept fading slowly and repeatedly between Kundry and Klingsor. It exposes a dual nature of the subject, as shown to great effect in *Jew Süß*. With a technique perfected in Nazi films, Syberberg again alludes to German cinema of this era. Of course this also awakens a number of associations related to Wagner and ideology. But more importantly, the double exposure draws attention to the symbol exposing the hidden nature and identity of Parsifal. The tableau coincides with the call of the invisible chorus for the uncovering of the Grail, "Enthüllet den Gral!" And here it stands: the dual Parsifal. A stone from heaven according to Wolfram; development to a Christ-like balanced Self with wisdom and insight, perfection and completeness according to Jung; transmutation to the most precious material according to alchemy; completion of the *tikkun* process in the righteous individual according to the Kabbalah; and attainment of power to heal and redeem according to Wagner.

The variants even find a parallel in the ancient Hermetic text "Isis to Horus." Here the elements implore God to stop the wrongdoing of humankind. God finally declares, "Another shall now come down to dwell among you, an efflux of my being" (Scott, 1:491). The Grail is the most significant, but not the only, object symbol for the subject of this process, as the following images reveal. Nor is the importance of the *krater* exhausted with the dual identity.

Syberberg could have chosen a variety of chalices for the double exposure. Several others have already appeared in the film. But he selected one that is particularly endowed with evocative power. The *krater*, or mixing bowl, figures in ancient Hermetic literature. Wider than deep, this footed vessel apparently inspired Wagner's Grail, to judge from the sketches that Joukowsky prepared for the 1882 production. The Hermetic sources describe how God endowed humans with two gifts besides the body, namely reason (speech, *logos*) and mind (*nous*): "Now speech, my son, God imparted to all men; but mind he did not impart to all. . . . He filled a great basin with mind, and sent it down to earth" (Scott, 1:151). The divine gift apparently inspired Wolfram's text, which differs noticeably from the French versions. He does not mention a Eucharistic chalice associated with the Bible. The Hermetic treatise explains why the *krater* was sent: "Hearken, each human heart; dip yourself in this basin, if you can, recognizing for what purpose you have been made, and believing that you shall ascend to Him who sent the basin down" (Scott, 1:151). This baptism would not so much serve as a rite of purification or ceremony of admission as an act of absorbing, acquiring, or becoming more like, the substance in which one immerses oneself. The content of the basin conveys a coveted boon, as the quoted passage explains. "Now those who gave heed to the proclamation," the treatise reads, "and dipped themselves in the bath of mind, these men got a share of *gnosis*; they received mind, and so became complete men" (Scott, 1:151). This *gnosis* has been bestowed upon the dual Parsifal, and, as Parsifal proclaims, also Amfortas and Kundry have become "complete" or "whole."

The Hermetic texts use a variety of expressions for gaining *gnosis*, such as "arrival at the House of Knowledge" or "knowledge of God." The experience resembles the biblical story of the Holy Spirit descending on the apostles at Pentecost. Wagner had already treated that subject in "Das Liebesmahl der Apostel." Jan van Eyck included it in his *Ghent Altarpiece*, which informs the film. The right panel visible when the altarpiece is closed includes a representation of a stone statue. This grisaille portrays John the Evangelist holding a flaming chalice. Used perhaps also for the Eucharist, it is wider than most goblets. Its contents bestowed special gifts on those present at Pentecost. The shape of this painted vessel creates an associative link to the Hermetic *krater*.

Syberberg is, of course, also familiar with another famous Grail from German cinema. Arnold Fanck included a *krater* in his 1926 silent movie *Der heilige Berg* (*The Sacred Mountain*, a.k.a. *Peaks of Destiny*). Leni Riefenstahl made her debut as a movie actress in it. Actually, Syberberg borrows his Grail from Fanck's plan for the movie. The consulted video version contains several shots that include the vessel, but the particular image used by Syberberg is apparently a sketch for one of Fanck's scenes, not a still from the movie.[19] In black and white, as its original, Syberberg's Grail is oversized, standing on a stepped altar, and is surrounded by stalactites, stalagmites, and complete columns of ice in a cave of ice formations. The place is an ice cathedral. That concept should be familiar to students of the Third Reich era. Hitler's architect Speer could claim his share of glory in the aesthetic designs of mass events. Especially famous were his ice cathedrals of searchlights pointed upwards at night. Michael Zimmerman describes the effect: "On the great parade grounds (thirty square kilometers), surrounded by skyward-trained searchlights forming a 'cathedral of ice,' a million people would be assembled both to witness and to serve as the constituent elements of totalitarian 'art' at its finest."[20] The ice cathedral returns the motif of the Third Reich, winter and coldness from Syberberg's grid of associations. Riefenstahl's role in the ice cathedral segment reinforces the connection. But as with *Karl May* and its elderly actors, the "quotation" does not only evoke Nazi cinema, but also the history of German cinema in general. After all, Fanck's movie predates the Third Reich. Adding to these associations is the function of the *krater* in *Der heilige Berg*. Not only does it appear in the hallucinations of a dying man, it also represents death. The timing suggests that reaching the basin on its pedestal amounts to taking leave from the old way of life, maybe from life itself. The Hermetic texts elicit similar assumptions. To reach the House of Knowledge, one reads there, one must cast off the limitations of the body: "But first you must tear off this garment which you wear, . . . this living death, this conscious corpse, this tomb you carry about with you " (Scott, 1:173). Another example is provided by Zosimos, as summarized by Richard Reitzenstein.[21] Zosimos dreams that he ascends the fifteen steps up to an altar shaped like a giant basin or bowl. It is filled with boiling water and many people. Here, he learns, humans are separated from their bodies and become spirits, *pneumata* (9). The destruction of the body in death does not mean the end, according to Hermetism, but the return to a process of transformation. So while Parsifal I slowly learns to accept his mortality as an individual, one recognizes that the next alchemical step, *nigredo*, is starting. All the other characters in the Grail Hall except the Parsifals are already dead. Whether taken literally or metaphorically, gaining the Grail entails the end of a quest and the beginning of a new stage in a cycle. One cannot help wondering if the tableau with a glimpse of the ice cathedral also serves as a quasi-musical return of the conclusion in *Götterdämmerung*. Liberties of the satyr play may account for the transformation from fire to ice. But since the *krater* in the ice cathedral disappears quickly from view, the following camera takes weaken the impression.

The double exposure focusing on the embracing Parsifals and the Grail changes almost immediately to a view that includes increasingly more of the surroundings. One recognizes, for example, Faith/Synagogue to the left, holding both a chalice and the broken lance draped in black gauze. She looks immobile, resembling the statue that inspired her role. That again evokes Riefenstahl's techniques. She perfected the stone-like effect of subdued colors and sculptured treatment of faces and bodies, resulting in a biographer's term "statues on film."[22] For good measure, Syberberg includes the sculpture of the swan on the right side. While the camera continues to zoom away, the double exposure fades out, as does the Grail motif in the music. A number of objects become visible. The viewer recognizes most of them as symbols appearing repeatedly in the film, such as the open book with the score and Wagner's portrait, the throne, the Parsifal statue, the imperial crown, etc. They are all carriers of themes and motifs found in Wagner's score or Syberberg's narrative. The objects appear in a subtly controlled arrangement. Several of them stand in symmetry or balance to each other, some in groups. For instance, the holy lance stands next to the cross-tipped staff, and the Parsifal statue and/or the polyhedron from *Melencolia I* pairs with the rough ashlar across the room. The latter may actually represent the Omphalos, or Omphallos, of the Apollo temple in Delphi. It replaces the phallic monument from Delos. Similarly the open book showing the score prefigures another book held by Kundry/Herzeleide lying on her bier. Looking like statues on sarcophagi, Kundry and Amfortas become petrified works of art, while the rest of the Grail society is reduced to skeletal remains and scattered clothing. Clearly, the quest for the Grail is a story from the past, and this past is dead. At least sometimes. The viewer remembers the eery effect of Herzeleide's effigy closing the book in her hands in the first prelude. The last detail among so many to catch the viewer's attention is the curtain. White gauze has been draped so as to frame the tableau like a theater curtain. To the last strains of "Redemption for the Redeemer" this arrangement fades into a black screen. Since the embracing Parsifals disappear from view before the petrified scenario fills the screen, one assumes at first that the quester escapes the general demise. But the function of the Grail as *krater*, especially in Fanck's movie, dispels this *Wahn*, as Wagner would have expressed "hope" or "illusion." It is all a matter of knowledge and wisdom about the end. Undoubtedly, this is how many read *Parsifal*. The Kabbalah may not be more encouraging, but shifts the focus to redemption or restoration of a divinely conceived order through human effort. The completion of the task may not promise happy rewards for the redeemer in this life. However, pious and ethical striving is linked to transcendental results. The emphasis lies more on the general purpose than on the individual end. And both the Kabbalah and ancient Hermetism share with other heterodox schools of thought a sense of continuity beyond the individual's demise. Accordingly, the black screen concluding the tableau of petrified elements is not the end.

The orchestra continues, and so does Syberberg's narrative. As the camera again zooms away, the black screen turns out to be a close-up of the eye socket of a human skull. This object was prefigured by the skeletal remains. A similar skull appears close to the end of *Karl May*, when the protagonist pays his respects to Emperor Death a week before he dies physically. The repeated introduction of death echoes *Ludwig*, where the king suffers multiple deaths. To say nothing of *Hitler*, where the dead also have the nasty habit of emerging from their coffin or grave. This time the skull marks the coda of a visual composition. As Emperor Death, it wears an ossified copy of the imperial crown, replete with the orphan stone. It rests or floats on the surface seen in the initial phase of the film with the credits: a murky water or oil with patches of ice and drifting fog. There also the floating photos show a dead world in ruins. The skull can be found in various systems of symbolism thanks to its power of polyvalence. Freemasonry, for example, includes it among its imagery. Connecting it to the biblical Golgotha, Wilmshurst concludes his discussion with the remark, "[T]he cranium or skull is given prominence in the Master Mason's Degree."[23] One may wonder if the film includes a hint to Masonry here. The skull is, of course, the most obvious symbol of death. It also identifies the alchemical stage of *nigredo*. In this phase of transmutation the substance decomposes, and its elements are recombined, resulting in a transformation and new life. The end stage is also a beginning. Known in alchemy as the *os occiput*, the skull encloses the brain, considered the seat or center of the divine part of human nature and therefore close to spiritual transformation. Especially the rounded shape of the skull led alchemists to assign to it the mystical properties of the globe, sphere, and ball. Jung summarizes: "According to tradition the head or brain is the seat of the *anima intellectualis*. For this reason too the alchemical vessel must be round like the head, so that what comes out of the vessel shall be equally "round," i.e. simple and perfect like the *anima mundi*" (*Psych. and Alch.*, 87–88). Jung refers here to an ancient Harranite text and includes an illustration of a skeleton standing on a black sun called *rotundum*. He continues: "The work is crowned by the production of the *rotundum*, which, as the *materia globosa*, stands at the beginning and also at the end, in the form of gold" (88). Jung's interest in alchemical imagery relates to his study of the human psyche. Syberberg resorts to a parallel approach when he begins the plot of *Parsifal* with the sibyl or seer holding a crystal ball. The round skull brings the film to its end and completes the cycle.

The final scene functions as a postlude. The skull fades into another spherical vessel, a crystal globe with the Bayreuth opera house in it. As on the side panels of *The Garden of Delights* when closed, one sees a lit world in the middle of the globe, while the lower half remains dark and invisible. This crystal half sphere was included among the objects in the tableau before the skull appeared, but then resting on a tall foot, making it look like the tree-footed Grail in the first prelude. The effect of the half globe had also been prefigured in the tree in a labyrinth at the beginning of act 2. Syberberg presents, then, Wagner's stage first among the symbols of a dead world. Now it returns in a Grail that is also a vessel of transformation. Furthermore, it marks end and beginning. Only gradually does one realize that the globe is the crystal ball of the prophetess. The wavy material surrounding it is her hair. As Edith Clever slowly raises her head, the hair recedes and unveils all of the Bayreuth theater. As on two occasions before, she looks seriously into the camera lens, probing the reflection for what the future holds in store. When the music ends, she closes her eyes and lowers her head, letting the hair cover up the globe. Her head is the concluding image of the film.

A sibyl is a prophetess, seer, or oracle. According to Cosima Wagner's diaries, her husband was familiar with the sibyls painted by Michelangelo and with the fate of the Sibylline Books (July 15, 1881). He also considered the task of the artist close to that of a prophet, both in the sense of seeing the future and of communicating a needed change to others, as did the prophets of the Hebrew Bible. He calls such a man with a mission an "artistic poet" and a "poet priest." He admonished his readers, "[L]et ourselves be gently led to reconcilement with this mortal life by the artistic teller of the great World-tragedy. This poet priest, the only one who never lied, was ever sent to humankind at epochs of its direst errors, as mediating friend."[24] Syberberg depicts him in this role in the first prelude as a puppet piercing an ear. He is impatiently trying to get the public to pay attention to his message. Prophesy also plays an important role in *Parsifal*. True to Wagner's gradually increasing preoccupation with the feminine in human nature, Syberberg chose a prophetess for the introductory and the concluding images. She happens to share the face with Parsifal's mother, Kundry, the temptress, and the penitent. She is (or should be) easily recognizable as the Anima and prominent archetype. As such she predates and succeeds the story about any individual.

Syberberg was probably inspired to this positioning of the sibyl by Jan van Eyck's *Ghent Altarpiece*. When closed, the polyptych displays on the uppermost sections paintings of two prophets and two sibyls. These four predicted the coming of a savior. Considering the Christ-like mission of Parsifal, the parallel becomes visible. Syberberg has created a cinematic altarpiece, and his sibyl figures on the outer side of the side panels. Also belonging to the external sides are the first camera takes with credits before the beginning of the first prelude, as well as the skull at the end. But for what sanctuary did the director create this work? One may assume for a cathedral built of living stones, or rather, for a temple of the heart. That would be more in line with the emphasis on the "inner God." Although the film has been shown to mass audiences, Syberberg appears to have translated the work for the only suitable stage, the privacy of home viewing. The film calls for repeated viewings and contemplation.

Chapter 10

Epilogue to *Parsifal*

This discussion of *Parsifal* has so far differed from other printed studies of movies and operas. The selected approach became necessary for several reasons. First of all, the subject has inspired a wealth of variants, culminating with Wagner's version of it. Many of the critical examinations, especially of Wagner's *Parsifal*, have arrived at drastically different conclusions. Twentieth century politics and criticism have further burdened his music drama with a cloak of ideology. Since Syberberg preserves every word and note of the work, his film must bear the same scrutiny as any stage production of *Parsifal*. Especially those features viewed by many as proto-Nazi call for alertness. Besides, Syberberg's oeuvre invites misunderstanding and noncomprehension. The counterpoint produces ambiguities, encouraging even painful misconceptions by critics and the public. To that comes his reputation of being difficult, uncompromising, provocative, untimely (*unzeitgemäß*), and always demonstratively politically incorrect. Syberberg and his work require a different approach. Already in the *Filmbuch* he discussed the importance of musical concepts for his aesthetics. This preoccupation reached its culmination in *Parsifal*. But Syberberg also draws inspiration from other sources not identified in his publications. In view of the surrealistic setting and surprising details of the film, any viewer would need to see his *Parsifal* repeatedly, preferably in short segments, to gradually comprehend the film. This need for elucidation dictated the choice of a partially descriptive approach similar to the *explication de texte*. Even with such a detailed commentary, many facets remain to be explored. The Parzival/Parsifal story has been enigmatic from the beginning. Syberberg adds his interpretation, superimposing it on Wagner's work while trying to uncover some of its secrets.

The director began his German Cycle with *Ludwig*, calling it a requiem. He ended the cycle with *Parsifal*, which also includes a requiem of sorts. The third act concludes with a ritual blessing of the mortal parts of human nature and celebrating the immortal components. Just before that Amfortas pleads with his dead father to intercede for him, allowing him to be released from misery. The idea of intercession is strengthened by the visual references to van Eyck's altarpiece and the statue of Uta. Both of these artworks were donated for the same purpose: intercession through mass and prayers. Did Wagner have the same intention with his last work? If so, that might turn the audience into a congregation of participants. With Wagner's presence palpable throughout the film, one is at least inclined to attribute that intention to the cinematic version. But as already mentioned, the film may even possess an additional dimension. It is itself an altarpiece.

In spite of the commonly held view that *Parsifal* is a vehicle for Wagner's proto-Nazi *Weltanschauung*, many have interpreted it as an expression of the composer's return to Christianity. Nietzsche was an early and passionate disseminator of that view. But his hate-love relationship with Wagner resulted in the most conflicting statements. For example in *Der Fall Wagner* he describes the composer as "the man who is by far the most related to me" (621) and as a "righteous atheist and immoralist" (423). Condemning Wagner's presumed relapse into Christianity, he warns his readers," For what you hear [in *Parsifal*] is Rome—Rome's faith without words!" (232). Reminiscing about his conversations with Wagner, he sees only an "intellectual lack of character" in the composer's reverence for the Eucharist (417, 425). He dismisses the "old magician, this Klingsor of all Klingsors" (122), claiming that the composer ended by solving "all problems in the name of the Father, the Son, and the Holy Master" (123). Playing on the concluding words in *Parsifal*, he asks, "[W]ho redeems us from this redeemer?" (454). Nietzsche presents *Parsifal*, then, as being, or pretending to be, a Christian work. But he also knew Wagner's enthusiasm for the ancient Greek theater and the spiritual function of drama in the pagan festivals. In the same collection of statements about Wagner, Nietzsche wonders if the composer was serious about *Parsifal*; was it perhaps rather a conclusion and satyr play? (141)? If so, one might assume a different intention behind the pious façade. The question insinuates duplicity in the author and an unrecognized dimension in his last work. Syberberg accepted, or at least "quoted," Nietzsche's remark in the film. This appears most conspicuously in the third act when the Grail society gathers for the ceremony. Some of the members wear masks that transform them into corpses and satyrs. But many other details fit the characteristics of the satyr play, some of them even for Wagner's stage version. Usually the fourth play following a trilogy, the ancient Greek satyr play rounded off the sequence.[1] But if one enlarges the trilogy to a tetralogy, one could view both the *Meistersinger* and *Parsifal* as satyr plays added to a sequence of four plays. The stock characters include a villain who controls the satyrs (Beckmesser among the *Meistersinger*, Klingsor in his world and as a threat to the Grail community). The leader of the satyrs is Silenos (Hans Sachs, Amfortas). The villain is overcome and the satyrs liberated by a hero (Walther von Stolzing, Parsifal). Sexuality is a noticeable theme (toned down in *Meistersinger*, retained in *Parsifal*). The satyrs love to dance (apprentices, St. John's Day festivities; flower maidens, at least according to the libretto, moving knights). Spook and theft, especially of weapons, are common themes (mischief during midsummer night, theft of contest song; fighting, theft of holy lance). Other typical features of satyr plays recur in *Parsifal*, such as transformation (metempsychosis; swan and lance in the film), love of food and wine (Eucharist-like Grail ceremony), and appearance of deities (luminosity of Grail, light from above, Grail Carrier). Although mostly identical to tragedy in form, the satyr play always has a happy ending. Most Wagnerians would agree that also that criterion applies to the *Meistersinger* and *Parsifal*, at least in Bayreuth, since the protagonists achieve what they yearn for.

With Parsifal finding back to the Grail and redeeming Amfortas and Kundry, the hero has fulfilled the prophesy and achieved the highest level of personal attainment. The luminous Grail from heaven corresponds to the magic ring of the Nibelungen treasure. The man who Wotan hoped would relieve the curse and set things straight again failed to achieve the goal. But Siegfried was reborn as Parsifal, who succeeded. Brünnhilde's counterpart is Kundry, the regal Anima who loves but also tries to destroy the hero. The fiery cataclysm of *Götterdämmerung* finds its contrasting counterpart in a display of divine mercy at the end of *Parsifal*, at least in the stage versions. Syberberg counters the fire with ice, but retains the theme of end and demise, *Untergang*.

Wagner's admiration for Aeschylus and Greek theater nourished his vision of Bayreuth as a special center. It also informed his work. In his book *Wagner and Aeschylus,* Michael Ewans agrees with Nietzsche and points out a number of characteristics qualifying *Parsifal* as a satyr play to the *Ring*, inspired by the *Oresteia*.[2] He includes several of Cosima's diary entries suggesting that Wagner might have harbored such an idea (Feb. 19, 1878; Aug. 8, 1878; April 29, 1879; Sept. 8, 1881). It is also fitting that Syberberg incorporates a few "satyric" features in the film. Early on he had selected a quotation about Sisyphos as the motto for his dissertation. Sisyphos was one of the most popular characters of the Greek satyr plays.[3] Viewed within the German Cycle, *Parsifal* can be seen to function as a satyr play in two distinct settings. First, *Parsifal* functions as a satyr play to the trilogy. Thematically and visually, it borrows features from all three films. But one can also draw a parallel between Wagner's *Parsifal* following the *Nibelungen Ring* and Syberberg's *Parsifal* following the seven-hour *Hitler*. Divided into four parts, it is also a tetralogy. Actually, this is how Syberberg apparently wants the public to consider his *Parsifal*. Without being specific, he points out in the book to the film that the word *Grail* appears prominently both at the beginning and at the end of *Hitler* (34). It is true that especially the fourth part prefigures elements in *Parsifal*, e.g. Harry Baer in his Amfortas wrap and the enigmatic girl in the teardrop globe. Even a Wagner is present in the guise of André Heller. Still, Syberberg's German Trilogy provides a more easily recognizable foil for his satyr play.

Perhaps viewing the concepts *satyric* and *satiric* as interchangeable, Syberberg seems to use Wagner's death mask to treat the composer as irreverently as a satyr would.[4] Cosima recorded on June 21, 1881 that Wagner had such masks of Beethoven and Weber in his home. He disliked them so acutely that she removed them on that day. He compared them to "playing games with the crucifix." Not only does the director reintroduce a death mask. It was even made of the composer himself. Furthermore, the film does create a link between Wagner's features and a crucifix through the crucified Wagner doll. Neither satyric nor satiric, however, is the main function of the death mask in the film. It reminds the viewers that the originator, or creator, of this story is dead. What the viewers witness is a recreation, or translation, of his original. Although score and libretto guarantee fidelity to the original, the visual treatment amounts to more than an interpretation. As a new creation displaying ever so obliquely its insights, it pushes back the limits of established interpretation. In this respect Syberberg's work transgresses the limits of convention and language of translation. He both revives and goes beyond the function of the ancient satyr play.

The Greek drama inspiring Wagner's and Syberberg's works dates from pagan times. Almost as old are the Hermetic scriptures that inform the Grail texts. Syberberg gives them the most conspicuous homage in the final presentation of the Grail as a *krater* and through the *organon*. The latter appears in several variants throughout the film: first as the carrousel-like structure in the first prelude, then repeatedly as the *Gestell* and watchtower behind Klingsor, and finally as the heart/violin, fan, and fountain motor in act 3. Most of the extant Hermetic literature hails from the syncretistic age of Hellenism. It entered the underground movements of religious and philosophic thought later, mingled with Gnosticism and heretical Christian movements, e.g. Catharism and Manichaeism, only to surface occasionally to inspire Christian mysticism during the Middle Ages. Not until the Renaissance did the attempt begin to reconcile Hermetism with Christianity. As mentioned before, Wagner knew this literature. Always siding with the rebels, he must have been attracted by its condemnation as heresy or paganism.

Wagner was a voracious reader. One impetus for studying the Hermetic texts may have been his preoccupation with Freemasonry. The information about his association with the fraternity is sketchy, since the Nazis confiscated the library and destroyed the archives of the lodge in Bayreuth.[5] Actually, Bayreuth was home to both the grand lodge "Zur Sonne" and the lodge "Eleusis zur Verschwiegenheit" (Eleusis to Confidentiality), one of thirteen St. John lodges under the leadership of the grand lodge in Wagner's days. The grand master of the grand lodge, Friedrich Feustel, was instrumental in persuading Wagner to settle in Bayreuth. He was a banker and prominent citizen who later served in the Bavarian legislature and then in parliament in Berlin. This admirer, friend, and pillar of society was in a unique position to promote Wagner's plans for a festival theater. At least one memoir documents Wagner's regular contacts, visits, and discussion sessions with Freemasons.[6] Obviously, Wagner would have had to familiarize himself with the legacy of Western literature, philosophy, and comparative religious studies for admission to a lodge. But he was no neophyte in such readings. Already his choice of Senta as a name in *Der fliegende Holländer* reveals familiarity with metaphysical literature, possibly also with Masonic studies. Paul Nettl mentions that Liszt introduced Wagner to Masonry in 1841 and then adds: "But Wagner's interest was aroused even more by his brother-in-law, the husband of his sister Rosalie, Dr. Oswald Marbach, member of the Leipzig lodge 'Balduin zur Linde' and editor of a Masonic periodical, *Am Reissbrett*" (128). Although it still remains unclear when Wagner took up his Masonic studies systematically, they inform *Parsifal* unmistakably. Nettl only comments that some Masonic terms and ideas appear in *Parsifal*, for example the expression "high noon" and the responsorial organization of the Grail scene (128). Another component is the initiatory function of the seduction scene, especially the interplay of the spousal and filial roles expected of Parsifal. Nettl observes that also an initiation belongs to typically Masonic features of some operas: "The final secret of the Craft is symbolized by the Hebrew password, *Makbenak* (he lives within the son). It represents the principle of resurrection and regeneration, symbolized by the initiation which in its most lofty form is shown in the *Magic Flute*" (80). Also important is the quest of the hero. This "widow's son" personifies the intellectual principle or Logos, W. L. Wilmshurst explains. He characterizes it as "[t]he Christ-principle immanent in every soul; crucified, dead and buried in all who are not alive to its presence, but resident in all as a saving force" (199). This clearly corresponds to Parsifal's gradual awakening from fool to wise guardian of the Grail in Christ-like imagery. The film also adds a few visual Masonic touches not called for in the libretto. Apparently the director recognized and preserved this dimension of the work. But, did Wagner ever really join Freemasonry? Nettl reports that "Wagner intended to join, but was prevented by considerations of private matters, such as his relationship to Hans von Bülow and a disinclination to offend Bavarian Catholic circles" (128). Both reasons may have concerned Wagner, especially since he and his festival idea still depended on the king's patronage. The king's mental instability made his position increasingly precarious. The Catholic, "ultra-montan" party dominated Bavarian politics. Wagner's conduct had already caused his exile from Bavaria once. He could not afford a second confrontation with authorities. And Freemasonry was rejected by the Catholic Church. Throughout the nineteenth century the Vatican condemned Freemasonry repeatedly in bulls and edicts. For example in 1864 Pope Pius IX referred to the fraternity as the "Synagogue of Satan" (Beyer, 2:167). One wonders if this use of the word *synagogue* informs the character of that name in the film. Wagner's conduct may, however, also have complicated his admission to the lodge. His past private life and public statements could offer ample reason for rejection. Admission was decided by secret balloting in the lodge. So even if Wagner should have been a member elsewhere in his younger days, admission to the lodge in Bayreuth was a local decision. The guidelines of the grand lodge "Zur Sonne" of 1901, for example, require that members must have a good reputation (Beyer, 3:16). Beyer also emphasizes on the same page that all lodges under the grand lodge must practice religious tolerance. Not knowing if these guidelines were in effect when Wagner "intended to join," one can only surmise that he might have been rejected for several reasons. His anti-Semitic diatribes in the *Bayreuther Blätter* during the genesis of the *Parsifal* score were a matter of record. And his attempts at meddling into the king's political actions as well as his very belated marital respectability should have run counter to the principles of the fraternity. He may also have foreseen the obstacles and declared his change of heart to avoid the embarrassment of rejection. Regardless whether Wagner really was accepted into Freemasonry at some point in his life or not, the declaration of not joining may also have been a subterfuge. It is possible he did not want *Parsifal* to be known as a Masonic celebration on stage. Syberberg's film weaves in a number of Masonic hints that in any case point to the impact of Masonic studies on the composer.

It is difficult to reconcile Wagner's intolerance with the ideals of Freemasonry. But during his Masonic studies, possibly early in life, he became acquainted with

Jewish mysticism and related religious legacies, especially Gnosticism, ancient Hermetism and post-Renaissance hermeticism. These systems of thought and faith influenced each other. Therefore Wagner may also have drawn much of what looks like Kabbalistic elements in *Parsifal* from non-Jewish sources. To judge from Cosima's diaries, her husband's anti-Semitism amounted to an obsession. Inconsistencies abounded, however, e.g. in his infatuation with Judith Gautier. Nor did his dreams of "regeneration" for (Gentile) Germany last throughout the composition of *Parsifal*. According to the diaries he stated for example on December 17, 1878, "We do not hope, but we should like to;" on December 27 of the same year, "Germany is finished," and on December 17, 1881 that "the races have had it." On December 14, 1881, he emphasized that *Parsifal* was his most conciliatory work. Who might be the intended target of reconciliation? Most critics assume he aimed at the Catholic Church. The Church may have seemed an obstacle in those years, perhaps as a threat to the success of *Parsifal* and the future of the Bayreuth Festival. This concern may relate to the composer's repeated remarks that he really did not want to present *Parsifal* on a stage (e.g. October 13 and 24, 1878). And then there is Cosima's much quoted entry of January 5, 1881 about Wagner and *Parsifal*: "He then hints at, rather than expresses, the content of this work, 'salvation to the savior'—and we are silent after he has added, 'Good that we are alone.'" Why the sudden discretion in Cosima's diary? She otherwise recorded every diatribe, be it ever so offensive. Apparently Wagner's true intention with the work was too sensitive to be divulged even to his wife's (= their) diary. This precludes an anti-Semitic statement. If he had attributed an anti-Semitic dimension to *Parsifal*, he would certainly have felt free to mention it to his wife, who shared his bias.[7] Two other, related possibilities come to mind. First, Wagner's association and friendships with Freemasons in Bayreuth continued unabated from the time he moved there. The most prominent among them, Friedrich Feustel, was a frequent guest in the Wagner household. He even served as a pallbearer at the composer's funeral. If Wagner's admission to the lodge in Bayreuth was supposed to be kept secret, then he could, of course, not allow it to be included in Cosima's diary. She also treated his participation in a weekly discussion group discreetly (Beyer, 2:143). The Masonic dimension of *Parsifal* might point to Wagner's homage to Masonry, or even have served as a test or documentation qualifying him for acceptance, possibly even for advancement within the fraternity. Or it may merely express the impact of Masonic studies, which would have included the Kabbalah.

The other possibility is that Wagner's obsession with Judaism led him to study the Kabbalah at his own initiative. It would not have escaped the sympathizer of heretics and rebels that much in the Kabbalah runs counter to rabbinical Judaism. Some of its branches were even condemned as sectarian and heretical. When one also considers the Neoplatonic, Gnostic, and Hermetic elements informing it, the Kabbalah should have appealed to Wagner as a source of inspiration. To understand what he appropriated from it, it becomes necessary to recapitulate briefly a few Kabbalistic tenets. Unless explained in the notes, the information is drawn mainly from chapter 3, "Basic Ideas," of Scholem's *Kabbalah*.

A central concept is the Sefirotic Tree. As an image or paradigm it refers variously to creation by emanation, aspects of the Godhead, or process of manifestation. Like a flash of lightning the symbol zigzags from a point in the distant heavens "down" to earth. In its original or anthropomorphic form it is also known as Adam Kadmon. The zigzag pattern consists of ten points (vessels or *sefirot*). They are connected by 22 lines or paths named after the letter-numbers of the Hebrew alphabet. With the lines drawn, the paradigm is also known as the Labyrinth, and in an extended form, as the Jacob's Ladder. The line reaching from the tip to the bottom is the central pillar. It runs through and connects four *sefirot* (Keter, Tiferet, Yesod, Malkhut). Three *sefirot* on the left side and three on the right side form the left and the right pillars. As a process, this symbol begins with the unrevealed, transcendent Godhead and "ends" with manifestation as created matter. The point of origin is known as Ein-Sof (Infinite). Kabbalists often refer to this unknowable and therefore undefinable concept as "No-Thing" (*Ayin*) or "Nothingness." It remains totally immaterial and in concealment.

Did Wagner pattern his oeuvre for the stage on the Sefirotic Tree? That would suggest that he was familiar with this symbol quite early. The first indication of such a possibility is the decision to limit his works to be performed in Bayreuth to ten. Ten is a significant biblical and Kabbalistic number. But at the same time the selection helps obliterate the traces of his potential source of inspiration. Wagner wanted to include only the music dramas beginning with *Der fliegende Holländer* and ending with *Parsifal*. His early works and the first operatic success, *Rienzi*, were excluded. One might at first assume that the canon of ten comprises the ten *sefirot*. But *Rienzi* is really the first in the sequence. In true Hermetic (and hermetic) fashion the composer selected a title to serve his purpose: Embedded in *Rienzi* one finds a French word, *rien*. It means "nothing." When treated as analogous with the first *sefira* (Keter as Ein-Sof, "No-Thing") in a process of emanation, this work should not materialize on even the creator's own stage.[8] Consequently, it should be, and was, suppressed. But according to this counting, *Götterdämmerung* is the tenth work. Like *Rienzi*, it too ends with a fiery cataclysm. The three music dramas placed in the right column (*Der fliegende Holländer, Lohengrin, Rheingold)* share water as a characteristic. On the left side one finds *Tannhäuser, Tristan und Isolde,* and *Die Walküre.* Their shared fiery element materializes gradually from passion to an unmistakably manifest wall of fire surrounding the sleeping Brünnhilde. In the middle column, the *Meistersinger* fills the place of Tiferet. To its "correspondences" count the suffering son, the sun, and Leo among the Zodiac signs. The protagonist is Hans Sachs, who as his name reveals, hails from Saxony. And so did Wagner. This middle-aged widower sacrifices his romantic inclination to let the young lovers marry each other. The plot unfolds at St. John's Feast, which coincides with the summer solstice under the sign of Leo. Further "down" on the central pillar stands *Siegfried* in the place of Yesod. When the Sefirotic Tree is viewed anthropomorphically as Adam Kadmon or Primordial Man, Yesod is the location of the genitals. Wagner observed this dimension in the exuberant love aria between Brünnhilde and Siegfried before their union as the curtain falls.

Götterdämmerung takes the place of Malkhut, also referred to as the Shekhinah, Binah in exile, or the Divine Daughter. Brünnhilde is the divine daughter condemned to exile. Since Siegfried failed in his mission, it is only through Brünnhilde's action that the Nibelungen ring is returned to its guardians. This event enables the symbolic action to continue in a separate drama centered on Parsifal.

The need for continued action stems from an unexpected development that gave rise to evil. Kabbalistic variants of the biblical fall of Adam and Eve include the exile of Binah as the heavenly queen, and the breaking of the vessels. The three topmost *sefirot*, or vessels, remained intact, and the tenth, Malkhut, cracked, but kept its shape. But the remaining six shattered as the divine light or efflux flowed into them. Their shards nourished the dark forces, and much of the divine light fell with the shards and became mingled with gross matter in the world of the *kelippot*. As Scholem explains, "The entire world process as we know it, therefore, is at variance with its originally intended order and position. Nothing, neither the lights nor the vessels, remained in its proper place, and this development . . . was nothing less than a cosmic catastrophe" (*Kabbalah*, 138–39). One can easily recognize the exiled or fallen feminine aspect of divinity in Brünnhilde, likewise the particles of divine light in the treasure mined and forged by the Nibelungs. The six broken vessels must be restored for the process to continue, so that the scattered sparks of divine efflux can continue their course. The restoration process is called *tikkun*. It is the subject of *Parsifal*.

Whereas the imagery of emanation comprises ten *sefirot*, it changes to a system of five *parzufim* in the restoration process. The four intact *sefirot* or vessels function under different names and now represent a new stage in the process of catharsis and reconstruction. Of special importance is one *parzuf*, Ze'eir Anpin, which is reshaped from the six shattered vessels. Thus the original ten vessels still participate in the dynamics, but they are reconfigured so that the fifth one becomes the center of the cathartic processes. This protagonist corresponds to Parsifal. Even the hero's name points to this role. Wolfram von Eschenbach had spelled it Parzival with the *v* being pronounced as an *f*. Each of the five structures in the restoration process is a *parzuf*, meaning "face" or "countenance." The similarity between *parzuf* and the hero's name can be no coincidence, especially when considering the meaning attributed to it in Wolfram's narrative. Wolfram did not translate it simply as "face." That would have made his source of inspiration too transparent and dangerous. After all, he lived in an age of crusades and ruthless persecution of non-Christians and heretics such as the Cathars. Parzival is told that his name means "right through the middle," or "rehte enmitten durch." But that approximates the translation of *tikkun*, the restoration process. Brown's dictionary spells the word with *tau*, *yod*, *kaph*, and *nun* and gives the meaning as "middle." The use of *tikkun* for the restoration process probably refers to the development taking place along the central or middle column of the sefirotic symbol. It emerges also in the film's motifs of the Irminsul, phallus, pillar of the universe, tree, and the upright person supporting the celestial mantle. Wagner's death mask, which is another *parzuf* or *persona*, provides the setting and helps identify the action as *tikkun* in a *mise en abyme*. His death mask evokes the Kabbalistic Adam Kadmon of the restoration process. During that stage Adam Kadmon is the name of the totality of the five *parzufim* (*Kabbalah*, 142). The film underscores the importance of the numeral five for the *tikkun* in the first prelude. Here it presents five human actors and five variants of the Wagner doll. Surrounding the five Wagner miniatures are five recurring object symbols: Grail, crown of thorns, crucifix, pillory, and the polyhedron from *Melencolia I*. Like the broken *sefirot*, so also Wagner's death mask is fractured into segments when functioning as the setting for the action. However, also syncretist ideas pointing to Masonry enter the picture. Not only do the fourteen fragments of the mask landscape remind one of the parts of the dead Osiris' body, but this number recurs also in the puppet play: seven puppets of human characters, five object symbols (Grail, spear, wound, bow, arrow), plus two birds (swan, dove).

When attempting to equate Wagner's characters with the damaged *sefirot* that undergo the redemption process in Ze'eir Anpin, or Parsifal, one could take a hint from van Eyck's *Ghent Altarpiece*. It displays Kabbalistic dimensions. The artist presents several *sefirot* as groups. Both sides of the main panel contain many individuals in tightly packed formations. Therefore, in spite of their large numbers, the groups function as units. Wagner's libretto treats the flower maidens and the Grail knights similarly. As extensions of Kundry and Klingsor, the flower maidens are still present as flowers and in the dialogue of act 3. Referring to the *Wunderblumen*, Parsifal wonders, "I saw them wilt who once laughed at me; do they languish for redemption today?" And as Gurnemanz explains, all parts of creation, including plants, share in the miracle of renewed innocence of Good Friday. With Parsifal assuming a Christ- or Messiah-like role of redeemer, both the groups held captive by Klingsor's magic and those surrounding Amfortas are included as units in the *tikkun* process.

Parsifal is easy to identify as the active component of the restoration. Amfortas and Gurnemanz also fit the design. But what about Titurel? He died before the beginning of act 3. But he appears visibly as a doll in the penitent's bundle. He is also physically present in the coffin and the text. And significantly, Wagner had planned his revival as part of the miracle during the Grail ceremony. That suffices to identify Titurel as one of the fragments or parts of the Ze'eir Anpin.

Regardless whether one insists on ascribing the Kabbalistic influence only to Wolfram's text or to Syberberg's cinematic presentation of the work, Wagner himself has nonetheless added some elements not found in the medieval romances. For example, he lets Gurnemanz assert that grass and flowers are aware that they are not trampled to death by human feet on this particular day [= Good Friday]. The activity of crushing tender vegetation underfoot belongs to Kabbalistic variants of the biblical fall. Scholem lists several examples, including the trampling of young plants in paradise.[9] Faithful to the Kabbalistic pattern, Wagner endows Parsifal with all the qualities of the active Ze'eir Anpin composed of the six broken vessels. That leaves one major character, Kundry. Since she shares her face and knowledge with Herzeleide, she might also be that queen's manifestation in exile. She portrays the role of Binah, who later functions as the *parzuf* Imma. In Wolfram's version, she moves with her son from the court to a remote location that resembles exile. As noted earlier, the consequence of the breaking of the vessels is a displacement of Binah and all lower elements in the symbolic structure. Nothing remains in its proper place (*Kabbalah*, 138). So even if Binah (Herzeleide) remains intact, she is thrown into "exile." This condition lasts until the restoration process has been completed successfully. Until then she suffers banishment from her heavenly abode. Richard Wagner presents her in that predicament as Kundry. The Grail Carrier/Synagogue parallels her daughter, known as the *sefira* Malkhut, the lower Shekhinah, or heavenly daughter. Her other aspect in the *tikkun* process is the female Parsifal. All of these feminized symbols share the same letter *he* in the four-letter Holy Name. The hidden identities of these aspects of the Divine help present them as closely related. Wagner retains vestiges of Kundry's exalted status. Only through her mysterious knowledge is Parsifal repeatedly reminded of his mother. As a princess of the Grail dynasty and Amfortas' sister, Herzeleide became a queen through marriage, according to Wolfram. Only Kundry knows her history and feelings. And as a maternal force Kundry empowers Parsifal to prevail. Both the music and the words confirm that Herzeleide, Kundry, and the temptress are manifestations of the same figure. Her confession in the temptation scene indicates that she became vulnerable to evil powers a long time ago. The liberation and return of this *sefira/parzuf* depends on human action, or symbolically, on the actions of Ze'eir Anpin, who now is called Parsifal I. The struggle and conclusion of the *tikkun* process have, so Scholem explains, been reserved for man: "These are the ultimate aim of creation, and the completion of *tikkun*, which is synonymous with redemption, depends on man's performing them" (*Kabbalah*, 142). Wagner's redeemer completes the task. He even brings Kundry to the Grail ceremony.

Maybe the composer decided he had followed the Kabbalistic blueprint too closely. At the end of act 3, just before the curtain falls, he introduced two obfuscating details in the stage instructions. They do not affect the music or the dialogue, but veil the Kabbalistic dimension. First, he suppressed Titurel's resurrection, which had been included in the 1877 edition of the libretto as drama. From a Kabbalistic perspective, Titurel would be a *zaddik*, a righteous man of utmost piety. Lawrence Fine quotes the early Kabbalist Hayyim Vital on how it is possible for an adept to commune with the soul of a departed *zaddik*.[10] The contemplative efforts "activate" the bones of the dead person "so as to revive him temporarily, as if he were actually alive" (80). Fine explains that the objective of the activity is the ascent of the supplicant's soul with that of the *zaddik* to higher realms. That describes rather closely Amfortas' situation and prayer to his father. Titurel's revival confirms Wagner's familiarity with Kabbalistic literature and his intention to let Amfortas die as he pleads for. As already noted, Syberberg relocates a reminder of this detail to the end of *Ludwig*. He also varies it in act 1 by letting Titurel sit in his grave chamber during the ritual before returning to "sleep" again. Then, in the libretto, Kundry slowly collapses and dies while Parsifal holds up the Grail. Especially Kundry's death has nourished the prevailing view of *Parsifal* as being an expression of anti-Semitism: Not only could she as a woman not survive the male atmosphere of the Grail society; she was also "Jewish" and therefore did not belong there. What these interpreters fail to ask is: Why does Parsifal bring Kundry to the Grail Castle?

Syberberg's film answers that question and many others by often ignoring the stage instructions, by translating musical leitmotifs into visual equivalents, and by accentuating or adding Kabbalistic hints. Of course the director also retains Wagner's libretto and includes psychological and alchemical imagery wherever possible. His "production" amounts to both a reinterpretation and unmasking. By far the most complex component of the Kabbalistic pattern is Kundry. The apparent contradiction of having her appear both as the supernal mother and as her exiled manifestation vulnerable to evil conforms to Kabbalistic symbolism. Thus Scholem can refer to the third *sefira* as a feminine element within God, a demiurgic upper mother and upper Shekhinah, and to the tenth *sefira* as the lower Shekhinah and dwelling place of the soul (*On the Kabbalah*, 115). Actually, all the *parzufim* of the *tikkun* process contain within them secondary aspects. Louis Jacobs, for example, reports: "There are two aspects of the *Shekhinah* in Lurianic thought, two *parzufim* (each of the five *parzufim* is further divided into two, making a total of ten) known as *Rahel* and *Leah*."[11] Therefore the "younger" Shekhina can adopt different manifestations when she emerges as Grail Carrier, Synagogue, Voice from on high, and as Parsifal's feminine counterpart later. As the Ecclesia of Israel, the Grail Carrier both emits and reflects divine light. The Nukba de Ze'eir (Parsifal II) only reveals reflected light in her glittering eyes. Syberberg does not use Scholem's term "Ecclesia of Israel," but varies it as "Synagogue" and "Church." Scholem explains elsewhere how the hypostasis of the Synagogue or *Kenesseth Jisrael* was adopted and transformed by the early Church fathers into the personified Church (*Von der mystischen Gestalt*, 141). The young woman who emerges apparently from nowhere in the temptation scene is her other aspect who actively helps Parsifal I/Yesod. Only one interpreter of the film appears to have recognized that Parsifal II represents also an "other" side of Kundry, however without resorting to the Kabbalistic frame of reference. Marie-Bernadette Fantin-Epstein notes: "Nonetheless the choice of an actress instead of an actor to assume the development of the role is ambiguous. Isn't it rather an image of the young Kundry, the one before the fall, who appears there as a reflection before the other? Double of Parsifal or double of Kundry?"[12] Without mentioning it, Fantin-Epstein may be taking her cue from the moment when Kundry's and Parsifal II's faces appear as a double profile. The constellation might justify the assumption that these two characters represent two aspects of the same *parzuf*. Perhaps that was the director's intention., but more likely is the mother-daughter constellation. That view lets the two maternal manifestations, Herzeleide as queen in heaven and Kundry as queen in exile, share Clever's face. The tenth *sefira* is represented by the two younger ones, the Grail Carrier who comes from the Juno Temple and Parsifal's alter ego who confronts the temptress. Regardless how one aligns them, they represent Kabbalistic forces and ideas derived from the same two identical letters in the Ineffable Name. They should, then, represent strongly related concepts and at least partially identical qualities. Jungians will, of course, recognize that Kundry, as the (upper) Shekhinah in exile, also possesses another aspect. The anima can appear in a younger version as the daughter or Kore. This virginal figure is indeed the Nukba de Ze'eir. In this manifestation she becomes an active helper in the restoration process.

Nukba de Ze'eir (Parsifal II) is, as Scholem explains, "'the female of Ze'eir,' and represents the latter's complementary feminine aspect" (*Kabbalah*, 141). The male Parsifal, imitating the active component of Ze'eir Anpin, is comprised of the six broken vessels. The actor's name, Kutter, even means "vessel." In accordance with the Kabbalistic frame of reference he had to experience a maturation process before the restorative work can begin. He had been united with his feminine half in the first prelude, as the two huddled together in embryonic form. The mission is only completed when the two are reunited at the end of act 3. A reminder of the progressing work occurs in the Good Friday scene when the octagonal fountain comes into view. The sound of the water from the dragon mouths can barely be heard. It does not intrude to disturb the music (The sound has been relocated to the nightmare scene in *Ludwig*). In the consulted video version one cannot hear the water. A Kabbalist would compare the jets in the fountain with the "female waters" of the Nukba de Ze'eir, since the water rises through the column to circulate. For a harmonious union both "male" and "female" waters should flow (Fine, 69). These "male" waters should come from the male Parsifal, as the equivalent of Ze'eir Anpin. Although absent in person, he appears symbolically in the statue of St. Michael on top of the pillar of the fountain. This namesake of Michael Kutter holds two amphoras in his hands. Significantly, no water flows out of them. That is, not until after the kiss. The renewed flow suggests that the Yesod aspect of Parsifal has been restored. However, not until their embrace at the end of the film is the reunion of the two Parsifals consummated in the Kabbalistic sense. That concludes the *tikkun* process.

At this time one can recognize two other dimensions of the name of the Parsifal I actor. *Michael* means "like unto God." Parsifal develops into a redeemer with Christ-like qualities. His parallel Kabbalistic mission assumes messianic proportions. As the agent of redemption he fulfills the prophesy and becomes the symbol of a Messiah of sorts who restores wholeness and harmony and the return from exile. This restoration applies to all things and characters in exile, but most conspicuously to the return of Kundry and the lance and the healing of Amfortas. The other connection between the actor's name and that of the archangel also leads back to Jewish sources. Richard Reitzenstein notes in *Poimandres* that, " in the Talmud Michael, created first of all angels, frequently appears as [the] angel of snow, Gabriel as [the] angel of fire. . . . Michael is then probably [the] angel of winter" (280n). The comment identifies an additional source of inspiration for the director's fondness for snow. He rarely misses an opportunity to surround Michael Kutter with snow. Already Wolfram did that with Parzival. Syberberg had, of course, introduced the nexus coldness–Nazi mentality in the *Filmbuch*. Thanks to his consistent use of counterpoint that link recurs with variations in his books and films. Now one discovers its contrapuntal "contrasting" variant: the archangel Michael as angel of winter in Jewish scriptures. Both variations inform Parsifal I. Syberberg uses the actor's name as a connecting link in his semantic *Sprachgitter*.

Another attribute or association linking the male Parsifal with Yesod is the column of the universe. Scholem quotes from mystical sources that equate the righteous individual with such a pillar: "'A column ascends from earth to heaven, and Righteous is its name, after the righteous ones [on earth] . . . it supports the whole world . . . .' The symbolism of the column . . . corresponds to the Tree of Life . . . [and] the phallus" (*Von der mystischen Gestalt*, 90). As noted previously, also the images of the celestial pillar and the phallus accompany Parsifal throughout the film. Some Kabbalists might object to the connection between Yesod, the pillar, and the name of Michael. While all consulted books on Jewish mysticism assign the archangel Michael to a *sefira* on the middle column of the Jacob's Ladder, not all place it in Yesod. Z'ev ben Shimon Halevi's *A Kabbalistic Universe* can serve as an example.[13] Trying to systematize a wealth of unclear and evolving descriptions in older literature, Halevi presents several charts of the Jacob's Ladder. This is an extended form consisting of four overlapping Sefirotic Trees. It suggests the gradual changes from the purely spiritual origin in the top unit, or "world" (Azilut), down via the creation level (Beriah), then to the formation level (Yezirah), onto the world of making called Asiyyah. Since the levels overlap, several *sefirot* also overlap and function with multiple names in adjoining "worlds." Thus in fig. 12, showing the second world from the top, the name Michael appears in the center place of Tiferet, sharing the spot with Adonai and Messiah (Adonai = Malkhut). A comment in the margin identifies the location as "Malkhut of Azilut, Tiferet of Beriah, Keter of Yezirah" (49). Fig. 21 shows this location to be no. 7 from the bottom of the middle column on the Jacob's Ladder (169). Of interest here is the shared location of Michael and Messiah, although they function in different "worlds" of spiritual purity. The apparent conflict of associating Parsifal with Yesod disappears when one remembers that the character represents Ze'eir Anpin, a construct of six (broken) *sefirot* that include both Tiferet and Yesod. The director may have drawn his inspiration from the *Ghent Altarpiece*. It presents the archangel on top of the column of the fountain. It forms the vertical central axis of the composition. Since the sculpture is a part of the fountain, it appears to "belong" to it (Malkhut) while retaining its "watering" mission in the *tikkun* process as Yesod. Actually, Syberberg's use of this quotation from the altarpiece amounts to a reinterpretation of a famous and enigmatic artwork.

In contrast to Parsifal, Amfortas remains incapable of independent action. During the seduction scene, Parsifal I refers to him as *Elender* (miserable man). Soon after, Parsifal II deplores the *Elend* (misery) of the predicament of the Grail society and Kundry. Wagner chose these words with care. In Middle High German the noun *elend* had several meanings, among them "exile," "homelessness," and "captivity." The adjective *elend* meant, a.o., "abroad," "in exile," and "banished." The archaic meanings of the term still reverberate through the text, imbuing it with a Kabbalistic dimension. Amfortas is not only a broken vessel. As the other fractured *sefirot* he also fell from his intended position in the divine scheme. He can neither sit on the throne nor wear the celestial mantle. Without the healing of his wound, he cannot "return" or be "redeemed." He is still "in exile," as a broken *sefira* awaiting *tikkun*. While Amfortas corresponds mostly to the shattered and displaced *sefira* Tiferet, Syberberg makes Parsifal borrow the larger share of his active energy or quality from the ninth *sefira*, Yesod. Of course the main characters all share some visible qualities, as one would expect of stages in an emanation process. One example is the color black. The color is an attribute of the third *sefira*, the upper mother who brings forth the lower *sefirot*. Titurel's spear is wrapped in black; Amfortas has several blackened teeth; some of his young attendants, Gurnemanz, and Parsifal II wear black leather armor; Parsifal I has a black mole on his neck; the Grail Carrier has a beauty spot on her cheek; and finally, Klingsor wears a black leather outfit. When Wolfram von Eschenbach let Herzeloyde dress her departing Parzival in a leather outfit, she did not only make him look ridiculous to sophisticated court society. She also equipped his ethereal body with coarser skin suitable for a world of manifest matter. Similarly in the film, the black attributes indicate the process of gradual transformation into manifestation. But of the six *sefirot*, Parsifal I has also inherited the most from Yesod.

All the consulted sources on Jewish mysticism agree that the active role in bringing about the restoration process resides in Yesod.[14] A prominent but less important symbolic attribute of this *sefira* is the sun. Scholem lists numerous cosmological images as attributes of the *sefirot*, assigning the moon to Malkhut and the sun to "Tiferet or Yesod" (*Kabbalah*, 111). The film equips the male Parsifal with several solar symbols including the swastika. Most conspicuous is the phallic replica from the Delos Temple of the sun god Apollo. It links the solar imagery with the sexual symbolism that characterizes the lore about *tikkun*. Scholem associates the ninth *sefira* not only with the phallus, but also with circumcision, vitality, and virility (*Von der mystischen Gestalt*, 100–101). Significantly, Yesod represents "the Righteous One" who controls and channels the sexual energy into a religiously sanctioned restorative and redemptive activity. As Joseph resisted Pharao's wife and John the Baptist resisted Herodias, so Yesod does not indulge in the sex act as primitive procreation. He transforms the union into a spiritual embrace of the "upper" and "lower" elements that have been separated. This process is clearly outlined in *Parsifal*. As a redeemer Parsifal is the "Foundation of the World" and the "Tree of Life" (*Von der mystischen Gestalt*, 90). He restores harmony, repairs and helps the displaced components to their rightful positions, and enables the Shekhinah to return the lost sparks to the upper realms. With Kundry wearing her sparkling crown returned to Amfortas' side, the film presents a parallel to the reunion of the exiled Shekhinah and Tiferet. Her other aspect, Nukba de Ze'eir as Parsifal II, is united with her male alter ego. Since the model for the Parsifal character, Ze'eir Anpin, is composed of fragments from all six broken vessels/*sefirot*, Parsifal and Amfortas share many qualities. This allows the film to reunite one part of the dual Shekhinah with quasi-Tiferet (Amfortas) and the other part with quasi-Yesod (Parsifal I). The consulted literature on the Kabbalah agrees that reunion represents a prominent symbol of the *tikkun* process. However, not all Kabbalistic overviews give the same combination for the reunion, nor do they state what happens to these agents when they complete their mission. Some, e.g. Fine (70), view the reunion as being only of Ze'eir Anpin and Nukba de Ze'eir. The director chooses to unite the figures as two couples. One might view this as a sequential reunion of all aspects of the *parzufim*. Wagner only hints at the possibility of reunion in his libretto. The film completes the pattern.

Admittedly, several symbolic frameworks account for a confusing eclecticism of imagery in the film. However, a Kabbalist would recognize every little hint and detail as fitting seamlessly into a coherent whole. For example, one usually thinks only of Parsifal when referring to the redeemer in the text. But the film equips Kundry with a crown of thorns upon her arrival in act 1 and lets her be baptized like Jesus in "Jordan" later. This blurs the distinctions. A crown of thorns is in Christian tradition reserved for the crucified Jesus. This symbol signifies the Christian Redeemer. But within the context of Wagner's plot, also Kundry contributes to Parsifal's development. She helps him acquire an identity by giving him a name and other information. She prods his memory activating self-scrutiny. Even when posing as danger she helps empower him (as does Heidegger's *Gestell*). From a Kabbalistic perspective she is a four-fold force participating in the *tikkun* process. As a Shekhinah figure she assumes an active role. As the maternal *parzuf* Imma she has brought forth both Nukba de Ze'eir and Ze'eir de Anpin, including their potential as redeeming forces. Her own contribution, tribulations, as well as her partial identity with them entitles her to wear the symbol of a redeemer. Scholem is even more explicit. In a chapter on the Shekhinah he states, "After all, she [the upper Shekhinah] is for good reason and *expressis verbis* . . . transcribed as the sphere of redemption. As the "lower mother" Shekhinah remains present in the work of creation, as "upper mother" she is the opportunity for its redemption" (*Von der mystischen Gestalt* 170–71). And as mentioned in Halevi's figure 21 of the *sefirot* on the Jacob's Ladder, the archangel Michael shares a location with Adonai and Messiah. This location is identified as "Malkhut of Azilut, Tiferet of Beriah, Keter of Yezirah" (49). Malkhut (lower Shekhinah) and Messiah appear, then, in the same location on the chart. This overlap suggests an identity from a Kabbalistic point of view. The crown of thorns should not be alien from that perspective. Scholem writes about the Shekhinah in exile, "Thus she is also the rose that is surrounded by thorns and thistles, which are precisely those powers of the demonic that hold her captive" (*Von der mystischen Gestalt*, 184). But perhaps the most compelling parallel between the Shekhinah and the Christian Redeemer relates to the idea of creation by expression in Genesis: "And God said . . . .." Binah as the upper mother speaks or brings forth the lower *sefirot*. Scholem describes her as "an active power that becomes expression," adding: "The lower Shekhinah, however, carries this power that collects in her downwards and permeates as the living 'word' all worlds that stand outside the pleroma of the *sefirot*."[15] Such formulations about an aspect of the divine being the "living word" easily remind one of the Gospel of John which begins with, "In the beginning was the Word, and the Word was with God, and the Word was God." Verse 14 connects then to the theme of the Redeemer, "And the Word was made flesh, and dwelt among us." The Kabbalistic *Logos* is as closely linked to the redemption of individual souls as the Christian Word.

Like the Christian Redeemer, so also the Shekhinah in exile suffers tribulations on earth. The end of her banishment and return to her heavenly abode becomes the task of righteous believers. As they restore the perfection of their individual spiritual condition, they contribute to the *tikkun* on a cosmological scale. In other passages the Shekhinah is described as the soul, which, if further explored, would quickly lead to Freud and Jung's Anima. One notes with interest that the idea of the soul as Shekhinah in exile is linked to the lore of metempsychosis. Scholem observes, "But the exile of the body in outward history has its parallel in the exile of the soul in its migrations from embodiment to embodiment, from one form of being to another. The doctrine of metempsychosis as the exile of the soul acquired unprecedented popularity" (*On the Kabbalah*, 116). While Wagner may have found his inspiration for Kundry's transmigrations in mythical and Gnostic texts, e.g. in Catharism, the Kabbalah is also a strong possibility. Another detail supporting that assumption is Kundry's last rebirth as a penitent. Wagner's stage instructions prescribe a penitent's garment for her, and like the biblical "sinner," she washes and anoints Parsifal's feet and dries them with her hair. Of course, Mary Magdalene prefigures her in "Jesus of Nazareth." But the sequence of events evokes the Shekhinah as the model. About the upper Shekhinah Scholem states, "'Repentance' (literally 'return' in Hebrew) is a name for the third [*sefira*], because all things 'return' to its womb in the end" (*On the Kabbalah*, 49n). Syberberg retains the role of the penitent, but adds the visual-semantic Hebrew meaning of "return" as *Kehre* during the return to the Grail Castle. And there he "corrects" Wagner's version by restoring the penitent to her status of queen.

Just as popular tradition has merged several of the biblical Johns, so also several Marys experienced a similar fate. Their echoes balance those of Christ and John in *Parsifal* as if to provide a feminine counterpart. Syberberg draws on Van Eyck's paintings to allude to the Virgin Mary in her crowned glory and as the mother of a divine child. At the same time her avatar functions as a temptress endangering the hero while also appearing as a penitent sinner and repeating the pose of Mary the Magdalene. Both Wagner's fondness for Mary of Magdala and the merger of several Marys in the film suggest that Syberberg is obliquely pointing to the unorthodox literature. For example, the Gospel of Philip includes several passages about the Magdalene, mentioning that Jesus kissed her often on the mouth, provoking the other disciples to ask, "Why do you love her more than all of us?"[16] Three pages earlier a passage notes that there were three women among Jesus' close associates. They were his mother, his sister, and the woman from Magdala, "the one who was called his consort. His sister and his mother and his consort were each a Mary. In this connection it is worth noting that this view of Mary Magdalene has provided the framework as well as the title for the Gospel of Mary," Hans-Martin Schenke points out.[17] The allusions in *Parsifal* belong to several frames of reference. Most obviously, they reveal an undercurrent of spirituality outside the

Church. Less obviously, they draw attention to similar overlays in the roles of the Shekhinah. With that they establish a bridge to the Kabbalistic and Gnostic traditions. The Kabbalah, at least in its popular versions, operates with feminine concepts for aspects of the Divine. But independently of the Kabbalah, the allusions hint at the suppressed role of the feminine in Christian theology. Thus the mother of a part of the Trinity is not divine. Mary Magdalene suffered worse, as Jane Lampman observes: "The perception of Mary as a prostitute originated in 591, when Pope Gregory the Great falsely identified her with an unnamed sinful woman in the Bible. Almost 1,400 years later, in 1969, the Church officially corrected its error, though it lingers in public consciousness."[18]

Kundry as the penitent, or "Return," combines Kabbalistic and Christian elements. By returning her to the Grail court, Wagner hinted at a restoration in the Kabbalistic sense. By endowing her with a crown and resting place next to the Grail king, Syberberg restores her to the dignity of her original position. And, one might add, he strengthens the psychological interpretation. In the process he "corrects" the theological suppression of the feminine aspect. The fact that the characters die at the end of the film marks the end of a fugal evolution. As in the imagery of the Kabbalah, the symbols recombine and undergo transformations. It is worth noting that the sibyl, who shares her features with Herzeleide, Kundry in exile, and the crowned penitent, remains alive at the end. Little does it matter whether one considers her as Binah/Imma, Mother Nature, the Great Mother, *Anima mundi*, or the second half of Schopenhauer's Will and Representation. She is also the Kabbalistic Word creating the world by giving expression. She is immortal. The crystal globe in her hands is also variant of the Grail. In Wolfram's version, the Grail is an oracle. Written pronouncements appear briefly on its surface. A sibyl pronounces oracles. At the end she holds the crystal sphere, a carrier of divine intent and in itself an example of perfect shape. As a symbol of attainable perfection it should guide human aspiration. The combination of the sybil and her globe attribute reveals her hidden identity with the other representations of the Shekhinah, especially the Grail Carrier. The sibyl's face bending down over the sphere appears to represent the completion of the restoration process.

The central concern of *Parsifal* is undoubtedly redemption for the redeemer. The Christian veneer of the work obscures the fact that Wagner's idea is not so central in Christianity as the viewer might assume. Medieval mystics, heretics, and believers in the "inner God" relate easily to the concept of redemption for the redeemer. But mainstream Christians would not automatically link redemption as being also "for" the redeemer. The Christian Redeemer died for others without the need to redeem himself. "Imitation of Christ" has historically been a pious ideal for many believers, but it did not guarantee a redemption for themselves or others. However, Jewish mysticism links the concepts exactly as suggested in the drama. As a symbolic process, the work presents the gradual restoration of a world in need. Much of the preceding story can be gleaned from Wagner's other music dramas. *Parsifal* begins after the collapse of the world. Now comes the repair stage. As in the Kabbalah, the restoration process outlined in *Parsifal* has far-reaching consequences, but centers on human efforts. Psychologically and ethically it tells the story of a righteous one who succeeds in fulfilling human potential: Impious elements are overcome, damaged and displaced components are restored and returned to their intended order, harmony is reintroduced. And, in accordance with Kabbalistic lore, the Shekhinah is restored to her dignity, returning the holy sparks that had gone astray when the vessels fractured. The broken vessel AMFORtAs is reconfigured. The male Parsifal who accomplishes much of this also has "vessel" built into his name. Perhaps one should spell the title and protagonist's name Parzufal. His completed mission, as for every person, is the individual *tikkun*, the striving for perfection as intended in God's creation. The striving on a personal level results in *tikkun* on higher levels, uniting the upper and lower parts of the worlds. This results in redemption both for the composite redeemer and the world being saved. The perfect vessel for the divine emanation that the righteous individual aspires to become is a central ideal and symbol, the Grail.

Of course it does not escape one's attention that Kundry also functions as a redeemer who needs and achieves redemption. As the Kabbalistic aspect of the Godhead that creates by expression, she/it becomes the Word in the manifest world. She contributes to her own and other's redemption, first by bringing forth the saving agent who will carry out the action, then by empowering him. As an aspect of the lower Shekhinah, she eventually becomes an active partner. The director underscores her redeemer qualities most strikingly by letting her wear a crown of thorns and being baptized in "Jordan" as Jesus was. And Jungians will nod in agreement, recognizing in her the archetypal Anima and her powers.

But, one might object, does this still describe Wagner's *Parsifal*? To a considerable extent, yes. Syberberg elaborates and translates everything into images. He preserves the music and the libretto, but strengthens the Kabbalistic reading in the visuals. Needless to say, his interpretation challenges the prevailing understanding of the work. That understanding consists mainly of two hopefully conflicting views: *Parsifal* as a Christian drama and as an anti-Semitic statement. To judge from the secondary literature about the film, the viewers do not recognize the director's intent. Syberberg's own book on the film offers little help in this respect. Only after becoming aware of the mystical features can one detect some oblique hints in the text. Readers or viewers unfamiliar with the Kabbalah cannot recognize them in the film either. They must remain oblivious to its unique interpretation of the work. This interpretation seems incompatible with what we know about Wagner. If one assumes that his obsession with and aversion to anything Jewish was not his persona, but the real Wagner, why did he compose a redemptive saga? And what did he mean by *Parsifal* being his most conciliatory work? And what did he confide to his wife about it on January 5, 1882, something so sensitive that he said, "Good that we are alone"? His conciliatory intent may, of course, have been directed at the Masonic community. Perhaps he wanted to prove that he had acquired the insights and knowledge expected of members. Another possible constituency might be Jews who were familiar with the mystical tradition. Unlike most totally assimilated Jewish Germans, these might still adhere to their old traditions. Their practices and beliefs might even have been dismissed by the Jewish majority, much like mystical heretics by the Catholic Church. But could one also read the work as a disguised *mea culpa* and plea for forgiveness? As an admission of identification? As a statement of recognition? Although farfetched, the possibilities remain viable, especially in view of Syberberg's revelations in his *Richard Wagner Parsifal*, as the title screen (also) identifies the film. He does not make such claims in his book. However, he does attribute a related issue to Wagner's intent: The composer supposedly counted himself among those redeemed through *Parsifal*. This elevates the music drama to a self-redemption work. Syberberg states, for example, "Wagner created his self-redemption work for himself, viewing himself as [a] world to be redeemed by means of this story and [this] music." (12). Syberberg "translates" this declaration by turning Wagner's head into the world of the plot. Since the action is the *tikkun* process, the fractured head with its contents becomes the Adam Kadmon, the totality of the *parzufim*. The successful completion of their restoration efforts restores Adam Kadmon (*Kabbalah*, 140, 142). The process should, then, be repeated with every performance of *Parsifal*. From a Kabbalistic perspective, this would resemble the Christian prayer of intercession for the deceased. As Syberberg subjects *Parsifal* to a Kabbalistic reading, he carries out what Wagner may have been aiming at but could not bring himself to express openly. Syberberg's attempt amounts to a call for reevaluation. After all, the characters appear as forces in Wagner's head. They add up to his mind and inner world.

It may be just an unintended effect, but the characters moving around in Wagner's head invite also a very different association. Amfortas and, in a few scenes, Gurnemanz and Kundry are seen enveloped in a blond blanket. When Gurnemanz and Kundry drop it, they appear to emerge from it like butterflies from a cocoon. But while wrapped, they, and Amfortas, look like larvae. A larva or caterpillar reminds one of maggots and worms. That comparison revives the memory of a scene in Syberberg's *Scarabea* with the head of a dead horse full of maggots. His *Parsifal* features the head of a dead man with many moving little figures resembling such worms. The reader may remember his mention of *Wurm* in the passages about his early film, *Fritz Kortner probt Kabale und Liebe*, in the *Filmbuch* (70). The word also relates to the dragon, *Lindwurm*, that Siegfried slew and contrapuntally to Wagner's use of it. Cosima's diary entry of July 20, 1881 begins as follows: "R.[ichard] had a somewhat restless night, he dreamed first of all that I did not love him, then that he was surrounded by Jews who turned into worms." Syberberg revives the *Gewürm*. Throughout his *Richard Wagner Parsifal* they animate a dead man's head. And they hail from Jewish mysticism.

One of the Jewish writers informing Syberberg's *Parsifal* is Heinrich Heine. As Wagner's "bad conscience" he already made his presence felt in *Hitler*. This presence continues in *Parsifal* through numerous associative echoes from his writings. Also here Syberberg engages in a game of hide-and-seek. The reader may remember that in the book to *Hitler* the author describes a planned episode around Heine's poem "Die Grenadiere" and the "Marseillaise" by Wagner, but omitted it in the finished movie (Engl. ed., 61). In the fourth part, however, Heine appears as Wagner's antipode in the anonymous role played by Harry Baer. The name is suppressed, as it had been during the Third Reich. That continues in *Parsifal*, in accordance with Wagner's treatment of his former friend. He mentions him by name as a Jew in *Judaism in Music*, but omits their friendship and Heine's importance to him in his published memoirs. Tacitly, Syberberg erects a monument of sorts to him in *Parsifal*. But again, it does not wear Heine's name or even features. The monument is the death mask landscape. Of course the book to the film identifies it unmistakably as modeled on Wagner's death mask. It describes the idea to its use as being borrowed from Syberberg's planned film about Wagner that he had to abandon (22). The author does not mention how he got the idea to use a death mask as the location for a cinematic plot. One may wonder if not Heine's death mask is somehow related.

On February 17, 1981, 125 years after Heine's death, a memorial to him was unveiled on the Schwanenmarkt Square in Düsseldorf, the city where he was born. The city had neither commissioned it nor paid for it. It was a gift from a banker in Munich, Dr. Stefan Kaminsky. The artist who created this bronze monument is Bert Gerresheim. Like Syberberg, he too was born in 1935. Resting on a platform of concrete and surrounded by the metal outline of a box (a glass display box?) lies a head modeled on Heine's death mask. A "net" covers the lower part of the face. This memorial measures less than half the size of the Wagner mask landscape in *Parsifal*. Children love to climb all over it, making it as inhabited as Syberberg's creation. Of special interest here are the artist's comments on his work. Gerresheim maintains that it has become impossible to create traditional-looking memorials after World War II.[19] He had to seek a different approach to captivate the personality of a man whose persona differed from his private nature. The task required a form of polyvalence challenging the viewers' perception. He opted for a dead man's face with a covered mouth. In his article Gerresheim coins new terms for this kind of work. A "memorial" translates to German as *Denkmal*. Gerresheim's monument is a *Fragemal*, or an "inquirial." Other terms he uses are *Vexiermal* and *Vexiermonument*, best understood as a monument that confuses, misleads, deceives, distorts, teases, mocks, irritates, or provokes the viewer. It should achieve the same effect as Heine's persona. A thoughtful beholder should be sufficiently puzzled to reexamine Heine and his writings. An article by Ekkehard Mai in the same publication mentions several of Gerresheim's early studies for the monument.[20] He includes a photo of a bronze bas-relief showing a Lazarus- or Christ-like head in triple profiles (12). Another mentioned sketch includes a portrait of Heine imitating the face of Christ on the Shroud of Turin, replete with a crown of thorns (16). Obviously, Heine's years of suffering before he died assume the status of a passion. The parallel uses of Heine's and Wagner's death masks as landscapes and monuments are remarkable in their complementarity. Developed over several years and completed almost simultaneously, neither work seems to be inspired by the other. Syberberg's public comments on the importance of the face as landscape date back to the *Filmbuch* of 1976. But in view of Heine's and Wagner's personas and effect on the world, Gerresheim's and Syberberg's choices amount to a rare occurrence of synchronism and synchronicity. Syberberg does not exhibit Heine's features in his film, only those of Wagner. But thanks to the numerous hints and allusions, one recognizes the Wagner mask to be a Janus-face. The invisible "other"side with the wound resembles Heine. On the Wagner side Kundry functions as the wound.

Only an interpretation of *Parsifal* drawing on Jewish mysticism recognizes Kundry's importance in the plot. Parsifal is not the sole redeemer in this drama. Several forces contribute, most noticeably the Shekhinah and her avatars. The restoration and return of Kundry becomes the counterpart to the "healing" of Amfortas. Her multiple manifestations reflect faithfully that the Shekhinah not only corresponds to Jung's Anima, and maybe inspired it, but also sets in motion and participates in the *tikkun* process. Several of these manifestations share the face of Edith Clever. *Parsifal* is the first film in a series of stage and video/film productions with Edith Clever as the only actress and Syberberg as director. Clever is a star artist in a class by herself. As a movie actress she can look back at a long list of distinguished roles. She also portrayed *La Marquise d'O . . .* (1976) by Eric Rohmer, based on Kleist's novella of the same name. Years later she reinterpretated the same role, this time in a film directed by Syberberg. As a stage actress she established her fame on the Schaubühne in Berlin with roles ranging from ancient to contemporary characters. Her Clytaemnestra from Aeschylus' *Oresteia* trilogy is quoted visually in *Parsifal*. She has also increasingly toured with solo performances and readings. One of her one-woman productions was *Gertrud* based on a book by Einar Schleef in 2002. She has also been active as director with full ensembles, e.g. in *Medeia* in 1996, where she played the title role as well. Her groan and scream at the beginning and end of the performance caught the attention of all reviewers. But not one of them recognized the similarity to Kundry's vocalizations in Syberberg's film. Also worth noting is Clever's involvement with the marionette theater during the Salzburg Festival in 1997. Acting as Titania in Carl Maria von Weber's *Oberon*, she varied the interplay of marionette and mute actress in *Parsifal*. She spoke her part as the fairy queen whereas the humans were presented by puppets moving to the sound of invisible singers. Considering the importance of Kleist's essay "On the Marionette Theater" and its relevance to Syberberg's films, especially *Parsifal*, it appears that Clever and Syberberg have progressed aesthetically and philosophically on parallel paths. Her willingness to collaborate with Syberberg in *Parsifal* and the following films was serendipitous for his oeuvre. Her contribution goes far beyond that of Marlene Dietrich in her series of roles in Josef von Sternberg's movies.

With Edith Clever, Syberberg secured a famous and uniquely qualified professional actress for the central role(s). Equally impressive is the invisible Yvonne Minton, who lent her voice. In the other important roles only Martin Sperr was an established actor. The Grail Carrier and the two adult Parsifals, as well as many minor parts, were portrayed by amateurs. A special case was Armin Jordan, who played Amfortas and conducted the orchestra. That leaves only two major roles, Gurnemanz and Klingsor, in the hands of professional opera singers. But also their voices were dubbed and synchronized as in silent movies. That may be the film's strongest reference to the history of cinematography, in particular to the 1904 *Parsifal*. Other reminders include the old technique of front projections that often serve as backgrounds, as well as the selective use of Riefenstahl's innovations. The contrapuntal variations of these "quotations" suggest that the development of cinematography continues to inform the German Cycle. With its dead swan and dead Grail society at the end, *Parsifal* may constitute a swan song, also of cinematography.

As a feature film, *Parsifal* marks the end of a cycle and of a long series of varied movies by Syberberg. Thanks to its layering system of interpretations and aesthetic boldness, it defies labeling. "Opera film" does not do it justice. It is the only one of its kind. Sooner or later literary and film scholars will want to examine many topics left unexplored here. For example, Eric Rohmer made *Perceval le gallois* in 1978, based on Chrétien's romance. Rohmer has also been writing about his aesthetic theories, turning to Clever to portray his Marquise d'O . . . on screen, and directing another play by Kleist on stage and television. And in the spring of 2004, the Palais de Chaillot in Paris housed a retrospective of his work called "Eric Rohmer: l'Art de la fugue." He and Syberberg seem to be kindred spirits in at least some areas of their work. This deserves a closer scrutiny. To say nothing about the implications of visual counterpoint in *Parsifal* and the German Cycle. Syberberg refers to fugal structure as early as in the *Filmbuch* in the discussion of *Fritz Kortner probt Kabale und Liebe* (70). His cinematic work as music by other means awaits analysis. The list could go on.

If one restricts the scope to the German Cycle, it becomes obvious that the four main films, *Ludwig*, *Karl May*, *Hitler*, and *Parsifal*, relate to each other in a musical fashion besides functioning as tragedies plus satyr play. The remaining two, *Theodor Hierneis* and *Winifred Wagner*, may at first glance appear unsuitable for such comparisons, since they do not include music. That is, they do not contain audible music. However, the editing and the handling of topics continue the musical structure by other means, as Syberberg had announced repeatedly in his *Filmbuch*. His work amounts to a quasi-musical composition with ample use of counterpoint. One might be tempted to call it the "German Fugue" with *Theodor Hierneis* and *Winifred Wagner* as the episodes (*intermezzi, Zwischenspiele*). Some structural elements may be easy to recognize. For example, the final movement should return to the initial key. As Wagner's *Ring* cycle begins and ends with the Rhinemaidens, so also Syberberg joins beginning and end of his German Cycle into a ring. Both the early part of *Ludwig* and the final segment of *Parsifal* play in unusual, enclosed surroundings. They resemble caverns, either underground or in mountains. The earlier scale-covered, chtonic mother figure corresponds to Kundry, the "pythian seer," as Syberberg calls her (*Der Wald*, 278). The captive child Ludwig prefigures several male characters in *Parsifal*. Syberberg also borrowed the presence of all three norns in *Ludwig* from Wagner. They add two important dimensions echoing throughout the Cycle. First, they introduce the theme of prophesy. Such a divine, or divinely inspired, announcer of the future wears many names, e.g. *moira, vala,* norn, *parca* (German: *Parze*), Fata, sibyl, Destiny, prophet/ess, or fortune-teller. In Wagner's "regeneration" essays, even the poet turns into a priest-seer. Syberberg includes such voices in *Ludwig* with the norns, Tiresias, and the artist-priestess. He even lets the king make prophetic pronouncements. *Karl May* warns of the "wrong man." After the arrival of the wrong man, part 2 of *Hitler* continues the theme with an astrologer plus quoted predictions from speeches. In *Parsifal* the prophesy returns as Titurel's vision (*Traumgesicht*) on the Grail. Syberberg adds the mysterious sibyl. What do these seers usually predict? Apparently, that lives and societies undergo cyclic developments ending with demise and reconstellated fresh beginnings. Amfortas knew it all along when comparing the promised healer with Death.

The second dimension of the norn component lies in the presence of all three appearing at the same time. As their names in Nordic mythology relates them to past, present, and future, their simultaneous appearance blurs the concept of time (Grimm, 1:335–46). Such synchronous occurrences usually reveal themselves in Syberberg's details, for example the grey-haired child in *Hitler*. More ominous is the semantic implication. One wonders if the merging of past, present, and future results in only a brief simultaneity, or whether this phenomenon equates timelessness or eternity. Does it recur intermittently, or does it last forever? Such ruminations return the concepts of "always" (*immer*) and "perpetual," "everlasting" (*ewig*). In the ghost scene of *Hitler* they exhibited a subversive and frightening associative grid pattern extending to the Holocaust. On the other hand, liberation from the constraints of time might promise the bliss of Nirvana. Beyond the threshold of sorrows, suffering, and death lives Joy, Daughter of Elysium, taught Schiller and Beethoven, as Syberberg reminds his viewers in part 4 of *Hitler*. This realm should, then, also be the Grail Kingdom in its restored condition.

As these examples indicate, the films from *Ludwig* to *Parsifal* all relate to each other. *Parsifal* may function as a satyr play to the four-part *Hitler*, but it is equally important in the larger cycle. It may not be coincidental that the cycle consists of six films. The broken *sefirot* also number six. At a far remove the films do present some badly shattered *sefirot* in need of redemption. Several characters represent faint echoes of the creation process. Some particles of the divine efflux have remained close enough to inspire them to a diminished form of creative activity. King Ludwig is shown designing his lavish sled (to say nothing about his castles). Theodor Hierneis favors the culinary arts. Karl May creates new worlds in his books. Winifred Wagner manages a creative legacy. Hitler had first aspired to being an artist before embarking on "greater" projects. And Wagner, hiding as a subject behind Parsifal, harnessed his musical creations to drama and other arts, aspiring to a *Gesamtkunstwerk* with ambitious objectives. His final objective concerns Parsifal's mission. And the latter appears in the right position as Yesod, the righteous restorer. The four main films also contain references to esoteric systems. *Ludwig* contains Masonic symbolism, *Karl May* offers occult parlor games and a Gnostic quest with Kabbalistic overtones (mainly in paintings and names, e.g.

Emma, Klara, and Rosenroth). *Hitler* reveals the occultism thriving in the Third
Reich while introducing the Grail theme. And *Parsifal* presents a spiritual parable
borrowing from several traditions. A related theme weaves through all of them, the
human quest for paradise, a longing, a dream. The characters either yearn explicitly
for a release resembling paradise or redemption, or they suffer from melancholy.
The title characters are "de-ranged" (*ver-rückt*) like the broken *sefirot*, King Ludwig
most obviously. But Karl May also inhabits a borderland between imagination and
reality, and the others clearly exhibit a "fallen" condition. With Parsifal's mission
completed, the restored *sefirot* should theoretically be ready to be reborn in
harmony, but Syberberg chose to show only the final stage of the cycle.

Very little of this comes to the fore in the book to *Parsifal*. Rather, Syberberg
offers scattered reflections on his struggle surrounding the preparation and actual
shooting of the film. He, and not his Parsifal, is the protagonist. In some respects
one might compare his companion book to Thomas Mann's *Die Entstehung des
Doktor Faustus* (*The Genesis of Doctor Faustus*), written to accompany his novel
Doktor Faustus.[21] Like Mann, so also Syberberg reveals very little about the real
structure and nature of his work, but they both drop hints and identify a long list of
shared motifs and inspirations. This should come as no surprise, considering their
shared preoccupation with the "German problem," Wagner, *Parsifal*, Hitler,
Goethe, Heine, Kleist, Dürer, but also Dante and others, all mentioned in Mann's
companion book. And both refer to Adorno, whom Mann consulted extensively
while writing *Doktor Faustus*. Among other shared characteristics one notices
Mann's references to counterpoint (96), the themes of laughter and coldness (55),
apocrypha (113), and repeatedly, eschatology (69, 112, 158). But, of course, Mann
is the more disciplined writer, as always concerned with a lucid and elegant style.
Syberberg, by comparison, indulges in the first signs of "stream of consciousness"
prose and an "artistic" license in syntax, organization, and vagueness.

The book is dedicated to Edith Clever. It contains an abundance of
photographs, most of them taken during rehearsals. As complements to the stills
from the film they serve to record the evolution of the work and to supplement it.
They belong to the film as apocrypha, Syberberg remarks (30). His choice of
expression imbues the film with the nimbus of a gospel. But later on he refers to it
as a satyr play (34). He does not identify the comedy features of his satyr play.
However, he describes his *Parsifal* as a totality, "in the sense of eschatological
yearning as tragedy, which also encompasses comedy" (34). Seven chapters later
the author reverses the order: "A comedy that includes the tragedy of the world"
(57). On the same page he also uses the expression "Satyrspiel des Untergangs"
(satyr play of the demise), possibly playing on Wagner's use of *Untergang*.[22] But
the literary concepts, in particular "satyr play," remain out-of-focus for most
viewers. Only from Hermetists and Kabbalists will Syberberg's *Parsifal* elicit
chuckles of recognition. For what else is this interpretation so imbued with Jewish
mysticism if not a satyr play? Both the composer's anti-Semitism and Hitler's
admiration for him and especially for *Parsifal* are largely responsible for the
ideological reading of Wagner's artistic testament. A Kabbalistic interpretation

therefore comes as a shock. Those who view Amfortas and his society as representing Wagner and his fellow Germans would neither recognize nor acknowledge Herzeleide-Kundry's child as the redeemer Yesod. The ramifications give food for thought, both within Syberberg's German Cycle and for *Parsifal* within Wagner's scheme.

Operating with such terms as satyr play, tragedy, and comedy, Syberberg reminds the reader that his film unfolds within the given parameters of libretto and score. His own contribution must therefore reside to a considerable degree in the visual treatment. Here and again throughout the book he mentions his aesthetics, but only hints at the core of his thoughts. A fragmentary idea emerges in his previous publications, especially the early comments on *Ludwig* in the *Filmbuch*. They basically amount to a program of emulating music by other means. But since music is a given component of *Parsifal*, it acquires new functions. In the interplay of music, voice, and face, for example, the music turns into a unifying agent (55). The dubbing reverses the situation of the ancient theater where actors spoke their lines while wearing masks. Now the mask is a face that must express what comes from another source. The result resembles animation when the mask or face (*persona, parzuf*) reveals the singer's voice and music in turn enriches the face with sound. Syberberg ties this discussion to Kleist's comments on marionettes, but without clarifying his thoughts on the subject. In retrospect one discovers that the pantomime in the first prelude and the intermittent appearance of dolls play their parts in this dynamic. Actually, dolls and ventriloquists' dummies figure prominently already in *Hitler*. In *Parsifal* the actors function as dummies miming disembodied voices. The idea may derive from Wolfram's *Parzival*. In book 7 he introduces the sisters Obie and Obilot. The Hebrew echo in their names points to a ventriloquist or necromancer (*aleph, vau, bet*). Especially little Obilot, who still plays with dolls, speaks to Gawan as if endowed with the wisdom of a divine teacher. The girls' father is Count Lyppaut. As his name reveals, his castle faces the world of the *kelippot*, an important concept in the Kabbalah. Wagner settled for a necromancer from the *kelippot* side. Syberberg reintroduces the doll aspect. His characters move and act to the sounds of unseen forces. Like marionettes they can achieve a balance of grace for only a short time. Most of the time, however, the Voice or Word that animates them comes from a separate entity. The actors and their characters are fragments fallen from their proper positions. Or, as in the case of Nukba de Ze'eir, fallen and just slightly cracked. The fracture shows in her voice, which she shares with Rainer Goldberg and Parsifal I. Even her maternal aspect, Kundry, is deprived of her own voice, signaling the *Riss*. A voice belongs to the creative dimension of the Godhead. Much like the light of the divine emanation, it passes through, or is refracted, respectively reflected, by the receiving vessels. It appears, then, that the doll-like muteness resembles the condition before the refraction. Actually, all the voices in the film have been separated from the visible actors. Syberberg does not explain why he chose two professional singers for the roles of Gurnemanz and Klingsor. It looks at first as if they do not need to first establish the unity granted by the music to miming actors and disembodied voices.

But even their voices come from a separate soundtrack, introducing the same division and a dose of irony. For Kundry the division was a welcome device. The complexity of this character represents the rift (*Riss*), the director notes (54). One concludes that her silence in the third act expresses a new unity in which the voice part has already been absorbed or gathered by the surviving mute, pious virgin and queen. Musically, her silence also assumes a different dimension. Starting as the enframing sibyl with a voice and continuing in her miming appearance as Herzeleide in the first prelude, the character undergoes a series of quasi-contrapuntal metamorphoses, also in relation to the use of her voice. The wailing and laughter constitute variations of distress over her exile and helplessness. Klingsor may have appropriated part of her voice. But when screaming, she may also display some power of creativity, bringing forth the redeeming child, who arrives soon after. Not only does the queen at the end of the drama find her peace, but she also illustrates the longed-for return of the Shekhinah. This would entail the restoration of both Shekhinahs and their dual aspects, the end of exile and divisions, and the regaining of wholeness and completeness. The *Riss*, one remembers, appears in one form or another (e.g. Heine) throughout the German Cycle. As the wound, Kundry in particular personifies this predicament and its healing.

The author describes his own contributions in terms compatible with Jewish spirituality, but, as usual, without admitting any affinity or indebtedness. He states that his imagination is not of the inventive kind (48). Modestly he sets himself apart from creative artists who can act, read music, or write poems. The activities chosen for comparison probably contrast him and the unnamed Wagner. Since the latter aspired in his essays to the prophetic leadership of a poet-priest, his festival would presumably serve as the center for communal mysteries. Syberberg contrasts such ambition with his own limitations. With unsuspected humility he points to the predecessors in the arts. Their accomplishments resulted in the legacy on which his own work builds. For example about film he remarks, "Thus without the invention of cinema I would be nothing " (49). The recognition of and respect paid to a tradition characterizes the Kabbalah. As if emphasizing the difference between himself and Wagner further, Syberberg describes his own talent as the ability to recombine existing elements to a new entity (48). With perhaps false modesty here, he suggests that this resulting recombination might be something "optical-acustical" or something to be smelled or tasted. The Kabbalistic implication is clear. A creation perceptible to the senses belongs to this world, far removed from divine forces. But at the same time the effort imitates the *tikkun* process, even if at a remove. By collecting shards and displaced fragments and combining them into new or restored forms, the artist emulates the activity of the righteous individual, who on a personal level contributes to the divine restoration process. And the vessels in need of restoration appear in the director's *Parsifal* and the German Cycle. They are primarily his compatriots, secondarily humanity in general.

While the first section of the book (pp. 8–60) contains mostly the author's rambling reflections, the second part (60–231) follows the divisions of the film. The author shares his experiences with the preparations, dilemmas, and working on the set. Once in a while he identifies visual details not likely to be recognized by viewers, but not as often as one might wish. Much of the commentary takes its cues from the technical challenges of moviemaking. However, much of it sounds also like verbal applications of the director's famous fog machines. On such occasions one suspects that the meaning of the statement belongs to a different and unidentified frame of reference. The third section (234–69) reverts to reflections. Although Syberberg again emerges as a topic, he does not dominate the content here. At least initially the tone is no longer humble. "His" *Parsifal* represents such an anomaly in the sex-and-profit oriented movie fare that he calls the film a "counterworld." Yet for this work he selected Cannes as the site of its world premiere. The incompatibility of *Parsifal* and Cannes as center of the movie festival, the "brothel of cinema," is the real satyr play, he states (235). One also remembers the connection of his work to Monte Carlo with its casinos. Measuring himself against Wagner, who wanted to withhold this work from other opera houses, Syberberg plans to ignore the movie distribution system, aiming instead at the video market. Defiance replaces humility. He even refers to himself as "this Parsifal" and "old fool" who consciously resists the temptation of the movie business world (236).

The author's comments provide a wealth of informative nuggets, often wrapped in seemingly unrelated reflections. He confirms having taken a few liberties with the sound track, such as introducing bells after the music ends in act 2 (e.g. 244, 245) and sounds of water elsewhere when the music is silent. But one cannot hear Kundry wail at the end as he claims. Perhaps he knowingly included erroneous statements similar to the "Hermetic glitch." The reader cannot always rely on the author's accuracy. But in his next book of 1984 he complains repeatedly about cuts made in the videos of *Parsifal* distributed by Gaumont, the French co-producing company that provided much of the funding. These may affect the added sound effects.

Nowhere in his book does Syberberg mention how unique his interpretation is in Wagner criticism. Most studies of Wagner's *Parsifal* do not include examinations of the medieval Grail and Arthurian literature. Nor could any works on connections between the opera and Jewish mysticism be found for this study. However, such literature exists on the medieval Grail texts. For example, Anne Marie D'Arcy's *Wisdom and the Grail* touches upon the correspondences between the Shekhinah and the Grail (288–94). And Eugene Weinraub claims in *Chrétien's Jewish Grail* that "according to the Montpellier MS the female Grail Bearer is Jewish (a descendant of Israel): 'Cele ki porta le Gréal, Si est du lignage Israel Pucile virgene; . . .' which may indicate that the Fisher King is also of the Jewish persuasion."[23] Syberberg does not identify the sources that inspired him. However, readers aware of the Kabbalistic dimension of the film will recognize hints throughout the book. For example, the focus on Kundry suggests a different reading of the "cursed, the redeemed [female] redeemer" (240). This makes only sense from a Kabbalistic perspective. About the Grail Carrier one reads very little, but the few comments include the characterization "figuration of faith and eventual reunion of old, opposing worlds" (243). These "old, opposing worlds" refer to her double function as Church (Faith/Glaube) and Synagogue, also their representation in the Strasbourg Cathedral and van Eyck's works, including some not used in the film. One needs to be aware of the author's lacunae and omissions. To German readers, of course, persecution would form the primary frame of reference for "old, opposing worlds," but it might not explain "opposing" as a mutual stance. The author uses the rare word *entgegenstehend* here, and that can mean both "hostile" and "facing." However, the Kabbalah operates with such concepts as conflicting worlds as well as being face to face when united. Sometimes Syberberg's use of words induces as many meditations as his images, but also opportunities for misunderstandings.

Another example of the author's hints appears in the reference to the starry lining of Wagner's robe, "a sign of his [Parsifal's] origin and destination" (244). Apart from their heterodox function here, stars on clothing still elicit painful memories. A final example is a long sentence enumerating cases of "reunions" and "restored wholeness" in the plot, such as the reunion of Amfortas and Kundry, the embrace of the two Parsifals, and, enigmatically to most readers, the marriage of the "old and the new Law" (251–52). This amounts to Syberberg's definition of healing and wholeness. This kind of reunion may have been the motivating factor behind making the film. More so, perhaps, than a Kabbalistic interpretation of Wagner's work is the director's attempt to reach out and reconcile communities of related faiths separated by a history of intolerance, discrimination, persecution, and the Holocaust.

Another apparently unrelated emphasis in the book also fits into the pattern of oblique hints. The author uses words for "transgressing" (*hinausgehend, grenzüberschreitend*) several times about the film (e.g. 244, 246). For example, he identifies two art forms as transgressing while being mutually exclusive, namely the experiment and the total work of art. He distances himself from the experimenters, since their work had deteriorated to a prevailing fashion in Germany of the 1980s. With his *Parsifal* he embraces the total work of art, "in spite of rejection in Germany" (247). Within the film he uses, for example, sounds of water to "break" the self-imposed frame of the given music (244). One searches in vain for a justification or explanation. Syberberg may have in mind Walter Benjamin's thesis in "The Task of the Translator." Benjamin is, of course, talking about translating literary texts. Syberberg is translating a total work of art into a new medium as well as trying to express its hidden language. That which cannot be communicated in straight-forward words but only in symbols, says Benjamin, that is the core of "pure language."[24] The translator's task is to liberate and redeem this captive element. To accomplish this he must "break through the decayed barriers of his own language" (80). That seems to describe Syberberg's intention with *Parsifal*. In this process "language" does not refer only to German. The expression encompasses here also music, the language or conventions of moviemaking, the prevailing interpretations of the work, and a reading linking the end with the beginning of a cultural legacy.

By incorporating and preserving Wagner's music and score, Syberberg appears to assume a subservient role in the filming of *Parsifal*. But obviously he does not offer just another recording of a familiar work. He makes motifs and themes in the score visible, thus stepping into territory uncharted in cinema and on stage. He translates the movements of the music, while subjecting it to a new interplay with faces and bodies. He continues his own cinematic program while in turn appropriating, and sometimes renouncing, moviemaking techniques. His treatment of the visuals incorporates practically all known interpretations of the Grail story. And finally, he reintroduces an unexpected source of its mystical dimension. Every detail that makes this version of *Parsifal* Syberberg's own work amounts to a transgression beyond convention. And the very act of transcending limits is at the heart of the Kabbalah. The *tikkun* process consists of overcoming the barriers of the world to raise it to an ethically and spiritually perfected condition.

Walter Benjamin would have approved of Syberberg's film. Being Jewish and familiar with Jewish mysticism, he would have recognized its emphasis. In several respects he seems to emerge as an invisible partner in dialogue. Or at least, the director took Benjamin's insights to heart and applied them in the film. One might even wonder if Benjamin played a role similar to that of Adorno for Mann's *Doktor Faustus*. One text likely to inspire Syberberg is Benjamin's "The Work of Art in the Age of Mechanical Reproduction."[25] The second half of the essay discusses cinema, which at the time of writing was technically the most advanced form of art. Several comments here resonate in the film. For example, movie actors do not play to an audience, only to a camera. "The film actor," writes Benjamin, quoting Pirandello, "feels as if in exile—exiled not only from the stage but also from himself" (231). That is roughly the predicament of the *sefirot* and their fragments in *Parsifal*. In the course of rehearsing a scene, the movie actors face tests different from those on stage or in an arena, Benjamin asserts. These performance tests he compares to barriers to be overcome.[26] As already noted, the concept of transgressing is central to *Parsifal*, most literally in Amfortas' fall and Parsifal's arrivals. And central to Benjamin's argumentation is that true art originally had its place in cultic service: "It is significant that the existence of the work of art . . . is never entirely separated from its ritual function. In other words, the unique value of the 'authentic' work of art has its basis in ritual, the location of its original use value" (225–26). Ritual dominates the plot of *Parsifal*, not only in the two Grail ceremonies, but also in the initiation-like temptation sequence. When the genuine or authentic work of art was embedded in tradition and ritual, Benjamin claims, it also possessed an aura. This magically radiating but invisible nimbus surrounding the artwork he defines as "an unusual web of space and time."[27] As civilization separated art from its liturgical use, its aura grew dimmer, especially when the artwork became reproducible: "[T]hat which withers in the age of mechanical reproduction is the aura of the work of art" (223). Perhaps inspired by Wagner's use of time turning into space in act 1, Syberberg retains the rituals, even adds one in the puppet play, and seems to restore the aura, in spite of its presence in a film. Benjamin implies several times that the cinema constitutes the end of the move of art away from a religious function. It has lost the aura. The emphasis on ritual in *Parsifal* is unusual for any dramatic work.

Regardless what interpreters have wanted to read into it, Wagner imbued *Parsifal* with a spiritual component. So even if not a copy of a Eucharistic liturgy, ceremonies restore a ritual setting for much of the work. To this Syberberg adds the Kabbalistic and Hermetic dimensions that meet Benjamin's prerequisite for an aura. This accounts for his play with luminosity and reflections. The resulting impression suggests that the director adheres to Benjamin's characterizations of art with aura, challenges the limits of its existence in film, and deliberately deviates from prevailing cinematic conventions (e.g. with miming actors) by establishing a new category of art. It is film, but not entertainment and distraction for the masses. It is Wagner's legacy, but not the message a Hitler would like. The Kabbalistic interpretation "overcomes" and transcends the ideology attributed to the work, thus redeeming it. Both the Kabbalah and Benjamin's writings operate with the idea of a fallen state. It displays the condition of chaos, decay, brokenness, and shattered objects. Especially the fragments become conspicuous in *Parsifal*. Syberberg expands the metaphysical notion of brokenness in numerous visual equivalents. Not only Adam Kadmon and the six *sefirot* have been reduced to fragments. Also easily recognized as fragments in exile are the cropped details removed from their context in famous works of art. The absent context invariably contains, or points to, a spiritual or symbolic dimension. It ranges from religious representations (e.g. iconic Christ face, gilded Christ sculpture on crucifix, head from *Last Supper*) to symbolic renderings from mythology (e.g. Zeus, hand and face of Venus). But also objects have been added that one no longer thinks of as possessing spiritual significance, e.g. Charlemagne's crown or the polyhedron. Syberberg recognizes their lost auratic dimensions and adds them as fragments of the past. Or, one might say, as components of memory at home in the mind. They have all been dislocated, reappear in isolation, often in petrified form, only to be collected in a tentative new constellation at the end. This would equate Benjamin's "dialectical images" that possess epistemological importance. Furthermore, Syberberg's emphasis on eschatology parallels Benjamin's and the Kabbalah's view of messianism. This entails, as both Scholem and Jennings explain, an apocalyptic demise with everything in this world being in transience.[28]

As if pointing to Benjamin's influence, Syberberg endows the human face with an unexplained significance both in his films and publications. He mentions repeatedly the "face as landscape." Of course this reveals also that he planned the set for *Parsifal* years in advance. However, Benjamin's essay on the artwork mentions a pertinent detail. In the gradual secularization of art and its loss of aura, photography demands a middle position, Benjamin states. He says there about the cultic value of art that it retires into an ultimate retrenchment, the human countenance: "It is no accident that the portrait was the focal point of early photography. . . . For the last time the aura emanates from the early photographs in the fleeting expression of a human face" (227–28). In motion pictures the aura has been lost for several reasons, among them political abuse and "consumption" by mass audiences seeking entertainment. Syberberg seems to challenge that claim in an attempt to "save" also cinema from its predicament. Hence the emphasis on the king's face in *Ludwig* and its contrapuntal return in *Parsifal*, this time with an identifiable spiritual dimension. Again the camera dwells at length on certain faces. Close-ups of e.g. Herzeleide or the Grail Carrier reclaim their aura as manifestations of *parzufim* (= countenances). Others, among them Parsifal I and Amfortas, also possess this invisible nimbus as fractured *sefirot* to be combined into a new *parzuf*. Both categories represent stages in divine manifestations. One could therefore imagine *aura* to equate the halo-like radiance of divine forces. If viewed as vessels for the emanation, the sparks or efflux still cling to them. One remembers that also Wolfram described the beauty of Herzeloyde, Parzival, Conduiramurs, and Repanse de Schoy as luminous. The characters are still associated with a spiritual context. Although fictional, and now cinematic, they function as artworks in the kind of ceremonial environment Benjamin outlines. He probably was inspired to his own thoughts on the aura by Kabbalistic lore.

The occasional dwelling on faces in *Parsifal* appears at times in some unusually long camera takes. These seem to disregard the potential of available technology and moviemaking conventions. In other words, the camera is sometimes used as if to evoke still photography or at least the early stage of cinematography of Edison or Méliès. The renunciation of bravura work with the camera recurred in *Hitler* and was partially explained in *Die freudlose Gesellschaft*. One remembers Syberberg's dismissal of Riefenstahl's innovations. The entanglement of politics and cinematic sophistication prompts his separation of politics and art. This art, he appears to imply, must return to its roots for "healing" and reorientation. That, of course, would parallel the restoration process of the Kabbalah.

The return from a politically tainted cinematography to spiritual art in a ritual context may seem far removed from Wagner's death mask. And still, it too is a countenance hailing from the composer's face. Significantly, Benjamin would remind us, from a dead man's face. A mask is even mechanically reproducible. It actually *was* reproduced in several sizes for the film. Its origin as an imprint of a face bars it from being considered a real work of art. But unlike its mortal origin, the copy may survive for a long time. In chapter 8 of his essay on the artwork Benjamin mentions that the ancient Greeks could mass produce bronzes, terracottas, and coins.[29] But every other type of artwork was unique and therefore had to be made to last. Somehow Wagner's death mask seems to stretch and play with Benjamin's assertion. All the small versions of it are shown intact. When the face functions as the moon in a black sky, it even radiates reflected light. However, the huge mask landscape is reduced to fragments. This suggests the presence of a larger frame of reference. On the one hand it represents the composer's public face, his *persona*. On the other hand, as a set and landscape the mask also serves as the homeland of the music and characters, who, of course, originated in their creator's head. Thus this imitation of the fallen and broken Adam Kadmon constitutes the totality of the quasi-*parzufim* involved in the plot. Not only do their successful efforts recombine and restore the symbols they represent individually. They also restore Adam Kadmon. Therefore the symbol of totality bearing Wagner's features is the ultimate beneficiary of the redemption process. The setting may not be the sanctuary Benjamin stipulates for auratic art, but it shelters action leading to redemption according to Kabbalistic imagery. This relocates Benjamin's ritual function of authentic art from a temple of stone to the sanctuary of the righteous individual's person. Addressing the viewers' heart and mind, Syberberg has turned the development of art back towards its spiritual function, restored the aura that Benjamin could not detect in movies, and contributed to "redeeming" Wagner.

Wagner himself put in numerous supportive details that form the basis for the director's treatment. They surface in the music and in the voiced parts of the libretto. But in spite of his studies, he was unable to recognize Judaism in public any more than accept female equality. Also the feminine in human nature preoccupied him until his last hour, but there too, his prejudice blocked a breakthrough. With the two issues being combined in Kundry, she becomes the main carrier of that liberation in the film. And as for the title hero being "neither male nor female," as Wagner told his wife, how did he plan to present that idea on stage? Syberberg changed Wagner's negated expression into its opposite, "both male and female." Short of finding a hermaphrodite for the part, he translates Wagner's wish by observing the notions of the ideal in alchemy and psychology. And surprisingly, this complementarity harmonizes with the imagery of the Kabbalah. The male Yesod may be the active force in restoring the broken *parzufim*, but it is the female *parzuf* that enables him to complete the task of uniting the fragmented whole.

Syberberg did not abridge or alter the music and the sung dialogue. The parts of the orchestra and the singers are the audible components that constitute the composition. However, he did take liberties with Wagner's stage instructions and added sound when the music is silent. The stage instructions should serve only one purpose: to shape the visual presentation. A listener can ignore them while viewers in the opera audience must filter the sound through its visual impact. The burden of *Parsifal*'s anti-Semitic reputation lies primarily in the composer's other writings and in the stage instructions, not in the music and singers' lines. Nowhere do the audible parts imply Kundry's death and Amfortas' survival. By liberating the work of Wagner's instructions Syberberg removes the ideologically tainted dimension. Not only does this open the possibility for a new interpretation and for Syberberg's own visual creation. It may even fulfill the composer's wish. Wagner had already relegated the orchestra to invisibility in the pit. He also remarked to Cosima repeatedly that he really did not want to present the action on stage, e.g. on September 23, 1878. If carried out, that would have reduced a performance to a purely audible experience. The composer's stage instructions would no longer distort the reception. Perhaps *Parsifal* should have been a symphony with a chorus, or an oratorio. Not only does Syberberg's film relieve the composition of the problematic stage instructions. He also removes it from the stage and returns it to Wagner's head. One of several possible interpretations might view the outcome as the demise of *Parsifal* as well as its composer and presumed German Grail society. Another reading would see it as a saving strategy or a second chance. Ending with Kundry as the immortal Great Mother, the film awakens the hope for a new birth.

Chapter 11

Parsifal Encounters the Outside World

For many years Richard Wagner had struggled to promote performances of and secure royalties from his music dramas. But when ready to present his last work, *Parsifal*, he no longer wanted to release it to the opera stages of the world. He decided to reserve it for his own stage in Bayreuth. Although this proved futile, Wagner's attempt endowed the work with the nimbus of a sacred treasure to be protected from the profanity of ordinary opera business. A hundred years later Syberberg tried to emulate the composer's attempt on a reduced scale. But due to Gaumont's majority share in the funding for the film, the director had only limited control over its distribution. Nonetheless, the circumstances surrounding *Parsifal*'s premiere allowed him to adopt a Wagnerian pose.

The premiere of *Parsifal* took place at the film festival in Cannes. This annual event is, of course, a major international media spectacle attracting, beside legitimate creators and artists of cinema, hordes of publicity- and business-hungry visitors with interests incompatible with spiritual concerns. One might therefore assume that Syberberg would have fought to avoid this setting for the premiere of his *Parsifal*. But had he not let the soundtrack for the film be produced in Monte Carlo? In that mecca of casinos and gamblers Nietzsche had heard the first prelude played in concert as early as in 1887. Syberberg may have found Cannes to be an equally suitable and unlikely scene for his film. The festival atmosphere would parallel Klingsor's world of temptations and empty pursuits. The potential for international publicity would not hurt either. Through two strategies Syberberg "saved" *Parsifal* from the defilement of mixing with the mundane movie fare and crowds at the festival. The film was shown outside of competition, releasing it from comparisons. And it was shown at night, starting at one o'clock. That guaranteed an appreciative and determined audience different from most festival attendees. Numerous French and Italian newspapers and journals had published articles about the film throughout 1981 and spring of '82, preparing the public for an event of significance.[1] Many devotees flocked to Cannes primarily to see *Parsifal*. Regardless of attire, they were admitted free of charge to the old Palais where the screening took place. A problem caused a last minute panic: The film copy sent from Munich was incomplete. A private plane came to the rescue, bringing the missing rolls from Paris, where *Parsifal* was scheduled to premiere on the Champs Elysées the next day.[2] This *nuit blanche* between the 19th and 20th of May continued after the performance with breakfast on the beach at sunrise.[3] Syberberg's strategies proved successful, allowing him to introduce *Parsifal* with a celebration.

Much of the information about the film's reception and related events can be found in Syberberg's next book, *Der Wald steht schwarz und schweiget*. There one reads, for example, that the major funding company, Gaumont, marketed *Parsifal* as a regular movie, showing it everywhere in movie theaters. Syberberg retained the right to present the film in Germany and at special events. His printed comments reflect his own experiences showing it mostly on such occasions internationally. The French company marketed also the video and through its subsidiary, Erato, recordings of the music. Syberberg complains repeatedly that the Gaumont film and video versions had been trimmed of some sound effects, probably Kundry's cries at the end. But *Parsifal* was launched, and Syberberg spent much time traveling with his copy of the film, giving lectures and participating in discussions about it. He knew from experience that he could not rely on the German press to provide unbiased coverage. He had long been a persona non grata, and the choice of subject invited further distortion. Hitler had admired Wagner, whose anti-Semitic statements became notorious. Syberberg had made a film called *Hitler*, then a documentary about the incorrigible Winifred Wagner, and now a cinematic version of Wagner's last music drama. It did not take much effort to present Syberberg in the press as a Nazi. In the meantime he had also given up on the majority of his compatriots. He refers to them as "the Hitler people and the following generation." But, he assures his readers, it was especially for them he had undertaken the *Parsifal* project. Hitler understood *Parsifal* as his Bible and had announced that he wanted the work performed as part of the victory celebrations ending World War II, under the directorship of Wieland Wagner. For that reason, Syberberg maintains, it became "necessary to make this *Parsifal* and especially today" (*Der Wald*, 84). But since he does not reveal his interpretation and how it might change perceptions, few people bothered to consider the not so obvious possibilities.

Syberberg knew that he could best reach "his" German audience at special events. They would attract those familiar with his other work, those interested in Wagner, and art and music lovers. The first opportunity came with the seventh "documenta" art exhibit in Kassel a month later. The German premiere of *Parsifal* coincided with the opening of this international event. More than 350,000 visitors attended the exhibit as a whole. Not only did many of them also view the film as part of the art on display, but they also visited the rooms devoted to the film. Syberberg had secured four adjoining rooms in the basement of the Fridericianum (part of the exhibit complex) for many of the objects seen in the film. With dead leaves on the floor, visitors got close-up views of the Zumbusch copy of Parsifal, the Van Eyck fountain, the puppets, Charlemagne's throne and crown, and much more. The objects were now in different groupings, provoking thoughts on German history. The phallus from Delos, at 3.5 meters, would not fit through the door. It therefore went on display outside under a huge razor blade by Oldenburg. Syberberg mentions this constellation, but refrains from commenting on it (*Der Wald*, 69). The periodic "documenta" attracts an international public. Syberberg must have rejoiced in the interest shown his exhibit, since several of the rooms with his display needed to be cordoned off to keep the throngs of visitors under control (*Der Wald*, 69).

Parts of the Syberberg exhibit traveled on to Zurich and Vienna for the exposition on the *Gesamtkunstwerk*. In retrospect the display attracts attention. At least in Vienna it consisted of two parts: on one floor six rooms of props from the film, and on the floor beneath three rooms with eight television sets playing *Parsifal* in staggered timing. The sound was low enough to allow the viewer to concentrate on one screen at a time. "Like a fugue," Syberberg describes it, "different stages of the same action in different niches of a cathedral" (*Der Wald*, 234). The use of multiple screens anticipated another exhibit he created many years later for another "documenta." It was larger and more ambitious in scope, but had evolved from this fusing of technology and association with spiritual traditions.

Eventually most of the objects appearing in *Parsifal* found their way into the film museum of the Cinémathèque in Paris. But the concrete head landscape of Wagner's death mask was more difficult to move. It resided for a while outside on the grounds of the Bavaria Studio. There it became one of the attractions for tourists taking the tram ride of the studio tours. Two years later it was transported in five railroad cars to Berlin for another art exhibit called "Der Hang zum *Gesamtkunstwerk*" (The Penchant for the Total Work of Art). There it was placed in the park of the exposition site, Charlottenburg Palace, near the Berlin Wall. Although the exhibit catalog neglects to mention Syberberg's films and the organizers relegated his section of the display to an annex, he still managed to put his stamp on the event. The Wagner head in its fourteen parts (a still from the film) adorned the title page of the catalog. The resting place of this enormous object elicited conflicting ruminations in Syberberg (*Der Wald*, 531–32). As a composite representation of the master of the composite *Gesamtkunstwerk* it had found its rightful place. But the proximity of the Wall triggered the most disparate reflections. Finally, the weatherbeaten head rested now in Berlin, the capital of Wagner's admirer whom Syberberg had shown rising from the composer's grave. The concrete head deteriorated from the exposure to the elements and eventually disintegrated. In that it repeated the demise of the Grail society in the film.

Syberberg had created his *Parsifal* in time for the centennial of the music drama. Of course he wanted to show it in Bayreuth. Both a contribution to the commemoration and a provocation to the "Bayreuth" establishment, his *Parsifal* ran in matinee performances in a downtown theater while the festival pilgrims filled the town in July. As expected, Wolfgang Wagner and the mayor did not honor this counter-*Parsifal* with their presence. Wolfgang Wagner had not forgotten the scandal surrounding *Winifred Wagner*. His efforts to prevent Syberberg from using the music from Bayreuth recordings had not stopped the project, but his influence could still hamper Syberberg's plans. However, one cannot help wondering if he studied the film privately and was inspired by it. Seven years later, when he again included *Parsifal* in the festival season, he introduced a significant change at the end of the third act. He let Kundry survive, clearly against the composer's stage instructions. In 1994 he again changed the conclusion to let Kundry conduct the final Grail ceremony much like a female savior.[4] One remembers that Kundry as the sibyl or "Pythian seer" is the only surviving character in the film. As the pagan, psychological, and Kabbalistic Great Mother she is immortal. Somehow Wolfgang Wagner realized that and disobeyed his grandfather's instructions.

While *Parsifal* continued to run for four months at a movie theater in Paris and the videos sold briskly, Syberberg traveled with the film to special events. One of the highlights was the success in Rome. On August 27 and 28, 19982, the film was presented under the open night sky in the Circo Massimo to a capacity crowd. In October he showed it in the opera house of Barcelona to a sold-out house. Not so overwhelming was the screening at the Telluride festival in September. Contributing to the half-full house there was the timing. Unlike the audience in Cannes, the cineastes in Telluride did not like movies after midnight, only rest or parties. In Germany the director took *Parsifal* to Berlin as part of a retrospective of his work. It took place in the Arsenal during the annual fall arts festival, "Berliner Fest-wochen," in September. The film was shown for three days towards the end of the event. This run was scheduled as an "Homage to Edith Clever." Earlier on the same days the public could also see Eric Rohmer's movie *Perceval le Gallois* of 1978 in the same theater. That gave the audience the opportunity to compare two films on related subjects. The word had gotten out in spite of no advance ads or other publicity. Sold-out houses resulted in additional midnight performances. Also in Munich the director decided to show the film without publicity, starting in September in the Arri. Within a few screenings word-of-mouth spread the news, and the film soon attracted capacity crowds and continued later for a long time in Sunday matinees. This set the pattern for *Parsifal* in Germany—no advance publicity, no ads, no press conferences. Not surprisingly, the pattern also influenced the reception in the German media. Coverage was sparse and often jaundiced. One may wonder if the director did not want this result. After all, he reports that French journals and newspapers published over 800 articles and reviews of *Parsifal* by the fall of 1982. More than fifty articles appeared in Italian outlets after the two screenings in the Circo Massimo, and two dozen reviews followed the one event in Barcelona (*Der Wald*, 148–49). In other words, his accomplishments received ample recognition abroad, but not at home. His disregard for the German movie distribution and media business showed no sign of softening. Syberberg even added a nuance in his stand-off with the opinion makers. Not only the press, but the country as a whole has suffered the fate of the Grail society: "We live in a dead country," he reiterates. The German media establishment had written him off as a brown rightist after the *Hitler* film, and it continued to ignore him or distorted his work. For example, *Parsifal* was denied consideration for the Federal Film Award (*Bundesfilmpreis)* two years in a row. Presumably it was "only" a filmed version of a Wagnerian performance, but "not a movie" (*Der Wald*, 579). In view of Syberberg's interpretation and adherence to aesthetic principles, this must have hurt him as well as confirmed the notion about Germany being a dead country. Nonetheless, the film did receive the Critics' Award (*Kritikerpreis*) for 1982. This annual prize is granted in seven categories of artistic achievement, and *Parsifal* won the distinction for "film." This was the second Critics' Award for Syberberg, the first coming in 1968.[5] He apparently received it with mixed feelings, calling it an *Alibi-Farce* (*Der Wald*, 242). At least it must have been a consolation for him that Clever received the Bavarian Film Award for her performance in *Parsifal*.

The year 1983 brought more travels and speaking engagements related to *Parsifal*. In New York it played for eight weeks to a full house, first in Alice Tully Hall of Lincoln Center under Francis Ford Coppola's aegis, later at the Guild Theater. The premiere ended with a standing ovation for the director, spiced with boos. The following day he addressed the Wagner Society of New York, where he apparently enjoyed a friendly reception and lively debate. As expected, *Parsifal* was also present for the commemoration of the centennial of Richard Wagner's death in Venice. The composer had died there on February 13, 1883. As then, the carnival celebrations dominated the streets. Nonetheless, the film attracted a full house in the Fenice-Malibran Theater in the evening. That is the theater Wagner rented in 1882. He directed his Symphony in C Major there on December 24, in honor of Cosima's birthday on Christmas Day (Gregor-Dellin, 834–35). Syberberg knew what venues to select! Whenever possible, he avoided cinemas in favor of opera houses and theaters for such events. Due to the contract with Gaumont, the film circulated in regular movie theaters as well, but Syberberg upheld his non-conformist screening regimen also at events in Germany, for example in the Old Opera in Frankfurt am Main and the State Opera in Hamburg, invariably to capacity crowds. On numerous occasions later, screenings occurred in connection with symposia, Goethe Institute conferences, or retrospectives of Syberberg's films. This schedule could be quite hectic for him. For example, at a four-day event in Toulouse entitled "Syberberg, le Cinéaste et l'Écrivain," he participated on six occasions with lectures, discussions, and public interviews (*Der Wald*, 357). Another trip brought him and *Parsifal* to San Francisco and Los Angeles for the Filmex festival.

While staying busy with similar engagements for a couple of years, Syberberg harbored hopes of showing *Parsifal* in two locations of importance to him. One was Delphi in Greece. Obviously the connection Wagner-Aeschylus influenced this wish. The religiously inspired drama festivals in ancient Greece had nourished Wagner's plans. Syberberg had already presented the film in an open-air ancient setting in Rome. But he had to settle for a more realistic venue: a movie theater named Delphi in Berlin in connection with the exhibit on the *Gesamtkunstwerk*. The other desired location was Israel. At the time, Wagner's music could not be played in Israel. His name was too closely associated with National Socialism. Without ever hinting at his Kabbalistic "redemption" of *Parsifal*, Syberberg still thought his film could contribute to righting old wrongs. He viewed his film "as a political manifestation of atoning for moral guilt, a guilt accumulated over centuries" (*Der Wald*, 249). He had even received an invitation from Israel and could have shown the film in the Goethe Institute in Jerusalem. But the German ambassador intervened and put a stop to the preparations (*Der Wald*, 356).

Such disappointments and irritation over the German media were muted by printed accolades and appreciative reviews abroad. Occasionally Syberberg could also recognize that his film influenced how others viewed Wagner's *Parsifal*, although probably without touching on the central dimension of his interpretation. For example, the renowned stage director Ruth Berghaus directed *Parsifal* in Frankfurt in the 1982–83 season. Either she miraculously came up with many of the same visual details that occur in Syberberg's film, or she adapted and adopted it as an inspiration, perhaps as a silent tribute to his work. The German newspaper reviews did not recognize the indebtedness, including the end with a dead Grail society. Both Ruth Berghaus and Wolfgang Wagner count as celebrity directors in the world of German theater and opera. It is intriguing that their startling changes in *Parsifal* productions occurred only after Syberberg's *Parsifal* became known.

Over the years the literature about Syberberg's *Parsifal* has swelled to a library. Not only was the film eagerly awaited among the director's admirers, especially in France, but articles about it began to appear before the shooting was completed in the studio. One example is Guy-Patrick Sainderichin's report.[6] He contributes information, observations, reflections, and photos not appearing in other publications. He quotes Syberberg in action on the set, for example when citing Ernst Bloch with "One needs to be modest when facing Wagner" (25). Or, when Syberberg makes two statements about the work in one breath: "*Parsifal*, that is Wagner himself, it is a monument of Wagner to himself" (26). Sainderichin observes how the crowds move around in the head like vermin swarming in a cadaver, however, without further references to Syberberg's or Wagner's use of that imagery (27). He also informs the reader that the two Parsifal actors are a couple in real life, a detail fitting nicely with the idea of complementary manifestations of a composite whole. Balancing history and elucidation with description and reporting, the writer concludes with a warning to Wagnerians: "Tremble, ye pilgrims to Bayreuth! A plot is brewing in Munich" (29). Sainderichin's article exemplifies much of the literature about *Parsifal* appearing in other European countries. It accepts the surrealistic dimensions as meaningful means of expression, while appreciating the fidelity to Wagner's text and music.

In an interview published in *Cinématograph* in May 1982, Syberberg states that his *Parsifal* was not influenced by other movies with themes from Arthurian literature.[7] He claims not to know John Boorman's *Excalibur*. And although he finds Eric Rohmer's *Perceval le Gallois* intellectually interesting, he prefers a different approach. The text and music had prevented him from deviating as much from his source as Wagner did from his medieval sources. He calls his own version "a continuation and an evolution" (14). When asked if he identified with any of the title figures of his films, he points to a poster of *Parsifal* showing three names prominently: Parsifal, Wagner, and Syberberg. Apparently the film has something to do with all three, but he does not give a clear answer (14). He had already hinted at his own affinity with Parsifal and his quest when referring to himself as "this old fool" in the book to the film. In the same interview he also reveals a detail that must puzzle readers who have not seen the film. Discussing Edith Clever as Kundry and archetype, he describes her attempted seduction as an act of refusal (16). The temptress refuses? Then one remembers her bared breast and Parsifal's position as a suckling infant. Yes, Syberberg found a way to make the hero's reaction comprehensible, both mythically and psychologically. His French interviewers knew Wagner's music drama, Syberberg's oeuvre, and had seen the film. They were informed and appreciative.

The German reviews were much more diverse and predominantly critical. They are few by comparison, and many tend to suffer from a mixture of ignorance, animosity towards Syberberg and Wagner, and conformity to the prevailing views. Typical, and unfortunately influential in setting the tone, is the early review by Klaus Umbach in *Der Spiegel*.[8] Several members of the editorial staff had served on a commission that evaluated Syberberg's request for funding of the film. For this and other similar applications the director had prepared sixty non-returnable packets of detailed descriptions of the project, including plans for props and names of cast members and technical ensemble. The journalist probably had access to this information, because he mentions a detail that does not appear anywhere in the film or the book about it. He reports twice that the male Parsifal actor is Swiss. His membership on or closeness to the commission that rejected Syberberg's application might also account for the negative tone of the review. An appreciative assessment would have amounted to an admission of the commission's poor judgment. One also needs to be aware of the prestige *Der Spiegel* enjoys. Founded under the auspices of the American occupation forces after World War II, the publication prides itself of being Germany's leading news magazine, fiercely independent and democratic. The review does not meet the proclaimed standards of the magazine. One cannot even be sure if the reviewer actually watched the film or at least most of it. He claims, for example, that the title hero arrives riding his white horse (226). Not so. Nowhere in the film does Parsifal appear on horseback. Furthermore, Umbach lets a flock of angels sing from a gigantic Bible (226). He means the sopranos "from on high." Perhaps he owns a Bible with the *Parsifal* score and a Wagner portrait in it? And maybe Syberberg's packet of information did not describe or explain the dead that Parsifal must pass on entering the Grail Castle. Umbach refers to them as a boothful of ghosts. He also reproaches Syberberg for presenting "a solemn Eucharist." The reader may remember that the only glimpse of the traditional Grail ritual is a reflection of Joukowsky's sketch on the Grail Carrier's dress. The film is "painfully boring" and, worst of all, more than four hours long. This last fact the reporter ascribes to the "monomaniac" director's fondness for films of excessive length. Of course the film leaves Wagner's music intact, but Syberberg gets blamed for its length. The reviewer regrets that Syberberg did not turn Wagner's work upside down. He should at least have turned it into a comical opera (227). He did not even a single time try to spit into the Grail (226). No, Syberberg certainly did not spit into the Grail. Unfortunately, other critics continued the negativity and careless handling of facts. The symbiosis of Third Reich ideology, Hitler, and Wagner was now expanded to include Syberberg's name in much of the German press, even in scholarly circles (with a few exceptions). If the director had wanted to present himself as the victim of a new ideology as hateful and intolerant as Nazism, he had succeeded.

By and large, the reviews of *Parsifal* belong to the shorter and less important publications about the work. That includes also most of the reviews published in the English-speaking world. To be sure, they are not aggressive and distorting as so many appearing in Germany. But many of the reviewers tend to suffer from lack of understanding. Complicating their task, Syberberg incorporates several critical approaches as subtexts in *Parsifal*. Of these Brecht's theories of epic drama and alienation were recognized only in a handful articles. One of them is Gunnar Iversen's "Brecht + Wagner = Syberberg."[9] Although the bulk of this article assesses Syberberg's total cinematic oeuvre up to 1985 and hence does not focus only on *Parsifal* or dwell long on the Brechtian dimension, it recognizes it. The article also appreciates the setting as the geography of the soul. And, the text points out, "no doubt Syberberg transgresses boundaries with this beautiful film" (26). Similarly John Rockwell remarks, "It's as if Wagner's hypnotic allure and Brecht's intellectual alienation have been somehow mystically united."[10] He also realizes that this *Parsifal* will not appeal to everybody, being a bit too weird for that. But, he predicts, it has the potential for becoming a cult film (46). Marcia Citron, who devotes a chapter to *Parsifal*, sees Brechtian influence in numerous features, such as the disjunction between voice and actor, the division of the title hero, and the existence of Amfortas' persona inside and outside the narrative.[11] The second half of her chapter focuses on memory. It notes that beginning and end meet, closing a circle and inscribing memory in several forms. This leads beyond Brecht to Citron's question: "As we view Germany after reunification, we see a new social order that has led to strained and dashed visions of utopia. Is this predicted in the purification ritual that is the film itself?" (158). Also Jeremy Tambling's chapter on the film examines the alienation devices. For instance, he finds the fact that Kundry is kneeling and pleading with a woman to be "radically disturbing."[12] As for the historical allusions, especially to the Third Reich, he disagrees with Syberberg's premise: "The 1967 Mitscherlich thesis of the German 'inability to mourn' might seem to necessitate the need to exorcise the image of Hitler: but that cannot be done by using Wagner: there is no separation from what needs to be deconstructed" (210). Syberberg had stated in his book to the film, "One does not combat Hitler with statistics from Auschwitz, but with Richard Wagner" (224). He also uses *Parsifal*'s words that only the spear that caused the wound can heal it. The destructive potential of the spear is transformed when presented by the transformed bearer, whose insight into and experience of suffering, *Mitleiden*, becomes the prerequisite for the healing process. Tambling does not accept it.

The political and historical dimension of the film elicited more criticism than approval in the English-speaking world. In some cases one can recognize echoes of German reviews, which often consider any references to Nazi history as a sign of Wagner's and Syberberg's presumed sympathies with Third Reich ideology. Others consider such visual hints superfluous and disturbing. George Movshon, for instance, thinks, "But it soon becomes clear that we are to watch an allegory, that Wagner's composition will be made the skewer for a shish-kebab of recent German history."[13] The writer prefers *Parsifal* untainted and unburdened by that kind of subtext: "In sum, I found the political elements in the film to be irrelevant and distressing, like moustaches on the Mona Lisa" (20). Both he and Andrew Clements think all the referentiality of so many visual elements make the film "a notable failure."[14] Most non-German critics do not share the obsession with joining Wagner and Nazi ideology, and therefore prefer a less challenging and more traditional visual treatment. Even Ronald Holloway's mostly positive review from Cannes concludes, "The trick is to identify the motifs as the images pile one upon the other to the point of mental exhaustion —the interpreters of irony among the elite intellectual class of critics will have a field day."[15] At least one critic writing about Syberberg's film-cum-exhibit at the "documenta" found the references to history a proof of the filmmaker's "obsession to be taken seriously as an artist, while also cashing in on the media's current success at toying with fascism under the guise of historical introspection."[16] The reviewers did not recognize the function of the historical and political dimension as an important foil for the director's interpretation of the work. On the one hand, the objects and references in the film function within Benjamin's framework of auratic and non-auratic symbols. The aura is restored through the connection with Jewish mysticism. This relationship undergoes a fugue-like transformation through the Nazi veneration for many of the same symbols.[17] On the other hand, a reading on a different level sees the imagery as fragments and allegories accompanying the demise of the Grail society. It, in turn, illustrates the decline beyond regeneration of modern German society. After all, the film's concluding Grail ceremony differs starkly from expectations. But at least Jack Kroll's article appreciates Syberberg's deviation from prevailing ideas about *Parsifal*: "The film performs the extraordinary feat of both splendidly presenting and forcibly challenging a consummate work of art."[18] With appreciative comments on many aspects of the film, he also remarks, "Certain to infuriate Wagner purists, Syberberg's film is a bizarre masterpiece in its own right, arguably the best movie version of an opera ever made" (49).

An article by Manfred Schneider concentrates on aspects in Wagner's and Syberberg's *Parsifal* that most other studies leave out.[19] Focusing on the gaze, he ignores the Medusa's eyes. He considers the gaze a sign of insight and knowledge. This he links with the simultaneity of objects from various periods and places that blur the concept of time and space. The result, he claims, is a film that functions as the medium of historical memory. The characters, plot, and montage of objects all serve to transform knowledge into the ultimate insight with music as the main carrier. The gaze also reveals the blind will inherent in everything and the finite nature of everything, or, as Schneider calls it, "a theological, rather: a philosophical elementary given" (892). Kundry is the embodiment of this absolute consciousness independent of time and space. Thus, both the characters and the symbols contribute to endow cinema with a new mission: the preservation and transmission of historical memory.

Michael Walsh does not share that view. He takes issue with the director's method that relies on associations: "Syberberg's problem is symbols: there are too many of them . . . Syberberg employs symbols the way others use props; in fact he uses them *as* props."[20] Although overall critical, the writer recognizes some of this imagery as being Freudian. In view of Wagner's emphasis on chastity and sexuality, the Freudian dimension in the film is easy to recognize. Quite a few of the studies refer to Freud. One example is the review by J. Hoberman, who had attended the premiere in Cannes. He describes the bleeding wound as "a portable gash that's the very image of [a] vagina as castrated phallus."[21] He considers *Parsifal* a most blatantly Freudian movie, but quotes Syberberg as being rather reticent about his methods. When asked if he thought of the film in psychoanalytic terms, Syberberg had responded evasively (64). The director may assume too much. But at least Hoberman and a few others recognize Freud as an inspiration behind the visual narrative. Hoberman describes Syberberg admiringly as a "vocational German," a "useful political lightning rod," and an "anti-modern modernist." More often, reviewers quickly invoke Freud when referring to the film's surprises, but do not elaborate. David Denby, for example, calls Kundry's bared breast in the seduction scene a "Freudian shocker."[22] When, however, he dismisses the division of Parsifal, one gets the feeling the writer does not recognize how faithfully this illustrates Freud's theories. Just such a psychoanalytic elucidation of Parsifal's transformation is offered by Oskar Sahlberg.[23] His scholarly study interprets the hero's rejection of the seduction as "absorbing the mother in himself" (343). By accepting the feminine in himself he can preserve his masculinity, as evidenced by the continuing male voice. The feminine manifestation is his alter ego from his early childhood. Sahlberg also recognizes the mask landscape as the inner world. He describes Parsifal's entry into it as a descent into a past which is our present: "It is the descent to the roots of the evil, from which actually salvation, healing should have grown, and through which work of memory, of insight can still develop; a work that only became possible with the means of film" (344–45). He also sees the quest for the Grail as the search for one's Self and one's roots. Similarly Thomas Elsaesser does not shy away from the demands Syberberg places on the viewer. He states that the film is not merely a "send-up of a classic ripe for plucking."[24] While some of the ideas are shocking, he admits, "they derive from Syberberg having worked through the elements of the myth and Wagner's ideological use of them, rather than out of iconoclasm or the need to dazzle with cinematic effects" (137). After considering the psychological implications of Wagner's libretto (with the composer's instructions), he remarks that its Christian veneer allowed Wagner to "bypass" the Oedipal drama and tragic guilt. Syberberg changes that by making "Parsifal, the saviour, male *and* female, and his saving grace the recognition of both as parts of the same self" (138). Elsaesser also points out that the globe with the Bayreuth theater in it alludes to Edison's Black Mary, as seen in *Hitler*.

Clearly, Syberberg's film poses many challenges to viewers. Not all of them recognize his frames of reference or are willing to explore the visual surprises. At the division of the title hero, for example, the critics divide into separate camps. Some refer to a psychological dimension, while others remain descriptive and often dismiss what cannot be plainly understood. To this group belongs Stanley Kauffmann, who thinks the division is only intended to jar preconceptions and provoke new scrutiny.[25] Other reviewers, who may not have recognized the psychological implications either, took the precaution to refer to Freud, perhaps for two reasons. Some early reviews contained such references. And, Syberberg's book *Die freudlose Gesellschaft* includes a pun on Freud's name in the title.

While Sahlberg and Elsaesser refer to both Freudian and Jungian concepts in their articles, most critics display less familiarity with Jung's thought. This is rather surprising, considering the popularity of Jungian approaches to literature barely a generation ago. Paul Coates' study will serve as an example among the scholarly examinations.[26] He observes, "Syberberg's Grail is the reintegration of the personality that split in the moment of crisis, playing dead as it were in order to secrete the threatened (male) portion of the personality elsewhere, for later recovery" (128). Taking his cues from Syberberg's book to the film, he emphasizes two central ideas: The film tries to eliminate the "sexist polarity of male redeemer and female temptress," and also "the notion that the female and the Jew (linked in Kundry, whom Wagner compared to the Eternal Jew) require redemption *from without*" (127). Syberberg elaborates on this concern repeatedly, e.g. on pp. 56–57 in his book.

Also relatively ignored in secondary literature is Syberberg's aim to create a *Gesamtkunstwerk*. With Wagner's thought on the topic culminating in *Parsifal*, this possibility beckoned. And of course his film combines a long list of components associated with Wagner's concept. Tambling notes," If film is the *Gesamtkunstwerk*, what Syberberg perpetuates is the nineteenth-century ideology of art itself as the privileged bearer of meanings in the absence of religion: art as the new metaphysics" (207). Syberberg would probably dispute the "absence of religion" but confirm the link to metaphysics. By reintroducing spiritual components, he has transformed (his) film into auratic art.

Not so much metaphysics as philosophy attracted Norman Fischer to his study of the film.[27] It examines Syberberg's interpretation against views by Wagner, Nietzsche, and Marx, with emphasis on the treatment of Kundry. It concludes, "Syberberg's emancipated film version of *Parsifal* allows this dialogue and philosophical reconstruction to begin" (151). Fischer does not recognize to what extent Syberberg has already subjected Wagner's work to a new interpretation. Since the director has not commented on his most revolutionary contribution, the debate about *Parsifal* continues along the established paths. Thus Wagner's misogyny and anti-Semitism still remain the basis for modern studies. In some minds, any interpretation running counter to this prerequisite is dismissed. Therefore also Jean-Jacques Nattiez takes exception to Syberberg's statement about having solved the problem of antifeminism and anti-Semitism.[28] But he also discusses Wagner's concept of androgyny in the title hero. Quoting Cosima's diary of June 27, 1880, he reminds the reader that Wagner wanted Parsifal to be "sexless, neither man nor woman." A male and a female manifestation do not correspond to Wagner's statement, according to Nattiez. He comments, "In spite of what Syberberg suggests, womankind perishes so that Parsifal's sanctity is not corrupted by the female element. Parsifal is asexual, and it he who saves Kundry" (290). More focused on anti-Semitism is Marc Weiner's book on Wagner mentioned in chapter 7. His "afterword" includes comments on the film (349–53). Taking his cue from the death mask set, he sees the characters as trapped in Wagner's body. This implies that they too have become lifeless and sterile, since the body is literally the "embodiment of Wagner's ideological agenda" (350). The film shows it as a tool that also provokes new questions. One of them is "whether the icons of ideology in Western culture have so changed since the nineteenth century that we must speak of a fundamental break between Wagner's intentions, the initial reception of his music dramas, and our own twentieth-century perception of them" (351). Thanks to the cultural distance between Wagner's thought when published and our reception of it, it becomes possible to reexamine the ideas of racial and sexual exclusion in his music dramas. And their "meaning," Weiner reminds the reader, has only been evoked, not explicitly stated. Without attempting an assessment of the film, Weiner welcomes the unorthodox visual treatment precisely because it provokes questions.

To a different category altogether belongs the growing literature on *Parsifal* as an Arthurian film. A good introduction to Arthurian themes on the screen is *Cinema Arthuriana*, edited by Kevin Harty.[29] The editor's overview reveals that Wagner's *Parsifal* started the genre with Edwin Porter's version for Edison in 1904. He adds a description and history of this early work (3–4). His bibliography includes a select list of early reviews and articles about Syberberg's *Parsifal* (237–39). A chapter by Ulrich Müller in the same volume deals in more detail with Syberberg's film.[30] Although it is not being discussed explicitly, one realizes that very few movies with Arthurian themes have been made in Germany. Richard Blank's *Parzival* of 1980 appears to be the first one. This non-traditional version of Wolfram von Eschenbach's romance mixes the Middle Ages with modern society. In 1981 followed *Feuer und Schwert: Tristan und Isolde*, directed by Veith von Fürstenberg. Apparently Syberberg's *Parsifal* is only the third Arthurian film and the second one focusing on the Grail seeker in Germany, not counting filmed stage productions. Müller places Blank's and Syberberg's films in their respective histories of development and debate. One observes with interest, however, that both films dispense with realism and resort to artificial conceits that deviate from Hollywood traditions. Müller accepts the duality of the title hero and concludes: "A film of the highest quality, it furthermore is a valuable treatment of a Wagnerian opera, with whose innovative qualities no other screen adaptation (even from Bayreuth) can compare. . . . Occasionally shocking or controversial, it is in all events extraordinarily exciting" (164). The editor, Harty, includes the same bibliography in a later book, *The Reel Middle Ages*, but does not add anything new to the summary of plot and characteristics.[31]

Another study by John Christopher Kleis contains more nuances.[32] He too considers the film as belonging in the Arthurian tradition. While operating with such concepts as deconstructionism and fetishism, Kleis views the text's misogyny as a moral flaw that Parsifal must overcome. However, he does not accept the divided hero: "This transformation is Syberberg's one big misstep in the film" (117). He refers to the director's "subsequent feminist readings" as unconvincing, since the conflict takes place in a man. Therefore, Kleis avers, "Syberberg is here attempting to cover his confusion and to throw his problem back at the audience that agrees with his feminism and is willing to get it in any form" (117). Similarly, he dismisses

Kundry's role at the end, declaring that the director has given her "undue prominence" (119). The central issue in the Parsifal story, he claims, is the (Protestant) debate of salvation achieved through faith alone or through good deeds resulting from faith. Overall, Kleis considers *Parsifal* "a brave film." He concludes that "Wagner surely would have applauded this sort of technological/philosophical *Gesamtkunstwerk*. . . . Whatever its flaws, it makes us look at—and, more important, think about—not just Wagner but about the way the issues of the Arthurian tradition are reflected in our own struggles" (120).

The last article to be included in this selection of studies is one by Donald Hoffman.[33] It discusses and compares three "Arthurian" films, Rohmer's *Perceval le Gallois*, *Parsifal*, and the American *Fisher King*. Especially the juxtaposition of Rohmer's and Syberberg's films invites further exploration due to similar subjects and different aesthetics. Examining the devices and mechanisms chosen to achieve Brechtian alienation, Hoffman declares Syberberg close to both Brecht's spirit and style (51). Especially the division and the reunion of male and female convinces him that the film does not glorify a Nazi-inspired utopia. He concludes that "[the embracing Parsifals] may be read as a Jungian allegory of the reunified soul" (50–51). He also reads it as a political allegory. His conclusion seems more optimistic than Syberberg's when he parallels the reintegration of the soul with a reunion of the two German states and a "victory" over the Nazi and communist ideologies so entrenched there. Noteworthy is his observation of the crowned skull at the end of the film. It echoes, Hoffman explains, the dead German ecclesiastics in Eisenstein's 1938 film *Alexander Nevsky* (50). This adds one more reference to cinematography in *Parsifal*. Throughout his text he pays also attention to cinematic techniques, especially framing and reframing the hero, their purpose and result. This insistence reminds the reader that *Parsifal* is not only a representation and interpretation of Wagner's work, but also a film with its own set of aesthetic criteria.

The sampling of secondary literature on Syberberg's *Parsifal* indicates interest from a large and varied public. Both journalists, artists, and scholars have shared their thoughts on the film. Initially, the reviews and interviews with Syberberg prevailed. Typical is an article cum interview by Ralph Schnell.[34] It offers an overview of Syberberg's aesthetics in the German Cycle interspersed with Syberberg's statements. Gradually, scholarly studies began to predominate. Apart from the interviews, the director's own statements on the film followed in the form of lectures and his next book. He gave, for example, his 1983 lecture, "Filmisches bei Richard Wagner" (The Cinematic in Richard Wagner), at a symposium at Castle Thurnau in Bavaria.[35] The interdisciplinary conference observed the centennial of Wagner's death, attracting speakers from East and West Germany, Austria, Great Britain, and Israel.

Syberberg begins by emphasizing that cinema based on an existing score must by definition deliver the visual component. Through close-ups, for example, it can offer more than the long-shot view from the rows in the opera house. Later he reminds the audience of the weekly newsreels from the war front that preceded every movie in German cinemas during World War II. They used primarily Wagner's music as soundtrack accompanying speech and image. This perverted music resulted in an "applied Wagner in the sense of the dream about world rule by the ideologically tainted (*völkisch gesinnten*) Wagnerians" (69). Syberberg wants nothing to do with that use of Wagner's music. But he does not aim at simple photography either. He returns to his emphasis on the human face and the wish to merge it with music and dialogue to a new unity, letting the face reveal or uncover the music. What he does not mention in this context is the Kabbalah's stress on the *parzuf*, the countenance, in the quest for restored wholeness. Therefore he only adds that he chose the death mask as the basis for the whole idea "for various reasons" (70). Similarly, he emphasizes his separation of voice and actor, comparing it with the division in the marionette theater between puppet and voice, but passing over the subject of fragmentation in the Kabbalah. The closest he comes to acknowledging the influence of Jewish mysticism is a reference to Walter Benjamin and the aura (71–72). Benjamin's writings may be more indebted to mysticism than Scholem and other biographers give him credit for. Syberberg's page about the aura forms the central topic of the lecture thematically and structurally. This is what his film is all about, he states (72). With the aura restored he hopes to achieve an ideal kind of theater that he calls art "in the service of political, relevant catharsis" (72). He introduces several expressions for the aura, such as "the third dimension," "the inner eye," and "the depth." In this, he notes cryptically, lie the reasons for the divisions and for not celebrating the Grail ceremony on screen.

Not quite so cryptic in retrospect are Syberberg's following thoughts on Wagner's *Ring*. As he outlines in the discussion with the audience after his lecture, he considers nature or creation subject to cyclic destruction, and that is the main subject of the *Ring* (74–78). After referring briefly to the elements involved in the cycle of transformations, he reduces them to the chiffre of "forest", *der Wald*. This mythic forest derived from Dante's world is dying in modern Europe, he reminds the audience. Of course, in the early 1980s, the effects of acid rain and pollution began to manifest in dying trees all over central Europe. One could hardly open a newspaper or magazine without encountering references to the "dying of the forest," *Waldsterben*. Now the dying forest serves him as a parallel to the destruction that concludes the *Ring*. The knowledge of an approaching demise, the end-of-time awareness, is then connected with Wagner, who declared *Parsifal* to be his last work for the stage, and who knew his own death was near. Syberberg finally connects the dimension of eschatology with the death mask as landscape (including forest). He does not mention that his next book will have the word *forest* in its title. Rather, one gains the impression that his next film may be his version of Wagner's *Ring*. In a world facing *Götterdämmerung*, or today also *Menschendämmerung*, Syberberg claims with Hölderlin in mind that art assumes the mission to save or redeem humanity by showing a vision of possibilities (73). In the ensuing discussion, where the division of Parsifal cropped up again, he responds that Parsifal as a couple united in love supports the idea of redemption as love. A bit later he explains that this Parsifal is his own version of the character: "I used Wagner for it just as Wagner utilized the texts of the Middle Ages. Thus a new creation" (76).

Syberberg's lecture in Thurnau was only one of many presentations he gave in the years following *Parsifal*'s release, but not much has been recorded of the contents. The other major source of information about the film is Syberberg's book of 1984, *Der Wald steht schwarz und schweiget*. This time he turned to the publishing house Diogenes in Zurich. The book continues where *Die freudlose Gesellschaft* leaves off. While the second half of the latter text includes much information about the film, all of the book to the film (*Parsifal: Ein Filmessay*) focuses on it, and *Der Wald* devotes about two thirds of its contents to it. The trio forms, as it were, a triptych in print to accompany the film. *Der Wald* keeps the format of the first volume, but mirrors it to create the symmetry. The subtitle, *Neue Notizen aus Deutschland*, confirms the continuation of a diary-like pro-gression of short text blocks. Mostly numbered, the units vary in length from a few lines to several pages. They are gathered into chapter-like clusters with individual headlines followed by a concluding *Register*, making it easy to look up specific data or names. Appearing in chronological order, the headlines consist of time and/or place references indicating the author's activities and whereabouts. This arrangement returns a faint echo of Gurnemanz' words about time turning into space. The first chapter returns to 1981 and the preparations preceding the shooting of the film. In other words, it links up with the contents of *Die freudlose Gesellschaft*. The following 22 chapters cover the period from *Parsifal*'s premiere to the spring of 1984. Not by chance does this list of 22 include the word *night* in its first and last headlines. Thanks to them the list bends into a circle with beginning and end meeting. Although Syberberg's future engagements in all likelihood also included travels and lectures devoted to *Parsifal*, the book rounds off the subject and prepares for new endeavors. Towards the end it announces that the next film will be called *Die Nacht*. If one includes the introductory chapter and the index, the book comprises 24 units, much like the segments on a traditional clock face. Starting the count at midnight with the first unit, one arrives at the second chapter about *Parsifal* in Cannes at 1 a.m. Sure enough, the screening of the film started at 1 a.m. during the *nuit blanche* between May 19th and 20th, 1982. What at first glance looks like an artless recording of events and commentary reveals itself as a carefully structured text.

The main topic is *Parsifal*'s reception in Europe and the United States up through the spring of 1984. Syberberg traveled with his film to numerous events. Consequently, the chronicler emerges as a second and equally important subject. He and his title hero Parsifal become a divided protagonist in a nonfictional narrative set in the modern world. Sometimes the author reports in the first person singular, identifying the subject as Syberberg. On other occasions he refers to the subject as the third person pronoun *he*, raising questions in the readers' mind. As Goethe wrote about the two souls in Faust, Syberberg presents a divided modern mind. Much of the time the reader remains unaware of the author's dual nature, shrugging off the use of *he* instead of *I* as an attempt to appear less conspicuous in the text. The tendency to present the subject in the third person becomes stronger towards the end of the book where the focus shifts. The bulk of the book reports on travels with *Parsifal*, experiences during these activities, and reflections based on the writer's observations. These include more disenchantment with the German media. One may, then, read the grammatical shift in subject pronoun as a reflection of his image in Germany resulting from a diminished status. The writer sporadically adopts the reduced view of himself that others project on him. At the same time the subject continues to function as two variations in counterpoint. Regardless which form the writer chooses, the subject continues the critical reflections on German society. Interspersed with the reports on *Parsifal* are comments on a wide range of current affairs, especially as pertaining to the media. As opinion makers and powerful cogs in the machinery, the media representatives now display a dangerous conformity. Of course Syberberg has in mind the very same representatives who served on the public commissions that denied support for his film projects and who continued the boycott in their publications. They claim to be good democrats and paint him as an admirer of Nazism. He sees them as heirs to and practitioners of that same authoritarian rule. Not only does their conformity reveal the heel-clacking political correctness of yesteryear, he implies, but so do also the distortions and malice in their attacks. One passage describes the opinion makers as a pack of "dogs or hyenas or jackals" waiting in ambush for the caravans from which they draw their subsistence (558), The author avoids the term *wolves*, but any canine will suffice for a quasi-musical allusion to the Wolf and the pack of dogs references in the *Hitler* film. Sometimes the attacks on Syberberg take the form of neglect. This antagonism resurfaces throughout the book, much as the adversity Parsifal endures (e.g. 536).

Another recurring topic is the concern for the environment, with the focus on trees and forest. The Sefirotic Tree appears in its real-life German variants. They are damaged and dying. Of course their plight parallels the spiritual and ethical condition of the population surrounding them. The author juxtaposes the "damaged image of humanity" and the "covering of nature with concrete" (541). Symptomatic of the sorry predicament is Fassbinder, who functions as an example of those following the media industry (e.g. 544). His name continues to crop up repeatedly. Among other recurring German names one notices Hölderlin, who withdrew from the world in despair and madness, and J. S. Bach, whose music became an inspiration for Syberberg's aesthetics. Their works belong to the healing forces in German culture. The author also identifies negative and destructive figures whose appearance can become less threatening when presented as part of art. Hitler is an example, against whose dangerous influence Syberberg "saved" himself by not making him the subject of his *Hitler* film, but instead his voters and their descendants (116). Only that combination yields the "whole" Hitler, he adds. Among the hundreds of names mentioned, Jung is conspicuously absent. Freud, on the other hand, leads the list of frequently cited Jewish intellectuals and artists. They serve as the counterparts to Syberberg's spiritually moribund compatriots. Second in the list is Benjamin, whose influence is not always identified by name. Especially in discussions on aesthetics, his thoughts on symbolic art inform the text. Repeated references to ritual and restoration of the aura reveal his importance (e.g. 49, 115, 537). On numerous occasions references remain unidentified and therefore often unrecognized. For example, in an autobiographical passage written in the third person singular, the author describes how rebellion saved him from the death of stifling conformity. The insight about his predicament and choice came from reading something very different from [Heidegger's] *Principle of Ground*, he confides, "when he heard from old books how . . . ideas could become objects only through contemplative meditation" (559).[36] Syberberg does not indicate which old books he had "heard." But as a result he now aims at creating art as "objectification of ideas," that, by means of contemplative meditation, can become recognizable to the senses (560). In this connection he also sees the fulfillment of the laws of music as the highest stage of insight and of life. He appears to have harbored these objectives for some years. His composition of visual fugues does not only produce synaesthesia. But also the fugal subject undergoes a series of transformations in its progression away from and eventually towards its original key, as seen in a circular arrangement. It expresses the cycle of life.

More often than not Syberberg prefers hints and allusions over precise information. With the fugal procedure also characterizing his writing, his textual counterpoints allow room for misunderstanding. He takes it in stride. For unknown reasons he also withholds information that perhaps might change the public's view of him. In a passage describing himself, one reads: "And he wrote and wrote [while] moving in circles, contradicting himself, like crazy, to inform, . . . explaining, increasingly provoking in his search for the center, sometimes smiling, but still, he did not divulge the most important thing" (553–54). Whatever he was or is withholding, the act prevents the public from seeing the full picture. It might also prevent understanding and a fair judgment of the man as well as of his work.

The idea of partial visibility finds an echo in the poem that provides the title for the book. The title is the fourth line of Matthias Claudius' "Abendlied" (Evening Song), written in 1779.[37] It is one of the three best known evening poems in the German language, the others being Heine's "Nachtgedanken" and Goethe's "Wanderers Nachtlied." Syberberg made use of them in his *Hitler* book and film. There, lines from Heine's poem introduce and conclude the text, and the subtitle to part 1 includes the "Goethe Oak of Buchenwald." Legend reports that Goethe composed the first half of his poem sitting under a tree in what later became the grounds of the concentration camp. André Heller also recites both halves of the poem in part 4 of the film. All three of these poems are familiar to Germans. Allusion to any one of them easily evokes the others. In addition, Claudius' line now triggers the memory of Syberberg's *Hitler*.

Claudius' "Abendlied" begins with the description of nature at peace. The birds have stopped singing, making the forest silent. The darkness of the forest contrasts with the sparkling firmament. Up there one can see a half moon, but, the poet adds, it is really round and beautiful. And he reminds the reader, we laugh at so many things because our eyes cannot see them the way they really are. Stanzas 5 through 7 turn into a bed-time prayer. Peace and piety permeate the text. By taking the only line about the forest out of context, Syberberg subjects it to a very different range of connotations with jarring echoes. The black and silent forest points both to a dead nature destroyed by modern society and to the late hour in an eschatological sense. But simultaneously the words also retain their original meaning and atmosphere from the poem. This third dimension provides the bridge to the next film in the planning stages.

The quoted line as title ends with the poetic or achaic form of a verb. Modern German would say *schweigt* and not *schweiget*. Of course the poet selected the extended form to retain the meter. But the line has now been deprived of its context. It is just a fragment, Benjamin would remind us. And this fragment with an archaic form revives the memory of a similarly odd verb in a poem much closer in time. Paul Celan's "Todesfuge" also contains the archaic *träumet* (dreams). Since his "Death Fugue" plays out in a concentration camp, the association elicits a feeling of apprehension. Another concentration camp! Celan's verbal fugue links Hebrew and German to achieve its musical effects. The *-et* in the verb ending calls up two Hebrew homonyms, one of them meaning "time" (*'ayin, tau*).[38] In Syberberg's frame of reference, that word recalls eschatology, end-of-time, as at the end of *Parsifal*. Thus the black and silent forest is a dead forest heralding the impending demise or *Untergang* of humanity as well. True to his calling as an artist, Syberberg presents his insight as a veiled oracle that not everyone can interpret. Easier to discern is the emphasis on night. As another Parsifal, the author is about to descend into the dark realm of dreams and the subconscious. In terms of Freud's theories, budget, technical extravaganza, and cast, the next endeavor means a regression. The planned *Night* is a monologue with only one actress, Edith Clever. As the Anima, she had already appeared as the gate to the collective unconscious in *Parsifal*.

The German press showed relatively little interest in the book. Its chronicle of *Parsifal*'s reception appeals mainly to readers appreciating the film. And predictably, the criticism of current affairs in Germany provoked animosity among journalists and again resulted in rebuttals from the reviewers. Hans Christian Kosler, for example, reacted in a typical fashion.[39] His article reveals little about the book's content. Kosler presents it only as attacks and criticism nourished by Syberberg's resentment. He is seen as a man with the ambition of a Zarathustra who rants in anger foaming at the mouth ("mit Schaum vorm Mund," L 2). In a sad way, the review proves Syberberg right.

Chapter 12

The Monologues

The years between *Parsifal* and *Die Nacht* were a productive period for Syberberg. *Parsifal* was released on film, video, and records, along with the accompanying book, *Parsifal: Ein Filmessay*, in time for the centennial of the music drama in 1982. Then followed travels with the film, interviews, discussions, and lectures, such as the conference presentation in Thurnau. At least six articles by him appeared in 1982, and at least two more and a chapter in a co-authored book came out the following year.[1] During this time he was also writing *Der Wald steht schwarz und schweiget* and preparing the next film.

The articles supplement *Der Wald* as commentary on contemporary issues, mostly in Germany. Keeping the same format as the book, they were all printed in *Medium*. As the name implies, this magazine focuses on the creative media. Writing in a journal devoted to the media as someone active in the same field, Syberberg criticizes the media and everything they represent, while also presenting constructive ideas. One might describe him as a Wagnerian priest-seer dispensing insights coming from a medium. Most of the criticism on cultural life served by the media varies, but only rarely duplicates, the attacks in *Der Wald*. With amazement one acknowledges the range of observations, reflections, and conclusions of the author. The Germany these observations present is far removed from a perfect democracy. Rather, it emerges as the prostitution of an ideal through majority "correctness" and conformity, an incestuous interlacement and bureaucratization, and a resulting vulgarization as the lowest common denominator. Comparing current conditions with those of the Roman Empire, Syberberg states in "Die Falle ist zu," "Bread and circus equate consumerism and media today. Bread and circus were used to entertain, to distract, to deceive the people, the masses, the *plebs*, the Romans" (20). This statement seems to target the same society depicted time and again in surrounding notes of criticism. But on the next page follows a passage describing the media output received by an unidentified person. It simply lists what this individual "consumes," such as three newspapers in the morning, mail, hourly news on the radio, news broadcasts on television, etc. (21). Although a grammatical subject is omitted, the receiver and consumer can only be the author. As a critical outsider and simultaneously a depersonalized consumer of mass media, the writer is unable to extricate himself from the situation. More than an admission, the listing resembles a confession. His dual role also reveals the continuation of verbal counterpoint.

Three of the articles in *Medium* report on the reception of *Parsifal*. They appeared in the April, September/October, and December issues. While some passages duplicate information included in the books, much of the content expands on that material. Syberberg's comments in the books frequently establish parallels between the Third Reich and a contemporary continuation of its mentality and practices. However, the articles are less blunt. Only once does the author become more explicit. The occasion is a review that insinuates a connection between his *Parsifal* and National Socialism. This prompts the remark that his friends know "that they have to read between the lines, . . . as in *Neues Deutschland* or *Der Völkische Beobachter*, we are a trained people."[2] These newspapers, published respectively in the German Democratic Republic and the Third Reich, were of course censored and streamlined. Whenever he refers to his friends beyond Germany's borders, he invariably writes "beyond the walls of our borders." The expression includes the walls dividing Berlin and the two Germanys, as well as the mental wall blocking vistas and unbiased thinking. In this environment Syberberg presented his *Parsifal* as a counterworld. About Wagner one reads that he becomes interesting only through his work. The author makes fun of Richard Burton's portrayal of Wagner in the TV series *Wagner*, calling him the living "master from America" linking Hollywood and Bayreuth. Ever so faintly one detects the overtones of *U.S.A.* and Celan's and Syberberg's use of "a master from Germany." Without describing or explaining his own contribution to the debate about Wagner, he states only, "How can anyone speak about Richard Wagner and anti-Semitism without knowing this answer," meaning his *Parsifal*.[3] Unfortunately, the answer is not as easy to understand as he probably anticipated.

One of Syberberg's articles of 1982 focuses on Fassbinder ("Sie haben ihn"). After the latter was found dead in his home in June, the country experienced a Fassbinder mania. Countless articles in the print media, programs on radio and television, retrospectives, and symposia celebrated the man Syberberg considered his antipode. Yes, Fassbinder was a master of cinema in Germany, the article admits. But as the media's darling he became a symbol of his society with all its moral flaws. Using the artist as a seismograph of his time, Syberberg finds ample material for his somber conclusion. As a contrast to the media adoration surrounding Fassbinder's death, the article points to Romy Schneider and Alexander Mitscherlich, whose deaths the same summer received scant attention by comparison. Especially Mitscherlich, who in the sixties had co-authored the seminal study *The Inability to Mourn*, was too uncomfortable to be remembered, Syberberg implies (37). The article may have been one of very few texts, perhaps the only one, commenting critically on Fassbinder's passing.

The two articles in January and February/March 1983 continue the commentary with the emphasis being on Wagner, the *Parsifal* film, and more on current conditions in Germany. Especially the last topic identifies Syberberg as an indefatigable critic of German affairs. His unwillingness to compromise or soften his tone had caused controversies and earned him enough enemies to marginalize him in his own profession. It did not help either that his choice of cinematic subject matters and provocative statements earned him the reputation of a Nazi sympathizer, or at least an outspoken ultra-nationalist. This latter image may have contributed to the invitation to participate in a public lecture series held in Munich in November 1983. The topic was Germany, the occasion, the 50th anniversary of Hitler's ascension to power. The year 1983 had witnessed a flood of commemorative discussions and publications, not just in Germany. Now Syberberg was one of five speakers and co-authors of the proceedings volume. They were all well known to the general public.[4] Syberberg's lecture takes as its point of departure the Cold War with Germany serving as the buffer zone between the superpowers and as the planned site for neutron bombs and atomic weapons. The situation was tense. The crisis, the speaker maintains, does not have to lead to a confrontation. It also offers opportunities for constructive developments, inviting scrutiny of Germany's condition and possibilities for reunification. Summing up the situation, he identifies a cultural loss. The virtues that previously had been considered ideals were abused and debased in the Third Reich, and hence abandoned. Among these concepts he counts, among others, *Heimatliebe* (love of homeland) and *Pflichtgefühl* (sense of duty). Regrettably, the old *Treue* (loyalty) survives only as adherence to a political party. Also lost are other concepts, such as aura, taboo, and myth. The losses represent something that used to be central and characteristic of cultural consciousness. Instead the Germans adopted the values of the occupation powers. "We have now become the best Americans of Europe," one reads (39). The result is a lack of identity. Syberberg encourages also disobediance against the replacement virtues he sees as stifling personal growth. Such steps would include resistance to the industry creating and satisfying new needs.

Then, abruptly, the text sets off in a new direction, prompted by the observance of the events in 1933. Syberberg presents two hypothetical scenarios and lets his imagination fill in the developments. The first scenario considers what Germany might have looked like if there had been no Hitler. He wonders if there would have been an Israel. And what would all the artists and philosophers who fled into exile have created or written without the trauma? The second scenario is easier to imagine, it appears. It plays with the victorious outcome for Hitler's attack on the Soviet Union in 1941. That is, if the war had ended before Pearl Harbor, U.S.A.'s participation, and the Holocaust. Germany had already experienced several years under Hitler before the war broke out, enabling the hypothesis of a post-war continuation in practices and ideology. Here Syberberg indulges in a bit of malice directed at some of his attackers. In the imagined Nazi-ruled situation, the correspondents describing the festivities commemorating January 30, 1933 (the day President Hindenburg appointed Hitler chancellor) would have included Umbach and Zelinsky. The fourth unit of text includes a personal reflection. The author goes through a list of hypothetical fates for himself if he had lived under such conditions. Without Hitler, however, he would probably have followed in his father's footsteps, stayed in Nossendorf, and never have become a filmmaker. Unfortunately, the past events happened, and the trauma of those years reshaped the world and the heirs.

The readers familiar with Syberberg's quasi-musical style now begin to search for counterpoint in the text. It does not take long to recognize the variants of the subject." And if", the author asks, "every era consists of the burning of witches plus cathedrals, where would Hitler's cathedrals be? And if they did not exist, what would that mean for our time?" (43). One recognizes faith and persecution as two related issues, but fails to see a contemporary parallel. Then, half a line later he drops the scandalon: "And Begin and his Beirut? Has also Begin the right he takes for himself from his past? The fixation of the victim on his murderer through assimilating acts? And has not he also been elected democratically?" (43). The Israeli invasion of Lebanon, that would result in 18 years of occupation, was still in fresh memory. But after the Holocaust any German criticism of Israeli politics became impossible. Not only does Syberberg break the taboo and transgresses limits again. But the repeated *also* implies a juxtaposition of the Israeli general with Hitler's officers or the dictator himself. In the progression of contrapuntal composition one would expect the victim to perhaps become a perpetrator or victor and vice versa. Spurred by the commemorative occasion, the author chooses for his quasi-musical inversion the most sensitive, practically prohibited, variant. And on the same page he speculates that if the war had ended in 1941 with a German victory, there might have been no "final solution," adding "as revenge for the lost war?" (43). The tacked-on question was probably included to dampen the incendiary effect. But at least in Germany, the public reaction to such statements was and still is predictable. Fully aware of that, Syberberg continued to adhere to his aesthetic program, "music by other means." Sometimes one suspects that the shocking effect does not so much express a biased or unpopular opinion as an intention to stir up a reaction. Distance in time and the painful nature of the issue have brought with them forgetfulness and suppression of memories. Syberberg does not allow the past to be forgotten. Since it is a painful past, the method and result are also painful. The author turns around the dictum by Adorno that no more poetry is possible after Auschwitz. Not so, writes Syberberg, after Auschwitz only art can still save us, to keep alive in our consciousness the suffering and mourning (58): "Only art attends to the morality and conscience of the brutally progressing reality of history and moves, if we are lucky, the memories . . . for this commemoration of the dead—and also of the living" (59). This statement on the mission of art is a recurring theme in Syberberg's publications. Already in the German edition of his book to the *Hitler* film, the introduction consisting of seven essays is called "Art as the Rescue from Germany's Dismal Condition." The author's compositional technique probably accounts for the frequent shifts in perspective, but at the cost of textual coherence. He also notes that some preliminary sections of his presentation had been printed in *Libération* in Paris on January 30 and some in *Movie* in New York during the summer.[5] Actually, as early as on February 3, Wilfried Wiegand had commented on the text in *Libération* in *Frankfurter Allgemeine Zeitung* under the headline "Carnival license?" ("Narrenfreiheit?" 23). The liberal French daily had granted Syberberg no less than five pages, which he filled with the two hypothetical scenarios and the rumination about his own status under such circumstances. It appears, then, that the bulk of his lecture in Munich builds on material already published in the French paper. At the conclusion of the lecture series, Hans Schwab-Felisch reported on it in *Frankfurter Allgemeine Zeitung* on

December 1 (Feuilleton). He observes that the presentations met with extraordinary interest, that Syberberg's text was the only imaginary one, and, strangely enough, that none of the speakers referred to Heine's "Nachtgedanken." Syberberg has cited this poem on several occasions in his cinematic work. Considering the neutron bombs on German soil, the political tension, and Syberberg's use of the poem, especially in *Hitler*, the omission of it is noteworthy.

Also in the fall of 1983 all the films of Syberberg's German Cycle could be seen in Holland. A series of retrospectives brought them to Amsterdam, the Hague, Rotterdam, Utrecht, and Groningen. Erica Bilder's book about Syberberg appeared in time to coincide with the series.[6] Written in Dutch, the first half of the volume consists of six interviews with Syberberg conducted by Erica Bilder and Peter Ungerleiter. Most of the topics and information sound familiar at this point. Syberberg's statements on modern Germany, his position there, his films, and personal reminiscences vary other texts published earlier. But at least one of the interviews still offers material of interest. "Hitler in us—but not in the Jews?" addresses *Parsifal* and *Hitler*. Syberberg notes that the quest for paradise as a topic ended with *Parsifal*. Paradise as fulfillment can be found in or through art. The rest of the chapter focuses on his experiences in Jerusalem and Tel Aviv where he showed *Hitler* and had lengthy discussions with the audiences afterwards. The film was screened with its English title, *Our Hitler*. That directed the attention to the expression "the Hitler in us." Especially the young people in the audiences grappled with the ramification of the idea. A Hitler also in them? Yes, also in the nation of victims. An exclusion or exception would amount to racism, Syberberg declared (32). The potential for Hitlerian evil resides in human nature, he decided. Considering the circumstances, the discussion became more poignant than with most other audiences and locales.

The midsection of the volume contains three excerpts from Syberberg's *Filmbuch* and *Die freudlose Gesellschaft*, followed by photos from his German Cycle. The book refers to it as the Grail Cycle. The last section by Bilder offers an overview of the New German Cinema, Syberberg's position, and a discussion of his films up through *Hitler*, followed by a biography and filmography. For those able to read Dutch, this remains a handy introduction to Syberberg's early and best known works.

In spring 1985 a short essay by Syberberg appeared in English, "The Abode of the Gods."[7] It focuses on the concept of *Heimat*, usually translated as "homeland" or "home area," but in the text clarified as "the place where one belongs." With millions of Germans being exiled, expelled, bombed out, or otherwise uprooted during and after World War II, the term soon acquired a nuance of nostalgia and sentimentality. To that came a wave of kitschy *Heimat* movies in the fifties. The makers of the New German Cinema rebelled against this type of entertainment in the late sixties, avoiding everything associated with the debased concept. Except Syberberg. Now, in 1985, the tide was finally turning and the idea reexamined, for instance in Edgar Reitz' *Heimat*. Again Syberberg removed himself from the mainstream. The article explains how for a long time he thought, as had Ernst

Bloch, of *Heimat* as the place everyone yearns for but has not reached yet. One recognizes here the quest for paradise and the Grail Kingdom that permeates his German Cycle. Now, Syberberg says, for him the meaning has shifted somewhat towards Hölderlin's and Heidegger's use of the term, which is the "abode of the gods." He may also have in mind the elusive origin to which the seeker returns, as described in Hölderlin's hymn "Andenken," and Heidegger's book-length examination of it.[8] But one can also recognize a reference to *Parsifal*, with the return given a mystical interpretation as well as an eschatological dimension.

Die Nacht

As in the past, Syberberg was again frustrated by how the bureaucracy of the arts subsidy system treated his next film project. One can read more about the application process and disappointments in the last section of *Der Wald*. Somehow he persevered, but on a low budget. Making a virtue out of necessity, he embarked on a departure from cinema traditions. *Die Nacht* is not a regular "movie." It does not present a plot or action. That characteristic had of course been prepared as early as in *Ludwig* with its episodic structure, and continued in *Theodor Hierneis*, that focuses on one narrator acting as a tour guide. Similarly, *Winifred Wagner* features one person reminiscing; long sections of *Hitler* ignore action in favor of narrative; and even *Parsifal* conveys much of the plot information in epic style. *Die Nacht* is a monologue featuring one actress, Edith Clever. That is, much of the time she carries out a monologue reciting poetry or recalling what a letter said, or talking in a dreamlike state. But on other occasions she carries on a dialogue with the spectator or another mute and invisible interlocutor. And occasionally, she breaks into song. As in *Parsifal*, Clever gives an amazing performance with her face serving as a landscape of emotions. She slips in and out of male and female roles that often leave her unidentified until one recognizes the text. And frequently she remains as enigmatic as the Pythian seer alias maternal Anima in *Parsifal*.

The six-hour film consists of two major parts in black and white. Each part is preceded by a lengthy "prelude" in color. The fact that the first and third segments are identified as preludes and not as prologues or introductions suggests a musical structure. The titles, credits, and other information appear only *after* each prelude. The accompanying music is restricted to pieces from J. S. Bach's *Das wohltemperierte Klavier*, played by Svjatoslav Richter, and excerpts from Wagner's *Tristan and Isolde* as well as *Götterdämmerung*, directed by Furtwängler. Besides color and length, several features distinguish the preludes from the following longer sections: They take place in daylight inside a building, while the longer parts feature a small spotlit place of undefined ground surrounded by darkness, sometimes close to the steps of an ancient Greek theater. Besides, in both preludes Clever wears winter clothing. Initially it is even so chilly that one can see her breath as she speaks. The dark sections, in a "mental" environment, are warm enough to let her wear a long dress. Invariably, her clothing is black or dark. Also, each prelude consists of numerous, relatively brief, episodes, each presented in one stationary camera take. This orderly, controlled, "rational" structure contrasts with the arrangement of the longer sections. Their units vary greatly in length, intensity, genre, sophisticated camera work (by Xavier Schwarzenberger), and subject matter. They also differ by offering selections of texts from a long list of authors, even an autobiographical description of Syberberg's childhood world. This personal element is supported visually with stills from his room with a view of a storks' nest. Viewers unfamiliar with Syberberg's publications cannot recognize the allusions. It comes as no surprise that some of the textual selections also function as quotations from his other works. For example, Heine's "Nachtgedanken" needs only the first line to trigger memories of its occurrence in the *Hitler* film. And again, it elicits a bundle of connotations that mesh with other elements in the film, e.g. the condition of Germany, Syberberg's and Heine's relationships to this condition in their respective lives, Heine as an artist, as Wagner's friend and Janus face, as a Jew, plus everything related to anti-Semitism. Syberberg has woven a complex pattern of themes and has refined his visual equivalents. A look at some of these units will illustrate his procedure.

The film opens in medias res with Clever speaking as Chief Seattle, giving his speech of 1855. She is surrounded by daylight and the reality of decay. Each camera take shows her in another ruined part of what once was a palace. One cannot help thinking of the Hohenzollern City Palace in Berlin, at least in some of the episodes. The film does not identify a location. Occasionally, the sound of tools can be heard faintly, raising the question if the building is being restored or demolished. Clear is only that the magnificent interior at one time exhibited the refinement, wealth, and power of its owners. Their palace, and everything it symbolizes, now displays a story of downfall and ruin. This environment illustrates the situation of Chief Seattle, whose nation has faced defeat by the European invaders. Without passion or tears, the chief observes the cycle of vitality and decline. In what amounts to a prophesy, Seattle predicts that also the victorious invaders will experience the same loss: "One time your America will [also] have been." This echoes similar predictions by May as Tiresias in *Ludwig*. And of course, it does not stop there, as more recent history proves. Also a reminder that the past still lingers in the present, as Seattle warns (the spirits of the dead), resounds loudly in the form of graffiti defacing the wall behind Clever. The "oi-oi" text plus a symbol point to the neo-Nazi underground music scene, with other English words possibly being names of bands or gangs. The fact that the scribblers did not use German shows the influence of the Western powers and the subsequent decline of the German language. The director's introduction of *U.S.A.* in *Winifred Wagner* underscores the chordal effect of two simultaneous meanings of America as U.S.A. and *U.S.A.*, with the visible ruin being situated somewhere in Berlin. The city is indicated in script that precedes the prelude: "They divided the city right through the middle of us, they split the country right through the middle of me, and they felled the trees deep inside me. i am the tree." These lines alert the viewer to multiple dimensions of the visual composition. Several speakers may be involved: at first the citizens of divided

Berlin, then an unidentified German, or is it the country lamenting? The third voice could belong to the forest, the country, or Mother Earth, the Goddess herself. And finally, the fourth subject transgresses the rules of orthography by identifying itself as *i* in lower case and as "the" tree. Which tree? One of the felled trees, one assumes. Goethe's oak in Buchenwald? The Germanic Tree of Life? Or the Sefirotic Tree? The plight of the forest had been anticipated both in the book and the lecture of 1984, along with the symbolic power of the forest. And why does the text begin a new sentence with a lower case letter? Perhaps the infraction emphasizes the diminished status and condition of the subject. But Syberberg might also follow Celan's lead in the "Todesfuge." The latter's apparently arbitrary use of capital and lower case letters in line beginnings convey both quasi-musical and semantic information, as Olsen's study points out. Of interest here is the deviation from German convention signaling the possible presence of a second language at play. In Celan's poem, that language is Hebrew, which does not use capital letters. If Syberberg is hinting at a similar dimension in his text, then the tree may very well be the Kabbalistic symbol. Support for that possibility appears in the repeat of "right through the middle," *mitten durch . . . hindurch.* It brings back the *tikkun* process of *Parsifal* and Wolfram's interpretation of the hero's name. Furthermore, the spelling deviation also conjures up Martin Buber's *I and Thou (Ich und Du).*[9] Building on Jewish thought, Buber contrasts the "I-You" concept with "I-It" (e.g. 53–55). In the "I-It" constellation, the It is a separate entity, an object to be used, something worldly and distinct from the ego-oriented I. The "I-It" constellation does not express reciprocity or a personal relation. The diminished subject identifying itself as "the" tree appears to reflect the attitude of the surrounding powers. It is "only" a commodity, nuisance, or serviceable material. It may also be a symbol of fragmented human nature in need of redemption. Chief Seattle speaks for a nation vanquished and removed to make room for new settlers. Syberberg may be presenting a stage that precedes or imposes the experience of "I-It." The conscious, ego-oriented I has only recently erected a barrier separating itself from a perceived It. In Germany, such a barrier became a reality during the Cold War, but it had also assumed other forms, as the following sections show.

Separating the prelude from the first longer part are still frames of title and credits. In between one also sees other stills of motifs and props as if they belonged in the list of credits. Two in particular attract attention: an ancient Greek theater and the skeletal wooden frame of a house. Both appear in successive enlargements that finally show only a detail of the original image. In the *Hitler* film such simple, old-fashioned photography functions as a contrast to Riefenstahl's zooming and moving cameras. Each sequence of enlargements might, then, repeat the protest against a political or ideological dimension. Besides, each depicts a subject that once served as an early stage in a development and as an inspiration for artists later. Here one thinks primarily of Richard Wagner and his indebtedness to Aeschylus and of Syberberg, whose childhood home assumed the place of paradise after it was lost. That the house timbers represent the barn in Nossendorf is suggested by the accumulation of twigs on the roof where other photos in the film and the *Filmbuch* show a storks' nest. Among the other objects in the line-up one notices a crystal ball, a phallic cupola covered in crisscrossing chains, a copy of Goethe's *Faust*, and a tiny teddy bear. Compared to Syberberg's *Parsifal*, the props are few and the setting simplified.

Clever's first episode in the first long part simulates a gathering of concepts related to "night," e.g. *Heilige Nacht*, as in the Christmas carol, *Umnachtung* (madness), *Nacht der Seele* (night of the soul), and *Nachtgesang* (lullaby). With her eyes closed as if in a state of dreaming or unconsciousness, she collects, as it were, vocabulary that will be acted out in subsequent units. A few lines borrowed from the penultimate chapter of Nietzsche's *Also sprach Zarathustra* confirm that the speaker is located in a realm where "deep midnight speaks." Her awakening resembles that of Kundry early in act 2. When she later also laughs like Kundry during her confession, the identity of the two figures becomes almost certain. Clever represents a power from the deepest layers of the collective unconscious that overlaps with the female symbols of the Sefirotic Tree.

As other segments follow, one notices passages resembling Syberberg's criticism of current society. At one point Clever reenacts Penthesilea's immolation from Kleist's play of that name, but she soon sits up again. This force cannot die. The viewer, who has searched in vain for more elements promising coherence, is soon relieved. At about this point Richard Wagner emerges as a character around whom such coherence can accumulate. Most episodes, including the lengthy ones, quote statements by, and sometimes about, him. This long sequence begins with a quotation from Cosima's diary. She records that the night before he died Wagner had dreamed about all the women in his life, "alle seine Weibsen." From then on the text weaves together quotations from his operas, letters, *Brown Book*, and other publications, all with the emphasis on his loves in art as contrasted with the passions in real life. For a while the recorded voices of Tristan and Isolde can be heard, both yearning for night, love, and death. Clever sings along. Less united in feeling and reciprocity are the excerpts from Wagner's letters to his lady loves describing longing and desire. They are monologues based on written sources, not mutual and simultaneous declarations of devotion. Clever's enactment presents these statements as erotic fantasies, caressing herself for lack of a lover at her side. But other episodes are interspersed, such as statements about the king and how he listened to Wagner. Of course the composer had his reason for impressing the young monarch favorably, since so much depended on him. His own behavior towards the king was guided by ulterior motives. That knowledge relativizes the passionate declarations. And when Clever eventually quotes from Wagner's letters to Judith Gautier, his egocentric nature takes center stage. His ardent declarations soon turn into requests for luxuries from Paris, such as slippers, perfumes, or silks.[10] At one moment he wants six meters of yellow silk with a rose pattern for his chaiselongue, soon after he specifies six meters of pale pink satin for a house robe. They were both evoked in the *Parsifal* film. In return he is sending an excerpt of the score from the Grail ceremony. These and other examples underscore the lack of true love in Wagner's affair. He was using Judith. She may have functioned as an inspiration for Kundry, perhaps also for the flower maidens. But his feelings apparently bore no resemblance to unquestioning devotion. The following quotations from Cosima's diary string entries recording Wagner's declarations of love and his betrayal (e.g. February 12, 1878). The latter theme is varied in the next long passage from the end of *Götterdämmerung* where Brünnhilde prepares to join Siegfried in death. He had betrayed her unwittingly. Again, the characters of Wagner's musical work exhibit feelings that are unconditional and deep. This love represents an ideal, while the composer did not live up to it in his own life. In the Brünnhilde episode, Clever first sings alone, then along with a recording, finally listens only. She does not appear to mime singing as in *Parsifal*. Also this segment ends with death.

The next episode returns to Wagner's real life, although the scene is unbelievably theatrical. Clever impersonating Wagner is groveling on the floor pleading with an unseen gentleman to make him his slave. "Buy me!" he entreats. Eventually rising to his feet, he retreats submissively, bowing three times in exaggerated humility. The text stems from Wagner's letters to Meyerbeer begging for the latter's help (Gregor-Dellin, 148). This is the same benefactor he would soon malign in letters and publications. The following excerpts provide the inversion when Wagner declares himself to be Meyerbeer's contrast. This culminates in lines from his letter to King Ludwig of November 22, 1881. Here the composer considers the Jewish race the born enemy of pure human nature (Strobel, 3:229–30). "Maybe I am the last German," he adds, soon sighing, groaning, and collapsing. This chilling culmination of part 1 awakens the memory of the spirit slumbering in Wagner's grave from which Hitler's ghost rose. The Wagner impersonation represents, then, the best and the worst of his nation. As a creative genius he could even envision nobility and pure feelings. As a flawed human being he treated others as means to an end, created barriers of distinctions, and propagated hatred, thus becoming a forerunner of the Anti-Christ who admired him so much. Again one is struck by how closely the selections in part 1 illustrate Martin Buber's concept of "I-It." Wagner's I is an ego-centered entity who creates differentiation (Buber, 111–12). The constellation is not a relationship as much as a proximity involving use and egotism. Buber published his *I and Thou* in 1923. He might have chosen harsher descriptions after 1945.

Although the text draws on several other authors as well, Wagner dominates part 1. This endows him with a representative function. Clearly, the downfall and ruin presented visually in the prelude is a consequence of what unfolds in the long section. The prelude could also be a postlude.

The second half of the film exhibits the same structure as the first half. The introductory frame of script describes an explosive destruction of the familiar world, leaving nothing as it used to be, neither the "word" nor the "world." The final phrase follows a period, but begins with a lower case letter, perhaps again suggesting a different language involved. The following prelude in color starts with a transitional episode. Clever is sitting on the stones of a Greek amphitheater, implying an open-air environment. But she leaves this location, disappearing into the background. It and the "sky" are dark, except for an area of diffused light promising a dawn or heralding the dusk. The subsequent, relatively short, episodes take place indoors with daylight entering through windows. Only in one unit does Clever straddle the borders of the indoor-outdoor world by sitting of the floor in the door opening of a barn, while a rooster can be heard in the distance. The prelude shows details of the interior in an intact building. Clever remains in focus, though, regardless whether she is leaning against a wall, standing freely, or seated contemplating a cut flower or leaf, and regardless from what angle she is photographed. The poetry she recites hails from "Book Suleika" in Goethe's *West-Östlicher Divan*, written between 1814 and 1819, when the poet was in his sixties.[11] Most of the recited sections were inspired by Marianne von Willemer, a married teenager who also contributed some of the poems. This mutual but platonic love affair rejuvenated Goethe. His *Divan* is not to be confused with Wagner's *chaise longue*! And as Goethe's lengthy notes, paralipomena, and added essays prove, he had studied Persian culture and poetry thoroughly. However, the poetry of the *Divan* does not consist of Goethe's original translations. It was mostly inspired in form and content by the work of Hafiz († 1389). The love and wisdom infusing these verses include a spiritual component. Even when the poem's voice does not address the beloved Other, that person is present in the text. One would be hard pressed to find poetry besides the Song of Songs that better illustrates Buber's concept of "I-You." The association between the I and the You is a mutual relationship of strong feelings. The reciprocal activity involves the whole person and results in "the unification of the soul" (Buber, 137). That portal leads to a spiritual relation, Buber notes: "The relation to a human being is the proper metaphor for the relation to God—as genuine address is here accorded a genuine answer. But in God's answer all, the All, reveals itself as language" (151). Unlike Wagner's ego-centered, passionate voice, the I in an I-You relation sees the Other as a person and part of the I. Where Wagner contrasts himself with Meyerbeer, erects mental distinctions between "Germans" and "Jews," and approaches his women as means to gratification, Goethe's poems overcome differences of sex and individuality, aiming at the glimpse when dualism yields to unity. The two sections of the film thus function as contrasts, revealing related and yet very different worlds of thought, much like the variation of a musical subject.

The subsequent interruption with title, stills, and credits repeats the series of step-by-step enlargements of the amphitheater and the house frame. The list of quoted authors is longer: The last Pythia of Delphi, Pythagoras, Aeschylus, Plato, Sophocles, Goethe, Hölderlin, Schiller, Jean Paul, Claudius, R. Wagner, Heidegger, Beckett, and Ingeborg Bachmann, besides the mentioned Marianne von Willemer. Omitted are the unknown author of the fairytale "Ilsebill" and Syberberg.

The long section of the second half reverts to black and white. The surrounding is again the darkness of night, with the sphere of activity restricted to a lit circle. There the gravel-like black ground is covered with a blond and a darker skin, the former engraved with the Greek theater on the underside. The accompaniment of Bach's fugues on the piano no longer suffers competition from Wagner's music, only from Clever's singing towards the end. In spite of the restrictions of her movements and acting, her performance requires the viewers' full attention. Maybe *recital* would be a better term, considering the constant interaction of music and words. In segments of uneven length the fairytale about Ilsebill (in Low German) still includes God, while soon after a sleepwalking Clever deplores the absence of God.

The most famous text is the cave parable from book 7 of Plato's *Republic*, which is recited in its entirety. Playing with her own shadow, Clever illustrates details in the narrative. The original, by the way, presents the text as a dialogue. Of interest is primarily the artificial difference between the prisoners kept down in the shadow world and the individuals who experience daylight and sun above ground. Due to their limited exposure, the prisoners' thinking is restricted and full of misconceptions. They might even kill someone who enlightens them or tries to lead them into daylight. The distinctions setting the prisoners apart result from conditions over which they have no control. But occasionally, exceptions occur and an individual can gain a different insight. One can easily recognize the segment as a variation on perceived differences between humans and the difficulty in establishing an I-You relationship to others. The hostility towards someone with different views might also echo the ostracism Syberberg experienced in Germany.

Other sections return to the topic of trees and forest. Sounding like a newspaper report on the dying of the forest, the *Waldsterben*, Clever finally personifies an afflicted tree that snaps and breaks in a storm. One also thinks of the Sefirotic Tree in its distress. The episode ends with the recitation of Claudius' line "Der Wald steht schwarz und schweiget," as used in the title of Syberberg's book. With increasing frequency the recited texts also contain statements sounding like quotations from Syberberg's publications, including autobiographical fragments. The excerpts weave together the ecological disaster with symptoms of decay in a modern society pursuing socalled rationalism and pluralism. There is no more room for the holy, *das Heilige*, or poets, in such a secularized and sick world. "Once upon a time there was a star," one hears, but then the fairytale turns into a horror story. This star, our world, had lost God Father and betrayed Mother Earth. Its inhabitants caused the earth to look like their souls. Similarly, when they abandoned beauty, they soon lost liberty and a list of cherished ideals. The man who "screamed" against this is, of course, Syberberg. An abrupt switch to Goethe's *Faust* sounds at first as being entirely unrelated. But Faust's descent to the Mothers to fetch Helen might parallel Syberberg's attempt to face dangers to bring back ideals of beauty, even to an indifferent world. Of course, *Faust* made a deep impression on Syberberg as a schoolboy. The recited texts continue, like disjointed memories, with fragments of narrative of his childhood impressions. When he lost this paradise after World War II, music and poetry became his surrogate home in art. He plays on the semantic links of "art," "artificial," and "artistic" here, for his *künstliche Heimat*.

An era has reached its end. After Pythia of Delphi pronounces her final message, one hears that "Europe's legacy is squandered." Even the Christian God has died. Clever proceeds to bid goodbye to the pagan gods as inspiration of art and imagination, and to her "children," the tiny objects she "guarded," and prepares to die. This sequence of several episodes ends with Clever singing a number of lullabies to her "children," including the song by Claudius. The ritual is no funeral, although one hears that death is near. When she herself beds down for a return into night, one remembers that this force from the depth of the soul does not die. But for now, she withdraws from the world which is about to face extinction, as Chief Seattle had warned would happen.

The very last camera take pans up into the darkness and stops at a bright lamp. An artificial sun has risen. It is probably the sun of enlightenment, rationalism, and secularism. It also looks like a visual quotation from Buber's *I and Thou*, where it is called an "electric sun" (120). A glance at Buber's context confirms the allusion. Towards the end of part 2, Buber supplements the I-It and I-You constellations with a demonic kind of I who produces the You-feeling in others, but does not reciprocate. For such an individual all others remain Its. Writing in 1923, Buber, like Hegel, uses Napoleon as an example, referring to him as "the lord of the era," which was a fateful time ending in a downfall, an *Untergang*. This ability to use other people by activating their You-feelings is called *cathexis* by Freud. When the followers under the spell of the one-way constellation fail to activate their You in the target of their focus, it may turn inside. "Thus the confrontation within the self comes into being" (Buber, 119), and this produces a crisis, such as a split personality or an alienation between I and the world (120). Someone trying to cope with the conflicting psychological forces often resorts to one of two solutions. One is to summon "thought," the same intellectual power alluded to in the "electric sun" illuminating the dark chamber of the soul. But, Buber points out, this choice pacifies the torment only as long as the individual cannot see the whole picture. The other way to combat the horror is usually avoided, although the individual knows in what direction to move, "deep down in the unloved knowledge of the depths—the direction of return that leads through sacrifice. But he rejects this knowledge; what is 'mystical' cannot endure the artificial midnight sun" (120). It appears that Clever embodies the "mystical" and the "unloved knowledge of the depths." By preparing to die or sleep she seems to be withdrawing from consciousness, leaving the field to the electric sun. Her presence also illustrates Hölderlin's lines from "Patmos," "But where there is danger, there also the saving force grows" ("Wo aber Gefahr ist, wächst das Rettende auch"). Like Kundry, she represents both danger and help. In *Parsifal* she is associated with the *Gestell*, the term borrowed from Heidegger.[12] But in act 3 she appears as a penitent, which links up with his *Kehre*, seen in the Good Friday segment and during the second walk, the *return*, to the Grail Castle, making a *turn* in the road (*umkehren*) as the group passes a pile of swept-up refuse (*Kehricht*). As mentioned in chapter 9, Scholem states that Jewish mysticism associates the return with the maternal *sefira* Binah, or upper Shekhinah: "The *Sefirah Binah* is the 'supernal Jubilee,' in which everything emerges into freedom and returns to its source, and therefore *Binah* is also called *Teshuvah* ('return')" (*Kabbalah*, 112). He elaborates on the concept in *On the Kabbalah and Its Symbolism*: "'Repentance' (literally 'return' in Hebrew) is a name for the third [*sefira*], because all things 'return' to its womb in the end" (49n). It means, then, that the mystical concepts of "return" and "repentance" apply to the same symbol on the Sefirotic Tree. This symbol materializes as the penitent Kundry in the third act of *Parsifal*. Buber makes use of the same concept, obviously also translating the Hebrew term for "return", *teshuvah*, into German. However, he calls it *Umkehr*, not *Kehre*. The word appears in the quoted passage mentioning "the direction of return that leads through sacrifice " ("die Richtung der Umkehr, die über das Opfer führt," Gm. ed. 73). Walter Kaufmann's introduction to the English edition of *I and Thou* points out that *Umkehr* is one of the central concepts in the book (35–37). He does not refer to its significance in the Kabbalah. Suffice it here that most people struggling under the alienation between I and world, according to Buber, do *not* choose the "direction of return" and the mystical, which must yield to the "electric sun." Like Syberberg, Buber also speaks about the sickness of our age and the need for a return (104). It would appear, then, that mysticism and Buber's work inform the film.

The film also incorporates a musical dimension, as suggested by the subtitles "Präludium." Taking a cue from the audible fugues by Bach, one might view the film as a visual composition in four movements. *Der Wald* refers to it as an oratorio for one voice (561). The introductory frame of script presents the subject as suffering a separation or rift. The subsequent movements go through the variations of division and union, longing to heal the *Riss*. The film is a unique cinematic work of art, but obviously not a movie likely to draw big audiences. As *Parsifal*, it needs to be viewed in sections and repeatedly. The first impression of a simple recitation deceives. The work is quite complex. This overview barely scratches the surface.

Syberberg had alerted the public that his next film would differ from the movie norms. In *Der Wald* he devotes an entire page to the description of his cinematic work (501–2). He describes the "crime" for which he already feels condemned. It consists of film without a plot, dialogues, or linear structure. He uses music, also monologues in the "dialectical form of the masked I." Furthermore he strives for "beauty as ethos and form as [the] morality of the daily task in a classical sense." It was predictable that such language would be lost on the average movie critics. But they were not likely to read his book either. Nor would they be inclined to see this lengthy performance on stage in a theater. *Die Nacht* actually existed as a work for the stage first, as a few lines of text among the credits in the film point out. In September 1984 it was performed in Paris during the "Festival d'Automne," supported by the French Cultural Ministry. Clever gave several performances in the Théatre des Amandiers in Nanterre. Since she recited in German, French subtitles were projected onto the dark background above her. Not surprisingly, the program was divided over two evenings. Syberberg may have chosen the theater in Nanterre for its location. Situated on the western fringe of metropolitan Paris, Nanterre boasts a pre-Revolution obelisque marking the meridian.[13]

The film version was created in Berlin later, while more stage performances followed in Berlin and Hamburg in the spring of 1985. Most subsequent reviews of *Die Nacht* refer to the screen version. It had its film premiere in Berlin during the commemoration of May 8, 1945, Germany's capitulation. It screened soon after at the Filmfest in Munich. On May 15 Syberberg showed it in Cannes during the festival, and as could be expected, at night. But as *Parsifal* before, *Die Nacht* did not enter the competition. Also this film has traveled internationally, usually with its director, to special events, often under the auspices of German cultural centers, universities, festivals, and retrospectives. During 1985 both Syberberg and Clever accompanied the film to Chicago, Montreal, and New York. There were four special screenings at the Public Theater in NewYork, with Syberberg and Clever addressing the spectators on each occasion.[14] The film has also been shown on television in many countries (with subtitles). In Germany it aired first on the station Arte, then on ZDF.

A thorough and appreciative review appeared in *Der Spiegel*.[15] Peter Wapnewski, who has written many books on Wagner, devoted four pages to the film. Unlike most critiques, his text does not focus exclusively on Clever. It expresses admiration for her performance, to be sure, but it also examines the film as a whole. Clever's recitation of male and female roles leads to the conclusion that she really represents the human voice. And the film is very German, Wapnewski observes about its scope, comparing Syberberg with Mann's Dr. Faustus, a composer (127). This leads to comments on the function of Bach's music in the film. The writer sees its architecture as a "disciplining countervoice" to the lack of moderation in the "soul spaces" presented by Clever. He means the sections on Wagner, which he finds too long. Actually he questions the selections of Wagner's letters as fitting in the concept of a dying culture. He does not see their role as contrast and counterpoint to the Goethe selections. Not only the Wagner section is too long, also the six hours' duration receives a comment. However, Wapnewski mutes his criticism by stating that the film does not let the viewer go so easily (128). He softens this further by expressing the desire to compare the film version with its live performance on stage. One learns here that the two prelude sections were missing in Paris (129). And these two parts plus Plato's cave episode he considers the most memorable parts of the whole. He also tips his hat to Syberberg for pursuing his ideal of art in contrast to prevailing trends (128).

Manfred Schneider wrote an equally appreciative and knowledgeable review in *Die Zeit*.[16] He ends by characterizing Syberberg as exploring, even transgressing, the borders of film as a medium. A review by Angelika Kaps reports that the earliest theater version in Nanterre included a monitor on stage for "projections" of the external world, whereas the text by Sibylle Wirsing avoids an assessment of the film by concentrating on Clever's performance.[17]

Many of the consulted reviews and other studies share three characteristics. The reviewers have difficulty grasping the thoughts and statements, in part due to language problems, or due to the unidentified content, or due to the length of the work. Many admit to being overtaxed. Second, they emphasize the film's function as a swan song to Western culture. Not only Germany's defeat and cultural decline, but also the decline of an era is recognized. Third, without exception Edith Clever receives praise for her impressive performance. Stanley Kauffmann even assumes that "*Die Nacht* must have been conceived with the prospective collaboration of

Edith Clever."[18] He also quotes Syberberg as remarking that she never needed a prompter during the stage performances (25). Ronald Holloway refers to Clever's cinematic appearance as "outstanding" and "enchanting."[19] Eric Santner concludes that Clever stands in "for the last member of many civilizations: the last American Indian, the last Greek, the last German, the last European, the last human. The monologue is a tapestry of textual citations primarily from Western literature and philosophy including, in a central position, the German metaphysical and Romantic tradition" (*Stranded Objects*, 192).

It should be clear, even without Syberberg's comments, that he was exploring new territory for cinematic arts by incorporating the theater. On the one hand, the move might have been dictated by fiscal restraints. On the other hand, he had long expressed criticism of the direction German cinema was taking. Years before computer-generated action spectacles, he already distanced himself from the movie fare aimed at entertaining mass audiences. His films reveal an inward development. When the emphasis is on the movements of conscious and unconscious components of the psyche, one does not need elaborate sets or hundreds of extras. He retreated to the interior theater. He clarified his thoughts on this interiorization in an interview with Christopher Sharrett in 1987.[20] Asked about the disappearance of frontal projection in *Die Nacht*, he responded that the idea is still present, but has been transformed. He described it as a projection onto one figure, with her face and the viewers serving as screens (20). As the transmitter of the idea, the actress functions literally as a medium while she recites the final words of the Pythia of Delphi. In other contexts she relays the message like a mirror refracting a beam of light. The visual component appears restricted compared to six hours of verbal recitation. This is deliberate, Syberberg explained, elaborating on the interaction between word and image. The process starts with words. When pronounced, they are so to speak projected and become images in the viewers' mind (20). In other words, the translation or transfer from word to image is only suggested on the screen, but completed in the viewer. Syberberg softens the apparent pessimism of his message by pointing to the relaying character being a woman, whom he associates with birth and life.

For many years Syberberg had addressed the public both with images and with words. The publications continued to exhibit more obvious continuity in style than the films. But without fail, they echo the same concerns that the films convey less explicitly. One example is his essay "Ende der europäischen Zeit" (End of the European Era), published in spring 1985.[21] The occasion was the commemoration of Germany's capitulation on May 8, 1945. Forty years had passed, and for several reasons, this milestone became a topic of intense debate throughout the spring. Syberberg's essay was apparently written early in the spring before the debate heated up. It is one of eleven chapters in a volume called *Die Unfähigkeit zu feiern* (The Inability to Celebrate). *Feiern* means primarily "to celebrate." One honors an occasion with a ceremony or festivity. The date in 1945 marked the end of Hitler's dictatorship and the end of fighting and of the devastating allied bombardments. That should have been reason enough to celebrate, even if it meant a military defeat.

But for many it also belongs, or still did in 1985, to a traumatic complex of guilt, involvement, suffering, and/or loss. The end of warfare resulted in massive loss of German territories, expulsions of millions, starvation, chaos, and then division of the remaining country. A painful period, then, and no reason for celebration, many Germans would say. The title of the book containing Syberberg's essay plays on the Mitscherlich study *The Inability to Mourn*. It deals with the psychological aftermath of World War II in Germany. Not only the grieving process was stunted, but, so the book of 1985 now claims, also joy and celebration. Syberberg takes as his starting point that the war that Hitler launched had to be stopped for moral reasons. But the victors squandered their claim to moral superiority. He then points out how the Allies took revenge and advantage of the situation. Only France showed moderation. "What have you," he asks, "what have we, made of the moral victory?" (61). The peace and opportunities gave way to an era of atomic weapons and fear. Germany became gradually wealthy and influential, but it did not regain the unsullied condition of its pre-Hitlerian culture. From now on one recognizes the themes and arguments that recur with variations in many of Syberberg's publications. What is new is the expansion of the moral decline to affect the other participants of World War II as well. And art, especially film, becomes the mirror of society's condition. He deplores art used as a vehicle for ideology and for "consumption as a sign of democracy" (63). The apocalyptic tone of *Die Nacht* resounds with added nuances and dominates the conclusion. The European downfall is for him the apocalypse predicted in the Bible. Syberberg reminds the reader that the European culture died on its own, not through external influences (68).

Syberberg's criticism and somber view differ from the tone in the other chapters. But by and large, they too express the difficulty with the occasion, which turned out to be primarily a West German problem. The German Democratic Republic had adopted the expedient formula of "liberation" by the Soviet army and a distinction between the "fascists," who had all fled to the West, and the innocent remaining Germans. Adding fuel to the debate in West Germany was the announced visit by President Reagan. His visit should serve as a symbolic act of reconciliation between the United States and West Germany. His ceremonies for this purpose caused an international furor. On May 5th, President Reagan balanced his public appearance with Chancellor Helmut Kohl at a former concentration camp with another on the same day at a German military cemetery. One might have expected that an American president would have chosen Dachau near Munich, located in the former American occupation zone. But he selected Bergen-Belsen in the former British zone. If his public commemoration had stopped with his speech and wreath-laying in the concentration camp, many critics would have remained silent. But from there he and his group continued on to the military cemetery in Bitburg. It contains the graves of about 2,000 fallen German troops. Among them were some 47 SS officers. The presence of their graves sparked worldwide indignation.[22] In the flood of literature resulting from this public event one also finds a statement by Syberberg.[23] His reaction expressed nuances and was therefore offensive to many. On the one hand he agreed with the protesters that especially the commemoration in Bitburg did nothing to further reconciliation, as had been intended: "[T]he actual event itself was indecisive, demagogic and more like a military-historical farce of fear, with armored cars between the graves, with jet fighters, military bands, people in uniform and timid speeches" (37). But this hardly amounts to a condemnation. He does not even refer to the event as a photo opportunity or media event, as other contributors did in the same collection of statements. "I would simply have wished," he writes, "that Reagan had held his concentration camp speech by the graves of the dead whom public opinion must hold responsible for these things. What happened in the past is too monstrous for us to be able to forget it or to domesticate it" (37). Only the last sentence of his article refers to the Jewish victims of the concentration camp indirectly: "Beside the two Christian priests present at the ceremony the Jewish one was missing amongst his own dead—a picture that renews a two-thousand-year-old tradition" (37). The text (possibly abridged by the editor) fails to mention Bergen-Belsen in this context. Jewish protesters held a commemorative ceremony in the concentration camp after Reagan and his entourage had left. The president's speech in Bitburg was too conciliatory for the critics, including, for example, references to the young age of some of the dead buried there. Without mentioning the source, Syberberg picks up the comment: "The dead SS men in Bitburg were as old, I hear, as my own daughter's schoolfriends are now; and they are supposed to be responsible for the hell we all know. Who is responsible however?" (37). He points to the young men's fathers, teachers, and superiors who now had become respected business partners. Such comments did not endear him to either the protesters or the defenders. And he adds about the controversy surrounding the president's itinerary well before the trip, "The fact that he then held out stubbornly to the end was a show of courage of which I would not have believed him capable" (37). The actor from Hollywood who resisted the storm must have appealed to Syberberg, who recognized a variation of his own stance in Germany. One can only wonder if the president who acknowledged, or at least did not exclude, the dead SS members, did not also evoke the other *U.S.A.*? However, readers not well informed about Syberberg's work would never suspect such a connection. They would only see his article as a wishy-washy statement that failed to make a clear point.

Molly

Late in 1985 Syberberg made his next film, the first for video from the start. In color and three hours long, it is a monologue divided into two parts. Known as *Molly*, the official title reads *Edith Clever liest Joyce* (Edith Clever Reads Joyce). This time the ensemble consisted of only two individuals, Clever in front of the camera, Syberberg behind it. James Joyce provided the entire script: the concluding chapter of his novel *Ulysses*. Syberberg had written most scripts for his earlier films. Even in the documentaries he controlled the direction of the content through interviewing techniques and editing, as in *Winifred Wagner*. In *Parsifal* he added visual prelude sections supplementing the libretto, and in *Die Nacht* he selected the quotations and combined them with his own texts. Now departing from that level of control, he relinquished the position of screenwriter and apparent director. The retrenchment affects also several other aspects of filmmaking. Not only does the screen show one person delivering a monologue, but this time she reads all of it. Her book remains visible most of the time. She represents the same character throughout. Furthermore, she stays in the same chair throughout. Boring? Not at all.

Most of the time the camera remains directed against the corner of a room. The wall on the right side is unadorned and painted white. Placed against it, near the corner, stands the armchair on which Clever sits reading the book. It is a hardback Suhrkamp edition translated by Hans Wollschläger. Clever wears a black pullover or caftan, later on adding a shawl. The wall to the left of the corner has a window without curtains. A radiator under the window supports a candlestick with a lighted candle. The interior provides, then, sources of warmth and a little light in a *mise en abyme* relationship to the exterior light. As daylight gradually yields to darkness, the diminishing candle becomes the main source of illumination. But during the first half of the film, daylight streams in through the window. It does not offer much of a view. Instead of pedestrians and street traffic one sees only suburban trains going in opposite directions at short intervals. They move through an indistinct white landscape where the tracks are barely visible. One assumes snow covers the ground. The trains appear to pass the building right outside the corner, adding a faint rumble to Clever's recitation. Obviously, the surroundings do not offer many distractions. A similar focus had been achieved in *Die Nacht* with darkness enveloping a small spotlit circle. Now one realizes that also white can produce the same effect. The location is part of Edith Clever's apartment in Berlin, meaning that not even a studio was needed.

The pared-down setting limits the range of activity both for the cameraman and the actress. A few visual interruptions may have been dictated by the length of film in the camera or punctuation in the text. Most of the time the photography consists of very long takes. The variations are subtle, such as zooming closer to Clever's face, or panning to the window to catch two trains passing each other. With few exceptions, Clever remains in focus, and the camera follows her movements. She may curl up in the armchair, sit up straight, lean her head against the wall, slide her fingers through her hair, turn the pages, or hold up the book to catch the waning light, etc. The changes in position often echo her reactions to shifts in the narrative she is reading. But the acting dimension of her presentation rests primarily on her face and voice. More so than in the previous films by Syberberg, the human face functions as a landscape of expression and emotion. This could easily have resulted in exaggerated dramatization. But the fact that Clever is reading from a book prevents her total identification with the text's subject. The book functions as a filter. She conveys the thoughts by vocalizing the words; she may share and mimic the feelings or show empathy; imagination even lets her slip into the role of the fictional subject some times. Still, she remains a reader. Her voice competes with the facial nuances as a medium reflecting a drama taking place out of sight. Rich in modulations, this voice can also read entire passages in brisk monotony. But when the words touch on the memory of an intimate encounter, the voice slows down, changes to express or react to the sensuality suggested in the text, or somehow transforms itself in unison with the literary episode. One might compare Clever's voice and face with two instruments used to play Joyce's composition.

So what is Clever reading? The last chapter of *Ulysses* is the "Penelope" unit that also concludes the "Nostos" section of the book. Joyce constructed his novel around Homer's epic. Homer's final section includes Odysseus' homecoming from the Trojan War. His wife, Penelope, has faithfully waited for him while warding off other suitors. Joyce reduces the years of Odysseus' wanderings into a single day, June 16, 1904. His Odysseus, or Ulysses, is Leopold Bloom, who spends the day wandering around Dublin, tormented by his wife's anticipated adultery. Most of the book conveys Bloom's inner monologue throughout his experiences that day. Only the final chapter focuses on his wife, Molly. Her husband has returned home and gone to bed. Before she also goes to sleep, the text shares her recollections, experiences, and reactions to the day as another inner monologue. It reveals a strain of thoughts and feelings with many abrupt shifts in direction. They are triggered by associations and account for the lack of coherence in the text. Structurally, the text runs on for pages without interruptions. Less grammatical than stream-of-consciousness writing, Joyce's chapter consists of only eight "sentences." Still, this style leaves much room for the interpreter. Molly has not remained faithful to her husband. She is a sensual, earthy woman, yet sensitive, romantic, and vulnerable. The chapter reveals a portrait of a twentieth-century Penelope with many nuances.

Although Penelope is a rare name in Germany, it occurred before in one of Syberberg's films. In *Karl May* one finds a young girl by that name, portrayed by another bearer of the name, Penelope Georgiou. She plays the androgynous Mignon figure. She is about as old as Molly's daughter. The Penelope in Joyce's novel has developed into a woman who appears to be less enigmatic. She has also dropped the name and calls herself Molly. Molly is a pet form of Mary. Her husband's name, Bloom, brings to mind the rose and its significance in symbolism. The Virgin Mary is the Rose of Heaven, and also the Shekhinah is known as the Rose.[24] Syberberg's Kundry is the Rose of Hell plus Mary Magdalene plus Queen of Heaven, etc. Would by any chance this Molly also serve as the mystical symbol fallen into exile? She shares her face and voice with Kundry who most unmistakably represents that concept. Also in *Die Nacht* Clever's roles include the Anima aspect of the Shekhinah. One is tempted to view Clever's roles, also in the following monologues —through the reflection and filter of literature—as embodying the image of something originally holy and sublime now languishing in degradation. Molly Bloom fits into the Madonna-whore dualism of Mary-Eve and Herzeleide-Kundry.

In spite of the simplicity of the set and execution, Syberberg observes a number of characteristics outlined by Joyce, but others he ignores. The author had prepared a plan for *Ulysses* with a list for each chapter.[25] For example, the novel takes place on June 16, known to Joyce's admirers as "Bloomsday." Syberberg apparently moves the time to winter. Likewise, Molly's ruminations during the night are being read between afternoon and nightfall. Another deviation concerns the bed. Besides the title "Penelope," Joyce specified that chapter 18 should have a bed as its setting. This is not shown visually, since Clever reads the book in an armchair. However, the bed figures in the text read to us and indirectly through Molly's recollections of sexual encounters. From a list of physical organs characterizing each chapter Joyce selected "Flesh" for this unit. He also referred to Molly in faulty German as "The flesh that always affirms," playing on Goethe's Mephistopheles, who calls himself "the spirit that always negates," and indirectly on Gretchen (Fargnoli and Gillespie, 20). Syberberg retains the allusion to flesh in the way he handles color. Only Clever's skin and the flame of the candle display natural color. The surrounding is practically black or white. The color of her skin draws attention to the face of the actress. Among Joyce's list of techniques one finds "Monologue" for this chapter, and among correspondences, "Movement." The trains take care of that. More importantly, in his handling of the visuals, Syberberg preserves the psychological nature of the inner monologue. The fictional Molly Bloom does not talk aloud while letting all this go through her head. The people and places, experiences and feelings reside in her mind. The reader conveys her words to us as a medium would. Any other moviemaker tackling this subject would have sent the actress through a series of realistic flashbacks, and without a doubt, would have exploited every sexual episode visually. Syberberg dismisses such temptations.

Remembering how Martin Buber's *I and Thou* informs *Die Nacht*, one wonders about the I-You relation in *Molly*. The author's words come as thoughts of a subject that communicates only indirectly via the reader. Actually, the subject does not address anyone, making this soliloquy a true monologue. But the thoughts are perceived in spite of, or thanks to, their preservation in print. They are even endowed with a voice. Somehow, Molly, who only thinks everything we hear, has found a surrogate mother who gives birth to her words. It appears that Clever as the reader accepts actively and with full attention what is conveyed to her. She, in turn, relays the words to us. The text has also passed through a translator. Strangely, the Kabbalah operates with a similar concept of separations, mirrors, filters, or facets in the four worlds, with some reflections of the divine light penetrating through the layers. Even in the lowest world of matter, a vestige of such refractions functions. Also, among the *sefirot*, Binah is the aspect of the Divine that creates through expression, and the lower Shekhinah is the Word on earth. In this particular case of projection, the word/Word is relayed through several intermediaries. In spite of Molly Bloom's human shortcomings, the transmission process of her thoughts also evokes—at a far remove—an I-Thou relationship, with the receptive viewer being the new partner addressed. The process also hints that the artist (Joyce) gives shape to an inspiration, transforms and preserves it in a work of art (the book), which, if good fortune allows, will enrich the perceptive receiver via Clever's recitation. This view of art is becoming more noticeable in Syberberg's work. Also, the technology of frontal projection has changed. Still in *Parsifal* projections would fill the background. They have been replaced with a system of projections focusing on the human apparatus. It does not matter whether one calls the process a projection, transmission, refraction, translation, or relay, the principle remains the same. Something from a distant source undergoes weakening, even alienating transformations, in the process of being conveyed through filters, stages, or different channels. But one can still recognize an ever so faint relationship to its source. In *Molly* the process is barely visible, having become internalized.

Syberberg's ideas of art stem from the age of mimesis. It runs counter to current views on art, especially in Germany, where Syberberg has repeatedly been labeled a modernist as well as a postmodernist. For him art is still a reflection or reminder of the sacred. Without that dimension it ceases to be art. In an interview of 1987 he elaborates on this, curiously without mentioning Benjamin.[26] Something new is developing, he deplores there. This new development reflects modern society with its throw-away consumption. It does not know the old concepts, such as catharsis, truth, aura, or myth, he asserts. But for him there has to be a world theater or cosmos in the old sense. This anchoring in a tradition based on largely abandoned religious and philosophical views may surprise many, since much of his cinematic work defies film tradition. He now presents himself as a nonconformist to an age that no longer conforms to tradition. Many other interviewers and critics have interpreted his cherished tradition to be the ideology and aesthetics of the Third Reich. They ignore the dimension he mentions here, something related to aura and mediative purposes and origins. It includes at least a hint of a loftier context. His chosen topics are grounded in that context.

Compared to Syberberg's earlier films, there have been relatively few published studies and comments on *Molly*. One reason may be the format. A videocassette does not compete with new movies for attention. The fact that *Molly* deviates so much from the usual moviefare undoubtedly also contributed to its being almost ignored in film literature. Another reason is the triple authorship of the work. The credits do not mention a director. Clever's name appears in the title, *Edith Clever liest Joyce.* Then Syberberg lists himself as the photographer. This renunciation of authorship was modified in 2004, when an exhibition book cum catalogue included a brief chapter on the film.[27] It is introduced without specifying the director or creator, but lists Edith Clever and Syberberg as co-responsible on top of the page, followed by the title that reveals Clever's appearance of the screen. The book accompanied a commemorative exhibit on Joyce's *Ulysses* in Vienna throughout summer 2004 in the Atelier Augarten (Österreichische Galerie Belvedere). The occasion was the one hundredth anniversary of "Bloomsday," June 16, 1904. A long list of international artists contributed works of visual art related to the book. This list includes such distinguished names as Joseph Beuys and Man Ray. The exhibit collected a "visual compendium" highlighting the translation of a literary source into a visual medium.[28] Sebastian Huber, the author of the commentary on *Molly* in the book, concludes that "Syberberg is employing a strictly anti-illusionistic, anti-illustrative procedure" (22). Clever does not try to portray Molly Bloom, he emphasizes. Rather what is shown is the process of reading as a process of consciousness (23). She conveys the activity of reading Joyce, not acting Molly's part.

The film's first presentation to a larger audience took place with its debut on Austrian television on Dec. 20, 1985. It was also shown the following year in Berlin at the International Forum film festival. *Molly* receives considerable attention in the Italian book on Syberberg by Stefano Socci, along with the other monologues (93–100). Since Clever was the only artistic partner also in the following monologues, her collaboration with Syberberg became the topic of an article by Manfred Schneider.[29]

Fräulein Else

This video film bears a copyright date of 1987, with the preparations starting the fall before. In several respects it continues and varies Syberberg's exploration of a new mode in visual art. Again, the work saw its early phase on a stage, the Odéon, in Paris. However, it is not clear if Edith Clever performed before a live audience there. She is the only person on screen. She again wears black and reads from a book. And again, darkness surrounds her performance. The differences emerge only gradually.

This time the title and credits appear in two places. But unlike *Die Nacht*, the first identification shows up rather early, between a brief introduction and the film itself. The second title occurs at the end along with the credits. Arthur Schnitzler's name appears first, followed by the title, *Fräulein Else*. This beginning indicates that the film will remain close to its literary source. Schnitzler (1862–1931) was a Viennese playwright, novelist, psychoanalyst, and medical doctor. Some of his novellas, among them *Fräulein Else*, refine the "inner monologue" that Syberberg already explored with Joyce's novel. Only after the title does one see Edith Clever, then her name. As the camera zooms away from her, one recognizes the dark surrounding as the stage of an empty theater. It is not a Greek amphitheater, but its European enclosed successor. All the seats, even in the balconies, are covered with sheets of white fabric. Obviously, the theater location must be important, since the work could easily have been filmed in a studio or other environment, perhaps even in a naturalistic setting. Also emphasized is the emptiness of the interior. Clever does not present a public performance, at least not in the filmed version. This is the interior theater of the psyche. Actually, the dimly lit theater can only be recognized in the two brief showings of the credits. During the performance itself the camera focuses on Clever, an island of light surrounded by darkness. Only after this view does Syberberg's name appear, presumably in the capacity of photographer and director. The brief presentation of credits in subdued color is preceded and followed by an introductory episode with voice-over. One assumes the voice belongs to Syberberg. Black and white snapshots in an album show the area and site where *Fräulein Else* takes place: forest and the towering mountains of the Dolomites surrounding the resort hotel in the story. The real-life hotel was destroyed during World War II, leaving only a few ruins in the landscape. The voice-off scene provides this information. It also adds that the novella was considered old-fashioned

when Schnitzler published it in 1924. A few comments of description and interpretation serve as a transition to the story. One hears, for example, that we are about
to witness an *Untergangsmonolog*, a monologue of downfall, with the process in
the title heroine's mind providing a parallel to the demise of the Austrian monarchy.
It is the old drama of a struggle between temptation and purity presented in the
interior of one person. It is also, the voice concludes, the drama of lost innocence.
The historical parallel may not seem so obvious to non-Europeans. When the
Austrian monarchy was abolished at the end of World War I, crowned heads of
several other countries also had to seek exile. Europeans saw the political outcome
of the war and the accompanying social upheavals to be the external manifestation
and conclusion of a long-time moral decline. It meant the end of an era. Miss Else
presents herself as an individual and as the symbol of a past but not distant age. It
does not require much imagination to see the connection to the predicament of
modern Europe, and especially Germany. The moral and political decline has
entered a second phase, and the end is predictable.

The story is Else's inner monologue during her final hours. The nineteen-year-
old girl from Vienna is spending a vacation with relatives at a resort hotel when she
receives an urgent letter from her mother. Her father, a lawyer and passionate
gambler, is facing imminent arrest and ruin unless Else can persuade an acquaintance, who is also a guest at the hotel, to come to the rescue with a loan of 50,000
gulders. The man agrees, on the condition that he may see Else naked. The narrative
ends with her self-exposure and suicide by overdosing on sleeping powder. The
story unfolds in the time set by Else's inner monologue, all within a few hours. The
text has been abridged to pare it down to two hours' recitation.[30]

From this outline one may conclude that the film follows the formula of *Molly*,
since both render the inner monologue of a literary character, even presented by the
same actress. And yet there is a major difference in the treatment of the situation,
as signaled by the environment. While Clever is reading and vocalizing Molly's
thoughts, she is for much of the time surrounded by daylight. She remains a reader,
as the title of the film also indicates. But when sharing Else's thoughts, she
identifies with the character and assumes the part of acting as Else. The dark theater
interior suggests a stage performance, and Clever's eyes confirm it. When the
camera backs away from her, one can see her holding up the book and turning the
pages. But in close-ups, her eyes do not rest on the paper. Her facial expressions,
body language, and voice all imitate Else coping with her thoughts almost as a stage
actress would portray her on stage.

The inner drama takes place while Clever remains seated at a small table on the
stage. Other cinematographers would have capitalized on a rich text by showing
interesting characters, beautiful surroundings, and all-too-human behavior. With the
exception of the old photos in the album, Syberberg moves the action into the
imagination. The viewers have to visualize everything with Clever's help. For the
first time in Syberberg's films they also have to imagine the music heard and
identified by Else (at least the consulted video did not contain any audible music).
For example, towards the end Else slips off the only garment she is wearing, an

ankle-long evening coat, in the music room, where the wealthy acquaintance waits for her while listening to another hotel guest playing Schumann's *Karneval* on the piano. Carnival marks the end of the ancient year, and it also accompanies the end of Else's life. But we can only hear it in our imagination. Syberberg does not allow any audible impressions besides the human voice. Although the film is in color, he eliminates most sensory enrichments and distractions. Most of the time the camera focuses on Clever's face in close-up. Only when it occasionally zooms away very slowly, can one see the table, chair, and book. A glass of water on the table is the only other object. Of course, one thinks, Clever will need a sip after talking so long. After a while one begins to wonder, though. Does the glass contain merely water for the actress? Or is it a prop? Is it the glass into which Else dissolves the fatal dose of Veronal? Clever does not touch the glass.

This minimalism aims at concentration. The focus on Clever builds to a climax at her (Else's) degradation. Rarely does one experience such an intense exposure while the actress remains fully clothed! Critics may question the logic in presenting Else's inner monologue as an oral performance. After all, the poor girl is not speaking into a microphone, and everything we hear goes through her mind until the moment of death. Syberberg emulates here the author who also enters the character's mind, then records and shares it with the readers. However, Clever also recites other people's voices as they engage in conversation with Else. The printed story distinguishes them from Else's silent and spoken words through italics. Thus strictly speaking, some passages are dialogues and conversations with others. The text simply offers a running record of what Else's mind registers and produces in "real time." Clever must bring out these distinctions by modulating her voice. This presents a problem for viewers not familiar with the novella and for the average moviegoers unused to sustained concentration.

Fräulein Else is the fourth film by Syberberg in which Edith Clever plays a lead or only role. One can recognize a connection between her metaphysical identity as Kundry and the psychological equivalent in *Die Nacht*. Even as Molly the figure could be viewed as a modern incarnation of the idea. Else shares the same face and voice. Yes, she belongs to the same group. Arthur Schnitzler was Jewish and might very well have been familiar with Jewish lore and mysticism. As the reader may remember, the Shekhinah symbol occurs in two variants on the Sefirotic Tree, the maternal, creative *sefira* and her filial duplicate on earth. The "upper" symbol creates or gives birth to the lower seven ones through expression, and the "lower" Shekhinah (the daughter) functions and suffers as the Word on earth. The Kabbalistic Word is, at least in its popular, non-theological form, viewed in feminine terms. Else appears to assume some of the characteristics associated with this imagery, and again only at a far remove, as a faint reminder with modern twists. She is young and still virginal. She receives a call from her father via her mother's letter to save him. She understands that this mission will require sacrifice. She suffers an extended agony vaguely comparable to the stay on the Mount of Olives. She accepts the sacrifice for her father. Her self-exposure amounts to a public revelation. Her inner struggle resembles at times the better known plea "Remove this cup from me." In the end she empties not a cup, but a glass, causing her death. Blasphemy? Perhaps, if one calls the work "Else's Passion." In that case Schnitzler and Syberberg would have to share the blame. But the parallels are by no means as obvious as in *Ludwig*. One cannot, however, deny the relationship of *Fräulein Else* with Syberberg's other films, especially from *Parsifal* and on. One could easily compile a list of vocabulary items in *Fräulein Else* that also express concepts central in the other films, especially *Parsifal*. Actually, the numerous expressions shared with the libretto amount to a dictionary. Parallels in content include, a.o., a pharmacon that can poison and heal, characters hoping for intercession and compassion, even a stretcher for the sufferer is not missing. The amazing overlap in vocabulary and ideas may stem from related topics rather than coincidence. On the last page of the novella, when Else's cousin frantically calls out her name, she is losing consciousness, as shown by shorter and shorter fragments of text. She can register "Else!" repeatedly, but the last time only "El ..." before her mind shuts down. The syllable is identical with the ancient Semitic name of God. Nowhere does Syberberg intimate that he includes a spiritual dimension in this film. But the parallels are too numerous to be ignored. This observation does not nullify the historical references in the film's introduction.

Fräulein Else appeared on Austrian television (ORF), which had commissioned it. Producer is Syberberg's company, listed as HJS Filmproduktion this time. It also appears from the acknowledgments that the Goethe Institute in Paris provided assistance. In February 1987 the film saw its German premiere at a festival in Berlin called "Internationales Forum des jungen Films."

Penthesilea.

Syberberg did not rest on his laurels. In November 1987, he and Edith Clever again participated in the Festival d'Automne in Paris with a stage version of *Penthesilea*. At first glance the formula looks similar to that of the preceding film: Clever is the only actress on stage. She performs the work of an author as a monologue. The performance is subsequently filmed on location in an empty theater. But the viewer soon discovers numerous differences. *Penthesilea* is a more ambitious undertaking than the other monologues.

The theater, Peter Brooks' Bouffes du Nord, surprises the viewer by being a run-down establishment, to judge from the battered walls of the stage area. Again all seats are covered with sheets, and Clever reads from a book whenever seated at a small table on stage. This time some props find their way back into the image, all of them assuming symbolic value. Besides a glass and pitcher of water, a rose, candles, and several books clutter the table top. A varying number of candles supplement the sparse illumination, resulting in subdued colors. As in the previous films, the light is focused on Clever, who wears black. Standing out against the dark surrounding are several white sculptures: the death masks of Napoleon and Frederick II, a statuette of Goethe and several busts of him, the Prussian sisters

Queen Luise and Princess Friederike, the reliefs of an eagle and a genius with the torch turned down, plus a column. Later on several floor pillows create the illusion of a friendly environment, plus a few other objects enhance the theatrical effect. Apparently, the theater no longer serves only as an inner space. The setting is still bare and far removed from realism, but has moved away from total minimalism.

In *Penthesilea* the text develops into a real drama with several characters presented by one actress. However, teichoscopy removes all events off stage that can be remotely considered visibly dramatic. Everything is inner drama, abridged to four hours' of encounters and dialogues in the form of a monologue. At times this monologue is read at the table, at other times it is acted out somewhere on the stage.

Heinrich von Kleist (1777–1811) published his tragedy *Penthesilea* in 1808, the same year Goethe released the first half of *Faust*. A Prussian nobleman and officer, Kleist experienced Prussia's defeat during the Napoleonic War. The kingdom that Frederick II (the Great) had elevated to a European power declined to a shadow of its former glory. Kleist was a troubled and restless soul. Grounded in the age of Idealism, his work spans the period from Classicism and Romanticism to modern literature, in spite of his short life. He committed suicide at the age of 34. His literary output comprises mostly essays, plays, and novellas.

Penthesilea takes place during the Trojan War. The title heroine is the queen of the Amazons, arriving in Troy with her army. Both the Greeks and the Trojans think the Amazons come as their allies, but confusion ensues immediately when these engage in battle with both parties. The real purpose of their involvement is to capture men for their rose festival, a hymeneal celebration for procreative purposes. Penthesilea wants to capture Achilles, but finds herself overcome instead upon the sight of him. In the course of the events, he pretends to be her prisoner when she recovers from her swoon. They instantly fall in love, but are soon separated when the fighting continues. Penthesilea is overwhelmed to learn the true situation. When she receives another challenge from Achilles to face him in battle, she thinks he has betrayed her and only wants to prove his superiority. She meets him with full military force, including attack dogs, while he, alone and equipped with only a spear, intends to succumb so as to be her consort for the rose festival. Not recognizing his intention, she injures him with an arrow and then attacks him with her dogs, literally biting and devouring him to death. As she later comes to her senses, she commits suicide without any weapon, simply by imagining that she is stabbing herself.

Except for the gentle scene when Penthesilea and Achilles get to know each other, every episode is highly charged emotionally. Penthesilea proves herself volatile and unpredictable, easily paralyzed or fainting when overcome by emotion. The experience of instant love unleashes passion, which turns into rage in face of presumed betrayal. Thus, without any battles fought on stage, the monologue conveys a series of confusions and shifting feelings. Since most of the text renders Penthesilea's lines, the viewers share her inner developments. Not only is the queen of the Amazon state not allowed to lead the life of an ordinary woman, but her emotions and reactions also strike a modern audience as pathological. In this abundance of *pathos* one finds both passion and suffering. So far removed historically as to become legendary, the protagonist assumes qualities of a mythic figure. As in Kundry's case, the story of her passion ends in death. She even conducts a ritual cleansing that helps her overcome her confusion and guilt before dying. The white cloth serving as her towel envelops her body for a while, the color change in clothing suggesting the inner effect of this baptismal rite.

Edith Clever delivers a tour de force. While Penthesilea's role frequently requires intensity in expression, the other characters tend to be calm. Clever also distinguishes the characters by voice pitch and, sometimes, by moving a few steps to a different spot. Occasionally she sits down and reads a few passages from the book. These variations supply all the modulations needed to make the play come alive. One does not even miss the realism attempted by most movies and theater performances. Actually, the language of this tragedy might not endure a realistic staging. Kleist's iambic verse is so loaded with imagery that it would be out of place in natural surroundings. But in spite of the reduction in stage props, the performance offers more than just the play. It also includes Kleist himself. Just as *Parsifal* abounds in visual references to Wagner's life and German history, so *Penthesilea* incorporates allusions to Kleist's life and Prussian history. This is the dimension that justifies the few props. The introduction to the film provides a hint. The first frame shows "Paris 1987 / Bouffes du Nord," followed by "Heinrich von Kleist / *Penthesilea*." The third frame offers some silent background information. One reads that Kleist sent the play to Goethe in 1808, "on the knees of his heart," and that Goethe did not like it. Subsequently the image switches to a statuette of Goethe facing several larger busts of him and a relief in the distance. One wonders if they are engaged in some form of debate of the drama. Another cut presents the death mask of Frederick II. More script relates that Kleist was almost ten years old when the monarch died in 1786, and with him Prussia's time of greatness. One also reads that Queen Luise, the dominating figure in those years, was revered by Kleist and his contemporaries. It was the time after the French Revolution and Napoleon's victory over Prussia. The camera continues to move until it rests on the statue of the royal sisters. Another camera take presents the duo from behind when suddenly Edith Clever steps into view and addresses them with the first line of the play, "Greetings, Your Royal Highnesses!" The sculptures are scattered at first, with the Goethe group on stage, the Prussian sisters at the edge or at the first row of seats, and the king's mask in the back behind the rows. Goethe, the intellectual and literary giant of his time has joined the royals to provide a frame and an audience for which the drama unfolds. One assumes, then, that this addition to the few props relates to the play. And yes, on a superficial level one can recognize the theme of decline, for Prussia as well as for royalty and what it signifies. Also for Kleist and his soul sister, Penthesilea, the end was approaching. Neither of them earned recognition from the royals of their time. The bas-relief of the genius with the lowered torch conveys grief over their deaths.

Among the smaller objects the rose plays its role as a visible reminder of the rose festival. Also the glass of water does its duty when Odysseus receives a refreshment. More enigmatic are the candles. Clever lights a number of them, staying occupied while reciting entire sections of text. Instead of using matches, she repeatedly tears a page out of the book she reads from, folds up the paper, ignites it in one of the flames, and uses it to light other candles. Since they are not strictly needed for illumination, one assumes they represent the element of fire, love, life, and, not the least, "inner light," as well as the mentioned Helios. Later in the play Penthesilea blows out the flames, now more obviously related to life and love. The pitcher and glass represent the element of water; the books, the human spirit replacing the element wind, and the rose represents earth. But the burning pages also refer to Kleist's destruction of his manuscripts before he died. While Penthesilea narrates the history of the rose festival to Achilles, she also wets torn-out pages in the pitcher and covers the faces of the death masks with them. Does she try to eliminate historical constraints? Does her story douse Achilles' ardor? Or does the element of water play in counterpoint to the fire of love being told? Penthesilea's attempt to cover up the sculptured faces may also relate to the intimacy of the scene. She does not want witnesses, as she proceeds to cover up the busts with cloth. However, this action also eliminates the historical dimension created by the sculptures. Furthermore, their visibility amounts to a reminder of societal expectations and code of conduct. Penthesilea has hunted down the lover mentioned by her dying mother. This conflicts with the rules of the Amazon state. The choice should be random, without passion dictating the selection. When Achilles is called back to the continuing combat and she finds out that her victory was an illusion, her world collapses. Several cuts in the subsequent scenes condense her reaction, which includes the extinction of candles. When she receives Achilles' challenge, she overturns the column. Goethe's figurine had been standing on it earlier. Placed in the middle of the stage, it reminds the viewer of the "middle pillar" of the righteous individual's ascent in Freemasonry. Its fall may announce the decision not to pursue that path. But it obviously also signifies ideal masculinity. In her preparation for a fight unto death, one hears the first of only two hints of music in the film. Clever is humming a few bars from the choral conclusion of Beethoven's Ninth Symphony ("Freude, schöner Götterfunken"). The grim resolve apparently fills her with joy, as she takes leave from her surroundings, extinguishing more candles. The book from which she had read and torn pages she places at Goethe's feet, declaring "Triumph!" This change in the historical relationship and use of Beethoven's music during such somber circumstances again suggest a fugal handling of themes. This is the same composition Syberberg used to great effect in the fourth part of *Hitler*, there personified as little Joy (*Freude*), the daughter of Elysium. The girl returned in *Parsifal*, again embodying a symbolic presence. In the mystical frame of reference, she and Kundry represent two manifestations of the same symbol (or two closely related symbols, depending on how one interprets the two *he*'s). And Kundry shares the face with Penthesilea. One should also remember the significance of Beethoven's composition in German history, as hinted in Mann's *Doktor Faustus* and more recent events. At the time this film was made, Germany was still divided and Prussia already removed from the map. Besides, the uplifting music does not fit the situation. Penthesilea is preparing to fight to death. Is she also taking away the cherished music, thus depriving the Germans of *Freude*, as she just had denied Goethe the text of the drama? Syberberg's interpretation of the classic work opens up as many questions as Kleist's play has elicited in book form.

Now the drama is practically over, leaving only Penthesilea's self-immolation. The attention has been so focused on her that one could easily overlook the subtlety of the directing. The camera follows the moves of the actress more so than in the previous films. But scene 15 is photographed from the back of the stage, transforming the rows of the empty theater into a background. It literally marks a turning point in the plot. Other directing techniques used sparingly include zooming and panning, change in perspective, and variety in lighting. Kleist's printed text is divided into 24 scenes. On many occasions Syberberg marks the transition from one scene to the next with a new camera take. But the cuts in the text blur the divisions, as do the panning and other sudden shifts. When one factors in the camera takes of the sculptures and script, one is left with the impression of more than 24 visual units, probably closer to 34.

After Penthesilea's self-immolation and final comments by the High Priestess and Prothoe, Clever sits down at the table, resting her head in her hands. She has just concluded a performance like the one Kleist himself witnessed. The only public performance of *Penthesilea* during his lifetime was a pantomimic monologue. So one learns from another frame of script at the end of the film. That kind of premiere undoubtedly contributed to Syberberg's decision to handle the drama as a monologue. It may also account for Kleist's suggested presence. His name and the title appear again first among the credits that conclude the film. Only then follow the names of Clever and Syberberg. This arrangement suggests three co-authors of the film, but does not identify a director or co-director. Syberberg's name appears further on again as the photographer. This time the list of credits comprises many names and a number of co-producers.

After the run on stage in Paris during fall 1987, work on the film was completed in the winter, with a copyright date of 1988. More stage performances followed in Germany, including the Hebbel-Theater in Berlin, the Schauspielhaus in Frankfurt am Main the following spring, and the Munich Residenztheater in June. The film premiered in Berlin in April 1988. It has also appeared on television in several countries.

Penthesilea is the second of three Syberberg films based mainly on Kleist's works. Other moviemakers have also been drawn to Kleist, e.g. Eric Rohmer, Volker Schlöndorff, Helma Sanders, and Hans Neuenfels.[31] By comparison, Syberberg's version is classical in its unity, letting Kleist's drama unfold on stage without interruptions. His own commentary frames the work but does not intrude into it. Even orchestral music must yield to the human voice.

Also worthy of an examination is Syberberg's *Penthesilea* and Riefenstahl's plans for a movie of that drama. With his books and previous films incorporating quasi-musical structure and references to movie history, one almost expects some hidden similar components in this work too, and be it only in counterpoint. One could, for example, imagine an intent to save or purify the drama from any asso-ciation with Riefenstahl and the Third Reich aesthetics. Or could it be a quasi-intercession for Riefenstahl? In *Die freudlose Gesellschaft* he explicitly discusses his programmatic avoidance of the innovations of Riefenstahl and her "master." And *Parsifal* includes a background projection of a sketch for a movie by Fanck in which she made her debut as an actress. Now he completed the film of *Penthesilea* that only World War II prevented her from making. This was the project she talked about for years, for which she developed elaborate plans and script, and which would probably have crowned her career.[32] She intended to play the title role, stating in her production notes: "If there is a transmigration of souls, then I must have lived her life at some previous time. Every word that she speaks is spoken from the very depth of my soul—at no time could I act differently from Penthesilea."[33] And one reads there, "Also, in *Penthesilea* I found my own individuality as in no other character" (194). Somehow, then, Clever's and Syberberg's Penthesilea throws a shadow with Riefenstahl's profile due to his contrapuntal procedure and system of associations. But is this the work Riefenstahl dreamed about?

In some respects Syberberg's film and Riefenstahl's plans agree. They both pay homage to Kleist. Syberberg does this by stressing Kleist in the credits and frames of script, and by restoring the historical forces influencing his life in the form of visible sculptures. Riefenstahl describes Kleist in her notes as being "maligned and misjudged like no other artist by his own people," and resolves, "to him this film shall be a memorial" (195).

They both agree on making a film of Kleist's play using his words, not a movie merely inspired by the play. It means that the text has to be abridged (Riefenstahl, 199). Syberberg's cuts result in a focus on the title heroine at the expense of external, or visual, drama. Riefenstahl also agrees that some parts of the text can dispense with cinematic action: "There are passages in *Penthesilea* that one should primarily only listen to—where the visual must be moved entirely into the background. Thus the accoustical [*sic*] and the visual factors must, in wonderful composition, alternate reciprocally, must enhance each other or combine intimately" (199). Syberberg also introduces a pattern of alternation when Clever periodically stops acting and sits down at the table to read aloud select passages.

Riefenstahl does not want to present the drama simply as a documentary of a theater performance. She does not even think *Penthesilea* can succeed on a theater stage: "Then it is for me still preferable as a radio drama, only spoken, when I then can fully enjoy the language without being continually disturbed by the all too human Amazons whom I must look at on the stage" (196–97). It is intriguing that also Syberberg devoted attention to the radio as the *Urstimme*, or "voice from earliest times."[34] Although not echoing Riefenstahl's statement about her project, he refers in that article to the previous monologues made with Clever as focusing on the inner voice captured by the *camera obscura* (72). Through semantic branching he arrives at *Kammerspiel* and alternate modes of communication. This leads to reminiscences linking the importance of radio in his early life with the emphasis on language and acoustical reception in his monologues. One also remembers his use of radio broadcasts in *Hitler*.

Riefenstahl mentions in her notes how she wanted to introduce the elements of nature in her movie. She plans to incorporate a full spectrum of them, the sun, moon and stars, etc. (203). Syberberg also retains the elements, but reduces them to four in symbolic form on the table. Both filmmakers opt for subdued colors for their project. Riefenstahl states in her memoirs, "In no way was the film to resemble Hollywood technicolour spectacles. I wanted to use the colours sparingly. These were to be subtle nuances between beige and brown, like the colours of the pyramids on the Nile."[35] Syberberg does not comment on his sparing use of color. The setting is dark. With the exception of a few props and the actress, the colors run towards a monochrome reddish-brown. This reduction of the palette continues the emphasis on the inner world, starting with *Die Nacht*.

On several points Riefenstahl and Syberberg agree, but choose different paths of implementation. Both did not want to interrupt the play with additions of their own material. But since the narratives call out for visualization, Riefenstahl planned to add a prologue showing the Amazons at home before departing for Troy, then Achilles in action as the *Iliad* describes him, and subsequently a section centered on Hector's funeral. Only after the funeral would the herald announce the Amazons' approach: "Here Kleist's poetic style begins" (198). Syberberg created his own mini-introduction with the sculptures of Kleist's contemporaries and some brief quotations as Clever opens the other books on the table, one by one, before deciding on the volume containing *Penthesilea*. From then on the text comes from the play.

Both filmmakers agree on the importance of music. Riefenstahl first refers to the rhythm of the visual impressions, calling it a wild melody (201). She subsequently envisions her film as a film opera with the added prologue having very little dialogue, but mostly chorus songs and dances (202). Her composer would be Herbert Windt, she adds in her memoir (250). Her description points to a traditional handling of music in historical movies. Obviously Syberberg did not want to emulate Riefenstahl's handling of music. Nonetheless, his idea of music in *Penthesilea* resembles the first part of Riefenstahl's outline. More importantly, in his book to the film he repeats Kleist's thoughts on music in relation to his texts: "Everything is music, and the texts, the *basso continuo*."[36] The bass accompanies the melody, he explains there. It determines the tone and rhythm of the whole composition. The action on stage is the melody in the form of song, something both audible and visible. His "chamber music" has been relocated to the internal stage, *nach innen*, with such shows of visible rhythm as the periodic burning of pages brimming with the textual imagery that caused Kleist difficulty on stage. Both Riefenstahl's wild melody and Syberberg's internalized melody sound related but remain vague and unconvincing, even with his film available for examination. The rest of Riefenstahl's plan relating to music obviously differs greatly from Syberberg's final version.

Both Riefenstahl and Syberberg recognize in *Penthesilea* a framework pointing beyond the human. In her production notes Riefenstahl describes Penthesilea as a goddess and a human at the same time (203). The reference to divinity may not be so out-of-place for an Amazon queen who is known as the "daughter of Ares." Syberberg does not evoke this mythic connection. However, in his book to the film he repeatedly imbues the work with a higher dimension, using the term *das Hohe* (the high, the sublime) and *spirituality*. On one level his terminology echoes the era of the plot. Penthesilea and Achilles did not only believe in the gods. They were descended from them. But one also remembers that all the characters in Syberberg's films who share Clever's face embody a spiritual dimension, be it ever so faintly. Syberberg does not identify Penthesilea as the manifestation of this component, but refers to the play and the culture from which it arose. That era, German Idealism, professed faith in transcendental values. Its philosophy and aesthetics provided the foundation for most intellectual and artistic accomplishments in Germany in the late eighteenth and much of the nineteenth century. Of course, Idealism was anchored in the Western tradition with roots reaching back to antiquity. For two generations following World War II, most German artists and intellectuals have ignored or rejected this cultural legacy. The Third Reich had extolled its version of "German" culture, and that sufficed to make also Idealism anathema, or at least suspect. Anything the Nazis admired had simply become too contaminated with ideology. Syberberg knows the risk when he professes allegiance to German Idealism. He explicitly does not proclaim any manifesto or formulate new theories [23]. His film distances itself from contemporary aesthetics, he writes, because it is indebted to the aesthetics of German Idealism [26]. It remains faithful to "the structures of thought and feeling that do not question the sublime and thus ourselves in our loftiest potential, but serves purposes that correspond to the Idealist period of German cultural history" [26]. He attempts to present "art in its divine potential" [34]. If this should succeed, it would touch realms that earlier times called the Holy [34]. With this formulation Syberberg moves away from Riefenstahl. One can begin to recognize his grounding in art history and literature. Especially Walter Benjamin's writings on auratic art, although unidentified, inform his thought here, or at least share in this legacy. Without mentioning Benjamin's name or using his terminology, Syberberg's objective is to restore the aura.

     In two related respects Syberberg appears to adopt Riefenstahl's aesthetic ideas, but develops them in contrasting ways. Her notes repeatedly point to statues, both as inspiration and as "live" parallels. For example, she envisions the transition between her prologue and the play-based part in words evoking art. Here, seen against a rising sun, Penthesilea on her white horse should stand like a statue (198). Aha, one may conclude, such remarks induced Syberberg to include statues in his film. Maybe so. He even introduces a classical relief of a genius with a torch. Her text also mentions something similar: "I see before me the classical reliefs—where, above all, the body speaks and the costume is unimportant" (201). The figure in Syberberg's relief is almost nude. Its posture and attributes also speak—of grief. However, being a genius with angel wings it does not represent an ordinary mortal. And Syberberg's sculptures of Kleist's human contemporaries do not display nudity. He even drapes a towel over one of the Goethe busts that reveals bare shoulders. Also Edith Clever wears a demure black suit covering most of her person. In contrast, Riefenstahl's notes emphasize the sculptural quality of the human body, extolling its beauty. She links this beauty to art, especially Michelangelo's sculptures (201). Of course also her Achilles must be handsome, like a lion when angry, and then "gleamingly divine" again. If such statements in Riefenstahl's notes inspired Syberberg, they produced a corrective reaction, not imitation. He saw no need to display Clever's attractiveness, since her face and gestures function as the screen on which the drama is shown. The sculptures are admittedly beautiful, but they portray mostly dead people with covered bodies. Nor does their appearance command the kind of attention Riefenstahl propounds. She wants to visualize the qualities of Kleist's language in the bodies. That transfer takes place in Syberberg's film too, but he concentrates it all on one actress and a few symbols. His ideal of beauty aims at bringing the text closer to its sacral roots. He may even be suggesting a literal aura with the candles glowing around the protagonist. He refers to them as "inner illumination" [19].

Riefenstahl's notes criticize an earlier film made of Kleist's comedy *Der zerbrochene Krug* (*The Broken Jug*, 200). The disturbing factor is the clash between a naturalistic setting and Kleist's poetry as dialogue. His language requires a stylized setting, she emphasizes: "Not a single scene dare be realistically photographed (the light)" (201). She envisions the stylization to be conveyed through light, the composition of the frame, and a rhythm alternating between Dionysian frenzy and classical serenity. Syberberg also observes the need for stylization with similar means, but carries it out with full consistency. He pares down the visual trappings to a minimum, requiring the viewers to activate their imagination. Just as Penthesilea's feelings, so also her world must come alive in the viewers. He introduced this expectation most explicitly in *Molly*, where the spectators observe a reader react to a text, and, maybe, share the reactions. *Penthesilea* has moved beyond that and even *Fräulein Else* by presenting the drama as action. But still the spectators must also become listeners and activate their inner soundingboards, so as to experience the sympathetic reverberations and visualization. Syberberg reduces the external dimension in favor of the inner drama. In his book to the film he uses the term "representation of the world in one person" [23]. This intent transforms the title heroine into a microcosm. Since he also restricts the physical arena to a mostly dim, bare stage, he creates the non-realistic handling for which Riefenstahl develops only a partial concept. His frame does not distract from the language and focuses the viewers' attention. In this setting Kleist's verse and imagery can succeed. But would it have had a chance in Riefenstahl's planned film? How stylized and non-realistic would the result have been with its huge battle scenes and Amazons on 1,000 white horses in the Libyan desert? Her planned extravaganza in 34 episodic units would have looked too much like the Hollywood spectacles she disparages. Syberberg's contrast may very well be the only viable alternative to save a dramatic work so far removed from our language.

The richness of Kleist's verse has been an obstacle to its success on stage. Syberberg pays attention to the language. His gestures are so imperceptible as to be easily overlooked. A glance at the printed text may not suffice. For example, his use of *mise en abyme* sometimes functions as a mirror *of* the text. The statue of the royal sisters finds its reflection in Penthesilea and Prothoe. One of the royal sisters was Queen Luise, who shared the fate of her country and died at a young age. Likewise Penthesilea was an ill-fated queen who died young. Her confidante, Prothoe, addresses her frequently as *Schwesterherz* (sister heart). Perhaps not related by blood as Princess Friederike to Queen Luise, she exhibits a comparable devotion. Another mirror *of* the text is the column that Penthesilea overturns. With the pillar reflecting Achilles, its toppling foreshadows his death. A broken or fragmentary column also appears in the funerary relief with the mourning genius. Penthesilea is herself facing the abyss more than once physically, emotionally, morally, and politically. When she gradually regains her mind after Achilles' death, Prothoe asks if she has "ascended" from the realm of shadows. A strange question, since Elysium or the Underworld does not usually relinquish the dead. Syberberg also indulges in at least one playful elaboration on Kleist's language. When Penthesilea learns that she personally killed Achilles through her bites, she asks, "Did I kiss him to death?" Relapsing into mental confusion, she soon after remarks, "Kisses, bites, it rhymes." Syberberg adds a visible rhyme to *Küssen* and *Bissen* with the *Kissen*, "cushions," on the floor. For the most part, though, his directing is discret, giving center stage to Edith Clever and Kleist. The film even withholds his name until the end.

This self-effacement continues in the book to the film. Technically, the hefty volume is a program for the theater performances. Syberberg's game of hide-and-seek may induce librarians to catalogue it under Kleist or Clever, and not under Syberberg as the author. The outside cover lists the title, *Penthesilea*, followed by "Heinrich von Kleist." Under a photo of Clever appears her name, and on the bottom "Hans J. Syberberg." Part of his given name has shrunk to an initial. Similarly, on the title page Kleist's name precedes *Penthesilea*. On the bottom the disappearance act continues with the initials "HJS," then "Fotos / Text" and "1988." However, the book does not contain only excerpts of the play, and Syberberg is undoubtedly the author. The softbound volume is unpaginated, consisting of a 37-page-long introduction of photos and text, followed by 214 pages of photos from the play with Syberberg's handwritten, practically illegible captions from Kleist's lines. The pictures stem from rehearsals. The introduction includes photos from *Molly* and *Fräulein Else* as well. The inside back cover shows a picture of Syberberg in the Paris metro followed by his full name. What appears at first as modesty and self-effacement assumes a different character in the concluding paragraph of the introduction. After outlining plans for a changed lighting system during the scheduled performances in Berlin, the author makes fun of himself. Such measures are the strange results of the "omnipotence of director vanity," he writes, with the director assuming the "role of a demiurge." Syberberg is playing with the concepts of creativity and creation. In the three-step chain of authorship, he gives first place to Kleist, who himself adapted and transformed ancient sources. Clever continues the creation process by interpretating the text and giving it life with words and action. Syberberg puts himself in the third place as the force who prepares and transforms it to film and video for life in a material world. This process reflects on a human level the creation mystery in ancient philosophy and several undercurrents of Western spirituality. Plato, for example, considered the demiurge the creator of the visible world (*Timaeus*, 41, 42). The word has, then, a venerable tradition. Syberberg as a human demiurge is aware of his place in the hierarchy, of his mission, and of the pitfalls of "director vanity" and assumed "omnipotence." The use of this terminology confirms the presence of a spiritual component also in the film.

If the biblical creation suffered a glitch in the Garden of Eden, then a human creator should not presume to compete with it and produce a perfect work. Some form of imperfection reflects the creator's humility. This line of thought manifests in the film as one overlong pause between two scenes. In the book it shows up as the amateurish lack of a publisher's standards. The text is reproduced from a typescript containing corrections and typos. Of the thirteen numbered mini-chapters numbers 9 and 10 are missing.

Although the introduction touches upon many topics, it does not discuss or mention other films of or about *Penthesila*, nor the plans by Riefenstahl. It does refer frequently to the age of German Idealism. Presumably the ideals of renewed spirituality, of the holy and the sublime are concepts at home in the philosophy of that age, but the text remains vague about attributions or clarification. The same applies to the "guilt" that gains importance for the author's objective. He does not mean only Penthesilea's guilt here. Due to the references to Idealism, the guilt might point to original sin and related concepts. However, more likely is the legacy of the twentieth-century disaster that Syberberg shares. He describes himself as "knowing, at least contemplating, the guilt that led to all of this, for which atonement requires rituals and exercises that lead to the tragic in an art that this era has lost, or just now, or still, makes possible?" [27]. In spite of the author's vagueness, one thing is clear: his aesthetics is inseparable from moral issues involving guilt and atonement.

Not so clear is whether also the style of Syberberg's prose expresses aesthetic or philosophical principles. This volume contains numerous passages in stream-of-consciousness and inner-monologue style. Conspicuously many sentences consist of a series of fragments. That may result from reading too much Kleist. But unlike Kleist, Syberberg loses the grip on grammar. He lets the thoughts drift and intertwine, as if dreaming. His prose abhors periods. He often replaces the period with a question mark, as in the quotation in the previous paragraph. This characteristic shows up with increasing frequency. The question marks tend to conclude narrative statements that normally should end with a period. The effect is twofold. The monologic flow of thought transforms itself into a dialogue pretending to induce the reader to an active response. Also, the question mark weakens the authority of the writer, as if the asking for consensus might make him less threatening or provocative. In either case, the question mark signals awareness of a potential interlocutor whom the writer wants to engage.

Syberberg published basically the same text as a chapter in a *Festschrift* the following year.[37] He added a new first mini-chapter, reshuffled passages, made some corrections, and omitted the last paragraph, for a total of 12 numbered units of text without any photos. The new version retains the characteristics of his style.

One of the first reviews appearing in Germany reported on the performances in Paris. Joseph Hanimann describes the experience as neither expressive nor realistic, but magic.[38] He admits that the performance expects more of the audience than regular theater fare. In Germany the stage version premiered in Frankfurt am Main (Großes Haus) on April 16. It then moved to the Hebbel-Theater in Berlin as part of the city's celebration of being honored as the "cultural city of Europe" for 1988, and later on to the Residenz Theater in Munich. The German stage versions were half an hour longer than the performances in Paris. A reviewer in Frankfurt mentions that the audience applauded both Clever and Syberberg enthusiastically.[39] The performances in Munich led to an interview of both of them with the *Süddeutsche Zeitung*, a text that appeared later also in a book.[40] Emphasizing the tension and exhausting experience, the article states that Clever enchants and mesmerizes audience and critics alike (91).

Also in April 1988 an article about Syberberg and Clever appeared in *Der Spiegel*.[41] The occasion was the German premiere of *Penthesilea* in Frankfurt am Main. The text reminisces, reports, and describes, with focus on the collaboration of the two artists. The frame is the few hours that Clever and Syberberg share with Matthias Matussek, one of the editors of *Der Spiegel*. The evening begins in a studio at the Wannsee in Berlin, where Syberberg completes the editing of a video version for French viewers. The first part of the article concentrates on Clever's Penthesilea, concluding that other portrayals are all failures by comparison. From now on Penthesilea has a face, that of Edith Clever (218). One learns about an invitation from Vienna to perform the work in a theater there. The reporter writes with more sympathy for her than for Syberberg. When referring to the *Hitler* film, he also reveals that he has probably not seen it when claiming that André Heller plays the title role (219). He includes Syberberg's criticism of current cultural conditions and describes it in terms of religious fanaticism, "awfully German," and not afraid of ridiculousness (221). He paraphrases Syberberg's statements on politics, calling him stupid and "dandylike with aesthetic judgments" (223). This reaction was elicited by Syberberg's observation that Hitler considered himself an artist and also created something (223). Never mind that young Hitler really had been rejected by the Art Academy in Vienna, and that his creation, the Third Reich, was a disastrous achievement. Any comments about Hitler short of condemnation entail a provocation, and Matussek reacts predictably. Syberberg also comments on Kurt Waldheim and Chomeini. Thus Matussek describes this "harmless" man with whom he chats over dinner as a secret terrorist. But instead of throwing bombs, he directs Kleist. For that Matussek is relieved (223). He thinks that *Penthesilea* is Syberberg's most beautiful and mature work to date. Ironically, he is making the kind of aesthetic judgment for which he criticizes Syberberg. The article concludes with a visit the three of them make to Kleist's grave at the lake. He committed suicide at the Wannsee in 1811 and was buried on that spot. The studio where the editing takes place is in the vicinity. The article ends with Syberberg's disparaging remark about the new buildings along the lake. The Wannsee, provocative political statements, buildings at the lake—could there be a connection? It was in a villa at the Wannsee that a conference of high-ranking Nazi officials formulated the "Final Solution" in January 1942. Many would think that a discussion of Third Reich topics at the Wannsee without mentioning the Holocaust would indeed amount to a provocation, Kleist or no Kleist. It is a place where a thinking person might easily despair when pondering German history. Did Matussek report everything truthfully or did he present a distorted image of Syberberg? Did Syberberg display a persona most people would reject? Throughout his films and books one can observe contrapuntal principles of composition. Does this procedure also apply to himself? If so, one might recognize a counterpoint in his behavior: the simultaneously ostracized, persecuted, and celebrated artist speaks without condemnation about the persecutors of the recent past. But a suspicion about the accuracy of the article lingers, especially in view of Syberberg's statements on similar topics elsewhere. In a French publication, for example, he discusses Hitler the artist as belonging to a "mephistophelian avant-garde."[42] Still, taking delight in roughing feathers at home, he constantly provoked irritation. One journalist stated in reference to Syberberg's published opinions that one should not allow such texts to be printed.[43] The difference between his image at home and abroad became more pronounced as the years passed. Actually, his prestige abroad continued to climb. For example, in 1988, he was invited to speak at a conference in Rotterdam.[44] It was an international symposium on the Frankfurt School and critical theory, with prominent philosophers and critics attending. Syberberg participated in a session on postmodernism and the *Gesamtkunstwerk*. Considering himself antimodern, he wanted art to give expression to suffering and the tragic. He also proposed a "new austerity" as a countermeasure against the millions squandered on mass entertainment "art." The comments amount to a description of his own work.

Die Marquise von O . . .

In Edith Clever Syberberg had found the perfect artistic partner. He refers to her in the program book to *Penthesilea* as a "giant of the stage." Her portrayal of Penthesilea soon led to another Kleist heroine in 1989, Julietta, an Italian noblewoman. She is the title character in *Die Marquise von O . . .*, a novella that appeared in 1808, the same year as *Penthesilea*. Again Syberberg and Clever collaborated on a monologue that transgresses the definitions and traditions of artistic genres. It combines the narrative genre of the novella with the dramatic art of the theater and the cinematic art of the screen. Not quite so strictly minimalist as the other monologues, it still omits all unnecessary details in favor of a focal point, the narrator cum actress.

The film has a subtitle, *vom Süden nach dem Norden verlegt* (Relocated from the South to the North). The Napoleonic wars, when French troops invaded Prussia, apparently inspired the story. Of course the political situation at that time precluded a recognizable treatment of the circumstances. Therefore Kleist relocated the plot to the south, letting Russian troops invade an Italian location. Syberberg shifts the action back to northern Germany and chooses settings that Kleist knew well. This change does not affect Kleist's text, which Clever recites in its entirety. But it does imbue the work with an added dimension, since Russian troops invaded North Germany again in 1945. The German locations figure only as theater-style backdrops. Maybe some of them are projections, but in that case they imitate backdrops to perfection. Since these images remain in view much of the time, they become the main carriers of the relocation. Only in the first sentence of the story does Kleist mention that the hometown of the marquise is Italian. Its name, and all other place names and family names are reduced to initials. That facilitates the relocation to northern Germany. And in 1989 the people living in that part of the country would not have forgotten the fighting, chaos, and fate of the women in 1945. Therefore the events in Kleist's novella divide and transform themselves into mirroring stories. One belongs in Kleist's world of ca. 1808, the other reflects northern Germany in 1945 and after. Thanks to the stylized simplification of clothing and props, the story becomes timeless. Kleist's novella takes place basically in three locations: the fortress that the Russians attack, the home of the marquise and her parents in the same town, and the country estate of the marquise. The backdrops combine the fortress and the home in town into one building, the Hohenzollern Palace, known as the *Stadtschloss*, in what later became East Berlin. It was heavily damaged by bombardment in 1945 and torn down in 1950. The film uses several views of it in ruins, thus emphasizing the rubble as a projection of inner conditions. For the country estate Syberberg chose Friedersdorf in the eastern province of Oderbruch. This palatial estate was also destroyed in spring 1945 and later razed.

The marquise is a young widow with two little daughters. At the death of her husband three years earlier she vowed not to remarry and moved back to her parents' home. During the attack by the Russians, a group of soldiers drag her away, and only the intervention of a young Russian officer saves her from gang rape. He leads her to a safe spot where she faints. When peace is restored, life appears to return to normalcy, albeit under Russian control. Her rescuer, Count F., is exceedingly attentive and soon asks her to marry him. Torn between her vow and debts of gratitude, she hesitates. War-related events separate them for several months. When it becomes certain that the marquise is pregnant and she maintains her "innocence," not knowing how she could possibly have come into such a condition, her parents evict her and cut all contact with her. She moves to her country estate. Out of duty to her unborn child, she decides to advertize for the unknown father and promises to marry him for the child's sake. This leads to reconciliation with her parents. On the announced day of identification, Count F. appears, humble and contrite. They do get married, but live apart until their son is a year old. The contrast between his appearance as a saving "angel" and his behavior as a "devil" was too much for her. Only with the passage of time can she reconcile herself with reality and accept him as her husband. The narrative begins with the advertizement, then moves back to the marquise's return to her parents' home after her husband's death, and follows the events chronologically from there.

The film adheres faithfully to the text of the novella. It avoids, however, a period recreation. A neoclassical bench is the main concession. Other furniture includes a convertible sewing/tea table and four chairs. Gottfried von Schadow's statue of Queen Luise and her sister reappears. Other props are restricted to a few objects. The background consists of three projections or theater backdrops in U-formation, and of which the center image occasionally changes. Most of the time only one of the pictures or the darkness between them is visible. This arrangement creates the illusion of a theater setting, although the filming took place in a studio. Of course Clever also gave this performance on stage in several theaters. Syberberg could easily have filmed everything on a stage again, but abandoned that idea in favor of some help from a technical crew. The arrangement remains sparse and deliberately artificial. It becomes Clever's challenge to activate the viewers' imagination and make the plot come alive.

This time music occasionally joins Clever's voice. Passages from Beethoven's String Quartet No. 13 in B flat Major, opus 130 and his Great Fugue, opus 133 can be heard intermittently throughout. In view of Syberberg's fondness for contrapuntal composition, one may assume that also the visual part of the film contains fugal characteristics.

Heinrich von Kleist's name and the complete title appear before the film, followed by "Berlin Spandau 1989." His name and the short title reappear again at the end, where they head off the credits that include the names of Clever and Syberberg, in that order. The title is, however, not the first thing to appear on the screen. While it heads the list of printed credits at the end, it trails a series of still photos in the beginning. Both of these framing sections are in black and white, contrasting with Kleist's story in color. The frame clearly represents the present, or at least recent times, while the fictional content hails from the past. The initial section comprises 17 stills in black and white followed by five transitional stills and camera takes in color. These 22 units add up to an introduction. But what do they convey? The first photo shows a jet in the sky, accompanied by the sound of the engine. Perhaps the plane indicates the modern age. Or, maybe the sky and not the plane is the important part. If so, the film begins with a glimpse of the celestial realm. The next two photos show the earth. The patch of ground is overgrown and marred with debris. Does Syberberg still play with the Kabbalistic concept of *Kehricht-Kehre*-return here? If he is weaving in his concern for ecology, one wonders about a connection to the main story. This little part of the earth suffers chaos and destruction. An invaded sky and a destroyed earth? They belong together, since the plane engine still roars. The sound strikes one as odd, since the plane is not shown moving. Maybe the correlation between sound and image adds to the narrative. That might point to a contrapuntal treatment. The inclusion of Beethoven's fugue makes that even more likely.

The next cluster of photos depict the door leading into the studio, an overview of the studio with the backdrop, and technicians at work. One picture shows an interior shot of a ruin. One cannot tell yet if this view represents another backdrop or part of the studio. There is less noise during this sequence. Then follow four shots accompanied by motor sounds plus the barking of invisible dogs. Two are exterior photos, one interior, all messy and neglected sites. The fourth shows a road. This was filmed in Berlin before the Wall came down. Do the dogs belong to the East German border guards, or perhaps guards in a concentration camp? The sound indicates the presence of living animals, although the photos show no sign of life. Or does Syberberg again introduce a pack of dogs for the purpose he did in *Hitler*? There he plays an inaudible fugue on an invisible organ using the visual pun involving the pack-*Koppel*-coupler to change the sound. With the next still the sound does change back to that of only a plane seen in the sky outside the studio. The sound continues in the following picture showing the surface of a road. Half of it is a narrow country road paved with cobblestones, the other half widens it in unpaved terrain showing tire tracks. The view is directed to the ground that does not even show the shadow of a plane. The sequence repeats that of the beginning: from heaven to earth. The sound accompanying the pictures changes from the plane engine to subdued noise on to barking, followed by another plane engine and finally silence. If the jet suggests warfare or noise pollution, the debris on the ground might be the result of the destruction. The views from the studio depict perhaps the artist's attempt to cope with the experience, and the repeat leads the artist away into the countryside. The next picture is the silent photo of an agricultural field reaching to the horizon, allowing heaven and earth to meet. At this point the title appears superimposed on the landscape. The last view in black and white, number 17, shows a painting of the Friedersdorf estate that replaces the country estate in the novella.

Up to this point the pictures have followed each other abruptly, much as if joined as cuts. The next few units switch to color and form a gradual transition to live film. Friedersdorf reappears, now in color, followed by another view of it with the identification and date, 1811. For the first time the camera zooms and pans. Some units of this transition are linked through fade-outs and fade-ins. The first fade-in opens to Clever sitting at a table, where she takes out a cup with the Friedersdorf painted on it. It is a nice little *mise-en-abyme*. Beethoven's music occupies the soundtrack until scene or take 22. Only then does Clever begin to narrate and act out Kleist's story. The transition from the introduction to the text itself takes the form of a lengthy double exposure. As a visual fugue, the black and white sequence corresponds to the exposition, and the following section with fade-outs to the first episode or *Zwischenspiel*. The next major section uses double exposure to separate the scenes. It continues to roughly unit 34. This section renders the events of the attack. Towards the end one loses track of the counting and identification of scenes. When a unit fades out and the next unit fades in, one can usually tell if the film introduces a new camera take. But when this transition takes place in the darkest area of the set featuring Clever covered in a foot-long black cape, the visibility dwindles and the procedure escapes analysis. One cannot distinguish a cut from a fade-out or double exposure. This indeterminacy characterizes the transition to the next major section. It also appears to constitute the second episode that includes the marquise's fainting spell. The mystery surrounding her impregnation repeats itself in the uncertaincy about technical procedures. This little unit is a memorable episode. It begins with a dark double exposure continuing the view of the silent marquise, dressed only in her long white gown, outstretched on the floor. A closer, equally dark image of an upright, silent Clever emerges superimposed. She has wrapped herself in a black cape, making only her face recognizable against the black background. Then, slowly, her hand reaches out of the cloak, seeming to grope the body lying on the floor. Music accompanies this and the following unit of Clever in black. She remains silent for a long time. The next major section continues with fade-outs marking the inner divisions. Usually, but not always, they correspond to new paragraphs in Kleist's text. This section of approximately 22 scenes comprises the rest of the novella. At the end of the narrative the image transforms itself into a still. With her back to the camera, Clever stands immobile looking at the backdrop of Friedersdorf. This unit appears to revert to the transitional takes that follow the exposition. The credits form the coda.

Four hours long, *Die Marquise von O . . .* requires the viewers' full attention to be appreciated. With no book in sight, Clever follows the text, alternating narrative with dialogue. When for example several people talk around the table, she moves to the chair on which the speaker sits. Such shifts in location or direction supplement voice modulation, gestures, and facial expressions. Subtle variations suffice. Compared to Penthesilea, the marquise acts and reacts as a noblewoman. Her passion is also a tale of suffering and confusion, but ends with forgiveness and life. The spiritual overtones are embedded in Kleist's text. Her savior appears as "an angel from heaven," she has previously been "the goddess of good health," her unborn child seems to be "more divine" than other children because of the mysterious conception. When finally the mother visits her, she calls her daughter "purer than angels." With Gnostic and Kabbalistic parallels the marquise suffers degradation, exile, and suffering. The reconciliation with her father is "heavenly joyful", and they kiss and behave as lovingly as newlyweds. Syberberg's visual addition is Kabbalistic: a fragment. This piece of a sculpture lies on the ground at the heroine's country estate where she withdraws in her banishment. She moves the heavy chunk with her, a gesture repeated at the end, when she carries it to the statue of the sisters. The *tikkun* process entails the collection and recombination of the sefirotic fragments. At the same time, the broken remnant may also represent the predicament of the Prussian and/or German cultural and spiritual condition. Another detail may point in the same direction. Near the end of the story the marquise leaves the room and, at the door, sprinkles her family members with holy water. This gesture so familiar to Catholics undergoes a baffling change in the film. Instead of blessing them with water she throws dead leaves at them (= the viewers). The leaves again cover the ground as in so many films by Syberberg. He may long ago have abandoned the concept of *Trauerarbeit*, or "work of mourning," but perhaps not *Trauerkunst*, "art of mourning." Mourning or grieving is associated with leaves, as formulated by Hölderlin. Syberberg's visual signature borrows the poet's *Laub der Trauer*, or "leaves of mourning." To judge from the locations chosen for the plot, the grief concerns a loss related to Prussian history, its culture, way of life, ideals, in brief, a homeland that no longer exists. But the leaves also signify a second source of mourning, as established in the discussion of *Parsifal*. And hermetically, this connection is the Holocaust. Through the power of associations, the trauma of the twentieth century intrudes into the plot, joining the ruins from World War II. More recognizable is the mourning of the fallen state of Germany, both in its amputated and divided condition, and in its cultural and spiritual decline.

The ruins find their most obvious expression in the backdrops, respectively background projections. Various exterior and interior views of the bombed-out Hohenzollern palace supposedly illustrate the destruction wrought by the Russian attack in Kleist's novella. They also reflect the fall and confusion of the characters. This occurs most poignantly when the soldiers grab the marquise and the count rescues her. Here the background shows the rotunda in an interior shot directed upwards, revealing the sky through the remains of the cupola. The phallic ramifications of cupola-*Kuppel-kuppeln* were discussed in connection with *Hitler* and *Parsifal*. The image reappears later, and again with the same connotation. The count's abuse of phallic power parallels the ruined condition of the cupola.

Another detail from the same palace assumes more significance. The statue of Queen Luise and her sister remains on the set much of the time, although the camera does not always include it. Before the rape, the statue is covered up, but afterwards revealed. It is unmistakably a single piece of art. However, it represents two figures with their arms around each other, looking in different directions. The duality inherent in the sculpture expresses confusion for the title heroine: is she promiscuous or not? But contrapuntally, the statue also represents something royal that survived intact while the rest of the palace was destroyed. A projection shows the original location of the statue. It is a piece of wall between two doorways. This site appears in its ruined condition as the background for much of the action. Syberberg places his copy of the life-sized sculpture before this view between the doors. With also the light concentrated on the two sisters, the white statue emerges visually and symbolically as unscathed in a ruined environment. In that sense it also functions as a projection of the marquise's personality. She is a pure soul. But the statue also supports the action in more tangible ways. When the marquise discusses her baffling condition with a midwife, she addresses one of the marble sisters as if she were the midwife. More dramatically, when her mother visits her at the country estate, that lady merges with the other half of the sculpture. In the sustained balance of narration and acting, Clever resorts to every imaginable nuance to approximate illusion. While the figures of the sculpture suggest a whiff of make-believe, they also function as her inner voices. Especially the overlay of the mother with the statue underscores the esoteric dimension of the story. Symbolically and psychologically, the sculpture functions in several capacities: as an art work of something revered in a lost or different world, as a combination of unity and duality, as a projection of the marquise's inner condition, and as a representation of the mother and the midwife. It recalls aspects of several spiritual traditions, most clearly the Kabbalah's upper Shekhinah and lower Shekhinah. As the maternal aspect of the Divine symbolizes the first *he* of the Holy Name, so her divine daughter on earth does the second *he*. Her exile figures prominently in the sefirotic lore, as does the restoration of the fragments. Whether viewed as two parts of the Holy Name or just a double feminine aspect of the Divine, these symbols reverberate through Kleist's story and find a visual representation in the film. This dimension could easily be overlooked in favor of a political or historical lament over Germany's and Prussia's fate. On one level, the film appears to tell and intertwine two or even three stories. On another level, the black and white sections and props merge with Kleist's text into a coherent fugal composition.

Among the props, the backdrops especially create the illusion of a stage setting. As the previous monologues, so also *Die Marquise von O . . .* played in several theaters. During the spring of 1989 it ran in the Hebbel-Theater in Berlin, in June in the Bockenheimer Depot (Schauspiel Frankfurt), and in October as part of the Festival d'Automne in Paris. Vienna and other locations followed. The numerous reviews report an enthusiastic reception by audiences, but mixed response by the critics.[45] While Sibylle Wirsing plays it safe by focusing on Clever, Gerhard Rohde almost chokes on his allergy against anything Prussian. Calling the monodrama a Prussian séance, he uses a variant of this expression 15 times and cannot understand the "paradoxically" appreciative audience (37).

The most significant comment on the work remains Syberberg's own text.[46] It is again a program to accompany the performances and thus without the usual bibliographical information. Contrary to the book to *Penthesilea*, this volume of 83 pages is exquisitely printed. Syberberg's essay appears scattered over 33 pages. With photos on every page, many of them by Syberberg, the pictorial content with lengthy captions conveys much of the information. As expected, rehearsal shots of Clever in the title role fill quite a few pages. The pictures tell the story of glory days and downfall. Especially stark are the contrasts of pre- and post-war photos of the palace in Berlin, followed by its demolition. Much space is devoted to separate histories of Friedersdorf and the Berlin palace, also letters, e.g. by Kleist and the aristocratic family von der Marvitz, who used to own Friedersdorf. The letters and excerpts range from 1811, the year Kleist visited his friends at Friedersdorf, to 1917. These personal statements illustrate the life, ideals, and philosophy of a Prussian elite superceded by more plebeian forces of recent times, first democracy, then Nazi rule, occupation with Soviet-style socialism, and Western-style democracy in the Federal Republic, and at the time of writing, a divided system with dead or moribund culture. The ideal world of the old system, the essay explains, declined after the French Revolution, but survived for several generations in the communities centered on country estates. The upholders of that culture formed a counterworld to the Nazi ideology. On two occasions Syberberg mentions the Prussian officers' failed revolt on July 20, 1944 (50, 74). With them, the old world, for which he uses Prussia as a model, perished. Now all of Europe is suffering a similar fate. Old-fashioned ethics, sense of responsibility, and culture are being replaced with new technologies and different ways of thinking. This shift also affects art. Against this background of change and loss, Syberberg's comments on art assume the outline of a program. Oblivion threatens the cherished world that has been lost, unless art can preserve the memory of it: "What does not become form, has not lived" (39). Syberberg emphasizes that he does not mean museum-style preservation or commercialization: "Where art turns into business, it is dead," he maintains. The art he calls for needs an artist with a recognition of loss, sense of alienation from present society, and a desire to create without regard to usefulness or profit (39). Syberberg obviously describes himself here. Two pages further he characterizes this work as a merging of film and theater. Of course he does not mean a movie aiming at entertainment, but film as a combination of Brecht's alienation plays and Kortner's intensity.

Towards the end of the essay, the text defines the first monologue, *Die Nacht*, as "the night of Europe" and "counterworld" to the present (73). The passage does not connect it with *Die Marquise* or the other films made between them. It serves mainly to underscore the eschatological development of thought throughout the book. But here and on the following pages the question marks again replace the periods with increasing frequency. The plea for contradiction, questioning, or at least response, weakens the gloomy predictions. Running parallel to this tendency is the growing length of stringed sentence fragments without a verb. In one such incomplete, questioning statement over five lines, the text wonders if the marquise, this "serene sister" of Penthesilea, may not appear to us as a "redemption" (76),

One perceives perhaps from the preceding pages that Syberberg's film differs dramatically from Eric Rohmer's treatment of the same novella in 1976. Filmed in German, it too stars Edith Clever as the marquise. Wherever possible it keeps Kleist's words in dialogue and voice-over, or it translates descriptive or narrative passages into visuals. Overall, the result is a beautiful and unusual film, but close to a regular movie. And yet one can only marvel at the differences between the two versions, both works of art treating the same novella with the same actress in the same role! A comparative study of them by Leonardo Quaresima appeared in 1990.[47] He characterizes Syberberg's aesthetic formula as "from Brecht to Wagner, from Kortner to Clever" (101).

Additional comments by Syberberg appeared in 1989 as a chapter in a book published for a Kleist commemoration.[48] In June 1989, Frankfurt am Main celebrated Kleist with a symposium and a week of cinema devoted to movies about Kleist or of his works. This went on concurrently with the stage performances of Syberberg's and Clever's *Marquise*. Syberberg acknowledges the presence of Rohmer and his version in one summarizing statement: "If one compares the last of the works [his monologues] with the present movie version [Rohmer's] . . ., we see an orchestra of characters merged into one instrument that already fourteen years ago played a remarkable solo in it, [now] directed as a soloist who combines all voices of the orchestra" (40). Comparing the *Marquise* and *Penthesilea*, he points to an important shared feature, the statue by Schadow. In the previous film the sisters stood on the periphery, now they rest in the center background, "as a yardstick for composure" (42).

Many thoughts from the program-book recur with the point of departure being modern society. This European society speaks loudly of liberation and means the end of exploitation of humans by other people. Unfortunately, this exploitation has been replaced by different ones, that of nature by humans, and that of art for profit purposes. People think of themselves as free, but have really only been liberated to become consumers, like "slaves in the colonies of the opinion industries" (39). Similarly, the subsidy system of the arts has created the illusion of a utopia of art and culture. But these streamlined activities have been adjusted to suit an entertainment and leisure time mentality. True culture is dead or dying, the author announces. Only the awareness of loss and its expression as protest or counterculture might assure its survival. Syberberg describes two opposing forces. One has matter as its center, surrounded by materialism, "progress," enlightenment, and profit-driven business. Against this he establishes spirit (*Geist*) and its art, faith in God, and "lamenting beauty." Art can only arise from a sense of identity, he claims, and this art must lament all the losses. It does not level accusations (*Anklagen*) or express sympathy (*beklagen*), but it formulates the lament (*Klage*), which nourishes poetry and music (44). This art draws on memories of one's culture and the awareness of "the curse." In combining or reconciling the past with the present, it must strive to find the center, *die Mitte* (37). He means an equilibrium, one assumes, a Janus-faced balancing of tradition and innovation. But one should also remember the importance of the center in Parzival's "rehte enmitten durch," pointing to the *tikkun* process.

During his stay in Frankfurt for the Kleist festivities Syberberg also gave a lecture at the university.[49] According to a newspaper comment, he presented his "revolutionary" thoughts calmly and without "fanaticism" (41). Contemporary artists have failed to act as the conscience of history, he stated. Instead they cater to the abject and worthless, neglecting the real topics, namely "Auschwitz," the fate of Germany, including Prussia, and the mass deportations. He does not care for a pluralism that abdicates responsibility and conscience.

More and more Syberberg's publications focus on a few related topics. The focus may shift from one to another, but their number remains limited. Already a year earlier he had published an article which summarizes many of his thoughts on art and culture, "Die enthauptete Kunst" (The Decapitated Art).[50] It describes his reaction in the Cluny Museum in Paris when he stood facing numerous large and newly excavated heads of statues depicting royalty. The statues had adorned a sanctuary until the French Revolution. The revolutionary masses in search of liberty and democratic rights marked the beginning of a new era by destroying the ideals of the past. They started by demolishing art of royalty. They were the kings of the Old Testament. This decapitation signaled the execution of the human royals, the victory of enlightenment, and the end of so-called royal culture. That means, the author adds, the end of the royal in human nature. The remains of the statues have now been relegated to a museum. The death of art will spell the end of Europe, he states, which will be deprived of memory and history. It appears, then, that Syberberg attributes much significance to art for preserving a link with the past.

Historic records are composed by victors of war, but surviving art reveals the true facts, even when dressed up as myth. And, he concludes, art also grants death a meaning by giving expression to the tragic. The tragic is the home of art, "Heimat der Kunst."

Ein Traum, was sonst?

While writing his next book, Syberberg took time to prepare another monologue with Edith Clever. It premiered in December 1990 at the Hebbel-Theater in Berlin. *Ein Traum, was sonst?* (A Dream, What Else?) borrows its title from a line in the fifth act of Kleist's *Prinz Friedrich von Homburg* (1809–10). This indicates that the project draws on Kleist's text, but only to a limited extent. The following observations are based on the video version, which bears a copyright date of 1994.

The opening image seems familiar, a black and white still of a field where heaven meets earth on the horizon. As in the *Marquise*, the image soon serves as the background for the title. This time the names of Edith Clever and Hans Jürgen Syberberg, in that order, complete the frame. The information appears again at the end, heading a list of scrolling credits. But unlike the previous work, the film starts immediately *in medias res*. Aside from being a theater-cum-film project and a monologue with Clever, it shares several characteristics of the previous works. Clever is wearing dark clothing in a black environment, concentrating the effect of color on her face, or *parzuf*. The props have been reduced to a minimum. Occasionally one sees a large chest the size of a coffin, a chair, a stack of books on the dirt-covered floor, a small sculpture fragment, a filled wine glass, and a cigarillo. Most important of all is a mound of soil with a shovel stuck in it. Music by Beethoven supplements the soundtrack. It is his Symphony No. 6 in F Major, the "Pastorale," of 1808, in a 1952 recording. The music accompanies much of the second half of the film. It alternates with periods of silence and, to some extent, periods when Clever recites Euripides, Kleist, and Goethe. The first half presents a very different sequence of acoustical impressions. They are sounds from real life. But after a while they begin to resemble units of audible elements that might have inspired some sections of the music. When the symphony takes over, the human voice offers the only competing sound. Or viewed differently, the music surrounds the voice. In an intricate interplay of sound effects, the real life additions function as the material or experience from which art (here literature and music) arises. That experience includes pain and loss. This is interwoven with two strands of visual narrative to form a rich composition. The first impression of minimalism deceives. Artistically, this film equals *Hitler* and *Parsifal* in sophistication.

The visual story unfolds on two levels. In the background, changing projections of stills in black and white fill the screen. These views serve in part as a window into reality with a coordinated soundtrack. Mostly, though, they function as psychological projections of what Clever experiences, visualizes, thinks, feels, remembers, or longs for. During these sections the soundtrack will often run in counterpoint to the visuals, especially in the first part of the film. The interplay of two sets of visuals in Syberberg's films dates back at least to *Ludwig*. In *Ein Traum* the background visuals assume a major role in spite of being merely stills. The change of images takes the form of fade-ins, usually with ongoing double exposures involving Clever, or new camera takes of her.

The title screen fades to Clever, who covers her face with her hands. The only other item visible is a pile of soil with a shovel. Since the title information was superimposed on the picture of an agricultural field, the connection emerges automatically. The mound of dirt resulted from a hole being dug in this field. Although the viewer does not see the hole, one soon realizes that it will serve as a grave. The plot of the film, if one may use such a term for the activities of the mind, takes place at the site of this open grave. Clever, the only live character, probably expects to die soon. The film does not name her, but the text on the video sleeve identifies an inspiration for her. There one reads that she or her model is mentioned in the memoirs of Marion, Countess Dönhoff.[51] Syberberg thought highly of the countess and dedicated the film to her.[52] At the end of World War II she lived at Friedrichstein, one of the family's rural castles near Königsberg, now Kaliningrad in Russia. As the Soviet army approached in early 1945 and the roads were clogged with refugees fleeing westward, she mounted her horse and joined the trek. She made a brief stop in Varzin, an estate owned by the widowed daughter-in-law of Bismarck. This old lady inspired the character played by Clever. The cigar-smoking Sibylle, Countess Bismarck treated her young visitor to the finest wines, savoring the last few days of her life to the fullest. She had decided not to flee, but harbored no illusions about the fate of herself and her property once the Russians arrived. She had her grave dug, since there would be noone else around to help her when the moment came. Unfortunately, Countess Dönhoff does not mention what happened when the Red Army did arrive, but one assumes that the old lady did not survive the event. Clever's character borrows some features from Countess Bismarck. Although much younger, she displays the same refinement and elegance. Countess Bismarck's resolve to stay and await the inevitable reveals courage. Both she and Countess Dönhoff belonged to the nobility living on country estates in a Prussia that no longer exists. Her predicament assumes a representative function.

This role reveals only one aspect of the situation. More central to the film as a whole is the waiting at the open grave. Like Beckett's *Waiting for Godot*, it grapples with the issue of eschatology. Perhaps the old lady in Prussia had attained sufficient wisdom and serenity to face the ultimate. In the film a comparable acceptance is present from the beginning, but the literary figures that animate the protagonist's mind react to imminent death in different ways. Every time a strain of thought returns Clever's consciousness to the current situation, the field fills the background.

Reality dominates the projections and the soundtrack during the first long segment of approximately 17 scenes or units. The time is early 1945. The ravages of World War II show in mountains of rubble on bombed-out streets, people working on clearing debris after bombardments, or burned buildings. Contrasting with the images of destruction are country roads lined with trees, intact rural estates, and beautiful interiors, many of them reproduced from Countess Dönhoff's memoirs. The projections convey conflicting worlds, one of war and destruction, the other of peace and normalcy. Intruding into both worlds is an equally disparate cacophony of sounds. Snippets of radio broadcasts in several languages may hint at Syberberg's father tuning in to foreign news on his illegal radio during the war. Other broadcasts offer political speeches in German. These authentic radio excerpts continue the technique introduced in the *Hitler* film. Variety occurs with the noise of war, such as artillery, explosions, or alarm. Occasionally sounds of an opposing world try to penetrate in the form of church bells and fragments of music, but not for long. All the while Clever is waiting. Her movements and activities are restricted. She can pull up a chair, sit down, walk over to the chest, put on her coat, pick up a wine glass, or move the chair again. At times close-ups emphasize her reactions to the sounds. For example, her face reveals fear as she listens to the whining sound of falling bombs, anticipating the explosions when they hit. During this section of the film the noises of war assault the ears and dominate Clever's mind. As projected in background images, her thoughts and memories attempt in vain to focus on happier days. When the church bells return for a moment, they conjure a memory from before the war: the picture of a little boy playing with toys at the foot of a Christmas tree. This is Syberberg as a child. It appears, then, that Clever's character shares the filmmaker's memories, perhaps even functions as his mother or alter ego. The happy intermezzo fades away when the church bells of Nossendorf yield to howling wind. Throughout this long section Clever does not utter a word.

Storm sounds begin and conclude the following sequence. It too consists of roughly 17 scenes. It shows how Clever's mind succeeds to block out the war for increasingly longer periods. When the war enters visually, the sound no longer relates to it. Even the war itself has been transmuted to a photo of refugees on the road. Winter alternates with summer in the pictures, just as farming activities alternate with rural nature and more elegant interiors from Countess Dönhoff's memoirs. Other visual links to the first section are the cigarillos Clever begins to smoke (Countess Bismarck smoked cigars) and the shovel. At one point the memories elicit a smile on her face. During most of this section one notices only one soundtrack, but on at least one occasion also footsteps become audible. The sound has changed to a series of domestic activities carried out by one person. This unseen person opens and closes a drawer, walks up a staircase, pours water, moves around, etc. These everyday sounds indicate an unhurried routine. When Clever closes her eyes briefly, silence takes over, indicating the transition to the next sequence.

Fade-ins and double exposures introduce most new scenes. There are 22 of them in the following segment. The storm has swept away the peaceful memories, and the ensuing silence cannot stop an onslaught of new images of wartime ravages. One street in ruins is followed by the projected memory of it before the war.

Another photo shows bombed-out Dresden from the roof of the Zwinger. This well-known picture documents the Allied bombardment of Dresden in February 1945, during which at least 35,000, perhaps as many as 135,000, refugees and inhabitants perished. Its inclusion may also function as another self-reference, although not as a self-quotation. In *Die freudlose Gesellschaft* Syberberg distanced himself from the technological innovations of Riefenstahl and her "master." One such innovation appears in *Jew Süß*, namely double exposure. Syberberg uses it deliberately in the second act of *Parsifal*, and gradually more in the monologues. *Jew Süß* originally included a curse involving fire from heaven. Germany experienced the realization of the curse during World War II in the form of massive bombardments and resulting firestorms. Since double exposure appears throughout *Ein Traum*, the technique carries with it an implied connection to the Third Reich and the "curse," of which Syberberg speaks repeatedly. As such a carrier the technique becomes the main marker for one of the quasi-musical variations in the cinematic composition. And in this film the collapse of the Third Reich also sets the frame for the "plot."

During the first part of this segment the soundtrack offers a contrast to the projections. Again and again birdsong accompanies the views of dismal reality. The incompatibility of the two tracks of information underscores the fugal use of counterpoint, but also illustrates how a soothing influence of nature interferes with the effect of the destruction. Its attempt to heal suffers a setback at the sight of civilian casualties littering a street after a bombardment. The conflict finally erupts into words. For the first time in the film Clever speaks. For a short while the birds fall silent as Clever assumes the identity of Hecuba, the queen of Troy. She is a prominent character in two of Euripides' plays, *Hecuba* and *The Trojan Women*. In the latter she faces the deaths of her 19 sons and her husband, King Priam. She laments her loss and pain, which coincides with another view of war casualties. Besides lending her voice also to the grief over the German dead, she introduces an element of classical literature, that is, art, into the narrative. She is able to articulate her feelings. Somehow, the outburst of vocalized pain becomes a channel for healing as well as art. This episode is brief. It interrupts the longer segment accompanied by birdsong. Structurally it functions as a *stretto* in a fugue.

With Clever turning silent and the bird singing again, the long section continues. Several views of a church in ruins serve as a transition to a series of rural images unaffected by war. Here the birdsong harmonizes with happy moments. Does the memory of a church bring with it consolation for the soul? A prewar view of the church in Syberberg's childhood village sets the stage for other photos of a "normal" life in the countryside. Some of these pictures hail from the director's family albums and have appeared in his printed works. For example, one recognizes his mother among the people leaning against a car. That photo appeared in the French special issue called "Syberberg" (80). Also the straw-covered roof with the storks' nest makes a comeback. Not only do Syberberg's personal memories supplement the projections of historical reality, but his own childhood world also acquires representative qualities. It functions as an idealized antidote both to the political reality of National Socialism, the war, and post-war society. It represents the wholesome countryside that for a long time escaped the wartime destruction of the cities. And, as the base for memories, this lost paradise nourishes the spirit, provides strength, and beckons for a return. Compared to the tragedy characterizing several of the other sections, this segment borrows features from a fugal *intermezzo* (*Zwischenspiel, divertimento*). Clever's actions at the end signal a transition to another long unit. She picks up the shovel and eventually sticks it into the pile of soil. On the one hand she may identify with the rural world just depicted and act out an activity typical of farm life. On the other hand she may be contemplating her grave. The bird has stopped singing.

The following long segment comprises approximately 22 scenes. Clever smiles as happy memories cheer her mind and form the sequence of background projections. These images of rural life in summer continue the autobiographical component. Some of them have appeared on Syberberg's Web site and include him as a child. Throughout this section Beethoven's Pastorale fills the soundtrack while Clever remains silent. In addition to the pile of dirt her most important prop is now a small sculpture that she pulls out of her pocket. It is the lower half of a human body mounted on a plinth. The fragment may suggest the broken condition resulting from the destruction of war. But since Clever smiles while pulling it out, it probably points beyond the pain. It remains a treasured piece of art even as a fragment, testifying to a culture lost in history when such things of beauty were created. It also reminds one of Benjamin's words about early art and the sacred as well as the aura. Last, but not least, the sefirotic fragments await restoration.

The next major unit takes the viewer by surprise due to the reversal in tone and form of delivery. The music fades away for a while as Clever begins to recite and act from several scenes in Kleist's *Prinz Friedrich von Homburg*. Putting on a military jacket she transforms herself into the young prince, who is an officer in the army of the Prince Elector of Brandenburg. During the battle of Fehrbellin (in 1675) he led his troops into combat prematurely and against the orders of his commander. In spite of victory he has now been courtmartialed to death. Having seen the open grave waiting for him he pleads for his life (3.5). If not before, then at least now the viewer realizes that the mound of soil blocks the view of a grave. The prince's fear of death contrasts with his courage in battle and with the resignation of Countess Bismarck witnessed earlier. In the following excerpt Clever assumes two additional roles, that of the Prince Elector and of his niece, Natalie. She pleads for mercy for the prince (4.1). Her uncle agrees to call off the execution if the prince considers the verdict unjustified. At the beginning of this episode the commander had been reading a book on the Hohenzollern Palace in Berlin. As a visual quotation from *Die Marquise*, this oversized volume revives the viewers' memory of the former splendor and subsequent ruin of the palace. Its destruction parallels the downfall of the young prince. One of the background projections underscores the symbolic function of the building: it shows several views of the cupola. Starting with *Hitler*, the director has consistently associated a cupola with the male member, and it again with the Kabbalistic Yesod. This active element in the restoration process must, of course, restore its own ideal Self in order to effect the repair of the other broken vessels. The view of the waiting grave has shattered the prince, who must learn to overcome his fear and restore his wholeness. He realizes that a pardon does not right the wrong he has committed, and accepts the verdict as a matter of honor. His decision pleases the Prince Elector, who annuls the verdict. Before the news reach the prince, he is already standing blindfolded at the edge of his grave, ready for the execution. He has overcome his fear of death and utters the most famous lines of the play, "Nun, o Unsterblichkeit, bist du ganz mein!" (Now, o immortality, you are altogether mine! 5.10). During this and the following episode Beethoven's music accompanies the action softly. The Prince Elector arrives with his retinue and announces the unconditional pardon (5.11). The prince asks overwhelmed if this was all a dream. The joking answer is, "Ein Traum, was sonst?" (A dream, what else?). This line became the title of the film.

A gesture by Clever indicates the transition to another segment. She simply takes off the military jacket, revealing her black dress, and replaces the book back on the stack of other volumes. To the sound of a bird in Beethoven's symphony the projection changes to the garden view of Friedersdorf, familiar from *Die Marquise*. The 34 projected pictures of this section represent a medley of nature, intact buildings, and ruins. Gradually they shift to Goethe's home. Easiest to recognize are the oversized sculpture of Juno's head from his house in Weimar, his bed, and the drawing of him with his secretary, Eckermann. The soundtrack continues to play the symphony, but usually stops when Clever recites. The dramatic excerpts come from the fifth act of Goethe's *Faust II*. As the song of Lynceus shifts into teichoscopy describing the fire of Baucis' and Philemon's home, the viewers witness Faust's last sin. He wanted to get rid of the old couple, their cabin, and the irritating bell on their chapel. Mephistopheles and his helpers carry out the wish in their own fashion, resulting in fire and death. Their report to Faust conjures up visible ruins and a pause in the music. The silence suggests that the Pastorale is incompatible with the massacre. But unforgettable is Clever giving the report as Faust's alter ego, Mephistopheles, and his helpers. Only a few seconds long, the episode presents Clever in double exposure with the effect of several animated devils talking simultaneously. Her suddenly exaggerated facial expressions, rapid speech, and gestures certainly match the performance of Gustaf Gründgens, the most famous Mephistopheles of German stage and cinema. Again history informs the use of double exposure and the acting: Gründgens, at one time Thomas Mann's son-in-law, thrived as an actor in the Third Reich. The music remains silent as Faust is blinded and describes the night penetrating his world. The projection visualizes this as the interior of a house in ruins. But as he goes on mentioning the shine from his "inner" light, one sees a door opening with light shining through it and hears the music again. Also the last lines spoken by Faust before he dies begin in silence against a black background, but end with the harmony of music and another view of the light-filled door opening (door = *daleth*). It is worth noting that Faust dies at the site of his open grave. Being blind, he thinks the workers are digging a ditch, but Mephistopheles' aside makes clear it is not a *Graben* but a *Grab*. Most German viewers are so familiar with this scene that Clever can omit any gestures to the grave. The last quotation from *Faust II* is the brief statement by the *chorus mysticus* that concludes the play, ending with, "The eternally feminine inspires us to higher realms," or, literally, "moves" or "pulls us up" ("Das ewig Weibliche zieht uns hinan"). Recited last and out of context, this may sound enigmatic to some. But as so often in Syberberg's work, he expects the viewers to possess a minimum of knowledge about German culture, thus they should be able to fill in the gaps. This *post-mortem* episode ends with an apotheosis of the *Mater Gloriosa*. Christians interpret her as the Virgin Mary. But as presented, this spirit would also be compatible with the Shekhinah. Goethe was a Freemason and familiar with comparative religious studies. Within the framework of the film, the concluding lines appear to console the reciting Clever, who ends the recitation with a serene face.

The remainder of the film forms the coda. As Clever gathers the items that had functioned as props and puts on her coat again, the music enters its final phase. The visuals concentrate on Nossendorf, at first the Syberberg estate, then other views including the church. The recent image of it with its amputated tower is finally replaced with an old photo showing the pre-war church. And it, of course, displays the symbolic spire intact. By now Clever has sat down on the pile of dirt. She is still waiting as the credits scroll over the screen.

Since Syberberg includes so many autobiographical reminders, why did he choose an actress and not an actor to project the images? Either Clever portrays him, or a genderless mind reliving a generally shared human history, or she represents a maternal idea, or maybe all three. The director was separated from his mother early in life, but includes both of his parents in the photo projections. Whatever else one might wish to read into the pictures, those from Syberberg's childhood convey a sense of roots and legacy. The child also grew up with an awareness of a mother missing but living far away. Furthermore, all three literary excerpts in the film refer to the feminine. Hecuba appears as a mother, Natalie intervenes to reverse the verdict, and at the end Faust's immortal parts are surrounded by spirits. One of them was "formally called Gretchen." Another is the *magna peccatrix*, known in Luke 7.38 as the sinner who wetted Jesus' feet with her tears, anointed them with balm, and dried them with her hair. They and the other feminine spirits praise the *Mater Gloriosa*, who, the *chorus mysticus* jubilates, is "[t]he eternally feminine that inspires us to higher realms." Their words conclude the spoken part of the film. This center of veneration is glorified in Goethe's text by the *doctor Marianus* as Queen of Heaven, highest ruler of the world, virgin, mother, and equal of gods. This full list of aspects fuses the Virgin Mary with the two Shekhinahs. If the main character of the film is related to this feminine force, she would welcome the end of her exile on earth. She would also be a link in the chain reaching back to Kundry, as this is the seventh appearance in a row for Clever in the twelfth film since the "radical" beginning with *Ludwig*, the virgin king. This dimension of Clever's nameless character is strengthened by the sculptural fragment and the great care given the glass she moves around. As the Grail, so also this glass is a vessel and a feminine symbol. The care devoted to it underscores its importance.

Somehow, the characterization of *Ein Traum* as a monologue seems inaccurate. It certainly continues the series of one-woman films with Clever; it shares several characteristics with the others, and Clever is the only one speaking. But she only lends a voice to the figures from literature as they come to mind. The protagonist does not speak as an individual. Obviously, Countess Bismarck only inspired the scenario, as shown through the increasing emphasis on the director's own memories. Clever embodies both everyman and everywoman. With a few exceptions her strain of thought takes her and the viewer from the last days of World War II back in time. The literary characters share her loss and predicament and serve as models for facing the end. Art, in the form of literature, music, and sculpture, surrounds and enriches her last hours. In her mind she has returned to her (= the) childhood paradise while preparing for death—an archetypal journey.

But, the viewer may wonder, what about the title, *Ein Traum, was sonst*? Most people would associate it with the concluding images of the childhood world: Syberberg expresses the hope to return to his earliest home in East Germany. But he also knows it may very well remain just a dream. The process of reunification began in 1989, kindling his hope. The film version of *Ein Traum* was shot in 1994, four years after the stage version premiered in theaters. At that time he had probably inquired about the possibilities of reacquisition. The purchase of the remains of his father's confiscated property became both a dream and an obsession in the following years. This wish explains one aspect of the title. A cynic might also interpret the title as an admission of lost faith and ideals. Both Kleist's and Goethe's heroes believe in something beyond death linked to personal striving in life. To many, faith in transcendental values would indeed be a silly dream. For others it becomes a beacon. To this comes Syberberg's own statement. In the theater program he identifies the topic as Prussia's end. Prussia was declared out of existence by Allied decree on February 25, 1947, he points out (6). He focuses on what disappeared, "[n]ames that nobody mentions anymore" ("Namen, die keiner mehr nennt"). This happens to be the title of one of Countess Dönhoff's books. His intent is to present a piece of memory reviving naïvete, art, dream, and life in a world that perhaps never existed. It sounds like a threnody to a lost past. However, viewers who have not read the text will easily miss this point. The more immediate impression of a "dream" arises from Clever's and the literary characters' confrontation with death. It is not known if Countess Bismarck believed in life after death. Perhaps life itself looks like a bad dream to many. For Queen Hecuba life brought sorrows in excess, while Kleist treats the confrontation with finality as a shock promoting character development. He chooses a more drastic event for his "dream" than Calderón de la Barca in *Life Is a Dream* (*La vida es sueño* of 1635). Presumably Kleist found the source in Frederick II's *History of Prussia*. Goethe, however, let the *chorus mysticus* proclaim towards the end, "All things transitory are but a parable," as Clever reminds the viewer. Without declaring Faust's quest a dream, Goethe both ends his work on a more uplifting note and implies that his character serves as an *exemplum*. Syberberg selected the literary excerpts to serve as quotations supporting his own views. The destruction has also assumed cultural and ecological dimensions. It would appear, then, that on one level the main character is waiting for a personal end while remembering the experiences that shaped her life. But the predicament extends also to German culture, Prussia's, Germany's, and Europe's decline, and the fate of the earth. In such a situation art preserves the memory of the past. Art may even assume a new mission. By confronting society with memories of its atrocities, accomplishments, and wisdom of the past, maybe, just maybe, art can slow down or halt the decline.

Being two hours and ten minutes long, *Ein Traum* is shorter than most Syberberg films. As indicated, it shares many characteristics with the other monologues. For example, it also introduces the four elements first noticed in *Penthesilea*. But in several respects this film differs from the others. Although Clever stays in view throughout the film, she remains silent more than half the time. She only lends her voice to the literary characters of the quoted texts. Benjamin might have said she only speaks through art. Furthermore, the music on the soundtrack is restricted to one symphony. Its beauty elicits a visible response in Clever on several occasions. Nowhere else in Syberberg's films except *Parsifal* does one hear so much of only one composition throughout the film. It amounts to an apotheosis of Beethoven's creation. And most strikingly, much of the film consists of visuals in double exposure. Occasionally darkness surrounds Clever, but usually she appears in front of or superimposed on shifting projections that fill the screen. One wonders how this was handled in the stage version. Even with a film of the stills projected in the background or a TV monitor on stage, the effect could hardly match the soft merging of images characterizing the film. On some occasions Clever walks into the background and practically becomes a part of the projected environment. Unlike a performance on stage, the film can take advantage of zooming and panning, with new camera takes showing Clever from different perspectives. The refinement of double exposure and the extent of its use are unique in Syberberg's oeuvre. While in the following years he often dismissed cinema as business, entertainment, or propaganda, he has quietly transgressed, or at least changed, the concept of film technology and created cinematic art for the theater of the soul. He transformed, maybe he would say "redeemed," Riefenstahl's innovations by adding a spiritual dimension.

When the theater version premiered in Berlin in 1990, Marion, Countess Dönhoff was a guest of honor. Syberberg includes a photo of the two of them on his Web site.[53] To judge from the title page of the theater program, *Ein Traum* was scheduled for performances on at least four European stages (Hebbel-Theater in Berlin, Kaaitheater in Brussels, Festival d'Automne in Paris, and Szene Salzburg).[54] It also ran in Frankfurt an der Oder during a Kleist symposium in 1991. Syberberg participated in the conference, emphasizing the idea of downfall and end.[55] The video sleeve mentions other performances in Lisbon, Edinburgh, Moscow, and Parma before the video became available. As with all of Syberberg's works, the film version has also been screened at numerous special events internationally, beginning with the 1991 International Film Festival in Berlin and including the Festival Du Nouveau Cinéma Montréal in 1996. This time Syberberg restricts his published statements on the work to a 23-page essay cum theater program for the stage version. It includes photos of Clever, who again appears as a co-author on the title page. The verso identifies Syberberg as the author of the text. It presents the film as he wants it to be understood. Conceived before the reunification, it supposedly was meant to focus on the downfall of Prussia. But with the political developments, this became only one of the topics. The director did not make a German *Gone With the Wind* or TV documentary, but rather a poetic threnody in pictures. He calls it emblematic art and a "winter trip of lost dreams" (8). Separate sections focus on, e.g., Goethe and Prussia, Kleist, or the symphony, all linked together and to their function in the work. He points out that the storm in the music anticipates the disaster ensuing from Faust's order: "But this is followed by the composer's prayer of thanks to the Deity in the last movement after the storm. The prayer will save also this Faust" (10). Syberberg emphasizes repeatedly that action and guilt engender tragedy (*Tragik*): "No heroes without tragedy, without heroes no tragedy" (18). Speaking in generalities, he does not identify the evil connected with human action, but calls it only "devil's work," *Teufelswerk*, as in Faust's case. His kind of striving has resulted in modern "progress." In the face of death, both the wrongdoing of Kleist's prince and the guilt of Goethe's Faust experience pardon, respectively redemption. This experience Syberberg surrounds with Beethoven's music, "the saving music" ("Musik . . . die rettende," 9). In a variation of themes, the author returns to the notion of art as a redeeming force, as in this film, which he no longer describes as a monologue, but as an "inner dialogue." This art, to which he counts his stage and film version, aims at recovering the lost aura. Every time one reads "new aura," "myths" follow in the same sentence (e.g. 15).

For many Germans of Syberberg's generation and even younger ones, the trauma of the Third Reich caused a repression and dismissal of all German history as tainted. Syberberg's cinematic works attempt to restore the memory of the past, the good and the bad. His "myths" in *Ein Traum* aim at reviving the memory of an era with the faith and ideals still nourished by the age of Idealism. The pastoral and aristocratic Prussia this film conjures up also still lived in harmony with nature. It serves as a counterworld to the Third Reich and post-war society. But this old world no longer exists, hence the director-author's attempt to endow it with mythic qualities. The myths of the ancients included the gods. One therefore expects Syberberg to include a spiritual component in the material of his myths. Indirectly he does that through Kleist and Goethe, more directly but almost imperceptively, with images of the village church, and artistically and most convincingly, by letting the music assume redemptive qualities. When Clever smiles and embraces the "light" of the music, she too experiences a transfiguration similar to Faust's. This effect illustrates the view of art's mission. Besides keeping memories alive it must also link up with, or at least point back to, something sacred. The German reunification gave new impetus to this thought. Only art can help seal the new unity, Syberberg writes. And there is guilt that needs to be dealt with actively and productively. It must become form (*Ein Traum* 22). To reach out and become effective art must support consciousness about loss as well as guilt.

Ein Traum, was sonst? concludes the series of films with only Edith Clever before the camera. They are usually referred to as monologues, but obviously this term fits only to the extent the format observes a one-person delivery. Examining the sequence one discovers considerable variety and even development within the format. It also shares features with Syberberg's earlier works. For example, a "monologic" pattern occurs repeatedly in his German Cycle. And as *Parsifal* is the sixth film of the German Cycle, *Ein Traum* concludes the monologues as number 6. Both series consist of four films with music and two with speech functioning as a score. In the book to *Parsifal* the author mentions the "saving" tones of the music (252). Beethoven's symphony assumes this function in *Ein Traum.* In *Parsifal* the frontal projections play their role, only to disappear in the following monologues. Now, in *Ein Traum,* they reappear with full force. They convey the story when Clever remains silent. While also being projections of the mind and thus imagined environment as well, they develop into a system of double exposure, the most conspicuous technical characteristic of the film. And finally, one is left with a question. In the *Parsifal* book, Syberberg refers repeatedly to the opera as Wagner's self redemption work (e.g. 12, 263). The concept of redemption, healing, and saving gains strength also throughout *Ein Traum.* Does Syberberg hope for a similar redemptive effect that includes himself with this film? Remembering Buber's contrasting ways of his "electric sun" versus the "return" (penitence, *teshuva*), one recognizes that Syberberg opted for the less attractive and more difficult quest through the depth of the soul.

The metaphysical and spiritual dimensions of Syberberg's work tend to go undetected, since he does not comment on them, at least not in terms understood as such by the general public. While earlier films became known as the German Cycle, the Grail Cycle, or the German Trilogy, the monologues display similar characteristics. Most conspicuously, "German" topics remain central. Admittedly, like Winifred Wagner, Molly Bloom does not have a German origin. But the names given her and her husband by the author, Penelope and Ulysses, tie her to a mythic past. Myth remains a central ingredient in Syberberg's oeuvre. Furthermore, the concept of a German trilogy finds an equivalent in the monologues based on works by Kleist. The plots about them evolve around guilt, overcoming, and forgiveness. The characters undergo a development towards a higher level of personal attainment. Kleist showed up early in Syberberg's films. His novella *The Engagement in St. Domingo* provided the basis for *San Domingo,* and his essay on the marionettes echoes through *Parsifal.* Kleist was not only an adherent of Idealism, he was also a Prussian. His struggles and works contribute to a new variant of the "German" subject in Syberberg's use of counterpoint. The two-pronged emphasis on Prussia focuses on the palace in Berlin as a center and symbol of an aristocratic past and on the rural culture lost to history. Especially the latter allows Syberberg to reenter his cinematic work. He had already appeared recognizably in several early documentaries, for example the one on Brecht's productions that includes the *Urfaust.* Now also the Faust theme returns in the final monologue, even in the concluding segments of it, giving the impression of a circle closing. In some cases, the "inner" theater of the monologues takes place on a stage. Syberberg started out with films of Brecht's and Kortner's work on stage. With *Parsifal* as the transition, the monologues mark a distinct development towards concentration and the inner world. Gone are the fog machine, big budgets, and controversial subject matter. But unlike the stage versions, the videos and films of the monologues received more critical attention abroad than in Germany. Leonardo Quaresima's article is one of the more thorough assessments.[56] One reason for the discrepancy may be that, chronologically, the films followed the stage versions and were neither theater performances nor regular movies. Not fitting into a category, they ran counter to expectations. And as the camera usually focused on Clever, so did many reviews. The director's contribution receded into the background.

Syberberg is by no means the first or only artist to break away from the conventions of his field. Early in the twentieth century the theatrical arts underwent revolutionary developments. Brecht's works had taught Syberberg a great deal about such innovations, e.g. episodic structure or narrative plot. Most conspicuous in his own explorations is the monologue format. His stage productions beginning with *Die Nacht* belong to "postdramatic theater," an increasingly important development in the world of theater. It encompasses a long list of characteristics that differ from traditional drama. Actually, many of Syberberg's films beginning with *Ludwig* display some of the features. Hans-Thies Lehmann's book on postdramatic theater examines these characteristics as seen on European stages in the eighties and nineties.[57] Syberberg's monologues fit right in. For example, the monologue structure is considered symptomatic (233). The script often consists of poetry or narrative prose, even fairytales, but not necessarily plays (197). The list continues. Lehmann mentions Syberberg by name only four times, but appears to describe examples of characteristic features seen in his works quite frequently.[58] Perhaps the author refrains from crediting him due to the controversy that raged about him in the early nineties. One begins to wonder if Syberberg should be considered merely a representative artist of postdramatic theater or a pioneer in some areas. His emphasis on, e.g., the tragic, guilt, catharsis, memory, music and requiem, as well as his use of such visual effects as tableau and montage, occur early in his career. An examination of Syberberg and postdramatic theater would fill a book. But in two areas he undisputedly emerges as a pioneer. First, he has adapted postdramatic theater to the cinematic medium. Or one might say, he has enriched or infused cinema with features of postdramatic theater. Concentrating on soul drama in a sparse setting, he offers one way out of an overly commercialized and vulgarized art world. Second, his cinematic theater has reestablished the aura. While resorting to Jewish spirituality in *Parsifal*, he later also incorporated the Gnostic and ecumenical Christian legacy of Idealism. With the links to spiritual sources, and be they only an overtone in his compositions, he has reintroduced the aura that Benjamin considered indispensable for art and lost in cinema.

Chapter 13

Turbulence

A review of Syberberg's cinematic work up to the early nineties reveals three phases. After a period of "apprenticeship" with television came the first group of movies. Some of them conform to the definition of movie, such as *Scarabea* and *San Domingo*. Others carry the label of "non-fiction films," for example the interview portraits of Romy Schneider and Count Pocci. But already the first full-length film transgresses established norms of reporting, interviewing, and moviemaking with the treatment of Kortner. From the beginning Syberberg seems to defy classifications. The second phase is the German Trilogy, respectively German Cycle, also known as Grail Cycle. Of these *Karl May* comes close to being a regular biographical movie, but it too includes non-realistic elements and obeys laws that differ from prevailing cinema. Two deceptively simple documentaries, *Theodor Hierneis* and *Winifred Wagner*, interrupt the trilogy, which is followed by *Parsifal*, like a satyr play. Of this list, *Ludwig* became an underground cult film early on. So did *Parsifal*, which also became an object of interest to music lovers, pro- and contra-Wagnerites, and the Arthurian community. It was *Hitler*, however, that became associated with Syberberg's name in his homeland. His treatment of the subject broke a taboo. The third phase consists of the monologue with Edith Clever. Anyone familiar with the principles underlying Syberberg's aesthetics will recognize the consistency throughout his work for the screen. Even when a stage is not visible, his films have not moved far from the theater. Although his opinions on cinema and art changed some over the years, the standards or guidelines for his own films have remained faithful to ancient traditions. Best reflecting his thoughts on his work during the years he created the monologues is the interview of 1987 ("Mit kleinsten Mitteln"). Appearing as a chapter in Rötzer and Rogenhofer's *Kunst machen?*, the interview took place between the work on *Fräulein Else* and *Penthesilea*. It differs from other interviews with the director in the late eighties by taking his most recent films into consideration and by asking informed questions about his views on art and film. Discussing art in general, Syberberg makes a distinction between traditional art and its modern successor. "Art," as people understand it today, possesses a market value and a museum value, but it has been deprived of its mission, he maintains. It has lost its iconography, and thus its connection with issues beyond daily life. It used to function as memory, including both irrationalism and "*ratio* of the strict form" (173). A central concept was guilt, as in tragedy, and original sin leading to the need for atonement and redemption. All this has yielded to a different aesetics based on vulgarity, meanness, brokenness, and destructiveness. Obviously, Syberberg deplores the shift to a secularized and impoverished understanding of art. He reminds the interviewer that the ancient theater arose from religious rituals. It fulfilled a communal and spiritual function in a system where the ego was viewed as a "world theater" (173). In such ideas one can recognize echoes both of Richard Wagner in his earliest plans for a festival theater, and of Walter Benjamin on art and its origin in sacral ritual. These thoughts found their expression in the monologues. *Die Nacht* even includes glimpses of an ancient amphitheater. *Fräulein Else, Penthesilea, Die Marquise von O . . .*, and *Ein Traum, was sonst?* exist in stage and film versions, with several of them incorporating a stage and theater interior as the set. At the time of the interview, the last three works were still in the planning stages. Thus some statements do not apply to all of the monologues, since they differ from each other in content and aesthetic means. Thanks to the question and answer format, however, Syberberg's comments on his latest works are more concise than in the printed programs.

The interviewer also wanted his reaction to Adorno's dictum about poetry being impossible after Auschwitz.[1] To some extent, Syberberg agrees. The old art is dead, and what counts as art today does not deserve the name, he thinks. But nonetheless he feels provoked to contradict Adorno, because it affects him as an artist. He would like to exempt himself from Adorno's analysis, since his own views and aspirations differ thoroughly from the prevailing notions. It appears that the interviewer recognized Syberberg's position. After all, the director had repeatedly made similar pronouncements during the eighties, offering them as variations on Adorno's statement.

Syberberg elaborates on the characteristics of film versus theater in an article of 1988, "Seeing the Light."[2] Supposedly a review of a book about the stage designer Adolphe Appia, it deals mostly with Syberberg's ideas and theater-related work. About his earlier films he states, "There was a mixture of theater and film in that work, and it showed itself to be as absolute in its rejection of the status quo as was Adolphe Appia when he envisioned his new stage" (32). He goes on to describe how he transformed the studio into an empty stage, concentrating the entire repertoire of expression and effects onto one human being. He admits an affinity for Appia's most revolutionary innovations, but not dependency or inspiration. The discussion of his cinematic oeuvre centers on two points. The films express his inner world and thoughts. Also, he feels called on to defy the existing order (33). Many of Syberberg's cherished views discussed in this article also find expression in other publications. But one formulation occurs here probably for the first time. He comments on the "fragments" into which our world has split: "[A] fragmentation or atomization of which film is one expression— we must build the world up again, we must make it whole" (34). He outlines how he tries to contribute to this in his art through concentration on the actor and exclusion of distracting and superfluous elements. The restoration of the fragments was at the heart of his *Parsifal,* but he does not refer to it in this context. Apparently, Syberberg's exploration of the stage in symbiosis with film is his attempt to save both from the fate of the prevailing subsidized "art" as entertainment business.

During the years Syberberg devoted to his monologue projects, his name continued to crop up in interviews, book chapters, and articles. The overwhelming majority of these texts, however, ignore his later work. Two examples will illustrate the prevailing assessment at home. In 1987 Anton Kaes devoted a chapter to Syberberg and the *Hitler* film in his book *Deutschlandbilder*.[3] He examines the film from the perspective of "posthistoire." While he arrives at a nuanced-to-critical evaluation of the film (more exactly, of the book to the film), he shares most Germans' view of it as a "manic self mirroring of the author" (138). He also thinks that Syberberg knows no limits in his assessment of himself (167). Be that as it may, but the chapter remains one of the most scholarly and helpful studies of the film. The consulted text suffered from having eight scattered blank pages.[4] These lacunae do *not* hint at censorship, as the complete English version proves in the author's *From "Hitler" to "Heimat"* (37–72).

The other example is an interview first published in *Die Zeit* on September 30, 1988, and subsequently as a chapter.[5] André Müller, a freelance journalist, apparently wanted to present Syberberg's his opinions and personality. Little is said about him as a filmmaker, author, or theater director. Many of the statements are interesting enough to be quoted, were it not for the circumstances surrounding the interview. The reader can only wonder: What did Syberberg actually say? Which parts did Müller doctor or invent? The interview presents a friendly, soft-spoken man with an inner rage and killer instinct. Some of his views vary statements published elsewhere, others sound farfetched or peculiar. He declines to answer some questions, for example about his relationship to women. Others he does address, but not with a yes- or no-reply. The text gives the impression of a dangerous megalomaniac with terrorist potential. Two factors modify this impression: the interviewer's four-page introduction, and Syberberg's "Declaration," a loose two-page insert, both in the book. The introduction objects to Syberberg's condition of reviewing the final script of the interview. Müller adds insinuations by dropping hints of topics not included in the final version. When Syberberg received the script four days before printing and objected to something, Müller was "in despair," his nerves in uproar. He pleaded for acceptance of the text, writing later," My spirit was frazzled, my body exhausted" (185). Müller does not mention if he honored Syberberg's objections. The interview appeared under the title "Man will mich töten" (They Want to Kill Me). Syberberg's "Declaration" ("Erklärung vom 12. Juli 1989") confirms that Müller rushed the text to print without the desired changes. Syberberg's protests appeared twice in *Die Zeit*. He also resorted to legal assistance to prevent any reprint of a text he found offensive. Müller's shortening of the answers supposedly resulted in a montage of deceiving combinations, omissions, and falsifying changes. The result was tendentious, "not authentic," and aiming at confirming an already prejudicial view of him, the "Declaration" claims. Not only did Müller ignore Syberberg's objections before the interview appeared in *Die Zeit*, but he also ignored the legal injunction against reprinting it. He included it as a chapter in a book of interviews, and Syberberg found out about it after the volume had been published. The publisher agreed to include the "Declaration" as an insert in the remaining copies and promised to omit the chapter if the book should see a second edition. Obviously, Syberberg found the printed interview unacceptable and fought back vigorously. But he learned, again, that even when suffering defamation or shabby treatment in the media, he had little recourse to protect his name. Nor were his printed protests likely to change the public's image of him. And yet, he had earned the respect of many, both in Germany and abroad, mainly through his cinematic work. In spite of the enemies in the press, Syberberg was honored in 1989 with the Federal Cross of Merit, the *Bundesverdienstkreuz.*[6] It is one of the highest distinctions a civilian citizen can earn at the federal level in Germany.

   The years 1989 and '90 were a turbulent time for Germany and Eastern Europe. The economic foundation of the Soviet Union was gradually collapsing. It was no longer in a position to impose its will on the satellite states behind the Iron Curtain. Their economies suffered even worse. Social unrest spread in the Warshaw Pact countries, including East Germany. Tension escalated, but for the first time, bloody reprisals did not materialize in the G.D.R. Without the orders and support from the Soviet leadership, the East German politicians dared not intervene. Contrary to the brutality used in crushing the workers' revolt in 1953, the protests in the fall of 1989 became a bloodless revolution. Reunification was in the air, although not as the wish of everyone, at least not for right away. With East Germany's economy a basket case, many predicted that reunification would cause gigantic problems for West Germany as well, unless the political changes followed in increments. But euphoria prevailed. The reunification of the Federal Republic of Germany and the German Democratic Republic took place officially on October 3, 1990. Deprived of much of its pre-World War II territory in the east, the reunited country took the shorter name of Germany. Needless to say, numerous issues animated the public debate at the time, but the events also encouraged a preoccupation with national affairs at the expense of other topics. Already in the eighties some German historians began to reassess the past shaping the present and were denounced as revisionists. The resulting historians' dispute, or *Historikerstreit*, characterizes the polarization gripping public discussion on any issue concerning Germany. For many the trauma of the Third Reich blocked the view of the past, obliterating all nuances.The prevailing, politically correct view considered modern Germany a good, indeed very good, and progressive democracy in harmony with its Western protector, the United States. As always skeptical of majority trends, Syberberg did not join the chorus, although he too welcomed the reunification.

   In the summer of 1990 he published another book, *Vom Unglück und Glück der Kunst in Deutschland nach dem letzten Kriege* (Munich: Matthes & Seitz). The clumsy title might be translated as "About the Misfortune and Good Fortune of Art in Germany after the Last War." The spine of the volume shortens the title to *Kunst in Deutschland.* Of course the "last war" refers to World War II. The 199 pages fall into an introduction and three long sections, each preceded by an illustration with caption. The text and its organization share several characteristics with Syberberg's previous books. For example, it continues to divide the material into chapters of uneven length, much like Adorno's *Minima Moralia.* The 158 units listed in the index show individual subtitles. However, the numbers deceive. In part 3, 41 of the listed chapter subtitles only appear in the text as the beginnings of new paragraphs. That reduces the total to 117 units resembling chapters. To that come three distinct texts by Syberberg in the introduction, for a total of 120 original units. Why the inconsistency? Either it indicates a remarkable sloppiness in the writing and/or editorial process, or it was done deliberately. The subtitles often seem to have little to do with the main topic of art. One reason for that may be the author's habit of commenting on current conditions in diary style. Actually, the content is a compendium of commentary and opinions on art in a German context, interspersed with autobiographical passages. But the diary style has morphed into a chronicle. It can mainly be recognized in the temporal progression of the three major sections. The first was composed before the political unrest started, with one chapter dated as late as June 1989. It bears the title "Aus einem verlorenen Haus: Zu einer Nachkriegs-ästhetik in Deutschland" (From a Lost House: About a Post-War Aesthetics in Germany). The second part was written during summer and fall 1989, as the situation was becoming tense, as the title suggests: "Aus dem letzten Sommer: Vor dem Fall des Vorhangs" (From Last Summer: Before the Fall of the Curtain). The last word refers to the Iron Curtain dividing Europe, including the Wall in Berlin. The third segment is called "Die deutsche Katharsis ist die Kunst: Das wieder-gefundene Haus" (The German Catharsis is Art: The Found-again House). To what house do the first and third titles refer? Perhaps it means the author's childhood home. It was lost through expropriation. But since a house can also function as a home, Syberberg may have had in mind that word, *Heim*. A very short path leads from *Heim* to *Heimat*, meaning "home," "home area," and "homeland." And this *Heimat* is Germany as well as Prussia, as the introduction indicates. Syberberg was born in western Pomerania, a part of Prussia. Berlin was the capital of Prussia. With the introduction being written after the rest of the book, the author may have hoped for a restoration of his home area, at least in name. The Allied Control Council had formally dissolved the state of Prussia on February 25, 1947.[7] That decision still stands. Also the territories assumed by Poland and the Soviet Union remain "lost." But in 1989 the author may have harbored a hope for more changes than just the reunification of the G.D.R. and the F.R.G., although the introduction does not state so explicitly. The very first page of the book shows a familiar photo: The interior view of the ruined palace in East Berlin, but without the princess statue. The accompanying text gives the history of the ruin after 1945, a development that sets the tone for other remarks later. This text is followed by two quotations by Frederick the Great, King of Prussia, and Carl von Clausewitz, a Prussian general, theoretician, and contemporary of Kleist. Their comments on honor, peace, and duty remind the reader of a past when a code of conduct meant more than empty words. Three other distinct texts make up the bulk of the introduction. First comes an essay on the aesthetics of post-war Germany. It is followed by a piece of prose printed to look like a modern poem identifying a quest for identity. The conclusion is another essay six and a half pages in length, "About the Author Who Wrote Here." Although only one paragraph is autobiographical, the subtitle opens the door for more subjective statements. This collection of short pieces outlines the author's premise and perspective, as well as the topics. Many reviewers did not read any further, especially critics who already disliked the author. As he knew well, the introduction contains numerous statements inviting misunderstandings, distortions, and attacks. The public looking only at the reviews would conclude that the author was at best an ultra-rightist, at worst a neo-Nazi.

The first red flag is the emphasis on Prussia. Most Germans have adopted the Allies' notion of Prussia as a center of militarism, political ambition, and an aristocratic, anti-democratic way of thinking. Besides, Prussia enjoyed a position of hegemony among the German states in the 18th and 19th centuries. This resulted in the Prussian king being offered the imperial crown when the states reunited as a (second) empire in 1871. And then there is the awareness that so much of Prussia and other areas were lost in 1945. These events belong to a period of painful memories, such as expulsion for millions, loss of property, systematic rape, and numerous other retaliations. This entire complex of issues had been repressed, officially distorted as "liberation" by the Soviets, and become a taboo topic. Any restoration of a Prussian state within the new Germany would necessitate a confrontation with the past. The nostalgia for a Prussian homeland also sent out other signals. Not only are the 15 million displaced Germans and their descendants a powerful political force, but they have also hoped for a return to their respective home areas or at least compensation. Whether deserved or not, this longing to turn around the course of history has also earned their organizations the reputation of regressive political views. They, and any whiff of revisionism, were and still are decried as unwelcome.[8] Syberberg's inclusion of the palace ruins, King Frederick, and General Clausewitz plays right into a field of suppressed history and taboos.

The second transgression occurs in the pages on the aesthetics in post-war Germany. In the East as in the West, foreign political powers swept away old traditions along with the Nazi system, creating a new kind of conformity. In the vacuum that Syberberg calls "lack of culture," the Jewish emigrés became the founding fathers of aesthetics in West Germany, while Karl Marx, who also was Jewish, assumed that role in East Germany. Much in their thought was based on German Idealism, as the author notes: "The aesthetics of Adorno to Bloch and Benjamin, Marcuse and Kracauer, in the heritage of German Idealism, determined cultural life in Germany after 1945. Being free of the Hitler stigma, they became the intellectual founding fathers of Germany's post-war history" (14). So far, so good. Syberberg had revealed his own allegiance to German Idealism in the program to *Die Marquise* (40). He is familiar with the literature of the emigrés, even shares many of their tenets. Their influence should, then, have provided a bridge leading the Germans back to their pre-Nazi cultural legacy, while serving as an example of possible paths to pursue. This kind of fruitful encounter did not take place, Syberberg implies. Instead the "Germans" resorted to mimicry and conformity, adopting international trends and anything foreign. The author sees a danger for the future in this. While still "embracing" the founding fathers, he denounces their followers and the ensuing development. One factor contributing to the shift away from roots was the "curse of guilt" (14) which made the majority susceptible to manipulation, he claims. The emphasis on German guilt paralyzed what could have become a rebirth of cultural life. The author places much of the blame for this on the "leftists." The parties to the left of center, including the Social Democrats, were prohibited during the Third Reich and their members persecuted. For example, one prominent member was Willy Brandt. Upon his return from exile after the war, he became the mayor of West Berlin and subsequently chancellor of West Germany. He and his party members were considered "good" Germans who did not share in the national guilt. Many younger Germans opted for the party too, perhaps identifying such affiliation or sympathies with a badge of guiltlessness and a political statement against the past system. The arrangement also turned out to be profitable, encouraging self-righteousness and, as Syberberg claims, intimidation of others. The "leftists" found it advantageous to ally themselves with the "Jews," resulting in a "Jewish-leftist aesthetics against the guilty ad nauseam" (14). The author concludes this paragraph thus: "Whoever joined the Jews and the leftists was successful, and it did not necessarily have anything to do with love or understanding or even inclination. How could Jews tolerate that, it be then that they only wanted power."[9] This passage became the most frequently quoted and distorted words in the reviews and sealed Syberberg's reputation for a long time. Even when one considers the context, one is tempted to wonder about the author's intent. But one needs to read carefully. Soon the text makes a distinction between the influential forces just mentioned and the "founding fathers" or intellectuals. The message out of emigration was one thing, it states, but the vulgarity of the untalented (*bedürftigen*) German stewards something else (14). The author claims that the moral advantage enjoyed by the emigrés stifled any development in cultural life. This status in Germany is what he wants to challenge, adding that to succeed, "help will be needed from the founding fathers themselves or their true successors" (15). He hopes to "save" something from the ossification and carry it further, perhaps even to "old positions." The last words may sound paradoxical, being both regressive and progressive. Literally, they can be both. He either wants to return to a stage from where a fresh beginning can take a different course. Or he intends to struggle forward in a quasi-musical fashion. When one proceeds along a circular arrangement of tones, for example an octave ring or circle of fifths, the end eventually meets the beginning at the "old position." Syberberg has remained faithful to the aesthetic program outlined in his first book, namely composing music by different means. He may, then, have a tonal progression in mind. Incidentally, accomplishing something "by different means," or *mit anderen Mitteln*, is Syberberg's twist on Clausewitz' dictum about waging war by different means. And he quotes Clausewitz in this introduction.

General Clausewitz was a contemporary of many philosophers and artists important in Syberberg's work, one of them being Friedrich Hegel. One might even expect the book to adhere to Hegel's dialectical progression of thesis, antithesis, and synthesis. The titles of the three major sections invite such expectations. But one is hard pressed to recognize such a development except towards the end, where art as the catharsis emerges as the envisioned equivalent of a synthesis. But in a less obvious way, a dialectical thinking permeates the book. The thesis is both the cultural stagnation described at great length, and the grappling with Adorno's statement about no poetry after Auschwitz. The author now wants to counter the dictum, drawing on the older German legacy as one part of the antithesis. The other part has grown out of the painful experiences, guilt, and losses resulting from the Third Reich. The envisioned art as the synthesis should combine elements of both areas while emerging as a new and different power. Such dialectical progression is not new in Syberberg's work. The *Hitler* film presents an earlier example of this procedure. In the last segment of the film, the two complementary characters played by Heller and Baer disappear into the Black Mary. Faust and Mephistopheles, the two halves of the human soul, have been transformed into the *famulus* Wagner and Harry (Baer) Heine. This grappling produces the child who completes the process by stomping on the toy dog with the moustache. Her act of overcoming, and later contemplating, this unwelcome legacy illustrates the Hegelian synthesis. She represents the third stage. Now the author envisions a new art to grow out of the disparate premises. And as did Paul Celan in his "Death Fugue," so also Syberberg resorts to musical principles to provide the "*ratio* of strict form." But having described the crisis of the present in such dire, even apocalyptic terms, he presents his vision of the catharsis merely as a hope and suggestion.

The introduction includes also a third item attracting the attention of many reviewers. Syberberg writes that he had been requested to give his opinion on Hitler as a mass murderer. Although the dictator is not the main topic of the book, his name crops up on at least every second page, and enough confusion about and distortions of the author's thoughts about him had arisen in the wake of the *Hitler* film. The two pages addressing the issue should make it clear that the author abhors the dictator. If he had been an adult during the Third Reich, he would probably not have survived, he states (19). Nonetheless, the reply proceeds in such a way as to allow new distortions and even doubts among readers unfamiliar with his other work. One can identify a series of details that contributed to renewed attacks on him. First, the statement on Hitler as a mass murderer does not materialize. The fact that the author fails to deliver a clear condemnation was interpreted by many as evasion or possibly tacit refusal. Little does it help that he refers to the dictator as a "horrible figure" and his guilt as being beyond measuring in human dimensions (18). In this discussion he does not mention the Holocaust, genocide, or mass murder. The term *Holocaust* is reserved for the American-made television series of that name, as on page 55. He condenses the horror to the chiffre of *Auschwitz*, adding that Auschwitz made art available (18). This linking of art and Auschwitz in a paragraph of unclear and convoluted prose satisfied nobody. Syberberg apparently tries to combine Adorno's statement on Auschwitz and the latter's use of the name as a chiffre with his own challenge of the dictum in something akin to a thesis and antithesis as well as a verbal counterpoint. The result is at best a dissonance, at worst a failure. It fails by diverting attention from the reality of Auschwitz. Also infuriating many is his reminder that Hitler rose to power through democratic elections, making the people share responsibility for his success and its con-sequences. In a similar vein he refers to the victims of Stalin, the atomic bomb, and the peace time nuclear disaster in Chernobyl. By spreading around the blame for such staggering catastrophes, he seems to reduce the dimension of the Hitler-related terrors. Finally, the author's reluctance to formulate a condemnation of the dictator reveals itself in his use of vocabulary. To many readers the terms made little or no sense. Most revealing is the repeated use of *Weltgeist*, meaning "world spirit." Hitler, the author writes, was a medium of the *Weltgeist*, a horrible "apparition," and a concentration of energy catapulting itself into the world arena. Such expressions date back to the age of Idealism, more specifically Hegel's philosophy of history. Known for its dialectical principle, it divides the three stages of historical processes into the subjective, objective, and absolute spirit (*Geist*). The first of these relates to the individual, the second to society and the epochs in which societal forces evolve. The *Weltgeist* manifests in the second stage, the realm of the objective spirit, through the "great personalities." They are movers and shakers who arise to power and change the world, or at least human history. Such leaders are not necessarily great men, but they rise to significance as on a tidal wave unleashed by their society. Hegel sees them as the tool of the *Weltgeist*. Syberberg uses the same word about Hitler. Hegel's thought on the supra-individual function of the medium, or tool, accounts for Syberberg's assessment of the dictator. Whether or not one accepts such terms for the Third Reich terrors, it becomes clear that the author adheres to the dialectical principle. He wants to proceed to the third stage, to develop a synthesis, in the realm of the absolute spirit. Of course the dialectical process does not stand still. It continuously evolves in a series of three-step dynamics. According to Hegel the realm of the absolute spirit also leads through three stages, namely art, religion, and philosophy. His philosophy of aesthetics attributes to art a mission or place above and beyond political history. This is the stage Syberberg wants to prepare. Hence the book's main topic is art, its status and potential.

The first of the three major sections includes a gathering of topics already explored in Syberberg's recent publications and interviews. Dealing with post-war aesthetics in Germany, this section also elaborates on the points made in the introduction. The author soon manages to offend more readers. In a listing of the "central topics of our time," presumably as pertaining to Germany, he first mentions the collapse in 1945, rape as liberation, reeducation, division of the country, and the disappearance of Prussia. Then as number two, Auschwitz and the exodus of the European Jews to Israel and America (33). Then follows the forced migration of 15 million expelled Germans in the East. Apparently, at the time of writing, the Holocaust had faded from the primary to the secondary position of preoccupation. Foremost remains the trauma the author experienced personally and was still facing. Many readers would have expected a different sequence. Especially alienating is the consistent use throughout the book of *Auschwitz* as a chiffre for the complex of the Holocaust. Of course, Syberberg can refer to Adorno as his model here. But the exodus does not compare with the concept in horror.

The author refers to Adorno's statement repeatedly, always in an adversarial tone (e.g. 30, 34). He also expands Adorno's *Gedichte*, "poetry," to encompass all the creative and performing arts. But before he can point the way towards refuting Adorno, he devotes much space to describing the current condition and identifying its taboos in art. One of them concerns the rural culture which Syberberg considers his legacy. Another is Hitler as an artist. Only after several references to the dictator's politics, war, even Reich, as art, and his promotion of art in the service of politics, does one learn about Hitler as a moviemaker through his involvement in t he weekly newsreels (37). Syberberg had introduced the dictator's projectionist as a character in the *Hitler* film. The historical man behind that character probably provided Syberberg some of the information about the newsreels. Without revealing his source(s), Syberberg claims that Hitler edited the newsreels, provided the commentary, or corrected them (37). Another comment on the dictator points out that he drew on thoughts from German Idealism when envisioning his Reich as a work of art (29). The association with Hitler burdenend Idealism so badly that its reputation still had not recovered in 1990. And precisely this philosophy nourishes Syberberg's thought and arguments. He continues, for example, to refer to the *Weltgeist* (e.g. 39, 101, 120). But his inspiration does not appear to derive only from Hegel, but also from Hans Sedlmayr. The art historian was his most influential university teacher. Syberberg does not identify him by name, but refers to him obliquely early on (28). This Idealist concentrates on the history of Western painting, sculpture, and architecture, observing the changes, eventually identifying the present status as a diseased condition. As a symbol or mirror of its time, Sedlmayr concludes in *Verlust der Mitte* (mentioned in chapter 1), the current art scene represents a total catastrophe and, perhaps, the beginning of regeneration (204). A number of Sedlmayr's observations provide the base for Syberberg's comments, including the words of the title, "loss of the center." Not only did Syberberg find a kindred spirit in the art historian, but his book could even be considered a tribute to him, although the author suppresses the name.

Some of Sedlmayr's concepts found their way into Syberberg's work quite early. One is the notion of chill or coldness to describe a condition in modern society (Sedlmayr, 159). It should be noted that Syberberg adds several dimensions to this idea, as mentioned in previous chapters. Another observation by Sedlmayr is the trend toward synthetic materials (147). Love for the anorganic results in a move away from nature and the natural (147, 158). Syberberg expands this to environmentalism, a concern that had become much more acute since Sedlmayr published his book. It also accounts for his frequent use of "plastic" as a pejorative epithet for the current way of life in the West. And while Sedlmayr associates the *dies irae* with the melancholy outlook of modern humanity, Syberberg borrows the context of this *sequentia* of an anniversary requiem for a fuller requiem in his films, beginning with *Ludwig*. The most central of the shared concepts is probably the rift, *Riss* (Sedlmayr, 169). Syberberg both presents it visually in his German Cycle and as division, separation, melancholy, and lack of harmony in his writings. To Sedlmayr the *Riss* means the disturbance in or destruction of the relationship between human beings and everything important, such as their own psyche, other people, nature, the spiritual world, and most of all, God. With a widespread loss of faith, people forget the Thou and the awareness of being created in God's image (172). This disturbance forms the thrust of Sedlmayr's examination. For him the loss of the center, *Verlust der Mitte*, is the crisis of having lost the soul-to-God relationship. Syberberg adopts Sedlmayr's thesis of decline and loss, also in art as a symbol of the human condition. But writing for a secularized public, he tones down the emphasis on the religious. Thus his loss of a center points quite literally (also) to a divided country without a capital as center (45). Somewhat vaguely he describes the move away from the center as the ex-centric. He views the shift on the scale of values from high to low as corresponding to that on the horizontal plane. The focus has moved away from central ideals to the lateral and ephemeral as well as the lowly and abject (45). And yet, he includes the concept of the spiritual in a roundabout way. He discusses over several pages the loss of the aura in photography and cinema, only mentioning Benjamin towards the end. The downplayed attribution can only be recognized by readers familiar with Benjamin's writings. And only Benjamin traces the aura back to the origin of art in the service of the sacred. Syberberg concludes this discussion by formulating his program, namely to find and reintroduce the aura or the spiritual, even in film and photography (50). The German word for "spiritual," *geistig*, encompasses also the "intellectual" and "mental," a wide area relating to the mind and soul as opposed to the body. This broader applicability makes it tempting to render the expression just quoted as "of the spiritual and intellectual dimension." The choice of *geistig* rather than *religiös* obscures the connection to the sacred as the setting and purpose of auratic art. But still, it includes it. That brings Syberberg's program close to Sedlmayr's hope and Hegel's third dialectical stage (art, religion, philosophy) of the absolute *Geist*. Furthermore, Syberberg states, unawareness of the loss of the center has resulted in a culture without identity paralyzed in the non-authentic (50). Being without awareness and identity means having no present or future and thus disappearing from history. Therefore the thinking person's—and artist's—insight must lead to a countermove. In such a reaction Syberberg sees his task or mission, namely of leaving a trace in history, of really having existed, thus of making a difference (51).

The art serving that mission must be one of lamentation. It must lament that which has been lost so as to preserve its memory for posterity. Here again Syberberg conjures up the taboos, especially the mass deportations, not only of Germans after 1945, but also of eastern Poles and others. These events rival the disasters recorded by Homer and Virgil, he notes. But no Hecuba was heard this time. In the middle of these passages stands a line that sticks out and attracts attention: "To say nothing about the chapter of the Jews. For this is probably a different case" (65). And that is it. No elaboration, no lamentation. Perhaps this "chapter" needs to be treated in a separate unit or genre? Or does it mean that persecution with genocide belongs to a different category? Or that lament must be composed by surviving victims? Or did the founding of Israel change everything?

Syberberg's enemies were quick to denounce this line as another proof of his presumed ideology. But it deserves a closer look. So much in Syberberg's work displays quasi-musical structure. Also this book follows the pattern. The isolated line reveals the presence of a Jewish variant of the subject. In this "movement" it can barely be recognized because it is being played simultaneously with another form of the subject. But here, for just a moment, it emerges alone from the chords that change the overall sound. It is as if Adorno's voice penetrates with a reminder that any kind of "poetry" would be impossible. But he did not say poetry for whom. And Syberberg objects to his statement repeatedly. Somehow this conflict surfaces as Adorno's silencing of mourning in words along with Syberberg's attempted remembrance. The subject and its inversion are playing simultaneously. In connection with remembering and commemoration, Syberberg's emphasis on the requiem comes to mind. Much of his work incorporates elements of the mass for the dead. In the chapter called "Prohibition Against Lamenting," *Klageverbot*, the Jewish variant crops up again in the brief mentioning of "Christ, the distant God from the Orient," "Jerusalem conquered," and the "God of the Old Testament." The stress remains on the need to erect cathedrals of memory and achieve catharsis through atonement of the guilt. But as in this chapter, the Jewish variant remains present, often without name or clear reference, and often peripheral to the central topic. The recognizable variant of the "melody" is the "German" subject. Thus the author quotes at length Schiller, Kant, and others, while Jewish names are barely mentioned or not identified. One exception is Freud (31, 58, 71), whose study on Moses serves to vary the theme of suppressed expression (71–72). More often the author only weaves in vague references, such as the statues of biblical kings destroyed in the French Revolution (69) or the golden calf (51). Syberberg also treats himself in a similarly circumspect manner. In the chapter on censorship through silence he describes how the system can suppress unwanted voices by ignoring them, but without stating that he himself experiences this fate (52–54). In a passage on objections, one reads that it takes an outsider to deliver the needed resistance. The author does not mention his own status as an outsider. And when he describes examples of how current aesthetics favors the small, ugly, and sick elements, he includes, "The servant is more important than the facts in reference books to characterize a dictator who rules or destroys the world, from Caesar to Hitler. The cook turns into a key figure for a king " (38). Caesar, of course, points to Brecht's novel *The Affairs of Mr. Julius Caesar*, as chronicled by his secretary and slave, Rarus. Syberberg himself uses a servant's perspective to great effect repeatedly. At least one of Syberberg's early films also fits into the category dealing with abject subject matter, namely *Sex Made in Pasing*. Thus he includes his own work in the criticism of current aesthetics, but without identifying himself or his films. Clearly, Syberberg is a variant of the subject. But in the first major section he keeps a low profile and does not appear either in the first person singular or as a named subject.

The author's unidentified presence changes in the second section. His first inclusion does not yet name him, but describes only his next project, *Ein Traum, was sonst?* (82–83). It too remains nameless. But from then on the author emerges, usually in the first person singular, sometimes in units dealing with other topics. At times one can also recognize his own work when he outlines his priorities. For instance, the fat, subsidized art scene in Germany needs to undergo asceticism of simplicity (e.g. 101). This describes his own monologue projects. Whether he created them that way by choice or by necessity is not revealed.[10] A variation on the topic of self-accusations fills the chapter "Confession" (103–8). With himself as an identified subject, Syberberg outlines here his own career as an ongoing accommodation to a system he abhors. He too is guilty.

The second section introduces a long list of names, both German and foreign. Among the rulers and politicians Hitler's name occurs most frequently, but only occasionally as the tool of the *Weltgeist* or influence on art. Surprisingly often the name appears more like an historical marker, as in "before Hitler" or "after Hitler." He functioned as an accelerator of the downfall of Germany, the center of Europe, and thus of the West. The pessimism noticeable in Sedlmayr's book continues here. Clearly, the Western democracies are facing a cultural decline heralding the approaching end. Several times the author uses expressions like "five minutes to twelve." One name omitted is that of Oswald Spengler, whose *End of the West*, however, is mentioned by title (*Untergang des Abendlandes*, 90). Reminders of the present condition recur in almost every chapter.

The topics of the introduction and first section crop up regularly in new variations. But there is a distinct shift away from the juxtaposition of "leftists and Jews." The leftists disappear as they blend in with the German majority. The negative connotation of the founding fathers' influence and their inept German followers assumes a new constellation in the "axis U.S.A.-Israel" (78–79). The author avoids explicit recriminations or anti-Semitic remarks. But the chapter is called "Lost Prussia and Gained Israel," suggesting not so much a complementarity as polarization and counterpoint. Pointing out the preeminence of Marx and Freud in much of the world, he concludes that since they were Jewish, their systems were determined by it, and people (at least in Germany) are living in the Jewish era of European cultural history. But while enjoying the pinnacle of technical power, they are on the verge of facing their last judgment (79). And he warns against the resistance provoked by power, a development leading to a bundle of problems (*Knäuel von Problemen*, 80). The choice of words resorts here again to Hermetic double layering.. The Hebrew equivalent of *Knäuel* is *golem*, well known from literature and film as a creature with destructive tendencies. In other words, the dominating powers are likely to provoke war or violent counter-measures. This description of polarization is blurred by the reference to how Europeans have adjusted to feeling, thinking, and acting according to the new development. In the book the blurring continues in a barely perceptible way. One reads about countries without land (e.g. 81), and lost territories, cuts, and reductions. And in the relation between man and woman, the latter is of equal rank and without incisions or reductions, *unbeschnitten* (122). The concept played with throughout the book is that of the cut, emasculation, and circumcision: *Beschneidung*. The male Germans have suffered emasculation just like their country. At the same time the "Jewish" motif of circumcision plays along.

The chordal interplay with Jewishness goes one step further in a passage that was often distorted by reviewers. In deploring the modernization and "progress" in his favorite Alpine vacation spot, the author mentions some of the famous guests who in the past spent their summers here. They included Freud, Herzl, Hofmannsthal, Broch, and Mahler, all of them Jewish. They would turn in their graves if they saw what had been made of their thoughts and their environment, one reads (125). Literally, Syberberg quotes a local farmer saying that they would ride out of their coffins and enter the chimney like lightning ("aus der 'Truhn aussi reitn und wie der Blitz in den Schornstein einifahrn'"). For many readers, associations with chimneys awaken the specter of concentration camps and their crematoria. The combination of Jewish dead and chimneys would also evoke Celan's "Death Fugue" in German readers. So, from one perspective, the distinguished summer visitors would only be highly dismayed at the changes. From another perspective, the combination of Jewishness, death, and chimney awaken Holocaust associations, supposedly revealing the author's lack of sensitivity. But another association adds two other, equally divergent links, namely Heine's *Der Doktor Faust: Ein Tanz-poem*. More specifically, his appended "Elucidations" (28). Syberberg was apparently inspired by Heine's comments here on Mephistopheles. Heine's devil is, for instance, a high-ranking member of hell, comparable to a *Reichskanzler*. That was Hitler's title before he declared himself *Führer*. One recognizes him in Vitzliputzli, who in Heine's version left for Europe to take revenge, much like the tool of the *Weltgeist*. Heine's devil can also assume any shape, e.g. a beautiful woman (Syberberg's Scarabea) or even the Wandering Jew. He is a master of dance, *Tanzkünstler*, providing a precedent for Hitler as an artist, *Künstler*. But like his diabolical underlings who frolic with the witches at this *Reichstag*, his embraces are icy cold. Heine's hell is a chilly place, adding a nuance to Syberberg's metaphor of coldness. Of interest to the quotation about the dead riding out through the chimney is Heine's description of the witches. Some of them are dead sinners who have no peace in their grave (48). They are happy to leave their coffin to ride to the witches' sabbath. Also, they ride primarily on broomsticks, even up through the chimney (47–48). In Heine's context, the German riders from the coffins going through the chimney belong to the devil's followers and have nothing to do with Judaism. Heine himself, however, was raised as a Jew. In Syberberg's quotation, the riders refer to the Jewish dead just named as being shocked. The associative overlay covers or includes divergent categories in counterpoint to each other. Syberberg is still composing by different means. Besides, this example returns Heine as the author's alter ego. His name appears otherwise only a few times in the book. Since the quotation represents a conversation from Syberberg's own life, he enters the field as a player-variant himself.

Reading Syberberg's prose without being familiar with his work poses difficulties with comprehension. His adherence to musical principles causes additional barriers. It accounts for constant variations and transformations of the subjects. Also the coherence suffers. The quasi-musical progression forces the author to divide the material into short segments with "notes" entering new constellations as "chords." One finds, for instance, a constant chain of contrasting concepts in close proximity. If the text mentions losses, gains will often follow within the same paragraph (e.g. 77). Other examples include silence versus lamenting art (repeatedly), freedom versus slavery (102), or war versus peace (86). The contrasts function as inversions. Different variations include comparisons of aristocracy with, e.g., the media nobility of film, television, and sports. The modern ennoblement consists of fame and awards, such as Oscars or Nobel (98). Furthermore, quasi-musical crab arrangements imitate the backward movement in words such as "love without consequences, the consequences without love" (125). And in the chapter called "Pommern II" he is playing the organ using the coupler repeatedly. This time the coupler is first *Koppel* in the meaning of "pasture" (94). The context had concentrated on Tolstoy in his rural retreat. The activation of the coupler changes the sound to include Syberberg who, without transition, suddenly joins the Russian as the subject (94–95). Then, in the next paragraph, *Hunde*, or "dogs" (pack of dogs = *Koppel*), cause Tolstoy to disappear from the text, leaving Syberberg as the only subject. One remembers his use of stuffed dogs in the museum in the *Hitler* film. Their visual and spoken presence had a similar effect on the sound. Syberberg may have borrowed this feature from Celan's "Death Fugue." The fact that the quasi-tonal subjects are heard simultaneously often results in disparate elements appearing in close succession or mixed together. That may account for the emphasis on symbiosis of Jews and Gentiles (79) as well as for the semi-shade preferred to sun or shade alone (112). It should be clear, then, that the author adheres to strict formal criteria, also in his publications. This will strike many as surprising, since the first impression shouts disregard for structure and disciplined style. It so happens that the form Syberberg observes applies to music, not to language based on everyday grammar and syntax. The result is an unusual form of poetry challenging Adorno's dictum.

Compared to Syberberg's previous books, this volume shows no improvement in style or organization. Some sentences go on for 12–14 lines. Many passages consist of incomplete sentences with some statements being mere lists of nouns. Even grammatical errors crop up. Then, while wondering, one remembers the description of old Tolstoy in the strange interplay with the Syberberg subject. He no longer cared about elegant style, one reads, his prose was downright sloppy, with errors, irregularities, and without corrections (94). Why did the author include such comments about Tolstoy's late writings? One also reads that the old man composed his confessions, even denounced his early work, and concentrated on the simple things in life. Apparently, the stylistic symbiosis sets in as soon as Syberberg enters the text in the sentence containing *Koppel*. Right there, in the same sentence, occurs the first grammatical error, a verb in the singular following three subjects. He also refers to his own films, without mentioning their titles, as examples of the prevailing aesthetics that he dismisses (38), and even includes confession-like self-recriminations (103–8). Another Tolstoyesque liberty occurs in *Gründe* as referring to land or property (100, 106). This plural form of *Grund* (ground) is today used mainly in the sense of "grounds" or "reasons." The singular still denotes "ground" as earth, soil, land, or property. Syberberg's use of the word in the plural goes against current usage. At the same time he reveals his allegiance to two other giants normally seen at opposite ends of the spectrum, not in any symbiosis: Celan and Heidegger. As discussed in Olsen's study on the "Death Fugue," the poet also plays with the inter-lingual semantics of *earth* (*Erde, Schwa:+ r + z = eretz, Adam, man/Mann*). And Heidegger's *ground* is a central concept in his philosophy. Other implied references to Heidegger occur, e.g., in *Geschick* (64) and the numerous derivations of *eigen*, most notably in *das Eigentliche* in every definition of the word. So although Syberberg's prose would hardly earn him a literary prize, one finds an amazingly consistent system in the apparent sloppiness.

This style continues in the third section of the book, as do the variations of the subject matters. Written between November 1989 and April '90, the segment discusses a turbulent time, but ending before the official reunification on October 3, 1990. The tone alternates between vague hope for the future and skepticism. Containing several dated chapters, the text approaches the definition of a chronicle. But since it also contains many other reflections, it falls short of actually being one. True to its musical principles, the subjects reappear, recombine, and undergo transformations. Thus the *Weltgeist* returns to Germany, at first unnamed as something dark and unredeemed threatening humanity (178). On the following page an earlier manifestation of this force gains a name in a reference to Hegel's comments on Napoleon. And now it transforms itself into a leaderless population as the tidal wave of a peaceful revolution (180). One senses the author's concern for the continuation. Will another tool of the *Weltgeist* materialize, as Napoleon did in the wake of the French Revolution or Hitler following the Versailles Treaty? Throughout the third part Gorbachev appears as the leader of a super-power. His peacemaking obviously prevented the East German authorities from resorting to military suppression, as it had before. However, Syberberg does not refer to him in terms of the *Weltgeist*, and writing in 1990, could not predict the arrival of such a force. The reader may, however, infer that the benevolent power broker represented such a variation on the theme.

Although the author usually refrains from predictions, he does at least once slip into the role of Cassandra, the prophetess of Troy who warned her people in vain. Three times in the chapter "Antigone" he issues warnings beginning with *Vorsicht* (Watch out! 162–63). The changes in Germany so far resulted from a popular movement in the East only, Syberberg observes. The intellectuals on both sides of the border remained silent, fearing the change. Those in the East stood to lose their politically founded privileges, those in the West would have to face the suppressed taboos. Many of these taboos surface in vocabulary anathematized since the Third Reich, such as *Volk* or *Blut und Boden* (blood and soil). With the East German banners proclaiming "Wir sind das Volk," the noun lost its stigma and became acceptable again. Syberberg claims the same for *Boden*, referring throughout to the soil and rural culture he identifies with. But, he also observes, the East Germans gained their freedom through a revolution. The West Germans, who did nothing to help them, were given theirs by the Western powers. But their freedom did not unfold, it developed into dependency and cultural imitation. So, Syberberg wonders, what will the West Germans choose now that they face reunion and unity? The liberation of the (West) Germans is still ahead, he claims (151). Their predicament had deteriorated into being without "authenticity," a term by Adorno used frequently in the book as a substitute for consciousness about indigenous or native qualities, or also identity. They are without identity. And will the East Germans help lead the move out of stagnation, or will they just succumb to the "inauthentic" ways of the West Germans? In spite of the emotional response to the development, Syberberg's apprehension surfaces repeatedly. For example, in the chapter "10. November 1989," he outlines the loss of German identity in three stages (again) to arrive at the present events, the breaching of the Berlin Wall the night before. Rejoicing in the regained identity, he remarks that in the past only Hitler could awaken such feelings. The wound has healed, he declares (148). The reminder that one had to go all the way back to Hitler's public appearances to find a comparable euphoria underscores the parallel of the *Volk* in revolution and the medium of the *Weltgeist*, as well as the question where this will lead. The reference to Amfortas' wound pulls in the memory of Parsifal. The hero has, one remembers, often been interpreted as a Hitler-like redeemer figure who cures the ills of German society. Syberberg had also put on the mask of Parsifal when he refers to himself as "this fool" in the book to the film. Now he repeats the role play, again as the fool. And again one can only marvel at the density of referentiality in his writings. For example, the title of the unit "Offene Gegend" (Open Area) paraphrases the still shorter scene in *Faust I* called "Open Field." The second sentence refers to recent scornful treatment of him in the press, while mentioning also Kleist. The next statement says only "At the pillory of today's markets" (189). Here he tacitly identifies with Richard Wagner, whom he had shown as a doll in such a position in *Parsifal*. And that pillory was modeled on one in Van Eyck's painting as an instrument of Christ's Passion. Finally follows the question "Where was I?" Parsifal makes that remark in act 2 as Kundry awakens the memory of his mother. Now it is Syberberg who is coming to his senses. Taking leave of the fool's role, he avoids the *Weltgeist* association in favor of the artist's mission. With the wisdom of insight he lists some of the possibilities ahead. The first steps are conceived in negative terms. Not through lamentation over losses does the way go, and not via the "Auschwitz of the dealers." Nor does it go to the left or the right: "Nicht nach links, nicht nach rechts geht der Weg" (190). While one certainly can read it as a political admonition, it also refers to Wolfram von Eschenbach's "rehte enmitten durch," or "right through the middle." He has paraphrased this statement in several texts. This should, then, remind of Parsifal's path towards wisdom. But in Wolfram's case, the center path also contains spiritual connotations. These have survived in esoteric systems to this day, especially as the middle of three columns. Syberberg invokes also the memory of the column by mentioning the pillory. A musician might read it as a manipulation of leitmotifs.

The program Syberberg envisions for art undergoes a number of different formulations in the book. In the third part the concept of *Glück* (good fortune) is gaining ground. The opportunity has arrived to create art with a mission. It relates closely to the concepts of identity and authenticity, of center and middle. The Germans are now the people of the center. They must learn to strive towards constructive commemoration and a new aesthetics. Only art, the author maintains, can bring forth the kind of catharsis that results in renewed innocence and redemption. This art must restore the aura. It is representative and has "more heart." This "heart" draws its nourishment from the soil and culture. It is "at home" and in harmony with itself (156). But while most art reflects its society, high art , *hohe Kunst*, helps elevate it (176–77). It often represents a counter world to reality. It does not so much express dreams or ideas as it relates to a sanctuary, devotional images, or music. Thus the author reintroduces the connection between art and the sacred, but without mentioning the aura in this context. To him music, especially Beethoven's work, functions as an uplifting force with a spiritual dimension. One recognizes an example of this function in *Ein Traum*, which at the time of writing only existed in the stage version.

Another mission of art is suggested in the major subtitles but is not clearly developed in the text: Art can become a second home (172). The first home had been lost, now art must replace it. And of course, he reminds the readers repeatedly, only that reality, memory, or suffering that gains the form of art will survive in history. Along with the prospect of art as a second home resounds the memory of the lost home from Syberberg's childhood. As in *Ein Traum*, it reappears also here (e.g. 152, 188). First the hope to reacquire the property emerges. The expropriated estate that should have been his inheritance informs the use of *verlorenes Haus* throughout the book. Gradually, the idea of restoring the home and the village supercedes the thought of acquisition. Saving and restoring it turns into a substitute art, an envisioned effort described as "art that becomes culture" (188). This differs from the past when art grew out of culture. Besides serving as a quasi-musical transformation, the reference to art as rural culture belongs both to the variations of art's mission in the new era and to Syberberg's own program. In the years to come, his attention turned more and more to the childhood home that had become a lost paradise.

As already observed in the comments on Tolstoy, Syberberg mentions him only as the old author who turned his back on high society and city life in favor of rural simplicity. Syberberg appears to undergo a similar change in his own outlook. It remains unclear, however, whether he feels ready for such a change in his personal life. Also, while devoting much space to the opportunities and ideal mission of art in his book, doubts and skepticism break through time and again. His apocalyptic premonitions take their cues from the dismal state of cultural life in the West. But while at least holding up Tolstoy's choice as a model and praising rural life, the author takes leave of the culture business of his society (157). One assumes, then, that Tolstoy serves as a model for Syberberg, not only in the choice of lifestyle, but also in his disregard for style and rules in his writings, as well as for society's judgment of him. The effect of this ideal on Syberberg's prose was already noted. But he had indulged in a similar disregard for years. And it does not account for all the peculiarities of the "style" in this book. The most conspicuous deviation from common usage is the separation of elements that belong together. It can, for example, affect the noun + genitive expression. Modern German keeps these elements together, as in "die Flagge meines Landes" (my country's flag, the flag of my country). He often separates the elements with a verb or an adverb, as on page 96: "Ich weiß, daß ich nun Gegner bin dieser Zeit" (I know that I am now an opponent of this time). Another type of division affects an adjective + noun sequence. As in English, the German adjective precedes the noun. But occasionally Syberberg adds it as an afterthought, as in "jene Ode der Freude, der wiedergefundenen" (that Ode to Joy, the found-again, 173) or "die Natur, die geschändete" (nature, the violated, 168). This unusual syntax could easily be seen as an emulation of Hölderlin's or Kleist's style. Sometimes both poets resorted to such expressions, e.g. Kleist in *Penthesilea*. They were both grounded in the classics. They were also familiar with Johann Heinrich Voss' translations into German of Homer's *Odyssey* (1781) and *Iliad* (1793). Often, but not always, Voss retains Homer's word order, which includes such sequences as noun + article + adjective.[11] His texts remain close to the Greek originals and still enjoy the lead among Homer translations in Germany. It appears, then, that Syberberg may have been inspired to at least some of his stylistic idiosyncracies by the ancient epics as well as their influence on the German authors of the Idealist era, especially Hölderlin and Kleist.[12] Such emulation in style would run parallel to his numerous references to *Untergang*, including the downfall of Prussia, Germany, Western culture, Troy, the deaths of the ancient heroes, and their commemoration in Homer's art. On occasion he even sounds like Cassandra.

But Homer's Greek is not the only language displaying the mentioned characteristics. One finds them also in Hebrew. Actually, a number of other features in Syberberg's book appear to resemble Hebrew more than classical Greek. Three possible sources of inspiration come to mind: Martin Buber's translation of the Hebrew Bible into German, Paul Celan's poetry, and Klaus Reichert's study on Hebrew characteristics in Celan's language.[13] Reichert's text serves as the main guide for the following examples.

1. Separation of elements that belong together grammatically. Reichert describes two types of usage, of which one occurs both in Syberberg's prose and in Homeric Greek and Hebrew. This is the sequence of noun + article + adjective, as already mentioned.

2. Revival of old-fashioned or archaic vocabulary. Here one notices Syberberg's use of *so* as a relative particle instead of a relative pronoun (167), also repeatedly the plural *Gründe* in the sense of "land" or "property" (e.g. 100, 106). According to Reichert such word choices in Hebrew awaken the memory of old and new meanings by functioning as means to "rescue" the forgotten (162).

3. Transformation of words into other grammatical categories, especially infinitives and participles used as nouns. One example is Syberberg's "alle in sich

Irrende, in die Irre geführte Menschen" (all those fooling themselves, people led astray into confusion, 54). *Irre* is the curse Kundry calls down on Parsifal.

    4. Parataxis. Three forms of it occur so frequently that they may characterize Syberberg's prose. One is the asyndetic juxtaposition of sentences or words. In the chapter "Glück" one reads about New Year's Eve 1989: "Leipzig, Gewandhaus, live zum Ende dieses Jahres Beethoven, 9. Symphonie, Kurt Masur, ist es Einbildung, Dank" (Leipzig, Gewandhaus [= concert hall], Beethoven live at the end of this year, Ninth Symphony, Kurt Masur [= conductor], is it imagination, thanks, 173). These blocks do not unite into sentences, and as so often, the verbs are missing. But still, the list tells a story. Sometimes the blocks do not add up to a list, as in "Rundum Leere. Depression der Niederlage. Alles falsch und anders?" (All around emptiness. Depression over defeat. Everything wrong and different? 192). More frequent is the string of short elements, especially nouns (e.g. 70). They form the second type of paratactical junctions that Reichert calls "tectonic" constructions (158). Quite often this jumble of fragments ignores syntactical links in spite of reaching great length. Up to 14 lines long, such accumulations remain grammatically incomplete. Maybe Tolstoy inspired the liberties, maybe Celan, or perhaps even Reichert's study on Celan. The third form of parataxis is also mentioned by Reichert, namely the numerous sentences beginning with a capitalized *And*. These structures form the most striking feature of Syberberg's style in this book. Excluding quotations, captions under illustrations, and *und* used *within* a sentence, one finds the following: In the two essays of the introduction with ten pages of text there are 11 cases of *Und* in initial position, of which one begins a new paragraph. Part 1 contains 35 uses of *Und* over 43 pages, while they increase in part 2 to 52 cases of *Und* on 54 pages of text, with four of the cases introducing new paragraphs. Part 3 reaches a climax with 91 times *Und* over 59 pages, with 12 of them beginning new paragraphs. They tend to accumulate in conspicuous clusters of frequency (p.124: 7 cases; p.108: 6 cases; p.164: 6 cases). Reichert points out that *and* is the most frequent word in the Hebrew Bible (157). He also mentions that Adorno in his essay "Parataxis" describes the paratactical style as anticlassicist.[14] Therefore, besides incorporating Hebrewisms in his prose, Syberberg may also play on the contrast between classicist and modern or non-classical style. This would serve the contrapuntal composition of his text.

    Another aspect of that procedure is the prominence of specific vocabulary items, such as "Jews," Jewish names, Israel, and expressions from the Hebrew Bible or literature by Jewish authors. Since Syberberg mentions Gretchen (121), he also includes Sulamith (17), but not together as in the "Death Fugue." Readers aware of the importance of counterpoint in his work soon suspect that the constantly shifting tone accompanying the Jewish and the Gentile elements reflects the progression of counterpoint. Obviously, he sees Jews and Gentile Germans as two subjects or variants of the same subject, *Mensch*. They are "ineinander verschränkt" or "intertwined", he remarks (79). But as usual, he also includes himself as a topic. All of his books contain some autobiographical features. Logically, then, the Syberberg theme will at times sound along with a variation of the Jewish one. The progression of transformations continues until the subject(s) return(s) to the original key at the end of the composition, if it is a fugue. This emphasis on being "intertwined" might account for the Hebrewisms in the prose. But, one wonders, does this style restrict itself to merely proceeding quasi-musically? On several occasions in the past, Syberberg made statements inviting questions about a Jewish side of him:

1. In the *Filmbuch* Syberberg quotes the postscript attached to the *Winifred Wagner* film (284–85). Here Mrs. Wagner states that the public may be surprised that she had remained silent for so long and then suddenly agreed to talk. She counters such speculation with the question "why not?" Syberberg had suggested the phrase, which Wolfgang Wagner accepted with the remark that it was really a Jewish conclusion (285). When some old Nazis saw the film, they asked if the director was Jewish (292). The author does not reveal what else in the film might have prompted such an inquiry. He merely reports the reaction to this phrase.

2. In *Die freudlose Gesellschaft* Syberberg mocks the current, often insincere but obligatory, philo-Semitism and also the politically correct pride in a modest family background. Apparently he does not qualify in these categories. He asks rhetorically how he and his *Hitler* film would have been treated if he had been the illegitimate child of a Jewish mother and his father had been a day laborer. With "Einmal angenommen " he ends the speculation (Just assuming , 153). The book includes passages about his father's position and estate, but says only about the mother that she left after a year. One assumes, then, that the question is merely rhetorical. However, his father did become a laborer on his former estate for a while after the expropriation.

3. *Der Wald steht schwarz und schweiget* contains another strange passage: "He [= Syberberg] knew a woman who did not tell anybody that she might have a Jewish background, today and here, during the good days, which would have made many things easier for her, her everyday battles and the realization of many a plan. And so she rather struggled on, even suspected by the children with the Nazi fathers of being a Hitler supporter" (557). Who was she? Someone close to him?

And now in *Vom Unglück und Glück,* the author includes a brief text that invites related questions. For the first time in his books he tries his hand at poetry. A poem that reads like his prose in 23 lines precedes the autobiographical essay of the introduction (16). Untitled, unrhymed, and divided into three blocks of 12, 2, and 9 lines, it expresses a personal quest for memory and identity. Both the content and the poetic structure link it associatively with the three older passages just mentioned. Especially the uniqueness of the poem in the author's work attracts attention. He has tried on many professions before, but by writing a poem he aspires also to being a poet. That designation brings to mind a poem by Paul Celan, "Und mit dem Buch aus Tarussa."[15] More precisely, one thinks of the motto preceding the poem, "All poets are Jews." Syberberg knows Celan's work well. Perhaps the reference to exile in Celan's poem elicited the response. Most frequently in the last section of the book, Syberberg refers to himself as an emigré. He may identify with Celan's status, although the latter wrote as a Jewish survivor of the Holocaust, both in exile and in diaspora. Syberberg only lost his childhood home, became later an East German "exile" in West Germany, and eventually a self-proclaimed emigré in his own country through ostracism. Although the circumstances differ, he emphasizes the experience of exile. And as a "poet" he also shares the status of a Jew, according to Celan. In that connection one is reminded of the pre-1945 photo from Syberberg's childhood home on his Internet diary on January 1, 2004. It shows the living room, *Damenzimmer*, with a menorah on a cabinet. How many German households kept a Jewish symbol in plain view during the Third Reich? *Vom Unglück und Glück* also includes numerous references to losses, reductions, cuts, and incisions in a variety of contexts, often using the verb *beschneiden*, the basis for *Beschneidung*, or "circumcision." In his study of Celan, Reichert mentions circumcision as a ritual with two meanings (166). Apart from the common meaning of the term, the preparation of a child for admission into a community, it also has a transferred meaning. Here Reichert refers to Paul's stress on the "circumcision of the heart" to designate the pure of heart and sinless (Rom. 2.29). This sense of the word establishes a close proximity of circumcision and catharsis as processes of purification. Besides, the Jewish theme appears as important in the book as that of German identity. Together they function as the premise for the synthesis of "catharsis" through art. Moreover, the Jews and the "Germans" function as the two subjects of a double fugue, as defined in Prout's *Fugue* (182). They both appear in the first essay of Syberberg's introduction. First, as a group, one "hears" the Gentile Germans from film and theater, with Adorno mixed in towards the end (13). Then, in quick succession, follows a list naming Adorno, Bloch, Benjamin, Marcuse, and Kracauer (14). They are the "founding fathers" imposing their stamp on the heritage of Idealism after 1945. They function as the second subject or countersubject introduced early in the exposition. After the codetta consisting of the poem, the third stage reintroduces them intertwined with the Gentiles in the paragraph on Jews and leftists. The poem-cum-codetta modulates to the "answer" segment. This answer is the essay on the author, who devotes as much space to Hitler as to himself. They, Hitler and Syberberg, relate somehow to the two subjects introduced in the first essay. According to classical fugal principles, they sound "in imitation." That is, they run more or less parallel with the original subjects, but transposed higher or lower in the register. However, the two subjects introduced earlier do not go silent. They continue to sound in counterpoint. Obviously, more than two voices, here four, are needed in the answer section. Also, according to Prout, the transposed versions of subject 1 and subject 2 begin in reversed order in the answer: "The answer will in the first instance be given by whatever voice has the second entry" (3). The voice that introduced the first, Gentile subject should follow, not lead, in the answer. Consequently, a transposed variant of the Jewish subject should begin the answer. This voice sounds along with Syberberg, who starts the essay with an autobiographical passage. But he avoids the identifying first person pronoun until line 7. If this had been written in Hebrew, there would have been no need for a pronoun, since the subject would have been identified in the verb ending. The German prose contains a Hebrew characteristic.

The paragraphs concentrating on Hitler and the *Weltgeist* follow as the second voice. The original sequence is recognizable in the contrapuntal presence of the subjects, especially on p.17.[16] Together, the texts of the introduction correspond to a fugal exposition consisting of subjects, codetta, and answer. The quasi-musical treatment also reveals how Syberberg prefers to align himself. Since his book contains as many obstacles to comprehension as Celan's poetry, its Jewish and musical dimensions have been ignored or downright misunderstood. As the author also plays with expressions leaning on Heidegger, e.g. *das Eigene, das Eigentliche, Enteignung*, and others associated with the Third Reich, such as *Volk* and *Blut und Boden*, readers will only register what they recognize. To that come statements that are unclear, ambiguous, or intended to provoke. It comes as no surprise, then, that the reception of the book ranged from faint appreciation to total rejection. In view of the quasi-musical handling of language and topics, Syberberg obviously wants to make his book a work of art. Unfortunately, words are not notes. When they layer up, imitating chords, clarity suffers. He would have done his readers and himself a service by presenting his thoughts in simple prose. Perhaps much would have sounded differently. But that would have deprived the book of its provocative edge, and Syberberg of his place in the limelight.

One of the first reviews appeared in *Die Zeit*.[17] Here Günther Nenning chooses a sarcastic-funny approach for two purposes. It both helps soften his rejection of the book and conceal his insecurity. Half the review consists of quotations. This procedure results in scattered conclusions characterizing Syberberg as a fool, a reactionary, and a madman. But he can also be a wily man, a *Schlitzohr*. Riding the "German steed," he knows he is destined for a hero's death at the hand of the reunited German *Intelligenzija*. Calling him a mannerist and latecomer of modernism, Nenning eventually identifies him as a precursor of the art of the future.

Soon after two review articles appeared on the same day in *Frankfurter Allgemeine Zeitung*.[18] Werner Fuld dismisses Syberberg's book as a mixture of culture chauvinism and nationalism combined with an attack on democracy and art. He concludes that Syberberg has no business being where culture is debated ("Wo über Kultur gesprochen wird, hat Syberberg nichts mehr zu suchen," 33). His colleague Frank Schirrmacher lends support by turning rejection into distortion and *ad hominem* attacks. Thus Syberberg is a postmodernist and anti-Semite whose words might have sounded ridiculous a year ago, but now assume a more dangerous tone. Schirrmacher concludes his comments with another distortion. He draws on the interview with André Müller that Syberberg fought against. To bolster his view, he claims that Syberberg in that text "was allowed" to praise Hitler, using this interview as reliable source material. In brief, Syberberg with his anti-Semitic invectives has produced a worthless piece of trash, a *Machwerk*. Syberberg's rejoinder appeared two weeks later.[19] As expected, he rejects the accusations of anti-Semitism. Trying to shift the attention to his main topic, he reminds the readers, "Art is politics, for aesthetics is not only the form in which one sees the world, but also the form through which one influences the world, therefore something important is determined" (36). But some journalists try to prevent the different, *das*

Andersartige, from being heard. He thinks the "socalled free democratic culture" tends towards suppression of dissenters (36). The readers' letters to the editor on September 21, 22, 24, 26, and 28 defend the book and criticize the reviewers. One of them even suggests that the strong condemnation of the book was just the newspaper's attempt to stir up a controversy during the summer lull.

Since *Der Spiegel* prides itself of being the leading news magazine in Germany, its book reviews receive attention beyond the national borders. As a result, the equally negative review by Hellmuth Karasek set the tone for many others that appeared later.[20] The word on top of the page above the title summarizes the writer's assessment: Neo-Nazism. He quotes liberally from Syberberg's sentences, only to weave in his own phrases that support his thesis. Thus he explains *Vom Unglück und Glück* in the book title as follows: "'About Misfortune: The Jews are our misfortune. 'About Good Fortune:' Syberberg is our good fortune. For the fact that we don't realize the good fortune we have in Syberberg, well, of course, the leftists and the Jews are to blame again" (240). Karasek refers to Syberberg as a Nazi and desk criminal and to his book as also being criminal. "One can hardly be insane in a more dreadful way," he warns (240). While cleverly distorting through stitching together and adding his comments as if they were Syberberg's, Karasek also reveals his own professional shortcomings. He does not understand what he has read, and he has probably only skimmed through the introduction. At least he restricts his comments and quotations to the introduction. To fill up two and a half pages he resorts to two expansion tricks. First, he ridicules two other reviewers whose approaches differ from his own (Günther Nenning in *Die Zeit* and André Heller in *Abendzeitung*). Second, he too quotes extensively from the 1988 interview with André Müller that Syberberg had protested against. He also includes a long passage from a speech by Himmler to the SS as if it were part of the Müller interview. It is the passage in the script book to *Hitler* about the need of the SS officer to overcome his human feelings and remain "decent" in his duty to kill. All this he cuts and pastes for his conclusion about Syberberg: "A Hitler for a psychiatric hospital" (242). The shockwaves from this review were predictable, as confirmed by the readers' letters to the editor three weeks later (September 24: 12+). Syberberg's protest also appears among these letters. He points out three fallacies. 1. The Müller interview was not authentic. 2. The Himmler quotation had no relation to the interview. 3. Karasek had only read the first few pages. He ends by suggesting that Karasek and the readers see his *Hitler* film to contemplate his intent with and the effect of the Himmler quotation. This intent is to overcome "the Hitler in us." Obviously, too many of his compatriots either fail to recognize his intent, or refuse to acknowledge it.

Syberberg's book had certainly attracted the critics' attention. Their chorus of denunciation discouraged different assessments in the leading media outlets for a while. One exception was André Heller, who felt provoked to defend Syberberg publicly.[21] Ever since the *Hitler* film was released, he writes in the *Abendzeitung*, some reviewers have denounced Syberberg as a Nazi sympathizer. He refers to these journalists as "stutterers in thinking," *Denkstotterer*. Syberberg had committed a sin in revering such concepts as *Heimat*, beauty, and greatness. Heller considers him simply an "engaged anti-fascist" and "one of the most original and radical nomads in that cold desert that one might call the German climate." In a summary of the development in Syberberg's cinematic work, he points out that the films up through *Hitler* had been copied formally by other filmmakers dozens of times. However, the recent work with Clever has become taboo in the press, in spite of its "exemplary frugality" and "crystalline concentration." And now his latest book has made him a subject of ostracism, *Verfemung*. Heller hints that the animosity in the press may relate to the demands Syberberg makes on the viewers and reviewers. Referring to the colors of the German flag, Heller adds that it is one of the "black-red-golden national characteristics not to let oneself be robbed of one's prejudice by judgment." The article ends with a call for Syberberg's rehabilitation.

Many Germans may have agreed with Heller, but a certain intimidation grew along with the expansion of the public debate on Germany. Whoever defended people like Syberberg or broke the long-held taboos was suspected of a Third Reich mentality. Only those on the acknowledged political far right had nothing to fear. Therefore Syberberg experienced support from constituencies resembling underground movements. One example is the "Turbund" on its Web site.[22] This archaic name meaning "tower society" may remind some readers of Goethe's *Turmgesellschaft*, of which Wilhelm Meister becomes a member. The "Turbund" menu displays numerous links to esoteric topics popular (also) during the Third Reich, the *oi*-music scene, and a mix compatible with old and neo-Nazi thinking, although nothing anti-Semitic. One of the links leads to comments on Syberberg's *Hitler* film. Surprisingly knowledgeable, the anonymous site editor gives an analytical appraisal of the film surpassing many printed studies in perspicuity. One cannot help wondering if Syberberg contributed some sections of the assessment himself. That raises the question if he may have collaborated on other sections as well. The style, choice of vocabulary, and topics do not exclude the possibility, but neither do they prove it either. Certain is only that he had earned the sympathy of a community outside the main stream .

As the discussion about Germany continued to gain coverage in the media, Syberberg received an invitation to appear at a public debate in East Berlin. The East Germans did not share the phobias of the West Germans and had not yet been sufficiently westernized to react negatively to Syberberg's views. The event was a four-day affair focused on Syberberg and his book. The *Hitler* film ran on four consecutive days, Edith Clever played *Die Marquise* on stage in Deutsches Theater, and Syberberg appeared as the featured member on a panel of discussants in the Academy of Arts in East Berlin.[23] This event became a media event with a predictably biased coverage in numerous West German newspapers and magazines. *Der Spiegel* published a report by Matthias Matussek.[24] Compared to his article about Clever and Syberberg of 1988, the tone has changed. Following Karasek's example, the journalist abandons all semblance of civility. One learns very little about the debate, except that the panel faced a large and sometimes rowdy audience. The journalist's attitude reveals itself early in two ways. Trying to summarize the scope of the symposium, he writes that its topic was supposedly about the splendor and misery of irrationalism in Germany ("Vom Glanz und Elend des Irrationalismus in Deutschland"). That echoes the structure of the title of Syberberg's book. Instead, he corrects, the real topic was whether Syberberg is a great artist or only an anti-Semitic idiot (260–61). The other signal of the writer's intent surfaces in the title of the review, "Gefolgschaft erzwingen" (To Compel Fealty). The expression stems from Susan Sontag's "Syberberg's *Hitler*," reprinted in her book *Under the Sign of Saturn*. There she states near the conclusion, "Syberberg's film belongs in the category of noble masterpieces which ask for fealty and can compel it" (165). Matussek and his cohorts chose to acknowledge only what they recognized, namely a way of thinking compatible with the demands of Third Reich obedience to a Führer. Sontag's essay is denigrated as a Nazi-like (*Stahlhelm*) text and evil nonsense (264). Half of the review concentrates on Sontag, who was one of the panelists, ridiculing her comments, publications, and person. The writer ignores Syberberg's book, but pretends to have seen the film, which, he claims, celebrates the master race idea (264). Again he cannot refrain from attacking André Heller's appearance in the film ("the Roncalli-clown"). He reaches the nadir when he includes the critical comments of an old man in the audience who had lost his family in the concentration camps (266). The reviewer did not have the decency to reprint Syberberg's answer.

For a hint to this answer one can turn to Ian Buruma's article in the *New York Review*.[25] He states only: "The old man who stood up in the East Berlin Academy was wrong, of course; Syberberg does not like Hitler" (36). He too takes exception to some of Syberberg's opinions, for instance on American-style democracy and foreign influence. Familiar with the negative treatment in the German press, he retains a critical impartial tone, but with nuances. "Syberberg is not so much a crypto- or neo-Nazi," he writes, "as a reactionary dandy, of the type found before the war in the Action Française or in certain British aristocratic circles (whose spirit lives on in *The Salisbury Review* today)" (37). He recognizes Syberberg's ideal of a rural-based natural order as being related to his longing for a return to his childhood paradise. "Because this ideal community is an imaginary one," Buruma writes, "he must invent it, through the kitsch of his childhood: Hitler's speeches, Karl May's adventure stories, and echoes from Bayreuth" (43). Having actually read Syberberg's book, he describes the fascination with Kleist and the Romantics as a quest for a utopia, " in Syberberg's case a kind of kitsch, de-Nazified vision of Blood and Soil" (43). He concludes that Syberberg is an intellectual in search of the ideal community, but with the gloomy premonition of a unified Germany soon turning into a "rancid" democracy of old party politics. Buruma was right about that, as one recognizes in retrospect. Unfortunately, he had no influence on the German reviewers.[26]

The reunification brought with it an unprecedented public debate. It resulted in a breakthrough a repressed topics and concepts, among them Germany, nation, and identity. Through the negative reviews, Syberberg's name became linked with revisionism and dangerous nationalism. As expected, most of the contributions to this debate address the issues with concern, strong opinions, and often belligerence. What a surprise, then, to find an irreverent and often playful text among them! In a rather un-German book, Rembert Hüser devotes 65 pages to Syberberg and *Moby Dick*.[27] Apparently the impetus for the combination were two concurrent events in Bielefeld about these topics. The author uses this as a pretext to interweave them. Only after he mentions Paul de Man does a connection surface. De Man had translated Melville's book into Flemish as a young man. He later became the target of attacks for his wartime articles in a collaborationist newspaper in Belgium. Now the whale as a monster from the psychological depths and the reception of Syberberg's ideas alternate and overlap nonsensically and ironically. Hüser does not care for the director's *Hitler* film or latest book, but he is much more annoyed by the media figures denouncing him. Therefore Syberberg's case serves to unmask the journalists, especially Frank Schirrmacher. When the latter dismisses Syberberg's aesthetics as postmodern intellectualism, Hüser delves into a lecture on postmodernism, and especially on the difference between deconstructionism and postmodernism (118–21). It appears that Schirrmacher had published several articles using these concepts indiscriminately about Derrida and de Man. Finally the whale blows a lot of steam consisting of "postmoderndeconstructivistilistivism." Hüser points out how poorly researched Schirrmacher's article about Syberberg is (132n), and that Syberberg and postmodernism are mutually exclusive (126). In Syberberg's latest book he observes a penchant for lists similar to Homer's catalogues. At least he registers one of the subtexts. More important, he recognizes the emphasis on the caesuras in Syberberg's concept of time, November 9, 1989 marking the latest break between past and present (133). As for the denunciations, Hüser reminds the reader that one needs to read Syberberg's book and to read it carefully.

At least in some circles *Vom Unglück und Glück* met with more acceptance. In September 1990 Heimo Schwilk from *Rheinischer Merkur* interviewed Syberberg about the book.[28] Another review had appeared there earlier, but after the aggressive articles by Karasek and Schirrmacher, the interviewer wanted to probe Syberberg's reaction and clarify some of his ideas. The text is a welcome compendium to the book. It also distinguishes itself favorably from the attacks in its civilized tone and informative answers. Syberberg does not even comment on the negativity, but offers elaborations on several issues mentioned in his book. For example, the aesthetics of the ugly that had prevailed since 1945 has not resulted exclusively from marketing forces. In some cases it also grew out of suffering, giving form or expression to that condition. In response to his thoughts on the "Jewish spirit," he points to the desirability of retaining identity, of not being absorbed by the population at large. For both the Jewish and the Gentile populations in Europe he sees the ideal situation in preserving the minority status as an "intellectual and spiritual" (*geistig*) province in a mutually fruitful dialogue with the majority population. Any total merging or domination, as he thinks happened after 1945, does not serve either side (23). About the mission of art as a counterforce to prevailing entertainment, he emphasizes a modest format with a connection to cultural roots. In past centuries the church and the monarchy provided comparable centers of belonging, consolation, and sense of identity. He sees his recent work for the stage as continuing in this spirit. Incidentally, he points out that the productions with Edith Clever enjoyed full houses and standing ovations. This, he thinks, confirms that his approach is meeting a need.

In Schwilk Syberberg had found a sympathetic interviewer. Their contact led to another project a couple of years later when Schwilk edited a book to which Syberberg contributed a chapter.[29] *Die selbstbewusste Nation* quickly went through three editions. The meaning of the title can range from "the proud or self-confident nation" to "the self-conscious nation." A quick perusal eliminates the shade of pride or arrogance. Every chapter reveals a concern for German identity in the sense of becoming self-conscious about a problematic legacy or current condition. The volume is dedicated to "the patriots" of July 20, 1944 and June 17, 1953. The dates refer to the officers' revolt against Hitler and the East German workers' revolt against Stalinist rule. Still the book became branded as brownish ultra-rightist for several reasons. The introductory chapter reprints Botho Strauß' essay "Anschwellender Bocksgesang" (Swelling Song of the Goat). Duden's *Wörterbuch der Antike* gives *Bocksgesang* as "tragedy," a word derived from the Greek *tragos*, meaning "billy goat." The title refers, in other words, to a current, growing tragedy. The essay by Strauß criticizes modern Germany and caused its author the same ostracism that befell Syberberg. Another reason is the inclusion of Ernst Nolte, prominent in the historians' dispute in the eighties and decried as a revisionist. This overlooks the fact that the contributors to the volume represent a wide spectrum of opinions. Among them one finds, for instance, Michael Wolffsohn, born in Tel Aviv, and Brigitte Seebacher-Brandt, best known in Germany as the widow of Chancellor Willy Brandt. Syberberg's chapter appears in the section labeled "Identity." He writes about *Eigenes*, "that which is one's own," and *Fremdes*, "that which is foreign." To this he adds a subtitle, "On the loss of the tragic." With that he links on to the text by Strauß.

After the denunciations of his latest book, Syberberg apparently realized that offense is the best defense. He now enters the arena forcefully. The collapse of the Marxist power system caused an examination of many issues, political, economic, and aesthetic. Again the writer reminds the reader that collaboration with the occupying powers existed both in East and West Germany. Both parts of the country experienced their share of Quislings and collaborators in all fields, including the arts. Of course, Vidkun Quisling, who served as governor of Norway under German occupation, was executed as a traitor after World War II. By mentioning Quislings, Syberberg suggests that there exists such a thing as treason in the area of arts as well. Addressing those in former West Germany, he asks if not also they have betrayed their *Eigenes*. While softening the statement with a call for self-scrutiny, he makes his point quite clear: Any denunciators will from now on join the ranks of traitors of German culture.

Many things changed with the reunification, also in the language. As an example the author refers to *Volk* as a term rehabilitated by the popular revolution

in East Germany, and now joining *Gesellschaft*, or "society," as a viable concept
(125). Both in East and West, dogmas and beliefs are being questioned, including
the moral superiority of the Western system. But when the writer describes how "the
previous system" collapsed morally, politically, and culturally, the reader wonders
what system he refers to (126). The passage does not identify time or place. Does
he mean former West Germany that he criticizes in the previous paragraph, or
former East Germany discussed on the previous page, or both? Only towards the
bottom of the page can one recognize that he means the Third Reich. What looks
like poor writing soon reveals itself as continued textual composition containing
counterpoint.

The following pages return to a topic introduced in *Vom Unglück und Glück*,
namely the exiles who returned to Germany after the war. This time the author
makes a more careful distinction between the "victors with occupation interests"
and those returning. After the collapse, help from abroad was needed. The Germans
were fortunate, one reads, because the help did not come only from the victors, but
also from the emigrants who had fled, and they were people "from our midst"
("mitten aus uns," 127). The critics who had denounced his recent book had
interpreted these exiles as exclusively Jewish and Syberberg as an anti-Semite for
objecting to the effect of their influence. He does not call them founding fathers any
more, and the emphasis has shifted from influence to help. The few representative
names include also Gentiles, such as Brecht and Thomas Mann. But Brecht settled
in East Germany and Mann in Switzerland after the war, a fact that varies the
author's implied criticism of West German conditions. Instead of repeating the
condemnation given so much space in the book, he now uses him-self as an example
of a development gone astray. What looks like another autobiographical outline
serves several purposes. At first the overview reads like a self-confident assessment
of his accomplishments. He had succeeded in creating something authentic and
genuinely German, *Eigenes*. Also, his "work of mourning" commemorates not only
the victims, but also the nation of perpetrators. After *Parsifal* the emphasis shifts
to the latter. At this point a different tone becomes noticeable. The description of
the author's career turns into a confession and self-recrimination. He too had
succumbed to prevailing trends in topics and aesthetics and had benefited from the
subsidy system. Without stressing the implications, his self-scrutiny assumes a
representative function. These chords combine two variants playing concurrently,
Syberberg and the Germans. The following passages continue with a different
combination or emphasis. The arguments could easily be interpreted as a rejection
of Benjamin's and Adorno's writings, but again, one needs to read carefully.
Syberberg does not mention their names. He disagrees with the dictum about no
poetry after Auschwitz, also with its revised interpretation of no "high art" in the
old style. Now nuances have been added to this complex. While he dismisses the
materialistic sociology of art in its technical reproducibility, he deplores the loss of
the aura. He sees the restoration of beauty in art to be his mission or *Auftrag* (131).

The last two pages read like a manifesto. Aesthetics is politics. Only from the
strength of the authentically characteristic, *Eigenes*, can German art exert a

constructive influence in its own society and beyond. This art should take its nourishment from the lost culture of the past. Through reconciliation it should aim at redeeming guilt. The author compares this ideal function with art's service to earlier gods (133). One recognizes Benjamin's prerequisite for the aura. The tragedy of existence, Heidegger's concept *Da-sein*, as expressed in art is all that will remain when we are gone, Syberberg concludes, and modifying Bloch's term, this art, a silent smile, may be all that remains as the "heritage of this time." By drawing on concepts from the unidentified Benjamin, Heidegger, and Bloch, the conclusion tries to pull together the cultural legacies to be reconciled. At the same time repeated references underscore a predicament as well as support the thesis in Strauß' essay.

Although Syberberg continued to be active in the following years, his image was now linked to the furor surrounding *Vom Unglück und Glück*. He was neither the first nor the only writer to attract attention during reunification. But he already had many enemies in the media and became an easy target. Among the majority of German reporters and critics, the rejection of him remained unabated for a long time. It surfaces also in two studies that aim at presenting an overview of the situation. In an article of 1991, Lothar Baier supports the rejection of Syberberg and his book, calling it imbecility.[30] He points out that other authors, whose works appeared in the same publishing house as Syberberg's book, had expressed similar views in the eighties, e.g. Gerd Bergfleth and Jean Baudrillard. What Baier questions is the motivation of the critics who now cry "Nazi." Their socalled democratic antifascism is too selfserving and unconvincing (128). A contrasting example refers first to an unidentified article about Syberberg in the French newspaper *Libération* (123). The paper devoted much space to the controversy, concluding that Syberberg was denounced by German intellectuals as an anti-Semite while being defended by French and American intellectuals with a Jewish background. Baier then tries to prove the fallacy of that argument. Ending by belittling Syberberg through ridicule, he assures the readers that any danger of Nazisim from his subject could be averted through a prize, financial support, and recognition. Not once does he pay the respect to call Syberberg's publications "books." They are all "pamphlets."

Baier's article appears to have supplied much of the source material for the other study that aspires to a broader discussion of the issues. In 1992 Diedrich Diederichsen published his article in *October*.[31] Trying to place Syberberg within a context of German and European debate, it distorts and misrepresents two premises, and hence Syberberg's main thrust. The intellectuals targeted in his study have contributed to "an amnesia coinciding with the unification," the author claims (66). This really does not apply to Syberberg, who time and again emphasizes the need for memory. But the American readers of *October* are not likely to know that. Those trusting Diederichsen's overview are led to believe that Syberberg presents a basis for German identity that is too tainted with questionable ideology. Diederichsen also undermines Syberberg's arguments that the German leftists bore the responsibility for the development of an imitative, non-authentic art scene. He first includes Syberberg's most inflammatory statement from *Vom Unglück und Glück*, distorting it for his own purpose. The original translates as "Whoever went along with the Jews as well as the leftists, was successful" ("Wer mit den Juden ging wie mit den Linken, machte Karriere ," Syb., 14). It concludes with "How could Jews tolerate that, it be then they only wanted power" ("Wie konnten das Juden ertragen, es sei denn, sie wollten nur Macht"). Diederichsen concludes the passage as "Jews must have put up with this since they wanted power" (69). Red flags pop up. A few pages further he disputes the presence of German leftists and their influence by asserting that there had been no established left in Germany in the postwar period (70). He restricts the concept of *left* to the communists and anarchists, exempting the social democrats. His version of the political forces at work therefore contradicts and discredits Syberberg's use of *leftist* as scurrilous and out of touch with reality. When he also refers to Syberberg's enemy from *Der Spiegel* as "the rather harmless Mr. Karasek" (69), the writer's agenda becomes unmistakably clear. Other references to Syberberg include phrases like "a sensibility clouded by paranoia" (67) and "Syberberg is someone who has always been somewhat off balance" (82). This kind of characterization continues the defamation introduced in *Der Spiegel* and many newspapers. For if Syberberg is mentally unstable and ready for psychiatric treatment, who needs to take him seriously? With other journalists having set the tone, Diederichsen felt safe to continue with his own misrepresentations. A few years later he and Syberberg were scheduled to appear as speakers at a symposium in Munich.[32] The program on the Internet includes the note that Diederichsen canceled on short notice due to the participation of Syberberg. It could not have been for political reasons, as the titles of the presentations and the slate of speakers prove. It was not a convention by or for rightists. Had his defamation had a legal aftermath? Did he feign fear of a man "off balance"? Or was he too embarrassed?

Another study of 1992 by Eric Santner concentrates on Syberberg and the painter Anselm Kiefer.[33] While rejecting the author/director's late work, the writer tries to substantiate the accusations in the German press with his own assessment. Although oblivious to the counterpoint in Syberberg's book, he mulls over one occurrence of it: "The German [text] reads: 'Suchte ich nicht auch mich Liebkind zu machen bei der Generation der Emigranten.' By writing 'Liebkind,' Syberberg is, I suspect, saying, 'didn't I play at being the good Jewish son to the emigrés'" (15n). Santner does not know what to make of it, but translates it as "favorite son" in a longer quotation illustrating Syberberg's recantation of previous artistic efforts.[34] He should have consulted Grimm's dictionary. Prominent in his study is Alexander and Margarete Mitscherlich's *The Inability to Mourn*, on which he also bases his chapter on Syberberg in *Stranded Objects*. According to Freud, mourning is the normal processing of loss, while melancholy results when a very strong, identifying attachment, such as a cathexis, is suddenly shattered. The Mitscherlichs interpreted the Germans' relationship to Hitler and his visions as such a cathexis. Now Santner thinks that Syberberg's "work of mourning" has undergone a major shift and that his book reinterprets the Mitscherlichs' thesis in a disturbing way: the

Germans' work of mourning can only begin when they free themselves from the
Jewish influence (17). Also, blind to the dialectical principle at work, Santner sees
in the references to Antigone a displacement of an ethical model of mourning by an
aesthetic one: "Syberberg rejects, in other words, the ethical dimension of mourning " (18). It would have been repressively Oedipal and Jewish, he concludes.
Presumably, Syberberg's reference to Antigone and her devotion to her dead
brother must equate an unstated loyalty to a Nazi past. Similarly, Santner fails to
recognize the dialectical progression or shifting of the "caesura" in German history
from 1945 to 1989/90. Another point in his study builds on his understanding of
fantasy as meaning ideological fantasy: "The force of Syberberg's work as an artist
derives precisely from his programmatic insistence on the perverse perspective—as
a necessary condition of all aesthetic creation and reception" (22). Santner sees
Syberberg as presenting ideological constructions: "The reason for this would seem
to be that he is incapable of conceiving of fantasy except in deeply anti-Semitic
terms" (23). He summarizes the conclusion on Syberberg's aesthetics with one
word: obscene. With this condemnation Santner joined the German media.
Syberberg had been accused before of assuming the role of a persecuted Christ-like
prophet. Now he suffered the crucifixion.

A broader analysis of the issues is offered in Gerd Gemünden's study.[35]
Outlining the reexamination of national and cultural identity after 1990, the chapter
focuses on Syberberg, Wim Wenders, and Botho Strauß. These three artists all
became controversial for expressing views considered heretical in wide circles.
Gemünden distrusts the quest for identity related to Germany as a *Kulturnation*.
Referring to the three "neo-conservatives," he states, "Theirs is a nostalgia that is
deeply problematic because it invokes a unity that never existed in reality, and that
has outlived its usefulness as a model for the twenty-first century" (129). Worse,
Syberberg's stress on "the redemptive power of art and imagination in service of a
national and cultural identity" assumes a disturbing role: "In his deeply pessimistic
account, the postwar German malaise all but eclipses the horrors of the Third Reich
and the Holocaust; the real tragedy for Syberberg is not Hitler but what came after
him. . . . For Syberberg, art—and only art—is the true victim of the Holocaust"
(124). In retrospect he sees racism and nationalistic hybris in the films and finds the
book troublesome.

Influenced by the attacks on Syberberg is also the dissertation by Stephen D.
Slater of 1992.[36] Although devoting much attention to the concept of *felix culpa* in
the *Hitler* film, he concludes that the book of 1990 changed the public's
understanding of Syberberg's cinematic work. He thinks that "further ambiguity has
now been introduced into a film that thrives on multiplicity of meaning and the
contrast between image and sound" (233). Adopting the prevailing interpretation
of the book in Germany, Slater concludes that the ethical integrity of *Hitler* has
been undermined by anti-Semitism and nationalism (235).

The attacks on Syberberg continued for a while, also in scholarly circles. One
example is Bernd Kiefer's study on the use of montage in the director's films.[37]
Written in 1991 for an interdisciplinary lecture series, the text examines several of

the early films up to *Parsifal*. The first half offers a useful overview of the theory of montage in modernism, antimodernism, and posthistoire. But increasingly, the author takes his cues from Syberberg's publications rather than the films. In the second half he takes care to coordinate his conclusions with the views on Syberberg prevailing in the German press. Therefore, in spite of many helpful observations in the first half, the second part of the study invites objections. Kiefer concludes that Syberberg's quest for identity does not refer to the individual or subject, but to a collective (245). He considers Syberberg's aesthetics of montage to be authoritarian and totalitarian. As illustration he quotes in his concluding lines a phrase in *Vom Unglück und Glück*: "Das zum Kunstwerk gewordene Leben des zum Staat geronnenen Volkes" ("The life, turned into a work of art, of the people that flowed into a state," 184). This is posthistoric aestheticism, he thinks, and blind to any consequences on the political level and therefore alarmingly modern, that is, indebted to modernism. This implies, or so the readers will conclude, that Syberberg's aesthetics is close to the views on art in a totalitarian society, such as the Third Reich. Two details in the text strengthen that conclusion. A footnote states about Syberberg, "Especially his attitude to National Socialism must be seen as shameful for him" (230). That influences readers who might still be unfamiliar with the debate in Germany. And then the quotation contains two words, *Volk* and *Staat*, belonging to the taboo vocabulary popular in Nazi days. But unintentionally, the example also illustrates the pitfalls of quoting phrases out of context. Kiefer's text includes 48 footnotes documenting quotations from Syberberg's publications (six books, one interview). All but five of these refer to very short fragments embedded in Kiefer's sentences. By combining snippets so eclectically one can prove almost anything. Syberberg's prose requires consideration of the context. A closer look at the selected phrase above can serve as an example for how the context determines the meaning of a fragment.

The phrase appears in a context describing a chain of metamorphoses. First the artist reacts to loss and elevates it to tragic art. Of this arises theater that is now turning into film. The last sentence of this passage captures the transformation also in two words expressing stages in a process: the ephemeral theater, *das flüchtige Theater*, is solidifying into art, *zur Kunst sich festigt*. The theater turned film as art is the unstated subject of the next sentence: "Und erlöst im ewigen Jerusalem seiner Wünsche nach Totalität der Bilder und Töne und Bewegungen, endend in der Apokalypse der Auflösung? Das zum Kunstwerk gewordene Leben des zum Staat geronnenen Volkes, des in diesem Jahrhundert zum Krieg sich verhärtenden Reiches seines Untergangs" (184). A translation reads no better: "And redeemed in the eternal Jerusalem of its wishes for a totality of images and tones and movements, ending in the apocalypse of disintegration? The life [that was] turned into a work of art, of the people [that] merged to a state, [the people] of the Reich hardening for the war of its downfall in this century." This passage, which constitutes the central part of the transformation chain, contains the phrase quoted by Kiefer. Exasperating as prose, it is typical of Syberberg's composition in words. It consists of two statements showing several apparent parallels, but the first ends in a question mark, the second in a firm period. A conspicuous, repeated feature is the comma that divides each statement into distinct halves. The presence of Jerusalem in the beginning indicates that a variant of the Jewish subject can be "heard," although the name does not serve primarily as a geographic indicator. As the eternal Jerusalem of art's endeavors it represents a spiritual ideal, a restored paradise, while retaining the association of a community. At this stage, art is "redeemed" and has fulfilled its wishes, having become a total work of art. The second sentence also includes a work of art, *Kunstwerk*, that grew out of the life of a people. At this point several modifiers in the genitive vie for a link-up. I read it as the life of a people that first "flows" or merges into a state, and then, after the comma, as the people of the Reich that hardens or ossifies. Its life turned into a work of art in the second sentence may still entail tragedy, but it shows no link to a spiritual center comparable to Jerusalem. Its state, *Staat*, is a secular concept. The first sentence includes the past participle *erlöst*, "redeemed." It suggests the effect of art in its ideal state. The second sentence contains *gewordene* and *geronnenen*. They are also past participles indicating past actions or processes. *Geworden* (become) parallels *erlöst* by referring to a change, but without the spiritual dimension. *Geronnen* is a strange choice of verb, meaning "flowed" or "streamed." But moving like a river still expresses the progression of the process. If one accepts the resulting state to echo Jerusalem, then where in the first sentence is the element corresponding to the *Volk* or *Leben*? Suddenly the adjective *ewig* begins to pulsate, sending out signals. The reader may remember the discussion of *ewig* and *immer* in chapter 4 where the Hitler ghost speaks from Wagner's grave. By transgressing several language barriers (Hebrew, Greek), translation provided the chain of *ewig/immer-tameed-*burnt offering-*holocaust*. Syberberg reactivates it here. Behind the smoke of *ewig* hides the Holocaust suffered by the community that finds its contrapuntal correlate in *Volk*.

Stepping beyond the commas, one finds both continuations to lack a subject-verb structure. They are merely modifying phrases built around a present participle. In both cases, this present participle expresses a final stage of a development, "ending" and "hardening." *Sich verhärten* can also refer to the end stage of an organic process, such as becoming sclerotic or indurated. In either case, the participles point to a destruction of the condition in each first half. Although the *Untergang* of the *Reich* looks like a parallel to the *Apokalypse*, the latter borrows its term from Bible language, the other does not. Both second halves contain a temporal element, or so one thinks at first about "eternal" and "in this century." They might function as contrasts. And what in the first half expresses a wish for totality of the ideal *Gesamtkunstwerk*, hardens in the second half into the total war of a totalitarian *Reich*. In other words, on one level one recognizes several parallels between the two statements. But on another level they look quite different. The "German" variant does not sound like a simple repetition. The parallel dimension of the second structure suggests the fugal "answer" repeating the subject voice, while the differences reveal also the continuation of the subject voice in counterpoint. *Auflösung* functions as a codetta that modulates to a different key.

Actually, that word possesses three musical dimensions, namely the resolution of a dissonance, the cancellation of a signature, and the disintegration of a key or tonality. In any case, it introduces a change. Read merely at face value, the *Apokalypse der Auflösung* may entail death, or only dispersion, as in the diaspora, expulsion, and emigration. And as the last word of the first sentence, *Auflösung* relates to the last word of the second sentence, *Untergang*. *Auflösung* begins with a prefix that often indicates an upward movement. *Untergang*, on the other hand, expresses a downward movement. This contrast suggests the presence of a quasi-musical inversion in the second sentence. And finally, *Auflösung* shares its root forms, *Los* and *lösen*, with *erlöst* or "redeemed." This resembles the frequent transformations of Hebrew words, especially participles and nouns derived from them (Reichert, 158). Equally unusual in German prose are the absence of a subject in the first sentence, the pile-up of genitive forms, and overall convoluted syntax. Syberberg has added an overlay of Hebrew characteristics and selected vocabulary flexible enough to imitate musical dynamics.

As links in a chain of transformations, both sentences include the notion of art under changing conditions. Also noteworthy is the question mark following the destruction in the first statement. The section relates a disaster but leaves it open-ended. The other sentence seals the downfall with a period. Following these two sentences, the chain continues with art as film that deteriorates into business. Viewed in its context, the phrase containing *Volk* and *Staat* forms the step leading to the phase with a *Reich* and war. The progression refutes Kiefer's use of the quotation. He chose it to support his thesis, and it includes mainly the political dimension. His study targets not only montage in film aesthetics, but especially Syberberg's *Kulturmontage*. With such emphasis on the implications of its use in modernism and postmodernism, one may wonder why the author ignores Syberberg's book on photography in the thirties, in which he comments on modernism. One also wonders why he ignores the director's cinematic work following *Parsifal*. Does this contradict his conclusion too strongly? And why does he ignore the director's program in the *Filmbuch* that identifies music as the important factor shaping his work? This also affects Syberberg's use of the montage technique. When Kiefer presents Syberberg's aesthetics as "alarmingly" modern and entailing "dangerous" consequences, he chooses an interpretation supporting the accusations in the German media. Thanks to his scholarly overview and eclectic incorporation of mostly very short fragments, he distorts the facts more convincingly than the journalists were able to do.

Sometimes the disapproval assumed much more outspoken modes of expression. For example in mid-March 1993, Syberberg's appearance at a public event caused a protest demonstration.[38] The city of Düsseldorf held an exhibit on cultural identity, and Syberberg was invited to give the opening address. It examines if people in the West had betrayed their identity: "Haben wir im Westen Eigenes verraten?" His observations that many of the old ideals had been abandoned sound familiar by now. But they were of little interest to the protesters who demonstrated with a sit-down strike and calls for boycott.

A different assessment on the book of 1990 is offered by Stephen Brockmann.[39] He characterizes Syberberg as "one of the most prolific and persuasive thinkers about modern German identity." Taking his cues from the *Hitler* film and *Vom Unglück und Glück*, he offers an examination of the film, an overview of its reception, and the issues it shares with the book of 1990. Then he places the book in its historical context. He recognizes that Syberberg's thought had remained consistent over the years, and that his views on art echoes much in Nietzsche's *Birth of Tragedy*. Unlike most German critics, Brockmann takes Syberberg seriously in his description of West German art as promoting the ugly, abject, and sick. He outlines the condemnation of the book in the German press and concludes: "But this fact alone indicates neither that Syberberg is fundamentally wrong, nor that his thinking does not reflect important currents in contemporary Germany. On the contrary: Syberberg's marginalization and the allergic reactions to his thinking inside Germany may well indicate that he has touched a raw, but very live nerve" (57). As a self-proclaimed and now actual outsider Syberberg has embraced a tradition dating back to Nietzsche's *Unzeitgemäße Betrachtungen* and Thomas Mann's *Betrachtungen eines Unpolitischen*, and, Brockmann adds, also the conservative revolutionaries of the Weimar Republic. Without accepting all of Syberberg's ideas, he reaches the conclusion: "It is possible that what we are witnessing, then, and what Syberberg so bafflingly represents, is a postmodern rebirth of the politics of cultural despair" (59).

The reviews of *Vom Unglück und Glück* in Germany differ from many of the critical articles appearing later by being emphatically negative. In spite of Syberberg's unchanged views, the political development shifted his assumed position from the outside to the right. Sometimes called merely a confusionist, he became increasingly identified variously with neo-Nazism, ultra-rightism, neo-conservatism, and the "New Right." These terms have clarified somewhat in the public consciousness as the years passed. Hence many articles now refer to him as belonging to the New Right. The term applies to a relatively small faction in a surprisingly diversified political landscape. Neither close to the conservative leading parties, CDU and CSU, nor the handful parties on the far right, this group consists primarily of intellectuals and artists. By publishing extensively, they contributed to the debate on German identity far beyond their numbers.[40] Undoubtedly, Syberberg expressed many views shared by the New Right. He was, for example, disappointed with the conservative parties' refusal to redress the expropriations of 1945–49. This caused him to publish repeatedly an open letter of complaint to former Chancellor Kohl on his Web site.[41] As increasing numbers of journalists and academics began to examine such issues as identity and the taboo topics, these have gradually become part of the mainstream discourse, and in some areas the lines between the political right and left have blurred. Although Syberberg in the last decade has been grouped with the New Right, as have Botho Strauß, Wim Wenders, and Peter Sloterdijk, he may sooner or later again be seen as an outsider in opposition to a majority. He has reminded his readers on numerous occasions that the path does not lead to the left or the right, but right through the middle.

Chapter 14

From Tower to Cave

In the early nineties Syberberg no longer needed to assume the role of an unwelcome son in his homeland. Now he was one. It became more difficult to secure funding for his projects. He had long complained about that, for example in *Der Wald steht schwarz und schweiget* (585). In that book he also outlined the plan for a film project called "Tower Fragments," (586). Only parts of the outline could be included in later films. But the title attracts attention. What significance would the concept of a tower have for the film or its maker? One possible inspiration might be Goethe's *Turmgesellschaft* in the novels about Wilhelm Meister. But in history and literature a tower often functions as a prison or a retreat of isolation. One of the planned fragments in *Der Wald* focuses on Montaigne, who withdrew to the tower on his estate in Aquitaine. Another item in the list mentions Hölderlin, who, after his collapse, spent the second half of his life in the now famous tower in Tübingen. In these two cases a tower served as a residence of isolation. Maybe Syberberg also contemplated a withdrawal to a lofty refuge? The idea of a tower seems to fit the progression of his work. He returned to Hölderlin in the nineties and included some of his poetry written in the tower in the theater program *Hölderlin. Solo für drei Stimmen*. Edith Clever recited. The concept may even support the possibility of contributions to the "Turbund" Web site. *Tur* is the archaic form of *Turm*, with *Turbund* meaning "tower society." And if the tower has windows, the view may offer more far-reaching vistas than ground level. This position might support new combinations of outlook (*Aussicht*) and insight (*Einsicht*). A quasi-musical progression (and Syberberg has remained consistent in his compositional mode) might compare the elevation of a tower with a high pitch. A fugal progression makes one anticipate an inversion sooner or later. And it occurred in 1997, when Syberberg descended into Plato's cave with his *Cave of Memory*. But until then, he sought refuge in his metaphorical tower. While nurturing concentration and creative activity, it also brought him closer to stormy winds. The storm he himself had unleashed with his book in 1990 did not subside so soon.

Dozens of comments in Germany display a high degree of unanimity. Their reaction to Syberberg's views also reflects a widespread paranoia with the past and political correctness. As the years passed, the German search for identity began to gain more nuances. In 2004 when Bernd Eichinger produced a movie about Hitler's last days, *The Downfall* (*Der Untergang*), the press did not accuse him of being a Nazi. While one has to look long and hard in Germany to find any parallels to American flag-waving and flag-wearing as expressions of patriotism, a change in attitude manifests in many ways. Movies and television programs again explore German topics, including the problematic past. The same goes for literature, painting, and pop music. And still one finds reluctance to accept this trend in the German press. For example, a recent report about the move towards a normalized national identity in *Der Spiegel* still reveals suspicion and discomfort.[1] And yet, the tone is strikingly different from the treatment meted out to Syberberg and others sharing his views fifteen years earlier. In his case, the venomous reaction by the press had at least two reasons, the rejection of his presumed opinions as well as animosity against the man.

Although not alone in his views, Syberberg's publishing outlets at home were for a while restricted. But he remained in touch with the international community. For example, he published an article in *Cahiers du Cinéma*.[2] The autobiographical text relates how classic French movies by Cocteau and Carné influenced him in his teens. The author had mentioned them already in his *Filmbuch*. Considering his emphasis on roots as the nourishing element for identity and art, one notes with interest how the article runs counter to expectations: The movies that inspired him were not German, but French. Another part of the article deals with the recent past. He was, for instance, able to revisit his childhood home after 40 years' absence. Walking through the rooms of the house, he was overwhelmed with memories. The experience resulted in a script which he apparently had not been able to translate into a film yet. In retrospect one recognizes that this wish found at least a partial expression in the film version of *Ein Traum, was sonst.* The article also mentions his renewed interest in photography.

Other activities included travels to retrospectives or stage productions of the monologues. At the 1992 International Festival in Edinburgh, for example, one could see many of his films, while at the same time *Ein Traum, was sonst* ran in live performances in the King's Theatre.[3] After a screening of *Hitler* during his stay in London later that year, a discussion with the audience resulted in an audiocassette.[4] In hesitant English, Syberberg answers questions spanning his career as a filmmaker, but not as an author. Sometimes one cannot be sure if an evasive answer reflects unwillingness to discuss a topic, e.g. was the minimalism of the monologues planned or just necessary, or problems with understanding rapid-fire, lengthy questions. But most of the time he shares his opinions forthrightly and eagerly. That applies especially to topics he cares about. One can also observe that in the interview with Florian Rötzer mentioned earlier ("Mit kleinsten Mitteln"). There he elaborates on the aesthetic challenges of creating stage productions for one actress. Later, after the additional experience with more monologues, he was happy to reflect on the concept of space, *Raum*, in his film and theater productions for *Theaterschrift*.[5] Following a discussion with one of the editors, Gerhard Ahrens, Syberberg's ruminations on the theater as space take the form of four letters to Ahrens. Obviously, these thoughts evolved over several months. He recognizes a development in his artistic career. His earlier films took form in studios with few props against projections filling the background. These projections were powerful components of the image, guiding, supporting, or also contrasting the action. Several of the monologues abandon the use of projections. Similarly, he shifted the search for unity in the multiplicity of the *Gesamtkunstwerk* to the "world theater in one person" (156). He found traditional theaters well suited for this focusing, since their architecture can successfully minimize distractions. In his collaboration with Clever she functioned as the "space." The stage was reduced to housing a "system of coordinates" (162). Not until the fourth of these letters does Syberberg add, "Of course we move in spaces of the soul, where else. Where myths obtain and construct their images in art" (164). This might not have been so obvious to readers unfamiliar with his recent projects. *Projection* refers not only to a cinematic technique, but also to a psychological process. As his work probed deeper into the realm of the soul, it left the projections behind, at least for a while. They reemerge in the film version of *Ein Traum, was sonst.* Psychologists might describe the movement as a descent into the collective unconscious without projections, an ascent back through the personal unconscious, and an awakening.

Although Syberberg had devoted several years to the monologue projects, the public viewed him mainly as a movie maker and the writer of *Vom Unglück und Glück.* Either type of work appears to be of little interest in another interview he had with Marilyn Snell of the *New Perspectives Quarterly*, which was subsequently reprinted in *At Century's End.*[6] Knowledgeable about his work, Snell does not ask about his films or publications, only about his thoughts on modern Germany. A brief note introduces him to the readers as a filmmaker, mentioning *Hitler* and *Parsifal*, as a dramatist, essayist, and cultural critic, also as "the man German intellectuals and politicians love to hate." At the time of the interview, Germany had experienced an upsurge in neo-Nazi youth gangs, violence against foreigners, and, in response, wide-spread demonstrations expressing sympathy for the asylum seekers and other victims of discrimination. This situation determines the topics and direction of the interview. The brutality of the gangs and their extremism, which is also anti-Semitic, frightens Syberberg. While a threat, the anarchic violence has resulted, he thinks, from years of repression targeting much in German history. Unpopular opinions or facts have long been silenced. He sees the eruptions of violence as a protest of the disenchanted opting for the taboos as a form of protest. At the time of the interview, the unemployment, especially in the eastern half of the country, had not yet reached its destabilizing extent. Soon and still years later, it would exceed 20%. Wishfully Syberberg views the gangs only as a "wound" festering from long-time neglect, thereby minimizing their political implications. Later he would express his horror more directly. For instance in his Web diary of March 30, 2005 he states that "all is not well in Germany," mentioning hordes of skinheads (www.syberberg.de). The other topic of the interview with Snell concerns art and the demonization of aesthetics as something tainted by fascism. He reiterates that art should help conquer an ugly reality and point the way to something better. That includes linking up with a legacy despoiled by the Third Reich and reaching beyond it into the past. He wants his art to pass through it and to overcome the ugliness that characterizes much in contemporary society (*At Century's End*, 121). Again he emphasizes the necessity of art in a framework of catharsis and atonement (124).

Another interview-cum-article with John Rockwell appeared in the *New York Times* in 1992.[7] It demonstrates clearly the difference between Syberberg's treatment at home and abroad. In an introductory overview of his cinematic oeuvre, it also differs from the prevailing assessment by naming *Parsifal* the film with the widest distribution. Although the monologues represent a noteworthy artistic development, Rockwell thinks they have appealed to a smaller segment of the public. Syberberg admits that Clever's cooperation over several years may have hurt her career. But as a protest against the central value of money today, he will no longer market or promote his work. Rockwell mentions the director's book of 1990, the charges of anti-Semitism, and Syberberg's denial. The article characterizes him as "an aristocratic, Romantic German idealist and esthete who longs for his lost childhood on his father's estate" (C15).

The remains of Syberberg's childhood home would indeed preoccupy him more and more, as one can recognize already in *Ein Traum, was sonst*. Despite the aggression in the German media and his continued artistic endeavors, one notes a steady return or progression towards "old positions." In one publication of 1993 he looks back at the time when he filmed Bertolt Brecht's plays.[8] These amateur activities in 1953 when he was seventeen turned out to be formative experiences. Seventeen years later he created a film documentary of the old rolls, *Nach meinem letzten Umzug*. Another 22 years passed before he revised and reissued it on video under the title *Syberberg filmt bei Brecht*. This edition gained considerably more attention than the film version, as also the attitude toward Brecht was changing. Syberberg's texts appeared in the fourth issue of *Drucksache*, published by the Berliner Ensemble. This was the stage ensemble Brecht directed in East Berlin. The issue focuses on the *Urfaust* production that Syberberg filmed. The first of his texts in it, "Aus der Zeit der letzten Unschuld," reminisces and reflects on that experience. The author also weaves in the complementarity of Brecht and Kortner as two masters from whom he learned. He furthermore recognizes the return to the theater in his own work, the different aesthetics dictated by the stage as studio, and the opportunity for a fresh start in the cinematic arts in the form of a "new innocence." Another section of the issue contains a selection of his photographs from this period. The concluding text, "1971 — *Nach meinem letzten Umzug*," offers an excerpt from the soundtrack on which Syberberg's comments alternate with those by Hans Mayer. Barely three years after the release of this video, the German-speaking countries commemorated the 40th anniversary of Brecht's death. And in 1998 followed the 100th anniversary of his birth. Needless to say, Syberberg's video became a treasured component of the numerous symposia devoted to Brecht all over the world.

Syberberg's return to the Brecht documentary signals several shifts in his creative career. His interaction with the Berliner Ensemble had taken place in a theater, not a cinema. Although he had not strayed far from the stage in most of his films, he now appears to have left the movie theaters behind in favor of live acting and video recordings for home viewing or television. With many of the monologues planned for the stage as well as video, he retreated from the movie world. This withdrawal began with *Die Nacht*. Less conspicuous is his new role in this phase. For ten years, up until *Ein Traum, was sonst*, he both directed and, sometimes, worked behind the camera. But in the 1990s one observes a trend towards self-effacement as a director. Both in the film credits and in the theater programs Syberberg deemphasizes his name, at one time even reducing it to mere initials. While continuing to direct Clever in one-woman stage productions, he appears to have abandoned also the filming, or at least the claims to any credit for it. It looks as if he had reduced his contribution to that of photographer and documenting reporter, returning as it were to his status during the Brecht performances of 1953. For example, in 1993 he directed Clever's performance in *Hölderlin: Solo für drei Stimmen* and the following year in *Nietzsche*, but no video recordings of these productions are available on the market. He recorded at least part of the *Hölderlin* program, as evidenced by excerpts on his Web site. When one, for example, consults the Web site of the Hebbel-Theater (hebbel-am-ufer.de), where the performance premiered, one discovers in the archive links several other productions listed with Syberberg as director, e.g. *Edith Clever liest Thomas Bernhard* of 1990. However, he does not refer to them as his own work or even collaborative efforts. But at least the *Hölderlin* production followed the pattern of his previous theater projects by appearing on stage in Germany and at festivals and special events abroad, e.g. Paris, Rome, and Madrid.

The concept of *Hölderlin* continues the handling of literary texts in monologue style. The subtitle, "Solo for Three Voices," announces the multiple roles Clever assumes. She again slips in and out of the identities of Hölderlin's fictional characters Hyperion (= Hölderlin) and Diotima, and of Wilhelm Waiblinger, who describes his friend's condition in later years, which he spent in the tower of his caregiver's house. While this "soul drama" may thus consist of several figures, most of them express Hölderlin's words, relaying his thoughts. Friedrich Hölderlin (1770-1843) wrote most of his works in the first half of his life before his idealized Diotima, Susette Gontard, died in 1802. Then his illness struck. Syberberg commemorates the 150th year of the poet's death. A contemporary of Kleist, friend of Hegel and Schelling, and prominent representative of German Idealism, Hölderlin developed in his literature themes that also characterize Syberberg's works, e.g. Germany. Central is his emphasis on the tragic. The tragic presupposes faith in the divine. It presents the outcome of human action as divine force or will, often as punishment. This aspect of the tragic dominates Hölderlin's translation of Sophocles' *Oedipus*, where the title hero must come to grips with his guilt. In the translation of *Antigone*, where the title heroine transgresses the laws by burying her dead brother, the nature of the tragic gains more nuances. She does not think she has sinned against the gods, revealing her private view of her relationship to the divine. Many Hölderlin scholars also see a patriotic element in the treatment of the subject, e.g. Wolfgang Binder.[9] Furthermore, he recognizes in it a tacit shift from the ancient Greek to a "Hesperian," or Western, philosophy (197–98). Similar thoughts and references to Hölderlin's translations inform several of Syberberg's texts, most of all the notion of the tragic.

When Syberberg took the *Hölderlin* program to a retrospective in Madrid in the fall, Clever performed it live. The remainder of the event was a multimedia combination of films and exhibits. Viewers could walk through a series of rooms with props, projections, costumes, and three-dimensional recreations of settings of the other monologues, including some backdrops.

While Syberberg was preparing the *Hölderlin* project, he also devoted attention to an issue that stirred the passions in Berlin and far beyond the city's borders. The authorities decided to close the Schiller Theater in Berlin, the largest German stage coming close to being a national theater. Unlike most cultural institutions, it was funded at the federal level, not at the state level.

During the summer preceding the final decision, Syberberg joined other artists and intellectuals in protest. Einar Schleef was one of them. They spoke to the public in a series of lectures and debates in the foyer of the theater. The Berlin press regularly reported on these events and carried on the debate, but all the efforts could not prevail. The closing of the flagship theater became the loudest statement of the government in a newly reunited nation, Syberberg pointed out in several texts. Faced with formidable fiscal problems, the federal government decided that culture was expendable. A year later the Schiller Theater reopened, but now as a stage for musicals and light-weight entertainment. Thus the demise of the distinguished home for serious drama proved Syberberg right. As he had emphasized in *Vom Unglück und Glück*, the world of the arts in post-war Germany had deteriorated from an inspiring influence to escapism. The fate of the Schiller Theater served as a representative example. It also confirmed Syberberg's fears. The forces governing the reunited country had not reassessed and adjusted their thinking and policies. Western structures were imposed on the East, which was simply annexed. Worse, the majority of East Germans eagerly adopted the ways of West Germany, forgetting the ideals that had nourished their aspirations. The opportunities for a new beginning that Syberberg cautiously and faintly hoped for in his book evaporated. Except for the mounting economic woes, much remained the same after the reunification. This disappointment must have filled Syberberg with a grim satisfaction. The course of events made him a prophet whose predictions came true.

Some of Syberberg's thoughts triggered by the fate of the Schiller Theater found their way into his next book, *Der verlorene Auftrag* (The Lost Mission or Mandate).[10] One could describe it as volume 2 or the continuation of the book of 1990. But at 103 pages it is only half as long. It consists of three sections: photos of Clever in the monologues, including *Hölderlin*; ten chapters with individual titles, and a lengthy section called *Nachträge* or "addenda." The volume concentrates on the arts close to Syberberg's heart, with insights and comments updated to reflect the recent past. The ten chapters show more cohesion and a clearer style than the book of 1990. But the addenda section reintroduces the aphoristic structure of the previous book. Most text blocks in it are separated by an asterisk except for a numbered sequence, and only a few begin with individual headlines. Although not dated like diary entries, these passages were in part inspired by current events, bringing the commentary up to the summer of 1994, after the filming of *Ein Traum, was sonst*. Again Syberberg includes himself as a topic. One learns, for example, what happened to an 8-page-long interview ready for publication in *Stern* in June 1994. The new chief editor of the magazine, who had just left *Der Spiegel* after 25 years there, suppressed the article. Syberberg includes some of his statements from the interview at the end of the book. Apparently the interviewer had solicited his views on Jewish and Gentile Germans, the topic at the core of the furor in 1990. Syberberg recapitulates his earlier comments on traumatic history and loss of identity. He then points out the difference in experience affecting most Germans and the survivors of the Holocaust. While the latter might have experienced Auschwitz personally or through family members, the former's experience was linked to wartime traumas, such as bombardment or deportation, followed by the official suppression of the memories. When one speaks of German history, Syberberg maintains, one must include the experiences suffered by the Germans as well, since such large-scale suffering contributes to the formation of identity (102–3). But such views were still unwanted in a popular magazine, leading him to some more unwelcome conclusions. Writing in "Freudian style," he states that Nazism is tribal history. It has entered the souls of people and settled in their genes, even in those who may not have known their Nazi grandfathers. He also compares the current neo-Nazis with the Erinyes, the torturing spirits of revenge. He uses the ancient idea as something that goes on haunting people as long as they remain dishonest to themselves.

This return to the taboo topic clearly ensued from Syberberg's experience of the *Stern* interview. Other references to Jews or Israel occur peripherally, as for instance in the comments on the reopening of the Schiller Theater. Its debasement as a stage for pop entertainment revives the memory that the "liberators" had wanted a similar conversion of Wagner's festival theater in 1945. This was prevented by the returned emigrés, who "saved the culture" (101). Syberberg is now more careful in separating the influence of the emigrés from that of the "leftists" who courted them in the book of 1990. He places the blame for the malaise in cultural life on the Gentile Germans with no room for distortions.

Most of the book discusses cinema, theater, or art in general. In view of the recent controversies surrounding him, he observes that the democrats' inner emigration is now art that is different (47). Apparently he includes himself among the democrats in a non-democratic environment. Although removed from mainstream society as an artist, he is neither alone nor does he claim to be. As observed about the monologues in chapter 12, his work shares many characteristics with postdramatic theater, and one can recognize a similar outlook also in the book. With Hölderlin in fresh memory he repeatedly returns to *Oedipus* and *Antigone* and the issues associated with these tragedies. They may be central to the aesthetics of postdramatic theater, but somehow Syberberg appears to arrive at the topics independently. For example, while Lehmann's book stresses the importance of affect and breaking taboos in postdramatic theater, Syberberg does not brandish these elements in his late films and stage work. Of course he wants to provoke an affect in the viewer, but in a subdued way sparking reflection. And the taboo consists in transgressing the boundaries of traditional drama and cinema. He may move with the trend while exploring a field, only to create something new of the old, especially by combining the best suitable features of several arts. He may view his efforts as saving film and saving theater. In spite of the pared-down format, the result still retains echoes of the *Gesamtkunstwerk*. This concept carries the stigma of taboo, even today. In the eyes of the general public, though, he breaks the taboos more in his books than in his films and stage productions. However, *Der verlorene Auftrag* offers little that might arouse the same indignation as before.

The main topic is the mission of art. It has nothing to do with box office success, the author emphasizes. Nor is it related to the mandate (also *Auftrag*) claimed by politicians when pretending to fulfill the wishes of a majority. Instead he varies formulations already presented in several earlier publications: To keep alive the memory of the past, thus depriving death of its finality (78). That would enable art to survive and instill meaning in the history of life and country (14). While the author's works offer examples of possible strategies to revive the moribund arts, his remarks on the contemporary art scene reveal skepticism about the prospects for succeeding.

While still writing his book, Syberberg also completed the filming of *Ein Traum, was sonst* and worked on the preparations for a project on Nietzsche. Not quite incidentally, this took place in 1994, which marked the 150th year of Nietzsche's birth. The initial plan included Einar Schleef as performer, who died in 2001, was a recognized author, stage designer, painter, and director, but also a difficult person. Nonetheless, Syberberg admired his talents and put up with his human shortcomings, including unreliability. Presumably due to illness, Schleef canceled his appearance shortly before the premiere. He was supposed to recite from *Also sprach Zarathustra* in Weimar as part of the "Kunstfest Weimar" in June. The even more famous Heiner Müller agreed to replace him, but came down with the flu two days before the event. Undeterred, Syberberg turned to Hartmut Lange, who supposedly presented at least part of the program.[11] More recent photos on Syberberg's Internet diary suggest that he took part in the presentation himself (e.g. March 9, 2005). But since he does not identify the photos as hailing from the actual program for an audience, one can only assume they show him reciting to a public. The premiere took place in the Reithalle of the palace, a building with a long and checkered history. Not only did Nietzsche eventually live and die in Weimar. The town also ranks as the home of Goethe and a long list of other artists and intellectuals.

Perhaps in anticipation of seeing Einar Schleef or Heiner Müller perform, a number of television crews and reporters attended the event. It is not clear to what extent the program was adjusted, but at least Schleef's monologues from *Zarathustra* were replaced by the "Dionysos Dithyrambs." The program also included numerous letters by Nietzsche from 1888 and '89, the period preceding his mental collapse. Five video monitors supplemented the recital with films by Syberberg. They concentrated on the German stages of Nietzsche's life, e.g. the house in Röcken where he was born, buildings and places he knew in Weimar, archival manuscript pages of his "Dionysos Dithyrambs," even views from Buchenwald concentration camp near Weimar. The program concluded with Edith Clever appearing on the television screens, intoning the "Night Song" from *Zarathustra*. The event was preceded by a television interview of Syberberg and followed by a banquet with the dignitaries who also attended the festival in town.

To judge from Syberberg's fragmentary remarks in his Internet diary on March 5, 2005, Schleef appears to have approached him again, trying to make amends. They agreed to another collaborative Nietzsche program centered on *Zarathustra* in Salzburg during the "Sommerszene Festival," scheduled for August 1994. An announcement even appeared on the Internet, but again Schleef let him down in the last moment.[12] "It took place," Syberberg remarked ("Es fand statt"), making one assume that he had anticipated the problem. He again took Schleef's place and recited texts by Nietzsche. Unfortunately he does not elaborate. A similar episode occurred three years later, when Schleef failed to show up with the promised materials for the tenth "documenta" exhibit. Whether their friendly relations survived these tribulations remains unknown. Apparently Syberberg declined to engage in any further joint projects. He did, however, incorporate Schleef into his "documenta" installation of 1997. Also in June 2000 he filmed sections of Schleef's play *Verratenes Volk*, which includes Schleef reciting from Nietzsche's *Ecce Homo*. Syberberg recorded this from the audience, seemingly repeating his role in the Brecht documentary. In many respects, Einar Schleef serves a representative function in Syberberg's oeuvre. He was a mixture of genius and human frailty, a very German artist and a symptom of his time. Besides, the focus on Nietzsche not only includes the poet-philosopher's attack on Germany and the anti-Semitism of his day, but also dwells mostly on the period shortly before his collapse. This parallels Syberberg's pessimistic view of Western, especially German, decline in the arts and culture in general. Sadly, Schleef was also approaching his end, succumbing to heart disease the following year.

Another opportunity to discuss German film and his favorite topics offered itself in an interview of Syberberg by Edgar Reitz in 1994.[13] The German filmmaker Reitz may be best known for his three cycles called *Heimat*. The interview explores many topics, among them genius, real and inner emigration, and art with long-lasting relevance or value. Again one reads about art trying to overcome death, aiming at immortality (158). Also that the war-time memories of the German majority differ from that of the victims of the Holocaust, and that the memories of the former were suppressed and repressed for a long time (161–62). One recognizes a gentle rebuttal in Reitz' concluding remarks, which also touch upon his own *Heimat* films. But overall, Reitz agrees with Syberberg on many issues and expresses some of these shared views in the introduction to the book in which the interview appears.

The impetus for the interview was the commemoration of 100 years of cinema. It invited reflections on the history, current status, and future of cinema, especially German film. Reitz recorded 25 movie makers on digital video in his interview series and incorporated bits and pieces of them in the film *The Night of the Directors* (*Die Nacht der Regisseure*). It premiered at the Berlin Film Festival in 1994. Not only does the "documentary" include Syberberg, the other 24 filmmakers, plus older colleagues, but it also demonstrates the possibilities of digital manipulation of the screen image. For example, Syberberg and his colleagues do not really sit together on the first few rows of a fancy Kinemathek in Munich. Nor does Leni Riefenstahl really sit behind them. Many of the situations and constellations in which the "actors" appear were created digitally, pointing towards an entirely different era of visual arts and technology.

Over the course of a few years, the allergic reaction in the press to Syberberg subsided considerably. But a flare-up occurred in '95 at a symposium in Munich where Syberberg presented a paper. Also scheduled to participate was Diedrich Diederichsen, the pop-theoretician who had published a venomous article about him in 1992, as mentioned in chapter 13. He canceled because of Syberberg's presence.
[14] The title of the conference was "Das Rechte," not meaning the political right, as in right versus left, but the ethically, as in right versus wrong. The titles of the presentations and the speakers make it abundantly clear. The speakers included foreigners and Germans, some of them Jewish, all of them prominent. The reason for Diederichsen's cancellation therefore looks peculiar. Syberberg called his presentation "Das Rechte—tun" (To Do the Right Thing, or To Do What's Right). An expanded version was published the same year.[15]

The print version, *Das Rechte—tun*, consists of 22 oversized pages of tightly printed text. It continues the debate launched in 1990, but in a more academic style. Containing only one reference to his latest film, it is also considerably less autobiographical, at least on the surface. The author has arranged the material into ten numbered chapters, each more or less devoted to one issue. Identifying his topic right away as focusing on art, he also clarifies the title. He means it in the sense of the proverb, "Tue recht und scheue niemand," or "Do what's right and don't be afraid of anyone." Since the people of reunited Germany have all been "liberated," they enjoy much freedom of choice. Chapter 2 ponders on the nature of this freedom: Freedom from what? for what? Some sections develop opinions only hinted at in the previous books, but he emphasizes repeatedly that *das Rechte* means the morally right, not the political concept. To do what's right entails freedom from conformity as well as opposition to the mainstream (4). From then on he examines aspects of the artist's predicament. The prerequisites include such classical experiences as hubris, guilt, punishment, suffering, grief, the tragic, artistic form, and insight. Interwoven are also the negative forces and results, the "hell that needs heaven" (5). Without mentioning Martin Luther's name, the author introduces the word *Ablass*, or "indulgence," to evoke the abuses that led to the Reformation. Luther had initially protested against the sale of letters of indulgence by the Church. Such documents "granted" forgiveness for sin and replaced atonement. Now the term applies to the abuse and debasement of art that ought to promote redemption. It also marks the author as being in league with the reformer. Applied to the current state of affairs, Syberberg observes that German society and especially the artists have not dealt with the guilt and trauma of the Holocaust honestly and constructively: "And the consequence of this dealing with indulgences in matters concerning Auschwitz is the escape into the musical" (6). The fate of the Schiller Theater serves as his example. Going further back in history, the author uses the Bayreuth Festival to illustrate opposing forces affecting the arts. No longer called the founding fathers, the emigrés Adorno, Bloch, and Hans Mayer saved the festival after the war in spite of Wieland Wagner's closeness to Speer's aesthetics of light and the Wagner family's political history. One step still further back leads to a discussion of film in the Third Reich and "will to art." *Kunstwille*, a concept at home in German art history, is the urge to create art in a lasting, representative form. It elicits the question if the form of the *Kunstwille* during the Third Reich could also be "right" in the ethical sense, as in leading to catharsis. Without this question, Syberberg states, a number of movies, e.g. Riefenstahl's documentaries, must be considered remarkable milestones in cinematic history (10). He does not offer an answer, but introduces with the question another uncomfortable topic. And he asks provocatively if not also much in religious (Christian) art would look dubious when examined under the magnifying glass of the ethically good. This passage, incidentally, did not appear in the shorter conference paper.

Time and again Syberberg brings up topics bound to make mainstream Germans uneasy. He even quotes Mephistopheles' words as if they were his own, "I am the one who wants evil and always creates the good" (12). As this alter ego in human nature he wants to provoke action or at least anger. German readers may find something slightly irritating on every page. Nonetheless, his main points should not offend. Art should not function merely as a seismograph or mirror of its time, he thinks. And time has come to move beyond the traumas of German history, including the Holocaust. The "right" art today should present truthfully the hubris of its time and lament human blindness. Of course the artist must have gained insight into this situation to recognize the predicament. Also the divine remains a central concept, as does catharsis through art.

At times Syberberg sounds doubtful about the prospect of art with a mission, especially in passages describing the cultural decline. But the concluding paragraph introduces comments on recent technology. The computer in particular offers new possibilities. Having participated on screen in Reitz' digitally enhanced film, the author does not focus so much on tricks or aesthetics as on the practical opportunities opening up. The creating artist can now reach the receiving viewer directly. He or she can bypass the publisher, contract, control, and other restrictions. While recognizing the "cold loneliness" of such communication, Syberberg hopes the computer will offer a new freedom that may even support art with a mission. He soon found the new medium to provide exactly the artistic freedom he wanted.

During 1995, the year he turned sixty, Syberberg turned his attention to another artist with a representative value for his oeuvre. This man was the Austrian Oskar Werner (1922–84). As a stage and movie actor and director he early on became a star at home and in Hollywood. American audiences may remember him, e.g., in Kramer's *Ship of Fools*, a role that led to an Oscar nomination, and *The Spy Who*

Came in from the Cold, that earned him a Golden Globe. Against expectation, this phase in Werner's career did not interest Syberberg. He focused on Werner's declining years after he had returned to Europe. Although still appealing to his aging fans, he was treated savagely by the critics for his stage performances. As a consequence, he withdrew from the public for long periods at a time. His status as an uncompromising but suffering outcast appealed to Syberberg, who undoubtedly recognized parallels between Werner's predicament and his own status. He decided to write a book about him.

Oskar Werner and his acting style represented classical theater, now outdated amid waves of new trends. He also concentrated on the classical repertoire. But several factors contributed to the attacks on him. Not only had the classical theater style continued during and after the Nazi years, but also Werner's most influential mentor was Werner Krauss, who had played multiple Jewish roles in the infamous *Jew Süß.* Oskar Werner even honored him by adopting his first name as his own artist's name. Besides, Werner is easier to pronounce than Bschliessmayer. The link to a maligned past added poison to the critics' ink well. Werner's own shortcomings provoked more venom. Also, no longer young, the actor still portrayed such youthful characters as Hamlet and the Prince of Homburg. The latter role was his last public appearance on stage in 1983. It became a slaughter feast for the critics. Their scathing reviews could be collected easily for Syberberg's book project. More difficult to find and much more problematic were the other records of the artist's late career. His children in Austria and California decided after his death to obliterate all vestiges of their father's declining years, leaving for posterity only the memory of Oskar Werner's celebrated early career. They destroyed what they could find of tape recordings, photographs, films, records, videos, and other archival materials. They also imposed legal restrictions on the use and publication of any late works by their father. Syberberg managed to collect copies of some of these suppressed materials, but faced the repercussions of the legal constraints for his book-plus-audio project. He turned to the Internet for his solution. After withholding the manuscript for years and only preparing a few copies for friends, he published the text on his Web site hidden as numerous links in his diary entries of November 13 and 14, 2002. The title page includes Syberberg's name and "Munich, 1995," and the title "Oskar Werner: Von Letzten Dingen." The meaning, "Of Last Things," can of course also refer to ultimate matters in a philosophical or religious sense. Neatly typed and camera ready, the text lacks pagination. It consists of 97 numbered chapters of varying lengths. Hence the parenthetical reference numbers in the following comments point to the chapters, not pages.

Interspersed in the text are 24 polaroid photos of Werner in his last appearance in Kleist's *Prince Friedrich of Homburg.* The actor-director had prepared this production as well as the video recording of it at his own expense (2). In view of the legal constraints, Syberberg restricted the illustrations to these "indirect" snapshots from the video. Another possibility is that he took the pictures off the television screen when excerpts appeared on an ORF program. Obviously the book serves several purposes, foremost among them Werner's rehabilitation. A related objective emerges in the scattered comparisons between Werner's swan song in Kleist's play and Bruno Ganz' portrayal of the same character in a 1973 production in Berlin under the direction of Peter Stein. Syberberg distinguishes them as Werner's soul theater with aura and the other as a mere psycho-drama, in spite of the latter's critical success. Although Werner did not appear alone on stage in all of the snapshots, the focus rests on him as the title character. Much of his dialogue functions as a monologue, allowing Syberberg to draw connections to his own staging of the *Prince Friedrich of Homburg* in *Ein Traum, was sonst.* He too treats the seminal scene as an acceptance of death and the overcoming of it. One might at first wonder if Werner's portrayal influenced his own handling of the scene. But the text claims that he received a complete copy of Werner's video on December 8, 1994, his birthday (2). His own video of *Ein Traum, was sonst* had been completed earlier in the year. Another opportunity to study Werner in the grave scene may have occurred on October 23, 1994. On that day the Austrian television (ORF) and radio commemorated the tenth anniversary of Werner's death. Those programs included lengthy visual and audio excerpts from several of his late works. It would appear, then, that either the family's legal action affected only Syberberg, or the restrictions had been lifted, or that television and radio programmers ignored the prohibition. When Syberberg decided to publish his manuscript on the Internet, he also made the event a commemoration. November 13, 2002 would have been Oskar Werner's 80th birthday. Syberberg may have had one more reason for releasing the material. Early in 2002 Gitta Honegger had published a book in which she compares Oskar Werner and Thomas Bernhard, an Austrian author.[16] Syberberg had shared his Werner study with her, and she refers to the manuscript, quoting from it. She does not pay attention to his assessment, but accepts the condemning reviews of Werner, also there quoting freely from the documentation Syberberg had collected. It irritated him that she repeats as facts what he considers defamation, e.g. Werner's alleged alcohol abuse and Nazi aesthetics. This handling of sources amounts to an unacceptable selection of the "lethal weapons" and a renewed assassination years after Werner's death, he complained, calling Werner a tragic hero and deciding to publish the manuscript to restore the latter's reputation.[17]

Another parallel between Werner and Syberberg is their interest in *Faust.* Syberberg included the end of part 2 in *Ein Traum, was sonst*, letting Clever give voice to both Faust, the helpers, and Mephistopheles. Werner had only recorded an audio version of *Faust*, but with the same one-person treatment of the characters. His plans for a stage version did not come to fruition. Both directors place the opposing forces in human nature in the same person. This internalization is an important dimension of the "soul theater," or *Seelentheater*, as Syberberg mentions repeatedly. When one also considers Werner's place in cinema and theater as well as his rejection by the critics during his late years, Syberberg's empathy for him is understandable. He saw in him a fellow sufferer enduring ostracism by the same forces that Syberberg had to contend with. However, he does not gloss over Werner's human frailties. He portrays him as a vulnerable but gifted artist who refused to conform and give up a treasured tradition. And precisely this refusal endows Werner with the representative value that becomes Syberberg's main topic. The book does not focus on Syberberg as the outcast; Werner functions just as well as an alter ego in that role.

Not surprisingly, the text treats Werner's tribulations in depth, both in narrative form and through excerpts of reviews (e.g. 16, 31). Also the legal prohibitions imposed by the heirs amount to a posthumous assassination, he claims (30). The author even invokes a faint echo of Christ's passion by beginning chapter 84 with *Ecce Homo*, or "Behold this man," as Pontius Pilate said about Jesus. But of course the quotation functions as a quasi-musical chord that also includes the title of Nietzsche's book and Schleef's (and Syberberg's) use of it. As if this did not suffice, the passage mentions how the once celebrated star withdrew to the countryside and learned to love the rural simple life. And this is what Syberberg was in the process of relearning in his own life. Still, the focus remains on Werner's victimization by the press. The development and outcome of Werner's struggle present him as the flawed hero of ancient tragedies and as the representative of a dying culture. Especially the scene in which Werner as the Prince of Homburg takes leave from the world highlights this emphasis in Syberberg's discussion and illustrations. The author returns often to Werner's monologue-style aesthetics, which he of course shares (e.g. 15, 38). He characterizes it as an emblematic art that unites the whole idea symbolically in one person (38). This quest for in-gathering contrasts with the usual division of the poet's ego and human nature in multiple characters. One might wish that Syberberg had elaborated more on the ancient theater's treatment of such divisions. He points out that at one time the individual characters stepped forward from the chorus and engaged in a dialogue with it (48, 49). Perhaps he was inspired to these ruminations by the theater productions of Einar Schleef. More than any other contemporary stage director, Schleef reintroduced the chorus and revived its function in the dynamic between individual and collective (Lehmann, 236–37). But Syberberg does not mention him in this context, nor does he develop the topic further.

The text touches on many subjects. However, the focus remains directed at Werner and art in society. In that respect it continues the ongoing discussion in most of Syberberg's publications. It also shares many of their stylistic characteristics. The prose is relatively clear most of the time, but on occasion the author tests the reader's patience with sentences covering up to 19½ lines (93). A careful reading reveals the same subtexts as in previous books, including Kabbalistic or Neoplatonic concepts and quasi-musical counterpoint. The most obvious hint of the former is the fragment or broken piece (1, 34). The latter accounts for such paradoxes as "cage of a freedom once attained" (47), or inversion-like polyvalent changes like "knowledge that becomes acknowledgment" ("Erkenntnis, die zum Bekenntnis wird," 78). One may also translate it as "insight turning into confession." The theme of a *mea culpa* (but not *felix culpa*) returns repeatedly in the references to the public who did nothing to stop the attacks by the critics. Syberberg includes himself tacitly by choosing *we* as the subject on such confession-like occasions (e.g. 80). So, to a lesser extent, he continues to include himself as a subject variant, but avoids the *I* pronoun. Rather than referring to himself, he mentions, for example, his *Ludwig*, or weaves in the statement, "We live in a dead country," which served as the title of one of his early articles. Other statements modify the incendiary pronouncement of his 1990 book concerning the leftists courting the returning emigrés (93, 96). He also declares a need for entering the "arena" ready for combat, a word implied but not used in his chapter in *Die selbstbewusste Nation*. Many names and literary titles also serve as references to Syberberg's other works. The veiled self-referentiality points backwards in time. True to his music "by other means," he also includes elements pointing forwards. Memling, Mozart, the function of the chorus, and projections in space to be walked through all point to his next project (esp. 50). Actually, the book on Oskar Werner became the companion text and preparation for his next project, which shares the same subtitle.

This work is an installation at the tenth periodic international art exhibit "documenta." It took place in Kassel during summer and fall of 1997. The big companion book to the exhibit includes only an essay about Syberberg by Philippe Lacoue-Labarthe.[18] The smaller guide book refers to Syberberg's work by its English title, *Cave of Memory*.[19] Many reviews call it by its German title, *Höhle der Erinnerung*. Actually one official long version mixes the languages, *Cave of Memory in sechs Stationen: Ein begehbarer Film als Raum*. The "Film to Walk Through as Space" is, however, a cinematic kaleidoscope, or a cinematic experience with the viewer on the move. Syberberg's video based on the exhibit in Kassel uses both short titles and adds the German subtitle *Von den letzten Dingen* (About the Ultimate Matters). One notes that the big companion volume evokes Aristotle's main works in its title, *Politics Poetics*, while Syberberg's pages in the smaller guide relate to Plato. Not only does his title revive the memory of Plato's cave parable and the use of it in *Die Nacht*, but he also includes an excerpt of Plato's text in Greek in the guide book (220–21), as well as on the cover sleeve of the video cassette. Actually, the two facing pages in the guide book show only this cover, with a superimposed list of six names: Schleef, Kleist, Goethe, Raimund, Mozart, and Beckett, plus down in the corners, Plato and Syberberg. The six names represent the "stations" through which the viewers pass. The room was a darkened, rectangular hall with clusters of television monitors and projectors aimed at the walls. The viewers walked through a central corridor or paused in front of films, photos, and texts visible on the screens and the walls. In all, 21 monitors and 10 projectors showed 31 films, each about an hour long. In other words, to see all of Syberberg's exhibit, visitors would have to spend 31 hours in the room. While the viewers had a brochure to guide them through the experience, the following comments can only rely on printed reviews and Syberberg's own two videos. He produced the second one based on the installation's next exhibit venue in Berlin during the fall.

Many of the reviewers saw the arrangement as a slow walk through the center of a cathedral. With the hall being dark, the film projections on the walls resembled church windows or side altars. Such a comparison does not account for the monitors with equally luminous screens. But admittedly, both the layout, subdued light, and content of some of the visuals might support such associations. One also remembers that Syberberg had explored a related but less ambitious format for his exhibit based on *Parsifal*. Not to be overlooked, however, is his reference to Plato's cave. What the chained inhabitants in the cave see as shadow images on the lit wall constitutes an imperfect view of the world. This installation plays with similar ideas. The viewers are at home in a dark environment of limited insight. Their understanding of the world may be more restricted than some of the visuals they contemplate, and even these can only hint at a world beyond. To judge from the first companion video, several of the characters and views in the visuals face struggle, crisis, spiritual anguish, or physical decline. And still, in the second half of it, an increasing number of glimpses focus on a quest and concerns with life beyond death. Underscoring this impression are the sound effects and composition of the video. Assuming that it reflects what a viewer would experience on site, an additional dimension emerges in the second half. The installation is not only an homage to Oskar Werner, but also a requiem for him and what he represents. At least on the video, he can be seen or heard more frequently than any other component of the work.

The six names labeled "stations" represent the main authors, in one case composer, of the visual and audible materials. Visitors to the event benefited from additional identifying signs and screens, while the video offers only a handful identifications. One recognizes, for example, that many of the initial views on screen and monitor show Einar Schleef's production of *Faust* during the protests against the closing of the Schiller Theater. The actors performed at night in front of the building. But clearly this is not the only work shown associated with Schleef. Somewhat enigmatic is the view of people in black passing the camera in single file. Are they the actors directed by Schleef? The situation evokes the gathering of the Grail knights in *Parsifal*.

In contrast to that film, the camera does not stop for long at any one screen here. Perhaps carried by hand, it travels and pans frequently, moving in unpredictable patterns. Thus one cannot tell if all the segments shot from a car moving through Berlin, and that appear interspersed with other views throughout, belong to one film. Most of the views of the city are depressing: ugly tenement complexes, billboards, sections of the Wall, expanses of rubble, and fences everywhere. A sign announces a location as the "topography of terror," referring to the Third Reich political center where the old Radziwill Palace became the Chancellery and the structures on the Wilhelmstraße the home of Heydrich and the SS. Old shots intermingle with new film, making several layers of the past coexist with the present. The segments from Berlin dominate the views from the outside world, and they are not uplifting. Not so numerous, but different are views of stony paths through dense forest and rural landscapes. The only buildings in such segments are a country church and a lonely white house. When the camera does not travel, one cannot always tell if the view belongs to art work, still photography, or live film.

Many of the visual segments on the video derive from cinema, theater, and art. One might consider them extensions of the inner world as well. Oskar Werner appears on numerous occasions, both in stills and film segments, mostly as the Prince of Homburg. But one also sees him as the young Wehrmacht officer Wüst in Pabst's *The Last Ten Days* (*Der letzte Akt*) of 1955. The title refers to Hitler's final days in the bunker under the Chancellery. Especially the still of the young man's face with closed eyes seen from above haunts the exhibit. In his chapter on the movie, Marc Silberman characterizes Wüst's idealism as "redemption of Germany and the German people, and in particular an ideology of Germanness that is tied to traditional values of family, home, and integrity."[20] As a "sacrificial hero" who is killed by Hitler's guards, Wüst expresses in his final moments the message of the movie, "Don't ever say 'Jawohl!'" The handsome face with closed eyes turns into an apotheosis of peaceful death. Almost as often one sees a still of Oskar Werner in his last year, melancholy and frail. In addition to his frequent visual presence, one often hears only his voice reciting from the plays or also singing tunes from Vienna. Besides, his features appear in at least one portrait by Margarethe Krieger. This artist's work is represented with numerous drawings, many or all inspired by *Faust*.

Other still images of art include paintings looted by the Russians in 1945. The most important painting shown is Memling's *Last Judgment* of 1473, to which the camera returns repeatedly. If the camera basically moves along the central corridor and then back towards the door (the frequent fast panning blurs the direction), then the views of Memling's work appears near the "altar" of the imaginary sanctuary. As close-ups of the painting dwell on the condemned tumbling towards hell, one becomes aware that the soundtracks belong to or are closely coordinated with the visual impressions. Up until this point the sound accompanying the images surrounds the stations, be it Oskar Werner's voice, noise from Berlin traffic, or even bells from the country church. At times these soundtracks overlap as the camera moves between their sources. At some point music begins to intermingle. Eventually one becomes aware of the visuals to which the music belongs. A female singer (Hélène Delavault) and an unseen chorus with musicians perform Mozart's *Requiem* in one film. Occasionally her face alternates with another film showing Mozart's handwritten score and a finger following the notes as we hear the music played. It also accompanies the painting by Memling. Most poignantly, the section beginning with "Dies irae, dies illa" (That day, that day of anger) functions as a description of the visible images. And when the chorus intones "Lacrimosa dies illa" (That day will be a day of tears), the light dims as if reacting in horror. A requiem includes also numerous prayers for the person who prays, or in this case, sings. After all, it deals with the ultimate issues, *den letzten Dingen*, both death and judgment. But the text of a requiem does not only serve the prayer. It is primarily a mass for the dead. That purpose makes Mozart's composition a, perhaps the, central component of the work. The text contains six variations of "Requiem aeternam dona eis" (Give them eternal rest), referring to the dead. But which dead? Since Oskar Werner's voice speaks or sings from several soundtracks and mingles with the music, he appears to be the most obvious deceased person for whom the requiem is performed. But the text allows a broader application by referring to the dead in the plural, and they are not only the Christian dead. On two occasions it implores the Lord to grant "them" eternal life, adding "Quam olim Abrahae promisisti et semini eius" (Which once You promised to Abraham and his seed). Thus the Lord is asked to bestow his mercy both on Abraham's descendants and the other dead. The latter would include Werner, Schleef, and other Germans, many of whom had ample reason to fear Judgment Day. Besides, Syberberg has repeatedly described Germany as a dead country. It follows that the Germans and their world, as shown in the installation, and many of the visitors, are dead spiritually, ethically, and/or intellectually. But the darkened cave and most of the luminous images in it present an anguished world closer to death and hell than to heaven. The singer of the *Requiem* is French and thus not affected, it seems. Since the text of a requiem includes prayers for the intercessor as well, the appeal for mercy assumes a self-redeeming dimension. Viewed with detachment, the intercessors appear to be the singer and the audible celebrants of the mass. However, those familiar with a requiem or this composition may repeat the words in their mind or hum along as the finger shows the notes in the film. Such action would make them participants. The viewers who respond by participating become intercessors themselves. They might want to pray along with the singer, "Juste judex ultionis, donum fac remissionis ante diem rationis" (Fair judge of vengeance, make the gift of absolution before the day of reckoning). This *remissio* evokes the memory of the "indulgence" or absolution referred to sarcastically in the text on Oskar Werner. Forgiveness and mercy are not granted with the purchase of a letter of indulgence, but maybe through repentance and prayers. Nor will the government's payments of reparation to the victims of the Holocaust heal the wounds. Only a change of hearts can hope to come closer to forgiveness. And for those already dead, intercession may be the only hope. Syberberg hides the importance of the requiem in the subtitle of his installation. But it emerges as a continuation of a subtext in several of his films, beginning with *Ludwig: Requiem for a Virginal King*. The title character of that film may have enjoyed a privileged position, but he was as fragile and afflicted as, e.g., Amfortas, Hölderlin, Nietzsche, and Oskar Werner.

Syberberg's *Cave of Memory* contains more films and details than can be discussed here. But one more feature in the video from Kassel must be included. On a few occasions one glimpses a close-up of an enigmatic face among the projections. Just as Werner's face as Wüst, it is viewed from above, but with its eyes open. Due to the darkness of the image, one cannot tell if the face belongs to a person or a statue, a man or a woman. If it represents a female presence, it is one of only two female faces in close-ups, the other belonging to Hélène Delavault singing the *Requiem*. Considering the spiritual implications of the *Requiem*, one wonders if the same mystical subtext runs through the installation as in *Parsifal*. If so, then the two feminine units might relate to the versions of the Shekhinah, and the wall projections to the connecting lines of the labyrinth. The six "stations" consisting of monitors and projectors might be compared to the six broken *sefirot*.

The total of 31 lit surfaces does not add up to the 32 paths and *sefirot* of the Sefirotic Tree. But maybe the missing unit must be contributed by the viewer, making the viewer complete the pattern. That would indeed make the installation an "interactive" work of art. The darkened windows that only reveal a crack of light might hint at the "supernal" symbols not affected by the breaking of the vessels. But more convincingly, they serve as reminders of Plato's sun-filled world outside the cave. Syberberg's installation stimulates the imagination to explore several systems promising coherence. One might, for example, expand the imagery of the cave, sanctuary, and Sefirotic Tree with something as personal as an exploration of one's soul. Imagining walking through a hall of mirrors, one experiences the screens as reflections of one's innermost nature. The diversity ranges from one extreme to another in terms of conditions, aspirations, potential, and insight. As usual, Syberberg has not offered any explanation of the work, encouraging the viewer to contemplate the possibilities.

If the video offers a reliable impression of the overall arrangement, the work may exhibit some inconsistencies in nomenclature. For example, the six "stations" represent Schleef, Kleist, Goethe, Raimund (songs), Mozart, and Beckett. Of these creative artists whose works the actors and musicians perform, only Schleef was still alive in 1997. But the plays authored by Schleef receive scant attention on the video, compared to the man himself and his production of *Faust*. By contrast, the name of G. W. Pabst, in whose movie Werner plays the officer, is only mentioned in the concluding credits. Margarethe Krieger's artwork plays an even more dominant role than Memling's painting, but she does not belong to the "stations." Also, if Syberberg is still composing music "by other means," one might expect more leitmotivic use of counterpoint combining thematic variants. The possibility makes one wonder about the soldier seen early in an illustration or painting. A soldier is a warrior, a *Krieger*. Does this image refer quasi-musically to Margarethe Krieger's name? And furthermore, if the Kabbalah informs the work, then the "paths" may relate to the trump cards of the Tarot deck. One of the films actually concentrates on paths through dense vegetation. Several of the other film excerpts show situations comparable with the trumps. For example, the Magician might be Faust. The Last Judgment occurs also in Memling's painting, and other details point to more than one Devil. The car driving through Berlin might be the Chariot, while much in Berlin shows the effect of the Wheel of Fortune. Even the World, usually depicted as a nude woman, appears in one of Krieger's drawings. The soldier duplicates the Knight in the lesser Arcana, etc., etc. As suggested so far, Syberberg's installation invites multiple interpretations, or at least drifts of the imagination. At some point they seem to converge in the pursuit of ultimate questions.

At the end of the video the viewer realizes that it does not include all the films. Thus the impressions described above remain incomplete, perhaps not even accurate in reflecting the overall design. Various reviews suggest that some films appeared with slightly staggered timing on adjoining screens, creating a continuum of "time in space" as the viewer kept walking. The video cassette does not reveal, however, in what arrangement or sequence the 31 films could be experienced. Syberberg only mentions that all of them combined created the space he calls cave.[21] Unlike a film screened in a movie theater, the composite allows the viewer freedom of movement and choice of combinations when reflecting on them. But the viewer's choice is limited to whether or not to study the visuals and to the act of standing or progressing through the hall. In any case, Syberberg has selected what the viewer can see. So, without reminding the public of Plato's parable, the viewers are subjected to the same limited perception as the prisoners in the cave. But Syberberg does not comment on that, only that the "film" consists of the viewer's own combination of impressions.

This hour-long video is the first of two versions. The second video is based on the exhibit in Berlin. After the "documenta" closed in September 1997, Syberberg took his installation to Berlin during October the same year to coincide with the cultural festival "Berliner Festwochen." The companion video has the same German main title, *Höhle der Erinnerung*. The subtitle, however, has changed to *Im Hamburger Bahnhof* with "Live Variante" added. One also reads *Materialien aus dem Raum 'Höhle der Erinnerung'* (Materials from the Room, or Space, *Cave of Memory*) and "documenta 1997," leading one to expect a shorter excerpt. But this version is two hours long. The credits include Anton Radziwill as the composer of four songs on the occasion of the premiere of *Faust* in Berlin in 1819. They were performed in the Palais Radziwill that became Hitler's Chancellery. The songs were added in live recital on five consecutive evenings in the museum. But missing in the credits are three important components: Margarethe Krieger's drawings of Werner as Faust and her series on *Faust*, also Joseph Beuys' and Anselm Kiefer's works in an exhibit hall.

The Berlin video version consists of four lengthy segments of visual content interwoven with several soundtracks in a sophisticated editing process. The visual component dominating the first part explores an underground world, probably the basement of the building where the exhibit took place. A restless camera inspects the concrete surfaces that support pipes, wires, and ducts on an industrial scale. These spaces obviously belong to a huge complex. The setting relates to the title of the installation in several ways. It resembles a network of caves and tunnels. The name of the exhibit building, Hamburger Bahnhof, suggests a past function as a subway or railroad station. The tunnels of the subways of Berlin play a role in *The Last Ten Days*, when Officer Wüst tries to prevent the dynamiting and flooding of the tunnels. Thousands of civilians had sought refuge there against the bombs. Such associations of underground Berlin convert the shown location into an actual cave of memory. The spaces in the video are far from empty. Some halls apparently serve as storage areas, perhaps for the exhibit floors above. Stacks of crates, apparatus holding paintings (*Gestell*), and piles of various materials create a chaotic environment. It may be as chaotic as many people's minds and blocked memories. What the camera does not show is the exhibit room similar to the one in Kassel. On a few occasions the camera pans quickly to a television monitor or a projection surface, but the viewer remains as disoriented as with the first video.

After extensive traveling the camera makes a few short stops in a room that functions as a recital hall cum recording studio. It appears to provide the setting for a live performance of Radziwill's songs by Hélène Delavault, accompanied by Susan Manoff on the piano. This is not the first time the viewers see the singer or hear her voice. Besides, both her voice and the unseen chorus singing the *Requiem* and Oskar Werner's voice accompany the wanderings through the labyrinthine underground, sometimes simultaneously. Equally fleeting is the visual presence of Delavault. She constantly fades into double exposure. Here, near the piano, the first "scene" still plays the music of the *Requiem*. The camera cannot pause long enough to give the viewer an uninterrupted performance. It does, however, return to the singer for the *Faust* songs later. These repeated early glimpses only introduce her and her environment. One notices a series of drawings by Margarethe Krieger adorning the walls here. The *Faust* series, Oskar Werner's face, the female nude—they all appeared also in Kassel.

Via a television screen the camera seems to escape to new spaces while one still hears the *Requiem* and Werner's voice. They continue to accompany the visual meandering, sometimes with the voice strong and the music faint, or vice versa. The viewer's feeling of disorientation grows as both a television monitor and a large screen appear to show a new confusing environment. Not until several people begin to populate the view can one recognize the strange background as Anselm Kiefer's sculpture *The High Priestess*, as for the Tarot card. In German it is called *Zweistromland* (Land of Two Rivers). This marks the entry into the longest segment of the video.

The two artists whose works dominate this section are Anselm Kiefer and, to a lesser extent, Joseph Beuys. Syberberg had listed Kiefer's name in the concluding credits of the Kassel video. Kiefer and Beuys are perhaps the two most famous post-World War II artists in Germany. Especially Kiefer suffered the same attacks as Syberberg for including Third Reich taboo elements in his art. But as Syberberg he has also explored a wide range of history and metaphysical symbolism in his art.[22] Three of the works on which the video dwells relate to the Kabbalah and biblical or Jewish themes. The first is *The High Priestess*. It consists of two library cases holding ca. 200 huge volumes of lead. Set at a slight angle to each other, the bookcases (Euphrates and Tigris) measure 26 ft. long, 14 ft. high, and 3 ft. deep. It takes two strong people to lift one book. Almost half of them contain lead pages with applied photos and other materials. Difficult to access and presumably holding the wisdom of the Western world, this library has become emblematic of Kiefer's work. When consulted, the volumes reveal only oracles. Book 97, for example, contains 74 lead leaves with long hairs attached to them. This evokes memories of his earlier paintings *Margarethe* and *Sulamith*, inspired by Celan's "Death Fugue." He refrained then from presenting Sulamith's ashen hair, inscribing only her name on the canvas.[23] But here, in the depository of the High Priestess, it has been preserved. A smaller variant of the lead library not included in the video is *The Breaking of the Vessels* (Huyssen, 96). With its six labels identifying some of the *sefirot*, it may have served as an inspiration for Syberberg's installation in Kassel.

Another work alluding to Celan is an airplane of lead named *Mohn und Gedächtnis* (Poppy and Memory). That is the title of Celan's volume of poetry in which the "Death Fugue" appeared in its second edition. With stacks of more oversized lead books resting on the wings and dried poppy plants sticking out, this vehicle of memory may not be fit to take flight. And finally, the third emphasized work by Kiefer is a huge "painting" on lead, *Lilith's Daughters*. It features numerous small dresses attached to the surface. Based on Jewish lore, it receives more attention from Syberberg's camera than most of the other works.

The video also includes some sculptures by Joseph Beuys, among them *The End of the Twentieth Century*, an accumulation of stones with holes in them (dead soldiers?), and an unidentified column lying on the floor. One end is shaped like a human bust, making it an overturned herm. That could also suggest an *Irminsul*, as those mentioned in the discussion of *Parsifal*, act 2. With this symbol of emasculation and decline, the selections by Beuys express an apocalyptic, or at least, melancholy, view of the present age. Although not expressly pronounced, also the lead chosen by Kiefer as the material for his sculptures entails melancholy in alchemy and esoteric symbolism. He even made another lead airplane named *Melancholy*, replete with Dürer's polyhedron inside.

On several occasions during the stroll among the artworks, the camera pans quickly away from the screen and returns to other views, e.g. Margarethe Krieger's head of Oskar Werner as Faust. His voice can still be heard. This action of the camera reveals that the viewer observes a film of a film much of the time. The *mise en abyme* situation repeats a feature that is even more pronounced in the Kassel version. When one also considers the exoteric meaning of *mise en abyme*, "position at the abyss," and its implications, it becomes clear that much of what one sees reinforces the feeling of an impending fall, danger, threat, or end of a condition. Although this video lacks the subtitle of the other from Kassel, *Von den letzten Dingen*, the editing includes reminders of the same concerns with ultimate matters. One is therefore surprised at the next transitional episode. It introduces an apparently unrelated and banal view: a men's restroom. Perhaps the clogged-up sink being serviced points to disturbances in the circulation of divine efflux within the Sefirotic Tree? Such speculation is soon distracted by the reflection in the wall mirror: Syberberg with his handheld camera passing by. As usual, then, Syberberg includes himself in his work. But significantly, he does it in the most artless environment poised between an exhibit showing end-time or melancholy art works (those by Kiefer also possessing mystical dimensions) and the next major unit.

The segment showing the art of Kiefer and Beuys employs a range of editing techniques. While some of the panning involves disorienting shifts in visual worlds, most uses of panning are slow enough to seem natural. The occasional zooming, cut, and fade-out also follow cinematic tradition. But the linking of camera takes differs markedly in the following section where double exposure controls the visual progression. The soundtrack, however, moves in the opposite direction. When the visual impression results from one film, the sound often includes two tracks, usually Werner's voice and music. But when long double exposures begin to extend the transitions between takes, Werner's voice disappears, leaving only music to be heard. Beginning in the restroom, music by Radziwill takes over. The camera dwells more on the singer than the pianist. But regardless what else enters the field of vision, the image will alternate between one of the ladies and something else. Recurring most frequently among other views are Margarethe Krieger's drawings to *Faust* inspired by Oskar Werner's recording. This creates a dense composition with numerous "chords" of allusions and connections. One more fact adds to this impression. The singer, Hélène Delavault, exhibits a remarkable resemblance with Margarethe Krieger.[24] The latter was also a friend of Oskar Werner and contributed her copy of his *Faust* recording for Syberberg's installation. Both ladies feature with equal intensity on the other video through the singing of the *Requiem* and the presence of the drawings to *Faust* showing Werner's features. The painting is missing on the Berlin video, but one assumes a related constellation in words, image, and music to be at work. Everything also exudes referentiality, even Radziwill's name. Even if one did not know about the fate of his palace, one might recognize an allusion to the Third Reich in the use of double exposure. Syberberg's consistency imbues that technique with an historical and ideological function.

At this point the credits reappear, making one expect them to signal the end of the video. But no, the film continues with a segment focusing on Oskar Werner. Some of this material appears also in the Kassel version. A series of still photos show him singing the Viennese songs, with the written words attached under each picture like captions accompanying the soundtrack. A comparable effect occurs in the other video when a finger follows the score that one hears being played. The "doubling" of Werner's song makes it look as if the soundtrack invades the visual field, which this time only has room for still images. Even when the stills change to Werner in uniform in Pabst's movie, his voice resounds as if already disembodied. The haunting final image of Wüst with closed eyes accompanies the voice taking leave from this world, "und sag' der Welt Adieu."

The panning to a photo of Werner on the sofa shortly before his death marks a new stage in the sequence. Mozart's *Requiem* returns to the soundtrack. The visuals now alternate between the singing Delavault and Werner as the prince, the transitions consisting of double exposures. And they identify the presence of a Third Reich element. As Delavault sings "Dona eis requiem, amen," the prince accepts his death. But as soon as one hears "Quam olim Abrahae promisisti et semini eius," his voice kicks in again and the music turns faint. Werner reappears as the prince in the seminal late scenes and in strong color. No longer still images, these scenes alternate with glimpses of the singer. Finally, the blindfolded prince claims to have gained immortality, followed by the singer observing him in silence. The end of the *Requiem* coincides with the end of the video. Why did Syberberg not let the credits conclude the work? Did the final version result from sloppy editing? Did he think the video turned out too short and simply added the last segment as an afterthought? Or maybe he planned the final portion like this as a compositional unit from the beginning: The apparent end is not the end. And one remembers the three deaths of

King Ludwig in the film about him. Besides, the *Requiem* needs to be completed.

Some of the materials may be familiar from the other video, but they appear and sound in new constellations. The prayers from the *Requiem* obviously concern Oskar Werner. Not only does the film conclude with an homage to him, but also with an act of intercession in his behalf. Several times Syberberg has stated that his subject must possess representative or emblematic value. Werner clearly meets these criteria. The video shows him not only as Faust and the prince, but also in his frailty and in the role of Wüst. In that role he represents a maligned part of German history. When Syberberg made these videos, the current wave of movies about the Third Reich years had not started. But in the fifties a few movies defied political correctness, *The Last Ten Days* being one of them. And it shows the young officer as an idealistic hero. Therefore Werner as Wüst imbues his representative function with a positive historical dimension. Not all Germans of that era were bad, the video suggests, not even all those in uniform. The clips from the *Requiem* alternating with views of Werner amount to a prayer for divine mercy, maybe also human forgiveness, both for Werner and those he represents. This appeal emerges as the central idea of the installation, at least in the video. But it also presents the subject matter as flawed, moribund, or dead. It does not leave much hope for improvement in this life. The somber conclusion seems to apply to more than just modern Germany.

The two videos based on *Cave of Memory* include only a few hours of selections from some of the 31 films. Most visitors would not spend even that much time viewing it during the exhibit. The scope of the project discourages a proper assessment of its artistic value. But obviously the scope must have been important to Syberberg, as he could easily have reduced it. He had tested a similar but smaller format for part of his *Parsifal* exhibit 15 years earlier. He commented on it briefly in *Der Wald*, comparing it to a cathedral (234). Already in *Ein Traum, was sonst* he blurred distinctions of perception when Clever, who performs on a stage, walks towards the projected background, seemingly entering that environment. It consists of memories, feelings, and thoughts at home in the mind. The *Cave of Memory* presents a similar mindscape with the viewer doing the walking. Of course Syberberg is not alone about combining cinema and newer technology to an enhanced experience. Gary Hill, for example, also created intallations with a comparable physical arrangement: a corridor for the walking viewer through a darkened room with a number of projections on the walls (Lehmann, 436). In Hill's *Tall Ships* the projected images "react" to the spectator's presence by becoming live film. For instance, a distant figure in a projection comes closer to the camera to observe the spectator, then turns around and walks away when the spectator moves on. This "interactive art" dissolves the sense of borders, letting illusion transgress into reality or vice versa. Without mentioning Syberberg, his *Parsifal* exhibit, *Cave of Memory*, or quotation from Plato, Lehmann describes Gary Hill's installation as a Platonic cave, an Orpheus path, and a world of ghosts and shadows where the viewer's action becomes a component of the work itself (437). But this work and many others also exploring digital technology do not engage the viewer spiritually as does Syberberg's installation. Using only still photos and traditional motion pictures on video, he encourages the viewer to reflect on ultimate issues leading to shared prayers. His installation points also in opposite directions. In one respect it explores the latest ideas in the wrap-around experience of art. But it also revives the mission of a traditional sanctuary. The statues and paintings in a church serve pious purposes inducing self-scrutiny, prayer and worship. A cathedral from the Middle Ages constitutes an unsurpassed interactive work of art for its community. Syberberg's numerous statements on art with a mission have "advanced back" to his latest parallel. His installation restores the aura.

The "documenta" and the "Berliner Festwochen" assured the *Cave of Memory* a great deal of exposure, both in terms of viewers and coverage in the press, some of which found its way to the Internet. A reporter for *Die Welt* even claims that the Hamburger Bahnhof museum wanted to acquire the installation for its permanent collection starting in 1998.[25] But needless to say, very few reviews try to grapple with the complexity of the work. Most of them merely describe the physical characteristics of the arrangement. Nonetheless, they often include observations on other video or film exhibits, also at the "documenta," providing an idea of the direction in which Syberberg's art work is moving. Numerous reviewers recognize the work's significance. Although the tenth "documenta" comprised over 700 pieces by 120 artists, Peter Iden concludes his report on the huge exhibit: "Syberberg's *Cave* radiates everything that is missing everywhere else: The force of emotional appeal, lasting radiating power of the arrangement in space, awareness of history and its continued effect in the present."[26] Another appreciative assessment can be found in Jean-Pierre Faye's essay "Retour de mémoire," included on Syberberg's home page. He compares the work with a concert in four movements shaped around Plato's cave, the Faust theme, Kleist's *Prince Friedrich of Homburg*, and Mozart's *Requiem*. He draws associative links between the cave/*Höhle*, and hell/*Hölle*. A different assessment prevails in Karl Sierek's study, "La cathedrale."[27] While informative for its descriptive approach, the text soon reveals its author's bias. He has accepted the condemnation of Syberberg in the German media in the early nineties. When he also sees in the work references to Hitler's Berlin headquarters and Wüst's Wehrmacht uniform, he feels safe enough to characterize it in terms of Nazi "politaesthetics" and as inspired by Albert Speer's monumentalism. He repeatedly compares the layout with an electronic church, but without asking how the concept could guide the reception or viewer's interpretation. He finds only a "conceptual emptiness." The work, he claims, is a postromantic and post-Nazi hybrid that suffers under the load of education and lack of coherence. He cannot recognize any connection between the *Requiem* and the *Last Judgment*, for instance. Seeing only dysjunction, he considers the cathedral merely a blueprint for moving along a central axis. Certain ideas lie beyond the horizon of comprehension, e.g. Plato's cave, even when they are named and in plain view.

The mentioned essay by Philippe Lacoue-Labarthe, "Syberberg: On Germany after Hitler," in the big "documenta" book does not discuss the *Cave of Memory*.

Written in the eighties, it offers an assessment of Syberberg's early work and position in Germany. It functions more as an introduction to the artist. But it includes a statement that applies also to his installation at the "documenta:" "Syberberg's cinema has only one subject: Germany" (480). And as the *Cave* suggests, this Germany is in dire need of redemption. Also, as Plato's parable conveys, only in exceptional cases do individuals escape the fate of the majority. The others remain in the dark.

Syberberg would return to the format of installations several times in the years to come. At retrospectives and art events he would often ignore movie theaters in favor of exhibit halls. He might even add a display of costumes and props from the films shown. After the *Cave of Memory* with its slew of one-hour films, Syberberg appears to have shifted his attention to different creative endeavors. He has, however, continued to show his works at special events, usually with himself present. These often take place in other countries, such as an arts festival in Madrid in 1993, a retrospective there in 1994, a symposium in Buenos Aires in 1999, a comprehensive exhibit in Paris in 2003 or a similar one in Brussels in 2004, to name only a few. As the years passed, he also found more acceptance at home again. A few years made a remarkable difference in the public's reception of the taboo topics. For example, Günter Grass' novel *Im Krebsgang*, Jörg Friedrich's book *Der Brand*, or Bernd Eichinger's movie *Der Untergang* might even ride a wave of renewed preoccupation with the painful past. Fifteen years after Syberberg elicited such turmoil, he is still viewed by many as belonging to the New Right, but no longer as being provocative. The trend towards acceptance of the past resembles a return to normalcy in many areas. Even the question of identity may assume different nuances as the European Union keeps growing in size and power. Still far removed from functioning as a United States of Europe, the Union already wields considerable power over the member states. The Germans have long since given up their German currency and German passport in favor of the euro and European passport. This membership will undoubtedly influence the way German citizens identify themselves, if not tomorrow, then a generation down the road. Perhaps that development also informs Syberberg's requiem called *Cave of Memory*.

By 1997 Syberberg could again attract attention as an artist in his homeland. But one recognizes lingering antagonism in many published references to him. The tone has changed though. A few examples will suffice. In April 1997 Alban Nikolai Herbst presented a book review of Botho Strauss' publication *Die Fehler des Kopisten* in DeutschlandRadio.[28] Strauss had stirred up even more hysteria than Syberberg with his essay "Anschwellender Bocksgesang." Herbst reviews the book in the form of a three-way discussion among Strauss, Syberberg, and himself. The script does not make it clear if all three men actually participated in a conversation. Their statements appear to be, at least to some extent, quotations from their books with Herbst stitching it together. While the controversy looms in the background, they can state their views without interference or counterarguments. A second example is an interview with the exhibit curator Eckhart Gillen in 1997.[29] The occasion was the exhibit "Deutschlandbilder—Kunst aus einem geteilten Land"

(Pictures of Germany: Art from a Divided Country) in the Gropius Building in Berlin. Gillen explains that the included artists represent all aspects of the debate and confrontations about Germany since 1945. They place their finger in the wound, one reads, by disturbing and irritating. To the reporter's reproach that Gillen quotes Syberberg in the exhibit catalogue, he responds that Syberberg's work and Kiefer's mythological searches are central to the topic. Both of these artists say many things would be seen as positive if the Nazis had not also revered them. The art exhibit was supplemented with 70 movies shown over 12 weeks, with the *Hitler* film appearing in the category "German exorcism." A positive and weightier example is Jordi Ibáñez' book *Despues de la decapitación del arte*.[30] Only the subtitle reveals the main purpose of the study: *Una apología de Hans Jürgen Syberberg*. Completed in time for Syberberg's 60th birthday, the book surveys the situation of the arts in Germany over several chapters before focusing on Syberberg. Without discussing the films in much detail, the author analyzes his position within the field of aesthetics. Seemingly at the cutting edge of his chosen areas of activity, Syberberg eludes any labels, such as avantgarde. Ibáñez does not gloss over the statements in the book of 1990, but includes an overview of the feud and a few of the attacks against Syberberg in the following years. The author shows more interest in Syberberg's pronouncements on art than the application of them in his films. Only towards the end of the book does he offer conclusions based on Syberberg's late cinematic work, characterizing the four major monologues as a tetralogy of loss (137–38). Another recent example of renewed interest in Syberberg is Guido Goossens' book *Verloren zonsondergangen: Hans Jürgen Syberberg en het linkse denken over rechts in Duitsland*.[31] In many respects it resembles Ibáñez' study, taking its impetus from the feud following *Vom Unglück und Glück*. Offering a short biographical and cinematic survey, it concentrates on Syberberg's presumed shift in philosophy. The author devotes much attention to Europe's pre-fascist heritage and its fate after the war. Clearly, the development in Germany is observed with interest in the rest of Europe. Readers familiar with Dutch will find it a helpful and up-to-date survey of the intellectual and political scene in Germany.

It is still symptomatic of Syberberg's position in Germany that the most thorough studies about him have appeared abroad. When in February 1998 Germany commemorated the 100th anniversary of Bertolt Brecht's birth, Syberberg participated in the festivities in Berlin. A report in the *Berliner Zeitung* indicates that at least one speaker questioned the propriety of including Syberberg in the program.[32] He appeared nonetheless on the podium with Egon Monk, Brecht's assistant, reminiscing about his formative experiences when he filmed Brecht's rehearsals with the Berliner Ensemble. The four-day commemoration in Berlin included a most eminent public figure: the German president, Roman Herzog. Nothing could better illustrate the change in political climate. After all, Brecht had chosen to return to and settle in Soviet-occupied East Germany. Therefore, as long as the Cold War lasted, the West German schoolbooks and media denied him the recognition he enjoyed abroad. Syberberg undoubtedly considers him a fellow sufferer in that respect. Perhaps he also empathizes with Brecht for other reasons. At least readers might conclude that from an article he published about Brecht's late poetry in 1999.[33] Apart from the directing at the theater, these *Buckower Elegien* are Brecht's only literary expression from his last years in disillusionment. "Caught in his own trap," Syberberg observes ("In die Falle gegangen. Seine eigene"), while emphasizing the concept of wound and sad insight. Brecht no longer wrote about the people dear to him, feelings, or activities. Everything important remained unstated. One needs to read between the lines, Syberberg points out, quoting Brecht's underlined words of Ingeborg Bachmann, "Alles bleibt ungesagt" (Everything remains unsaid). Those words may apply also to Syberberg, functioning as an announcement of withdrawal from public debate. At the same time they remind the reader to look between the lines of Syberberg's texts as well. Considering how engaged Brecht's writings were, even when disguised in historical garb, Syberberg's selection for his own ruminations reveals a shared stage in life choices. As Brecht chose to move to the countryside in Buckow near Berlin, so also Syberberg began to contemplate a retreat from the city arena. His faint hope for rebirth or catharsis of German cultural life faded into disillusionment. He had already made his statement on that topic. Although by no means a taciturn recluse, he chose to disengage from the level of involvement characterizing his career so far.

Chapter 15

Homeward Bound

In April 1999 Syberberg gave an interview in the film journal *Revolver*.[1] The questions display a welcome lack of tendentious journalism, suggesting renewed acceptance of Syberberg by the movie profession and an increasing share of the public. The discourse offers an update of his philosophy as a filmmaker and artist. One learns about his fascination with the latest technology and its potential. Also how his own interactive film project for the "documenta" differs from other similar arrangements by being imbued with thought and intent, which he of course does not divulge. He still thinks that film, as the "music of the future," could function as Germany's voice in the "concert" of nations. The centrality of music in his work is confirmed by his comments on the *Cave of Memory*. The only film of 31 to which he refers with some detail is the one concentrating on Mozart's score. To the sound of a CD recording of the *Requiem*, a mostly invisible pianist reads the score at the piano by letting her finger follow Mozart's handwritten notes. This approach Syberberg considers an alternative to the usual format of televised concerts with their focus on the musicians and conductor. The positive reaction to his installation in Kassel surprised him pleasantly, one reads. Among other topics he reiterates that in the sorry state of contemporary culture, art must express opposition in order to contribute anything constructive. This is not possible when the ruling powers subsidize and thus control artistic expression. The artist must take risks and touch the wounds, he states. In conclusion he announces his disinterest in continued debates. He mentions pending trips to New York and Buenos Aires with his films and the intention to devote himself to his own affairs, not specifying what he means by that. Overall, the interview summarizes his philosophy and announces his withdrawal from the arena.

Of course Syberberg did not mean a complete withdrawal, neither from creative endeavors nor from pursuits involving confrontation. But the main focus of his activities was shifting to a new medium and a more personal project. He had found the Internet. He has not revealed when he decided to establish a home page, but his Web site, www.syberberg.de, has become his primary choice of publication venue. Beginning in 2000 he has constantly expanded it, adding also a Web diary. It supercedes the earlier books of commentary. They, of course, also show a diary-like progression in content. Like them, the diary combines observations on current events with autobiographical notes and information about his oeuvre. He has revised the site several times, updating the materials. Thus in addition to a catalogue in many languages of his books and films one can view clips, even long excerpts, of several of his films. Owning the rights to so much of his cinematic oeuvre, he can afford to ignore the movie business and its quest for profits. And the public has found his site. By early 2005 it had attracted over three million hits, the number increasing steadily. Visits peak during periods when Syberberg is involved in highly visible projects that receive much publicity. For example, on March 2, 2004 during his activities in Brussels, the home page saw 36,000 hits in one day.

One of the items listed currently on the cover page leads to material about such public events, e.g. reviews or commentary. One might wish for more accompanying information about authors, dates, or print sources, but at least the tidbits reveal the traces of continued exposure to the international public. Another part of the menu concentrates on Syberberg's autobiography. One soon recognizes the similarity with such information scattered in his books. It focuses on his early years in Nossendorf and the current situation. The earliest entries (2000–1) contain more text than photos. In some cases even the photos reproduce text, e.g. the father's typed memoirs of his years in Nossendorf during the war.[2] The big difference between the Web site and the books is of course the plethora of pictures now supplementing the texts. Or more precisely: An increasing portion of the information consists of photos while the text has been gradually reduced. The public may recognize some of the pictorial material from his earliest books and *Ein Traum, was sonst*. The oldest material hails from family albums that escaped the plunder in 1945. Since Syberberg indulged in photography from childhood on, he can still include live samples of his earliest home movies. He is less willing to share information about his private life as a husband and father. The material deemed suitable for public inspection draws a protective veil over his family and personal preoccupations. Thus the family cat receives more attention in the diary than his wife and daughter. Nowhere does he mention his daughter's university graduation or share much about his life and home in Munich. He probably decided on this silence to protect his family's privacy.

The section attracting most visitors is the Web diary. With few exceptions, Syberberg has entered some notes or added more pictures on a daily basis from the start. His digital camera accompanies him everywhere, even to the theater. But as with the other parts of the Web site, so also the diary offers a selective record of personal matters. Until late spring 2005 it was supplemented with frequent excerpts of online news, clippings from newspapers or magazines, and stills from television programs. The first few years Syberberg would comment on these additions, but later just include them. This parallels the observations in his article on Brecht. One has to learn to read between the lines. In his case, the viewer can often only recognize through an item's inclusion that the statement or event caught his attention. For lack of commentary the viewers are free to draw their own conclusions about why he found it important or how he reacted to the matter. He would, e.g., frequently include pictures of Palestinian-Israeli war scenes, inviting conflicting readings by his public. But at least on one occasion he did express sympathy for terrorists. The occasion was the theater tragedy in Moscow, when Russian police used poison gas to kill both the Chechen occupiers and hundreds in the audience. On October 28, 2002 the diary pointed out that the terrorists did not detonate the explosives strapped to their bodies. There were many women in the group. Syberberg decided to dedicate the big hall on his property to them and "other women fighters against tyranny." The diary also reflects his reaction to September 11, 2001, not in his own words, but in photos and as quotations of Chief Seattle's speech, first heard in *Die Nacht*, and published statements by Susan Sontag and Charles Simic. Television stills document his concern over the wars in Afghanistan and Iraq. In other words, he has expressed a critical attitude towards U.S. politics indirectly by including excerpts from newspaper articles, etc., for example about Abu Ghraib and Guantanamo Bay.

Some events have obviously lent themselves better than others to support Syberberg's compositional technique. One example of counterpoint developed in his entries in 2003. Occasional photos from the German press suffice to identify the scandals involving two prominent Germans: Michel Friedman and Jürgen Möllemann. The latter, a politician of the FDP, had published an election brochure containing criticism of Israeli politics. That cost him his political career. Branded an anti-Semite, he also came under scrutiny for illegal money transactions and tax evasion. Facing public disgrace and an impending indictment, he opted for suicide. Friedman, on the other hand, was an ex-president of the European Jewish Congress and, at the start of the scandal, a vice-president of the Central Council of Jews in Germany. He was best known to the public as the celebrity host of a television talk show, where he treated the guests as if they were facing the inquisition. This public model of decorum was revealed to indulge in a private lifestyle involving prostitutes and cocain. After paying a fine and staying invisible for a few months, he reemerged and has resumed a place in the limelight. Since Syberberg did not comment on the inclusions, many foreign visitors to his Web site may not even recognize the issues. Most of these copied inclusions referred to international as well as German politics. Gradually the international topics diminished in volume and frequency in favor of issues from the arts or German affairs. For example, on February 26, 2005 he reprinted clips from several online news items about a new luxury Intercontinental hotel opening on the Obersalzberg in the Alps. This happens to be the location of Hitler's mountain retreat, "Berghof." Nearby, tourists can visit the tunnels of his bunker complex.[3] Also in the vicinity stands a documentation center established in 1999 by the Munich Institute for Contemporary History ("Institut für Zeitgeschichte"). It includes a permanent exhibit on the history of Obersalzberg during the Third Reich. To this Syberberg adds some text from his script book to the *Hitler* film, including pp. 228–33 of the English edition and the corresponding pp. 255–61 of the German edition. The excerpts hail from part 4, "We Children of Hell," and concentrate on the opening of a Hitler museum on the Obersalzberg. One can now compare the speeches of the fictional mayor of Berchtesgaden and the tourist director of the museum from the film with the quotations of real-life spokesmen of 2005. The juxtaposition sends shivers down the spine. Now more than ever, Obersalzberg will become a sanctuary for pilgrims sympathizing with its past. Syberberg's sarcastic fantasy morphed into a fulfilled prophesy. He refrained from comments.

But on a few recent occasions, the diary references to current events have included Syberberg's opinion. Such events tend to concern individuals playing a role in his own life. When, for example, Susan Sontag died in late 2004, Syberberg wrote an obituary as only a friend could compose it (December 29, 2004). Another example is his concern for Margarethe Krieger. A few months after the artist suffered a stroke in early 2004, she was denied therapy; her recent art work disappeared while some of it mysteriously showed up on the Swiss market; her caregivers no longer grant Syberberg access to her (no visits, letters, phone calls), and she is being kept like a captive in isolation. Syberberg had promised to help her. Some of his correspondence appealing to various courts for intervention has been included in the diary (e.g. March 3, 2005). So far the legal system has displayed no compassion. Along with materials documenting his efforts to improve her circumstances (scattered letters, photos, narratives), the Syberberg home page also includes a display of her art work with numerous links and photos of her.[4] Some of her work which he owns, e.g. the *Faust* series, went on exhibit in Nossendorf during some cultural events he organized there. They now adorn the walls of the manor house. This concern for Margarethe Krieger and Susan Sontag translated into personal comments in the diary. How different, then, was his reaction to Leni Riefenstahl's death! She died at the age of 101 on September 8, 2003. Not until the 17th does one find a reprint of a brief obituary note in *Der Spiegel*. So yes, he remembered her, but no, he had nothing to add in person.

Syberberg's activities entail frequent travels. These experiences have resulted in numerous pictures in the diary. But not always has he mentioned the reason for the trip. Thus on the one hand he addresses a readership by sharing his entries on the Internet. On the other hand these records and comments are often fragmentary and unclear. In this respect the entries display a resemblance to his printed prose. As with the printed publications, one needs to read the entries with care. They often conceal important aspects. A series of photos with brief or no captions may look monotonous and thoroughly uninteresting to the casual viewer. To some extent they resemble the stills from early silent movies. If shown from a running movie projector, the sequence would yield a section of jerky moving pictures. This latent use of the material echoes Syberberg's earliest home movies as well as similar effects in his films, beginning with *Ludwig*. Another function may also be hidden in the photos: They some times serve as click-on links. More often links are buried in the captions as an obscured underlined word or an asterisk on the extreme right side of a wide format entry. Often these hidden pages contain the central part of the day's entry. Careful reading over several consecutive weeks leaves the impression that the pattern of composition continues, but it is camouflaged better. A certain theme, e.g. the rose, may recur in such variants as references to Kundry/Clever, blooming roses, Romy (=Rosemarie Schneider), or even Syberberg's cat Rosi. The sound-changing use of a coupler on the organ continues with references to dogs, cupolas and *Koppel*, now with the added semantic variant of "pasture." Periodic sexual references take, for instance, the form of male or female nudity, extraction of bull semen, clips about child pornography or the *Vagina Monologues* or *Talking Cock*. One may debate on whether to call this playing games or playing a composition. But one cannot deny Syberberg's consistency.

With no editor proofreading his texts, Syberberg's prose has not improved in syntax, spelling, or clarity. Typos and grammatical slips appear in almost every entry, while sentence fragments dominate the style. Sometimes his thoughts drift faster than his fingers can type, leaving gaps that the reader struggles to bridge. One may also remember the references in chapter 13 to a second language infiltrating Syberberg's German in counterpoint. That may account for the frequent omission of the subject pronoun *I*. He has also continued to refer to himself as *he* or the *child*, especially in the "child's room," when referring to his earliest years. Occasionally other languages will mix in, especially the local dialect he spoke as a child. The lack of concern for style parallels old Tolstoy's prose, which he described already in *Vom Unglück und Glück* (94). In his book of 1990 it looks as if Syberberg wanted to direct the readers' attention to Tolstoy's disregard for language to prepare them for his own liberties. At the same time his idiosyncrasies served counterpoint. Hermetists might also add a note about the significance of language, especially as the Word. But when Syberberg now indulged in the same lax handling of language as Tolstoy, he also established an additional parallel not visible when the book was published. Like the famous Russian, Syberberg has turned to rural pursuits. The childhood home in Nossendorf has become the focus of his interests. This return to roots completes a circular odyssey where end and beginning meet and overlap. One recognizes it in the content of the Web diary and in the preponderance of still photography echoing his picture-taking hobby as a boy.

During spring and early summer 2005, the Web diary underwent a further change. Reduced or gone were the excerpts of Internet materials, personal commentary on them, and clips from printed sources. The daily entries continued, but consisted primarily of snapshots of his childhood world. Perhaps this narrowing in scope resulted from other demands on Syberberg's attention and efforts. Time will tell if the simplification means a temporary curtailment or the retreat to an "old position" reflecting his childhood interests. Gradually, during late summer 2005, some commentary has returned. However, the topics concern only his own little world in Nossendorf. The first half of 2005 brimmed with events of commemoration, most of them related to 1945. But Syberberg, who has always been quick to share his opinion and linked his work to dates of commemoration, refrained from comments. His silence was conspicuous. Again one is reminded of his article on Brecht's *Buckower Elegien* and the statement "Everything remains unsaid." While the Web diary continues, its focus restricts itself to Nossendorf, at least for the time being.

When Syberberg sneaked out of East Germany, he had already spent several years away from the family estate. Soviet occupation and subsequent land reforms imposed expropriation and, for the Syberbergs, a new beginning in Rostock in 1947. The first separation amounted to an expulsion, while the departure in 1953 obeyed an inner urge to continue the wanderings. Repeatedly Syberberg has referred to his life in the West as a diaspora and to his home in Munich as a ghetto as well as a refuge. His tense relationship with the media business accentuated his feeling of being an outsider, or even an exile. Thus his chosen path does exhibit some similarity with the Jewish fate. It probably accounts for the Hebrew dimension in his use of verbal counterpoint. After the reunification the property in Nossendorf began to beckon like a Promised Land. Unfortunately, it no longer belonged to his family. The convoluted saga of reacquisition has received extensive coverage in the Web diary. Following years when the estate was a socialist cooperative, functionaries of the coop gained ownership. One of them even managed to buy several properties at a ridiculously low price, amassing almost 25,000 acres of land. This included most of the Syberberg estate. After the reunification, Chancellor Kohl's government took over vast areas of disputed East German land and drew a line under status quo. A class action suit challenged this ruling, but the verdict of the EU Court for Human Rights in Strasbourg upheld it on March 30, 2005. Its decision grieved Syberberg, but it may not have changed much in his case, since he already had invested large sums of his own money in the pursuit of reacquisition. His persistence paid off gradually, though, as he succeeded in buying back some portions of the former property. One half of the dilapidated manor house was the most important purchase at the time. Recognizing his zeal and tenacity, the current owners demanded unreasonable amounts. They could gain more by continuing to tear down the remaining buildings. The authorities contributed generous amounts to owners who wanted to demolish unsafe structures to make room for rebuilding. One does not find much incentive in such policies to rehabilitate older buildings. Most older real estate in the German Democratic Republic suffered neglect under communist rule. Few or no materials were available for repairs, and in every community people resorted to cannibalizing old structures for usable building materials to repair their homes. Now, after reunification, subsidies became available for clearing away the ruins. On the Nossendorf estate, most of the brick outbuildings and a large stable and barn were demolished as late as in 2000, but not replaced.

Syberberg's persistence engendered more than resistance. He has encountered fraud, sabotage, break-ins, and arson. Occasional vandalism is still occurring. Most conspicuous was the first fire in 2001, which destroyed the central staircase of the bricked-up and locked manor house. The arsonist had gained access through the roof. One can only surmise that a fire-damaged house would net the owner of the other half more in demolition subsidies or insurance compensation than a sale would. It was not the only suspicious fire in Nossendorf, but Syberberg did not give up. In October 2002 he became the sole owner of the core remains of the estate. The welcome was less than cordial. The day before the signing of the contract someone chopped down the only surviving linden tree in the front courtyard. The surrounding land includes the cobble-stoned courtyard in the front and some open land on the other sides. After securing a historic marker for the old house, Syberberg has spent much time and money on rehabilitating the property. Visitors to his diary have been able to observe these systematic improvements on a day-to-day basis. With the help of a few local workers, foremost among them a childhood friend, he has gradually returned the manor house to its historical condition. He places great importance on authentic, or at least historically correct, details. This includes a roof stand for a storks' nest on one building. As parts of the main house began to be inhabitable, he brought in furniture, Margarethe Krieger's framed drawings for the walls, plus the large statue of the Prussian princesses from his films.

With the rehabilitation progressing, he turned his attention to the surroundings and other structures. The neighborhood children helped him establish a kitchen garden, while professionals cleared mountains of rubble left from the recent demolitions by the previous owners. Trees and bushes were planted, while the borders were secured with stone fences and other authentic reconstructions. These measures might stop vandalizing vehicles, but not prevent destruction by humans. Undeterred, Syberberg continues the restoration step by step.

But why, the viewers and public may wonder. Why does Syberberg constantly commute to Nossendorf when his home in Munich offers a comfortable haven? And why all this struggle and expense? The return to his childhood home and its rehabilitation has become his most important current project, if not an obsession. Deeply personal, it represents an advanced stage in a quest. As in Parsifal's case, memories spur the quester on to return and heal the wound. And Nossendorf needs lots of healing, as do vast areas of former East Germany. Like Brecht in Buckow and Tolstoy on his estate, Syberberg also pays more attention to nature up close. Always an environmentalist, he can now contribute actively with constructive measures. He also continues to adhere to the Neoplatonic program that guides his Parsifal. Thus part of his energy has gone to restore the church in Nossendorf. As work progressed, the restorers uncovered medieval freskos that add to the structure's historical value. It can now again function as a sanctuary and center for cultural events. Pictures in the diary document both types of recent activities. When, for example, a White Russian youth orchestra gave a concert there in 2004, Syberberg's property just across the road served the crowd later as the site for refreshments, conviviality, and an exhibit. He had, of course, been instrumental in organizing the concert.

This private initiative to restore a shut-down church is unusual in a country where pastors are civil servants. The *Demminer Zeitung* published an article with photos of Syberberg and the altar.[5] It quotes his comment on the missing spire as a "circumcision of the church." But due to the cost and need for more donations, the first stage concentrated on the interior. Another article in a state journal for church affairs emphasizes Syberberg's wish to restore a "place of memory."[6] Not a cave, but a *place* of memory, a *Gedächtnisort*. Even the word for "memory" has changed from *Erinnerung*, as in his *Cave of Memory*, to *Gedächtnis*. Apparently Syberberg's project entails a related but different objective. He describes his endeavor as addressing the question on "how to heal the open wounds of recent history." With Nossendorf being a typical example of the decay of East German communities, Syberberg's efforts of revitalization hint at a philosophical program. One factor may be his sense of *noblesse oblige*. That may account for his interest in the children coming over to his house. They help him clean up the garden or bake in the kitchen or celebrate Christmas with a houseful of guests. By sharing time with them on constructive tasks he may hope to prevent an easy slide into vandalism and crime.

That may also explain his involvement in a nonprofit organization, the "Törpiner Forum," where he serves on a committee for work with young people. On a more philosophical level, his frequent fragments of text about Nossendorf have often consisted of musings inspired by the seasons, nature, and personal insights. It used to be that culture originated in the countryside, he writes, probably having in mind the etymological roots of *cultivate* and *agriculture*. With the village stagnant at best, time has come to return culture to the rural community. Similarly, nature is suffering due to human action, e.g. through too much concrete or blocking of natural drainage, calling for environmental rescue measures. Besides, sporadic hints "between the lines" in the diary suggest that Syberberg may also envision a more personal center for cultural activities. Not only might his property one day serve as a facility for workshops, symposia, retrospectives, concerts, or exhibits. It might possibly house his archive of films, photos, manuscripts, correspondence, and personal collections. A first step in that direction is perhaps the display of posters of all his films, now housed in the smallest building. But at the time of this writing he appears rather to be exploring possibilities than announcing definite plans. Besides, Nossendorf does not enjoy an ideal location for visitors. Not only does the village lack links to public transportation, but even Telekom considers it too remote and insignificant to provide the kind of technical support Syberberg needs for his webcam installations. Perhaps the restoration effort itself is more important than the result. And at this time much practical work remains to be done. Obviously, the project will take a while. A late stage in this project is the reconstruction of the spire on the church. The restored tower will parallel Parsifal's function as the *sefira* Yesod becoming the *parzuf* Ze'eir Anpin. The latter collects the fragments and completes the restoration process. Syberberg restricts his mission primarily to his own legacy, viewing it as an extension of himself.

With Syberberg present in most of his writings and much of his film work, it seems inevitable that his private efforts in Nossendorf should merge with plans for public programs of an aesthetic nature. An indication of such intentions appeared on his home page in 2000 or early in 2001.[7] These "aesthetic explorations" (*asthetische [sic] Forschungen*) outline a room installation similar to the *Cave of Memory*, but based on his work in Nossendorf. Technically, the new project would go beyond the arrangement at the "documenta," thus constituting a step forward in concept and execution. The viewers should be able to program the projections, getting a variety of possible combinations. Conceivably they could be surrounded simultaneously by visuals from the past, present, and future. Although Syberberg does not mention it, this virtual environment would also relate to his time tunnel in the first act of *Parsifal*. During the transformation music Parsifal and Gurnemanz proceeded forwards in space but backwards in time, as indicated by the flags. This experience can now gain more immediacy when live film and other visuals replace the flags in optional combinations. The views of Nossendorf, one may surmise, would function as a model for Prussia or Germany at large.

A more ambitious plan evolved also in the same year.[8] A 21-page masterplan for Nossendorf, it is actually an application for a grant from the Federal Foundation for Culture ("Kulturstiftung des Bundes"). Syberberg's hope proved futile. He may not have known that Diedrich Diederichsen served on the selection jury. The preamble to the application summarizes the plan as a "spiritual topography of history, to walk through, as the virtual landscape of a life and country." Perhaps the word *topography* raised fears. Most Germans associate it automatically with "topography of terror," for years the headline on a billboard in central Berlin, marking the area of rubble that previously housed the Nazi government headquarters. This sign features visibly in *Cave of Memory*. Another weakening factor may have been the cost of restoring the estate so as to serve as the site for the project. Furthermore, section 8 mentions the hope to establish a foundation that at some point might house the Syberberg archives. The jury chose not to fund the project.

Syberberg's plan envisions a permanent framework able to display both his current and past work as well as a variety of future installations and exhibits. This support structure would include the Internet, an open-air network of paths with "stations" of information, the interiors of the estate manor house and the church for screenings, projections, monitors, and three-dimensional arrangements, even the use of existing movie theaters in neighboring villages. In addition to his own films he wants to show older movies related to the history he concentrates on, including *Kolberg* of 1945, the wartime newsreels, and *The Last Ten Days* with Oskar Werner. He also wants to include films made by the children of Nossendorf. Furthermore, he hopes to display permanently some of his large projects, e.g. the installation about *Parsifal*, now on loan to the Film Museum of Paris. All aspects of these plans reflect present and past conditions while pointing to future possibilities. Thus his "topography" would form a counter-world to the infamous site in Berlin. Not only could Syberberg not realize this dream, but some of the buildings needed for the project were demolished before he could finalize their purchase.

The preoccupation with such concepts as heritage and identity found expression in Syberberg's films early on. In the last major one, *Ein Traum, was sonst*, his own legacy was interwoven closely with that of his home area and Germany. One building serving as a symbolic backdrop in that film is the war-damaged Hohenzollern palace in Berlin. The large copy of the princess statue from the palace even found a new home in Nossendorf. Ulbricht's regime had razed the remains of the old complex in the fifties, erecting a "Palace of the Republic" in its stead. In 2000, with Berlin again the capital, time had arrived to remove the replacement and erect a new symbol of unity. A prolonged and passionate debate erupted in all German media. Two questions dominated the discussions: What should the new "palace" look like, and what function should it serve? Berlin had long been the capital of Prussia before it became the capital of a united Germany. To many, the royal palace had retained the notion of a Prussian relic, and anything Prussian should be relegated to a closed history book. Syberberg felt compelled to contribute his views on the matter. They appeared as a series of three articles in the *Frankfurter Allgemeine Zeitung*. The first one takes issue with the prevailing desire of the politicians to erect the building as a new home for the non-European collections of the former Foundation for Prussian Cultural Legacy ("Preußischer Kulturbesitz").[9] Their main concern was to avoid making it a center for Prussian history, Syberberg concludes. But, he maintains, no center for a German legacy would mean a vacuum, a lack of identity, for the heartland of Europe. The new building should become a center promoting a sense of identity, but not a museum. It should become a virtual place. Since Prussia no longer is or has a country, its identifying center can only be an idea, a spiritual place. The writer visualizes this in terms familiar from the interview in *Revolver*. Projections could recreate every detail of the former palace. Such visuals could also present areas now absorbed by Russia and Poland, their people, languages, landscapes, literature, music, etc.

The second article addresses the appearance of the project.[10] In the meantime it had been decided to reconstruct only the façade of the complex, with the rest being new in design. Syberberg disagrees. The interior should determine the façade. The German planners could learn something from the Poles, who had restored and reconstructed several famous historical buildings. But if that is all the planners can think of, Syberberg adds an alternative suggestion guaranteed to infuriate many readers. One could direct the projections into the air, following the outline of the original complex. Most readers would not think of images in the air, but rather of beams as in Albert Speer's light cathedrals of the Third Reich. On the one hand, Syberberg invites the accusation of emulating Speer's aesthetics. On the other hand, he insinuates that such a solution would serve the way of thinking of people whose inner core cannot be reconciled with a "Prussian" reconstruction. As noted elsewhere, after the disaster of September 11, 2001, he included the light memorial at the World Trade Center in his Internet diary (e.g. March 12, 2002), with the caption "Speer revived. Under a different flag" ("Speer redivivus. Unter anderer Flagge"). One wonders if he also had in mind Winifred Wagner's *U.S.A.*

The inauguration of the rebuilt British Embassy prompted the third article.[11] Its location on the Wilhelm Street revives memories of the history of the neighborhood, later known as the "topography of terror." The author points out that the street had contained several city palaces hundreds of years old. It suffered drastic changes under the Nazis, then Allied bombardment, and finally leveling after 1945. He hopes the return of the first embassy will lead the Germans to consider reconstructing the neighborhood as a center with "history and form" for the future.

Syberberg's preoccupation with Prussia as a part of the German legacy sounded much more acceptable as the years passed. The debate about Berlin as an old and new capital centered largely on its Prussian past, which had been suppressed along with the Third Reich past. The discussion culminated in 2001–2, a year that commemorated Prussia's change to a monarchy in 1701. The new tone can be detected, for example, in the collective headline of three articles in *Die Welt*, "We Want All of Our History" ("Wir wollen unsere ganze Geschichte").[12] The sustained scrutiny of the German past brought with it a renewed interest in Syberberg, resulting in numerous notes, articles, and interviews in German newspapers, as well as public appearances. Gradually the public was also becoming aware of his Internet site. An indicator is, for example, a note in *Die Welt* on January 20, 2001, "Der vertriebene Sohn." It offers an update on his activities with emphasis on the work in Nossendorf, giving his Internet address as a special tip worth checking out. On October 7, 2001 he was the center of attention in a public debate in Berlin called "The Deletion of the Past." The event was part of a series of discussions in the Schaubühne Theater criticizing globalization. This gave Syberberg an opportunity to present his Nossendorf project and thoughts on the topic to an inquisitive audience. The program describes his lifelong theme as a grappling with Germany's fatal history and rebellion against the extinction of historic memory in a society that only knows the present.[13] The debate also touched on the concept of *Heimat* in an era of mobility and on what kind of past can still engender a feeling of identity. On October 9, the *Süddeutsche Zeitung* printed a review of the event that included so many quotations that it looks like an interview.[14] Soon after, the *Ostseezeitung* brought an article about Syberberg's endeavors in Nossendorf.[15] This may be the earliest publication besides Syberberg's home page to mention the less congenial relationship between the returning son and local power brokers. In *Welt am Sonntag*, Susanne Kunckel followed with "Pommern," a descriptive summary ending with Syberberg's Web address.[16] In brief, Syberberg had again emerged as a participant in the social and artistic discourse to whom the public paid attention. Both his aesthetic vision of Nossendorf and the practical efforts to revitalize the place even earned him a nomination for the 2001 cultural prize of the state of Mecklenburg-Vorpommern, in which his childhood village is located.

Throughout the years when Syberberg suffered the ire of the German media he continued to enjoy recognition in other countries. This can easily be recognized in the ongoing screenings of his films. After the retrospective in Buenos Aires, which included the monologues and *Cave of Memory* films in 1999, special events have featured his films every year, increasingly also in Germany. Sometimes it may be just one film that fits a specific framework for a series, on other occasions a cluster of films, or even a complete retrospective. For example, in November 2000 at the "Retour de Mémoir" series in Paris, Syberberg showed films from *Cave of Memory* with Oskar Werner and appeared for a discussion with Jean-Pierre Faye after the screening. He includes Faye's comments on the home page.[17]

It would appear, then, that Syberberg has regained a high-profile position as an artist and intellectual in his homeland as well. When Gitta Sereny published her book *The German Trauma*, she included a chapter on Syberberg.[18] Although it was written in 1978, it appears that many of her observations still apply. As in earlier years, the relationship between Syberberg and the media leaves him often grumbling. In November 2001 he had, for instance, published an article of reflections on current events in the *Frankfurter Allgemeine Zeitung*.[19] Clearly miffed, he reprints it in the Web diary on November 27 along with the much longer version he had submitted. Apparently the editors had not consulted him about the cuts. And when Brigitte Hamann published her book on Winifred Wagner in 2002, she devoted almost a chapter to the documentary Syberberg had made with the old lady in 1975.[20] Syberberg found a few things to complain about that, too, e.g. about how she handled a quotation and the way a television program treated an interview with him. One cannot help wondering if he was not actually pleased with so much publicity, especially since her book became a bestseller and the materials about Winifred Wagner on his Web site attracted more visitors than ever. He entered most of the materials about her as links to the diary in the summer of 2002, later incorporating them in the menu under "Central Pages" along with his film and numerous pictorial links. Whether justified or not, his commentary reveals that he interprets Hamann's book as Wolfgang Wagner's attempt to rewrite history. Hamann depended on him for much of the information. Syberberg had not forgiven him for interfering with his documentary when Wagner realized how revealing it was. Therefore Syberberg now retaliated by including lots of photos from old home movies of the Wagner household. He had gained access to them and apparently copied them while working on the documentary. Much of this material concentrates on Hitler's visits with the Wagners in Bayreuth. One may argue that Hamann's book by no means glosses over Winifred Wagner's friendship with Hitler, but Syberberg saw it as an opportunity to publish his cache of revealing documentation. He may have to wait a long time for an invitation to the Bayreuth dynasty.

The years 2001–2 kept Syberberg busy. His negotiations in Nossendorf required much of his time and energy. He also arranged for his films to be screened and shown on television. In spring 2002 he was invited to the Jewish Museum in New York, where the discussions centered on the *Hitler* film. A close reading of his Web site reveals a steady pattern of film screenings. In 2001 he also participated in a conference in Italy. "Il vento del cinema" is a prestigious periodic symposium devoted to film and philosophy. One of the better known participants, at least in Germany, was the philosopher Peter Schloterdijk. His presentation of Plato's cave as film must have pleased Syberberg in view of his own *Cave of Memory*. The organizers' letter of invitation emphasizes the importance of his films for the theme of the conference and for contemporary film. During this event in May and June 2001 in Lipari on Sicily, several film awards were given, and screenings took place in the old acropolis on the island. Another token of international recognition was an invitation to join the World Arts Council, meeting in Valencia. This entails nominating potential recipients of the award "Valldigna." What a letdown it must have been for Syberberg when he came home from Lipari and learned that arsonists had put the manor house on fire. Somebody obviously tried to prevent him from purchasing the other half of the building. Another disappointment soon followed. Einar Schleef died on July 21, 2001.

A search on the Internet will net a slew of articles and reviews, most written shortly before and after Schleef's death. The *enfant terrible* of the German theater scene had gained Syberberg's respect and friendship. However, Schleef caused Syberberg a series of disappointments when he let him down repeatedly for planned projects in Weimar, Salzburg, and Kassel. Perhaps Schleef's ego would not let him share the limelight with someone who might eclipse him. He was supposed to recite texts by Nietzsche in the Weimar program. His last minute illness did not prevent him from attending the event in the audience. Syberberg assumed some of the task, reciting Nietzsche himself. This may have inspired Schleef to imitate a similar arrangement in his own stage programs later. For example, he recited from Nietzsche's *Ecce Homo* in his *Verratenes Volk*. His novel *Gertrud*, with his mother as the protagonist, inspired Edith Clever to create a monologue theater program of it, with herself in the title role. And his book *Droge Faust Parsifal* shows clearly the centrality of Goethe's *Faust* and Wagner's *Parsifal* in his own thought, and also his kinship with Syberberg. Another peculiar touch of shared (purloined?) ideas surfaced in his direction of Elfriede Jelinek's *Sportstück* in Vienna in 1998. He used a film of a nude man running through the corridors in the basement of the theater, eventually continuing on the roof of the building. This man was surrounded by, or pursued by, a pack of dogs, a *Koppel*. His contribution to the collaboration on *Cave of Memory* in 1997 was supposed to have taken place in similar basement corridors. Syberberg had to complete that section on his own, incorporating the result in the second video from the Berlin exhibit of 1997. Much maligned in the media, Schleef stomped on, gradually gaining recognition from a reluctant press. At his death at 57, he became the center of widespread eulogies. Syberberg contributed an article about him in *Theater der Zeit*.[21] These pages combine memories with characterization. One learns, for example, that Syberberg had offered him six projection surfaces in a collaborative *Cave of Memory*. Schleef had entrusted him with some materials and was supposed to contribute more, including his version of *Faust* to function as a counterpart or variant to Werner's recording (5). As it turned out, Syberberg possessed sufficient film material by and about Schleef to name the first station after him. That inclusion suggests that he attributed to Schleef representative qualities. In the article he only summarizes it as "here in this case, in him, we have most beautifully before us the full richness and misery of a human being and his possibilities in this country today" (5). He also describes Schleef as the only man of theater since Brecht to develop his own aesthetics and one, who, like Kortner, was not able to secure a permanent director position anywhere. But this artist who transformed force and energy (*Kraft*) into form is not dead, Syberberg assures the reader. His legacy will enrich the world he left behind.

Syberberg's Web site includes a great deal more material on Schleef. First of all, the unabridged draft of the article from *Theater der Zeit*, which appeared later in *Einar Schleef: Arbeitsbuch*, is about twice as long as the early printed version, with photos accompanying each of the 13 sections.[22] Here one reads that Schleef and Clever had planned several joint productions, but due to Schleef they did not materialize either (segment 6). Section 8 discusses his aesthetics, unit 9 his personality; number 11 mentions a lost "Parsifal," and the final section concludes with a picture of Schleef's coffin at the graveside. Another group of texts in ten divisions offers more Schleef biography. After having included material about him on numerous occasions in the diary, Syberberg collected them to a Schleef memorial Web site in 32 sections, many of them with click-on links. His preoccupation with this artist indicates that he recognized Schleef's significance. With the latter's revival of the ancient chorus, emphasis on uncomfortable history, inclusion of himself in his work, provocations, passionate persona, and flawed, vulnerable personality, Schleef could serve as a counterpart to Oskar Werner and, one cannot help wondering, maybe to Syberberg. Aesthetically, Syberberg probably viewed him as a complementary or contrasting artist, especially after the monologues. Where Syberberg concentrated the action into one person, projecting the inner dynamics photographically as background, Schleef resorted to choral recitation and action. Where Schleef was loud, Syberberg employs silence or music.

While grieving the loss of this difficult friend, Syberberg was invited to contribute a visual component of an exhibit on Schleef in 2002. This exhibit ran from September 1 to November 9 in the Neuhardenberg Palace about an hour's drive east of Berlin. Already during the summer a retrospective of Schleef's work took place in Hannover. While that exhibit focused on Schleef's creative work, the homage in Neuhardenberg emphasized the tragic awareness of the artist. Named "Einar Schleef—deutsche Szenen," it contained some of the material from the first event. But added were the artist's archive of unpublished work and Syberberg's installation. Technically, the installation blended features explored in Madrid and the two "documenta" exhibits. The three-dimensional props were reduced to Schleef's bed. To create the needed surfaces for projected films, Syberberg resorted to a huge two-story cube standing within the larger hall. Visitors could view the films and stills inside these dark spaces, but their pattern of mobility was more restricted than for the *Cave of Memory*. The bed stood in the middle of the cube on the upper level, its upright pillow serving as an additional screen. Some of the visual material was photographed by Schleef, most significantly that of his dead mother. Other films included rehearsals from his theater work, the nude runner, and planned projects. Most of the material was, however, filmed by Syberberg. His diary of August 31, 2002 offers an overview of the included visuals. Most prominent among them are two excerpts from *Verratenes Volk*. The first hour-long unit features Schleef reciting passionately from Nietzsche's *Ecce Homo*, standing near the edge of the stage. Syberberg filmed it while in the audience and, one suspects, on more than one occasion. This was part of the material Schleef had promised to recite for the joint *Nietzsche* program in Weimar and Salzburg. Syberberg does not mention if Schleef had agreed to the filming or even knew about it. Somehow, then, he got the performance that Schleef had previously withheld from him. Another lengthy excerpt is the dance towards the end of Schleef's *Verratenes Volk*, called *Dies irae*, "the Day of Wrath," inspired by Mozart's *Requiem*. Here Schleef both directs and participates in the scene, with the chorus and himself dancing barefoot but otherwise dressed formally in black. His "play" starts with the expulsion of Adam and Eve from paradise and ends with the day of judgment. One can only wonder to what extent Syberberg's plan for Mozart's composition inspired Schleef's play, especially since the latter reneged on his contribution to the *Cave of Memory*. But he was made to keep his promise, so to speak, by being filmed like this. All the materials Syberberg used in his installations hail from the last few years of Schleef's life. And, he notes in the diary, they all relate to ultimate issues, "die letzten Dinge." This was the subtitle of his text on Oskar Werner and his "documenta" project. Another "tragic" element in his installation is the presence of the chorus. Its revival in Schleef's aesthetics links up with ancient tragedy and with twentieth-century experience. The use of the chorus shows clearly the similarities and differences between Schleef and Syberberg. Schleef does not only project the individual's inner dynamics onto the chorus but also presents it as the people or masses or military power against the individual. Especially the martial aspect characterizes his chorus. Therefore Syberberg could include clips of his *Parsifal* in this installation, especially those of the Grail knights in armor. These excerpts accompany Schleef's thoughts on the opera in *Droge Faust Parsifal* and his own Parsifal project. Would he have agreed to this use of Syberberg's film? On three occasions he had retreated from a joint project with him. It makes one wonder about a detail of the installation. Across from the bed stood a television set which ran a performance of Schleef's favorite German band, "Take That!" With "Take That!" being a group, it could easily represent the chorus addressing Schleef. Facing them, the Grail knights from *Parsifal* appeared on the pillow in Schleef's bed. The constellation suggests a confrontation, perhaps a conflict between his persona and inner nature. However, also typical of Schleef's provocative style and lack of concern for the public, the band's name epitomizes his attitude. Another projection? It could also function as Schleef's last greeting to the world. On the other hand, is it also Syberberg's greeting to the rascal who let him down? Not only had he managed to acquire films that Schleef had promised and denied him, but he had now introduced his own films to join the other's work, and being the survivor, had arranged the installation according to his own judgment, with Schleef unable to play any more tricks on him. Take that, old buddy!

The setting for the Schleef exhibit may have stimulated Syberberg's dreams for Nossendorf. Renamed Marxwalde under Soviet occupation, Neuhardenberg Palace and its surrounding community gained back the original name after the reunification. The restored palace has become a cultural center with ongoing exhibits and events. *Ein Traum, was sonst* was shown there during the summer. Among the festivities celebrating Andrei Tarkowsky's 70th birthday in October 2002 was one discussion program in which Syberberg participated. He holds Tarkowsky's movies in high esteem. Also the events at Neuhardenberg Palace enjoy high esteem in Germany, and the Schleef homage with Syberberg's installation was featured on ARTE on September 28 and with reviews and coverage in practically all media during the fall.

During the fall and winter Syberberg made available increasingly more of his cinematic work on his Web site. Likewise chapters of the manuscripts on Oskar Werner gradually found their way into the diary as links, a process completed on February 3, 2003. On March 27 he gave a talk on Werner in the Film Museum in Munich, illustrating it with the films and recordings he had used at the "documenta." He concentrated on Werner as Hamlet in 1979 and as the Prince of Homburg in 1983. He compared again the latter performance with that of Bruno Ganz in the same role in 1973. Along with such activities Syberberg continued his restoration work in Nossendorf and the preparation for what turned out to be his big event of the year, an installation in the Centre Pompidou in Paris. Named

Syberberg/Paris/Nossendorf, it ran from May 5 to June 6, 2003. It combined a retrospective of all his films with an ambitious use of technology. The on-site arrangement in Paris filled several large halls in the basement level (without windows). The walls alternated between surfaces onto which films were projected and expanses covered with printouts from his Web page, telling the story of Syberberg in Nossendorf. A large cube recreated the dining room as Syberberg knew it in his childhood, but with the windows still bricked up. Another enclosure showed his bedroom. A spotlight focused on several sacks of soil from Nossendorf in the middle of one of the halls, where scattered clusters of chairs invited the visitors to linger and view the films. What separated this installation from his previous ones was the use of webcams. Several monitors and surfaces showed live and in real time what three cameras in Nossendorf recorded, while four cameras at the installation allowed viewers in Nossendorf to watch the viewers and installation at the Centre Pompidou. This reciprocity created the impression of mirroring and virtual presence. Apart from a few technical glitches, Syberberg succeeded in bringing his home in Nossendorf, the "asshole of the world," as he has called the village, to Paris, and vice versa. And in Berlin, people going to the Hebbel-Theater could watch both sets of visuals on large screens in the foyer for an hour before each performance. As if this did not suffice, the Web diary included links to the webcam transmissions during the exhibit. That enabled countless people all over the world to share the views of the cameras through their computers via Syberberg's home page. The images transmitted via the Internet accomplished the blurring of time and space. When Gurnemanz told Parsifal "Here time turns into space," the music accompanied or suggested the "transformation." Syberberg competed with Wagner, since the visual materials represented several distinct eras. They included the Nossendorf buildings and the princess statue along with people at one end, and the films, exhibit spaces, and people at the other end. In both places viewers might even see themselves in the projections. On May 5, Syberberg stated in the diary that it was his objective to bring it all together, "the Third Reich era, the German Democratic Republic in the east, the Federal Republic of Germany in the west, and the reunited Germany." In part he accomplished this with family photos and films spanning 50 years. With the mutual reflections and mirroring he hoped to activate Nossendorf again with the projections of a spiritual and intellectual life. Only the future can tell if he succeeded in that. But his pioneering effort of harnessing *techne* for aesthetic purposes was readily acknowledged in wide circles. In part due to extensive coverage in the French media, in part through his computer-savvy fans, in part through word of mouth, the viewers on the Web exceeded the sizable numbers of visitors at the Centre Pompidou. During the month of the exhibit, Syberberg's home page registered almost half a million hits. The installation itself also attracted a steady stream of visitors, as did the separate retrospective. The films were screened in the cinemas of the Centre Pompidou in addition to those that were projected onto the walls. Syberberg attended the opening reception, later on participated in a discussion evening on May 17, and a radio interview on May 19 ("Tout arrive"). The German media showed fewer and more diverse reviews. While a text in the *Frankfurter Allgemeine Zeitung* on May 15 at least describes the installation and illustrates it with four photos, a review in the *Süddeutsche Zeitung* uses the event to renew the attacks from 13 years earlier. Willi Winkler called this piece "Our Little Farm" ("Unsere kleine Farm").[23] Not only does he find Susan Sontag quite crazy ("ganz schön verrückt") for having praised the *Hitler* film, but Syberberg is a Nazi, a madman, a little bit famous, and, so one reads three times, suffers from megalomania. Needless to add, the greater part of the article consists of an *ad hominem* attack.

The most voluminous publication appearing at this time is a French book published by the Centre Pompidou to coincide with Syberberg's installation.[24] He contributes about 100 pages of texts translated into French, five of them pieces from other publications, eight from his Internet materials, and a profusion of photographs. A 59-page introduction by Christian Longchamp provides an overview of Syberberg's life and oeuvre. It concentrates on the films. Not surprisingly, the bibliography section of secondary literature focuses on French studies. This book may be the only one to list a filmography that includes 100 of Syberberg's early short features for television. All parts of the works section contain more information than found elsewhere, making this book the most informative reference on Syberberg to date.

In a category by itself stands an article in *Sezession* with Syberberg's name listed as author.[25] After an anonymous introduction about him, his work in Nossendorf, and the project in Paris follows the main part of the text. It consists of excerpts of texts by Syberberg. Seven of these chunks hail from the Internet diary, three from his book of 1990, and four from an interview with Syberberg in May 2003, presumably by an unnamed journalist from the journal. The statements are arranged so as to give his view on contemporary Germany. The themes sound familiar. Against this negative assessment Syberberg sets his effort of rehabilitation to benefit everybody, victim and profiteer alike. And if the endeavor is doomed to defeat, he will at least have recorded the process of downfall, much as the ancient tragedies did. In the concluding passage he observes somberly that art does not possess the power to change the development. One can hardly mount effective resistance with civil means. His resignation has been noticeable for some time, but the montage of statements out of context accentuates the pessimism. The reader also questions if he collated the fragments himself. If not, how reliable is the text overall?

Syberberg's admirers in France appear to be less aware of his outlook. Nor did a retrospective of 22 of his films in Paris stop them from scheduling another series for the festival of documentaries in Lussas in the Ardèche during August. Each screening was followed by a discussion, and this intense preoccupation inspired one of the debate organizers, Rochelle Fack, to write an article on Syberberg and his use of memory.[26] Following his intent of dismissing the limitations of time and space, the writer ruminates on his films, occasionally addressing him with questions as if he were present. The approach yields an interesting review of the films. But the Internet project evokes also her irritation. Especially the focus on his personal situation as being representative for many elicits objections. The films and monologues engender admiration, while the use of the personal quest in Nossendorf as a continuation of aesthetic and creative pursuits hits the limit. At least Rochelle Fack reacted negatively. To that one can of course add that all of Syberberg's films contain topics of personal interest to him. But he has now dropped the guise of fiction or documentary, emerging as a visible subject of his continued pursuit.

At this time Syberberg still remains preoccupied with his project, dividing his time between Munich and Nossendorf. In October of 2003 an exhibit on Richard Wagner took place in Munich, with Syberberg contributing his films in which Wagner plays a role, namely *Ludwig, Winifred Wagner, Hitler, Parsifal,* and *Die Nacht* (diary, October 15 and 31). The exhibit space showed the films in their video or DVD sleeves, the Wagner dolls and other miniatures used as props, and the posters in the background. During the exhibit in the Film Museum and the month of November the films were screened in the Arri Cinema.

The next major event took place in Belgium during three weeks in March 2004. The Centre International de Formation en Arts du Spectacle (CIFAS) in Brussels issued the invitation. Syberberg and/or his work could be encountered in three different places. First, Syberberg himself gave a workshop in the CIFAS building, conducted in French and German. Aimed at people in the professions of film and theater, the program grew out of his recent experience: *Nossendorf as a Poetic Space—Cinema in the Age of the Internet.* His restoration of a "place of memory" concentrated on the church, since its interior was being restored concurrently with the workshop. Again several cameras transmitted their film live to Brussels. During these weeks Syberberg's home page received up to 36,000 hits per day. Also shown in the CIFAS building was an installation that combined features from the *Cave of Memory* of 1997, *Einar Schleef—deutsche Szenen* of 2002, and *Syberberg/Paris/ Nossendorf* of 2003. In the Brussels Film Museum one could see one part of a retrospective, the six films of the German Cycle. Several of the monologues made up the other part, shown in the Goethe Institute. Also on display there was a selection of the exhibit seen at the Centre Pompidou. It consisted mainly of printouts from the Internet showing various aspects of the Nossendorf project. The cover title of the entire undertaking was *Poetics of Nossendorf.* Only occasionally did Syberberg refer to the events in Brussels in his diary, e.g. on March 13 and 18, while the reports on Nossendorf continued with few interruptions.

It does not take long for the regular visitor to Syberberg's Web site to realize that the diary currently serves mainly one purpose: It documents his projects in Nossendorf. The larger goal has been subdivided. For example, the webcam component for the CIFAS workshop concentrated on the restoration of the church. With few exceptions, the diary entries included material from Nossendorf, relegating other notes on current events to links. Quite frequently one might search in vain for any text or caption. In May and June 2004, for instance, this silence continued for weeks while the pictures spoke for themselves. On many occasions the only text consisted of excerpts from other printed sources. Thus one learned through such photos that *Molly* was featured in an exhibit in Vienna in June 2004.

Sometimes the diary has ignored quite significant activities. The documentary film *The Ister*, for instance, received the silent treatment, although Syberberg appears in the film. It is inspired by Heidegger's wartime lecture series on Hölderlin's poem "Der Ister."[27] That was the ancient name for the Danube. *The Ister* film describes a journey from the mouth of the river back up to its disputed beginnings in Germany. In addition to Syberberg, the film weaves in lectures by the French philosophers Bernard Stiegler, Jean-Luc Nancy, and Philippe Lacoue-Labarthe. One may assume that Syberberg was included for two reasons, his *Hölderlin* theater program and his emphasis on identity, memory, culture, and roots. These issues are central in the film, as are Heidegger's other ideas about the poem, which centers on the Danube. Made by two young Australians, David Barison and Daniel Ross, *The Ister* began its round at international film festivals in Rotterdam in January 2004 to a reception of praise. But controversy erupted at the screening in Marseille, provoked by Heidegger and his status during the Third Reich. When it screened at the Filmfest in Munich on June 29 and 30, it attracted less attention, at least if the coverage on the Internet can serve as an indicator. But strangely enough, Syberberg too ignored it in his Web diary. Of course he could not claim credit for the work, but his statements contributed to its overall interest.[28] The film quotes his work intermittently before introducing him in person. First, accompanying a segment on the concentration camp Mauthausen, an excerpt from *Hitler* shows Himmler and his masseur. Like a musical theme, the Syberberg component reappears later with a still of the printed program to his *Hölderlin*. In another section it changes back to a clip from *Hitler* again, this time the starry sky with the tear-shaped globe. At one point Syberberg also leafs through the *Hölderlin* program, bringing photos of Clever into view. His long appearance occurs in part 5, presumably in his garden in Munich, although the location is not mentioned. Here he deplores the lost connection to the ancient tragedies, but does not care for "Valhalla" as an attempt to reintroduce a Greek presence in Germany. It is a nineteenth-century German hall of fame seen in the film. A Bavarian king built it as a Grecian temple overlooking the Danube, filling it with marble busts of famous Germans. Not much is said about Heidegger, Hölderlin, or the Danube. So much has been lost since the reunification, Syberberg remarks, including Heidegger and Hölderlin. They do not mean anything to modern Germans. Even the rivers have lost their poetic power. Maybe he is right. But at least the two filmmakers shared his concerns for roots and origins, as they pursued their search for the source of the river. The result is a work of art and a philosophical statement. *The Ister* garnered two awards in 2004, one at the Marseille International Documentary Festival, the other the Canadian Critics' Prize in October.

Occasionally Syberberg's name crops up in the media in connection with other celebrities. One example is his public appearance on August 12, 2004 in Berlin with Bernd Eichinger. Their friendship goes back many years. Eichinger, a scriptwriter, director, producer, and long-time mover behind the firm Constantin Films, helped finance several of Syberberg's projects, including *Hitler* and *Parsifal*. In 2004 and 2005 he caught the media's attention on two occasions, first as the producer of the

Hitler movie *The Downfall* (*Der Untergang*), then as the opera director of Wagner's *Parsifal* in Berlin. Many reporters asked for Syberberg's opinion. When some of them began to put distorted or fully invented statements in his mouth, he had to protest. One learns about this in his diary entries, e.g. of April 4, 200. There one also reads that the main ideas in Eichinger's Hitler movie came from Syberberg 27 years earlier. These ideas included the timing with the dictator holed up in his bunker, Bruno Ganz as Hitler, Goebbels' children providing the tragic element, and all this playing out underground under the Chancellery. But, so Syberberg claims, Germany was not yet ready for such a movie in the seventies, and Bruno Ganz was unavailable for the role, so his own film eschewed the historical portrayal of the dictator. But Eichinger remembered what he heard and used the ideas when the climate had become more receptive. Syberberg's public discussion with Eichinger about his *Downfall* took place just a few hundred yards from the bunker and the Holocaust memorial.[29] The other occasion of widespread media coverage came with the premiere of *Parsifal* in Berlin in March 2005 with Daniel Barenboim directing the Staatskapelle. Eichinger's interpretation became a sensation earning both cheers and boos. While many reviews compared it favorably to Christof Schlingensief's *Parsifal* of 2004 in Bayreuth, mockingly known as the *Hasifal*, some also remembered Syberberg's film and asked for his assessment. In an interview he praises Eichinger's production and points out that it by no means showed derivative or imitating features.[30] He even characterizes the setting in the third act in New York as genial. That act underscores a state of decline, even ruin. One wonders if he does not play on a detail in his film here after all. His *Parsifal* includes a photo of a toppled Liberty statue with a Manhattan background. Other possible signs of inspiration by Syberberg's film may be Amfortas' throne and toga-like draped garment, projections, avoidance of the Grail ceremony, and the non-seductive flower maidens and Kundry. Perhaps the most striking parallel can be seen in the sequence of Syberberg's and Eichinger's films. Both made a film on Hitler followed by Wagner's *Parsifal*. But with that the similarity ends at this time.

In vain does one look for indications of further plans for films by Syberberg. He has repeatedly declared cinema a defunct art, with theater close to the same fate. *Parsifal* apparently marks the turning point in his own cinematic oeuvre. In retrospect, the end of the film with the petrified remains of an icy cold Grail society begins to assume a role beyond the plot. The monologues that followed all contract the dramatic action into one person. In spite of ample drama, even multiple characters, this concentration suggests a philosophical statement. This is underscored by Edith Clever's continued presence beginning in *Parsifal* as Kundry, the immortal, maternal, enigmatic character of many names. In *Die Nacht* she bids farewell to German and Western culture, only to finally await the end at the conclusion of *Ein Traum, was sonst*. As an expression of Syberberg's aesthetic views, she represents a force nourished by the same insights that shaped Kundry, a force ready to disappear, but bound to reappear in a new cycle or world.

But what about the installations, one might ask. Syberberg did not end his creative work with the monologues. Perhaps not *Hölderlin*, but at least *Nietzsche* and the installations all incorporate film. Actually, Syberberg produced a large number of short films for his *Cave of Memory*, but not movie-length feature films. Some of them have been screened to larger audiences, e.g. *Ecce Homo* in Paris. In most cases, however, he assumes the more modest position of cameraman and documenting recorder. Also, in the installations each film constitutes a contributing element in a larger whole. One cannot even be sure if the individual films should be subjected to the same aesthetic standards as full-length features. They serve a different purpose. That applies even more to the visual recordings involving webcams. They are closer to the field work of a reporter. They do not provide the complete or only picture. Moreover, once installed the cameras do not even require a photographer. Not knowing if the results undergo any kind of editing, one is at a loss to apply aesthetic criteria to them. On the one hand, one senses a disappearing act by the creator of the materials. On the other hand, the integration of such visuals into a larger plan presupposes a framework deserving assessment. The visuals may in part claim a utilitarian purpose, such as illustration for the workshap at CIFAS. But the overall scope, integration, and intent somehow transgress into the territory of aesthetics. This is a new field of creativity with films as multiple components. Again Syberberg finds himself at the vanguard of an artistic development. To judge from his plan for an installation at Procida (Italy) in the summer of 2005, he continues to explore this territory. Whether the Nossendorf project will prove suitable for aesthetic purposes only the future can tell. Most of his feature films grew out of topics that interested him. The Nossendorf project affects him even personally. Although he often appeared on screen in the earlier films, e.g. as interviewer, he has now become a subject in the narrative. The home page and especially the diary provide a natural vehicle for including himself. Therefore, not content to feature clips of Clever in a monologue, he can publish photos of himself directing her during rehearsals. Thus, thanks to the visual component, Syberberg can include himself in a diary entry even when the content consists entirely of photos, clips from newspapers or Internet news releases.

The Internet has provided a direct, versatile, and accessible venue for Syberberg's publications. While one still can find articles and shorter statements by him in printed sources, his book-length texts now appear on his home page. What he refers to as a diary continues where the printed books leave off. It permits more variation of textual and visual materials and of hide-and-seek. He can often relay a published fact or opinion without expressing his own view in words. By and large, though, his opinions have emerged eventually, as some topics tend to recur. But unlike the books, the diary allows his personal story and pursuits to fill as much space as desired.

One assumes that Syberberg will be remembered primarily for his films, although he seems to view his published work as equally important. However, he earned his reputation as a filmmaker. It has been difficult to classify him from the beginning. Much of his work clearly disregarded popular trends (e.g. *Pocci, Karl May*), while revealing a critical stand (*San Domingo*) and even a good nose for wide appeal (*Sex-Business*). But the films do not conform to expectations.

Syberberg consistently went his own way. Only with the German Cycle did he begin to develop an image as a public figure. This image was closely associated with his turn towards taboo topics. The documentary on Winifred Wagner became a sensation because of her fondness for Hitler. Then followed *Hitler* and *Parsifal*. The press was quick to draw conclusions about the selection of the subject matter. Ironically, it was the German Cycle that established Syberberg's reputation internationally, without the tarnish of prejudice. Especially *Hitler* and *Parsifal* have engendered a substantial amount of critical literature and have entered university curricula in such varied fields as history, Holocaust studies, psychology, German film, music, German literature, Arthurian literature, and comparative studies.

For a long time Syberberg has been seen as different, difficult, and politically suspect. He likes to present himself as the ostracized victim of a society with an onerous history. Some of the factors accounting for this view of himself spring to mind. For instance, he was born too late to serve in World War II, a fact exempting him from the collective guilt imposed on the German nation by the Allies. Even his father could not easily be branded with that condemnation. So he had to find a different kind of guilt if he wanted to identify with the Germans around him. His repeated litanies of confession attest to such attempts. Besides, the curse pronounced by Jew Süß may apply both to the Germans and any anti-Semites. And, as the Catholic Church still maintains, being human entails a *felix culpa*. The topic of guilt recurs in much of Syberberg's work, often as a personal variant echoing a metaphysical predicament. Thus he is guilty as well as the victim of a guilty majority. His publications containing the confessions present them as failure or wrongdoing in the writer's judgment. They relate to the tragic ensuing from human action. Among the attacks levied against Syberberg have been numerous accusations of arrogance. This is one quality he has not admitted among his sins. In that respect he resembles Parzival and Parsifal. Wolfram's hero does not know the sins for which he is held responsible, suffers for years on his quest, only to emerge as a redeemer at the end. As Will Hasty observes, Parzival gains insight, but does not really change.[31] Only through perseverance can he redeem the Grail society. His tenacity is a defiance related to pride, or *superbia*. This concept remains important throughout the *Parzival*. As a quality in the service of an ideal society of chivalry, it develops into strength of character enabling the hero's mission. Not mentioned by Hasty is a related dimension in the medieval narrative. It affects not only Parzival, but many of the main characters. In the original versions of the story, *pride* and *proud* share an important syllable: *Orgueil* and *orgueilleux* contain *or*, meaning "gold" in several languages. The alchemical subtext presents the "proud" characters and those with *or* in their name as ores containing the precious metal and their mission as refining it to purity. Parzival/Parsifal achieves that through tenacity, confrontations, and transgressions. Like that hero, Syberberg confesses and continues his struggle intrepidly. His first literal transgression was his flight to West Germany. And there the proud man persevered by asserting himself.

Syberberg may have considered himself predestined to emulate the medieval hero, especially when considering his own name. Most American readers might associate the first part of his name with *cyber* and find it appropriate that he has chosen the cyber world for his activities. But the connection to Parsifal extends to his name as well. The Celtic versions of the Grail literature include the story of Peredur, a variant of Parsifal and Parzival. He is also called a fool. In his story, the ugly woman lives at Castell Syberw, translated as "Proud Castle."[32] In the continental parallels, the woman is Cundrie, the character with the many names in Wagner's version. When one also considers Syberberg's interpretation of this figure, several frames of reference merge her to a divine and mysterious symbol. Her Celtic Castell Syberw may be located on the mountain that makes up the last part of Syberberg's name (*syber* = "proud," *Berg* = "mountain"). And the proud element must be refined to pure gold. As Parsifal redeems Kundry when returning to the Grail Castle, so also Syberberg feels he must return to his place of origin to carry out an act of redemption. In doing so he completes the "return" or *teshuva*. That concept was mentioned in chapters 9 and 12. As Heidegger's *Kehre* and Buber's *Umkehr*, the *teshuva* is also associated with the maternal *sefira* Binah (Scholem, *Kabbalah*, 112). Embedded in the linguistic grid are, then, many of the concepts familiar from Syberberg's *Parsifal*, namely the struggle of a quest, remembering one's origins, a maternal or feminine element, and the restoration of broken vessels to new wholeness. The return was initiated with the first purchase in Nossendorf where the repairs continue at this writing. The rebuilt church spire will reflect Yesod's condition. Even the "mother earth" reappears gradually where concrete surfaces are removed. But, one may object, Syberberg does not divulge much about his mother or other maternal forces. Her absence actually fits the symbolic pattern. Edith Clever replaced her for a while, portraying related characters. Also his family members as well as a Nossendorf girl who often visits the Syberbergs may assume the function of the symbol. One may assume that the late stages of the return will include some feminine presence as a symbolic equivalent in addition to the sense of soil and grave. Perhaps even Syberberg's insistence on such vocabulary as *Boden* and *Gründe* in *Vom Unglück und Glück* fits into the pattern of transformation affecting the maternal earth symbol. Finally, almost as an afterthought, one remembers the pre-war picture of the livingroom with a menorah. Is it a genuine photograph or a digitally enhanced image? If original, it might hint at another reason for his demonstrative perception of otherness. One might even suspect that Syberberg's defiance at times wants to provoke attacks and discrimination. His choices suggest an identity at odds with mainstream Germany. He insists on playing the role of Heine as the conscience, even the bad conscience, of his compatriots. In view of his consistent use of counterpoint, this identity may even resemble a double subject. In any case, he has chosen to emphasize difference while drawing inspiration from unexpected, and therefore unrecognized, systems of thought and symbolism. His *Parsifal* offers the best example.

Syberberg's artistic consistency over the years indicates an early resolve. One part of his program, the quasi-musical mode of composition, was announced already in the *Filmbuch*. Another, unannounced component concerns the spiritual and symbolic dimension of his oeuvre. Both have gone largely unrecognized. Critics and scholars have tried to classify him according to popular criteria, assigning his work variously to modernism, postmodernism, and posthistoire. But the labels refuse to stick. One has to search much further back in history for the principles informing his work. Although aligned for periods with other contemporary artists, Syberberg defies classification. His work remains untimely, in Nietzsche's sense of *unzeitgemäß*. And that may be the quality that imbues his oeuvre with lasting significance.

Notes

Chapter 1: The Early Years

1. John Rockwell, "The Re-Emergence of an Elusive Director: Hans Jürgen Syberberg shows his past work and ponders his future," *New York Times*, Sept. 2, 1992.
2. Hans Jürgen Syberberg, "Du pays mort d'une société sans joie," in "Syberberg," ed., Serge Daney and Bernard Sobel, special issue, *Cahiers du Cinéma*, Feb. 1980: 77 (Paris: Éditions de l'Étoile, 1980); subsequent references to this volume list it as "Syberberg." The photograph appears also on his home page.
3. Gitta Sereny, "Hans Jürgen Syberberg: Germany's Most Feared Film-Maker," *Saturday Review*, April 28, 1979: 30.
4. Hans Jürgen Syberberg, "Da un'altra Germania," in *Syberberg*, by Stefano Socci, Il castoro cinema 143 (Florence: La Nuova Italia, 1990), 3.
5. Richard Grunberger, *The 12-Year Reich: A Social History of Nazi Germany 1933–1945* (New York: Holt, Rinehart and Winston, 1971), 127.
6. Hans Jürgen Syberberg, *Die freudlose Gesellschaft* (1981; Frankfurt am Main: Ullstein, 1983), 144.
7. Hans Jürgen Syberberg, *Die freudlose Gesellschaft*, 160.
8. Hans Jürgen Syberberg, interview by Betsy Erkkila, *Literature/Film Quarterly* 10 (1982): 206–18.
9. Judy Stone, "Hans-Jürgen Syberberg," in *Eye on the World: Conversations with International Filmmakers* (Los Angeles: Silman James, 1997), 265; reprint of "A Controversial Film: Seven Hours on Hitler," *Kino: German Film* 1 (1979), 70; and of "Seven Hours on Hitler," *San Francisco Examiner and Chronicle*, Datebook, July 15, 1979.
10. Frederic Ewen, *Bertolt Brecht: His Life, His Art and His Times* (New York: Citadel, 1969), 467–70.
11. Hans Jürgen Syberberg, *Syberbergs Filmbuch* (Munich: Nymphenburger Verlagshandlung, 1976), 63.
12. Sereny, "Hans Jürgen Syberberg: Germany's Most Feared Film-Maker," 30.
13. Buch- und Kunstauktionshaus F. Zisska & R. Kistner, advertisement, http:// www .zisska.de/kataloge/2/343.html (accessed March 25, 1997).
14. Hans Jürgen Syberberg, *Der Wald steht schwarz und schweiget: Neue Notizen aus Deutschland* (Zürich: Diogenes, 1984), 259–60, 466.
15. Hans Sedlmayr, *Die Entstehung der Kathedrale* (Graz: Akademische Druck- und Verlagsanstalt, 1976) and *Verlust der Mitte: Die bildende Kunst des 19. und 20. Jahrhunderts als Symbol der Zeit* (Salzburg: Müller, 1948).
16. Hans Jürgen Syberberg, interview by Erkkila, 210.
17. Eric L. Santner, *Stranded Objects:Mourning, Memory, and Film in Postwar Germany* (Ithaca, NY: Cornell Univ. Press, 1990), 106.
18. Richard Wagner, *Stories and Essays*, ed. Charles Osborne (La Salle, IL: Open Court, 1991), 56–79.
19. Werner Schulze-Reimpell, "Epitome of Artistic and Moral Rigour," *The German Tribune*, May 29, 1992.

Notes to Chapter 2: Name Recognition

1. Wolfgang Jacobsen, "Fritz Kortner: Schauspieler, Autor, Regisseur," in Cinegraph: *Lexikon zum deutschsprachigen Film,* ed. Hans Michael Bock (Munich: edition text + kritik, 1984–).
2. Roger Manvell and Heinrich Fraenkel, *The German Cinema* (New York: Praeger, 1971), 110.
3. W. Michael Blumenthal, *The Invisible Wall: Germans and Jews: A Personal Exploration* (Washington DC: Counterpoint, 1998), 154.
4. Sigrid Löffler, "Christiane Hörbiger: Noblesse, ihre zweite Natur," *Die Zeit,* March 20, 1992.
5. Sibylle Zehle, "Ein Mann, ein Theater: August Everding machte es möglich; München hat sein Prinzregententheater wieder," *Die Zeit,* Nov. 22, 1996.
6. "Romy Schneider: Beichte am Berg," review of *Romy, Der Spiegel,* Feb. 6, 1967, 94.
7. Russell A. Berman, "Hans-Jürgen Syberberg: Of Fantastic and Magical Worlds," in *New German Filmmakers: From Oberhausen Through the 1970s,* ed. Klaus Phillips (New York: Ungar, 1984), 362.
8. Thomas Elsaesser, *New German Cinema: A History* (New Brunswick, NJ: Rutgers Univ. Press, 1989), 25.
9. "Ich muß meinen Gegenstand oder das Thema lieben, um es darstellen zu können, das schließt polemische Filme und Agitationsfilme aus und läßt anderen Regisseuren viel zu tun übrig," Syberberg, *Filmbuch,* 60.
10. Walter Nigg, *The Heretics,* ed. and trans. Richard and Clara Winston (New York: Dorset, 1990), 377–99.
11. Barbara Bronnen and Corinna Brocher, *Die Filmemacher: Zur neuen deutschen Produktion nach Oberhausen* (Munich: Bertelsmann, 1973), 35.
12. Eitel Timm, *Ketzer und Dichter: Lessing, Goethe, Thomas Mann und die Postmoderne in der Tradition des Häresiegedankens* (Heidelberg: Winter, 1989), 22.
13. Hans Jürgen Syberberg, *Die freudlose Gesellschaft,* 242.
14. Rosemarie Puschmann, *Magisches Quadrat und Melancholie in Thomas Manns "Doktor Faustus": Von der musikalischen Struktur zum semantischen Beziehungsnetz* (Bielefeld: AMPAL, 1983), 14–16.
15. Ernst Bloch, *Heritage of Our Times,* trans. Neville and Stephen Plaice (Berkeley, Los Angeles: Univ. of California Press, 1991), 12, 154–57.

Notes to Chapter 3: International Renown

1. Stephen Howarth, *The Knights Templar* (New York: Dorset, 1991), 305–6.
2. Reiner Schürmann, *Meister Eckhart: Mystic and Philosopher; Translations with Commentary* (Bloomington: Indiana Univ. Press, 1978), 3–47.
3. "Ludwig im Atelier der Bildhauerin Elisabeth Ney." Syberberg writes her name here with *th,* since that is how she spelled it while still living in Germany. Her studio-turned-museum in Austin, TX includes a plaster copy of her statue of King Ludwig. Not far away one finds two of her bronzes flanking the entrance to the rotunda of the Texas State Capitol.
4. "Da wird der Künstler zum Priester, Kunst zum Gottesdienst und die Bühne zur Kanzel." This paraphrases Richard Wagner's words in his *Kunst und Revolution (Art and*

Revolution) of 1849, in *Sämtliche Schriften und Dichtungen*, 5th ed., vol. 3 (Leipzig: Breitkopf & Härtel, ca. 1911), 11.

5. Hainer Plaul, "Karl May als Teresias im Ludwig-Film von Hans-Jürgen Syberberg," *Mitteilungen der Karl May Gesellschaft* 12, no. 14 (1972): 33.

6. Peter Wapnewski, *Richard Wagner: Die Szene und ihr Meister*, 2nd ed. (Munich: Beck, 1983), 108

7. Jacob Grimm and Wilhelm Grimm, *Deutsches Wörterbuch*, 33 vols., reprint, dtv 5945 (1854–1971, Munich: Deutscher Taschenbuch Verlag, 1984).

8. Harry Baer, *Schlafen kann ich, wenn ich tot bin: Das atemlose Leben des Rainer Werner Fassbinder* (Cologne: Kiepenheuer und Witsch, 1982).

9. Hans Jürgen Syberberg, *Die freudlose Gesellschaft*, 161.

10. "Urteil im Mai: Sedelmayr-Mord; Lebenslänglich gefordert," *Sonntag Aktuell*, May 2, 1993.

11. Bertolt Brecht, *Die Geschäfte des Herrn Julius Caesar* (Berlin: Weiss, 1949).

12. The historical-critical edition of May's works with Greno Verlag in Nördlingen will comprise ninety-nine volumes, according to Jörg Kastner, *Das große Karl May Buch: Sein Leben, seine Bücher, die Filme*, 2nd ed. (Bergisch-Gladbach: Bastei Lübbe, 1992), 315.

13. Axel Mittelstaedt, "Zur Charakterentwicklung Karl Mays," in *Karl May: Leben und Werk*, by Thomas Ostwald, 4th ed. (Braunschweig: Graff, 1977), 309–30.

14. Annette Deeken, "Träume eines Geistersehers: Zur Ästhetik eines Syberberg-Films," *Jahrbuch der Karl May Gesellschaft*, 1984, 50.

15. Grosz contributed animated film, drawings for backdrops, and designs for marionettes; Roswitha Mueller, *Bertolt Brecht and the Theory of Media* (Lincoln: Univ. of Nebraska Press, 1989), 8–9. In his memoirs Grosz describes his visit to May's home, mentions the spiritual and mystical component in his books, and concludes by linking May's influence to his admirer, Hitler. George Grosz, *George Grosz: An Autobiography*, trans. Nora Hodges (Berkeley: Univ. of California Press, 1998), 72–75.

16. Klaus Jeziorkowski, "Empor ins Licht: Gnostizismus und Lichtsymbolik in Deutschland um 1900," in *The Turn of the Century: German Literature and Art, 1890-1915*, ed. Gerald Chapple and Hans H. Schulte, 2nd ed. (Bonn: Bouvier, 1983), 190.

17. Lucien Dällenbach, *The Mirror in the Text,* trans. Jeremy Whiteley and Emma Hughes (Chicago: Univ. of Chicago Press, 1989), 12–15.

18. Thomas Ostwald, *Karl May: Leben und Werk* (Braunschweig: Graff, 1977), 232–33.

19. Hans Jürgen Syberberg, "Ein deutsches Heldenleben: Karl May," *Die Zeit*, Oct. 18, 1974.

20. Frederick W. Ott, *The Great German Films* (Secaucus, NJ: Citadel, 1986), 20–21.

21. Ute Schneider, "Lil Dagover: Schauspielerin," in *Cinegraph.*

22. Cinzia Romani, *Die Filmdiven im Dritten Reich* (Munich: Bahia, 1985), 96–105.

23. Fritz Kortner, *Aller Tage Abend* (Berlin: Alexander, 1991), 401.

24. "Käthe Gold," obituary, *Die Zeit*, Oct. 24, 1997.

25. Information about the actor's life can be found in the Willy Trenk-Trebitsch Archive of the Stiftung Archiv der Akademie der Künste in Berlin.

26. George Lellis, *Bertolt Brecht, Cahiers du Cinéma and Contemporary Film Theory*, Studies in Cinema 13 (Ann Arbor, MI: UMI, 1982), 3.

27. Georg Seeßlen, "Helmut Käutner: Regisseur, Schauspieler," in *Cinegraph.*

28. Bazon Brock, "Er war wirklich Old Shatterhand," *Der Spiegel*, Oct. 28, 1974, 186–87.

29. Friedelind Wagner and Page Cooper, *Heritage of Fire: The Story of Richard Wagner's Granddaughter*, 3rd ed. (New York: Harper, 1945), 217.

30. Unidentified passage from Albert Speer's memoirs quoted in Frederic Spotts, *Bayreuth:*

A History of the Wagner Festival (New Haven, London: Yale Univ. Press, 1994), 168.

31. Gottfried Wagner, *Wer nicht mit dem Wolf heult: Autobiographische Aufzeichnungen eines Wagner-Urenkels* (Cologne: Kiepenheuer und Witsch, 1997).

32. Eleonore Büning, "Hier gilt's der Kunst: Schluß mit der Wagnerei in Bayreuth," *Die Zeit*, Feb. 28, 1997.

33. http://www.germany-live.de/gl/Artikel/Kultur/1995-12 (accessed Nov. 15, 1997).

34. Hans Jürgen Syberberg, "Je n'ai jamais fait de politique," *Théâtre / Public* 13 (1976): 40–43.

35. Marcia Landy, "Politics, Aesthetics, and Patriarchy in *The Confessions of Winifred Wagner*," *New German Critique* 18 (1979): 151–66.

36. Hans Jürgen Syberberg, "Eine Zeugin und eine Schuldige," *Der Spiegel*, March 10, 1980, 234–35.

37. One example is Stephan Herbert Fuchs, "'Wenn der Hitler zur Tür reinkäme': Gedenkstunde für Winifred Wagner in Bayreuth," *Frankenpost*, June 23, 1997.

Notes to Chapter 4: *Hitler: Ein Film aus Deutschland*

1. Hans Jürgen Syberberg, *Hitler: Ein Film aus Deutschland* (Reinbeck bei Hamburg: Rowohlt, 1978); *Hitler: A Film from Germany*, pref. Susan Sontag, trans. Joachim Neugroschel (New York: Farrar, 1982); *Hitler: un film d'Allemagne*, pref. Jean-Pierre Faye, trans. François Rey and Bernard Sobel, Collection Change (Paris: Seghers-Laffont, 1978).

2. Susan Sontag, *Under the Sign of Saturn* (New York: Vintage, 1981) 135–65.

3. Otto Strobel, ed., *König Ludwig II. und Richard Wagner: Briefwechsel*, 5 vols. (Karlsruhe: Braun, 1936–39), 3:257.

4. Pierre Grimal, ed., *Larousse World Mythology* (London: Hamlyn, 1973), 461.

5. Dusty Sklar, *The Nazis and the Occult* (New York: Dorset, 1977), 119–22.

6. Reinald Schröder, "Welteislehre, Ahnenerbe und 'Weiße Juden': Kuriosa aus der Wissenschaftspolitik im 'Dritten Reich'," *Die Zeit*, April 26, 1991.

7. Reverberating through Syberberg's statement is the subtitle in Hannah Arendt's book, *Eichmann in Jerusalem: A Report on the Banality of Evil*, rev. ed. (New York: Penguin Books, 1980).

8. Syberberg incorporated the statement in his *Filmbuch* (107) and repeated it in the text and title of an article, "L'histoire de la musique de Wagner est écrite en lettres de sang," in *Théâtre/Public* 20 (1978): 15–18.

9. Gustave Doré, *The Doré Illustrations for Dante's "Divine Comedy": 136 Plates* (New York: Dover, 1976) 30. A fine English edition is Henry Wordsworth Longfellow's translation in four vols. (New York: Bigelow, 1909). The corpse in the grave is that of Farinata, a Florentine involved in the war between the Guelfs and the Ghibellines. Dante places him among the damned heretics for his lack of faith in the immortality of the soul (1: 172).

10. Cosima Wagner, *Cosima Wagner's Diaries*, ed. Martin Gregor-Dellin and Dietrich Mack, trans. Geoffrey Skelton, 2 vols. (New York: Harcourt, 1978), 1:172.

11. Richard Wagner, *Judaism in Music and Other Essays*, trans. William Ashton Ellis (1894; Lincoln: Univ. of Nebraska Press, 1995), 75–122.

12. Thomas Mann, "Bruder Hitler," in *Politische Schriften und Reden*, 3 vols. (Frankfurt am Main: Fischer, 1968), 3:53–58.

13. Neil Powell, *Alchemy: the Ancient Science* (New York: Doubleday, 1976), 64–65.

14. The presence of black American occupation soldiers at Wahnfried were noted by Wagner's daughter-in-law, Winifred Wagner, and other Germans: "[S]oldiers had actually been seen jitterbugging on Wagner's grave, . . . black soldiers danced in the Wahnfried garden with blonde German girls," Spotts, 201.

15. "Doch einmal angetreten gegen eine Riefenstahl und ihr System und ihren dahinterstehenden Meister, mußte auf ihrem Gebiet ihr Meister und sein System widerlegt werden, wenn es ging," Syberberg, *Die freudlose Gesellschaft*, 70.

16. Cosima Wagner, *Diaries* 1:620.

17. Heinrich Heine, *Deutschland: Ein Wintermärchen*, in *Werke*, Tempel-Klassiker (Berlin: Tempel, 1968), 607–69.

18. Syberberg's idea proved prophetic. After the American military had run Hitler's mountain refuge as a recreation center for the troops, they eventually turned it over to the Bavarian authorities in 1995. The initial plan to convert the site into a Hitler museum met with enormous criticism. Instead, the authorities decided to erect a center for Hitler documentation there. See Marion, Countess Dönhoff, "Wallfahrt zu Hitlers Refugium? Ein Dokumentenhaus auf dem Obersalzberg — welch ein Unfug," *Die Zeit*, Nov. 28, 1997.

19. Solveig Olsen, "Celan's 'Todesfuge': The Musical Dimension of a Verbal Composition," in *Literature and Musical Adaptation*, ed. Michael J. Meyer, Rodopi Perspectives on Modern Literature 26 (Amsterdam, New York: Rodopi, 2002), 207–8.

20. Heinrich Heine, "Aphorismen und Fragmente," in *Werke und Briefe*, 10 vols. (Berlin: Aufbau, 1962), 7:413.

21. Gershom Scholem, *Kabbalah* (New York: Dorset, 1974), 138–39.

22. Walter Wadepuhl, *Heinrich Heine: Sein Leben und seine Werke* (Cologne: Böhlau, 1974), 16.

23. Heinrich Heine, *Der Doktor Faustus: Ein Tanzpoem nebst kuriosen Berichten über Teufel, Hexen und Dichtkunst*; in *Werke und Briefe*, 7: 7-53.

24. On black Ma Kali doing the cosmic dance, see Pierre Grimal, ed., *Larousse World Mythology*, 223–26; on the black many-breasted statue of Diana of Ephesus, Erich Neumann, *The Great Mother: An Analysis of the Archetype*, 2nd ed. (Princeton, NJ: Princeton Univ. Press, 1974), pl.35; and on Isis as Earth Mother and the black earth of Egypt, Plutarch, "Isis and Osiris," in *Moralia*, trans. Frank Cole Babbitt, 15 vols., Loeb Classical Lib. 306 (Cambridge, MA: Harvard Univ. Press, 1993), 5:83, 137.

25. René Querido, *The Golden Age of Chartres: The Teachings of a Mystery School and the Eternal Feminine* (Edinburgh: Floris, 1987), 24–25, and Adele Getty, *Goddess: Mother of Living Nature* (London: Thames, 1990), 26–27.

26. J. L. E. Dreyer, *A History of Astronomy from Thales to Kepler*, 2nd ed. (New York: Dover, 1953), 38; Thomas L. Heath, *Greek Astronomy* (New York: Dover, 1991), xxvi; and Richard Hinckley Allen, *Star Names: Their Lore and Meaning* (New York: Dover, 1963), 468n.

27. Ptolemy, *Tetrabiblos*, ed. and trans. F. E. Robbins, Loeb Classical Lib. 435 (Cambridge, MA: Harvard Univ. Press, 1994), 41.

28. Charles Seltman, *The Twelve Olympians and Their Guests* (London: Parrish, 1956),99, as quoted in Paul Friedrich, *The Meaning of Aphrodite* (Chicago: Univ. of Chicago Press, 1978), 71.

29. Syberberg uses two excerpts from Beethoven's revised and abridged version of 38 lines; Schiller's "An die Freude" consists of 96 lines.

30. Lynn Thorndike, *A History of Magic and Experimental Science*, 8 vols. (New York: Columbia Univ. Press, 1923), 3:360.

31. George Ashdown Audsley, *The Art of Organ Building*, 2 vols., 1905 (New York: Dover, 1965), 1:529.

32. The stamp is reproduced on p. 22 in the English ed. of *Hitler* and on p. 32 in the German version. An autographed photograph of Mary Pickford in the same pose appears in "Syberberg," 66.

33. Thomas Mann, *Doktor Faustus: Das Leben des deutschen Tonsetzers Adrian Leverkühn erzählt von einem Freunde* (Frankfurt am Main: Fischer, 1067), 651.

34. Stephanie Barron, *"Degenerate Art": The Fate of the Avant-Garde in Nazi Germany* Los Angeles, CA: Los Angeles County Museum of Art, 1991), 56, 373, and 224.

35. Henry Pachter, "Our Hitler, or His?" *Cineaste* 10, no. 2 (1980): 25.

36. "Protesters Berate Haider as 'Fascist'," *Denton Record Chronicle*, Feb. 3, 2000.

37. Peter Kern, interview, "Lautes Bellen aus der vierten Reihe," *Der Spiegel*, Oct. 21, 2002: 197.

38. Hans Jürgen Syberberg, *"Hitler: A Film from Germany* or The Greatest Show of the Century," interview on French television during the Film Festival in Cannes, trans. Ian Christie, *Framework* 11, no. 6 (1977): 13–15.

39. Hans Jürgen Syberberg, "Wir leben in einem toten Land," *Die Zeit,* June 20, 1977; repr. as "The Syberberg Statement: We live in a Dead Land," trans. Barrie Ellis-Jones, *Framework* 11, no. 6 (1977): 11–12; quoted from repr. "We Live in a Dead Country (1977)," in *West German Filmmakers on Film: Visions and Voices*, ed. Eric Rentschler (New York: Holmes, 1988), 17–20.

40. Wolf Donner, *"Hitler* nach Deutschland!" *Die Zeit*, Dec. 23, 1977.

41. Hans Jürgen Syberberg, *"Hitler* — noch nicht für Deutschland," *Die Zeit*, Jan. 13, 1978.

42. Sereny, "Hans Jürgen Syberberg: Germany's Most Feared Film-Maker," 30.

43. Hans C. Blumenberg, "Träume in Trümmern," *Die Zeit*, July 7, 1978.

44. Karl-Heinz Janßen, "Wir — zwischen Jesus und Hitler: Mit Vernunft allein läßt sich der Judenmord nicht erklären," *Die Zeit*, July 7, 1978, Politik. Another report on this symposium is Gitta Sereny's "Building up defences against the Hitlerwave," *New Statesman*, July 7, 1978, http:// www.fpp.co.uk/Legal/Discovery/Di/0631.html (accessed Nov. 14, 2003).

45. Hans Jürgen Syberberg, interview by Betsy Erkkila, 211.

46. Robert Di Matteo, *"Our Hitler: A Film from Germany,"* Kino: German Film, Oct. 1979, 72.

47. Hans Jürgen Syberberg, "Mein Führer — Our Hitler: The Meaning of Small Words (1980)," in *West German Filmmakers on Film*, ed. Rentschler, 141.

48. Michel Foucault, "Les quatre cavaliers de l'Apocalypse et les vermisseaux quotidiens," interview by Bernard Sobel, in "Syberberg," 95–96.

49. Alberto Moravia, "Massez Himmler!" in "Syberberg," 96.

50. Susan Sontag, "Syberbergs Hitler," trans. Kurt Neff, in *Syberbergs Hitler-Film*, 7–32; "Eye of the Storm," *New York Times Review of Books*, Feb. 2, 1980, 36–43, and "Syberberg's Hitler," *Under the Sign of Saturn*, 135–65. An excerpt of her "Aventures dans la tête" and a letter to Syberberg appeared in "Syberberg," 93–95, and an abridged version prefaces the Eng. ed. of Syberberg's *Hitler* book, ix–xvi.

51. Sontag, *Under the Sign of Saturn*, 165.

52. Matthias Matussek, "Gefolgschaft erzwingen," *Der Spiegel*, Oct. 22, 1990: 260+.

53. Klaus Eder, ed., *Syberbergs Hitler-Film* (Munich: Hanser, 1980). The anthology contains Susan Sontag, "Syberbergs Hitler" (7–32), Jean-Pierre Faye, "Faust, Teil III" (33–35), Jean-Pierre Oudart, "Verführung und Terror im Kino" (37–50), Christian Zimmer, "Hitler unter uns" (51–68), Michel Foucault, "Die vier Reiter der Apoka-

lypse und die alltäglichen kleinen Würmchen" (69–73, interview), Alberto Moravia, "Massiert Himmler!" (75–76), Vito Zagarrio, "Der Nazi-Tyrann als Vorwand, um von den Dämonen von heute zu sprechen" (77–80), and Heiner Müller, "Die Einsamkeit des Films" (81–82).

54. Hans Rudolf Vaget, "Die Auferstehung Richard Wagners: Wagnerismus und Verfremdung in Syberbergs Hitler-Film," in *Film und Literatur: Literarische Texte und der neue deutsche Film*, ed. Sigrid Bauschinger, Susan L. Cocalis, and Henry A. Lea (Bern: Francke, 1984), 124–55; Anton Kaes, "Mythos Deutschland, Revisited: Historie und Posthistoire in Hans Jürgen Syberbergs *Hitler: Ein Film aus Deutschland*," in *Deutschlandbilder* by Anton Kaes (Munich: edition text + kritik, 1987), 135–70; and John Sandford, "Hans Jürgen Syberberg: Regisseur," in *Cinegraph.*

55. John Sandford, *The New German Cinema* (1980; New York: Da Capo, 1982), 116–31; Timothy Corrigan, *New German Film: The Displaced Image* (Austin: Univ. of Texas Press, 1983), 144–71; James Franklin, *New German Cinema: From Oberhausen to Hamburg* (Boston: Twayne, 1983), 163–77; Russel A. Berman, "Hans-Jürgen Syberberg: Of Fantastic and Magical Worlds," in *New German Filmmakers from Oberhausen through the 1970s*, ed. Klaus Phillips (New York: Ungar, 1984), 359–78; Anton Kaes, *From Hitler to Heimat: The Return of History as Film* (Cambridge, MA: Harvard Univ. Press, 1989), 37–72; Eric L. Santner, *Stranded Objects: Mourning, Memory, and Film in Postwar Germany* (Ithaca, NY: Cornell Univ. Press, 1990), 103–49; Anton Kaes, "Holocaust and the End of History: Postmodern Historiography in Cinema," in *Probing the Limits of Representation: Nazism and the 'Final Solution'*, ed. Saul Friedlander (Cambridge: Harvard Univ. Press, 1992), 206–22; Stephen Slater, "The Complicity of Culture with Barbarism: A Study of Thomas Mann's *Doktor Faustus* and Hans Jürgen Syberberg's *Hitler: Ein Film aus Deutschland*," PhD diss., Yale Univ., 1992; Manfred Schneider, "Medienpathetiker: Wagner und Syberberg," in *Das Pathos der Deutschen*, ed. Norbert Bolz (Munich: Fink, 1996), 173–88; and others.

56. Thomas Elsaesser, "Myth as the Phantasmagoria of History: H. J. Syberberg, Cinema and Representation," *New German Critique* 24–25 (1981–82): 108–54.

57. All three texts begin on p. 256 of *Vogue* 170 (May 1980); Syberberg, "What Can We Do with Hitler?", Susan Sontag, "*Our Hitler*, a Masterpiece from Germany," and Barbara Rose, "A Total Work of Art."

Notes to Chapter 5: A Chilly Climate

1. Hans Jürgen Syberberg, ed., *Fotografie der 30er Jahre: Eine Anthologie* (Munich: Schirmer/Mosel, 1977).

2. Hans Jürgen Syberberg, "Donnez-nous notre nostalgie quotidienne," interview by Jean-Michel Palmier, *Les Nouvelles Littéraires*, Feb. 5, 1976, 10–11.

3. Hans Jürgen Syberberg, "Form Is Morality: *Holocaust*, a Symptom of the Biggest Crisis in Our Intellectual Life (1979)," trans. Barrie Ellis-Jones, *Framework* 12 (1980): 11–15.

4. Ilse Koch was a female guard at the concentration camp, under whose surveillance, the remark implies, soap was produced from the victims' bodies.

5. Russell A. Berman, *Modern Culture and Critical Theory: Arts, Politics, and the Legacy of the Frankfurt School* (Madison, WI: Univ. of Wisconsin Press, 1989), chapter 6.

6. Alfred Dreyfus had been found guilty by a French court in 1894 of betraying military secrets to the Germans, but was eventually acquitted and rehabilitated years later. The case engendered widespread and passionate debate, while anti-Semitic feelings ran high. Zola's "J'accuse" in *l'Aurore* netted him a prison sentence for libel, which he escaped by fleeing to England and becoming a martyr in the pro-Dreyfus faction. Echoes of the case in French literature abounded, e.g. in Zola's *Vérité*, Anatole France's *M. Bergeret à Paris*, and Marcel Proust's *Jean Santeuil*.

7. David Welch, *Propaganda and the German Cinema 1933-1945*, rev. ed. (London, New York: Tauris, 2001), 99–109.

8. Heinrich Heine, *Französische Zustände,* in *Werke und Briefe,* 4: 368-83.

9. Heinrich von Kleist, "Über das Marionettentheater," in *Sämtliche Werke*, 4 vols. in one (Leipzig: Hesse, 1902), 3: 213–19.

10. Hans Jürgen Syberberg, "Hitler artiste de l'État ou l'avant-garde méphistophélique du xxe siècle," in *Les Réalismes 1919–1939,* ed. Pontus Hulten (Paris: Centre Georges Pompidou, 1980), 378–83.

11. Hans Jürgen Syberberg, *Die freudlose Gesellschaft: Notizen aus dem letzten Jahr* (Munich: Hanser, 1981). The unabridged paperback edition appeared with a slightly altered subtitle: *Die freudlose Gesellschaft: Notizen aus den letzten Jahren* (Frankfurt am Main: Ullstein, 1983). The French edition also has a different subtitle: *La société sans joie: de l'Allemagne après Hitler* (Paris: Bourgois, 1982). The citations are to the German paperback edition.

12. Theodor W. Adorno, *Noten zur Literatur* (Frankfurt am Main: Suhrkamp, 1981), 230–32.

13. Hans Jürgen Syberberg, interview by Judy Stone, *Eye on the World: Conversations with International Filmmakers,* ed. Judy Stone (Los Angeles: Silman James, 1997), 266.

14. Paul Celan, *Gedichte*, 2 vols. (Frankfurt am Main: Suhrkamp, 1986), 1:41-42.

15. André Heller, *Es werde Zirkus: Ein poetisches Spektakel* (Frankfurt am Main: Fischer, 1976), 146–59.

16. Hans Jürgen Syberberg, "Wer ist und was macht eigentlich André Heller?" *Du: die Zeitschrift der Kultur,* Schweizerische Monatsschrift 7 (July 1979): 69.

17. Klaus Jeziorkowski, "Das Glück der Wurzelbürste," review of *Die freudlose Gesellschaft, Der Spiegel,* July 10, 1981, 167.

18. Jörg Drews, "Die verfolgende Unschuld," review of *Die freudlose Gesellschaft, Merkur: Deutsche Zeitschrift für europäisches Denken* 36 (1982): 93–96.

19. Iso Camartin, "Ein Verletzter wehrt sich," review of *Die freudlose Gesellschaft, Neue Zürcher Zeitung,* Nov. 13, 1981.

20. Rainer Werner Fassbinder, "Homage to Werner Schroeter (1979)," in *West German Filmmakers on Film: Visions and Voices,* ed. Eric Rentschler (New York: Holmes and Meier, 1988), 198.

21. Hans Jürgen Syberberg, "Sie haben ihn zum lächerlichen Gartenzwerg ihres Selbstmitleids heroisiert," *Medium,* August 1982, 35.

22. Janusz Bodek, *Die Fassbinder-Kontroversen: Entstehung und Wirkung eines literarischen Textes* (Frankfurt am Main: Lang, 1991).

23. Hans Jürgen Syberberg, "Sie haben ihn . . . ," 36.

24. Hans Jürgen Syberberg, "Media Response to Fassbinder's *Berlin Alexanderplatz* (1980)", in *West German Filmmakers on Film,* ed. Eric Rentschler, 162–63.

25. Hans Jürgen Syberberg, "Sie haben ihn . . . ," 35.

Notes to Chapter 6:
Introduction and First Prelude to *Parsifal*

1. In 1882 Neumann established an itinerant company that presented the *Ring* in 135 opera houses, according to Spotts, 78.
2. R. Freiherr von Lichtenberg and L. Müller von Hausen, *Mehr Schutz dem geistigen Eigentum! Der Kampf um das Schicksal des "Parsifal,"* 4th ed. (Berlin: Curtius, n.d.,ca. 1914), 37.
3. "Ein sublimes und außerordentliches Gefühl, Erlebnis, Ereignis der Seele im Grunde der Musik . . .," Syberberg, *Parsifal: Ein Filmessay* (Munich: Heyne, 1982), 9.
4. Lichtenberg, 27, with more on this scandal 74–77.
5. Syberberg, *Parsifal*, 147.
6. Hans Jürgen Syberberg, *Parsifal: Notes sur un film*, trans. Claude Porcell, Cahiers du Cinéma (Paris: Gallimard, 1982).
7. Cosima Wagner, "An die Mitglieder des Deutschen Reichstages," 1901, in *Mehr Schutz dem geistigen Eigentum*, by Lichtenberg and Müller von Hausen, 70.
8. Paul Nettl, *Mozart and Masonry* (New York: Dorset, 1987), 128.
9. Detta Petzet and Michael Petzet, *Die Richard Wagner-Bühne König Ludwigs II.* (Munich: Prestel, 1970), illus. 725.
10. Petzet and Petzet's *Die Richard Wagner-Bühne* identifies the singer as female twice by using the feminine forms of the nouns *Gralsträgerin* and *Sängerin*, and including a photograph of her, 828.
11. "Wir haben Gralsträgerin, Knappe und Dr. Strecker mit Frau zu Tisch," Cosima Wagner, *Die Tagebücher*, ed. Martin Gregor-Dellin and Dietrich Mack, 4 vols. (Munich, Zürich: Piper, 1977), 4: 980.
12. Mary A. Cicora, *"Parsifal" Reception in the "Bayreuther Blätter,"* American Univ. Studies, Series 1, vol. 55 (New York: Peter Lang, 1987), 21.
13. Alfred O. Lorenz, *Der musikalische Aufbau von Richard Wagners "Parsifal,"* 2nd ed. (Tutzing: Schneider, 1966), 10–19.
14. Hans Jürgen Syberberg, ed., *Ein Mundkoch erinnert sich an Ludwig II*, by Theodor Hierneis (1953; Munich: Heimeran, 1972), 124–25, 126.
15. Wolfram von Eschenbach, *Parzivâl*, ed. Karl Lachmann, 6th ed. (Berlin, Leipzig: de Gruyter, 1926), 66–69.
16. The entry for "faith" is spelled with *aleph, mem, nun*, and *he* in Francis Brown, *The New Brown-Driver-Briggs-Gesenius Hebrew and English Lexicon with an Appendix Containing the Biblical Aramaic* (Peabody, MA: Hendrickson, 1979), 53, while Arabic *Imân* is given as "true faith" in Rudolf Kleinpaul, *Länder und Völkernamen* (Leipzig: Göschen, 1910), 124.
17. Urban T. Holmes, Jr. and Sister M. Amelia Klenke, O.P., *Chrétien, Troyes, and the Grail* (Chapel Hill: Univ. of North Carolina Press, 1959), 109.
18. Sumner McKnight Crosby, *The Royal Abbey of Saint-Denis from Its Beginnings to the Death of Suger, 475–1151* (New Haven: Yale Univ. Press, 1987), 205.
19. Henry Kahane and Renée Kahane, *The Krater and the Grail: Hermetic Sources of the "Parzival"* (Urbana: Univ. of Illinois Press, 1965), 1–7.
20. Wolfram von Eschenbach, 218–19.
21. Cosima Wagner, *Diaries*, ed. Martin Gregor-Dellin and Dietrich Mack, trans. Geoffrey Skelton, 2 vols. (New York: Harcourt, 1978), 2:898 (Aug.11, 1882). Subsequent cita-

tions refer only to the date of the entry.

22. Kleist, "Über das Marionettentheater," 213–19.

23. Wolfram von Eschenbach, 120–21.

24. Carl Fr. Glasenapp and Heinrich von Stein, eds., *Wagner-Lexikon: Hauptbegriffe der Kunst- und Weltanschauung Richard Wagners* (Stuttgart: Cotta, 1883), 633.

25. Many of the following remarks draw on Marion Meade, *Eleanor of Aquitaine* (New York: Hawthorn, 1977).

26. Part of the colonnade of the monastery found its way to the Cloisters Museum in New York, according to James J. Rorimer, *The Cloisters: The Building and the Collection of Mediaeval Art in Fort Tryon Park* (New York: Metropolitan Museum of Art, 1951), 16. Special thanks to Dr. Donald Vidrine of Denton, Texas for pointing this out.

27. Kahane and Kahane, 2 and 125.

28. The caricature is reproduced in, e.g., Robert W. Gutman, *Richard Wagner: The Man, His Mind, and His Music* (New York: Harcourt, 1974), illus.

29. Hans Mayer, *Anmerkungen zu Richard Wagner* (Frankfurt am Main: Suhrkamp 1966), 14–15.

30. Friedrich Nietzsche, *Thus Spake Zarathustra*, trans. Thomas Common, The Modern Library 9 (New York: Random House, n.d.), 10.

31. Richard Wagner, "Judaism in Music," 88.

32. Albrecht Dürer, *The Painter's Manual*, trans. and ed. Walter L. Strauss (New York: Abaris Books, 1977), 347.

33. Sigmund Freud, *The Interpretation of Dreams*, in *The Basic Writings of Sigmund Freud*, ed. and trans. A. A. Brill, The Modern Library (New York: Random House, 1966), 544.

34. C. G. Jung, "The Relations between the Ego and the Unconscious," in *Collected Works* vol. 7, 2nd ed., Bollingen Series 20 (Princeton, NJ: Princeton Univ. Press, 1977), 128.

35. C. G. Jung, *Symbols of Transformation*, in *Collected Works* vol. 5, 2nd ed., Bollingen Series 20 (Princeton, NJ: Princeton Univ. Press, 1976), 330.

36. C. G. Jung, *Symbols of Transformation*, 330.

37. C. G. Jung, *Psychology and Alchemy*, in *Collected Works* vol. 12, 2nd ed., Bollingen Series 20 (Princeton, NJ: Princeton Univ. Press, 1993), 19.

Notes to Chapter 7: Act One.

1. Helmut Börsch-Supan, *Caspar David Friedrich*, trans. Sarah Twohig (New York: Braziller, 1974), illus. pp. 31 and 80.

2. Börsch-Supan, 78.

3. Wieland Wagner, "*Parsifal*: Bayreuth, 1937. Decors: Wieland Wagner," http:// richardwagner.free.fr/wielandparsi.htm (accessed Dec. 14, 2001).

4. The British bass Robert Lloyd is reknowned for his range of repertoire. He has appeared on all the major opera stages in addition to pursuing a freelance concert career. He is also well known on British television and radio, and through numerous recordings. In 1991 he was made a Commander of the British Empire (CBE) by Queen Elizabeth II.

5. "Wilde Leute," in Richard Beitl and Klaus Beitl, *Wörterbuch der deutschen Volkskunde*, 3rd ed. (Stuttgart: Kröner, 1974), 972–73.

6. "Wilde Jagd," Beitl and Beitl, 970–72.

7. Cosima Wagner, *Diaries*, 2:1009–10; this statement is her last entry in the diary.

8. Petzet and Petzet, illus. 518–20.

9. C. G. Jung, *Psychological Types*, in *Collected Works*, vol. 6, Bollingen Series 20 (Princeton, NJ: Princeton Univ. Press, 1990), 470.

10. Richard Wagner, "Zur Entstehungsgeschichte," in *Parsifal*, ed. Michael von Soden, insel taschenbuch 684 (Frankfurt am Main: Insel, 1983), 89.

11. Stuart Holroyd, *Magic, Words, and Numbers* (London: Aldus, 1975), 63, and Israel Regardie, *A Garden of Pomegranates*, 2nd ed. (St. Paul, MN: Llewellyn, 1991), 63 and 68.

12. C. G. Jung, *The Archetypes and the Collective Unconscious*, in *Collected Works* vol. 9, bk. 1, 2nd ed., Bollingen Series 20 (Princeton, NJ: Princeton Univ. Press, 1990), 165.

13. Reuben Fine, *The Development of Freud's Thought* (Northvale, NJ: Aronson, 1987), 172–81.

14. Jochen Trüby, "Das teuerste Buch der Welt: eine Zierde für die Ewigkeit," *Scala*, Oct. 1994, 64 illus. The director's choice may also have been inspired by the king's similar mantle in the Bayreuth production of 1910. It displays a pattern in gold of Christ, saints, and angels, as shown in Charles Osborne, *The World Theatre of Wagner: A Celebration of 150 Years of Wagner Productions* (New York: Macmillan, 1982), 178.

15. C. G. Jung, *Aion: Researches into the Phenomenology of the Self*, in *Collected Works*, vol. 9, bk. 2, 2nd ed., Bollingen Series 20 (Princeton, NJ: Princeton Univ. Press, 1978), 213–14.

16. Fred Hoyle, *Astronomy* (London: Rathbone, 1962), 145–46.

17. Anselm Haverkamp, *Laub voll Trauer: Hölderlins späte Allegorie* (Munich: Fink, 1991), 93 and ch.4, and Anselm Haverkamp, *Leaves of Mourning: Hölderlin's Late Work — with an Essay on Keats and Melancholy*, trans. Vernon Chadwick (Albany, NY: State Univ. of New York Press, 1996), 78.

18. Scholem, *Kabbalah*, 344.

19. Scholem, *Kabbalah*, 346–50.

20. Cosima Wagner, *Diaries*, July 22, 1882.

21. Kahane and Kahane, *The Krater and the Grail* is still one of the best sources of information on this topic; see also Brian P. Copenhaver, *Hermetica* (Cambridge: Cambridge Univ. Press, 1996), 15, 131–35.

22. *Philo*, trans. F. H. Cohen and G. H. Whitaker, 2 vols., Loeb Classical Library 226 (Cambridge, MA: Harvard Univ. Press, 1991), 2:451.

23. James C. VanderKam, *Enoch and the Growth of an Apocalyptic Tradition* (Wash. DC: The Catholic Biblical Assoc. of America, 1984), 126.

24. Joseph Görres claimed historical roots for Titurel's ancestry. Belonging to an early priestly royal dynasty, Titurel got his name from a combination of his parents' names: Titurison, son of King Beryl (Parylle) of Christian Celtic France, and Elizabel, daughter of an Arragonian king. He supposedly died in India more than 500 years old. J. Görres, ed., *Lohengrin, ein altteutsches Gedicht*, "nach der Abschrift des Vaticanischen Manuscripts von Ferdinand Gloeckle" (Heidelberg: Mohr und Zimmer, 1813), xliii.

25. Richard Wagner, *Parsifal*, ed. von Soden, 92.

26. Richard Wagner, *Parsifal*, ed. von Soden, 119.

27. Richard Wagner, *Parsifal*, ed. von Soden, 101 and 124.

28. Richard Wagner, *Parsifal*, ed. von Soden, 89–90.

29. Petzet and Petzet, illus. 402.

30. Syberberg, "Utopies et projets," in "Syberberg," 44–45.

31. Eduard Hanslick, "Richard Wagners *Parsifal*," in Richard Wagner, *Parsifal: Texte, Materialien, Kommentare*, ed. Attila Csampai and Dietmar Holland (Reinbek bei Hamburg: Rowohlt, 1984), 150.

32. Herbert Silberer, *Hidden Symbolism of Alchemy and the Occult Arts* (1917), trans. S. E. Jelliffe (New York: Dover, 1971), 124.

33. Syberberg, "Utopies et Projets," 45.

34. Charles Walker, *Atlas of Secret Europe: A Guide to Sites of Magic and Mystery* (New York: Dorset, 1990), 174–75.

35. Robert Graves, *The Greek Myths*, 2 vols. (New York: Viking Penguin, 1986),1: 80.

36. C. G. Jung, *Alchemical Studies*, in *Collected Works*, vol. 13, Bollingen Series 20 (Princeton, NJ: Princeton Univ. Press, 1967), 331.

37. Homer Dickens, *The Films of Marlene Dietrich* (New York: Citadel, 1968), 112–15.

38. The original statue made for the king is supposedly lost, but a photo is included in Petzet and Petzet, illus. 651. Its pose is not identical with that of the copy used in the film.

39. Arrian, *Anabasis Alexandri*, trans. P. A. Brunt, 2 vols., Loeb Classical Library 236, (Cambridge, MA,: Harvard Univ. Press, 1989), 1: end map.

40. R. C. Zachner, ed., *The Concise Encyclopaedia of Living Faiths* (Boston: Beacon, 1967), 209.

41. H. E. Wedeck, *Dictionary of Gypsy Life and Lore* (New York: Philosophical Library, 1973), 367, 124–25, 409.

42. Wedeck, 409, 518, 125.

43. Mario A. Pei and Frank Gaynor, *Dictionary of Linguistics* (New York: Philosophical Library, 1954), 99.

44. Some examples are Paul Lawrence Rose, *Wagner: Race and Revolution* (New Haven: Yale Univ. Press, 1992); Leon Stein, *The Racial Thinking of Richard Wagner* (New York: Philosophical Library, 1950); Mark Weiner, *Richard Wagner and the Anti-Semitic Imagination* (Lincoln, London: Univ. of Nebraska Press, 1995) with an afterword on Syberberg's *Parsifal*, 349–53; Hartmut Zelinsky, "Der verschwiegene Gehalt des *Parsifal*," and "Richard Wagners letzte Karte," both in Richard Wagner, *Parsifal*, Csampai and Holland, eds., 244–51 and 252–56.

45. Wolfram's text is stanza 241. For other translations see Wolfram von Eschenbach, *Parzival*, trans. A. T. Hatto (New York: Penguin, 1987), 128; Wolfram von Eschenbach, *Parzival*, trans. Helen M. Mustard and Charles E. Passage (New York: Vintage, 1961), 131; and Stephen C. Harrof, *Wolfram and His Audience* (Göppingen: Kümmerle, 1974), 84–85. Harrof's discussion of the metaphor concludes, "Rather, the audience has been asked to experience the quest in large part with the hero" (86). See also Bernd Schirok, "Die senewe ist ein bîspel: Zu Wolframs Bogengleichnis," *Zeitschrift für Deutsches Altertum und Deutsche Literatur* 115, no.1 (1986): 21–36 and its bibliographical information; and Hans-Jörg Spitz, "Wolframs Bogengleichnis: ein typologisches Signal," *Verbum et Signum*, ed. Hans Fromm, Wolfgang Harms, and Uwe Ruberg, 2 vols. (Munich: Fink, 1975), 2:247–75.

46. Arthur B. Groos, "Wolfram von Eschenbach's Bow Metaphor and the Narrative Technique of *Parzival*," *Modern Language Notes* (*MLN*) 87 (1972): 399.

47. Kurt Ruh, *Geschichte der abendländischen Mystik*, 4 vols. (Munich: Beck, 1993–99), 2:461–67.

48. Donald N. Ferguson, *A History of Musical Thought* (New York: Crofts, 1935), 150–51.

49. Glasenapp and Stein, eds., *Wagner-Lexikon*, 898.

50. Martin Heidegger, "The Question Concerning Technology," in *Basic Writings*, ed. David Farrell Krell (New York: Harper, 1977), 301–7.

51. E. A. Wallis Budge, *Osiris and the Egyptian Resurrection*, 2 vols. (New York: Dover, 1973), 2:117, 128.

52. Felix Weingartner, "Erinnerungen an die *Parsifal*-Aufführungen 1882," In *Parsifal*, by Richard Wagner, ed. Csampai and Holland, 128.

53. Petzet and Petzet, illus. 515.

54. Hermann Rauschning, *Gespräche mit Hitler*, 4th ed. (Zürich: Europa Verlag, 1940). The quotations are supposedly based on the author's daily notes from 1932 to 1934.

55. Cosima Wagner, *Diaries*, e.g. Aug. 21 and 31, 1880.

56. Richard Wagner, "Das Liebesmahl der Apostel: Eine biblische Szene," (1843), *Sämtliche Schriften und Dichtungen*, 5th ed., 12 vols. (Leipzig: Breitkopf & Härtel, n.d., ca. 1911), 11:264–69.

57. "Blut und Leib der Opfergabe wandelt heut' zu eurer Labe der Erlöser, den ihr preis't, in den Wein, den nun euch floss, in das Brod, das heut' euch speis't," Richard Wagner, *Parsifal: A Festival D rama*, trans. H. L. and F. Corder, "at the theatre ticket office" (New York: Rullman, n.d., ca. 1913), 18.

58. "Blut und Leib der heil'gen Gabe wandelt heut zu eurer Labe sel'ger Tröstung Liebesgeist, in den Wein, der euch nun floß, in das Brod [,] das heut euch speis't," Richard Wagner, *Parsifal*, in *Gesammelte Schriften und Dichtungen*, 4th ed. (Leipzig: Ziegel, 1907), 10:344. The spelling differs slightly in more recent editions of the score *(*e.g. New York: Dover, 1986), 208–10.

59. Emma Jung and Marie-Louise Franz, *The Grail Legend*, trans. Andrea Dykes (London: Hodder, 1971), 297.

60. Richard Wagner, *My Life*, trans. Andrew Gray, ed. Mary Whittall (Cambridge: Cambridge Univ. Press, 1983), 309.

61. Heinrich Heine, *Atta Troll: Ein Sommernachtstraum*, in *Werke*, 600.

62. In "Leib und Seele" Heine spells the name Meyer-Bär, but denies the composer a position among the stars of the Big Bear (Big Dipper), Heine, *Werke*, 437.

63. Wagner did not know whether to spell it Petz, Pätz; Bertz, or Perthes, according to Martin Gregor-Dellin, *Richard Wagner: Sein Leben. Sein Werk. Sein Jahrhundert* (Munich: Goldmann-Schott, 1983), 40.

64. The Bavarian Martin Sperr achieved fame as a playwright, actor, and stage-director. He died in April 2002 at the age of 57.

65. The note still appears in German in Richard Wagner, *Parsifal in Full Score* (New York: Dover, 1986), 588.

66. Richard Wagner, "Parzival," in Richard Wagner, *Parsifal*, ed. von Soden, 96–124.

67. See for example the debate in Richard Wagner, *Parsifal*, ed. Csampai and Holland with polemics by Gutman, Zelinsky, Kaiser, and Dahlhaus, ch. 4, 214–69.

68. Erwin Panofsky, *Abbot Suger and Its Art Treasures on the Abbey Church of St.-Denis*, [*sic*] 2nd ed. (Princeton, NJ: Princeton Univ. Press, 1979), 203 and illus. 16. The cover has the correct title: *Abbot Suger on the Abbey Church of St.-Denis and Its Art Treasures*.

69. David J. Levin, *Richard Wagner, Fritz Lang, and the Nibelungen: The Dramaturgy of Disavowal* (Princeton: Princeton Univ. Press, 1997), 126.

70. Jean Markale, *The Celts: Uncovering the Mythic and Historic Origins of Western Culture* (Rochester, VT: Inner Traditions International, 1978), 46–47.

71. Polly Young-Eisendrath and Terence Dawson, eds., *The Cambridge Companion to Jung* (Cambridge: Cambridge Univ. Press, 1997), 318.

72. Richard Wagner, "Herodom and Christendom," in *Religion and Art*, trans. Wm. Ashton Ellis, (1897; Lincoln: Univ. of Nebraska Press, 1994), 279.

73. W.P. Campbell-Everden, *Freemasonry and Its Etiquette* (New York: Weathervane, 1978), 85.

74. Ignaz von Döllinger, *Geschichte der gnostisch-manichäischen Sekten im früheren Mittelalter*, vol. 1 of *Beiträge zur Sektengeschichte des Mittelalters*, 2 vols. (Darmstadt: Wissenschaftliche Buchgesellschaft, 1982), 1:131.

75. Moshe Idel, *Kabbalah: New Perspectives* (New Haven: Yale Univ. Press, 1988), 166–67.

76. Richard Wagner, "Jesus von Nazareth: Ein dichterischer Entwurf," (1848) in *Sämtliche Schriften und Dichtungen*, 5th ed., 11: 273–323.

77. Wolfram's claim that he does not know the "letters" ("ine kan decheinen buochstap," st. 115.27 between books 2 and 3), could refer to Hebrew symbols in magic. The negated expression also fits in with his compositional pattern of positive and negative pronouncements.

78. Another Hebrew equivalent of "recompense" is spelled with the same letters as *shalom* (*shin, lamed, mem*). Although the vocalizations differ for the several entries with this spelling, their definitions may also inform Wolfram's and *Parsifal's* context. They include: "be whole, complete, free from fault [*teleios*]; to reward, recompense; peace, contentment, completeness; perfect, complete, safe, at peace; peace-offering, sacrifice, thank-offering," and the noun "recompense." One might thus read Repanse de schoy's name as the "peaceful or rewarded joy." However, in the sense of sacrifice, the word approaches the meaning of the second part of the name, as the discussion will point out.

79. Petzet and Petzet, Joukowsky's sketch, illus. 683.

80. Gershom Scholem, *Von der mystischen Gestalt der Gottheit: Studien zu G rundbegriffen der Kabbala* (Frankfurt am Main: Suhrkamp, 1977), 143.

81. Franz Kampers, "Der Waise," *Historisches Jahrbuch* 37 (1919): 455–56.

82. Börsch-Supan, 158–59.

Notes to Chapter 8: Second Prelude and Act Two

1. Sigmund Freud, "Medusa's Head (1922)," in *Collected Papers*, authorized trans. by Alix and James Strachey, vol.5, The International Psycho-Analytical Library 37 (New York: Basic Books, 1959), 105–6.

2. Friedrich Nietzsche, *Der Fall Wagner: Schriften—Aufzeichnungen—Briefe*, insel taschenbuch 686 (Frankfurt am Main: Insel, 1983), 415.

3. Heinrich Heine, "Delacroix" in "Französische Maler," in *Werke und Briefe*, vol. 4 (Berlin: Aufbau, 1961), 308–12..

4. "Truth in Fiction?" *Bible Review*, Feb. 2004, 10.

5. Richard Wagner, "Shall We Hope?" in *Religion and Art*, trans. William Ashton Ellis (1897; Lincoln: Univ. of Nebraska Press, 1994), 115.

6. Richard Wagner, "Was ist deutsch?" in *Gesammelte Schriften und Dichtungen*, 4th ed., vol. 10 (Leipzig: Siegel, 1907), 53.

7. Jacob Grimm, *Deutsche Mythologie*, 3 vols. (Graz: Akad. Druck- und Verlagsanstalt, 1968), 1:95–99.

8. Sigmund Freud, *Totem and Taboo*, in *Basic Writings*, ed. and trans. A. A. Brill, The Modern Library (New York: Random, 1966), 854.

9. Young-Eisendrath and Dawson, 319.

10. Alexander and Margarete Mitscherlich, *The Inability to Mourn: Principles of Collective Behavior*, trans. Beverley R. Placzek (New York: Grove, 1995). Eric Santner examines at length the importance of this book for understanding Syberberg's *Hitler* in his *Stranded Objects*.

11. Eric Rentschler, *The Ministry of Illusion: Nazi Cinema and Its Afterlife* (Cambridge, MA: Harvard Univ. Press, 1996), 158–64.

12. Petzet and Petzet, illus. 672–76, also Weingartner, 128–29. The garden of the 1882 *Parsifal* production was presumably inspired by the landscaping of the Palazzo Rufolo near Ravello, which Wagner visited in 1880.

13. Carl Dahlhaus, "Parsifal," in Richard Wagner, *Parsifal*, ed. Csampai and Holland, 203; repr. from Dahlhaus, *Richard Wagners Musikdramen* (Velber: Friedrich, 1971).

14. The celestial cow was sometimes depicted as a goddess with only the head of a cow. She was considered a form of the primeval female creative principle. In some aspects she was identified with Isis and Hathor, in others with Mah-Urt, Nut, and Maat, the spouse and female counterpart of Thoth, according to E. A. Wallis Budge, *The Gods of the Egyptians, Or, Studies in Egyptian Mythology*, vol. 1 (New York: Dover, 1969; repr. of London: Methuen, 1904), 422–23.

15. Richard Wagner, "*Parsifal* at Bayreuth, 1882," in *Religion and Art*, 301–12; the article appeared first in the November-December issue 1882 of the *Bayreuther Blätter*.

16. Jung claims they symbolize wholeness, quoting Boschius: "The *cauda pavonis*, combination of all colors, symbolizing wholeness," *Psychology and Alchemy*, 223.

17. Perhaps Syberberg's treatment of the location inspired Pedro Almodovar to a much more explicit parallel in his *Talk to Her*, the movie that earned him an Oscar in 2003.

18. Richard Wagner, *Selected Letters*, ed. and trans. Stewart Spencer and Barry Millington (London: Dent, 1987), 877.

19. Kamran Talattof, "Persian or Farsi? The debate continues," http://www.iranian.com/Features/Dec97/Persian (accessed Oct. 12, 2002).

20. For a brief survey with bibliography of the Chrétien discussion see Chrétien de Troyes, *Le Roman de Perceval ou Le Conte du Graal; Der Percevalroman oder Die Erzählung vom Gral*, ed. and trans. Felicitas Olef-Krafft, Universal-Bibliothek 8649 (Stuttgart: Reclam, 1991) 587. Chrétien does not reveal the meaning of the name, but many scholars read it as *perce-val* (penetrate the valley). Wolfram von Eschenbach lets Sigune tell Parzival his name, with its meaning being *rehte enmitten durch* (right through the middle, 75). This reading points to a Kabbalistic derivation to be discussed at the end of the *Parsifal* chapters.

21. Hans von Wolzogen, "Der Name 'Parsifal' (1888)," in *Wagneriana: Gesammelte Aufsätze über R. Wagner's Werke vom Ring bis zum Gral* (Walluf: Nendeln, 1977), 163–66.

22. Wolfram uses this noun as a veiled equivalent and variant of the name in stanzas 407.10, 428.19, 434.6, 478.16, and 481.29. Wagner does not retain the esoteric dimension of the name.

23. Friedrich Hölderlin, "Patmos," in *Sämtliche Werke*, Tempel-Klassiker, vol.1 (Wiesbaden: Vollmer, n. d.), 342.

24. Lucie Lamy, *Egyptian Mysteries: New Light on Ancient Knowledge* (New York: Thames, 1989), 25–26.

25. R. E. Witt, *Isis in the Ancient World* (1971; Baltimore: Johns Hopkins Univ. Press, 1997), 153.

26. "According to Herodotus, the Sorrowing Wife and Mother was shown in pantomime

by female mummers in their tens of thousands, men and women alike beating their breasts," Witt, 41–42. Even Bayreuth has been known to play on Mime's name with pantomime. For example in 2001, the singer portraying Wotan in *Siegfried* lost his voice and mimed the role on stage while his cover provided the voice, standing at the side of the stage. Similarly, one of the valkyries acted out her role silently while one of the norns sang her lines, also in plain view.

27. Walter Benjamin, "Über den Begriff der Geschichte, ix," in *Gesammelte Schriften*, vol. 1, bk. 2, ed. Rolf Tiedemann and Hermann Schweppenhauser (Frankfurt am Main: Suhrkamp, 1991), 697–98.

28. Richard Wagner, "Am Abgrund," in *Sämtliche Schriften und Dichtungen*, 5th ed., 12: 387.

29. Peter Wapnewski, *Der traurige Gott: Richard Wagner in seinen Helden*, 2nd ed. (Munich: Beck, 1980), 188 and Hans Mayer, *Anmerkungen zu Richard Wagner*, 33. Mayer refers to a letter from Wagner to Liszt of Feb. 11, 1853.

30. Elisabeth Frenzel, *Stoffe der Weltliteratur: Ein Lexikon dichtungsgeschichtlicher Längsschnitte*, 3rd ed., Kröners Taschenausgabe 300 (Stuttgart: Kröner, 1070) 358–63.

31. Arthur Edward Waite, *A New Encyclopaedia of Freemasonry* (New York: Weathervane, 1970), 1.

32. Peter Zagermann, *Eros und Thanatos: Psychoanalytische Untersuchungen zu einer Objektbeziehungstheorie der Triebe* (Darmstadt: Wissenschaftliche Buchgesellschaft, 1988).

33. C. G. Jung, "The Relations between the Ego and the Unconscious," 162.

34. C. G. Jung, "On the Nature of the Psyche," in *Basic Writings*, The Modern Library (New York: Random House, 1959), 94.

35. Henry Wadsworth Longfellow, *The Complete Poetical Works*, Cabinet ed. (Boston: Houghton Mifflin, 1901), 531–32.

36. Cosima Wagner, *Diaries* 1: Notes 1126.

37. Celan, *Gedichte* 1: 242–43.

Notes to Chapter 9: Third Prelude and Act Three

1. Walter Scott, ed., *Hermetica: The Ancient Greek and Latin Writings which Contain Religious or Philosophic Teachings Ascribed to Hermes Trismegistus*, vol. 1 (London: Dawsons, 1968), 483–85.

2. Hartmut Zelinsky, "Rettung ins Ungenaue: Zu Martin Gregor-Dellins Wagner-Biographie," *Musik-Konzepte* 25 (May 1982): 74–115.

3. Hermann Levi, "Brief an seinen Vater über die letzte Aufführung des *Parsifal* im Festspielsommer 1882," in *Parsifal*, by Richard Wagner, ed. Csampai and Holland, 132.

4. Theodor W. Adorno, "Über den Bergen," in *Minima Moralia: Reflexionen aus dem beschädigten Leben*, Bibliothek Suhrkamp 61 (Frankfurt am Main: Suhrkamp, 1988) 157.

5. Celan, *Gedichte* 1: 285.

6. Richard Wagner, "Die Sarazenin: Oper in drei [= fünf] Akten (1843)," in *Sämtliche Schriften und Dichtungen*, 5th ed., 11: 238.

7. Donald Dickson, *The Fountain of Living Waters: The Typology of the Waters of Life in Herbert, Vaughan, and Traherne* (Columbia: Univ. of Missouri Press, 1987), 124–65.

8. Carol J. Purtle, *The Marian Paintings of Jan van Eyck* (Princeton, NJ: Princeton Univ. Press, 1982), 106.

9. Kurt Ruh, *Geschichte der abendländischen Mystik*, vol. 1 (Munich: Beck, 1990–99), 253.

10. Martin Heidegger, *Die Technik und die Kehre*, 8th ed., Opuscula 1 (Pfullingen: Neske, 1991), 37–47.

11. Heidegger, *Die Technik und die Kehre*, 40.

12. Heidegger, *Die Technik und die Kehre*, 20.

13. Heidegger, *Die Technik und die Kehre*, 47.

14. Werner Vordtriede, *Heine-Kommentar*, vol. 1 (Munich: Winkler, 1970), 69.

15. August Friedrich Gfrörer, *Die Geschichte des Urchristentums*, 2nd ed., 5 vols. (Stuttgart: Schweizerbart, 1838). Wagner may also have known Adolphe Franck, *Die Kabbala, oder die Religionsphilosophie der Hebräer*, ed. and trans. Ad. Gelinek (Leipzig: Hunger, 1844). The translator later spelled his name Adolf Jellinek.

16. Theodor W. Adorno, "Zur Partitur des *Parsifal*," in *Parsifal*, by Richard Wagner, ed. Csampai and Holland, 194.

17. Wagner admired Meister Eckhart so much that he insisted the mystic's writings be included in his son's reading list (C. Wagner, *Diaries*, Aug. 16, 1878). One reason for the composer's admiration may have been the Inquisition's condemnation of the mystic's teachings as heretical. The pope upheld the verdict when Meister Eckhart appealed. Wagner always sided with the rebels. He also shared the mystic's belief in the "inner God" (e.g. C. Wagner, *Diaries*, June 12, 1878).

18. The extremes of interpretation range from Hans Küng's appreciation of Wagner's God as a "light from within us" to Hartmut Zelinsky's condemnation of Wagner's "new" religion of redemption as annihilation: Hans Küng, "Wagner's *Parsifal*: A Theology for Our Time," *Michigan Quarterly Review* 23, no. 3 (1984): 311–33, and Hartmut Zelinsky, "Die 'feuerkur' des Richard Wagner oder die 'neue religion' der 'Erlösung' durch 'Vernichtung,'" *Musik-Konzepte* 5 (1978): 79–112.

19. It is reproduced in Renata Berg-Pan, *Leni Riefenstahl*, Twayne's Theatrical Arts Series (Boston: Twayne, 1980), facing p. 62.

20. Michael E. Zimmerman, *Heidegger's Confrontation with Modernity: Technology, Politics, and Art* (Bloomington: Indiana Univ. Press, 1990), 100. Syberberg "quotes" the effect years later. His Web diary of March 12, 2002 reproduces a photo showing the site of theWorld Trade Center with searchlights forming the columns of a memorial. He restricts his comments to "Speer redivivus. Under another flag,"

21. Richard Reitzenstein, *Poimandres: Studien zur griechisch-ägyptischen und frühchristlichen Literatur* (Leipzig: Teubner, 1904), 9.

22. David B. Hinton, *The Films of Leni Riefenstahl*, 2nd ed., Filmmakers 29 (Metuchen, NJ: Scarecrow, 1991), 42, 114.

23. W. L. Wilmshurst, *The Meaning of Masonry* (New York: Bell, 1980), 150.

24. Richard Wagner, "Religion and Art," 247.

Notes to Chapter 10: Epilogue to *Parsifal*

1. The comments on the ancient Greek satyr play are based on Bernd Seidensticker, "Das Satyrspiel," in *Satyrspiel*, ed. Bernd Seidensticker, Wege der Forschung 579 (Darmstadt: Wissenschaftliche Buchgesellschaft, 1989), 332–61.

2. Michael Ewans, *Wagner and Aeschylus: The Ring and the Oresteia* (Cambridge: Cam-

bridge Univ. Press, 1983), 252–55.

3. Bruno Snell, "Aischylos' 'Isthmiastai,'" *Satyrspiel*, ed. Seidensticker, 87.

4. Paul Merker and Wolfgang Stammler, *Reallexikon der deutschen Literaturgeschichte*, 2nd ed., 5 vols. (Berlin: de Gruyter, 1977), 3:601.

5. Bernhard Beyer, *Geschichte der Grossloge "Zur Sonne" in Bayreuth*, vol. 1 (Frankfurt am Main: Bauhütten, 1954), 24.

6. The daughter of Carl Kolb, a prominent member, recorded that Richard Wagner met with a discussion group every Wednesday (Beyer, 2:143).

7. Gutman's biography and the quoted articles by Zelinsky belong to the most condemning interpretations of *Parsifal* as a racial ritual and anti-Semitic weapon. Reprints of two equally famous rebuttals to Zelinsky are found in Csampai and Holland's edition of *Parsifal*: Joachim Kaiser, "Hat Zelinsky recht gegen Wagners *Parsifal*?" 257-59, and Carl Dahlhaus, "Erlösung dem Erlöser: Warum Richard Wagners *Parsifal* nicht Mittel zum Zweck der Ideologie ist," 262-69.

8. As for the names of the first *sefira*, Scholem concludes a lengthy discussion by quoting Hebrew sources: "It is called *Ein-Sof* internally and *Keter Elyon* externally . . . ," (*Kabbalah*, 92). In the new constellation during the restoration process the *sefirot* are converted into *parzufim*: 1. Ein-Sof / Keter into Arikh Anpin; 2. Hokhmah into Abba; 3. Binah into Imma; while 4. Hesed, 5. Gevurah, 6. Tiferet, 7. Nezah, 8. Hod, and 9. Yesod are all converted into Ze'eir Anpin, and 10. Malkhut into Nukba de Ze'eir.

9. Gershom G. Scholem, *On the Kabbalah and Its Symbolism*, trans. Ralph Manheim (New York: Schocken, 1965), 115.

10. Lawrence Fine, "The Contemplative Practice of Yihudim in Lurianic Kabbalah," in *Jewish Spirituality from the Sixteenth-Century Revival to the Present*, ed. Arthur Green, World Spirituality 14 (New York: Crossroad, 1987), 80.

11. Louis Jacobs, "The Uplifting of Sparks in Later Jewish Mysticism," *Jewish Spirituality*, ed. Arthur Green, 109–10.

12. Marie-Bernadette Fantin-Epstein, "De Wagner à Syberberg: Parsifal ou le masque éclaté," in *Mises en cadre dans la littérature et dans les arts*, ed. Andrée Mansau (Toulouse: UP Mirail, 1999), 260.

13. Z'ev ben Shimon Halevi, *A Kabbalistic Universe* (New York: Weiser, 1977).

14. Scholem's *Von der mystischen Gestalt der Gottheit* devotes an entire chapter to Yesod, "Zaddik; der Gerechte," 83–134.

15. "Die untere Schechina aber trägt diese Kraft, die sich in ihr sammelt, nach unten und durchdringt als das lebendige 'Wort' alle Welten, die außerhalb des Pleroma der Sefiroth stehen," Scholem, *Von der mystischen Gestalt der Gottheit*, 176. Also important in this context is Anne Marie D'Arcy, *Wisdom and the Grail* (Portland, OR: Four Courts, 2000) on the Shekhinah and Grail literature (289), Shekhinah as Logos/ Sophia (288), indwelling of Logos/Shekhinah in the Grail (288), Shekhinah as divine Wisdom and Torah (290–91), Gnostic Sophia and Kabbalistic Shekhinah (290n–91), Mary and Shekhinah (294–95), Mary as Wisdom (298), and bibliography (369–95).

16. James M. Robinson, ed., *The Nag Hammadi Library in English*, 3rd ed. (San Francisco: Harper, 1988), 148.

17. Hans-Martin Schenke, "The Function and Background of the Beloved Disciple in the Gospel of John," *Nag Hammadi, Gnosticism, & Early Christianity*, ed. Charles Hedrick and Robert Hodgson, Jr. (Peabody, MA: Hendrickson, 1986), 122.

18. Jane Lampman, "The true 'Gospel' of Mary explored," *Denton Record Chronicle*, Nov. 21, 2003.

19. Bert Gerresheim, "Die Plastik als Protokoll der Wahrnehmung," in *Das Düsseldorfer Heine-Monument*, ed. Hans-J. Neisser, 2nd ed. (Düsseldorf: Presseamt, 1981), 5.

20. Ekkehard Mai, "Das Leidenslager wird zur Landschaft," in *Das Düsseldorfer Heine-Monument*, ed. Hans-Joachim Neisser, 10–17.

21. Thomas Mann, *Die Entstehung des Doktor Faustus: Roman eines Romans*, Stockholmer Gesamtausgabe (Amsterdam: Fischer / Querido, 1949).

22. A Kabbalist might read *Untergang* also as "descent" or "going down," as still used about the setting sun. The ascent up the middle pillar starts from the bottom of the chart in Malkhut.

23. Eugene J. Weinraub, *Chrétien's Jewish Grail*, North Carolina Studies in the Romance Languages and Literatures 168, Essays 2 (Chapel Hill: Univ. of North Carolina, 1976), 61.

24. Walter Benjamin, "The Task of the Translator," in *Illuminations*, ed. Hannah Arendt, trans. Harry Zohn (New York: Harcourt, 1968), 80.

25. Walter Benjamin, "The Work of Art in the Age of Mechanical Reproduction," in *Illuminations*, 219–53. Zohn's translation is based on the third version of the text, which deviates considerably from the previous ones.

26. Walter Benjamin, "Das Kunstwerk im Zeitalter seiner technischen Reproduzierbarkeit," in *Gesammelte Schriften*, vol. 7, bk. 1 (Frankfurt am Main: Suhrkamp, 1991), 365. The passage is missing in Zohn's translation, which without comments reduces the two-page chapter to a half-page summary. The lines are included in Benjamin's second version.

27. "Ein sonderbares Gespinst aus Raum und Zeit," Benjamin, *Gesammelte Schriften*, vol. 7, bk. 1, 355. The translation replaces Benjamin's definition with a quite different sentence in *Illuminations*, 224.

28. Gershom Scholem, *The Messianic Idea in Judaism* (New York: Schocken, 1971), 6, and W. Jennings, *Dialectical Images: Walter Benjamin's Theory of Literary Criticism* (Ithaca, NY: Cornell Univ.Press, 1987), 58–59.

29. Walter Benjamin, "Das Kunstwerk im Zeitalter seiner technischen Reproduzierbarkeit," 361-62. The section is missing in *Illuminations*.

Notes to Chapter 11:
Parsifal Encounters the Outside World

1. Syberberg does not provide any bibliographical information, but cites articles about the *Parsifal* film printed before March 20, 1982 in *Le Monde*, *Les Nouvelles Littéraires*, *Le Nouvel Observateur*, *L'Express*, *Humanité Dimanche*, *Le Figaro*, *Cahiers du Cinéma* (8pp.), *Libération*, *L'Avant-Scène d'Opéra*, *Connaissance des Arts*, *Lespresso*, *L'Europeo*, and *La Repubblica;* he also refers to three television programs, two mentions in French news broadcasts, a half-hour program in a cultural program, and a one-hour program on Swiss television, all in Syberberg, *Der Wald steht schwarz und schweiget*, 32.

2. More about this can be found in Jean-Luc Douin, "19 mai 1982—la nuit messianique de *Parsifal*: Une rétrospective des grands moments du Festival de Cannes," *Le Monde*, May 10, 1997.

3. Emmanuel Decaux, "La nuit de *Parsifal*," *Cinématographe*, June 1982, 68.

4. Gottfried Wagner, *Wer nicht mit dem Wolf heult*, 281-82.

5. "Die Kritikerpreisträger 1951-2004," http://www.kritikerverband.de/ preise.htm.
6. Guy-Patrick Sainderichin, "Voyage à Munich: Hans Jürgen Syberberg tourne *Parsifal*," *Cahiers du Cinéma* 331 (Jan. 1982): 22–29.
7. Hans Jürgen Syberberg, interview by Jean-Claude Bonnet and Michel Celemenski, *Cinématographe*, May 1982, 14.
8. Klaus Umbach, "Gesalbte Primeln," review of *Parsifal*, *Der Spiegel*, May 24, 1982, 226–27.
9. Gunnar Iversen, "Brecht + Wagner = Syberberg," *Z* 3, no. 3 (1985): 23–27.
10. John Rockwell, "Film: Hans [sic] Syberberg's Adaptation of *Parsifal*," *New York Times*, Jan. 23, 1983, Sun. ed.
11. Marcia J. Citron, *Opera on Screen* (New Haven: Yale Univ. Press, 2000), 141–60.
12. Jeremy Tambling, *Opera, Ideology and Film* (New York: St. Martin's, 1987), 203.
13. George Movshon, "Opera: *Guntram* in concert, *Parsifal* on film," *High Fidelity*, June 1983, 19.
14. Andrew Clements, "Grail Chase," review of *Parsifal*, *New Statesman*, March 25, 1983.
15. Ronald Holloway, "Non-Competing at Cannes: *Parsifal*," *Variety*, May 26, 1982, 16.
16. Benjamin H. D. Buchloh, "Documenta 7: A Dictionary of Received Ideas," *October* 22 (Autumn 1982): 117.
17. For a succinct survey of Nazi preoccupation with occultism and Grail legends, see Mary Baine Campbell, "Finding the Grail: Fascist Aesthetics and Mysterious Objects," in *King Arthur's Modern Return*, ed. Debra Mancoff (New York: Garland, 1998), 213–25.
18. Jack Kroll, "Cinematic *Parsifal*," review, *Newsweek*, Jan. 31, 1983, 49.
19. Manfred Schneider, "Der ungeheure Blick des Kinos auf die Welt: Die Wissensmächte Musik und Film in Wagner / Syberbergs *Parsifal*," *Merkur* 38 (1984): 882–92. The author discusses some of the same ideas in "Das Kino als kompaktes Medium: Logik und Strategie des Zitierens in Wagner / Syberbergs *Parsifal*," *Freiburger Universitätsblätter* 85 (1984): 79–96.
20. Michael Walsh, "Through the Looking Glass," review of *Parsifal*, *Time*, Jan. 24, 1983, 84.
21. J. Hoberman, "His *Parsifal*: Following the Syberbergenlied," review, *Village Voice*, Feb. 22, 1983, 60+.
22. David Denby, "Marx and Freud Meet Wagner," review of *Parsifal*, *New York*, Jan. 31, 1983, 54.
23. Oskar Sahlberg, "Wagner heute — Syberbergs *Parsifal*," *Neue Deutsche Hefte* 178 (1983): 342–46.
24. Thomas Elsaesser, "*Parsifal*," review, *Monthly Film Bulletin* 50 (May 1983): 137.
25. Stanley Kauffmann, "Far from Bayreuth," review of *Parsifal*, *New Republic*, Feb. 14, 1983, 25.
26. Paul Coates, *The Gorgon's Gaze: German Cinema, Expressionism, and the Image of Horror* (Cambridge: Cambridge Univ. Press, 1991), 126–29.
27. Norman Fischer, "Hans-Jürgen Syberberg's Opera Film, *Parsifal*: Visual Transformation and Philosophical Reconstruction," *Film and Philosophy* 3 (1996): 145–53.
28. Jean Jacques Nattiez, *Wagner Androgyne: A Study in Interpretation*, trans. Stewart Spencer (Princeton, NJ: Princeton Univ. Press, 1993), 290.
29. Kevin J. Harty, ed., *Cinema Arthuriana: Essays on Arthurian Film* (New York: Garland, 1991).
30. Ulrich Müller, "Blank, Syberberg, and the German Arthurian Tradition," in *Cinema Arthuriana*, ed. Kevin J. Harty, 157–68.
31. Kevin J. Harty, *The Reel Middle Ages: American, Western and Eastern European,*

Middle Eastern and Asian Films about Medieval Europe (Jefferson, NC: McFarland, 1999) 202–4.

32. John Christopher Kleis, "The Arthurian Dilemma: Faith and Works in Syberberg's *Parsifal*," in *King Arthur on Film: New Essays on Arthurian Cinema*, ed. Kevin J. Harty (Jefferson, NC: McFarland, 1999), 109–22.

33. Donald L. Hoffman, "Re-Framing Perceval," *Arthuriana* 10, no. 4 (2000): 45–56.

34. Ralph Schnell, "Hans Jürgen Syberbergs filmische Mythologie: Syberberg und die großen Symbole," *Ästhetik und Kommunikation* 56 (1984): 105–11.

35. Hans Jürgen Syberberg, "Filmisches bei Richard Wagner," in *Richard Wagner: Mittler zwischen Zeiten*, ed. Gerhard Heldt, Wort und Musik 3 (Anif/Salzburg: Müller-Speiser, 1990), 66–74; his discussion with the audience, 74–78, 206–7, and 212.

36. The contrast is between ideas recognizable through the senses and through rational thinking, as outlined in Heidegger's *Principle of Ground* (*Satz vom Grund*). Syberberg is probably aware of the importance of mysticism in Heidegger's work. See, e.g., John D. Caputo, *The Mystical Element in Heidegger's Thought* (New York: Fordham Univ. Press, 1986).

37. Matthias Claudius, *Sämtliche Werke*, 7th ed. (Darmstadt: Wissenschaftliche Buchgesellschaft, 1989), 217–18.

38. Olsen, "Celan's 'Todesfuge'," 199.

39. Hans Christian Kosler, "Augenmensch mit Schaum vorm Mund: Hans Jürgen Syberbergs neue Notizen aus Deutschland," review of *Der Wald steht schwarz und schweiget*, *Frankfurter Allgemeine Zeitung*, Dec. 11, 1984, Literatur.

Notes to Chapter 12: The Monologues

1. Hans Jürgen Syberberg, "Die Falle ist zu," *Medium*, February 1982, 20–21; "Nur der Kranke hält es aus," *Medium*, April 1982, 27–29; "Wir sollen den anderen ins Gesicht spucken," *Medium*, July 1982, 40–41; "Sie haben ihn zum lächerlichen Gartenzwerg ihres Selbstmitleids heroisiert," *Medium*, August 1982, 35–37; "Ohne Neugier und Lust und Informationsredlichkeit," *Medium*, September–October 1982, 78–80; "Vorführen braucht soviel Energie und Phantasie wie Machen," *Medium*, December 1982, 31–33; "Welcher Sumpf von Pseudodemokratie," *Medium*, January 1983, 42–45; "In der Konformität des Vorurteils," *Medium*, February–March 1983, 71–73; Stefan Heym, Hans Jürgen Syberberg, Alexander Kluge, Gerd Bucerius, and Günter Gaus, *Reden über das eigene Land: Deutschland* (Munich: Bertelsmann, 1983), 36–61.

2. Syberberg, "Nur der Kranke hält es aus," 29.

3. Syberberg, "Ohne Neugier und Lust und Informationsredlichkeit," 79.

4. The lecture series was organized by the publishing house Bertelsmann and the Munich *Kulturreferat*. The other speakers were the author Stefan Heym, the moviemaker and author Alexander Kluge, the politician and later publisher Gerd Bucerius, and the media man and later diplomat Günter Gaus.

5. Syberberg also refers to two other recent articles of his that presumably appeared in the summer of 1983: "Wer Richard Wagner hat, hat Deutschland" in the French *L'Express* and "Fassbinder als neuer Mythos," in *New York*.

6. Erica Bilder, ed., *Hans Jürgen Syberberg* (Amsterdam: Barbar Events, 1983).

7. Hans Jürgen Syberberg, "The Abode of the Gods (1984)," in *West German Filmmakers on Film: Visions and Voices*, ed. Eric Rentschler (New York: Holmes, 1988), 245.

8. Martin Heidegger, *Hölderlins Hymne "Andenken,"* vol. 52 of *Gesamtausgabe*, (Frankfurt am Main: Klostermann, 1982).

9. Martin Buber, *I and Thou*, ed. and trans. Walter Kaufmann (New York: Scribner, 1970) and *Ich und Du* in *Das dialogische Prinzip* (Darmstadt: Wissenschaftliche Buchgesellschaft, 1984), 7–136. Parenthetical page references refer to the New York edition.

10. The only prop used during the sequence involving Wagner is a tiny glass bottle. Unlike the vial of balm for Amfortas or oil for Parsifal's anointment, this tiny flask serves mundane purposes. It doubles as an inkwell for Cosima's diary and for Wagner's perfume sent by Judith Gautier. In his book to *Parsifal* Syberberg mentions that he had planned "the next film on Wagner as a monologue by Judith Gautier" (241). Since that film did not materialize, her importance was reduced to a few visual references in the *Parsifal* film. If Syberberg wanted to include her as a Jewish force in Wagner's life, that role was subsumed by the metaphysical dimension of the film as a whole.

11. Johann Wolfgang von Goethe, *West-Östlicher Divan*, Grossherzog Wilhelm Ernst Ausgabe, 16 vols. (Leipzig: Insel, 1920), 11:644–932.

12. Heidegger, "The Question Concerning Technology," 301–7 and *Die Technik und die Kehre*, 37–47.

13. Francis Ambrière, *Paris*, Les Guides Bleus (Paris: Hachette, 1949), 401.

14. Stanley Kauffmann, "Into the Night," review of *Die Nacht*, *New Republic*, December 1985, 26.

15. Peter Wapnewski, "Hymnen an die Nacht," review of *Die Nacht*, *Der Spiegel*, July 15, 1985, 126–29.

16. Manfred Schneider, "Eine ganz neue Dunkelheit," review of *Die Nacht*, *Die Zeit*, Nov. 29, 1985.

17. Angelika Kaps, "Das Gesicht der Edith Clever: Hans Jürgen Syberberg drehte in Berlin *Die Nacht*," *Tagesspiegel*, Dec. 23, 1984, and Sibylle Wirsing, "Die Entdeckung einer Tragödin: Edith Clever in Hans Jürgen Syberbergs sechs-Stunden Film *Nacht;* Uraufführung in Berlin," *Frankfurter Allgemeine Zeitung*, May 11, 1985, DII, Feuilleton.

18. Kauffmann, "Into the Night," 24.

19. Ronald Holloway, "*Die Nacht*," review, *Variety*, May 22, 1985, 20.

20. Hans Jürgen Syberberg, "Sustaining Romanticism in a Postmodernist Cinema," interview by Christopher Sharrett, *Cineaste* 15, no. 3 (1987): 18–20.

21. Hans Jürgen Syberberg, "Ende der europäischen Zeit," in *Die Unfähigkeit zu feiern: Der achte Mai*, ed. Norbert Seitz (Frankfurt am Main: Neue Kritik, 1985), 59–72.

22. One of the best books about President Reagan's visit and the international reaction remains Ilya Levkov, ed., *Bitburg and Beyond: Encounters in American, German and Jewish History* (New York: Shapolsky, 1987). President Reagan's speech in Bergen-Belsen appears on pp. 131–35, and the one in Bitburg on pp. 168–71.

23. Hans Jürgen Syberberg, "Bitburg," *On Film* 14 (1985): 37; his text is one of five short essays by filmmakers and critics with the cover title "Reagan at Bitburg: Spectacle and Memory," 36–40.

24. Scholem, *Von der mystischen Gestalt der Gottheit*, 179.

25. A. Nicholas Fargnoli and Michael Patrick Gillespie, *James Joyce A to Z: The Essential Reference to the Life and Work* (New York: Oxford Univ. Press, 1996), 247–48.

26. Hans Jürgen Syberberg, "Mit kleinsten Mitteln sehr Anspruchsvolles offerieren," interview, in *Kunst Machen? Gespräche und Essays*, ed. Florian Rötzer and Sara Rogenhofer, 2nd ed. (Munich: Boer, 1991), 172–84.

27. Sebastian Huber, "Edith Clever liest Joyce: Der Monolog der Molly Bloom, 1985," in

Ulysses: Die Unausweichliche Modalität des Sichtbaren, ed. Thomas Trummer (Vienna: Brandstätter 2004), 20–25.

28. http://www.atelier-augarten.at/ausstellungen/ulysses/ulysses_texte.html (accessed June 2, 2004).

29. Manfred Schneider, "Dal libro al corpo: Hans Jürgen Syberberg e Edith Clever," in a special issue on Syberberg, *Cinema e cinema* 57 (January–April 1990): 81–87.

30. It is not known if Syberberg used an early version of the novella, but the text in the film contains many cuts that do not alter the context, compared to the edition in Arthur Schnitzler, *Fräulein Else,* in *Die Erzählenden Schriften,* 2 vols. (Frankfurt am Main: Fischer, 1981), 2:324–81.

31. A list of movies about Kleist or his works shows 46 titles in *Kleist in Frankfurt, Kleist im Film: Ein Arbeitsbuch,* ed. Leonhard M. Fiedler (Dierdorf: Margot Lang, 1989), 106–11. See also Irmela Schneider, "Aktualität im historischen Gewand: Zu Filmen nach Werken von Heinrich von Kleist," in *Literaturverfilmungen,* ed. Franz-Josef Albersmeier and Volker Roloff (Frankfurt am Main: Suhrkamp, 1989), 99–121.

32. Hinton, *The Films of Leni Riefenstahl,* 110; the author devotes an entire chapter to the *Penthesilea* plans (109–120).

33. Leni Riefenstahl, "Why Am I Filming *Penthesilea*?, *Film Culture* 56–57 (1973): 195.

34. Hans Jürgen Syberberg, "La radio come *Urstimme,*" trans. Elfi Reiter, special issue, *Cinema e cinema* 57 (January–April 1990) 68–74.

35. Leni Riefenstahl, *A Memoir* (New York: St. Martin's, 1993), 251.

36. Hans Jürgen Syberberg, *Penthesilea,* program (Berlin: Werkstatt Berlin, 1988), [16].

37. Hans Jürgen Syberberg, "*Penthesilea,*" in *Opern und Opernfiguren: Festschrift für Joachim Herz,* ed. Ursula Müller and Ulrich Müller, Wort und Musik 2 (Anif–Salzburg: Müller-Speiser, 1989), 211–26.

38. Joseph Hanimann, "Die Königin: wer sonst?" Review of *Penthesilea, Frankfurter Allgemeine Zeitung,* Nov. 17, 1987, DII, Feuilleton.

39. Hendrik Markgraf, "Liebesgeflüster und Kriegsgeschrei: Hans Jürgen Syberbergs *Penthesilea*–Inszenierung mit Edith Clever im Großen Haus," *Frankfurter Allgemeine Zeitung,* April 18, 1988, Lokales.

40. Hans Jürgen Syberberg and Edith Clever, "Sie hat den Glauben, ich das Bild," interview by Evelyn Roll, *Süddeutsche Zeitung,* June 25, 1988, repr. in *Kleist in Frankfurt, Kleist im Film: Ein Arbeitsbuch,* ed. Leonhard M. Fiedler, 91–92.

41. Matthias Matussek, "Ich hielt bei Peter Stein um ihre Hand an," *Der Spiegel,* April 11, 1988, 218+.

42. Hans Jürgen Syberberg, "Hitler artiste de l'État ou l'avantgarde méphistophélique du xxe siècle," in *Les Réalismes 1919–1939,* ed. Pontus Hulten (Paris: Centre Pompidou, 1980), 378–83.

43. "Schlimme Sätze," *Frankfurter Allgemeine Zeitung,* Oct. 3, 1988, Feuilleton.

44. Andreas Kuhlmann, "Auf dem Abstellgleis: Ein Kongreß über die 'Frankfurter Schule' in Rotterdam," *Frankfurter Allgemeine Zeitung* Dec. 6, 1988, Feuilleton.

45. Sibylle Wirsing, "Mein lieber Schwan," review of *Die Marquise von O . . .,* *Frankfurter Allgemeine Zeitung,* April 3, 1989, Feuilleton; *Marathon-Monolog,* review of *Die Marquise, Scala* 5 (Sept.–Oct. 1989): 20; and Gerhard Rohde,"Ruinenromantik und Abschiedsschmerz," review of *Die Marquise, Frankfurter Allgemeine Zeitung,* June 5,1989, Lokales.

46. Hans Jürgen Syberberg, *Die Marquise von O . . . (vom Süden nach dem Norden verlegt),* by Henrich von Kleist, Edith Clever, and Hans Jürgen Syberberg,program (Berlin: Hebbel-Theater, 1989).

47. Leonardo Quaresima, "*Die Marquise von O . . .*, Kleist, (Rohmer), Syberberg," special issue, *Cinema e cinema* 57 (January–April 1990), 97–108.

48. Hans Jürgen Syberberg, "Nach der *Nacht* und den Videofilmen *Fräulein Else* und der *Marquise von O . . .*," in *Kleist in Frankfurt*, ed. Leonhard M. Fiedler, 34–48.

49. "Streiter gegen Kulturbarbarei: Hans Jürgen Syberberg spricht in der Aula der Universität," *Frankfurter Allgemeine Zeitung*, June 6, 1989, Lokales.

50. Hans Jürgen Syberberg, "Die enthauptete Kunst," *Die Zeit*, June 3, 1988, Magazin.

51. Marion, Countess Dönhoff, *Before the Storm: Memories of My Youth in Old Prussia* (New York: Knopf, 1990), 197–99. The American edition is compiled from two of her books, with the mentioned episode coming from the earliest: *Kindheit in Ostpreußen* (Berlin: Siedler, 1988), and *Namen, die keiner mehr nennt* (Cologne: Diederichs, 1962).

52. Countess Dönhoff (1909–2002) lost many friends in the purge following the failed revolt of July 20, 1944. She became the editor of the weekly newspaper *Die Zeit* in 1968 and its publisher in 1973. A prolific journalist, author, and analyst of European politics and history, she received honorary degrees from Columbia, Smith, and the New School of Social Research.

53. http://www.syberberg4.de/12-Maerz.html (accessed March 13, 2002).

54. Edith Clever and Hans Jürgen Syberberg, *Ein Traum, was sonst?* Program (Berlin: Hebbel-Theater, 1990).

55. Jan Ross, "Der Dichter ist den Germanisten ausgeliefert: 'Kleist , die deutsche Nation und die Kunst heute': Ein Symposium in Frankfurt an der Oder," *Frankfurter Allgemeine Zeitung*, Oct. 23, 1991, Feuilleton.

56. Leonardo Quaresima, "Le cittá del cinema," review of *Ein Traum, was sonst*, http://www.syberberg.de/Syberberg3/italiani/italiani.html (accessed Nov. 29, 2004).

57. Hans-Thies Lehmann, *Postdramatisches Theater*, 2nd ed. (Frankfurt am Main: Verlag der Autoren, 2001).

58. E.g. pp. 55, 67, 116, 120, 197, 204, 226, 230, 276, 346, 350, 384, 405, and 437.

Notes to Chapter 13: Turbulence

1. "To write poetry is barbaric. And this corrodes even the knowledge of why it has become impossible to write poetry today," *Prisms*, by Theodor W. Adorno, trans. Samuel and Shierry Weber (London: Spearman, 1967), 34.

2. Hans Jürgen Syberberg, "Seeing the Light: *Adolphe Appia; Theatre Artist* by Richard C. Beacham," trans. Bert Cadullo, *New Republic*, Oct. 3, 1988, 32–36.

3. Kaes, *Deutschlandbilder*, 135–70.

4. The missing text affects pp. 145, 148–49, 152–53, 156–57, and 160.

5. Hans Jürgen Syberberg, interview by André Müller, in *Im Gespräch*, ed. André Müller (Reinbek bei Hamburg: Rowohlt, 1989), 183–203; with Syberberg's loose-leaf insert, "Erklärung vom 12. Juli 1989." Rev. repr. of "Man will mich töten," *Die Zeit*, Sept. 30, 1988, and Syberberg's protest, "Entgegnung," *Die Zeit,* Oct. 14. A second note was published among the letters to the editor on Nov. 18, 1988.

6. Michael Meyer, "Virtueller Weg nach Hause," *Ostseezeitung*, Oct. 26, 2001.

7. H. W. Koch, *A History of Prussia* (New York: Dorset, 1978), 288.

8. Konstantin von Hammerstein, et al," Vertriebene: Eine besondere Art von Heimweh," *Der Spiegel*, Aug. 9, 2004, 40–42, and Erika Steinbach, "Grandioses Versagen," interview by Hans Michael Kloth and Dietmar Pieper, *Der Spiegel*, Sept. 20, 2004: 36+.

9. "Wer mit den Juden ging wie mit den Linken, machte Karriere, und es hatte nicht unbe-
dingt mit Liebe oder Verständnis oder gar Zuneigung zu tun. Wie konnten das Juden
ertragen, es sei denn, sie wollten nur Macht," Hans Jürgen Syberberg, *Vom Unglück
und Glück der Kunst in Deutschland nach dem letzten Kriege* (Munich: Matthes und
Seitz, 1990), 14.

10. One notes with sad irony that the called-for asceticism arrived by 2004. With the German economy suffering, the subsidized arts are experiencing severe reductions in
financial support, resulting, for example, in 50% unemployment among actors.
Syberberg's criticism of the emphasis on the vulgar and worthless still remains valid,
as seen, e.g., in the 2004 production in Berlin of Mozart's *Abduction from the Serail.*
Its plot took place in a brothel, with corresponding costumes and acting.

11. Hartmut Erbse refers to the debate about Homer's formulations with, "But one can
very well bring in the cases in which the article stands after the noun with an explanatory or a qualifying adjective," in *Homer: German Scholarship in Translation*, trans.
G. M. Wright and P. V. Jones (Oxford: Clarendon, 1997), 315.

12. The following two examples from Voss' translation of the *Iliad* identify with
underlining the words separating elements that would appear together in standard
German: "EinerTochter vermählt des Adrastos . . ." (14. 121), and ". . . als er die
Stimme vernahm des redenden Gottes" (20. 380).

13. Klaus Reichert, "Hebräische Züge in der Sprache Paul Celans," in *Paul Celan*, ed.
Werner Hamacher and Winfried Menninghaus, suhrkamp taschenbuch 2083 (Frankfurt am Main: Suhrkamp, 1988), 156–69.

14. Theodor W. Adorno, "Parataxis," in *Noten zur Literatur*, suhrkamp taschenbuch 355
(Frankfurt am Main: Suhrkamp, 1981), 473.

15. Paul Celan, "Und mit dem Buch aus Tarussa," in *Gedichte,* 1: 287–89.

16. Reduced here to a list of names, these markers are: Th. Bernhard, A. Kiefer, Tarkovsky,
Gorbachev, K. Masur, V. Havel, Walesa, E. Jünger, Heidegger; followed by Hannah
Arendt, Sulamith, Salomo, Moses, David; then Rembrandt, biblical kings, prophets,
sibyls, Michelangelo, Pythagoras, and Plato (17).

17. Günther Nenning, "Auf deutschem Ross: Die deutsche Kunst ist groß, und Syberberg
ist ihr Prophet," review of *Vom Unglück und Glück, Die Zeit,* July 27, 1990.

18. Werner Fuld, "Hitler neu bedenken? An Syberbergs Unwesen soll die Welt genesen,"
review of *Vom Unglück und Glück, Frankfurter Allgemeine Zeitung*, Aug. 24, 1990,
Feuilleton, and Frank Schirrmacher, "Amerkungen zu einem Ärgernis," review of *Vom
Unglück und Glück,Frankfurter Allgemeine Zeitung,* Aug. 24, 1990, Feuilleton, also
printed as "Ein notwendiger Kommentar" in some editions of the newspaper.

19. Hans Jürgen Syberberg, "Wie man neuen Haß züchtet," *Frankfurter Allgemeine Zeitung*, Sept. 6, 1990, Feuilleton.

20. Hellmuth Karasek, "Frühling für Hitler?" *Der Spiegel*, Sept. 2, 1990: 240+.

21. André Heller, "Ein radikaler Nomade in der kalten deutschen Wüste," *Abendzeitung*,
Aug.18–19, 1990, Feuilleton.

22. http://home.t-online.de/home/turbund/ntrvw1.htm (accessed Nov. 27, 2000).

23. The other discussants were Susan Sontag from the United States, Bernard Sobel from
France, Heiner Müller from former East Germany, and Klaus Theweleit and Edith Clever from former West Germany.

24. Matthias Matussek, "Gefolgschaft erzwingen," *Der Spiegel*, Oct. 22, 1990: 260+.

25. Ian Buruma, "There's No Place Like Heimat," *New York Review*, Dec. 20, 1990, 34+,
repr. in *German Book Review* 2 (1990): 1–9.

26. Frank Schirrmacher, "Angst ist die Botschaft: Eine Syberberg-Debatte in der Akademie

im Osten Berlins," *Frankfurter Allgemeine Zeitung*, Oct. 17, 1990, Feuilleton. Other acerbic reviews appeared on Oct. 16 by Rüdiger Schaper in *Süddeutsche Zeitung*, Wilfried Mommert in *Frankfurter Rundschau*, Elke Schmitter in *Tageszeitung*, and onOct. 19, by Dieter Zimmer in *Die Zeit*.

27. Rembert Hüser, "Wale malen," in *Gelegenheit: Diebe; 3× Deutsche Motive*, by Dirk Baecker, Rembert Hüser, and Georg Stanitzek (Bielefeld: Haux, 1991), 101–66.

28. Hans Jürgen Syberberg, "Wir stehen fest im Sturm," interview by Heimo Schwilk, *Rheinischer Merkur*, Sept. 7, 1990.

29. Hans Jürgen Syberberg, "Eigenes und Fremdes: Über den Verlust des Tragischen," in *Die selbstbewusste Nation*, ed. Heimo Schwilk and Ulrich Schacht, 3rd ed. (Frankfurt am Main: Ullstein, 1995), 124–33. The chapter is a slight revision of a lecture he gave in March 1993, "Zu einer Definition des Eigenen,"repr. in *Deutschsein? Eine Ausstellung gegen Fremdenhaß und Gewalt*, ed. Jürgen Harten, Kunsthalle Düsseldorf, 14–25 Apr. 1993 (Düsseldorf: Meyer, 1993), 105–10. Only the last paragraph was replaced with a new page later. The occasion for the lecture was a symposium opening an exhibit confronting hatred of foreigners and violence.

30. Lothar Baier, "Eine ungeheuerliche Neuigkeit? Nachfragen zur Debatte um den Pamphletisten Syberberg," *Neue Rundschau* 102, no. 1 (1991): 117–30.

31. Diedrich Diederichsen, "Spiritual Reactionaries after German Reunification: Syberberg, Foucault, and Others," *October* 62 (Fall 1992): 65–83. A very different overview of Foucault's reception and impact in Germany is offered in Uta Liebmann Schaub, "Foucault, Alternative Presses, and Alternative Ideology in West Germany: A Report," *German Studies Review* 12, no. 1 (1988): 139–53. Although sharing many of Foucault'sviews, Syberberg does not refer to him in his publications.

32. "Das Rechte—Begegnung mit der Realität im Spannungsfeld zwischen Kunst, Philosophie, Wissenschaft und Politik," [symposium on July 1–2, 1995 organized by] Bayerisches Staatsschauspiel/Marstall in Co-Produktion mit der *Süddeutschen Zeitung* und dem Steirischen Herbst 95, http://www.stat.uni-muenchen.de/ philosophie/wis/ philo/rechtkon/ rechtepr.htm (accessed Nov. 26, 1997).

33. Eric L. Santner, "The Trouble with Hitler: Postwar German Aesthetics and the Legacy of Fascism," *New German Critique* 57 (1992): 5–24.

34. Grimm's dictionary defines *Liebkind* (love child) as *Jungfernkind*, meaning a "child born out of wedlock." Syberberg had played with a similar, unsanctioned status in *Die freudlose Gesellschaft*, 153. The passage in question posits the hypothetical situation of Syberberg being the child of an unwed Jewish mother. Of course, also Jesus' mother was a Jewish *Jungfer*, an association reviving the link to a Christ-like path of suffering.

35. Gerd Gemünden, "Nostalgia for the Nation: Intellectuals and National Identity in Unified Germany," in *Acts of Memory: Cultural Recall in the Present*, ed. Mieke Bal, Jonathan Crewe, and Leo Spitzer (Hanover, NH: Univ. Press of New England, 1999), 120–33.

36. Stephen Daniel Slater, "The Complicity of Culture with Barbarism: A Study of Thomas Mann's *Doktor Faustus* and Hans Jürgen Syberberg's *Hitler, ein Film aus Deutschland*," PhD diss, Yale Univ., 1992.

37. Bernd Kiefer, "Kulturmontage im Posthistoire: Zur Filmästhetik von Hans Jürgen Syberberg," in *Montage in Theater und Film*, ed. Horst Fritz, Mainzer Forschungen zu Drama und Theater 8 (Tübingen: Francke, 1993), 229–47.

38. "Online Nachlese 34 [352]: Deutschsein?" http://www.rep-berlin.de/on_0034.htm (accessed March 3, 1997).

39. Stephen Brockmann, "Syberberg's Germany," *German Quarterly Review* 69, no. 1 (1996): 48–62.

40. Besides a slew of articles on the Internet, one helpful overview and analysis is Jan Werner Müller, *Another Country: German Intellectuals, Unification and National Identity* (New Haven, CT: Yale Univ. Press, 2000), esp. 214–19 and the bibliography.

41. Hans Jürgen Syberberg, Home page, http://www.syberberg.de, e.g. diary 7-8-9 March, 2004 (accessed March 14, 2004).

Notes to Chapter 14: From Tower to Cave

1. Christoph Dallach, et al, "Patriotische Bauchschmerzen," *Der Spiegel*, Nov. 29. 2004, 184–87.

2. Hans Jürgen Syberberg, "S'approprier le monde," *Cahiers du Cinéma*, 443–44 (May 1991): 57.

3. Excerpts of the review in *The Guardian* and sections of the program notes appear on Syberbergs home page, http://www.syberberg.de/Syberberg3_2001/April/GB/gb.html (accessed Nov. 29, 2004).

4. Hans Jürgen Syberberg, "Talking Cinema," interview by Julian Petley, Sept. 7, 1992, audio cassette, ICA, 816.

5. Hans Jürgen Syberberg, "Briefe über Raum, Letters on space, Lettres sur l'espace, Brieven over ruimte," *Theaterschrift* (Sept. 1992): 154–64.

6. Hans Jürgen Syberberg, "Germany's Heart: The Modern Taboo," interview by Marilyn Berlin Snell,*New Perspectives Quarterly* 10, no. 1 (1993), http://www.digitalnpq.org/archive/1993_winter/ germanys_heart.html (accessed May 7, 2004); abr. repr. in *At Century's End:Great Minds Reflect on Our Times*, ed. Nathan P. Gardels, foreword Bill Moyers (La Jolla, CA: ALTI, 1996), 114–24, and as "El corazón de Alemania: El moderno tabú," in *Fin de siglo: Grandes pensadores hacen reflexiones sobre nuestro tiempo*, ed. Nathan P. Gardels, prólogo Bill Moyers, interamericana ed., (Mexico City: McGraw-Hill, 1996), 116–27.

7. Rockwell, "The Re-Emergence of an Elusive Director," C13+.

8. Hans Jürgen Syberberg, "Aus der Zeit der letzten Unschuld," *Drucksache* 4 (1993): 97–116, early photos, 117–28, 152, and "1971: *Nach meinem letzten Umzug*," 141–49.

9. Wolfgang Binder, *Friedrich Hölderlin: Studien*, ed. Elisabeth Binder and Klaus Weimar, suhrkamp taschenbuch 2082 (Frankfurt am Main: Suhrkamp, 1987), 196–97.

10. Hans Jürgen Syberberg, *Der verlorene Auftrag: Ein Essay* (Vienna: Karolinger, 1994).

11. Andreas Kilb, "O Mensch! Gib acht! Deutsche Szene: Hans Jürgen Syberberg feiert Friedrich Nietzsche in Weimar," *Die Zeit*, June 24, 1994, Feuilleton. The accompanying booklet or program was not available for consultation, Hans Jürgen Syberberg, *Nietzsche — Schleef — Syberberg* (Weimar: Kunstfest, 1994).

12. "Sommerszene Salzburg '94, " "Friedrich Nietzsche *Also sprach Zarathustra*," http://hirsch.casy.sbg.ac.at/altekultur/szene94/e18.html (accessed Jan. 3, 2005).

13. Hans Jürgen Syberberg, interview by Edgar Reitz, in *Bilder in Bewegung: Essays, Gespräche zum Kino*, ed. Edgar Reitz (Reinbek bei Hamburg: Rowohlt, 1995), 156–62.

14. "Diederich [*sic*] Diederichsen hat wegen der Teilnahme von Hans Jürgen Syberberg kurzfristig abgesagt," program notes, July 1, 1995, http://www.stat.uni-muenchen.de/philosophie/wis/philo/rechtkon/rechtepr.htlm (accessed Nov. 26, 1997).

15. Hans Jürgen Syberberg, *Das Rechte — tun* (Munich: Kronenbitter, 1995).
16. Gitta Honegger, *Thomas Bernhard: The Making of an Austrian* (New Haven, CT: Yale Univ. Press, 2002).
17. Hans Jürgen Syberberg, Home page, http://www.syberberg.de/Syberberg4/13_April .html (accessed Dec. 12, 2003).
18. Philippe Lacoue-Labarthe, "Syberberg: On Germany after Hitler," in *Politics-Poetics, documenta x: the Book* (Ostfildern-Ruit: Cantz, 1997), 480–82; a second title page changes the title to *Poleitics*; essay repr. as "Syberberg: de l'Allemagne après Hitler,"*Trafic* 25 (1998): 48–54.
19. *Short Guide/Kurzführer* (Ostfildern-Ruit: documenta-Cantz, 1997), 220–21.
20. Marc Silberman, "Late Pabst: *The Last Ten Days* (1955)," in *The Films of G. W. Pabst: An Extraterritorial Cinema*, ed. Eric Rentschler (New Brunswick: Rutgers Univ.Press, 1990), 213.
21. Hans Jürgen Syberberg, "Man muß so tief in die Wunde gehen, daß man in Verdacht gerät," interview by Benjamin Heisenberg, Christoph Hochhäusler, and Sebastian Kutzli,April 30, 1999, *Revolver: Zeitschrift für Film* 3 (2000), http://www.revolver-film.de/Inhalte/Rev3/html/ Syberberg.htm (accessed Nov. 14, 2003).
22. For an in-depth discussion of Kiefer's art, see Anselm Kiefer, *The High Priestess*, with an essay by Armin Zweite (New York: Abrams, 1989); for bibliographical references Andreas Huyssen, "Kiefer in Berlin," *October* 25, no. 1 (1992): 84–101, and Bernhard Schulz, "Wüstensand der Geschichte: Anselm Kiefer in der Fondation Beyeler in Basel," *Kulturchronik* 20, no. 1 (2002): 4–5.
23. Kiefer, plates and text xiii.
24. Margarethe Krieger suffered a debilitating stroke in January 2004. Syberberg tried to assist her and reported on her condition intermittently during the fall and winter in his Web diary. These reports include several photos of her, e.g. Dec.1 and 2, 2004. More about her can be found under "Central Pages" on Syberberg's home page.
25. Marc Hairapetian, "Oskar Werner Bonaparte: Im Tod wird der exzentrische Schauspieler wie ein Popstar verehrt," *Die Welt*, 12 Nov. 1997.
26. Peter Iden, "Finale im Mist: Die 10. 'documenta' scheitert an der Überforderung der Praxis durch die Theorie," *Frankfurter Rundschau*, http://www.superpeople .com/ smoker's-diary/fr.html (accessed May 5, 1998).
27. Karl Sierek,"La cathedrale: la construction vidéo de Syberberg engloutie dans la Documenta 10," *Trafic* 25 (1998): 54–67.
28. Alban Nikolai Herbst, review of *Die Fehler des Kopisten* by Botho Strauß, DeutschlandRadio, April 1997, http://www.dlf.de/literatur/gespraeche/ strauss.html (accessed April 15, 1998).
29. Eckhart Gillen, "Jede Generation die gleiche Scheiße," interview by Marius Babias about "Deutschlandbilder: Kunst aus einem geteilten Land," Sept. 7, 1997–Jan. 11, 1998, http://www.nadir.org/nadir/periodika/jungle_world/37/28a.htm (accessed May 7, 2004).
30. Jordi Ibáñez, *Despuéz de la decapitatión del arte: Una apología de Hans Jürgen Syberberg* (Barcelona: Destino, 1996).
31. Guido Goossens, *Verloren zonsondergangen: Hans Jürgen Syberberg en het linkse denken over rechts in Duitsland* (Amsterdam: Amsterdam Univ. Press, 2004).
32. Kirsten Klümper, "Brecht-Haus: Nächte mit Denkern," *Berliner Zeitung*, 12 Feb. 1998, Feuilleton.
33. Hans Jürgen Syberberg, "Mein Jahrhundertbuch: *Buckower Elegien* von Bertolt Brecht," *Die Zeit*, July 15, 1999, Feuilleton.

Notes to Chapter 15: Homeward Bound

1. Hans Jürgen Syberberg, "Man muß so tief in die Wunde gehen ."
2. Hans Jürgen Syberberg, Home page, http://www.syberberg.de/Projekt_Nossendorf/ Alltag2000/ verhandeln_uber_den_Rest/hauptei... (accessed March 15, 2001).
3. An intriguing documentary about this underground complex is Florian Beierl's video of 1992, *Hitlers Bunkeranlagen am Obersalzberg* (International Historic Films, Inc., 592). It exhibits so many of Syberberg's aesthetic characteristics that one cannot help wondering if he was involved in the project. But his name does not appear in the credits, unless, of course, he assumed a pseudonym. One notices, a.o., play with perspectives and a leader of the investigating team who always turns his face away from the camera. Reminiscences of *Parsifal* include protective outfits resembling medieval armor, scooping of water as in the Good Friday baptism scene, a rusty fan in a pile of debris near a turn, and Eva Braun's "throne" glimpsed through the bathroom door. Florian Beierl has also published several books about the same period.
4. Hans Jürgen Syberberg, Home page, http://www.syberberg.de/ Margarethe-Krieger.htm (accessedFeb. 25, 2005). In addition, the "Central Pages" in the menu include materials on Margarethe Krieger, Oskar Werner, Einar Schleef, Edith Clever, Fritz Kortner, Winifred Wagner, Romy Schneider, and more.
5. Christina Gest, "Nossendorfer Kirche ist live im Internet," *Demminer Zeitung* March 2, 2004.
6. Gert Holle, "Aus den Landeskirchen," *Glaube Aktuell*, Feb. 25, 2004.
7. Hans Jürgen Syberberg, Home page, http://www.syberberg.de/Projek_Nossendorf/ asthetisch_Forschungen/hauptteil_aesthetische_... (accessed March 15, 2001).
8. Hans Jürgen Syberberg, Home page, http://www.Syberberg3.de/Antrag/ Antrag1/ antrag1.html (accessed Sept. 7, 2001).
9. Hans Jürgen Syberberg, "Ein Preußen ohne Land, in den Lüften," *Frankfurter Allgemeine Zeitung,*June 8, 2000, Feuilleton.
10. Hans Jürgen Syberberg, "Die Polen sollen das Schloss aufbauen: Nicht von der Fassade, vom Innern her muss gedacht werden," *Frankfurter Allgemeine Zeitung*, July 14, 2000, Berliner Seiten.
11. Hans Jürgen Syberberg, "Und doch, ich erinnere mich an das Verbrechen, das der Wilhelmstraße widerfuhr," *Frankfurter Allgemeine Zeitung*, Aug. 2, 2000, Berliner Seiten.
12. Wolfgang Büscher, "Vertreibung: was war?", Johann Michael Möller, "Ein Akt der nationalen Selbstheilung," and Christoph Stölzl, "Preußen: was bleibt?" *Die Welt*, Feb. 16, 2002, Deutschland.
13. Hans Jürgen Syberberg, Home page, http://www.syberberg3.de/aktuelle_Termine/ aktuelle_termine.html (accessed Oct. 8, 2001).
14. Hans Jürgen Syberberg, "Kinderland: Wozu Heimat? Ein Gespräch mit Hans Jürgen Syberberg," *Süddeutsche Zeitung*, Oct. 9, 2001.
15. Michael Meyer, "Virtueller Weg nach Hause," *Ostseezeitung*, Oct. 26, 2001.
16. Susanne Kunckel, "Pommern," *Welt am Sonntag*, Oct. 28, 2001. Syberberg's Web page includes the much longer correspondence that was summarized in the printed note.
17. Hans Jürgen Syberberg, Home page, http://217.160.137.223/Syberberg1/Projekt Nossendorf/Alltag2000/Retour_de_memoire/hauptteil_retour...(accessed Dec.12, 2003).
18. Gitta Sereny, *The German Trauma: Experiences and Reflections 1938-2001* (London:

Lane, 2000), and *Das deutsche Trauma: Eine heilende Wunde*, trans. Rudolf Herm-stein (Munich: Bertelsmann, 2002), 298–306, Gm ed.

19. Hans Jürgen Syberberg, "Zulieferung für die Narren der Zeit," *Frankfurter Allgemeine Zeitung*, Nov. 24, 2001.

20. Brigitte Hamann, *Winifred Wagner oder Hitlers Bayreuth* (Munich: Piper, 2002), 613–28.

21. Hans Jürgen Syberberg, "Dionysos aus Deutschland, Ost: Für Einar Schleef," *Theater der Zeit*, Sept. 2001, 4–5.

22. Hans Jürgen Syberberg, Home page, http://www.syberberg.de under "Central Pages." With two changes it was printed as "Aus Dionysos Geschlecht" in *Einar Schleef: Arbeitsbuch*, ed. Gabriele Gerecke, Harald Müller, and H.-U. Müller-Schwefe, Arbeitsbuch 11 (Berlin: Theater der Zeit, 2002), 112–15.

23. Willi Winkler, "Unsere kleine Farm," *Süddeutsche Zeitung*, June 3, 2003. See also Katharina Voss, "Filme für die freudlose Gesellschaft," *Tageszeitung*, May 28, 2003.

24. Hans Jürgen Syberberg, *Syberberg/Paris/Nossendorf*, introd. Christian Longchamp (Paris: Centre Pompidou/Yellow Now, 2003).

25. Hans Jürgen Syberberg, "Das Projekt Nossendorf," *Sezession* 2 (2003): 30–34.

26. Rochelle Fack, "Hans Jürgen Syberberg—si ta mémoire se venge," *Trafic* 48 (2003): 70–88.

27. Martin Heidegger, *Hölderlin's Hymn "The Ister,"* trans. William McNeill and Julia Davis, Studies in Continental Thought (Bloomington: Indiana Univ. Press, 1996), 1–50.

28. The film does not yet circulate in movie theaters. The discussion of it here is based on a screening during an academic conference on April 21, 2005 at the University of North Texas in Denton. The distributor in the U.S. is First Run Icarus Films.

29. Hanns-Georg Rodek, "Der Untergang—Jetzt in Farbe," *Berliner Morgenpost*, Aug. 12, 2004, Feuilleton, and Stefan Reineke, "Hitler und Häppchen," *Tageszeitung* Aug. 8, 2004.

30. Hans Jürgen Syberberg, "Syberberg, der geniale *Parsifal*-Verfilmer, lobt die Insze-nierung seines Schülers Eichinger," interview by Hans-Werner Marquardt, *Berliner Zeitung*, March 21, 2005, Kultur.

31. Will Hasty, "Beyond the Guilt Thesis: On the Socially Integrative Function of Trans-gression in Wolfram von Eschenbach's *Parzival*," *German Quarterly* 61, no. 3 (1988): 366.

32. Jeffrey Gantz, trans., *The Mabinogion* (New York: Dorset, 1985), 249n.

Bibliography

1. Works by Syberberg

2. Publications about Syberberg

3. Other Cited Literature

1. Works by Syberberg

1.A. Filmography. Syberberg is the director except where noted. One finds a complete and descriptive list of his feature films, along with information on how to buy them, on his home page, http://www.syberberg.de.

1965	*Fritz Kortner probt "Kabale und Liebe"*
1965	*Romy: Anatomie eines Gesichts*
1966	*Kortner spricht Monologe für eine Schallplatte*
1967	*Die Grafen Pocci: Einige Kapitel zur Geschichte einer Familie*
1968	*Scarabea: Wieviel Erde braucht der Mensch?*
1969	*Sex-Business Made in Pasing*
1970	*San Domingo*
1971	*Nach meinem letzten Umzug*
1972	*Ludwig: Requiem für einen jungfräulichen König*
1972	*Theodor Hierneis, oder wie man ehem. Hofkoch wird*
1974	*Karl May*
1975	*Winifred Wagner und die Geschichte des Hauses Wahnfried von 1914–1975*
1977	*Hitler: Ein Film aus Deutschland*
1982	*Parsifal*
1985	*Die Nacht*
1985	*Edith Clever liest Joyce*
1987	*Fräulein Else*
1988	*Penthesilea*
1989	*Die Marquise von O . . . (vom Süden nach dem Norden verlegt)*
1993	*Syberberg filmt bei Brecht*
1994	Syberberg as performer: *Die Nacht der Regisseure (The Night of the Directors)*, dir. Edgar Reitz
1994	*Ein Traum, was sonst?*
1997	*Cave of Memory: 1. Höhle der Erinnerung: Von den letzten Dingen; 2. Höhle der Erinnerung: Im Hamburger Bahnhof*
2004	Syberberg as performer: *The Ister*, dir. David Barison and Daniel Ross

1.B. Theater Productions

1984	*Die Nacht*
1987	*Penthesilea*
1989	*Die Marquise von O . . .*
1990	*Ein Traum, was sonst?*
1993	*Hölderlin: Solo für drei Stimmen*
1994	*Nietzsche in Weimar*

1.C. Installations and Multimedia Exhibits

1982	*Parsifal*
1983	*Der Hang zum Gesamtkunstwerk*
1993	*Un monólogo de 20 horas, 10 años, 5 libros, 1 mujer*
1997	*Cave of Memory*
2002	*Hommage an Einar Schleef*
2003	*Syberberg/Paris/Nossendorf*
2003	*Richard Wagner*
2004	*Poetics of Nossendorf*

1.D. Publications by Syberberg. The texts are listed by year and alphabetically within each year. Except where noted, they were consulted for this study. The list does not make any claims to being complete.

1965

Interpretationen zum Drama Friedrich Dürrenmatts: Zwei Modellinterpretationen zur Wesensdeutung des modernen Dramas. Munich: UNI-Druck, 1965 (4th ed. 1979).

1972

Syberberg, ed. *Ein Mundkoch erinnert sich an Ludwig II.* By Theodor Hierneis (1953). Munich: Heimeran, 1972.

1974

"Ein deutsches Heldenleben: Karl May." *Die Zeit,* Oct. 18, 1974.
"Théâtre et télévision." Interview. By Bernard Sobel. *Théâtre/Public* 2 (1974): 3–5.

1975

Le film musique de l'avenir: un manifeste esthétique sur la base de mes films. Paris: Cinématèque Française / Musée Cinéma, 1975.

1976

"Donnez-nous notre nostalgie quotidienne." Interview. By Jean-Michel Palmier. *Les Nouvelles Littéraires,* Feb. 5, 1976, 10–11.
Syberbergs Filmbuch. Munich: Nymphenburger Verlagshandlung, 1976.
"Winifred Wagner: Je n'ai jamais fait de politique." *Théâtre/Public* 13 (1976): 40–43.

1977

Fotografie der 30er Jahre: Eine Anthologie. Munich: Schirmer-Mosel, 1977.
"Hitler: A Film from Germany; or, The Greatest Show of the Century." Interview on French television. Trans. *Framework* 11, no. 6 (1977): 13–15.
Interview. By Ian Christie. Oct. 12, 1977. *Framework* 11, no. 6 (1977): 16–18.
"Wir leben in einem toten Land." *Die Zeit*, June 20, 1977. Reprinted as "The Syberberg Statement: We Live in a Dead Land." *Framework* 11, no. 6 (1977): 11–12, and as "We Live in a Dead Country (1977)." In *West German Filmmakers on Film: Visions and Voices,* edited by Eric Rentschler, 17-20. New York: Holmes. 1988. Citations are to the Rentschler edition.

1978

"L'histoire de la musique de Wagner est écrite en lettres de sang." *Théâtre / Public* 2 (1978): 15–18.
Hitler: Ein Film aus Deutschland. Reinbek bei Hamburg: Rowohlt, 1978.
"Hitler – noch nicht für Deutschland." *Die Zeit*, Jan. 13, 1978.
Hitler: Un film d'Allemagne. Paris: Change, 1978.
Interview. By Manuela Fontana. In *Film und Drang: Nuovo cinema tedesco,* edited by Manuela Fontana, 140–48. Not available for consultation.
"Dem Teufel seine Chance geben: Ein Gespräch mit Hans Jürgen Syberberg über *Hitler: Ein Film aus Deutschland.*" *Süddeutsche Zeitung*, Dec. 9, 1978.

1979

"Alpträume akzeptieren." Syberberg's answer to Elfriede Heise's open letter to him, both printed together. *Frankfurter Allgemeine Zeitung*, Mar. 3, 1979.
"Wer ist und was macht eigentlich André Heller?" *Du: die Zeitschrift für Kultur*, July 1979, 68–72.

1980

"Un album de famille de cinéma (San Francisco, été 79)." In "Syberberg," edited by Serge Daney and Bernard Sobel, 8–29. Special issue 6, *Cahiers du Cinéma*, Feb.1980.
"Du pays mort d'une société sans joie." In "Syberberg," edited by Daney and Sobel, 72–89.
"Form Is Morality: *Holocaust*, a Symptom of the Biggest Crisis in Our Intellectual Life (1979)." *Framework* 12 (1980): 11–15.
"Hitler artiste de l'État ou l'avant-garde méphistophélique du xxe siècle." In *Les Réalismes 1919–1939.* Exhibit catalogue, 378–83. Paris: Centre Pompidou, 1980.
"Langer Abschied: Gegen die Gremien-Willkür." *Die Zeit*, Nov. 28, 1980.
"Le métier de cinéaste." In "Syberberg," edited by Daney and Sobel, 50–69.
"Utopies et projets." In "Syberberg," edited by Daney and Sobel, 32–47.
"What Can We Do with Hitler?" *Vogue*, May 1980, 256+.
"Eine Zeugin und eine Schuldige." *Der Spiegel*, Mar. 10, 1980, 234–35.

1981

"Au bout du chemin se tient l'enfant." *Théâtre/Public* 40–41 (1981): 69–73.
Die freudlose Gesellschaft: Notizen aus dem letzten Jahr. Munich: Hanser, 1981. Reprinted as *Die freudlose Gesellschaft: Notizen aus den letzten Jahren.* Frankfurt am Main: Ullstein, 1983.

1982

Interview. By Jean-Claude Bonnet and Michel Celemenski. *Cinématographe*, May 1982, 12–19.

Interview (1979). By Betty Erkkila. *Literature / Film Quarterly* 10 (1982): 206-18.

"Die Falle ist zu: Notizen aus dem Medienalltag." *Medium*, Feb. 1982, 20–21.

Hitler: A Film from Germany. Preface by Susan Sontag. Translated by Joachim Neugroschel. New York: Farrar, Straus, Giroux, 1982.

"Nur der Kranke hält es aus: Notizen." *Medium*, Apr. 1982, 27–29.

"Ohne Neugier und Lust und Informationsredlichkeit: 100 Jahre *Parsifal* in Bayreuth 1982." *Medium*, Sept.–Oct. 1982, 78–80.

Parsifal: Ein Filmessay. Munich: Heyne, 1982.

Parsifal: Notes sur un film.. Paris: Gallimard, 1982.

"Sie haben ihn zum lächerlichen Gartenzwerg ihres Selbstmitleids heroisiert: Zu Rainer Werner Fassbinder." *Medium*, Aug. 1982, 35–37.

La société sans joie: de l'Allemagne après Hitler. Paris: Gallimard, 1982.

"Vorführen braucht soviel Energie und Phantasie wie Machen: Eine Bilanz der *Parsifal*-Aufführungen mit Schlußfolgerungen." *Medium*, Dec. 1982, 31–33.

"Wir sollen den anderen ins Gesicht spucken: Notizen aus dem Medienalltag." *Medium*, July 1982, 40–41.

1983

"Alweer demokratie!" Interview by Erica Bilder and Peter Ungerleider. In *Hans Jürgen Syberberg,* edited by Erica Bilder, 19–24. Amsterdam: Barbar Events, 1983.

"Rede." Chapter without title or number. In *Reden über das eigene Land: Deutschland*, by Stefan Heym, Hans Jürgen Syberberg, Alexander Kluge, Gerd Bucerius, and Günter Gaus, 36–61. Munich: Bertelmann, 1983.

"Drie dagen Hollywood." Interview. In *Hans Jürgen Syberberg*, edited by Bilder, 63–66.

"Die Falle ist zu." *Medium*. Feb. 1982, 20–21.

"Film als muziek van de toekomst." In *Hans Jürgen Syberberg*, edited by Bilder, 61–62.

"Een groots resultaat." Interview. In *Hans Jürgen Syberberg*, edited by Bilder, 25–30.

"Hitler in oons, mar niet in de Joden?" Interview. In *Hans Jürgen Syberberg*, edited by Bilder, 31–34.

"Hollywood, Moskou en satellietstaten, en de landen ertussenin." Interview. In *Hans Jürgen Syberberg*, edited by Bilder, 7–18.

"In der Konformität des Vorurteils: Mediennotizen." *Medium*, Feb.–Mar. 1983, 71–73.

"Mijn films . . .." In *Hans Jürgen Syberberg*, edited by Bilder, 67–68.

"Nur der Kranke hält es aus." *Medium*, Apr. 1982, 27–29.

"Ohne Neugier und Lust und Informationsredlichkeit." *Medium*, Sept.–Oct. 1982, 78–80.

"Samenzwering of toeval?" Interview. In *Hans Jürgen Syberberg*, edited by Bilder, 47–60.

"Sie haben ihn zum lächerlichen Gartenzwerg ihres Selbstmitleids heroisiert." *Medium*, Aug. 1982, 35–37.

"Vorführen braucht soviel Energie und Phantasie wie Machen." *Medium*, Dec.1982, 31–33.

"Welcher Sumpf von Pseudodemokratie: Mediennotizen." *Medium*, Jan. 1983, 42–45.

"We waren drie vrienden in Rostock . . . en een bleef." Interview. In *Hans Jürgen Syberberg*, edited by Bilder, 35-46.

"Wir sollen den anderen ins Gesicht spucken." *Medium*, July 1982, 40–41.

1984

"An die Kinobesitzer." *Die Tageszeitung*, Jan. 30, 1984.

Der Wald steht schwarz und schweiget: Neue Notizen aus Deutschland. Zürich: Diogenes, 1984.

1985

"Bitburg." *On Film* 14 (1985): 37.

"Ende der europäischen Zeit." In *Die Unfähigkeit zu feiern: Der 8. Mai*, edited by Norbert Seitz, 59-68. Frankfurt am Main: Neue Kritik, 1985.

1986

"Im Herbst sterben die Eltern nach den Kindern." *Wiener*, Sept. 9, 1986.

1987

"*Penthesilea*: théâtre et film." *Théâtre/Public* 78 (1987): 125–28.

"Sustaining Romanticism in a Postmodernist Cinema." Interview. By Christopher Sharrett. *Cineaste* 15, no. 3 (1987): 18–20.

1988

"The Abode of the Gods (1984)." In *West German Filmmakers on Film*, edited by Rentschler, 245.

"Les chambres obscures du moi." *Trafic* 25 (1988): 45–47. Unavailable.

"Die enthauptete Kunst." *Die Zeit*, June 3, 1988, Magazin.

"Media Response to Fassbinder's *Berlin Alexanderplatz*(1980)." In *West German Filmmakers on Film*, edited by Rentschler, 162–63.

"Mein Führer—The Meaning of Small Words (1980)." In *West German Filmmakers on Film*, edited by Rentschler, 141.

"Seeing the Light." Review of *Adolphe Appia: Theatre Artist*, by Richard C. Beecham. *New Republic*, Oct. 3, 1988, 32–36.

"Sie hat den Glauben, ich das Bild." Interview of Syberberg and Edith Clever. By Evelyn Roll. *Süddeutsche Zeitung*, June 25, 1988. Reprinted in *Kleist in Frankfurt, Kleist im Film: Ein Arbeitsbuch*, edited by Leonhard M. Fiedler, 91–92. Dierdorf: Margot Lang, 1988

Penthesilea. Berlin: Hentrich, 1988.

"Man will mich töten." Interview. By André Müller. *Die Zeit*, Sept. 30, 1988, followed by Syberberg's "Entgegnung," Oct. 14 and a second protest on Nov. 18, both in *Die Zeit*. Reprinted in *Im Gespräch*, edited by André Müller, 183–203, with Syberberg's loose-leaf insert "Erklärung vom 12. Juli 1989." Reinbek bei Hamburg: Rowohlt, 1989.

1989

Die Marquise von O . . . (vom Süden nach dem Norden verlegt). By Heinrich von Kleist, Edith Clever, and Hans Jürgen Syberberg. Program. Berlin: Hebbel-Theater, 1989.

"Nach der *Nacht* und den Videofilmen *Fräulein Else* und der *Marquise von O . . . .*" In *Kleist in Frankfurt*, edited by Fiedler, 34–48.

"*Penthesilea.*" In *Opern und Opernfiguren: Festschrift für Joachim Herz*, edited by Ursula Müller and Ulrich Müller, 211–26. Anif/Salzburg: Müller-Speiser, 1989.

"*San Domingo*." In *Kleist in Frankfurt*, edited by Fiedler, 56–61. Reprint of "An die Kinobesitzer: Anstelle eines Werberatschlags (1970)."

1990

"Da un'altra Germania." In *Syberberg,* edited by Stefano Socci, 3–13. Il castoro cinema 143. Florence: La Nuova Italia, 1990.

"Filmisches bei Wagner." In *Richard Wagner: Mittler zwischen Zeiten,* edited by Gerhard Heldt, 66–78. Anif/Salzburg: Müller-Speiser, 1990.

"Im Rahmen des Nicht-Mehr." Interview. By Klaus Dermatz. *Die Tageszeitung,* Apr. 14, 1990.

"La radio come *Urstimme.*" *Cinema e cinema* 57 (Jan.–April 1990): 68–74.

Ein Traum, was sonst? By Edith Clever and Hans Jürgen Syberberg. Berlin: Hebbel-Theater, 1990.

Vom Unglück und Glück der Kunst in Deutschland nach dem letzten Kriege. Munich: Matthes und Seitz, 1990.

"Wie man neuen Haß züchtet." *Frankfurter Allgemeine Zeitung,* Sept. 6, 1990, Feuilleton.

"Wir stehen fest im Sturm." Interview. By Heimo Schwilk. *Rheinischer Merkur,* Sept. 7, 1990.

1991

"Mit kleinsten Mitteln sehr Anspruchvolles offerieren." Interview. In *Kunst machen?* Edited by Florian Rötzer and Sara Rogenhofer, 172–84. 2nd ed. Munich: Boer, 1991.

"S'approprier le monde." *Cahiers du Cinéma,* May 1991, 57. Not consulted.

1992

"Briefe über Raum, Letters on Space, Lettres sur l'espace, Brieven over ruimte." *Theaterschrift* Sept. 1992, 154–64.

Talking Cinema. Interview. By Julian Petley. Sept. 7, 1992. Cinema 816. Audio cassette. London: Institute of Contemporary Arts, 1992.

1993

"Aus der Zeit der letzten Unschuld." *Drucksache* 4 (1993): 97-116 and 117–28.

"Germany's Heart: The Modern Taboo." Interview. By Marilyn Snell. *New Perspectives Quarterly* 10, no. 1 (1993). Reprinted in *At Century's End: Great Minds Reflect on Our Times,* edited by Nathan P. Gardels, 114–24, La Jolla, CA: ALTI, 1996; and as "El corazón de Alemania: El moderno tabú," in *Fin de Siglo: Grandes pensadores hacen reflexiones sobre nuestro tiempo,* 116–27. Interamericana ed. Mexico City: McGraw-Hill, 1996.

"*1971—Nach meinem letzten Umzug.*" *Drucksache* 4 (1993): 141–49.

"Zu einer Definition des Eigenen." In *Deutschsein? Eine Ausstellung gegen Fremdenhaß und Gewalt,* exhibit catalogue, edited by Jürgen Harten, 105–10. Düsseldorf: Kunsthalle, 1993.

1994

Nietzsche—Schleef—Syberberg. Weimar: Kunstfest, 1994. Unavailable.

Der verlorene Auftrag: Ein Essay. Vienna: Karolinger, 1994.

1995

"Eigenes und Fremdes: Über den Verlust des Tragischen." In *Die selbstbewusste Nation,* edited by Heimo Schwilk and Ulrich Schacht, 124–33. 3rd ed. Frankfurt am Main: Ullstein, 1995.

Interview. By Edgar Reitz. In *Bilder in Bewegung: Essays, Gespräche zum Kino,* edited by Edgar Reitz, 156–62. Reinbek bei Hamburg: Rowohlt, 1995.

Das Rechte—tun. Munich: Kronenbitter, 1995.

"Eine Strafe der Götter: Hans Jürgen Syberberg über das Ende des Zweiten Weltkrieges, über Umerziehung und seelische Sklaverei, sowie den Verlust der Souveränität über die eigenen Bilder." *Die Tageszeitung*, Feb. 20, 1995.

1999

"Mein Jahrhundertbuch: *Buckower Elegien* von Bertolt Brecht." *Die Zeit*, July 15, 1999, Feuilleton.

2000

"Man muß so tief in die Wunde gehen, daß man in Verdacht gerät." Interview. By Benjamin Heisenberg, Christoph Hochhäusler, and Sebastian Kutzli. April 30, 1999. *Revolver: Zeitschrift für Film* 3 (2000). http://revolver-film/Inhalte/Rev3/html/Syberberg .htm (accessed Nov. 14, 2003).

"Die Polen sollen das Schloss aufbauen: Nicht von der Fassade, vom Innern her muss gedacht werden."*Frankfurter Allgemeine Zeitung* July 14, 2000, Berliner Seiten.

"Ein Preußen ohne Land, in den Lüften." *Frankfurter Allgemeine Zeitung*, June 8, 2000, Feuilleton.

"Und doch, ich erinnere mich an das Verbrechen, das der Wilhelmstraße widerfuhr." *Frankfurter Allgemeine Zeitung*, Aug. 2, 2000, Berliner Seiten.

2001

"Dionysos aus Deutschland, Ost: Für Einar Schleef." *Theater der Zeit*, Sept. 2001, 4–5.

"Kinderland: Wozu Heimat?" Interview. *Süddeutsche Zeitung*, Oct. 9, 2001.

"Zulieferung für die Narren der Zeit." *Frankfurter Allgemeine Zeitung*, Nov. 24, 2001.

2002

"Aus Dionysos Geschlecht." In *Einar Schleef: Arbeitsbuch*, edited by Gabriele Gerecke, Harald Müller, and Hans-Ulrich Müller-Schwefe, 112–15. Arbeitsbuch 11. Berlin: Theater der Zeit, 2002.

2003

"Das Projekt Nossendorf." *Sezession* 2 (2003): 30–34.

    Syberberg/Paris/Nossendorf. Introd. by Christian Longchamp. Paris: Centre Pompidou/Yellow Now, 2003.

2005

"Syberberg, der geniale *Parsifal*-Verfilmer, lobt die Inszenierung seines Schülers Eichinger." Interview. By Hans-Werner Marquardt. *Berliner Zeitung*, Mar. 2, 2005, Kultur.

2. Publications about Syberberg and His Work.

The list of texts cited or only consulted for this study is far from complete. One finds a growing number of studies, reviews, or interviews, many in non-Western languages.

Andrews, Nigel. "Hitler as Entertainment." *American Film* 3, no. 6 (1978): 50–53.

Anz, Thomas. "Die Wut des Hans Jürgen Syberberg: Seine Notizen aus dem letzten Jahr über *Die freudlose Gesellschaft.*" Review. *Frankfurter Allgemeine Zeitung*, Aug. 1, 1981, Literatur.

Baier, Lothar. "Eine ungeheuerliche Neuigkeit? Nachfragen zur Debatte um den Pamphletisten Syberberg." *Neue Rundschau* 102, no. 1 (1991): 117–30.

Berg, Robert von. "Deutschland: Ein Film von Hitler; Hans Jürgen Syberberg im Echo der amerikanischen Presse." *Süddeutsche Zeitung*, Feb. 28, 1980.

Berman, Russell A. "Hans Jürgen Syberberg: Of Fantastic and Magical Worlds." In *New German Filmmakers: From Oberhausen through the 1970s*, edited by Klaus Phillips, 359–79. New York: Ungar, 1984.

Bilder, Erica, ed. *Hans Jürgen Syberberg.* Amsterdam: Barbar Events, 1983.

Blumenberg, Hans C. "Träume in Trümmern: Hans Jürgen Syberbergs *Hitler* in Paris." *Die Zeit*, July 7, 1978.

Brock, Bazon. "Er war wirklich Old Shatterhand." Rev. of *Karl May. Der Spiegel*, Oct. 28, 1974, 186–87.

Brockmann, Stephen. "Syberberg's Germany." *German Quarterly Review* 69, no. 1 (1996): 48-62.

Brunette, Peter. "Ludwig: Requiem for a Virgin King." Rev. of *Ludwig. Film Quarterly* 34, no. 3 (1981): 58–61.

Buchloh, Benjamin H. D. "Dokumenta 7: A Dictionary of Received Ideas." Includes rev. of *Parsifal. October* 22 (Autumn 1982): 105–26.

Buruma, Ian. "There's No Place Like Heimat." Rev. of symposium on Syberberg and *Vom Unglück und Glück. The New York Review*, Dec. 20, 1990, 34+.

Camartin, Iso. "Ein Verletzter wehrt sich." Rev. of *Die freudlose Gesellschaft. Neue Zürcher Zeitung*, Nov. 13, 1981.

Chion, Michel. "L'aveu: *Parsifal* de Hans Jürgen Syberberg." *Cahiers du Cinéma*, July–Aug., 1982, 53–55.

Citron, Marcia J. *Opera on Screen.* Chapter on *Parsifal*, 141-60. New Haven: Yale Univ. Press, 2000.

Clements, Andrew. "Grail Chase." Rev. of *Parsifal. New Statesman*, Mar. 25, 1983.

Coates, Paul. *The Gorgon's Gaze: German Cinema, Expressionism, and the Image of Horror.* On Syberberg and *Parsifal*, 113–29. Cambridge Studies in Film. Cambridge: Cambridge Univ. Press, 1991.

Coppola, Francis Ford. "Vers un Bayreuth du cinéma." Interview about *Hitler*. In"Syberberg," 90–92. Special issue of Cahiers du Cinéma, Feb. 1980.

Corrigan, Timothy. *New German Film: The Displaced Image.* On *Hitler,* 144–71. Austin: Univ. of Texas Press, 1983.

Daney, Serge, and Bernard Sobel, eds. "Syberberg." Special issue of *Cahiers du Cinéma* (Feb. 1980). Paris: Éditions de l'Étoile, 1980.

Decaux, Emmanuel. "La nuit de *Parsifal.*" *Cinématographe* 79 (June 1982): 68.

———. "*Parsifal*: Hans Jürgen Syberberg." *Cinématographe* 79 (June 1982): 71–72.

Deeken, Annette. "Träume eines Geistersehers: Zur Ästhetik eines Syberberg-Films." About *Karl May. Jahrbuch der Karl May Gesellschaft*, 1984, 44–59.

Deleuze, Gilles. *L'image-temps*, vol. 2, *Cinéma*, 350–54. Paris: Minuit, 1985.

Denby, David. "Marx and Freud Meet Wagner." Rev. of *Parsifal. New York*, Jan. 31, 1983, 54–56.

Detje, Robin. "Taugt der Text noch? Taugen wir? Hans Jürgen Syberberg stellt im Hamburger Bahnhof aus und filmt im Keller." Rev. of *Cave of Memory. Berliner Zeitung*, Oct. 17, 1997.

Diederichsen, Diedrich. "Spiritual Reactionaries after German Reunification: Syberberg,

Foucault, and Others." *October* 62 (1992): 65–83.

Di Matteo, Robert. *"Our Hitler: A Film from Germany."* Rev. *Bay Guardian*, July 12, 1979, Day and Night. Reprinted in *Kino: German Film* 1 (1979): 72–74.

Donner, Wolf. *"Hitler* nach Deutschland! Ein offener Brief von 'Berlinale' Direktor Wolf Donner an Hans Jürgen Syberberg." *Die Zeit*, Dec. 23, 1977.

Douin, Jean-Luc. "19 mai 1982: La nuit messianique de *Parsifal." Le Monde,* May 10, 1997.

Drews, Jörg. "Die verfolgende Unschuld." Rev. of *Die freudlose Gesellschaft, Merkur* 36 (1982): 93–96.

Eder, Klaus, ed. *Syberbergs "Hitler"-Film.* Arbeitshefte Film 1. Munich: Hanser, 1980.

Elsaesser, Thomas. *New German Cinema: A History.* New Brunswick, NJ: Rutgers Univ. Press, 1989.

———. "Myth as the Phantasmagoria of History: Hans Jürgen Syberberg, Cinema and Representation." *New German Critique* 24–25 (1981–82): 108–54.

———. *"Parsifal."* Review. *Monthly Film Bulletin* 50 (May 1983): 137.

Fack, Rochelle. "Hans Jürgen Syberberg—si ta mémoire se venge." *Trafic* 48 (2003): 70–88.

Fantin-Epstein, Marie-Bernadette. "De Wagner à Syberberg: *Parsifal* ou le masque éclaté." In *Mises en cadre dans la littérature et dans les arts,* edited by Andrée Mansau, 257–64. Toulouse: UP Mirail, 1999.

Fassbinder, Rainer Werner. "Homage to Werner Schroeter (1979)." In *West German Filmmakers on Film,* edited by Rentschler, 198.

Faye, Jean-Pierre. "Faust, Teil III." In *Syberbergs Hitler-Film,* edited by Klaus Eder, 33–35. Appeared first as "Le troisième *Faust"* in *Le Monde,* July 22, 1978.

———. "Retour de mémoire." About *Cave of Memory.* http://www.syberberg.de.

Fischer, Norman. "Hans Jürgen Syberberg's Opera Film, *Parsifal*: Visual Transformation and Philosophical Reconstruction." *Film and Philosophy* 3 (1996): 145–53.

Fontana, Manuela. "Hans Jürgen Syberberg." In *Film und Drang: nuovo cinema tedesco,* edited by Manuela Fontana, 133–50. Florence, It.: Vallechi, 1978.

Foucault, Michel. "Die vier Reiter der Apokalypse und die alltäglichen kleinen Würmchen." In *Syberbergs "Hitler"-Film,* edited by Eder, 69–73. Appeared also as "Les quatre cavaliers de 'Apocalypse' et les vermisseaux quotidiens." In "Syberberg," special issue of *Cahiers du Cinéma,* 95–96.

Franklin, James. *New German Cinema: From Oberhausen to Hamburg.* Chapter 8 about Syberberg. Twayne's Filmmakers Series. Boston: Twayne, 1983.

Fuld, Werner. "Hitler neu bedenken? An Syberbergs Unwesen soll die Welt genesen." Rev. of *Vom Unglück und Glück. Frankfurter Allgemeine Zeitung,* Aug. 24, 1990, Feuilleton.

Gemünden, Gerd. "Nostalgia for the Nation: Intellectuals and National Identity in Unified Germany. In *Acts of Memory: Cultural Recall in the Present,* edited by Mieke Bal, Jonathan Crewe, and Leo Spitzer, 120–33. Hanover, NH: Univ. Press of New England, 1999.

Gerecke, Gabriele, Harald Müller, and H. U. Müller-Schwefe, eds. *Einar Schleef:Arbeitsbuch.* Arbeitsbuch 11. Berlin: Theater der Zeit, 2002.

Gest, Christina. "Nossendorfer Kirche ist live im Internet." *Demminer Zeitung* Mar. 2, 2004.

Gillen, Eckhart. "Jede Generation die gleiche Scheiße." Interview. By Marius Babias about the exhibit "Deutschlandbilder—Kunst aus einem geteilten Land." Sept. 7, 1997–Jan.11, 1998. http://www.nadir.org/nadir/periodika/jungle_world/37/28a.htm.

Glotz, Peter. "Die Bewaffnung mit Identität: Eine Analyse des deutschen Normalisie-rungs-Nationalismus am Beispiel Hans-Jürgen Syberbergs." *FrankfurterRundschau*, Jan. 22, 1994.

Göttler, Fritz. "Ein Leitstrahl für Kortner und Brecht: Hans Jürgen Syberbergs Begeg-nungen mit zwei Großen der deutschen Theatergeschichte." *Filmwärts*, Dec. 1993, 46–47.

Gommers, Luc. "*Parsifal*: Syberberg en Wagner." *Andere sinema* 76 (Nov.–Dec. 1986): 15. Unavailable for consultation.

Goossens, Guido. *Verloren zonsondergangen: Hans Jürgen Syberberg en het linkse den-ken over rechts in Duitsland*. Amsterdam: Amsterdam Univ. Press, 2004.

Hahn, H. J. "'Es geh t nicht um Literatur': Some Observations on the 1990 'Literatur-Streit' and Its Recent Antiintellectual Implications." *German Life and Letters* 50, no. 1 (1997): 65–81.

Hamann, Brigitte. *Winifred Wagner oder Hitlers Bayreuth*. Pp. 613-28 about Syberberg's film with Mrs. Wagner. Munich: Piper, 2002.

Hamilton, David. "Chéreau's *Ring*, Syberberg's *Parsifal*: Records as By-products." *High Fidelity*, June 1983, 67+.

Hamm, Peter. "Syberbergs Kampf: Der Regisseur des *Hitler*-Films als Autor." Rev. of *Die freudlose Gesellschaft*. *Die Zeit*, July 31, 1981.

Hanimann, Joseph. "Die Königin: wer sonst?" Rev. of *Penthesilea*. *Frankfurter Allge-meine Zeitung*, Nov. 17, 1987, DII, Feuilleton.

Heller, André. "Ein radikaler Nomade in der kalten deutschen Wüste." *Abendzeitung*, Aug. 18–19, 1990, Feuilleton.

———. *Es werde Zirkus: Ein poetisches Spektakel*. Heller's interview by Syberberg 146–59. Frankfurt am Main: Fischer, 1976.

Helm, Siegfried. "Ein aristokratischer Kohlhaas im Kunstbetrieb auf der Suche nach seiner verlorenen Zeit." *Welt am Sonntag*, Sept. 6, 1992.

Herbort, Heinz Josef. "Erlösung in der Totenmaske." Rev. of *Parsifal*. *Die Zeit*, May 21, 1982.

Herbst, Alban Nikolai. Discussion of *Die Fehler des Kopisten* by Botho Strauß, appar-ently with Syberberg and Botho Strauß. *DeutschlandRadio*, http://www.dlf.de/literatur/Gespraeche/strauss.html (accessed Apr. 15, 1998).

Hertmans, Stefan. "Syberberg als Amfortas: een pastorale wonde." *Etcetera* 9, no. 35 (1991): 42–43.

Hoberman, J. "His *Parsifal*: Following the Syberbergenlied." *Village Voice*, Feb.22, 1983, 60+.

———. "*Hitler*, a Script from Germany: The publication of Syberberg's screenplay is an occasion to reappraise his seven-hour antispectacle." *American Film* 8 (Nov. 1982): 76–81.

Hoffman, Donald L. "Re-Framing Perceval." *Arthuriana* 10, no. 4 (2000): 45–56.

Holle, Gert. "Aus den Landeskirchen: 25. 02. 2004." *Glaube Aktuell*, May 7, 2004.

Holloway, Ronald. "Exhibition Formula for Syberberg's *Parsifal* Follows 'Epic' Sce-nario."*Variety*, Oct. 20, 1982, 88.

———. "*Die Nacht*." *Variety*, May 22, 1985, 18+.

———. "Non-Competing at Cannes: *Parsifal*." *Variety*, May 26, 1982, 16.

Huber, Sebastian. "*Edith Clever liest Joyce*: Der Monolog der Molly Bloom, 1985." In *Ulysses: Die Unausweichliche Modalität des Sichtbaren*, edited by Thomas Trum-mer, 20–25. Vienna: Brandstätter, 2004.

Hursthouse, Annelene. "Hans Jürgen Syberberg: A Retrospective." In *Edinburgh Inter-*

national Film Festival Program, 18–22. Edinburgh: EIFF, 1992.

Hüser, Rembert. "Wale malen." In *Gelegenheit: Diebe; 3x Deutsche Motive,* by Dirk Baecker, Rembert Hüser, and Georg Stanitzek, 101–66. Bielefeld: Haux, 1991.

Ibañez, Jordi. *Despuéz de la decapitatión del arte: Una apología de Hans Jürgen Syberberg.* Barcelona: Destino, 1996.

Iden, Peter. "Finale im Mist: Die 10. 'documenta' scheitert an der Überforderung der Praxis durch die Theorie." *Frankfurter Rundschau,* n. d., http://www.superpeople .com/smoker's-diary/fr.html (accessed May 5, 1998).

Insdorf, Annette. *Indelible Shadows: Film and the Holocaust.* 2nd ed. Pp. 199–203 about *Hitler.* New York: Cambridge Univ. Press, 1989.

Iversen, Gunnar. "Brecht + Wagner = Syberberg." *Filmtidsskrift Z* 3, no. 3 (1985):23–27.

Jaehne, Karen. "Old Nazis in New Films: The German Cinema Today." *Cineaste* 9, no. 1 (1978): 32–35.

Jameson, Frederic. "In the Destructive Element Immerse: Hans-Jürgen Syberberg and Cultural Revolution." *October* 17 (Summer 1981): 99–118. Reprinted in *Signatures of the Visible,* by Frederic Jameson, 63–81. New York: Routledge, 1990.

Janßen, Karl-Heinz. "Wir—zwischen Jesus und Hitler: Mit Vernunft allein läßt sich der Judenmord nicht erklären." *Die Zeit,* July 7, 1978, Politik.

Jeziorkowski, Klaus. "Das Glück der Wurzelbürste." Rev. of *Die freudlose Gesellschaft. Der Spiegel,* July 3, 1981, 167–70.

Joch, Norbert. "An den Wurzeln des Übels: Zu Syberbergs *Hitler: Ein Film ausDeutschland." Tagesspiegel,* Mar. 17, 1979.

Kaes, Anton. *Deutschlandbilder: Die Wiederkehr der Geschichte als Film.* Munich: text+ kritik, 1987.

———. "Holocaust and the End of History: Postmodern Historiography in Cinema." In *Probing the Limits of Representation: Nazism and the "Final Solution,"* edited by Saul Friedlander, 206–22. Cambridge, MA: Harvard Univ. Press, 1992.

———. "Mythos Deutschland, revisited: Historie und Post-histoire in Hans Jürgen Syberbergs *Hitler: Ein Film aus Deutschland."* In *Deutschlandbilder: Die Wiederkehr der Geschichte als Film ,* by Anton Kaes, 135–70. Munich: text + kritik, 1987. Appeared also as "Germany as Myth: Hans Jürgen Syberberg's *Hitler: A Film from Germany."* In *From Hitler to Heimat: The Return of History as Film,* by Anton Kaes, 37–72. Cambridge, MA: Harvard Univ. Press, 1989.

Kaps, Angelika. "Das Gesicht der Edith Clever: Hans Jürgen Syberberg drehte in Berlin *Die Nacht." Tagesspiegel,* Dec. 23, 1984.

Karasek, Hellmuth. "Frühling für Hitler?" Rev. of *Vom Unglück und Glück. Der Spiegel,* Sept. 2, 1990, 240+.

Kastner, *Das große Karl May Buch: Sein Leben, seine Bücher, die Filme.* 2nd ed. Bergisch-Gladbach: Bastei Lübbe, 1992.

Kauffmann, Stanley. "Far from Bayreuth." Rev. of *Parsifal. New Republic,* Feb. 14,1983: 24–26.

———. "Into the Night." Rev. of *Die Nacht. New Republic,* Dec. 2, 1985, 24–26.

———. "Madnesses." Rev. of *Ludwig. New Republic,* Aug. 23, 1980, 24–25.

———. "Myths for Sale." Rev. of *Karl May. New Republic,* July 14 and 21, 1986:26–80.

Kesting, Jürgen. "Festspiel in der Schädelstätte." Rev. of *Parsifal. Stern,* May 27, 1982.

Kiefer, Bernd. "Kulturmontage im Posthistoire: Zur Filmästhetik von Hans Jürgen Syberberg." In *Montage in Theater und Film,* edited by Horst Fritz, 229–47. Mainzer Forschungen zu Drama und Theater 8. Tübingen: Francke, 1993.

Kilb, Andreas. "O Mensch! Gib acht! Deutsche Szene: Hans Jürgen Syberberg feiert

Friedrich Nietzsche in Weimar." *Die Zeit*, June 24, 1994, Feuilleton.

Kleis, John Christopher. "The Arthurian Dilemma: Faith and Works in Syberberg's *Parsifal*." In *King Arthur on Film: New Essays on Arthurian Cinema*, edited by Kevin J. Harty, 109–22. Jefferson, NC: McFarland,1999.

Kluge, Alexander. "Pact with a Dead Man." 1984. In *West German Filmmakers on Film*, edited by Rentschler, 234–41.

Klümper, Kirsten. "Brecht-Haus: Nächte mit Denkern." *Berliner Zeitung*, Feb. 12, 1998, Feuilleton.

Koch, Gerhard R. "Bußprediger als Mimose: Deutschestes Raunen—der Regisseur und Schriftsteller Hans Jürgen Syberberg wird sechzig Jahre alt." *Frankfurter Allgemeine Zeitung*, Dec. 8, 1995, Feuilleton.

———. "Der Unlustknabe und das Sex-Symbol: Syberbergs *Parsifal* und Ferreros *Mari-lyn* in Kassel." *Frankfurter Allgemeine Zeitung*, June 25, 1982, Feuilleton.

———. "Wer den Film hat, hat das Leben: Hans Jürgen Syberbergs Selbstbeweihräucherung." *Frankfurter Allgemeine Zeitung*, Dec. 18, 1976, Literatur. Rev. of *Syberbergs Filmbuch*.

Kosler, Hans Christian. "Augenmensch mit Schaum vorm Mund: Hans Jürgen Syberbergs neue Notizen aus Deutschland." Rev. of *Der Wald*. *Frankfurter Allgemeine Zeitung*, Dec. 11, 1984, Literatur.

"Die Kritikerpreisträger 1951–2004." http://www.kritikerverband.de/preise.htm.

Kroll, Jack. "Cinematic *Parsifal*." *Newsweek*, Jan. 31, 1983, 49.

Kuhlmann, Andreas. "Auf dem Abstellgleis: Ein Kongreß über die 'Frankfurter Schule' in Rotterdam." *Frankfurter Allgemeine Zeitung*, Dec. 6, 1988, Feuilleton.

Kunckel, Susanne. "Pommern." *Welt am Sonntag*, Oct. 28, 2001.

Lacoue-Labarthe, Philippe. "Syberberg: On Germany after Hitler." In *Politics–Poetics: Documenta X — the Book*. 480–82. Ostfildern-Ruit: Cantz, 1997. Reprinted as "Syberberg: de l'Allemagne après Hitler. *Trafic* 25 (1998): 48–54.

Landy, Marcia. "Politics, Aesthetics, and Patriarchy in The Confessions of Winifred Wagner." *New German Critique* 18 (1979): 151–66.

Langer, Lawrence. *Facing Hitler Facing Ourselves:* Syberberg's *Hitler: A Film from Germany*. Annual 1. Los Angeles: Simon Wiesenthal Center, 1997.

Lardeau, Yann. "La préhistoire du cinéma, à propos de *Parsifal*." *Cahiers du Cinéma*, July–Aug. 1982, 50–52.

Larsen, Jan Kornum. "Tyskland—et vintereventyr." *Kosmorama*, Apr. 1984, 18–25.

Lietzmann, Sabina. "Jedermanns Hitler: Syberbergs Film in Amerika." *Frankfurter Allgemeine Zeitung*, Mar. 3, 1980, Feuilleton.

Loney, Glenn. *Parsifal*. Rev. *Opera News*, Mar. 12, 1983, 42–43.

"Marathon-Monolog." Rev. of *Die Marquise*. *Scala* 5 (Sept.–Oct. 1989): 20.

Markgraf, Hendrik. "Liebesgeflüster und Kriegsgeschrei: Hans Jürgen Syberbergs *Penthesilea*-Inszenierung mit Edith Clever im Großen Haus." *Frankfurter Allgemeine Zeitung*, Apr. 18, 1988, Lokales.

———. "Sehnsucht nach Größe: *Penthesilea* und der Kampf gegen eine 'verkommene Kultur'." *Frankfurter Allgemeine Zeitung*, May 4, 1988, Lokales.

Matussek, Matthias. "Gefolgschaft erzwingen." *Der Spiegel*, Oct. 22, 1990, 260+.

———. "Ich hielt bei Peter Stein um ihre Hand an." *Der Spiegel*, Apr. 11, 1988, 218–25.

Meyer, Claus Heinrich. "Wider die Demokratie der Mittelmäßgen: Hans Jürgen Syberberg stellte sein Buch *Die freudlose Gesellschaft* vor." *Süddeutsche Zeitung*, May 2, 1981.

Meyer, Michael. "Virtueller Weg nach Hause." *Ostseezeitung*, Oct. 26, 2001.

Mommert, Wilfried. "Ein arischer Gartenzwerg mit Tränen wie im Wahnsinn: Heftige öffentliche Debatte um den Filmemacher und Buchautor Hans Jürgen Syberberg. *Frankfurter Rundschau*, Oct. 16, 1990.

Moravia, Alberto. "Massiaggiate Himmler!" *L'Espresso*, Dec. 9, 1979. Reprinted as "Massez Himmler!" in "Syberberg," special issue, edited by Daney and Sobel, 96, and "Massiert Himmler!" in *Syberbergs Hitler-Film*, edited by Eder, 75–76.

Movshon, George. "Opera: *Guntram* in Concert, *Parsifal* on Film." Rev. *High Fidelity*, June 1983, 18–20.

Müller, André, ed. *Im Gespräch*. Reinbek bei Hamburg: Rowohlt, 1989.

Müller, Heiner. "Solitude du cinéma – à Syberberg." In "Syberberg," special issue, edited by Daney and Sobel, 97. Reprinted as "Die Einsamkeit des Films." In *Syberbergs Hitler-Film*, edited by Eder, 81–82.

Müller, Ulrich. "Blank, Syberberg, and the German Arthurian Tradition." In *Cinema Arthuriana: Essays on Arthurian Film*, edited by Kevin J. Harty, 157–68. New York: Garland, 1991.

Nattiez, Jean Jacques. *Wagner Androgyne: A Study in Interpretation*. Translated by Stewart Spencer. Princeton, NJ: Princeton Univ. Press, 1993.

Naughton, Leonie. "Recovering the 'Unmastered Past': Nazism in the New German Cinema." In *History on and in Film*, edited by T. O'Regan and B. Shoesmith, 121–30. Perth: History and Film Association of Australia, 1987.

Nenning, Günther. "Auf deutschem Ross: Die deutsche Kunst ist groß, und Syberberg ist ihr Prophet." Rev. of *Vom Unglück und Glück*. *Die Zeit*, July 27, 1990.

Neunzig, Hans A. "Der standhafte Filmsoldat Hans Jürgen Syberberg: Des Regisseurs Notizen aus dem letzten Jahr: *Die freudlose Gesellschaft*." *Stuttgarter Zeitung*, Nov. 7, 1981.

Ott, Frederick W. *The Great German Films*. Pp. 279–84 about *Hitler*. Secausus, NJ: Citadel, 1986.

Oudart, Jean-Pierre. "Notes de mémoire sur *Hitler* de Syberberg." *Cahiers du Cinéma* Nov. 1978, 5–15.

———. "Verführung und Terror im Kino." In *Syberbergs Hitler-Film*, edited by Eder, 37–50.

Pachter, Henry. "Our Hitler, or His? *Cineaste* 10, no. 2 (1980): 25–27. Appeared also as "Unser Hitler, oder seiner?" *Frankfurter Allgemeine Zeitung*, Aug. 1, 1980, Feuilleton.

Persché, Gerhard. *Parsifal*. Rev. *Opernwelt: Die Internationale Opernzeitschrift*, Apr. 1983, 59–60.

Plaul, Heiner. "Karl May als Tiresias im *Ludwig*-Film von Hans Jürgen Syberberg." *Mitteilungen der Karl May Gesellschaft* 12, no. 14 (1972): 33.

Porter, Andrew. "By Compassion Made Wise." Rev. of *Parsifal*. *New Yorker*, Feb. 21, 1983, 112+.

Pym, John. "Syberberg and the Tempter of Democracy." *Sight and Sound* 46, no. 2 (1977): 227–30.

Quaresima, Leonardo. "Le cittá del cinema." Rev. of *Ein Traum, was sonst?* http://www.syberberg.de/Syberberg3/italiani/italiani.htm (accessed Nov. 29, 2004).

———. "*Die Marquise von O . . .*, Kleist, (Rohmer), Syberberg." *Cinema e cinema* 57 (Jan.–Apr. 1990): 97–108. Not consulted.

Reiter, Elfi. *La scena ottica: Cinema e teatro in Germania; il cinema di H. J. Syberberg*. Bologna: Univ. di Bologna / Unione Italiana Circoli del Cinema, 1990.

Rockwell, John. "Hans Syberberg's Adaptation of *Parsifal*." [sic] *New York Times*, Jan. 23, 1983.

———. "The Re-Emergence of an Elusive Director: Hans Jürgen Syberberg shows his past work and ponders his future." *New York Times*, Sept. 2, 1992, C.

Rohde, Gerhard. "Ruinenromantik und Abschiedsschmerz." Rev. of *Die Marquise*. *Frankfurter Allgemeine Zeitung*, June 5, 1989, Lokales.

"Romy Schneider: Beichte am Berg." Rev. of *Romy*. *Der Spiegel*, Feb. 6, 1967, 94.

Rose, Barbara. "A Total Work of Art." Rev. of *Hitler*. *Vogue*, May 1980, 256+.

Ross, Jan. "Der Dichter ist den Germanisten ausgeliefert: 'Kleist, die deutsche Nation und die Kunst heute'; ein Symposium in Frankfurt an der Oder." *Frankfurter Allgemeine Zeitung*, Oct. 24, 1991, Feuilleton.

Ruckhäberle, Hans-Joachim. "Hans Jürgen Syberberg." In *Reden über das eigene Land*, by Stefan Heym, Hans Jürgen Syberberg, et al., 35.

Sahlberg, Oskar. "Wagner heute—Syberbergs *Parsifal*." *Neue Deutsche Hefte* 30 (1983): 342–46.

Sainderichin, Guy-Patrick. "Voyage à Munich: Hans-Jürgen tourne *Parsifal*." *Cahiers du Cinéma*, Jan. 1982, 22–29.

Sandford, John. "Hans Jürgen Syberberg: Films from Germany." In *Syberberg: A Film-maker from Germany*, 5–12. Edinburgh: Edinburgh International Film Festival/BFI, 1992.

———. *The New German Cinema*. Pp. 116–31 about Syberberg. New York: Da Capo, 1982.

———. "Syberberg." In *Cinegraph: Lexikon zum deutschsprachigen Film*, edited by Hans-Michael Bock. Munich: edition + kritik, 1984–.

Santner, Eric L. "Allegories of Grieving: The Films of Hans Jürgen Syberberg." In *Stranded Objects: Mourning, Memory, and Film in Postwar Germany*, 103–49. Ithaca, NY: Cornell Univ. Press, 1990.

———. "The Trouble with Hitler: Postwar German Aesthetics and the Legacy of Fascism." *New German Critique* 57 (1992): 5–24.

Sauvaget, Daniel. "Aimer Wagner malgré . . . *Parsifal*." *Revue du cinéma*, July–Aug. 1982, 78–80. Unavailable for consultation.

———. "Syberberg: dramaturgie antinaturaliste et germanitude." *Revue du cinéma:Image et son*, 1979, 93–106.

Schaper, Rüdiger. "Der deutsche Frühschoppen: Eine Syberberg-Diskussion in der Ost-berliner Akademie. *Süddeutsche Zeitung*, Oct. 16, 1990.

Schirrmacher, Frank. "Anmerkungen zu einem Ärgernis." *Frankfurter Allgemeine Zeitung*, Aug. 24, 1990, Feuilleton. Appeared also as "Ein notwendiger Kommentar" in some editions of the newspaper.

———. "Angst ist die Botschaft: Eine Syberberg-Debatte in der Akademie im Osten Berlins." *Frankfurter Allgemeine Zeitung*, Oct. 17, 1990, Feuilleton.

Schmitter, Elke. "Der deliquent als Privatpatient." *Tageszeitung*, Oct. 16, 1990.

Schneider, Manfred. "Dal libro al corpo: Hans Jürgen Syberberg e Edith Clever." *Cinema e cinema* 57 (Jan.–Apr. 1990): 80–88.

———. "Eine ganz neue Dunkelheit." Rev. of *Die Nacht*. *Die Zeit*, Nov. 29, 1985.

———. "Medienpathetiker: Wagner und Syberberg." In *Das Pathos der Deutschen*, edited by Norbert Bolz, 173–88.

———. "Der ungeheure Blick des Kinos auf die Welt: Die Wissensmächte Musik und Film in Wagner/Syberbergs *Parsifal*." *Merkur* 38 (1984): 882–92.

Schümer, Dirk. "Pferdemist: Syberbergs *Nietzsche in Weimar*." *Frankfurter Allgemeine Zeitung*, June 21, 1994, Feuilleton.

Schwab-Felisch, Hans. "Wo liegt Deutschland? 'Reden über das eigene Land:' Zu einer Vortragsreihe in München." *Frankfurter Allgemeine Zeitung*, Dec. 1, 1983, Feuilleton.

Sereny, Gitta. "Building up Defences against the Hitlerwave." *New Statesman*, July 7, 1978.

———. *Das deutsche Trauma: Eine heilende Wunde.* Pp. 298–206 about Syberberg. Munich: Bertelsmann, 2002. Trans. of *The German Trauma: Experiences and Reflections 1938–2001.* London: Lane, 2000.

———. "Hans Jürgen Syberberg: Germany's Most Feared Film-Maker." *Saturday Review*, Apr. 28, 1979, 28–32.

Sharrett, Christopher. "Epiphany for Modernism: Anti-Illusionism and Theatrical Tradition in Syberberg's *Our Hitler*." *Millenium Film Journal* 10–11 (Fall–Winter 1981-82): 141–57.

Sierek, Karl. "La cathédrale: La construction vidéo de Syberberg engloutie dans la Documenta 10." *Trafic* 25 (1998): 54–67.

Silberman, Marc. "The Ideology of Form: The Film as Narrative." In *Film und Literatur: Literarische Texte und der neue deutsche Film*, edited by Sigrid Bauschinger, et al., 197–209. Bern: Francke, 1984.

Simeon, Ennio. "Il *Parsifal* di Syberberg e la aporie del film-opera." *Cinema e cinema* 57 (Jan.–Apr. 1990): 89–96. Not consulted.

Sirk, Douglas. "C'est toujours le pays du doute." Interview, in "Syberberg," special issue, edited by Daney and Sobel, 92-93.

Slater, Stephen Daniel. "The Complicity of Culture with Barbarism: A Study of Thomas Mann's *Doktor Faustus* and Hans Jürgen Syberberg's *Hitler: Ein Film aus Deutschland*." Phd diss., Yale Univ., 1992.

Socci, Stefano. "Hans Jürgen Syberberg: La frontiera e i sogni del viandante." *Cinema e Cinema* 57 (Jan.-Apr. 1990): 75–79. Not consulted.

———. *Syberberg.* Il castoro cinema 143. Florence: La Nuova Italia, 1990.

Sontag, Susan. "Aventures dans la tête." In "Syberberg," special issue, edited by Daney and Sobel, 93–95.

———. "Eye of the Storm." *New York Review of Books*, Feb. 21, 1980, 36–43. Appeared also as "Syberberg's *Hitler*" in *Under the Sign of Saturn*, 137–65. Vintage Book ed. New York: Random House, 1981; and as "Syberbergs *Hitler*, in *Syberbergs Hitler-Film*, edited by Eder, 7–32.

———. "*Our Hitler*: A Masterpiece from Germany." *Vogue*, May 1980, 256+.

———. Preface to *Hitler: A Film from Germany*, by Hans Jürgen Syberberg, ix–xvi. New York: Farrar, Straus, Giroux, 1982.

Spiel, Hilde. "Skandalon: Streit um Syberbergs *Hitler*-Film." *Frankfurter Allgemeine Zeitung*, Oct. 19, 1978, Feuilleton.

Stanbrook, Alan. "The Sight of Music." Rev. of *Parsifal*. *Sight and Sound* 56, no. 2 (1987): 132–35.

Stone, Judy. "Seven Hours on Hitler." *San Francisco Examiner and Chronicle*, July 15, 1979. Reprinted as "A Controversial Film: Seven Hours on Hitler," in *Kino: German Film* 1 (1979): 69–71; and as "Hans Jürgen Syberberg," in *Eye on the World*, by Judy Stone, 263–66. Los Angeles: Silman James, 1997.

Storm, Misa. "Un sogno: *Penthesilea*, Kleist e Napoli." *Esmeralda: Rivista di letteratura* 3 (2000): 10-27. Not available for consultation.

"Streiter gegen Kulturbarbarei: Hans Jürgen Syberberg spricht in der Aula der Universität." *Frankfurter Allgemeine Zeitung*, June 6, 1989, Lokales.

Tambling, Jeremy. "The Fusion of Brecht and Wagner: Syberberg's *Parsifal*." In *Opera, Ideology and Film*, 195–212. New York: St. Martin's, 1987.

Tindemans, Klaas. "'Was ist des Teutschen Vaterland?' De besmette woorden von Syberberg." *Etcetera* 9, no. 35 (1991): 46–52.

Thüna, Ulrich von. "Hitler und kein Ende: Zu Hans Jürgen Syberbergs *Hitler: Ein Film aus Deutschland.*" *Neue Züricher Zeitung,* Dec. 28, 1978.

Umbach, Klaus. "Gesalbte Primeln." Rev. of *Parsifal. Der Spiegel,* May 24, 1982, 226–27.

Vaget, Hans Rudolf. "Die Auferstehung Richard Wagners: Wagnerismus und Verfremdung in Syberbergs Hitler-Film." In *Film und Literatur: Literarische Texte und der neue deutsche Film,* edited by Sigrid Bauschinger, Susan L. Cocalis, and Henry A. Lea, 124–55.

———. "Ein kritisch-aufklärerisches Werk." Letter to the editor against the German version of Henry Pachter's article there of Aug.1. *Frankfurter Allgemeine Zeitung,* Aug. 30, 1980.

———. "Syberberg's *Our Hitler*: Wagnerianism and Alienation." *Massachusetts Review* 23 (1982): 593–612.

Voss, Katharina. "Filme für die freudlose Gesellschaft." *Tageszeitung,* May 28, 2003.

Wagner, Dave. "*Our Hitler.*" *The Progressive* 44, no. 8 (1980): 51–53.

Wagner, Gottfried. *Wer nicht mit dem Wolf heult: Autobiographische Aufzeichnungen eines Wagner-Urenkels.* 126–37 about *Winifred Wagner.* Cologne: Kiepennheuer und Witsch, 1997.

Walsh, Michael. "Through the Looking Glass: Fantastic imagery abounds in two new films of Wagner." Rev. of *Parsifal. Time,* Jan. 24, 1983, 84.

Wapnewski, Peter. "Hymnen an die Nacht." Rev. of *Die Nacht. Der Spiegel* July 15, 1985, 126–29.

Weber, J. "Rocker-Story nach Kleist-Muster." Rev. of *San Domingo. Stuttgarter Zeitung,* Aug. 28, 1970. Reprinted in *Kleist in Frankfurt,* edited by Fiedler, 62–65.

Wiegand, Wilfried. "Die Ausnahme unter den Filmregisseuren." *Frankfurter Allgemeine Zeitung,* Dec. 2, 1980, Politik.

———. "Die deutsche Mythologie: Ein Gespräch über Hans Jürgen Syberbergs *Parsifal*-Film." *Frankfurter Allgemeine Zeitung,* Apr. 3, 1982, Feuilleton.

———. "Doppelgesicht einer Epoche: *Fotografie der dreißiger Jahre.*" Rev. *Frankfurter Allgemeine Zeitung,* Jan. 21, 1978, Literatur.

———. "Endzeit und Erlösung: Hans Jürgen Syberbergs *Parsifal*-Film in Paris uraufgeführt." *Frankfurter Allgemeine Zeitung,* May 19, 1982, Feuilleton.

———. "Der "Hitler" in uns: Hans Jürgen Syberbergs Film in Berlin." Rev. of *Hitler. Frankfurter Allgemeine Zeitung,* Feb. 27, 1979, Feuilleton.

———. "Narrenfreiheit?" *Frankfurter Allgemeine Zeitung,* Feb. 3, 1983.

Wild, Andreas. "Wimpel im Nasenloch." Rev. of *Parsifal. Die Welt,* June 2, 1982.

Winkler, Willi. "Unsere kleine Farm." Rev. of *Syberberg/Paris/Nossendorf. Süddeutsche Zeitung,* June 3, 2003.

Wirsing, Sibylle. "Deutsche Kisten: *Ein Traum, was sonst?:* Syberbergs Berliner Nachkriegsmesse." *Frankfurter Allgemeine Zeitung,* Dec. 20, 1990.

———. "Die Entdeckung einer Tragödin: Edith Clever in Hans Jürgen Syberbergs Sechs-Stunden Film *Nacht*; Uraufführung in Berlin." *Frankfurter Allgemeine Zeitung,* May 11, 1985, Feuilleton.

———. "Mein lieber Schwan." Rev. of *Die Marquise. Frankfurter Allgemeine Zeitung* Apr. 3, 1989, Feuilleton.

Zagarrio, Vito. "Der Nazi-Tyrann als Vorwand, um von den Dämonen von heute zu sprechen." In *Syberbergs Hitler-Film,* edited by Eder, 77–80. Appeared first as "Il tiranno Nazista come pretesto per parlare dei demoni d'oggi." *Avanti,* Dec. 16, 1979.

Zimmer, Christian. "Hitler unter uns." In *Syberbergs Hitler-Film*, edited by Eder, 51–68.
Zimmer, Dieter. "Die Farbe Braun: Ignorant oder Wahnsinniger—zur Debatte um Hans Jürgen Syberberg in der Ost-Berliner Akademie." *Die Zeit*, Oct. 19, 1990.

3. Other Cited Literature

Adorno, Theodor W. *Noten zur Literatur.* Frankfurt am Main: Suhrkamp, 1981.
———. *Prisms.* Translated by Samuel Weber and Shierry Weber. London: Spearman, 1967.
———. "Über den Bergen." In *Minima Moralia: Reflexionen aus dem beschädigten Leben*, 157. Bibliothek Suhrkamp 236. Frankfurt am Main: Suhrkamp, 1988.
———. "Zur Partitur des *Parsifal.*" In *Parsifal*, by Wagner, edited by Csampai and Holland, 191–95.
Albersmeier, Franz-Josef, and Volker Roloff, eds. *Literaturverfilmungen.* Frankfurt am Main: Suhrkamp, 1989.
Allen, Richard Hinckley. *Star Names: Their Lore and Meaning.* New York: Dover, 1963.
Ambrière, Francis. *Paris.* Les Guides Bleus. Paris: Hachette, 1949.
D'Arcy, Anne Marie. *Wisdom and the Grail.* Portland, OR: Four Courts, 2000.
Arendt, Hannah. *Eichmann in Jerusalem: A Report on the Banality of Evil.* Rev. and enl. ed. New York: Penguin Books, 1980.
Arrian. *Anabasis Alexandri.* Translated by P. A. Brunt. 2 vols. Loeb Classical Library 236 and 269. Cambridge, MA: Harvard Univ. Press, 1989.
Audsley, George Ashdown. *The Art of Organ Building.* 2 vols. New York: Dover, 1965.
Baer, Harry. *Schlafen kann ich, wenn ich tot bin: Das atemlose Leben des Rainer Werner Fassbinder.* Cologne: Kiepenheuer und Witsch, 1982.
Barron, Stephanie. "*Degenerate Art: The Fate of the Avant-Garde in Nazi Germany.* Los Angeles, CA: Los Angeles County Museum of Art, 1991.
Beitl, Richard, and Klaus Beitl. *Wörterbuch der deutschen Volkskunde.* 3rd ed. Stuttgart: Kröner, 1974.
Benjamin, Walter. *Illuminations.* Edited by Hannah Ahrendt. Translated by Harry Zohn. New York: Harcourt, Brace and World, 1968.
———. *Gesammelte Schriften.* Edited by Rolf Tiedemann and Hermann Schweppenhäuser. 7 vols. in 15 bks. Frankfurt am Main: Suhrkamp, 1991.
———. "The Task of the Translator: An Introduction to the Translation of Baudelaire's *Tableaux Parisiens.*" In *Illuminations*, edited by Hannah Arendt, 69–82.
———. "Über den Begriff der Geschichte." In *Gesammelte Schriften.* Vol. 1, bk. 2, 691–704.
———. "The Work of Art in the Age of Mechanical Reproduction." In *Illuminations*, edited by Hannah Arendt, 219–53.
Berg-Pan, Renata. *Leni Riefenstahl.* Twayne's Theatrical Arts Series. Boston: Twayne, 1980.
Berman, Russell A. *Modern Culture and Critical Theory: Arts, Politics, and the Legacy of the Frankfurt School.* Madison, WI: Univ. of Wisconsin Press, 1989.
Beyer, Bernhard. *Geschichte der Grossloge "Zur Sonne" in Bayreuth.* 2 vols. Frankfurt am Main: Bauhütten, 1954.
Binder, Wolfgang. *Friedrich Hölderlin: Studien.* Edited by Elisabeth Binder and Klaus Weimar. Suhrkamp Taschenbuch Materialien. Frankfurt am Main: Suhrkamp, 1987.
Bloch, Ernst. *Heritage of Our Times.* Translated by Neville Plaice and Stephen Plaice. Berkeley and Los Angeles, Univ. of California Press, 1991.

Blumenthal, W. Michael. *The Invisible Wall: Germans and Jews; a Personal Exploration.* Washington DC: Counterpoint, 1998.

Bock, Hans-Michael, ed. *Cinegraph: Lexikon zum deutschsprachigen Film.* Munich: edition text + kritik, 1984–.

Bodek, Janusz. *Die Fassbinder-Kontroversen: Entstehung und Wirkung eines literarischen Textes.* Frankfurt am Main: Lang, 1991.

Börsch-Supan, Helmut. *Caspar David Friedrich.* Translated by Sarah Twohig. New York: Braziller, 1974.

Brecht, Bertolt. *Die Geschäfte des Herrn Julius Caesar.* Berlin: Weiss, 1949.

Bronnen, Barbara, and Corinna, *Die Filmemacher: Zur neuen deutschen Produktion nach Oberhausen.* Munich: Bertelsmann, 1973.

Brown, Francis. *The New Brown-Driver-Briggs-Gesenius Hebrew and English Lexicon with an Appendix Containing the Biblical Arameic.* Peabody, MA: Hendrickson, 1979.

Buber, Martin. *I and Thou.* Edited and translated by Walter Kaufmann. New York: Scribner's Sons, 1970.

———. *Ich und Du.* In *Das dialogische Prinzip.* 5th ed. Darmstadt: Wissenschaftliche Buchgesellschaft, 1984.

Budge, E. A. Wallis. *The Gods of the Egyptians: or Studies in Egyptian Mythology.* 2 vols. New York: Dover, 1969.

———. *Osiris and the Egyptian Resurrection.* 2 vols. New York: Dover 1973.

Büning, Eleonore. "Hier gilt's der Kunst: Schluß mit der Wagnerei in Bayreuth." *Die Zeit,* Feb. 28, 1997.

Büscher, Wolfgang. "Vertreibung—was war?" *Die Welt,* Feb. 16, 2002, Deutschland.

Campbell, Mary Baine. "Finding the Grail: Fascist Aesthetics and Mysterious Objects." In *King Arthur's Modern Return,* edited by Debra Mancoff. New York: Garland, 1998.

Campbell-Everden, W. P. *Freemasonry and Its Etiquette.* New York: Weathervane, 1978.

Caputo, John D. *The Mystical Element in Heidegger's Thought.* Athens: Ohio Univ. Press, 1978.

Celan, Paul. *Gedichte.* 2 vols. Frankfurt am Main: Suhrkamp, 1986.

Chrétien de Troyes. *Le Roman de Perceval, ou Le Conte du Graal: Der Percevalroman oder Die Erzählung vom Gral.* Edited and translated by Felicitas Olef-Krafft. Universal-Bibliothek 8649. Stuttgart: Reclam, 1991.

Cicora, Mary A. *"Parsifal" Reception in the "Bayreuther Blätter."* American University Studies, Series 1, vol. 55 (New York: Peter Lang, 1987).

Claudius, Matthias. *Sämtliche Werke.* 7th ed. Darmstadt: Wissenschaftliche Buchgesellschaft, 1989.

Copenhaver, Brian P. *Hermetica.* Cambridge, MA: Cambridge Univ. Press, 1996.

Crosby, Sumner McKnight. *The Royal Abbey of Saint-Denis from Its Beginnings to the Death of Suger, 475–1151.* New Haven, CT: Yale Univ. Press, 1987.

Dahlhaus, Carl. "Erlösung dem Erlöser: Warum Richard Wagners *Parsifal* nicht Mittel zum Zweck der Ideologie ist." In *Parsifal,* von Wagner, edited by Csampai and Holland, 262–69.

———. *"Parsifal."* In *Parsifal,* by Richard Wagner, edited by Csampai and Holland, 201–13.

Dallach, Christoph, et al. "Patriotische Bauchschmerzen." *Der Spiegel,* Nov. 29, 2004.

Dällenbach, Lucien. *The Mirror in the Text.* Translated by Jeremy Whiteley and Emma Hughes. Chicago: Univ. of Chicago Press, 1989.

Dickens, Homer. *The Films of Marlene Dietrich.* New York: Citadel, 1968.

Dickson, Donald. *The fountain of Living Waters: The Typology of the Waters of Life in Herbert, Vaughan, and Traherne.* Columbia: Univ. of Missouri Press, 1987.

Döllinger, Ignaz von. *Geschichte der gnostisch-manichäischen Sekten im früheren Mittelalter.* Vol. 1 of *Beiträge zur Sektengeschichte des Mittelalters.* 2 vols. Darmstadt: Wissenschaftliche Buchgesellschaft, 1982.

Dönhoff, Marion, Countess. *Before the Storm: Memories of My Youth in Old Prussia.* New York: Knopf, 1990. Based on *Namen, die keiner mehr nennt,* Cologne: Diederichs, 1962; and *Kindheit in Ostpreußen,* Berlin: Siedler, 1988.

―――. "Wallfahrt zu Hitlers Refugium? Ein Dokumentenhaus auf dem Obersalzberg― welch ein Unfug." *Die Zeit,* Nov. 28, 1997.

Doré, Gustave, *The Doré Illustrations for Dante's "Divine Comedy": 136 Plates.* New York: Dover, 1976.

Dreyer, J. L. E. *A History of Astronomy from Thales to Kepler.* 2nd ed. New York: Dover, 1953.

Dürer, Albrecht. *The Painter's Manual.* Edited and translated by Walter L. Strauss. New York: Abaris Books, 1977.

Ewans, Michael. *Wagner and Aeschylus: The Ring and the Oresteia.* Cambridge: Cambridge Univ. Press, 1983.

Ewen, Frederic. *Bertolt Brecht: His Life, His Art, and His Times.* New York: Citadel, 1969.

Fargnoli, A. Nicholas, and Michael Patrick Gillespie. *James Joyce A to Z: The Essential Reference to the Life and Work.* New York: Oxford Univ. Press, 1996.

Ferguson, Donald N. *A History of Musical Thought.* New York: Crofts, 1935.

Fiedler, Leonhard M., ed. *Kleist in Frankfurt, Kleist im Film: Ein Arbeitsbuch.* Dierdorf: Margot Lang, 1989.

Fine, Lawrence. "The Contemplative Practice of Yihudim in Lurianic Kabbalah." In *Jewish Spirituality from the Sixteenth-Century Revival to the Present,* edited by Arthur Green. World Spirituality 14. New York: Crossroad, 1987.

Fine, Reuben. *The Development of Freud's Thought.* Northvale, NJ: Aronson, 1987.

Franck, Adolphe. *Die Kabbala oder die Religionsphilosophie der Hebräer.* Edited and translated by Adolf Gelinek [Jellinek]. Leipzig: Hunger, 1844.

Frenzel, Elisabeth. *Stoffe der Weltliteratur: Ein Lexikon dichtungsgeschichtlicher Längsschnitte.* 3rd ed. Kröners Taschenausgabe 300. Stuttgart: Kröner, 1970.

Freud, Sigmund. *The Interpretation of Dreams.* In *The Basic Writings of Sigmund Freud,* edited and translated by A. A. Brill. The Modern Library. New York: Random House, 1966.

―――. "Medusa's Head." In *Collected Papers.* Authorized translation by Alix and James Strachey. 5 vols. The International Psycho-Analytical Library 7–10 and 37. New York: Basic Books, 1959. 5:105–6.

―――. "Mourning and Melancholia." In *On the History of the Psycho-Analytic Movement, Papers on Metapsychology and Other Works,* translated by James Strachey, 243–58. Vol. 14 of *The Standard Edition of the Complete Psychological Works of Sigmund Freud.* London: Hogarth, 1957.

―――. *Totem and Taboo.* In *Basic Writings of Sigmund Freud,* 805–930.

Friedrich, Paul. *The Meaning of Aphrodite.* Chicago: Univ. of Chicago Press, 1978.

Gantz, Jeffrey, trans. *The Mabinogion.* New York: Dorset, 1985.

Gerresheim, Bert. "Die Plastik als Protokoll der Wahrnehmung." In *Das Düsseldorfer Heine-Monument,* edited by Hans-Joachim Neisser. 2nd ed. Düsseldorf: Presseamt, 1981.

Getty, Adele. *Goddess: Mother of Living Nature.* London: Thames, 1990.

Gfrörer, August Friedrich. *Die Geschichte des Urchristentums.* 2nd ed. 5 vols. Stuttgart: Schweizerbart, 1838.

Glasenapp, Carl Fr., and Heinrich von Stein, eds. *Wagner-Lexikon: Hauptbegriffe der Kunst- und Weltanschauung Richard Wagners.* Stuttgart: Cotta, 1883.

Görres, Joseph, ed. *Lohengrin, ein altteutsches Gedicht.* Heidelberg: Moor und Zimmer, 1813.

Goethe, Johann Wolfgang von. *Faust.* Grossherzog Wilhelm Ernst Ausgabe, 16 vols. Leipzig: Insel, 1920, vol. 6

———. *West-Östlicher Divan.* Grossherzog Wilhelm Ernst Ausgabe, 11:644–939.

Graves, Robert. *The Greek Myths.* 2 vols. New York: Viking Penguin, 1986.

Gregor-Dellin, Martin. *Richard Wagner: Sein Leben, sein Werk, sein Jahrhundert.* Neu durchges. Aufl. Munich: Goldmann Schott, 1983.

Grimal, Pierre, ed. *Larousse World Mythology.* London: Hamlyn, 1973.

Grimm, Jacob. *Deutsche Mythologie.* 3 vols. Graz: Akad. Druck- und Verlagsanstalt, 1968.

Grimm, Jacob, and Wilhelm Grimm. *Deutsches Wörterbuch.* 1854–1971. 33 vols. Reprint dtv 5945. Munich: Deutscher Taschenbuch Verlag, 1984.

Groos, Arthur B. "Wolfram von Eschenbach's Bow Metaphor and the Narrative Technique of *Parzival.*" *Modern Language Notes* 87 (1972): 391–408.

Grosz, George. *George Grosz: An Autobiography.* Translated by Nora Hodges. Berkeley and Los Angeles: Univ. of California Press, 1998.

Grunberger, Richard. *The 12-Year Reich: A Social History of Nazi Germany 1933–1945.* New York: Holt, Rinehart and Winston, 1971.

Gutman, Robert W. *Richard Wagner: The Man, His Mind, and His Music.* New York: Harcourt Brace Jovanovich, 1968.

Hahn, H. J. "'Es geht nicht um Literatur': Some Observations on the 1990 'Literaturstreit' and Its Recent Anti-Intellectual Implications." *German Life and Letters* 50, no. 1 (Jan. 1997): 65–81.

Hairapetian, Marc. "Oskar Werner Bonaparte: Im Tod wird der exzentrische Schauspieler wie ein Popstar verehrt." *Die Welt,* Nov. 12, 1997.

Halevi, Z'ev ben Shimon (Warren Kenton). *A Kabbalistic Universe.* New York: Weiser, 1977.

Hammerstein, Konstantin von, et al. "Vertriebene: Eine besondere Art von Heimweh." *Der Spiegel,* Aug. 9, 2004, 40–42.

Hanslick, Eduard. "Richard Wagners Parsifal." In *Parsifal,* by Wagner, edited by Csampai and Holland, 134–61.

Harrof, Stephen C. *Wolfram and His Audience.* Göppingen: Kümmerle, 1974.

Harty, Kevin J., ed. *Cinema Arthuriana: Essays on Arthurian Film.* New York: Garland, 1991.

———, ed. *King Arthur on Film: New Essays on Arthurian Cinema.* Jefferson, NC: McFarland, 1999.

———. *The Reel Middle Ages: American, Western and Eastern European, Middle Eastern and Asian Films about Medieval Europe.* Jefferson, NC: McFarland, 1999.

Hasty, Will. "Beyond the Guilt Thesis: On the Socially Integrative Function of Transgression in Wolfram von Eschenbach's *Parzival.*" *German Quarterly* 61, no. 3 (1988): 354–70.

Haverkamp, Anselm. *Laub voll Trauer: Hölderlins späte Allegorie.* Munich: Fink, 1991.

———. *Leaves of Mourning: Hölderlin's Late Work, with an Essay on Keats and Melancholy.* Translated by Vernon Chadwick. Albany, NY: State Univ. of New York Press, 1996.

Heath, Thomas L. *Greek Astronomy.* New York: Dover, 1991.

Heidegger, Martin. *Basic Writings.* Edited by David Farrell Krell. New York: Harper and Row, 1977.

———. *Hölderlin's Hymn "The Ister."* Translated by William McNeill and Julia Davis. Studies in Continental Thought. Bloomington: Indiana Univ. Press, 1996.

———. *Hölderlins Hymne "Andenken."* Vol. 52, Gesamtausgabe. Frankfurt am Main: Klostermann, 1982.

———. *The Question Concerning Technology and Other Essays.* Translated by William Lovitt. New York: Garland, 1977. See also *Basic Writings*, 301–7.

———. *Die Technik und die Kehre.* 8th ed. Opuscula 1. Pfullingen: Neske, 1991.

Heine, Heinrich. *Atta Troll: Ein Sommernachtstraum.* In *Werke*, 537–606. Tempel-Klassiker. Berlin: Tempel-Verlag, 1968.

Heine, Heinrich. *Deutschland: Ein Wintermärchen.* In *Werke*, 607–69.

Heine, Heinrich. *Der Doktor Faust: Ein Tanzpoem nebst kuriosen Berichten über Teufel, Hexen und Dichtkunst.* In *Werke und Briefe.* Edited by Hans Kaufmann. 10 vols. Berlin: Aufbau, 1961–63. 7:7–53.

———. *Französische Maler.* In *Werke und Briefe,* 4:295–359.

———. *Französische Zustände.* In *Werke und Briefe,* 4:361–83.

Hinton, David B. *The Films of Leni Riefenstahl.* 2nd ed. Filmmakers 29. Metuchen, NJ: Scarecrow, 1991.

Hölderlin, Friedrich. "Patmos." In *Sämtliche Werke*, edited by Paul Stapf, 2 vols. Tempel-Klassiker. Wiebaden: Vollmer, n.d. 1:328–34.

Holmes, Urban T, and Sister M. Amelia Klenke, O. P. *Chrétien, Troyes, and the Grail.* Chapel Hill: Univ. of North Carolina Press, 1959.

Holroyd, Stuart. *Magic, Words, and Numbers.* London: Aldus, 1975.

Honegger, Gitta. *Thomas Bernhard: The Making of an Austrian.* New Haven, CT: Yale Univ. Press, 2002.

Howarth, Stephen. *The Knights Templar.* New York: Dorset, 1991.

Hoyle, Fred. *Astronomy.* London: Rathbone, 1962.

Huyssen, Andreas. "Kiefer in Berlin." *October* 25, no. 1 (1992): 84–101.

Idel, Moshe. *Kabbalah: New Perspectives.* New Haven, CT: Yale Univ. Press, 1988.

Jacobs, Louis. "The Uplifting of Sparks in Later Jewish Mysticism." In *Jewish Spirituality,* edited by Arthur Green, 99–126.

Jacobsen, Wolfgang. "Fritz Kortner: Schauspieler, Autor, Regisseur." In *Cinegraph,* edited by Bock.

Jennings, W. *Dialectical Images: Walter Benjamin's Theory of Literary Criticism.* Ithaca, NY: Cornell Univ. Press, 1987.

Jeziorkowski, Klaus. "Empor ins Licht: Gnostizismus und Lichtsymbolik in Deutschland um 1900." In *The Turn of the Century: German Literature and Art, 1890–1915,* edited by Gerald Chapple and Hans H. Schulte. 2nd ed. Bonn: Bouvier, 1983.

Jung, C. G. *Alchemical Studies.* In *Collected Works.* Edited by Herbert Read, et al. Translated by R. F. C. Hull. 20 vols. Bollingen Series 20. 2nd ed. Princeton, NJ: Princeton Univ. Press, 1954–93. Vol. 13.

———. *Aion: Researches into the Phenomenology of the Self. Collected Works*, vol. 9, bk. 2. 1978.

———. *The Archetypes and the Collective Unconscious. Collected Works*, vol. 9, bk. 1. 1990.

———. "On the Nature of the Psyche. In *Basic Writings of C. G. Jung.* Edited by Violet Staub de Laszlo, 37–104. The Modern Library. New York: Random House, 1959.

————. *Psychological Types. Collected Works*, vol. 6. 1990.

————. *Psychology and Alchemy. Collected Works*, vol. 12. 1993.

————. *Symbols of Transformation. Collected Works*, vol. 5. 1976.

Jung, Emma, and Marie-Louise Franz. *The Grail Legend.* Translated by Andrea Dykes. London: Hodder, 1971.

Kahane, Henry, and Renée Kahane. *The Krater and the Grail: Hermetic Sources of the Parzival.* Urbana: Univ. of Illinois Press, 1965.

Kaiser, Joachim. "Hat Zelinsky recht gegen Wagners *Parsifal?*" In *Parsifal*, by Wagner, edited by Csampai and Holland, 257–59.

Kampers, Franz. "Der Waise. Historisches Jahrbuch 37 (1919): 433–86.

"Käthe Gold." Obituary. *Die Zeit,* Oct. 24, 1997.

Katz, Ephraim. *The Film Encyclopedia.* New York: Putnam, 1982.

Kern, Peter. "Lautes Bellen aus der vierten Reihe." Interview. *Der Spiegel*, Oct. 21, 2002, 197.

Kiefer, Anselm. *The High Priestess.* With an essay by Armin Zweite. New York: Abrams: 1989.

Kleinpaul, Rudolf. *Länder und Völkernamen.* Leipzig: Göschen, 1910.

Kleist, Heinrich von. *Sämtliche Werke.* Edited by Karl Siegen. 4 vols. in 1. Leipzig: Hesse, n.d.

————. "Über das Marionettentheater." In *Sämtliche Werke,* 3:213–19.

Koch, H. W. *A History of Prussia.* New York: Dorset, 1978.

Kortner, Fritz. *Aller Tage Abend.* Berlin: Alexander, 1991.

Kracauer, Siegfried. *From Caligari to Hitler: A Psychological History of the German Film.* Princeton: Princeton Univ. Press, 1947.

Küng, Hans. "Wagner's *Parsifal*: A Theology for Our Time." *Michigan Quarterly Review* 23 (1984): 311–33.

Lampman, Jane. "The True 'Gospel' of Mary Explored." *Denton Record Chronicle*, Nov. 21, 2003.

Lamy, Lucy. *Egyptian Mysteries: New Light on Ancient Knowledge.* New York: Thames: 1989.

Lehmann, Hans Thies. *Postdramatisches Theater.* 2nd ed. Frankfurt am Main: Verlag der Autoren, 2001.

Lellis, George. *Bertolt Brecht, Cahiers du Cinéma and Contemporary Film Theory.* Studies in Cinema 13. Ann Arbor, MI: UMI, 1982.

Levi, Hermann. "Brief an seinen Vater über die letzte Aufführung des *Parsifal* im Festspielsommer 1882." In *Parsifal*, by Wagner, edited by Scampai and Holland, 132–34.

Levin, David J. *Richard Wagner, Fritz Lang, and the Nibelungen: The Dramaturgy of Disavowal.* Princeton, NJ: Princeton Univ. Press, 1997.

Levkov, Ilya, ed. *Bitburg and Beyond: Encounters in American, German and Jewish History.* New York: Shapolsky, 1987.

Lichtenberg, R., Freiherr von, and L. Müller von Hausen. *Mehr Schutz dem geistigen Eigentum! Der Kampf um das Schicksal des "Parsifal."* 4th ed. Berlin: Curtius, n.d., ca. 1914.

Löffler, Sigrid. "Christiane Hörbiger: Noblesse, ihre zweite Natur.: *Die Zeit*, Mar. 20, 1992.

Longfellow, Henry Wadsworth. *Christus: A Mystery.* In *The Complete Poetical Works of Henry Wadsworth Longfellow.* Cabinet Ed. Boston: Houghton Mifflin, 1901.470–686.

Lorenz, Alfred O. *Der musikalische Aufbau von Richard Wagners "Parsifal."* 2nd ed. Tutzing: Schneider, 1966.

Mai, Ekkehard. "Das Leidenslager wird zur Landschaft." In *Das Düsseldorfer Heine-Mo-*

nument, edited by Neisser, 10–17.

Mann, Thomas. "Bruder Hitler." 1939. In *Politische Schriften und Reden,* edited by Hans Bürgin. 2 vols. Frankfurt am Main: Fischer, 1968. 1:53–58.

———. *Doktor Faustus: Das Leben des deutschen Tonsetzers Adrian Leverkühn erzählt von einem Freunde.* Frankfurt am Main: Fischer, 1967.

———. *Die Entstehung des Doktor Faustus: Roman eines Romans.* Stockholmer Gesamtausgabe. Amsterdam: Fischer / Querido, 1949.

Manvell, Roger, and Heinrich Fraenkel. *The German Cinema.* New York: Praeger, 1971.

Markale, Jean. *The Celts: Uncovering the Mythic and Historic Origins of Western Culture.* Rochester, VT: Inner Traditions International, 1978.

Mayer, Hans. *Anmerkungen zu Richard Wagner.* Frankfurt am Main: Suhrkamp, 1966.

Meade, Marion. *Eleanor of Aquitaine.* New York: Hawthorn, 1977.

Merker, Paul, and Wolfgang Stammler. *Reallexikon der deutschen Literaturgeschichte.* 2nd ed. 5 vols. Berlin: de Gruyter, 1977.

Mitscherlich, Alexander, and Margarethe Mitscherlich. *The Inability to Mourn: Principles of Collective Behavior.* 1967. Translated by Beverley R. Placzek. New York: Grove, 1975.

Mittelstaedt, Axel. "Zur Charakterentwicklung Karl Mays." In *Karl May: Leben und Werk,* by Thomas Ostwald, 309–30. Braunschweig: Graff, 1977.

Möller, Johann Michael. "Ein Akt der nationalen Selbstheilung." *Die Welt,* Feb. 16, 2002.

Mueller, Roswitha. *Bertolt Brecht and the Theory of Media.* Lincoln: Univ. of Nebraska Press, 1989.

Müller, Werner. *Another Country: German Inellectuals, Unification and National Identity.* New Haven, CT: Yale Univ. Press, 2000.

Neisser, Hans-Joachim, and Werner Schwerter, eds. *Das Düsseldorfer Heine-Monument.* 2nd ed. Düsseldorf: Presseamt, 1981.

Nettl, Paul. *Mozart and Masonry.* New York: Dorset, 1987.

Neumann, Erich. *The Great Mother: An Analysis of the Archetype.* 2nd ed. Princeton, NJ: Princeton Univ. Press, 1974.

Nietzsche, Friedrich. *The Case of Wagner.* In *Basic Writings of Nietzsche.* Edited and translated by Walter Kaufmann, 603–53. The Modern Library. New York: Random House, 1968.

———. *Ecce Homo.* In *Basic Writings of Nietzsche,* edited by Kaufmann, 657–791.

———. *Der Fall Wagner: Schriften—Aufzeichnungen—Briefe.* insel taschenbuch 686. Frankfurt am Main: Insel, 1983.

———. *Thus Spake Zarathustra.* The Modern Library. New York: Random House, n.d.

Nigg, Walter. *The Heretics.* Edited and translated by Richard Winston and Clara Winston. New York: Dorset, 1990.

Olsen, Solveig. "Celan's Todesfuge": The Musical Dimension of a Verbal Composition." In *Literature and Musical Adaptation.* Edited by Michael J. Meyer, 189–212. Rodopi Perspectives on Modern Literature 26. Amsterdam: Rodopi, 2002.

Osborne, Charles. *The World Theatre of Wagner: A Celebration of 150 Years of Wagner Productions.* New York: Macmillan, 1982.

Ostwald, Thomas. *Karl May: Leben und Werk.* Braunschweig: Graff, 1977.

Ott, Frederick W. *The Great German Films.* Secausus, NJ: Citadel, 1986.

Panofsky, Erwin. *Abbot Suger and Its Art Treasures on the Abbey Church of St.-Denis.* [*sic*]. 2nd ed. Princeton, NJ: Princeton Univ. Press, 1979. The cover has the correct title: *Abbot Suger on the Abbey Church of St.-Denis and Its Art Treasures.*

Pei, Mario A., and Frank Gaynor. *Dictionary of Linguistics.* New York: Philosophical

Library, 1954.

Petzet, Detta, and Michael Petzet. *Die Richard Wagner-Bühne König Ludwigs II.* Munich: Prestel, 1970.

Philo. *Philo.* Translated by F. H. Cohen and G. H. Whitaker. 2 vols. Loeb Classical Library 226 and 227. Cambridge, MA: Harvard Univ. Press, 1991.

Plutarch. "Isis and Osiris." In *Moralia.* Translated by Frank Cole Babbitt. 15 vols. Loeb Classical Library 306. Cambridge, MA: Harvard Univ. Press, 1993. 5:83 and 137.

Powell, Neil. *Alchemy: The Ancient Science.* New York: Doubleday, 1976.

"Protesters Berate Haider as 'Fascist'." *Denton Record Chronicle*, Feb. 3, 2000.

Ptolemy. *Tetrabiblos.* Edited and translated by F. E. Robbins. Loeb Classical Library 435. Cambridge, MA: Harvard Univ. Press, 1994.

Purtle, Carol J. *The Marian Paintings of Jan van Eyck.* Princeton, NJ: Princeton Univ. Press, 1982.

Puschmann, Rosemarie. *Magisches Quadrat und Melancholie in Thomas Manns "Doktor Faustus": Von der musikalischen Struktur zum semantischen Beziehungsnetz.* Bielefeld: AMPAL, 1983.

Querido, René. *The Golden Age of Chartres: The Teachings of a Mystery School and the Eternal Feminine.* Edinburgh: Floris, 1987.

Rauschning, Hermann. *Gespräche mit Hitler.* 4th ed. Zürich: Europa Verlag, 1940.

Regardie, Israel. *A Garden of Pomegranates.* 2nd. ed. St. Paul,MN: Llewellyn, 1991.

Reichert, Klaus. "Hebräische Züge in der Sprache Paul Celans." In *Paul Celan.* Edited by Werner Hamacher and Winfried Menninghaus, 156–69. Frankfurt am Main: Suhrkamp, 1988.

Reitz, Edgar. *Bilder in Bewegung: Essays, Gespräche zum Kino.* Reinbek bei Hamburg: Rowohlt, 1995.

Reitzenstein, Richard. *Poimandres: Studien zur griechisch-ägyptischen und frühchristlichen Literatur.* Leipzig: Teubner, 1904.

Rentschler, Eric. *The Ministry of Illusion: Nazi Cinema and Its Afterlife.* Cambridge, MA: Harvard Univ. Press, 1996.

Riefenstahl, Leni. *A Memoir.* New York, St. Martin's, 1993.

———. "Why Am I Filming *Penthesilea?*" *Film Culture* 56–57 (1973): 192–215.

Robinson, James M., ed. *The Nag Hammadi Library in English.* 3rd ed. San Francisco: Harper, 1988.

Romani, Cinzia. *Die Filmdiven im Dritten Reich.* Munich: Bahia, 1985.

Rorimer, James J. *The Cloisters: The Building and the Collection of Mediaeval Art in Fort Tryon Park.* New York: Metropolitan Museum of Art, 1951.

Rose, Paul Lawrence. *Wagner: Race and Revolution.* New Haven, CT: Yale Univ. Press, 1992.

Ruh, Kurt. *Geschichte der abendländischen Mystik.* 4 vols. Munich: Beck, 1993–99.

Schenke, Hans-Martin. "The Function and Background of the Beloved Disciple in the Gospel of John." In *Nag Hammadi, Gnosticism, and Early Christianity,* edited by Charles Hedrick and Robert Hodgson, Jr. Peabody, MA: Hendrickson, 1986.

Schiller, Friedrich. *Kabale und Liebe: Ein bürgerliches Trauerspiel.* Grossherzog Wilhelm Ernst Ausgabe. 6 vols. Leipzig: Insel, n.d. 1:255–358.

Schirok, Bernd. "Die senewe ist ein bîspel: Zu Wolframs Bogengleichnis." *Zeitschrift für Deutsches Altertum und Deutsche Literatur* 115, no. 1 (1986): 21–36.

Schneider, Irmela. "Aktualität im historischen Gewand: Zu Filmen nach Werken von Heinrich von Kleist." In *Literaturverfilmungen.* Edited by Franz-Josef Albersmeier and Volker Roloff, 99–121. Frankfurt am Main: Suhrkamp, 1989.

Schneider, Ute. "Lil Dagover: Schauspielerin." In *Cinegraph*, edited by Bock.

———. "Romy Schneider: Schauspielerin." In *Cinegraph*, edited by Bock.

Schnitzler, Arthur. *Fräulein Else.* In *Die Erzählenden Schriften.* 2 vols. Frankfurt am Main: Fischer, 1981. 2:324–81.

Scholem, Gershom. *Kabbalah.* New York: Dorset, 1974.

———. *The Messianic Idea in Judaism.* New York: Schocken, 1971.

———. *On the Kabbalah and Its Symbolism.* Translated by Ralph Manheim. New York: Shocken, 1965.

———. *Origins of the Kabbalah.* Princeton: Princeton Univ. Press, 1987.

———. *Von der mystischen Gestalt der Gottheit: Studien zu Grundbegriffen der Kabbala.* Frankfurt am Main: Suhrkamp, 1977.

Schöning, Jörg. "Paul Hörbiger." In *Cinegraph*, edited by Bock.

Schröder, Reinald. "Welteislehre, Ahnenerbe und 'Weiße Juden': Kuriosa aus der Wissenschaftspolitik im 'Dritten Reich'." *Die Zeit*, Apr. 26, 1991.

Schulz, Bernhard. "Wüstensand der Geschichte: Anselm Kiefer in der Fondation Beyeler in Basel." *Kulturchronik* 20, no. 1 (2002): 4–5.

Schulze-Reimpell, Werner. "Epitome of Artistic and Moral Rigour." *The German Tribune*, May 29, 1992.

Schürmann, Reiner. *Meister Eckhart: Mystic and Philosopher; Translations with Commentary.* Bloomington: Indiana Univ. Press, 1978.

Scott, Walter, ed. *Hermetica: The Ancient Greek and Latin Writings Which Contain Religious or Philosophic Teachings Ascribed to Hermes Trismegistus.* 4 vols. London: Dawsons, 1968.

Sedlmayr, Hans. *Die Entstehung der Kathedrale.* Graz: Akad. Druck- und Verl., 1976.

———. *Verlust der Mitte; Die bildende Kunst des 19. und 20. Jahrhunderts als Symbol der Zeit.* Salzburg: Müller, 1948.

Seeßlen, Georg. "Helmut Käutner: Regisseur, Schauspieler." In *Cinegraph*, edited by Bock.

Seidensticker, Bernd. "Das Satyrspiel." In *Satyrspiel*, edited by Bernd Seidensticker, 332–61. Wege der Forschung 579. Darmstadt: Wissenschaftliche Buchgesellschaft, 1989.

Seltman, Charles. *The Twelve Olympians and Their Guests.* London: Parrish, 1956.

Silberer, Herbert. *Hidden Symbolism of Alchemy and the Occult Arts.* Translated by S. E. Jelliffe. New York: Dover, 1971.

Silberman, Marc. "Late Pabst: *The Last Ten Days* (1955)." In *The Films of G. W. Pabst: An Extraterritorial Cinema*, edited by Eric Rentschler. New Brunswick: Rutgers Univ. Press, 1990.

Sklar, Dusty. *The Nazis and the Occult.* New York: Dorset, 1977.

Snell, Bruno. : "Aischylos' *Isthmiastai*." In *Satyrspiel*, edited by Seidensticker, 78–92.

Spitz, Hans-Jörg. "Wolframs Bogengleichnis: ein typologisches Signal." In *Verbum et Signum*, edited by Hans Fromm, Wolfgang Harms, and Uwe Ruberg, 2 vols. Munich: Fink, 1975. 2:247–75.

Spotts, Frederic. *Bayreuth: A History of the Wagner Festival.* New Haven: Yale Univ. Press, 1994.

Stein, Leon. *The Racial Thinking of Richard Wagner.* New York: Philosophical Library: 1950.

Steinbach, Erika. "Grandioses Versagen." Interview. By Hans Michael Kloth and Dietmar Pieper. *Der Spiegel*, Sept. 20, 2004, 36+.

Stölzl, Christoph. "Preußen—was bleibt?" *Die Welt*, Feb. 16, 2002, Deutschland.

Strobel, Otto, ed. *König Ludwig II. und Richard Wagner: Briefwechsel.* 4 vols.

Karlsruhe: Braun, 1936.

Thorndike, Lynn. *A History of Magic and Experimental Science*. 8 vols. New York: Columbia Univ. Press, 1923.

Timm, Eitel. *Ketzer und Dichter: Lessing, Goethe, Thomas Mann und die Postmoderne in der Tradition des Häresiegedankens*. Beiträge zur neueren Literaturgeschichte 88. Heidelberg: Winter, 1989.

Trüby, Jochen. "Das teuerste Buch der Welt: Eine Zierde für die Ewigkeit." *Scala,* Oct. 1994, 64 –66.

"Urteil im Mai: Sedelmayr-Mord: Lebenslänglich gefordert." *Sonntag Aktuell* May 2, 1993.

VanderKam, James C. *Enoch and the Growth of an Apocalyptic Tradition*. Washington DC: Catholic Biblical Assoc. of America, 1984.

Vordtriede, Werner. *Heine-Kommentar*. 2 vols. Munich: Winkler, 1970.

Wadepuhl, Walter. *Heinrich Heine: Sein Leben und seine Werke*. Cologne: Böhlau, 1974.

Wagner, Cosima. "An die Mitglieder des Deutschen Reichstages." 1901. In *Mehr Schutz dem geistigen Eigentum!*, by Lichtenberg and Müller von Hausen, 70.

———. *Cosima Wagner's Diaries*. Edited by Martin Gregor-Dellin and Dietrich Mack. Translated by Geoffrey Skelton. 2 vols. New York: Harcourt, 1978.

———. *Die Tagebücher*. Edited by Martin Gregor Dellin and Dietrich Mack. 4 vols. Munich: Piper, 1977.

Wagner, Friedelind, and Page Cooper. *Heritage of Fire: The Story of Richard Wagner's Granddaughter*. 3rd ed. New York: Harper and Brothers, c1945.

Wagner, Richard. *The Authentic Librettos of the Wagner Operas*. New York: Crown, 1938.

———. "Jesus von Nazareth: Ein dichterischer Entwurf. 1848." In *Sämtliche Schriften und Dichtungen*. Edited by Hans von Wolzogen. 5th ed. 12 vols. Leipzig: Breitkopf und Härtel, 1911. 11:273–323.

———. *Judaism in Music and Other Essays*. Translated by William Ashton Ellis. 1894. Lincoln: Univ. of Nebraska Press, 1995.

———. "Das Liebesmahl der Apostel: Eine biblische Szene. 1843." In *Sämtliche Schriften und Dichtungen*. Edited by Hans von Wolzogen. 12 vols. Leipzig: Breitkopf & Härtel, 1911. 11:264–69.

———. *My Life*. Edited by Andrea Dykes. Translated by Andrew Gray. Cambridge: Cambridge Univ. Press, 1983.

———. *Parsifal*. Edited by Michael von Soden. insel taschenbuch 684. Frankfurt am Main: Insel, 1983.

———. *Parsifal: Ein Bühnenweihfestspiel*. Mainz: Schott, 1879.

———. *Parsifal: A Festival Drama*. Translated by H. L. Corder and F. Corder. New York: Rullman, n.d., ca. 1913.

———. *Parsifal in Full Score*. New York: Dover, 1986.

———. *Parsifal: Texte, Materialien, Kommentare*. Edited by Attila Csampai and Dietmar Holland. rororo Opernbücher. Reinbek bei Hamburg: Rowohlt, 1984.

———. "Parzival." In *Parsifal*, by Wagner, edited by von Soden, 96–124.

———. *Religion and Art*. Translated by Wm Ashton Ellis. 1897. Lincoln: Univ. of Nebraska Press, 1994.

———. "Die Sarazenin: Oper in drei [fünf?] Akten. 1843." In *Sämtliche Schriften und Dichtungen,* 11:230–63.

———. *Selected Letters*. Edited and translated by Stewart Spencer and Barry Millington. London: Dent, 1987.

————. Stories and Essays. Edited by Charles Osborne. La Salle, IL: Open Court, 1991.

————. "Was ist deutsch?" In Gesammelte Schriften und Dichtungen. 4th ed. 10 vols. Leipzig: Siegel, 1907. 10:36–53.

————. "Zur Entstehungsgeschichte." In Parsifal, edited by von Soden, 89–158.

Walker, Charles. Atlas of Secret Europe: A Guide to Sites of Magic and Mystery. New York: Dorset, 1990.

Waite, Arthur Edward. A New Encyclopedia of Freemasonry. New York: Weathervane, 1970.

Wapnewski, Peter. Richard Wagner: Die Szene und ihr Meister. 2nd ed. Munich: Beck, 1983.

————. Der traurige Gott: Richard Wagner in seinen Helden. 2nd ed. Munich: Beck, 1980.

Wedeck, H. E. Dictionary of Gypsy Life and Lore. New York: Philosophical Library, 1973.

Weiner, Mark. Richard Wagner and the Anti-Semitic Imagination. Lincoln: Univ. of Nebraska Press, 1995.

Weingartner, Felix. "Erinnerungen an die Parsifal-Aufführungen 1882." In Parsifal, by Richard Wagner, edited by Csampai and Holland, 127–31.

Weinraub, Eugene J. Chrétien's Jewish Grail: A New Investigation of the Imagery and Significance of Chrétien de Troyes's Grail Episode Based upon Medieval Hebraic Sources. North Carolina Studies in the Romance Languages and Literatures 168. Chapel Hill: Univ. of North Carolina, 1976.

Welch, David. Propaganda and the German Cinema 1933–1945. Rev. ed. London: Tauris, 2001.

Wilmshurst, W. L. The Meaning of Masonry. Reprint of 5th ed. 1927. New York: Bell, 1980.

Witt, R. E. Isis in the Ancient World. 1971. Baltimore: Johns Hopkins Univ. Press, 1997.

Wolfram von Eschenbach. Parzivâl. Edited by Karl Lachmann. 6th ed. Berlin: de Gruyter, 1926.

————. Parzival. Translated by A. T. Hatto. New York: Penguin Books, 1987.

————. Parzival. Translated by Helen M. Mustard and Charles E. Passage. New York: Vintage, 1961.

Wolzogen, Hans von. "Der Name 'Parsifal' (1888)." In Wagneriana: Gesammelte Aufsätze über R. Wagners Werke vom Ring bis zum Gral. Walluf:Nendeln, 1977. 163–66.

Wright, W. M., and P. V. Jones, eds. and trans. Homer: German Scholarship in Translation. Oxford: Clarendon, 1997.

Young-Eisendrath, Polly, and Terence Dawson, eds. The Cambridge Companion to Jung. Cambridge, Cambridge Univ. Press, 1997.

Zachner, R. C. The Concise Encyclopedia of Living Faiths. Boston: Beacon, 1967.

Zagermann, Peter. Eros und Thanatos: Psychoanalytische Untersuchungen zu einer Objektbeziehungstheorie der Triebe. Darmstadt: Wissenschaftliche Buchgesellschaft, 1988.

Zehle, Sibylle. "Ein Mann, ein Theater: August Everding machte es möglich: München hat sein Prinzregententheater wieder." Die Zeit, Nov. 22, 1996.

Zelinsky, Hartmut. "Die 'feuerkur' des Richard Wagner oder die 'neue religion' der 'Erlösung' durch 'Vernichtung'." Musik-Konzepte 5 (1978): 79–112.

————. "Rettung ins Ungenaue: Zu Martin Gregor-Dellins Wagner-Biographie." Musik-Konzepte 25 (May 1982): 74–115.

————. "Richard Wagners letzte Karte." In Parsifal, by Wagner, edited by Csampai and Holland, 252–56.

————. "Der verschwiegene Gehalt des Parsifal." In Parsifal, by Wagner, edited by Csampai and Holland, 244–51.

Zimmerman, Michael E. *Heidegger's Confrontation with Modernity: Technology, Politics, and Art.* Bloomington: Indiana Univ. Press, 1990.

Index

About the Author

Solveig Olsen came to the United States in 1965. Three years later she earned a PhD in Germanics at Rice University in Houston, Texas. In 1968 she moved to Denton as an assistant professor of German at the University of North Texas, where she remained until retiring as a professor of German in 2000 and from modified service (part-time) in 2005. Except for a stint as department chair, she devoted her energy to full-time instruction, research, and professional and university service.

Dr. Olsen's early research interests resulted in two books on Baroque topics, Christian Heinrich Postel and the Hamburg Opera, both published with Rodopi. In response to instructional developments and needs, her efforts shifted somewhat to include foreign language pedagogy, especially computer-assisted instruction. This preoccupation yielded a co-authored package of voice-based computer system materials, *VBLS/German* (manual and disks) for Scott Instruments and an edited volume, *Computer-Assisted Instruction and the Humanities*, published by the MLA. In addition she has also published numerous articles, chapters, and review articles.

Her interest in Syberberg's *Parsifal* grew out of the wish to incorporate video excerpts in an undergraduate course on medieval German literature that included Wolfram von Eschenbach's *Parzival*. The encounter led to years of related studies and resulted in this book.